# 1, 2, AND 3 JOHN

*Sacra Pagina Series*

Volume 18

# 1, 2, and 3 John

## John Painter

### Daniel J. Harrington, S.J.
### Editor

A Michael Glazier Book

**THE LITURGICAL PRESS**

Collegeville, Minnesota

www.litpress.org

A Michael Glazier Book published by The Liturgical Press.

Cover design by Don Bruno.

| 1 | 2 | 3 | 4 | 5 | 6 | 7 | 8 |
|---|---|---|---|---|---|---|---|

**Library of Congress Cataloging-in-Publication Data**

Painter, John.
    1, 2, and 3 John / John Painter ; Daniel J. Harrington, editor.
        p. cm. — (Sacra pagina series ; v. 18)
    Includes bibliographical references and indexes.
    ISBN 0-8146-5812-1 (alk. paper)
    1. Bible. N.T. Epistles of John—Commentaries.   I. Title: First, second, and
third John.   II. Harrington, Daniel J.   III. Title.   IV. Sacra pagina series ; 18.

BS2805.53 .P35  2002
227'.94077—dc21

                                           2001050587

*In memory of*

Gladys Lucy Painter   17.5.1897 to 14.4.2000

Edward Vincent Painter   28.5.1900 to 26.8.1968

Psalm 121

# CONTENTS

# 1 JOHN

## *Translation, Notes, Interpretation*

# 2 AND 3 JOHN

## 2 JOHN

## *Translation, Notes, Interpretation*

## *Translation, Notes, Interpretation*

## *Indexes*

# EDITOR'S PREFACE

Sacra Pagina is a multi-volume commentary on the books of the New Testament. The expression *Sacra Pagina* ("Sacred Page") originally referred to the text of Scripture. In the Middle Ages it also described the study of Scripture to which the interpreter brought the tools of grammar, rhetoric, dialectic, and philosophy. Thus *Sacra Pagina* encompasses both the text to be studied and the activity of interpretation.

This series presents fresh translations and modern expositions of all the books of the New Testament. Written by an international team of biblical scholars, it is intended for biblical professionals, graduate students, theologians, clergy, and religious educators. The volumes present basic introductory information and close exposition. They self-consciously adopt specific methodological perspectives, but maintain a focus on the issues raised by the New Testament compositions themselves. The goal of *Sacra Pagina* is to provide sound critical analysis without any loss of sensitivity to religious meaning. This series is therefore catholic in two senses of the word: inclusive in its methods and perspectives, and shaped by the context of the Catholic tradition.

The Second Vatican Council described the study of the "sacred page" as the "very soul of sacred theology" (*Dei Verbum* 24). The volumes in this series illustrate how biblical scholars contribute to the council's call to provide access to Sacred Scripture for all the Christian faithful. Rather than pretending to say the final word on any text, these volumes seek to open up the riches of the New Testament and to invite as many people as possible to study seriously the "sacred page."

DANIEL J. HARRINGTON, S.J.

# AUTHOR'S PREFACE

The Johannine Epistles emerged out of the obscurity of their second century history to become an essential part of the "Catholic Epistles" by the fourth century. The reasons for their early obscurity remain a mystery. Their emergence from that obscurity is explicable because of the recognition of their relationship to each other and the acceptance of the tradition of their Johannine origin. Once they emerged in this way they soon became part of the seven Catholic Epistles that were bounded by writings attributed to the brothers of Jesus, James and Jude. That the early church collected these writings as a corpus is significant as is the prominence given to the corpus in some major manuscripts. In recent times the Johannine Epistles have been viewed as an essential part of the Johannine literature, reasserting the importance of historical connections, without ignoring canonical connections, though the force of these has diminished. Both perspectives have been important for this commentary.

While the Johannine Epistles have not attracted the attention given to the Gospel, the "Historical Prolegomenon" sets out something of the rich history of tradition drawn on by this commentary. Indebtedness to that tradition is gladly acknowledged. Although there is not the wealth of commentaries that is to be found for the Gospel, there are, for example, the detailed commentaries of Schnackenburg, Brown and Strecker. The first and third of these are translations of earlier German commentaries and Brown's (over eight hundred pages) commentary is now twenty years old. The aim of this commentary is: (1) to be more accessible (shorter and hopefully clearer) without glossing over any of the problems that abound in the text. (2) To respond to recent criticisms and trends in scholarship on the Epistles. (3) To deal with the theology and relevance of the Epistles in Christian life and thought. Existing commentaries that are shorter inevitably fail to deal with many of the difficult problems posed by the text of these tantalizing little Epistles.

I am grateful to Linda Maloney for suggesting this contribution in the *Sacra Pagina* series and for her patient help in the completion of the task; and to Dan Harrington for his patience and his editing of the manuscript. In spite of all their support I am aware that imperfections remain.

I acknowledge my debt to St. Mark's for study leave in the first semester of 2000. The initial draft of the commentary was written while I was the visiting scholar at Asbury Theological Seminary. There I was given ideal facilities for the task at hand, including a friend to share my morning run. I am also grateful to Charles Sturt University for their support of my research and of this project in particular.

John Painter
St. Mark's National Theological Centre
Charles Sturt University
Canberra, ACT
Australia

# ABBREVIATIONS

## Biblical Books and Apocrypha

| | | | |
|---|---|---|---|
| Gen | Nah | 1–2–3–4 Kgdms | John |
| Exod | Hab | Add Esth | Acts |
| Lev | Zeph | Bar | Rom |
| Num | Hag | Bel | 1–2 Cor |
| Deut | Zech | 1–2 Esdr | Gal |
| Josh | Mal | 4 Ezra | Eph |
| Judg | Ps (*pl.:* Pss) | Jdt | Phil |
| 1–2 Sam | Job | Ep Jer | Col |
| 1–2 Kgs | Prov | 1–2–3–4 Macc | 1–2 Thess |
| Isa | Ruth | Pr Azar | 1–2 Tim |
| Jer | Cant | Pr Man | Titus |
| Ezek | Eccl (*or* Qoh) | Sir | Phlm |
| Hos | Lam | Sus | Heb |
| Joel | Esth | Tob | Jas |
| Amos | Dan | Wis | 1–2 Pet |
| Obad | Ezra | Matt | 1–2–3 John |
| Jonah | Neh | Mark | Jude |
| Mic | 1–2 Chr | Luke | Rev |

## Other Ancient Texts

| | |
|---|---|
| *Ant.* | Josephus, *Antiquities of the Jews* |
| *Apoc. Abr.* | *Apocalypse of Abraham* |
| *b.* | Babylonian Talmud |
| *B. Qamma* | *Baba Qamma* |
| 2–3 Bar | Syriac, Greek *Apocalypse of Baruch* |
| CD | Cairo Genizah copy of the *Damascus Document* |
| *Eccl. Hist.* | Eusebius, *Ecclesiastical History* |
| *Gos. Thom.* | *Gospel of Thomas* |
| *Ḥag.* | *Ḥagiga* |
| Ign., *Eph.* | Ignatius, *Letter to the Ephesians* |
| *Jub* | *Jubilees* |

| | |
|---|---|
| *Ketub.* | *Ketubot* |
| LXX | Septuagint |
| *m.* | Mishnah |
| MT | Masoretic Text |
| *Ned.* | *Nedarim* |
| NT | New Testament |
| OT | Old Testament |
| P. Oxy. | Papyrus Oxyrhynchus |
| Q | Sayings Source Q |
| 1QapGen | Qumran Cave 1 *Genesis Apocryphon* |
| 1QM | *War Scroll* |
| 1QpHab | *Pesher Habakkuk* |
| 1QH | *Hodayot* |
| 1QS | *Rule of the Community* |
| 1QSa | *Rule of the Community (Appendix)* |
| 4Q | Qumran Cave 4 |
| *Spec. Leg.* | Philo, *Special Laws* |
| *T. Levi* | *Testament of Levi* |
| *Test. Sol.* | *Testament of Solomon* |
| *Toh.* | *Toharot* |
| *Vit. Mos.* | Philo, *Life of Moses* |
| *Yad.* | *Yadayim* |

## Periodicals, Reference Works, and Serials

| | |
|---|---|
| AB | Anchor Bible |
| ABD | *Anchor Bible Dictionary,* ed. David N. Freedman et al. |
| BAGD | Walter Bauer, W. F. Arndt, F. W. Gingrich, and F. W. Danker, *A Greek-English Lexicon of the New Testament and Other Early Christian Literature* (2nd ed.) |
| BDAG | F. W. Danker, reviser and editor, *A Greek-English Lexicon of the New Testament and Other Early Christian Literature* (3rd ed.) |
| BDF | Friedrich Blass, Albert Debrunner, and R. W. Funk, *A Greek Grammar of the New Testament* |
| *Bib* | *Biblica* |
| Billerbeck | Hermann Strack and Paul Billerbeck, *Kommentar zum Neuen Testament aus Talmud und Midrasch* |
| *BTB* | *Biblical Theology Bulletin* |
| *BZ* | *Biblische Zeitschrift* |
| *CBQ* | *Catholic Biblical Quarterly* |
| EKKNT | Evangelisch-katholisches Kommentar zum Neuen Testament |
| *ETL* | *Ephemerides theologicae Lovanienses* |
| *ExpTim* | *Expository Times* |
| HNT | Handbuch zum Neuen Testament |
| HTKNT | Herders theologischer Kommentar zum Neuen Testament |
| *HTR* | *Harvard Theological Review* |

| | |
|---|---|
| ICC | International Critical Commentary |
| IDB | *Interpreter's Dictionary of the Bible* |
| Int | *Interpretation* |
| JAAR | *Journal of the American Academy of Religion* |
| JBL | *Journal of Biblical Literature* |
| JES | *Journal of Ecumenical Studies* |
| JR | *Journal of Religion* |
| JSNT | *Journal for the Study of the New Testament* |
| JSP | *Journal for the Study of Pseudepigrapha* |
| JSS | *Journal of Semitic Studies* |
| JTS | *Journal of Theological Studies* |
| MPL | Patrologia Latina, ed. J. Migne |
| NAB | New American Bible |
| NCE | *New Catholic Encyclopedia* |
| NIV | New International Version |
| NovT | *Novum Testamentum* |
| NRSV | New Revised Standard Version |
| NTS | *New Testament Studies* |
| OTP | *Old Testament Pseudepigrapha*, ed. J. H. Charlesworth |
| RB | *Revue Biblique* |
| RGG² | *Die Religion in Geschichte und Gegenwart; Handwörterbuch für Theologie und Religionswissenschaft.* 5 vols. 2nd ed. Tübingen: Mohr, 1927–1931. |
| RQ | *Revue de Qumran* |
| SJT | *Scottish Journal of Theology* |
| TDNT | *Theological Dictionary of the New Testament*, ed. Gerhard Kittel and Gerhard Friedrich |
| TS | *Theological Studies* |
| TU | *Texte und Untersuchungen* |
| USQR | *Union Seminary Quarterly Review* |
| WBC | Word Biblical Commentary |
| ZNW | *Zeitschrift für die neutestamentliche Wissenschaft* |

# HISTORICAL PROLEGOMENON

The Interpretation and Notes in this commentary do not report detailed debates with other commentators. They deal with the issues raised by the text directly and without detailed reference to other scholars. The aim of this chapter is to situate the commentary in relation to other scholarship. Scholars always build on the work of those who have traveled the path before them. In what follows it should become clear that this commentary is critically dependent on earlier work. It builds on an important tradition of Johannine scholarship and it is helpful for the reader to know this and to recognize the way this tradition has developed. A history of scholarship illuminates the way in which problems and issues dealt with in this commentary came to be recognized. This book builds on the tradition of interpretation found in the works of Theodor Häring, Robert Law, Alan E. Brooke and, more recently, C. H. Dodd (1946) and Rudolf Schnackenburg (1953). Raymond E. Brown (1982) has also worked out of this tradition and developed his own lines of interpretation. The commentary also outlines the variety of ways the Epistles have been read and points the way to future trends in scholarship.

Work on this commentary commenced with research done on *The Idea of Knowledge in the Johannine Gospel and Epistles* with Professor C. K. Barrett in Durham between 1965 and 1967. A popular version of aspects of my work on the Johannine Epistles was published as part three of my *John, Witness and Theologian* (1975) 101–28.

My interpretation of the Epistles drew attention to the implied Jewish audience of the Gospel and the non-Jewish context of the Epistles, which make no mention of Jews, do not appeal to Jewish Scripture, and call on the readers (in 1 John) to guard against idols (5:21). Nevertheless, the author of the Epistles continued to manifest a use of Greek influenced by Semitic language. As C. K. Barrett noted (*John and Judaism*, 1975), when the question of Jewish influence is dealt with we need to be clear what level or levels we are talking about. Telling the story of Jesus will have Jewish elements because the subject of the story was a Jew. If Matthew was a Jew writing for Jews, believers or otherwise, then Jewish elements might also enter the story because of Matthew or because of his prospective readers.

1

Jewish elements in the Johannine Epistles reflect the Jewish heritage of the author(s).

B. F. Westcott *(Epistles,* 1883) defends the authorship of Gospel and Epistles by the apostle John. He appeals to the thoroughly Hebraic nature of the writings but notes that the Epistles "do not contain one quotation or verbal reminiscence from the Old Testament" *(Epistles* xl). Though Westcott does not comment, this suggests a Jewish author writing to readers who were Christian but not dominantly Jewish. According to Westcott, by the time John wrote "Jerusalem had been destroyed," and the Church was an independent body through which the Holy Spirit worked. The danger from the world was not persecution but seduction to its values. Mission is no longer a focus *(Epistles* xxxiii). In the Epistles there is no sign of conflict between the advocates of the Law and the Gospel, or between Jew and Gentile, no problem concerning circumcision. The ethnic background of the readers is not an issue *(Epistles* xxxiv). For Westcott, acceptance of the common authorship of Gospel and Epistles was based on their common language and themes but "there is no sufficient evidence to determine the relative date of the Epistles and the Gospel as written." *(Epistles* xxxi). Nevertheless, Westcott was convinced that the Epistles presuppose that the readers were familiar with the truths communicated in the Gospel. This was possible because he thought that the Gospel "was shaped . . . in oral teaching long before it was published" *(Epistles* xxxi). In this respect Westcott already foreshadows the work of Raymond E. Brown who set out, in some detail, a reconstruction of the shaping of the tradition prior to the writing down and publication of the Gospel.

While Westcott was vague in relation to the details of the development of the Gospel tradition, he boldly identified the situation in which the Epistles appeared. They were written when the Church had become independent of Judaism and confronted issues specifically Christian rather than Jewish. Westcott notes that the Epistles contend with a Docetic error and identifies it as Cerinthian *(Epistles* xxxiv). He appeals to Jerome *(Dial. adv. Lucifer.* * 23); Ignatius *(Trall.* 9, 10; *Smyrn.* 2; *Eph.* 7); Polycarp *(Phil.* 7); Irenaeus *(Adv. haer.* 1.26.1; 3.3.4; cp. Epiphanius, *Haer.* xxxviii.1; Eusebius, *H.E.* 4.14) to support his position. Here he was bolder than Raymond E. Brown, who is reluctant to specifically identify the christological position of those opposed by the Epistles. Westcott names the error as the denial of the Incarnation and says, "Augustine *(ad loc.)* remarks characteristically that the denial of the Incarnation is the sign of the absence of love" *(Epistles* 143). In this way Westcott tied the second major problem in 1 John to the first. The failure to love was a consequence of the failure to confess the Incarnation, "Jesus Christ come in the flesh" (1 John 4:2; cf. 2 John 7).

Given that Westcott does not distinguish the situation in which the finished Gospel was published from the situation addressed by the Epistles, it seems that he thought them to be more or less the same. No attention is given to the way the developing Gospel tradition might have been shaped by earlier situations. Westcott is preoccupied with the identity of the author and uses the Jewish evidence as one strand of his argument to show that the author was the apostle John.

While the polemical nature of the Epistles is noted by Westcott, he does so in a way that minimizes it. First he generalizes the nature of the error opposed, saying "the Christological errors which St John meets exist more or less at all times" (*Epistles* xxxvi). He also generalizes the polemic as an essential function of truth:

> The pursuit of such a theme necessarily involves the condemnation and refutation of corresponding errors. But St John's method is to confute error by the exposition of the truth realised in life. His object is polemical only so far as the clear unfolding of the essence of right teaching necessarily shows all error in its real character. In other words St John writes to call out a welcome for what he knows to be the Gospel and not to overthrow this or that false opinion. (*Epistles* xxxix)

The understanding of the Johannine Epistles changes with the work of Robert Law (*The Tests of Life*, 1909). Like subsequent authors writing on the Johannine Epistles, Law made use of the detailed study of H. J. Holtzmann comparing in detail the evidence concerning the relationship of the Gospel of John to the Epistle (*The Tests of Life* 340–48). The evidence left Law with the view that either the two works were by the same author or the second was written by an author steeped in the knowledge of the first writing. Unlike Holtzmann, Law accepted the identity of authorship. While Holtzmann thought that this view necessitated acceptance of the priority of 1 John because the author must have moved from the lesser to the greater literary and theological achievement, Law argued for the priority of the Gospel. It was his view that the different nature of the two writings and the specific purpose of 1 John explain its more limited achievement. In particular he notes that the author was limited by the capacity of the readers for whom 1 John was written (*The Tests of Life* 360–63). For Law the Epistle is the author's defense of the meaning of the Gospel against Gnostic misinterpretation of it.

His work has been notable in three ways. First, his title captures the imagination, drawing attention to the characteristic language of 1 John ("By this we know") in a way that crystallizes the essence of Law's reading. Second, his analysis of the Epistle provides a resolution of many intractable problems involved in the reading of 1 John. Here Law was, coincidentally, in fundamental agreement with Theodor Häring's article of 1892 ("Gedankengang und Grundgedanke des ersten Johannesbriefes," in Adolf Harnack, et al., *Theologische Abhandlungen Carl von Weizsäcker zu*

*seinem siebzigsten Geburtstage, 11. December 1892.* Freiburg: J.C.B. Mohr
[Paul Siebeck], 1892, 173–200). That analysis continues to be influential,
being broadly adopted by Alan E. Brooke in his commentary in the ICC
series in 1912. Third, Law brought to light the pervasively polemical intention of the Epistle.

While Law says that "the polemical intention of the Epistle has been
universally recognised," he qualifies his approval of past views in two
ways. First, he reexamines the supposed object of criticism. Law notes
that the older commentators identified Laodicean lukewarmness as the
problem confronted by the Epistle. Law says that the Epistle gives no sign
of this intent, though it is full of passages that indicate another line of
polemic. He identifies a form of Gnosticism, instead, as the object of critique (*The Tests of Life* 25–26). Law's understanding of Gnosticism reflects
the work of Wilhelm Bousset (to whom he refers on p. 27). Bousset's
understanding of the nature and influence of Gnosticism was taken up
and developed by Rudolf Bultmann. While Law's monograph lacks the
detailed analysis of a commentary, the line of interpretation he lays down
is superior to the overall strategy of Bultmann's commentary on the Johannine Epistles, which is flawed by an improbable source theory.

Second, Law argues:

> Although explicit controversial allusions in the Epistle are few,—are lim-
> ited, indeed to two passages (2:18-19; 4:1-6) in which certain false teach-
> ers, designated as "antichrists," are unsparingly denounced,—there is no
> New Testament writing which is more vigorously polemical in its whole
> tone and aim. The truth, which in the same writer's Gospel shines as the
> dayspring from on high, becomes here a searchlight, flashed into a back-
> ground of darkness. (*The Tests of Life* 25)

Thus the whole Epistle is polemical, setting out tests that distinguish
the true from the false. Law's second chapter, in which this discussion occurs, is entitled "The Polemical Aim of the Epistle." In it Law addresses
the popular separation of the christological error from ethical problems,
arguing that they are united in one group of opponents (*The Tests of Life*
35–38). It should be noted that Law nowhere suggests that the polemic is
addressed to the "antichrists," the opponents of the author. Polemic like
this is seldom directed to those criticized. Rather it is addressed to those
who might otherwise be influenced by them. Further, though in response
to the errors of the opponents, which Law characterizes as Gnosticism,

> the whole presentation of truth in the Epistle widely overflows the limits
> of the controversial occasion. . . . St. John so little meets these with mere
> denunciation; . . . he so lifts every question at issue out of the dust of
> mere polemics into the lucid atmosphere of eternal truth, that his Epistle
> pursues its course through the ages. . . . Nevertheless, for its interpreta-

tion, the polemical aim that pervades it must be recognised. (*The Tests of Life* 35)

"Opponents" is my chosen nomenclature for those opposed by the author of 1 John. We may *assume* that they opposed him also. Other terms have been used to characterize them, such as adversaries, antichrist (2:18; 2 John 7), deceivers (2 John 7), false prophets (4:1), heretics, propagandists, secessionists, or schismatics. Three of these terms are used in the Epistles and the rest could be justified as a fair representation of what the author of 1 John said about them. That reminds us of the perspective of the evidence we have at our disposal. We can only guess at what the opponents said about the author of 1 John. According to Law, 1 John itself reports the claims of the opponents.

> When this, the general and most pronounced feature of Gnosticism, is borne in mind, a vivid light is at once shed on many passages in the Epistle. In those, especially, in which we find the formula "he that saith" (*ho legōn*), or an equivalent (*ean eipōmen, ean tis eipē*), it becomes apparent that it is no abstract contingency the writer has in view, but a definite recognised case. (*The Tests of Life* 29)

The commentary by A. E. Brooke published in the ICC series in 1912 builds on earlier commentaries and the studies by Holtzmann, Theodor Häring, and Robert Law. In his analysis of 1 John, Brooke favored Häring over Law where they differed. Häring perceived just two tests, ethical and christological, absorbing righteousness and love in the ethical test. He also separated 5:13-21 from the third cycle of tests, thus giving the Epistle a greater balance. In between the Introduction and the Epilogue are three cycles of the two tests. The analysis is followed in broad terms by both Brooke and Bultmann, though Brooke is somewhat critical, suggesting that "perhaps the attempt to analyze the Epistle should be abandoned as useless" (*A Critical and Exegetical Commentary on the Johannine Epistles* xxxii).

Brooke, like Law, concluded from a detailed analysis of the Gospel and Epistle (developed on the basis of Holtzmann's articles) that common authorship (*Commentary* xviii) and the priority of the Gospel (*Commentary* xix, xxvii) are the most likely conclusions. He argues that the Epistle appears to be a clarification of the Gospel for those who have not grasped its meaning adequately. At the same time Brooke echoes Westcott in recognizing that clarifying the content of the Gospel might not mean that the Gospel was already a published document (*Commentary* xxvii). Brooke is here alluding to the development of the tradition in John through oral preaching and teaching.

In dealing with "2. The Aim" of the Epistles (*Commentary* xxvii–xxx), Brooke notes (p. xvii) that "The more definitely polemical aim of the Epistles

is discussed in another section." (Section 5 discusses "The False Teachers.") Yet in discussing the "Aim" of 1 John he says:

> It is probably true that the writer never loses sight altogether of the views
> of his opponents in any part of the Epistle. . . . in spite of this, the real
> aim of the epistle is not exclusively, or even primarily, polemical. The edi-
> fication of his "children" in the true faith and life of Christians is the
> writer's chief purpose. (*Commentary* xxvii–xxviii)

For Brooke the errors of the opponents do not constitute the only danger.
There is the attraction of the "world." Further, the battle with the opponents is already over and the victory won (*Commentary* xxviii) by the time
the Epistle was written. One might ask: If this is true, why is it that the author of 1 John does not lose sight of their views in any part of the Epistle?

In his treatment of the false teachers Brooke examines the question
"One or Many?" He answers by suggesting there were many, but perhaps
"one special type of false teaching, or one special incident in the history of
his Church in connection with it" (*Commentary* xli). He then considers can-
didates for that main position, looking at Judaism, Gnosticism, Docetism,
Cerinthianism, and Ethical Errors (*Commentary* xli–lii). He concludes that
the errors are a combination of Jewish and Gnostic ideas such as are associated with Cerinthus.

Like Law, but in a less cohesive fashion, Brooke also recognizes what
he calls "false pleas," the three in 1:6, 8, 10 (*Commentary* 13), the second
group of false claims in 2:4, 6, 9 (*Commentary* 31, 37–38), and the final
"false claim" in 4:20 (*Commentary* 126). With Law, Brooke recognizes the
concrete nature of the danger faced by the author of 1 John:

> Throughout the Epistle he writes under a pressing sense of danger. He is
> not wasting his weapons on purely hypothetical situations, of the reali-
> zation of which he felt no serious apprehension. (*Commentary* 13)

Consequently his critique already foreshadows and rejects the current
tendency of some scholars (Pheme Perkins, Judith Lieu, Ruth Edwards) to
*reduce* the polemical style of 1 John to mere rhetoric. Nevertheless, like
Westcott he tends to generalize from the particular situation. Thus he describes 1:6, 8, 10 as "three false pleas often put forward by men to excuse
their 'love of the darkness'" (*Commentary* 13). Speaking of the form found
in 2:4, 6, 9, he writes:

> It is the direct and definite statement of the writer conscious of the fact
> that he is dealing with a real danger, and probably with a statement that
> was actually made, by men against whose influence he is trying to guard
> his *teknia*. If there is no reason to see in it an attack on any particular
> Gnostic teacher, it clearly deals with statements which they have heard,
> and to which they have shown themselves ready to listen. (*Commentary* 31)

Brooke rightly notes that the statements cannot be identified with any known Gnostic teacher. This need not mean that the views and practices opposed have no coherence. Of 4:20 he writes:

> The false claim is mentioned quite generally. At the same time, it is not improbable that the false teachers, who claimed to possess a superior knowledge of the true God, may also have laid claim to a superior love of the Father, who was "good" and not merely "just", as the God of the Old Testament. And the emphasis laid throughout the Epistle on the duty of mutual love makes it clear that their "superior" love had been more or less conspicuous in its failure. . . . (*Commentary* 126)

Here the reference to the "false teachers" makes the critique more specific and is consistent with the recognition of one specific crisis dominating the response of 1 John (*Commentary* xli). On this Law's position is more coherent and consistent with the evidence than that of either Westcott or Brooke.

Rudolf Bultmann began to lay down the lines of his interpretation of the Johannine Epistles in his "Analyse des ersten Johannesbriefes" (1927). This was followed by "Die kirchliche Redaktion des ersten Johannes-briefes" (1951). His position was then set out in his "Johannesbriefe" in *RGG*[3] (1959) and more fully in the Meyer commentary, the second edition of which (1967) was translated into English (*The Johannine Epistles*, 1973).

Bultmann argued that both the evangelist and the author of 1 John, whom he distinguished from each other, made use of common source material he designated the *Offenbarungsreden*, "the revelation discourses." Thus Bultmann interprets both the Gospel and Epistles against the background of and in conflict with early Oriental Gnosticism. This form of Gnosticism had already been influenced by Judaism but was not thought to be indigenously Jewish or Christian. Rather, its dualism revealed its Eastern origin. Bultmann saw both the Gospel and Epistles reinterpreting the Gnostic source, but in an adventurous way that was subjected to ecclesiastical redaction before these works became acceptable to the wider church.

An alternative to Bultmann's reading is to be found in the work of C. H. Dodd. In the 1945 Preface to his 1946 commentary on the Epistles, Dodd acknowledges indebtedness to earlier commentaries by Richard Rothe, B. F. Westcott, Bernhard Weiss, H. J. Holtzmann, Robert Law, Windisch, and A. E. Brooke. He goes on to say that his interpretation "has in large measure emerged from studies primarily directed towards the understanding of the Fourth Gospel in its contemporary setting." He indicates his indebtedness to Brooke's admirable introduction but differs from Brooke in distinguishing the author of the Epistles from the author of the Gospel.

Dodd agrees that the Gospel is prior to the Epistles but sees the author of the Epistles as "a disciple of the Evangelist and a student of his work."

While he "caught something of his style and manner," there is a difference (*The Johannine Epistles* lvi). On the whole Dodd considered the author of the Epistles to be more limited than the evangelist from a literary and theological perspective (*Johannine Epistles* xlvii–lvi). Dodd thinks the probability is that the Epistles were written by one author and in the canonical order, the second, dealing with similar issues to the first, soon after it, and the third, on another subject, some time later. He thinks 1 John to be a circular "epistle" addressed to a fairly wide public, and that 2 John is addressed to a particular local congregation while 3 John is a private letter to a friend, dealing with church matters (*Johannine Epistles* lxvi).

Dodd recognized and justified his vagueness in these matters, referring to the lack of detailed evidence relevant to the questions. Nothing has changed. His position is close to what is advocated by this volume, though 2 John need not be addressed to a particular church. The symbolism of "the elect lady and her children" might refer to any local church. Thus 2 John might have been written to accompany 1 John. Third John, though addressed to a named individual, is not about an altogether different subject than we find in 2 John. Second John deals with the Elder's instruction that no hospitality be provided for those who do not abide by his teaching. Third John responds to Diotrephes' refusal of hospitality to supporters of the Elder. Thus 1, 2, and 3 John appear to be addressed to a common situation, though 3 John was a little later than 1 and 2 John.

Dodd sees 1 John not as having a polemical purpose, but as an apologetic work, less successful and more open to distorted understandings than the Gospel. According to Dodd the Gospel was more successful in communicating the Christian message to the new culture encountered by Christianity at the end of the first century. In his commentary on the Epistles Dodd called the phenomenon Gnosticism. In *The Interpretation of the Fourth Gospel* (1953) he described it as the higher religion of Hellenism. He now saw both Gospel and Epistles as expressions of a dialogue with the higher religion of Hellenism, the intellectual and philosophical wing of the movement of which Gnosticism is the rather crude mythological expression. Law's analysis (*The Tests of Life*, 1909) of the study of Gnosticism is illuminating for an understanding of Dodd's thought, especially as Dodd (*Johannine Epistles* vii) acknowledges his debt to Law.

First, Law, drawing on the work of Wilhelm Bousset (*The Tests of Life* 27 n. 1), identifies the genesis of Gnosticism in "an irruption of Oriental religious beliefs into the Graeco-Roman world" that "sought to unite Western intellectualism and Eastern mysticism." He notes that scholars are divided about which of the two is primary and that "Church historians of the liberal school [tend] to glorify Gnosticism by giving chief prominence to its philosophical aspect." Dodd belongs to this group, though his position is somewhat more complex. In *The Johannine Epistles* (xvi) he recognized that

"The movement covered a wide range. Near the bottom of the scale it was little more than a way of making superstition respectable for the minor *intelligentsia*. Near the top, it took form in a high religion of mystical communion with the Divine." Here Dodd's position fits Law's description of "church historians of the liberal school." The elements important for Dodd's understanding of the Johannine tradition were the philosophical Stoic/Platonic motifs to be found in the movement "near the top."

Dodd came to distinguish this element from Gnosticism and to locate it in the higher religion of Hellenism (referred to as "this higher Paganism" in *Johannine Epistles* xvii). He then identified Gnosticism with the cruder mythological elements, seeing no essential connection between the two. Bultmann, for his part, was sharply critical of Dodd's Platonizing interpretation of the Johannine writings and the Gnostic problem. See his review of *The Interpretation of the Fourth Gospel* in *NTS* 1 (1954–55) 77–91 (English translation by W. C. Robinson in *HDB* 27 [1963] 9–22). See my "C. H. Dodd and the Christology of the Fourth Gospel" (1987).

In his *Johannine Epistles* Dodd fails to make the connection between philosophical elements and mythology in the Gnostic movement where the philosophy serves the mythology. This was more firmly grasped by Law. Nor does Dodd follow Law and Brooke in recognizing the claims of the false teachers (opponents) in 1 John 1:6, 8, 10; 2:4, 6, 9; 4:20. Thus he fails to grasp adequately the peculiar polemical nature of 1 John in confronting the false claims alongside its pastoral nurture of the faith of the community torn by schism. For a commentary that would build thoroughly on the insights of Law's *Tests of Life* we had to wait until 1953.

Rudolf Schnackenburg's commentary (*Die Johannesbriefe*) was first published in 1953, but English readers had to wait for a translation of the seventh edition in 1992. There is a strong affinity between Schnackenburg's work and that of Robert Law. Schnackenburg's full commentary provides a detailed introduction covering all-important questions, followed by a thorough analysis of the text. Writing of 1 John, Schnackenburg says:

> His purpose in writing is to strengthen true faith and mutual love, and the joyful certainty of fellowship with God (1:3) and of eternal life (5:13) which he brings. This general Christian goal of salvation is endangered by certain heretics and enemies of the faith. The polemic against the antagonists is by no means confined to the two sections 2:18-27; 4:1-6, but in fact pervades the entire document. (*The Johannine Epistles* 3)

In various places Schnackenburg makes quite clear that the literary duality of 1 John, combining pastoral concern and polemical intent, is addressed to those within the community who have been unsettled by the teaching of the "opponents" and by the rupture caused by the schism (2:18-19).

Only by refuting their errors could the disturbance be laid to rest and the community of believers encouraged on the way of faith and love.

The Johannine Epistles were addressed to Christian readers. Nothing in them suggests a dominantly Jewish Christian community. When I first wrote on John (1965–67), the dominant paradigms for interpreting the Gospel and Epistles were those developed by Rudolf Bultmann and C. H. Dodd. Scholarship at that time accepted the publication of the Gospel and Epistles late in the first century and assumed that they were addressed to Christians without any suggestion that those were predominantly Jewish Christians. The work of Schnackenburg, Dodd, Brooke, Law, and Westcott is in harmony with this position.

Interestingly, work on the Qumran texts was to change the understanding of the context of the Johannine writings. This was already beginning to happen in the mid-1960s when my research began. To this point those who, like Westcott, appealed to the Jewish character of the writings did so in order to affirm the Jewish identity of the author. They did not suggest that these works were written for Jewish or Jewish Christian readers. Impetus for this line of interpretation came from the recognition of the affinity of the Johannine writings and the Jewish texts from Qumran. It is difficult to say why interpreters did not adopt this approach earlier instead of following Westcott's preoccupation with the Jewish identity of the author. The content of John may draw attention to aspects of Jewish and Christian relations that suggest the Gospel is a manifestation of the process that led to the expulsion from the synagogue of those Jews who believed in Jesus.

This perspective was already featured by James Parkes in his study, *The Conflict of the Church and the Synagogue: A Study of the Origins of Anti-semitism,* first published in 1934. The book has a remarkable thesis for the time of its original publication. Parkes argues "that it was in the conflict of the Church with the Synagogue that the real roots of the problem [of anti-semitism] lay" (*Conflict* vii, Preface to the 1934 edition). In the Introduction he goes on to say:

> . . . the events following the destruction of Jerusalem in A.D. 70 made the conversion of the mass of the [Jewish] people less likely, and there is, consequently, a change in the tone of the literature. It is designed to confute rather than to convince. To this period belongs the Gospel of Saint John, with its complete lack of distinction between parties, and its condemnation of "the Jews" as a whole for actions which the synoptists had more specifically ascribed to the Pharisees or some other party. (*Conflict* ix)

Chapters 2 and 3 of Parkes' book are relevant to our discussion. Chapter 2, "The Clash with Christianity," deals largely with Mark and Acts. Parkes argues that during the ministry of Jesus and the relationship of believers with Judaism down to the destruction of Jerusalem there is an openness to the Jews and a desire to win them to the faith. He relegates his discussion of the Gospel of John to Chapter 3, "The Parting of the Ways" because, unlike the rest of the New Testament, it contains "more elements of the situation around A.D. 100 than of the situation in the lifetime of Jesus" (*Conflict* 28). The chapter title, "The Parting of the Ways," has caught popular imagination and is now, following Parkes, commonly used of the breakdown of relations between Jews and Christians, especially early Jewish Christians. See J. D. G. Dunn, *The Partings of the Ways* (1991) and J. D. G. Dunn, ed., *Jews and Christians: The Parting of the Ways AD 70–135* (1992). Parkes deals with the separation of Jews and Christians first in Palestine before turning to the Diaspora.

It is in the section on the Diaspora that Parkes treats the Fourth Gospel (*Conflict* 81–85). Patristic and Jewish evidence is used to set a context for reading the Johannine evidence. Parkes shows that after the destruction of Jerusalem that event was treated as a source of derision by Christian writers such as Justin (*Dialogue with Trypho*). He argues that whereas in Mark it is unclear at the beginning how Jesus' overture to the Pharisees will turn out, in John the reader is told at the very beginning, "he came to his own and his own did not receive him" (see *Conflict* 82). Jesus' conflict with the Jews soon develops to the point where they seek to kill him (5:16, 18) and Jesus says that they are of their father, the devil (8:44). Parkes specifically notes that the Jews in John determine to cast out of the synagogue any who confess Jesus as the Christ (9:22), so that people are afraid to speak openly of Jesus (7:13). He concludes: "All this is redolent of the atmosphere which must have existed at the end of the first century, when, indeed, confession of Christianity meant expulsion from the Synagogue . . ." (*Conflict* 83).

Nevertheless, Parkes' views did not become influential in the interpretation of the Gospel. Although he set the Gospel of John in the context of "the parting of the ways" at the end of the first century, this position did not become important for another thirty-five years. It may be that the book was ignored in 1934 because it dealt with the roots of antisemitism, which was not a problem the world was ready to handle. The republication date in 1969 is significant.

Other publications also drew attention to the probable relationship of events at the end of the first century and the language (in John) used to describe expulsion from the synagogue for the confession that Jesus is the Christ (9:22, 34; 12:42; 16:2). Here it is sufficient to note C. K. Barrett's 1955 commentary on the Gospel of John, 299–300. The second edition of the commentary in 1978 shows little change at this point other than the additional reference to the work of J. Louis Martyn, which adopts much the same position as Barrett's commentary (*Gospel According to St John*, 2nd ed.

361–62). An article by K. L. Carroll, "The Fourth Gospel and the Exclusion of Christians from the Synagogue" (1957–58) featured the Gospel of John and expulsion from the synagogue. The earlier work of Parkes and the specific essay by Carroll, along with other general treatments, were not enough to disturb the Johannine landscape, though the seeds of Martyn's thesis are to be found here.

This is illuminating because Martyn's book (*History and Theology in the Fourth Gospel*, 1968, 2nd ed. 1979) was instrumental in changing the approach to the Gospel. Earlier the language was viewed as evidence of a Jewish author. Now the Gospel itself came to be read in a way that implied that the story of Jesus was being told for Jewish believers somewhere in the Diaspora after the Jewish war, toward the end of the first century. This telling of the story of Jesus and his conflict with the Jewish authorities was now seen to reflect the story of the Jewish believers and their conflict with the synagogue, which ended with excommunication. It reflects the parting of the ways much as Parkes had outlined in 1934. Martyn's reading of the Gospel in the light of the merging of two stories caught the imagination in a way not even hinted at in earlier treatments. Part of this may have been due to timing. In the light of the Holocaust the problem of anti-Judaism was now recognized as a scandal. At the same time a good deal is due to the creative synthesis produced by Martyn, which systematically surpassed the earlier intimations of a solution to anomalies in the Johannine narrative.

Martyn's work did not take into account the Johannine Epistles, and scholars have not generally attempted to extend his thesis in their direction to argue for a specifically Jewish context for them. One reason may be that the finished Gospel is seen to be subsequent to the parting of the ways and set in a Christian rather than a Jewish context. If the Epistles followed the Gospel, they too would be set in a Christian rather than a Jewish context.

There are exceptions to this position. Prior to Martyn's book, research by John C. O'Neill (*The Puzzle of 1 John*, 1966) argued that 1 John was based on a *Vorlage* that can be understood in relation to the Qumran texts. He attempted to interpret 1 John from the perspective of the Judaism of the Qumran sect. Interestingly, although O'Neill's thesis has found no support, there is now a trend to interpret both the Gospel and the Epistles in the context of Judaism, with Jewish believers addressed in a common situation. See, for example, the work of Martin Hengel, *The Johannine Question* (1989); Judith Lieu, *The Second and Third Epistles of John* (1986); and Teresa Okure, *The Johannine Approach to Mission* (1988).

An alternative to this view is to recognize the linguistic similarities between the Johannine Gospel and Epistles and the Qumran texts as an indication of Jewish authorship. This is the view adopted by Westcott and others on the basis of the Jewish character of the Johannine language.

Whether or not the Epistles were written before the Gospel, by the time of their writing they were addressed to believers who were independent from Judaism, and the Epistles reflect no specifically Jewish problems. Even if the Gospel was written and published after the Epistles, it contains traditions shaped for Jewish believers who were working out their faith in relation to other Jews. No assumption of common authorship of Gospel and Epistles is made in this commentary and different contexts need to be taken into account when weighing the differences in the language and thought of Gospel and Epistles.

My reading of the evidence suggests that the Gospel was published between 85 and 90 C.E. If that is somewhere near the mark, the traditions in the Gospel had been shaped in changing situations in the five or six decades after the life of Jesus. I assume that the fundamental shaping of the traditions took place prior to the death of the primary author. By the time the Gospel was published the Johannine community contained both Jews and Gentiles. (See John 21:20-24 and my *John, Witness and Theologian* 14–16, and the more extensive discussion in *The Quest for the Messiah*, 1991, 2nd ed. 1993, 33, 66–87.)

My interpretation of the Epistles builds on the work of Theodor Häring, Robert Law, A. E. Brooke and, more recently, C. H. Dodd (1946) and Rudolf Schnackenburg (1953). In the 1960s, although I had the commentary by C. K. Barrett and Raymond E. Brown's first volume on the Gospel, there was no equivalent contemporary commentary in English on the Epistles. There was the earlier careful, detailed, and insightful commentary of Brooke (1912) and the brilliant, stimulating, and succinct commentary by Dodd (1946), but for an up-to-date detailed study the student needed to turn to the fine German commentary by Schnackenburg. Schnackenburg's treatment was sensitive and thorough and led the way for other great commentaries that have followed.

A note on the place and unsung influence, in the English speaking world at least, of Schnackenburg's commentary is useful here. In the preface to the 1992 English edition Schnackenburg graciously makes mention of the commentary by Raymond E. Brown in the following terms:

> As far as the Johannine Epistles are concerned, the most important event that has occurred [since Schnackenburg's previous German edition] is the appearance of Raymond E. Brown, *The Epistles of John* (Anchor Bible 30; Garden City, N.Y., 1982). This commentary takes note of and appropriates all the more recent literature. It runs to 812 pages. . . . Brown's interpretations are usually close to mine, though he sometimes takes a line of his own. It has not been possible for me [in the English edition] to enter into a detailed discussion of his views. His commentary represents a definite advance and is a high point of contemporary scholarship. (*The Johannine Epistles* [1992] xi)

The terms and tone of this compliment are illuminating. First, Schnackenburg saw Brown's commentary following his own line of interpretation fairly closely. This was laid down in the 1953 first edition. Perhaps because it was not translated into English until 1992, the place of Schnackenburg's commentary in Johannine scholarship has not received its due recognition from English-speaking scholars. To mention two works from eminent Johannine scholars from two sides of the Atlantic is illuminating. In her 1991 study, *The Theology of the Johannine Epistles,* Judith Lieu notes: "J. L. Houlden's commentary marks a new stage in commentaries on the Epistles, recognising as it does the importance of the polemical situation of the letters for their interpretation and the need to explain what the author was trying to do and the limitations of his approach. Raymond Brown's commentary develops this most fully . . ." (*The Theology of the Johannine Epistles* 121). This seems extraordinary until the bibliography listed on the same page is noted. There the date given for Houlden's commentary is correctly 1973, but the date for Schnackenburg's commentary is listed as 1979.

On the other side of the Atlantic, R. Alan Culpepper, in his brief treatment of "1-2-3 John" in the Proclamation series says: "Rudolf Schnackenburg, whose commentary was originally published in 1975, treats 1 John . . ." ("1-2-3 John," 113). Although this still places Schnackenburg's work prior to the publication of Brown's commentary, Culpepper goes on to say: "Like Brown, Schnackenburg finds the elder in debate with one group of opponents . . ." (ibid.) Given the magnitude and influence of Brown's commentary, it is not surprising that other works are measured against his. However, it is misleading if earlier works that paved the way for his commentary are made to look dependent on his. Had I not used Schnackenburg's commentary in the mid-1960s I might not have noticed. My point is to draw attention to the significant influence of Schnackenburg's commentary on English-speaking scholarship on the Johannine Epistles.

Of course Schnackenburg recognized points where Brown differed from his interpretation, but the main line of Brown's advance came from the massive detail of 812 packed pages. Brown left no stone unturned in his review of scholarship. His own interpretation was also developed exhaustively. Yet neither Schnackenburg nor Brown anticipated some of the turns soon to occur in Johannine scholarship. What seemed to be a "side track" became more of a main path when the reconstruction of the history of the Johannine community was put in question.

Schnackenburg's literary analysis builds on the observations of Law (*The Tests of Life* 29), who was broadly followed, though less clearly, by Brooke (*Commentary* 13, 17, 21, 31). Law recognized the claims of the false teachers, identified by a variety of formulae: "If we say . . ." (1:6, 8, 10); "The one who says . . ." (2:4, 6, 9); "If anyone says . . ." (4:20). (See

Schnackenburg, *The Johannine Epistles* 3 and n. 3, and p. 77.) The importance of these claims in constructing a profile of the opponents was an
aspect of my research and appears in my *John, Witness and Theologian*
(1975) 115–25, and more fully in "The Opponents in 1 John" (1986) 48–71.

Building on earlier work, Schnackenburg's commentary uses literary
analysis to demonstrate the scope and character of the argument in 1 John.
In this way he clarifies the struggle with "opponents," "secessionists," or
"heretics," whatever we choose to call those against whom the author of
1 John pits his wits. Like Law and Brooke (*Commentary* xxvii– xxx) before
him, Schnackenburg argued that this struggle largely determined the discussion of issues in the Epistles: "Only the conflict with the opponents
carried on all through the letter needs to be specially highlighted" (*The
Johannine Epistles* 17).

With his usual thoroughness, R. E. Brown drew on earlier work, building
on the tradition that recognized the polemical character of the Epistles. He
wove this together into a comprehensive and persuasive theory that provided a basis for his illuminating interpretation of the Epistles. Yet it is a
mistake to imply that the theory came first and the interpretation later.
The theory is constructed on the basis of a detailed and careful examination of all the evidence, both internal and external. The theory is tested
against the text to provide a detailed exegesis. Stated briefly, Brown's
position is that the Epistles were written about the same time in response
to a schism in the Johannine community. The schism also meant that those
who broke away formed a group that potentially sought to influence
other churches in the Johannine network. The Johannine Epistles are to be
understood as an attempt to deal with the aftermath of the schism and to
limit any further damage.

Brown argued that there is no evidence in the Epistles of any external
influence leading to a heresy among the schismatics. Rather, the conflict
between the Elder and the schismatics arose out of divergent interpretations of the Johannine tradition now found in the Gospel. Brown acknowledged that the Gospel might not have been published by the time
the Epistles were written, but he argued that the tradition had received its
fundamental shaping prior to the writing of the Epistles. Here he is close
to Schnackenburg's position:

> Most scholars today agree about the priority of the Gospel. Menoud's
> suggestion that the letter was composed between the dissemination of
> the gospel tradition in oral form and its completion in writing, has much
> to commend it. (*The Johannine Epistles* 39)

But Brown distinctively develops his own theory by arguing that the author
of the Epistles and the schismatics each formulated their positions on the
basis of their interpretation of the Gospel in whatever form they had it.

Although Brown recognized that priority of final composition could not
be demonstrated, he worked with the assumption that the Gospel was
known in more or less its present form. This was a control over the tendency to disregard parts of the Gospel if they did not fit the hypothesis.

Brown saw no evidence that there was more than one group of secessionists faced by the Elder. Careful analysis allowed him to reconstruct
the views of the opposition in a nuanced and credible fashion. In doing
this he resisted suggestions that were already being made to the effect that
the polemical form of the Epistles was simply a rhetorical strategy (*The
Epistles of John* 48–49). However, his brief critique has not held back the
growing tide of this approach.

There is now a trend to minimize the controversial nature of 1 John by
arguing that although there was a schism it was of minor significance,
past and over by the time the Epistles were written. Thus it is wrong to see
the Epistles as preoccupied with the controversy. It is also argued, against
the use of the formulae to identify the opponents, that (at least in some of
the formulae) reference is to what "we say" (1:6, 8, 10), not what "they
say." Hence the author cannot be talking of the secessionists. Schnackenburg had already foreseen this objection (*The Johannine Epistles* 77), arguing that the use of "we" does not mean that those who use the slogans are
still members of the community. Rather it indicates the perceived danger
of their views for those who remained in the community. The Epistle reflects the author's awareness that the schism, though now in the recent
past, still has the power to harm the community. Anyone who has experi-
enced a serious schism in a community will know of the trauma it leaves
in its wake.

In my summary treatment of 1975 I noted: "Though the heretics had
withdrawn, the community was in turmoil and continued to be threatened
by the false teaching" (*John, Witness and Theologian* 116). In light of recent
criticisms of the approach that makes the response to the schism central to
the purpose of 1 John, this brief statement needs to be supported in detail
in the commentary. Here a number of points can be made. Yes, the actual
schism is over, but 1 John reveals that the effects of the schism are every-
where to be found. Robert Law, A. E. Brooke, and Rudolf Schnackenburg
have made the point of the pervasive evidence of the conflict with the
schismatics in 1 John. It was a bitter and painful event and those who remained were traumatized by it. Their assurance was shaken. Were they
right to stay? Do the schismatics have the truth after all? Clearly 1 John
aims at damage control by seeking to show that those who seceded are
seriously in error. Hence there is polemic against their position. It also
seeks to assure those who remain with the Elder that they are abiding in
the truth and that they have eternal life. Thus the language of the Epistle
works in two ways: polemically against the *teaching* of the opponents, and

with a pastoral tone to reestablish the assurance of the readers. Using a series of tests concerning the true faith and love for one another, 1 John aims to expose those in error and assure those abiding in the truth.

Although 1 John is addressed to those who remain in the community of faith, not to the secessionists, it seeks to expose the error of the secessionists' way. There is an unmistakable polemical edge to 1 John. At the same time there is a pastoral concern for those whose faith has been badly shaken. This 1 John seeks to reestablish and confirm. The polemic is a necessary stage in dealing with the continuing disturbance and consequent uncertainty in the community, which could only be handled if the major positions of the opponents were seen to be refuted. The serious nature of the schism is revealed in 1 John 2:18-19:

> [18] Little children, it is the last hour, and as you heard, Antichrist is coming, and now many antichrists have appeared; from which we know, it is the last hour. [19] They went out from us, but they were not of us; for if they were of us, they would have remained with us; but that they may be revealed, because not all are of us.

It would be surprising if the whole Epistle did not revolve around the issues the schism raised. This is the position of Law, Schnackenburg and Brown. Yet the case for this position now stands under strong attack. It is not that the schism goes unrecognized by critics. Rather, critics argue that it is not central to 1 John. Other ways of reading the polemical material have been developed. Already in 1979 Pheme Perkins (*The Johannine Epistles* xxi–xxiii) was arguing for a more sensitive rhetorical understanding of the language. Brown responded to this approach, contending that the evidence of significant conflict, indeed schism, should not be reduced to rhetoric (*The Epistles of John* 48–49).

It remains to be seen whether these rhetorical alternatives can be as persuasive as an interpretation based on the recognition of the Epistle as a response to the aftermath of an actual schism. Of course it is a rhetorical response, but the rhetoric is aimed at the trauma left as an aftermath of the schism. Although the first shock is over, there was grave danger that those who remained might defect to the secessionists one by one. 1 John is not a communication seeking to win back the secessionists. They are branded as deceivers, antichrists, false prophets. This is not conciliatory language. The readers are left in no doubt that at the heart of the error 1 John attacks is the refusal to accept the Johannine christology. This is the first step in the strategy. It is aimed at galvanizing resistance to the secessionists and dispelling their attraction for the remaining believers. The second step is the pastoral building up of the assurance of those who believe what 1 John teaches, the assurance that they indeed are children of God and have eternal life.

We have no reliable external evidence concerning the author(s) of the
letters and the situations from which and for which they wrote. The letters
themselves provide the only clues we have. It has become common to attempt to reconstruct as much as possible about these issues from what is
written in the letters. Those critical of this approach refer to it as "mirror
reading" and emphasize the circularity of the process. This criticism is
more potent when directed against the reconstruction of community history reflected in the Gospel. The Epistles deal directly with the community and aspects of its life are explicitly the subject of what is written (see
2:18-27; 4:1-6). Nevertheless, caution is necessary in reconstructing the
situation for which 1 John was written, because it was not the author's
purpose to set out a systematic description of the situation. The author
presupposed much of the situation because it was well known to the readers of the letters. Further, we have only the point of view of the author(s)
of the Epistles. We should not expect to find a sympathetic presentation of
alternative views. It is of the faults of the opponents, rather than their
virtues, that we expect to read in these letters. At the same time, a gross
distortion of their views is not likely to be effective in turning the tide of
sympathy against the opponents.

Since the mid-1960s I have argued that the Johannine Epistles are collectively a response to the consequences of a schism impacting the local
churches under the influence of the Johannine tradition. This need not
imply a common authorship of the writings perceived as the Johannine
literature. An alternative to common authorship is the recognition of a
Johannine school. (See R. Alan Culpepper, *The Johannine School* [1975], especially 258–59, 287–88.)

In recent years I have become increasingly persuaded that common
authorship of the "Epistles" is more likely than their composition by multiple authors. A good case can be made for thinking 2 John was an introductory accompaniment to 1 John, sent to a number of local churches. The
general form of address "to the elect lady and her children" makes the
letter a suitable address to a number of local churches. Given the accompanying letter, which summarizes succinctly the central issues of 1 John,
the character of 1 John becomes less problematic. It deals with the issue of
the schism and the aftermath of trauma, confusion, and uncertainty. It is
in a form that could be used by the author in his own church, or sent with
a covering letter (2 John) to neighboring churches. This probably means
that 1 John was written first and 2 John was then written as an accompanying letter. But they were composed with the same situation in mind.

3 John was written still later but in relation to the same general crisis.
Addressing a specific problem that had emerged in one local community,
it is directed to one of the local churches in an area where Diotrephes
exercised leadership. Because Diotrephes refused to acknowledge the

authority of 1 John and forbade the giving of hospitality to supporters of the Elder, 3 John is an attempt to reestablish his authority in that church by calling on the support of Gaius and encouraging him to remain loyal. If this reading is correct the canonical order of the Epistles is the chronological order and only the third is a genuine popular *personal* letter, 2 John being a circular letter to a group of churches introducing 1 John.

It is sometimes argued that the subject of 3 John sets it apart from 1 and 2 John. This is true in a sense. But 2 John introduces the question of hospitality. Readers of 2 John are exhorted not to provide hospitality to those who do not agree with the Elder's teaching. 3 John deals with the reaction of Diotrephes and his refusal to show hospitality to the brothers who came from the Elder. Diotrephes excommunicated anyone in his community who provided them with hospitality (3 John 9-10). Gaius, to whom the letter was written, is commended for showing them hospitality. Obviously Gaius was under pressure and the Elder sought to strengthen his support in that area. That Gaius was able to resist the authority of Diotrephes suggests that he was not a member of his house church. He might have been one of those excommunicated by Diotrephes (3 John 9-10). Had this been the case the Elder would not have needed to inform Gaius of the situation, though the point could be to let Gaius know he was aware of how matters stood. Perhaps it is more likely that Gaius was the leader of another house church close to Diotrephes. The Elder was aware that Gaius might fall under the influence of Diotrephes and wrote 3 John in an attempt to guard against this possibility and to ensure continuing support in the area. Thus 2 and 3 John are not unrelated as they deal with the strategy of hospitality as it was used by each side in the conflict.

Recent studies have put in question the reading of the Epistles in a Hellenistic and Gnostic context. In 1966 John C. O'Neill (*The Puzzle of 1 John*) argued that the basis of 1 John is to be found in "twelve poetic admonitions" originally belonging to the writings of a Jewish sect similar to the community whose writings were found at Qumran. He has shown that the thought, language, and style of 1 John have important parallels with the texts from Qumran. His argument that the author of 1 John was a sectarian Jew is persuasive. But the suggestion that the opponents in 1 John were Jews who failed to accept Jesus as the Messiah (*The Puzzle of 1 John* 6-7) seemed to me, when I wrote my thesis (1965-67), to raise insurmountable objections. One of the points made by C. K. Barrett (*The Gospel of John and Judaism*, 1975) is that Jewish elements in a writing can be present for different reasons: because the subject matter is Jewish, or the author is Jewish, or the author is writing to a Jewish audience. Of course all of these conditions might apply. But the language of a writing could display Jewish influence simply because the author was Jewish. Had the Johannine Epistles been written to a Jewish audience we would expect appeals to the Jewish Scriptures. Quotations from the Scriptures are lacking in the Johannine Epistles. Appeals to Scripture do not demonstrate a Jewish audience because they became the Scripture of Gentile Christians also. But the absence of appeal to the Scriptures in a controversial situation would be extraordinary in writings addressed to Jewish readers.

O'Neill notes that the idea that the polemic of 1 John is directed against Jews is generally rejected. He names Rudolf Schnackenburg as one who had recently denied this possibility (*Die Johannesbriefe* [1953] 14–16, 137–38; second edition [1963] 16–17, 156). That the opponents were Jews had been advocated as long ago as 1904 by Alois Wurm *(Die Irrleherer im ersten Johannesbrief)*. Recent studies of the Epistles have again moved in this direction. O'Neill refers for support to John A. T. Robinson's essay, "The Destination and Purpose of the Johannine Epistles." This first appeared in *NTS* 7 (1960–61) and was reprinted in Robinson's *Twelve New Testament Studies* (1962).

O'Neill wrote from a context in which Gospel and Epistles were viewed in a common Hellenistic milieu. The Qumran discoveries were beginning to make an impact but the revolution in Johannine studies was yet to take place. The first edition of J. Louis Martyn's *History and Theology in the Fourth Gospel* appeared in 1968. While various earlier studies foreshadowed this development, it was Martyn's work that provided the catalyst for a paradigm shift in the study of the Fourth Gospel. Though aspects of his study have been questioned subsequently, recognition of the Jewish character of this Gospel remains secure. It may be that in time we will rethink what it means for this Gospel to be Jewish. It is unclear whether O'Neill thought that his argument concerning the Jewish context of 1 John would also involve a Jewish context for the Gospel and, if that were the case, how that might affect the order of composition and relationship between 1 John and the Gospel.

Awareness of the implications of the Qumran texts for the study of the Gospel and the situation in which it was shaped encouraged scholars, led by J. Louis Martyn and Raymond E. Brown, to a reading of the Gospel in a Jewish context of the late first century. The first volume of Brown's two-volume Anchor Bible commentary, *The Gospel of John*, was published in 1966. The shifting paradigm for the Gospel did not draw the Epistles with it. Brown went on to work out what happened to the tradition and to the believers subsequent to their exclusion from the synagogue. See his *The Community of the Beloved Disciple* and *The Epistles of John*, 1982. While Brown does not stress a move to a non-Jewish context, that is implied by the breakdown of the relationship with the synagogue. Certainly he allows for the entry of Samaritans and Gentiles into the Johannine community. The Johannine Epistles come at the end of this process, but so does the final editing of the Gospel. The shaping of the tradition by the relationship of believers with the synagogue took place before the publication of the Gospel.

Brown's approach refined his understanding of a process that had emerged in Johannine studies. The Gospel came to be seen in a dominantly Jewish context and the Epistles, after a rupture of relations with the synagogue, in relation to a Gentile context. That picture now becomes more nuanced because the evidence suggests that the Gospel itself was finally edited and published subsequent to the breach between the Johannine believers and the synagogue. Later strata of the Gospel may overlap the time of the writing of the Epistles.

Still, the nature of the Gospel separates it from the Epistles to a degree. The Gospel embodies Jesus tradition, even if that tradition has developed in a process of reflection and interpretation. The Epistles too contain tradition, but it is not so directly Jesus tradition. It is the teaching tradition concerning Jesus applied to the situation of the day. There is a subtle yet clear distinction between these two forms of tradition. In the Gospel the Jesus tradition is interpreted in the context of the life of the believing community. There the reflection, believed to be the product of the work of the Spirit Paraclete, takes its point of view from the resurrection or glorification of Jesus (John 2:22; 12:16; 14:16-17, 26; 16:13-15). The story of Jesus is told, illuminated by this perspective, and in a way that is relevant to the lives of Jewish believers toward the end of the first century C.E. The tradition in the Epistles is the transmitted Johannine teaching concerning Jesus. This is overtly directed to the issues affecting the faith and life of the Johannine community. It embodies the new command of Jesus, which is treated as old, indeed as the foundational commandment for the community.

Inasmuch as this approach involves a process in which the Epistles can be identified with the situation at the completion of the Gospel, it is possible to see Gospel and Epistles published more or less at the same time. Nevertheless, the most important factor shaping the development of the Gospel was the process of a changing relationship between believers and the synagogue. This became more and more of a struggle until at last the strain became too great and the relationship broke down. The struggle and the breach left deep marks on the Johannine Gospel tradition. Such marks cannot be found in the Epistles. This suggests that the Epistles were shaped in a later crisis. Indeed, they bear the marks of another breach, an internal schism (1 John 2:18-19).

Subsequent to O'Neill's study a number of scholars argued that the Epistles precede the Gospel or at least were written at about the same time, confronting the same issues. Those who advocate this view often fail to note that Brown and others have already allowed for overlap between the process of the composition of the Gospel and the writing of the Epistles. Although Brown published his commentary in 1982, Judith Lieu says of

Kenneth Grayston's commentary (*The Johannine Epistles,* 1984) that he alone presents a sustained argument that 1 John precedes rather than follows the Gospel. Grayston himself notes (*The Johannine Epistles* 10–11) that if the Gospel is thought to have been composed in a process it is possible to think of the situation confronted by the Epistles contributing to the composition of the Gospel. This is true of Brown's treatment in his *Johannine Epistles* (1982). Recognition of the process in the composition of the Gospel allows for its completion later in the more Hellenized situation of the Epistles, rather than pulling the Epistles back into the Jewish situation of the Gospel. Some scholars are now arguing for an earlier composition date for the Epistles in a continuing Jewish context. Alternatively it may be argued that in the first century there was no rupture of relations between Jewish Christians and other Jews and that the Gospel and Epistles were written in a Jewish context. Against this view is the absence of important Jewish evidence from the Epistles.

Judith Lieu's work on the Johannine Epistles has provided a new impetus for their study. Her books, *The Second and Third Epistles of John* (1986) and *The Theology of the Johannine Epistles* (1991) are among the most significant on the Johannine Epistles in recent years. From the beginning she has been an advocate of the distinctive witness of the Epistles, arguing that they have too often been subsumed as examples of the theology of the Gospel. Her aim was to allow the Epistles to speak for themselves. Given that the first of her books was on 2 and 3 John it comes as no surprise that this also means listening to the distinctive voices of each of those small Epistles. In this she is surely right, though I continue to think that with such scanty documents we have trouble making sense of them if they are unrelated to each other and any other document known to us, such as 1 John. Fortunately, the probability is that, even if not by the same author, the Epistles are related to each other and to the Gospel. I am inclined today to think that the evidence favors the acceptance of the common authorship of the Epistles.

Lieu does not suggest that each Epistle is a totally independent document unrelated to the rest. She acknowledges that the small letters (2–3 John) are part of the Johannine tradition (*The Second and Third Epistles* 125, 166). She also recognizes that the history and tradition of the Johannine community can be traced through the Gospel and Epistles. Nevertheless, at other points Lieu shows herself to be uneasy about the way circumstances or past history are "read off" from distinctively Johannine passages (*The Second and Third Epistles* 214; see also 208 n. 91 and 210–11 n. 97). In particular she questions whether the Gospel and Epistles represent different stages in the history of the Johannine community (*The Second and Third Epistles* 207), with the Gospel rooted in an external conflict with the synagogue of which there is no trace in the Epistles, while 1 John was born out of a schism in the community of which the Gospel knows nothing (*The Second and Third Epistles* 212).

Lieu questions the sequential view of the Johannine writings. She argues that the self-understanding and general context of the community is fundamentally the same throughout. What changes is the theological exponent, each of whom responds in significantly different ways (*The Second and Third Epistles* 207, 215). Only the Fourth Evangelist builds his theology centered on Christ, while the Epistles find their focus in the community. That this route leads to a dead end is suggested because the ultimate test is whether witness is borne to Christ alone (*The Second and Third Epistles* 215–16).

Much of this critique is persuasive. It begins by recognizing that the Johannine writings do not claim common authorship (*The Second and Third Epistles* 169). This paves the way for looking at the diversity of the Johannine witness in a variety of theological responses at different levels. Yet they are held together as the Johannine literature by the Johannine tradition. Here I think Lieu must go further in a number of directions. She recognizes the possibility that what links 1 John to the Gospel might be "community traditions behind the Gospel" (*The Second and Third Epistles* 210).

My own position may be summarized as follows:

1. I do not think that the Johannine tradition was shaped by a community; it was shaped in and for a community but not by a community. I think one foundational mind provides the essential character of the Johannine tradition. This teacher probably influenced a small group of "disciples" we can call, for the want of a better term, the Johannine School. In the index to Lieu's *The Second and Third Epistles* she lists three references to the Johannine School. There is no attempt to distinguish the Johannine School from the community. In my view the school sought to shape the community and worked in response to various crises through which the community passed. But without the formative tradition, shaped by the Johannine School, the crises would not have produced the Johannine community. Furthermore, we must assume some slippage between the School and the Community.

2. Given the development of the Johannine tradition prior to the publication of the Gospel, the view that the Johannine writings are different theological responses addressed to the same situation (*The Second and Third Epistles* 207, 216) conceals a multitude of complexities. One of these concerns the conflict in the synagogue in the Gospel. Given that this event lay some time in the past when the Gospel was published, it is possible that some traditions enshrined in the Gospel were decisively shaped in that context. I think the evidence suggests that the writing of the Gospel was a lengthy process and concede that much of the process might have been in the form of oral composition. Because the final breach was a serious traumatic event, wounds caused by the breach continued to be felt for some

time after the event and are pervasively evident in the Gospel. Very likely what I have called an event is better understood as a process, over a course of time. Though the Epistles were written subsequent to the breach that separated the Johannine believers from the synagogue, they show no sign of this particular trauma. Whether or not this breach has anything to do with *birkath ha-minim* is probably irrelevant. Lieu rightly recognizes that "9.22 etc. and John's hostility against the Jews undoubtedly imply the bitterness of the conflict" (*The Second and Third Epistles* 187 n. 44; see also C. K. Barrett, *John* 361–62).

3. The breach with the synagogue left evidence of trauma in the Gospel. The evangelist shaped the Gospel in response to this event. The Epistles provide no evidence of that breach, no evidence of a struggle with the Jews, no mention of the Jews at all.

4. The schism evident in the Epistles is one that rent the Johannine community (see 1 John 2:18-19). This is quite different from the struggle between those who believed in Jesus and the synagogue. The probability is that these two events occurred in order: breach with the synagogue followed by schism in the community.

5. There is no *clear* evidence of the schism in the Johannine community in the Gospel, though there may be clues that point to it (see John 6:60, 66). In the Gospel the rift between believers concerns those who sought to remain hidden within the synagogue by refusing to confess their faith openly (John 9:22; 12:42).

There is specific reference to a schism in the believing community in 1 John 2:18-19. Clearly this was no trivial event. The author refers to those who seceded from the Johannine community as false prophets, deceivers, antichrists. The bitterness that is apparent reveals the seriousness of the schism for the author and the community. The split is indeed over. The trauma remains. But that is not all. Those who went out were until recently members of the community, and the leaders at least were significant enough to be dubbed "antichrists." The danger still exists for the faithful who remain. The author of 1 John is sensitively aware that his readers may be seduced to follow those who have separated themselves from the community. That is the context for the writing of the Johannine Epistles. For a comparison of Lieu's work with the positions of Martin Hengel and Teresa Okure see my *The Quest for the Messiah* 80–87.

### For Reference and Further Study

Barrett, C. Kingsley. *The Gospel According to St John.* London: S.P.C.K., 1955, 2nd ed. 1978.

_____. *The Gospel of John and Judaism.* London: S.P.C.K., 1975.

Bousset, Wilhelm. *Kyrios Christos; Geschichte des Christusglaubens von den Anfängen des Christentums bis Irenaeus.* Göttingen: Vandenhoeck & Ruprecht, 1913. English: *Kyrios Christos; A History of the Belief in Christ from the Beginnings of Christianity to Irenaeus.* Translated by John E. Steely. Nashville: Abingdon, 1970.

Brooke, Alan England. *A Critical and Exegetical Commentary on the Johannine Epistles.* Edinburgh: T & T Clark, 1912.

Brown, Raymond E. *The Gospel According to John.* AB 29/29A. Garden City, N.Y.: Doubleday, 1967.

_____. *The Community of the Beloved Disciple.* New York: Paulist, 1979.

_____. *The Epistles of John.* AB 30. Garden City, N.Y.: Doubleday, 1982.

Bultmann, Rudolf. "Analyse des ersten Johannesbriefes," in *Festgabe für Adolf Jülicher zum 70. Geburtstag.* Tübingen: J.C.B. Mohr, 1927, 138–58.

_____. "Die kirchliche Redaktion des ersten Johannesbriefes," in Werner Schmauch, ed., *In Memoriam Ernst Lohmeyer.* Stuttgart: Evangelisches Verlagswerks, 1951, 189–201.

_____. "Johannesbriefe," in *RGG³.* Tübingen: J.C.B. Mohr, 1959, 837–40.

_____. *Die drei Johannesbriefe.* KEK 7th ed. Göttingen: Vandehoeck & Ruprecht, 1967. English: *The Johannine Epistles; A Commentary on the Johannine Epistles.* Translated by R. Philip O'Hara with Lane C. McGaughy and Robert Funk. Philadelphia, Fortress, 1973.

_____. "The Interpretation of the Fourth Gospel." Review of C. H. Dodd's *The Interpretation of the Fourth Gospel. NTS* 1 (1954–55) 77–91. English translation by W. C. Robinson in *Harvard Divinity Bulletin* 27 (1963) 9–22.

Carroll, K. L. "The Fourth Gospel and the Exclusion of Christians from the Synagogue," *BJRL* 40 (1957–58) 19–32.

Culpepper, R. Alan. *The Johannine School.* SBLDS 26. Missoula: Scholars, 1975.

_____. "1–2–3 John," in Gerhard Krodel, ed., *The General Letters.* Proclamation Commentaries. Revised and enlarged ed. Minneapolis: Fortress, 1995.

Dodd, Charles Harold. *The Johannine Epistles.* MNTC. London: Hodder and Stoughton, 1946.

_____. *The Interpretation of the Fourth Gospel.* Cambridge: Cambridge University Press, 1953.

Dunn, James D. G. *The Partings of the Ways between Christianity and Judaism and their Significance for the Character of Christianity.* London: S.C.M.; Philadelphia: Trinity Press International, 1991.

_____, ed. *Jews and Christians: The Parting of the Ways, AD 70–135: The Second Durham–Tübingen Research Symposium on Earliest Christianity and Judaism, Durham, September 1989.* Tübingen: J.C.B. Mohr [Paul Siebeck], 1992.

Grayston, Kenneth. *The Johannine Epistles.* NCB. Grand Rapids: Eerdmans, 1984.

Häring, Theodor. "Gedankengang und Grundgedanke des ersten Johannesbriefes," in Adolf Harnack, et al., *Theologische Abhandlungen Carl von Weizsäcker zu seinem siebzigsten Geburtstage,11. December 1892.* Freiburg: J.C.B. Mohr [Paul Siebeck], 1892, 173–200.

_____. *Die Johannesbriefe.* Stuttgart: Calwer, 1927.

Hengel, Martin. *Die johanneische Frage: ein Lösungsversuch.* Tübingen: J.C.B. Mohr [Paul Siebeck], 1993. English: *The Johannine Question.* London: S.C.M., 1989.

Holtzmann, Heinrich J. *Evangelium des Johannes.* Hand-Commentar zum Neuen
    Testament 4:1. 3rd ed. Tübingen: J.C.B. Möhr [Paul Siebeck], 1908.
_____. *Das Problem des 1 Johannesbriefes in seinem Verhältnis zum Evangelium.*
    *Jahrbuch für Protestant. Theologie* 1881, 1882.
Houlden, James Leslie. *A Commentary on the Johannine Epistles.* HNTC. New York:
    Harper & Row, 1973.
Klauck, Hans-Josef. *Der erste Johannesbrief.* EKK 23/1. Zürich: Benziger; Neukirchen-
    Vluyn: Neukirchener Verlag, 1991.
_____. *Der zweite und dritte Johannesbrief.* EKK 23/2. Zurich: Benziger;
    Neukirchen-Vluyn: Neukirchener Verlag, 1992.
Law, Robert. *The Tests of Life: A Study of the First Epistle of St. John.* Edinburgh: T & T
    Clark, 1909.
Lieu, Judith. *The Second and Third Epistles of John.* Edinburgh: T & T Clark, 1986.
_____. *The Theology of the Johannine Epistles.* Cambridge: Cambridge University
    Press, 1991.
Martyn, J. Louis. *History and Theology in the Fourth Gospel.* New York: Harper &
    Row, 1968, 2nd ed. 1979.
Okure, Teresa. *The Johannine Approach to Mission: A Contextual Study of John 4:1-32.*
    WUNT 2nd ser. 31. Tübingen: J.C.B. Möhr [Paul Siebeck], 1988.
O'Neill. John C. *The Puzzle of 1 John.* London: S.P.C.K., 1966.
Painter, John. *John, Witness and Theologian.* London: S.P.C.K. 1975, 2nd ed. 1978; 3rd
    ed. Melbourne: Beacon Hill, 1980.
_____. "C. H. Dodd and the Christology of the Fourth Gospel," *JTSA* 59 (July
    1987) 42–56.
_____. *The Quest for the Messiah.* Edinburgh: T & T Clark, 1991, 2nd ed. Nash-
    ville: Abingdon, 1993.
Parkes, James. *The Conflict of the Church and the Synagogue: A Study of the Origins of
    Antisemitism.* London: Soncino, 1934; repr. New York: Atheneum, 1969.
Perkins, Pheme. *The Johannine Epistles.* New Testament Message 21. Wilmington,
    Del.: Michael Glazier, 1979.
Robinson, John A. T. *Twelve New Testament Studies.* SBT 34. London: S.C.M., 1962.
Schnackenburg, Rudolf. *Die Johannesbriefe.* HThK 13/3. Freiburg, Basel, and
    Vienna: Herder, 1953. English: *The Johannine Epistles.* Translated by Reginald
    and Ilse Fuller. New York: Crossroad, 1992.
Westcott, Brooks Foss. *The Epistles of St John: The Greek Text, with Notes and Essays.*
    London: Macmillan, 1883.
Wurm, Alois. *Die Irrleherer im ersten Johannesbrief.* Biblische Studien 8/1. Freiburg
    and St. Louis: Herder, 1903.

# INTRODUCTION

## 1. A RHETORICAL AND HISTORICAL COMMENTARY

Writing a commentary on the Johannine Epistles is a somewhat more difficult task at the beginning of the twenty-first century than when the twentieth century began. In this instance it is not, as is the case with the Gospel of John, because of the proliferation of commentaries and other studies. Rather it is because the recognized paradigms for interpreting the Epistles have broken down. Changing interpretative paradigms are not always easy to explain. Sometimes a paradigm shift is the result of exhausting the potential of one paradigm so that attention is turned to another. There is an element of this in the development of Johannine studies. But the situation is more complex. Two great discoveries of ancient libraries have revolutionized our understanding of Second Temple Judaism and Gnosticism. As a result our understanding of both of these traditions is more firmly based but also less clear. The lack of clarity is a result of the evidence revealing that these traditions are more complex and pluralistic than had previously been understood. The result has been to situate the Johannine tradition more firmly in the traditions of Second Temple Judaism and to cast doubt on any Gnostic influence.

At the beginning of the twentieth century acceptance of the traditional view of Johannine authorship was quite widespread. On this view the Gospel and Epistles were the work of the apostle John. Today this is a minority view. In its place the idea of a Johannine school developed so that a number of anonymous leaders in the Johannine communities were thought to be the independent authors of the various works. The Johannine communities were believed to have shared something like a common history leading to a distinctive interpretation of the Jesus tradition. The various works were interpreted in the context of that history. Today there is a growing number of scholars who consider theories about the Johannine school and the history of the Johannine communities to be pure speculation. Their alternative is to read each of the Johannine writings "independently." Independently can mean each one in its own right and without reference to the others. It can also mean independently of history, so that each work provides something like its own whole world of meaning. This approach is literary rather than historical and may make use of rhetorical analysis in the process of interpretation.

This commentary proceeds on the assumption that literary analysis is the necessary point to *begin* the work of interpretation. The reading on which this commentary is based began with each work independently, making no assumptions about the order of the various Johannine works and their relationship to each other. But this is only the beginning. By giving priority to each writing in turn I am attempting to establish the order of the writings and their relationship to each other. In the end it is important to know as much as we can about the circumstances in which each of the works was written and the relation of each to the others. If such knowledge lacks certainty, the risk is necessary if we are to understand these texts. They clearly have a specific historical context. To read the texts quite independently of each other is in the end wrong if they have some relationship. To read them as purely literary phenomena is certainly wrong.

The texts deal with issues, actions and responses that belong to specific situations. To treat them simply as repositories of meaning to be unlocked in the head of the reader, without reference to any realities in the world, is manifestly mistaken. Readers need to do the best they can in relating what is written to events, issues, actions and responses. To do otherwise is to trivialize the texts and turn the process of reading into a game in which the reader is in control of the process.

Reading texts is often described in terms of a process that has moved attention from author to text and now finally to the reader. This is sometimes characterized as locating meaning behind the text, in the text, or in front of the text. Of course we have no access to the meaning of texts except through the process of reading, and readers are active agents in the process. That is not in dispute. The area of dispute concerns the way texts may convey meaning communicated by an author concerning life in the past. Hermeneutically the task of understanding an author from the past is not different, in principle, from coming to understand another person in the present. In practice there are some differences. The author from the past cannot respond directly to us to clarify and correct misreadings. But the careful author may foresee what needs to be said in order to make the intended meaning clear. Naturally difficulties increase as texts become more remote from the author and the circumstances of writing. Where those circumstances can be reconstructed with some degree of certainty and the text can be set in the context of other writings by the same author, the modern reader has resources for a good understanding of the text in its literary and historical contexts.

In the New Testament no texts are better placed than the letters of Paul. Even though there are problems, the existence of the Acts of the Apostles and other relevant evidence, archaeological and literary, enables us to frame Paul's mission with a considerable degree of accuracy. The Pauline corpus also provides a literary context in which there is broad agreement about the chronological order of the letters, though there is some debate and the authenticity of some letters is questioned. Out of this has come broad agreement about the *meaning* of Paul's letters. Of course there is dispute about the fine detail. The disputed areas are complex because they arise for different reasons. Some areas of the texts are linguistically resistant to clear meaning. Other aspects of the texts seem to be inconsistent, and readers have to decide whether we are confronted with self-contradiction, inconsistency, a self-conscious change of views, a tension in the author's views, or views that can be held together when the full circumstances are known. Different readings of Paul also emerge because readers approach the texts with a variety of evaluative stances. Nevertheless, a high degree of agreement is possible today among scholars working on the letters of Paul.

Turning to the Johannine Epistles, the reader is not in such a strong position. First, we are no longer able to appeal to the known author of these letters. We do not know that the Epistles were written by the author of the Gospel or even that they have a common author. That the Gospel and Epistles are products of the Johannine school is made probable by the shared language, style, and themes of these writings. Much of what they share sets them apart from other early Christian writings. Thus if these texts are not the product of a common author we need at least to recognize the influence of a common tradition in them. Whether the common tradition is transmitted by the Gospel, which influenced the letters directly, or underlies all of these writings in the form of a Johannine school, is a good question.

There is a growing diversity of views over the Johannine literature. One reason for this situation is the emergence of a literary criticism that is suspicious of a historical critical approach and in recent forms adopts a postmodern perspective. In extreme expression this approach may limit the meaning of reading texts to some form of autobiography. This kind of reading makes a virtue of a problem that has long been recognized, for example by Rudolf Bultmann in his 1957 essay, "Is Exegesis Without Presuppositions Possible?" While ruling out prejudiced conclusions being read into the text, Bultmann recognized that the exegete's mind is not a *tabula rasa*. The exegete brings questions and a way of reading the text to the task of exegesis. No exegete can avoid this. The question is, must we make a virtue of necessity? That is, do we simply affirm the interpretation as our own regardless of what others make of it? If this is the situation, then all exegesis is a form of autobiography. Or is what has been described as a necessity only the starting point from which the exegete seeks to move, a dilemma from which good exegesis may extricate us? Is it possible that good exegesis may develop from the particular point of view of one reader to increasingly grasp the point of view of the text as construed by the author? This commentary recognizes the difficulty posed by the pluralism of modern readings and seeks to find a way back to meaning conveyed in the texts of the Johannine letters.

Even when we are seeking to find the meaning of the text in its past context, the hermeneutical task inevitably involves self-consciously starting with our own present understanding. *We* can start nowhere else. Precisely in the awareness of the different understandings of others we have the opportunity for understanding the past. However difficult it is to grasp the meaning of another person, doing justice to their point of view, we manage the task daily with some degree of effectiveness. Of course there can be misunderstandings and in fact this is often the case. That we can recognize this is itself a sign of hope because we are at least aware of the difference between our own ideas and those of the other person. Misunderstandings are reduced and controlled by our efforts to understand the point of view of the other person.

The task is, in principle, the same when we seek to read texts from the past. We can only start where we are, but we can go out of our way to grasp the perspective from the past expressed in the text. The past is like another country, another culture, and all the effort that is necessary to understand a person from another country and culture is called into play to understand a text from the past. We need to learn the language of the text, including the particular nuances of the language found in the text. We need to learn about the subject that the text communicates, and so on. All of this leads us to some grasp on the text from the past. In our dialogue with the text from the past the only answers it can give to the questions we pose are the answers given in advance. For this reason the reader needs to be particularly sensitive to the nuances of the text in order to safeguard its integrity. Thus the reader of the Johannine Epistles needs to be sensitive to the way the text may correct and modify tentative interpretations.

The commentary that follows does not proceed via a detailed debate with contemporary scholarship. Such a debate is the basis of the reading expounded here and defended on the basis of the evidence of the text and other evidence more or less contemporary with the Johannine Epistles. To have debated all scholarly views on every point would have been tedious for the reader and would have expanded the scope of the commentary beyond reasonable limits. The commentary is outfitted with a "Historical Prolegomenon" so that the reader is made aware of where this commentary fits in the history of Johannine scholarship.

Because textual, grammatical, and syntactical problems abound in the texts of the Johannine Epistles it has been necessary to use quite extensive "notes." In this way the more technical discussion has been kept separate from the "Interpretation." Hopefully this allows the reader to follow the flow of the rhetoric of the Epistles. Thus the Interpretation can be read apart from the notes, but the reader should consult the notes in order to see alternative readings and the evidence and argument for the reading adopted.

In this commentary we are dealing with the sacred page, the page of Scripture. This alters nothing that has been said in terms of the process, and the struggle it involves, of understanding texts from the past. Rather it adds to the task. Because we are dealing with the sacred page there is a continuous tradition of reading that we can trace back to a time quite close to the writing of these texts. That tradition helps in many ways because we have access to interpretations by readers whose native language was Greek, and Greek from a period not very much later than the texts we are reading. This is certainly helpful, but it does not solve all problems, because differences had already emerged in these readings. Further, certain dominant traditions had developed that can no longer be accepted as unquestionably correct. These traditions were not uniformly accepted in the early church, but they provide a rich resource of evidence to be weighed by the contemporary reader.

Interpreting the sacred page in its historical context, using all means at our disposal, is the beginning of the task. Continuous reading of the text as sacred page is an expression of the conviction that the text continues to have vital meaning for us today. That meaning for the present is embedded in the pastness of the text. Only by wrestling with meaning in the past context can the reader discern the implications of the text for the present. Sometimes the implications are immediately apparent. At other times the reader has to struggle with the distinction between the culturally conditioned past and an abiding meaning for the present. No full account can be given of the way this can be done. The task of theology has always struggled with the problem of a living theology as distinct from a fossilized theology. By fossilized I mean the repetition of the same words given in the past without paying attention to the new contexts within which the words are spoken. This is not a live option because the words from the past are in other languages and even scholars who learn these languages do so from the perspective of the present time and cannot wipe out the knowledge this brings.

In the struggle to understand the sacred page and to discern the abiding meaning in the context of the culturally conditioned past there are some clues that may be helpful. The meaning of the text for the present is often to be found in the way the text modifies prevailing meanings and values (see Gal 3:26-28; Eph 5:15–6:9). The meaning of the text for the present is often to be found in the element that opens up the meaning for the future and that may be in tension with aspects that bind meaning to the past. Naturally, for the Johannine tradition meaning is rooted in the past. The witness of the Gospel and Epistles confesses that Jesus Christ has come in the flesh. But this event did not reestablish the old order. Rather, by it the old order was demolished. The Gospel proclaimed Jesus' triumph over the world (16:33), and 1 John affirmed that faith in this Jesus was the victory over the world (5:4). The old was passing away because the true light was already shining (2:8). Or, in the words of the book of Revelation, God says, "Behold, I make all things new!" (21:5). Thus we must expect the new reality of the Gospel truth to be in tension with the old order. When there is tension between meaning that opens up the future and the past that binds, the future seems to hold the key. Nevertheless, the new is embodied in the historically given witness to God in Christ. This is in tension with the world that is encountered by it. The new is grounded in the Gospel, in Christ, in God, not in the world and its values. Distinguishing the two can be complex, as in 1 John where the newness of the Gospel seems to have become what is old in the face of the novelty of worldliness.

Our study proceeds on the basis of a translation that seeks to stay in touch with standard translations to reinforce the sense of a fundamental consensus in the way these texts from the past are read. The reader should be aware, however, that the same English words are open to various interpretations, and choices need to be guided by the underlying Greek. The Greek is also ambiguous, so that the reader working with the English text needs to be alerted to the ambiguity of both the English and the Greek. It is the task of the commentary to make this path as clear as possible. Although the Johannine Epistles are written in simple Greek, with a limited and repetitive vocabulary and syntax (ordering of the words), the thought conveyed is often not simple or clear. It is the task of the translation and notes to work through this complexity to express the meaning of the Greek argued for in the commentary.

The Interpretation deals with a literary reading of the text in its first-century *sense*. As far as possible this reading does not assume specific historical reconstructions. The text is first treated as a literary phenomenon. Certainly intertextual and intratextual nuances and echoes are noted. This careful literary analysis is the basis of the next step. It is assumed that these texts are the expression of a particular historical context and that the meaning is best grasped in that context. The texts have a literary context and a historical context. The two should not be confused in the interpretative process. This is a complex point and some commentators think that a literary-rhetorical context is being confused with particular socio-historical contexts. The commentary raises the question of how far, in the case of the texts read here, it is reasonable to remove the literary-rhetorical phenomena from the socio-historical context. In a tradition that affirms the incarnation of the *logos* in history, at a particular point in time, in a specific place, and in a person of particular gender and race, there is a prima facie case for treating the historical context seriously. We might say that, in this case, there is an especially urgent need to do so.

## 2. PLACE IN THE CANON

The Johannine Epistles are included among the Catholic or General Epistles in the great fourth- and fifth-century codices containing the New Testament: *Sinaiticus* (ℵ) and *Vaticanus* (B) from the fourth century, *Alexandrinus* (A) and *Ephraemi Rescriptus* (C) from the fifth century. The 67 sheets that contained the Catholic Epistles between the Gospels and Acts are missing from the great Western codex *Bezae* (D). Thus, apart from a Latin fragment of 3 John 11-15, this important witness provides no evidence of the text of the Johannine Epistles. Nevertheless, the epistles are well attested in surviving manuscripts.

The naming of the collection as the "Catholic Epistles" can be traced back as far as Eusebius (*HE* 2.23.23-25), who says that James is the first of the seven Catholic Epistles. Obviously this is a reference to the order of the collection rather than the order of writing. With the 367 C.E. (Easter) Festal Letter of Athanasius the order of the Catholic Epistles is set out as James, 1 and 2 Peter, 1, 2, and 3 John, and Jude. This might have been the order presupposed by Eusebius, though we have no clear indication that it was, because he does not provide a listing of the other Catholic Epistles.

The category "Catholic" suggests that these works were addressed to the church universally. 2 and 3 John clearly have a more specific form of address. Our suspicion is that these works are bundled together in this way for want of a more suitable collection, and the number of seven epistles might have symbolic significance.

In the West, because letters in this group (like 2 and 3 John) were addressed to a specific individual, Gaius (3 John) or a specific church or group/network of churches (2 John), "Catholic" was taken as a reference to reception rather than the audience addressed. Reference to these letters as "Catholic" meant that they were universally received and in that sense "canonical." According to Eusebius this understanding of "Catholic" was also to be found in the East, where Origen appealed to the universal acceptance of 1 Peter but not 2 Peter (*HE* 6.25.5,8).

The uniform placement of the Gospels first in the canonical collection of the New Testament suggests that the order of the books was not guided by their supposed date of composition. The overall priority given to the Gospels might indicate that the fourfold Gospel was the first collection of early Christian writings to receive recognition. Although the Pauline Epistles are the earliest Christian writings, there is good reason to think that the Gospels formed the earliest public collection. Recognition of this collection became the basis for gathering together other early Christian writings. We would expect the Pauline corpus to follow the Gospels unless Acts had already attained recognition in its own right. Such recognition could be the basis for the canonical order of Gospels, Acts, then Paul.

Disturbing this theory is the evidence from *Vaticanus* (fourth century), the catecheses of Cyril of Jerusalem delivered around 348 C.E., the 59th canon of the Council of Laodicea (360 C.E.), and Athanasius' Easter letter of 367 C.E., which place the seven Catholic Epistles after Acts and before the letters of Paul. Almost certainly the collection of the Pauline corpus antedated the collection of the Catholic Epistles. Placement of them before the Pauline corpus might reflect a value judgment about the superior "apostolic" status of the authors of these works, the first three of whom might be identified with the "pillar apostles" mentioned by Paul in Gal 2:9 (James, Cephas, and John). If this is the case we note that in this group of "apostolic" letters, which some gave priority over the Pauline corpus, the letters of James and Jude are attributed to brothers of Jesus. Nothing in the earliest evidence suggests that they were numbered among "the Twelve," and we do not know if placing the Catholic Epistles before the Pauline corpus implied that they were. If it did, we find an interesting strand of evidence recognizing the support of Jesus by his family from the time of his ministry.

There is enough evidence to show that the Johannine Epistles were accepted and grouped with the Catholic Epistles by the beginning of the fourth century. Both the Pauline corpus and the Catholic Epistles are treated as the work of apostolic authors. The order of the two collections might have depended on the evaluation of whether Paul should be placed ahead of the "Catholic" apostles. The length of the Pauline corpus might also have a bearing on its ultimate priority over the Catholic Epistles in the canon.

The desire to give priority to the Gospels brought them together, giving expression to the fourfold nature of the Gospel. The early collection is attested by the appearance of the shorter titles, *According to Matthew; According to Mark; According to Luke; According to John*, by the last quarter of the second century. (See David C. Parker, *Codex Bezae*.) Acts connects the Gospels to the Pauline corpus (ordered from longer to shorter letters).

The canonical order of the Gospels is not based on their length. It could indicate the prevailing view of their chronological order at the time of the collection. Other evidence suggests that some (e.g., Clement of Alexandria) thought that both Matthew and Luke antedated Mark, but no testimony provides a solid basis for establishing the chronological order of the Gospels. The placing of John as the fourth Gospel seems to be based on the view that it was the last to be written. For the New Testament the canonical grouping of the Gospels is given priority over the unity of Luke and Acts, which had to be separated if John, rather than Luke, was placed fourth.

Once Acts was set adrift from Luke, its place in the collection of the New Testament books (before or after Paul) was not straightforward. Nevertheless, its canonical position is intelligible. Acts links the Gospels to the life and mission of the earliest church and the second half of Acts gives concentrated attention to the mission of Paul. It may be for this reason that, ultimately, the Pauline corpus follows rather than precedes Acts. Once the order in relation to Acts was settled there was still the question of the relation to the Catholic Epistles. Paul may follow Acts because his collection provides the largest corpus of works (after the Gospels), and his longer letters are longer than any following work except Revelation.

Paul's letters are collected in descending order of length. After the Pauline corpus the order of the works is only partly explicable. Hebrews is the longest of the remaining works apart from Revelation, which is appropriately the last book of the New Testament (see the conclusion in 22:16-21). Both fall outside the collection of the Pauline corpus and the Catholic Epistles. Hebrews may follow the Pauline corpus because of its length. That it is not regarded as Pauline is clear. It does not fit within the descending order of length of the books in the Pauline corpus. Nevertheless, it might have been placed next because some thought Hebrews to be Pauline in some sense.

In the Catholic Epistles, James (1749 words) is slightly longer than 1 Peter (1678 words). But 1 John (2137 words) is longer than either of them! James as a single work might have been placed first, but this does not explain why 1 and 2 Peter come before 1, 2, and 3 John. Perhaps the order of James, Cephas, and John, named in that order as pillar apostles in Gal 2:9, has influenced the order of the collection of the Catholic Epistles. Although 2 and 3 John are the shortest works (245 and 219 words respectively) in the New Testament, their place was secured ahead of the short epistle of Jude by their connection to 1 John. Thus within the Catholic Epistles the collection of Johannine Epistles was recognized (as was the connection of 1 and 2 Peter). In each case the collection was ordered from longer to shorter works. Jude, the shortest of the works standing alone, is the last of the Catholic Epistles and separates the Johannine letters from Revelation. The collection of the Catholic Epistles was more important than the connection between the Johannine Epistles and Revelation, even though tradition as early as Irenaeus acknowledged their connection. The collection of the Gospels was more important than the connection between the Gospel and Epistles of John. Interestingly, the Catholic Epistles are enclosed between two letters attributed to brothers of Jesus (James and Jude). Although the Pauline corpus was preserved with integrity, other collections took precedence over the Lukan and Johannine writings.

In modern times focus has fallen on the Johannine literature as an important collection within the New Testament, thus moving attention from the canonical collections of the Gospels and the Catholic Epistles. Ancient testimony going back at least as far as Irenaeus links the Gospel to the letters of John and Revelation by a common author, identified as the Beloved Disciple and named John the son of Zebedee. This view was not uncontested, but the major reason these books did not become a traditional collection within the New Testament was the drive to bring together the fourfold Gospel. This also led to the separation of Luke and Acts. The twentieth century has seen the restoration of both connections so that Luke–Acts is viewed as one important strand of the traditions in the New Testament along with the Johannine literature. In Luke–Acts the unity is undergirded by common authorship, common address to Theophilus, and a connected and continuing story from Luke to Acts. The connection between the books in the Johannine corpus is neither as neat nor as obvious as with Luke–Acts.

The principle of the order of the Johannine Epistles in the New Testament appears to be based on length, with the longest first and the shortest last. Thus the canonical order may imply nothing about the order of writing. There is something to be said for beginning the discussion with the shorter and more specifically addressed letters before turning to the longer and less specific 1 John.

FOR REFERENCE AND FURTHER STUDY

Brooke, Alan England. *A Critical and Exegetical Commentary on the Johannine Epistles.* Edinburgh: T & T Clark, 1912, lii–lxx.
Brown, Raymond E. *The Epistles of John.* AB 30. Garden City, N.Y.: Doubleday, 1982, 3–13.
Dodd, Charles Harold. *The Johannine Epistles.* MNTC. London: Hodder and Stoughton, 1946, xi–xvi.
Klauck, Hans-Josef. *Die Johannesbriefe.* Erträge der Forschung. Darmstadt: Wissenschaftliche Buchgesellschaft, 1991, 17–40.
Kruse, Colin G. *The Letters of John.* Grand Rapids: Eerdmans, 2000, 8–9.
Parker, David C. *Codex Bezae. An Early Christian Manuscript and its Text.* Cambridge: Cambridge University Press, 1992.

Schnackenburg, Rudolf. *The Johannine Epistles.* New York: Crossroad, 1992, 46–47.
Strecker, Georg. *The Johannine Letters.* Minneapolis: Fortress, 1996, xxix–xxxv.

## 3. EPISTLES OR LETTERS?

Since the work of Adolf Deissman it has been common to distinguish between the popular Greco-Roman letter and the literary epistle. Deissman concluded that the NT epistles belong to the genre of the more popular letters. His views came to be widely accepted. Since the publication of the commentary on Galatians by Hans Dieter Betz in 1979 scholars have increasingly turned their attention to a review of this judgment. What has emerged is a recognition of the merging influence of contemporary Greco-Roman rhetoric and the epistle genre in relation to some of the New Testament epistles. Epistles like Romans and Galatians have been carefully crafted and cannot easily be treated as popular letters. On grounds of length as well as form and structure they fall outside the scope of what we know of the popular letter.

With regard to the Johannine "Epistles" it can be said at once that 2 and 3 John fit the criteria of a popular letter admirably. In terms of length each of them fits easily on a single sheet. Each of them is specifically addressed by an author who identifies himself as *ho presbyteros*. That this designation is something of a puzzle to us does not weaken this recognition. (For the meaning of the term see the discussion of 2 John 1.) From this point it will be translated simply as "the Elder" and understood as indicating the recognition of the author as an authoritative leader in his own community and in a circle of surrounding, perhaps smaller, house churches.

Each of the letters (2 and 3 John) is addressed specifically, even if we suspect that "the elect lady and her children" is a metaphor for a local church or a network of house churches viewed individually. Reasons for this interpretation can be found in the discussion of 2 John 1. Each letter expresses the author's affection for the addressee(s). This is followed by a greeting or a prayer for their well being. At the end of each letter the author indicates that he has much to write but would rather communicate in person ("face to face"). The letters end with a closing greeting. Thus we could treat 2 and 3 John as popular "personal" letters and indeed this seems to be appropriate for 3 John. There is a slight problem with this classification if, as most think, 2 John is sent to a "neighboring" local church or individually to churches in a network. That "the elect lady and her children" is a metaphor for a local church is supported by v. 13 where the author sends greetings from "the children of your elect sister." This looks very much like the greetings of the members of one church being sent to another. In that case 2 John is not strictly a personal letter. The sender's use of the self-identifying "title," the Elder, also modifies the personal letter form in the direction of a more formal communication because this is not the name of the sender. It is a puzzling self-identification but appears to draw attention to the recognition of the author's authority by the readers.

1 John is another matter altogether. It is not a popular personal letter. It lacks the opening address and greeting and the closing greeting. Just what we are to make of the genre of 1 John has long been a matter of debate. In the NT the closest comparison is to be found in the Epistle to the Hebrews. Neither is a popular letter or a literary epistle. Despite lacking the specific form of address of a letter, 1 John is directed to a specific situation. That is evident by reference to the schism in the community (2.19) and the conditions surrounding that situation (see especially 2.18-27; 4.1-6). The nature of 1 John is best illuminated by reference to its relation to 2 and 3 John.

A note on the use of the term "Johannine Epistles" is needed to remove confusion. None of these three writings is formally an epistle. 3 John is a personal letter in Hellenistic, Roman form. Like 3 John, 2 John is written in the form of a personal letter but is apparently addressed to a church, or severally to a group of churches. 1 John is neither an epistle nor a personal letter. Often these works will be referred to by name, avoiding the problem of genre. 2 and 3 John can be spoken of as letters. How to describe 1 John remains a puzzle. Because of this, when the three works are spoken of together I will follow convention by referring to the Johannine Epistles.

FOR REFERENCE AND FURTHER STUDY

Betz, Hans Dieter. *Galatians: A Commentary on Paul's Letter to the Churches in Galatia.* Philadelphia: Fortress, 1979, 14–25.

Brown, Raymond E. *The Epistles of John,* 788–95.

Dahl, Nils A. "Letters," *IDBSupp* (1976) 538–41.

Deissman, Adolf. *Light from the Ancient East. The New Testament Illustrated by Recently Discovered Texts of the Graeco-Roman World.* London: Hodder and Stoughton, 1927.

Doty, William G. *Letters in Primitive Christianity.* Philadelphia: Fortress, 1973.

Hills, Julian. "A Genre for 1 John," in Birger A. Pearson, A. Thomas Kraabel, George W. E. Nickelsburg, and Norman R. Petersen, eds., *The Future of Early Christianity: Essays in Honour of Helmut Koester.* Minneapolis: Fortress, 1991, 367–77.

Kruse, Colin G. *The Letters of John,* 28–32, 40–41, 48.

Malherbe, Abraham J., compiler and translator. *Ancient Epistolary Theorists.* Sources for Biblical Study 19. Atlanta: Scholars, 1988.

Porter, Stanley E., ed. *Handbook of Classical Rhetoric in the Hellenistic Period 300 B.C.–A.D. 400.* Leiden: Brill, 1997.

Schnackenburg, Rudolf. *The Johannine Epistles*, 3–6.

Stowers, Stanley K. *Letter Writing in Greco-Roman Antiquity.* Philadelphia: Westminster, 1986.

White, John Lee. *The Form and Function of the Body of the Greek Letter: A Study of the Letter-Body in the Non-literary Papyri and in Paul the Apostle.* SBLDS 2. Missoula: Scholars, 1972.

_____. "New Testament Epistolary Literature in the Framework of Ancient Epistolography," *ANRW* II.25.2 (1984) 1730–56.

## 4. TRADITION

Perhaps the earliest evidence recognizing the Johannine literature is to be found in the titles of the books. The titles of the Gospels may be from the early second century, though evidence cannot be traced beyond the last quarter of the second century. The title "According to John" does not explicitly lift the veil of anonymity by identifying which John is meant. There is, however, little doubt that the apostle, son of Zebedee and brother of James is intended.

Because there are minor variations in the title of 1 John in the Greek MSS, all of which bear a title, it may be concluded that the original bore no title. The great codices of Vaticanus (B), Sinaiticus (ℵ) and Alexandrinus (A) have the title "The First Epistle of John." Codex Bezae (D) provides no evidence of the titles of the Johannine Epistles because it does not include the Catholic Epistles. A gap of sixty-seven pages between the Gospels and Acts provides evidence of where they once were placed. Other MSS add the descriptions "apostle" and "evangelist." The other Epistles are named "The Second . . ." and "The Third Epistle of John" respectively, but these titles cannot be traced back much before the end of the second century. Just how the name of John was associated with these books is unclear. Only the text of Revelation (1:1, 4, 9) lifts the veil on its author, naming him John. If tradition linked the Gospel, three Epistles, and Revelation, this might be enough to suggest the name of John as the author of all five books. Of course, Revelation does not identify this John, nor do the title of the Gospel or many forms of the title of the Epistles, though, as we have seen, some add "apostle" and "evangelist."

Irenaeus provides important information concerning John and the book of Revelation. Reference is generally to the Apocalypse of John (*Adv. haer.* 1.26.3) or what John says in the Apocalypse (*Adv. haer.* 4.17.6; 4.21.3; 5.28.2; 5.34.2), but on four occasions this John of the Apocalypse is described as "the Lord's disciple" (*Adv. haer.* 4.20.11; 4.30.4; 5.26.1; 5.35.2), a description Irenaeus regularly uses of the author of the Gospel and Epistle of John, which seems to include 2 John also. His references to Revelation are in the context of a discussion of imminent eschatological fulfillment. He was familiar with this theme in the letters of Paul as well as Revelation.

Thus the use of the titles needs to be illuminated by other literary testimonies. Before Irenaeus, in the last quarter of the second century, we have no certain reference to the Epistles, only possible allusions. These are set out chronologically beginning with *1 Clement* (ca. 96 C.E.), attributed to Clement, an early bishop of Rome. Allusions are noted in descending order of probability: 49.1 (cf. 1 John 5:1-3); 49.5; 50.3 (cf. 1 John 2:5; 4:12, 17-18); 27.1; 60.1 (cf. 1 John 1:9). In the final group of texts, reference to God who is faithful and righteous is so common in the OT that it is not possible to identify an allusion to 1 John on this basis.

The epistles of Ignatius, bishop of Antioch, are dated circa 110–115 C.E. He was familiar with and wrote to the churches of Asia Minor, the traditional area associated with John. That he mentions Paul but not John is puzzling if the Johannine tradition is associated with this region. Allusions may be another matter, but we are again in an area where lack of certainty has led to widely divergent views. Some allusions may be seen in Ign. *Eph.* 11.1 (cf. 1 John 2:18); 15.3 (cf. 1 John 3:2).

Many of the following works cannot be placed with any degree of probability with regard to time and place of authorship. The evidence of the *Didache* is marred by uncertainty as to its date and provenance. Some scholars hazard a guess at a very early date. Links between it and the Gospel of Matthew and Ignatius have encouraged some scholars to locate it in Antioch. A date around 120 C.E. (after Ignatius) seems marginally more probable than alternatives. Some allusion might be seen in *Did.* 10.5-6 (cf. 1 John 2:17). Reference there "to perfect it in your love" may draw on the negative "not perfected in love" of 1 John 4:18; see also *Did.* 11.7 (cf. 1 John 4:1); *Did.* 16.4 (2 John 7). The case for such allusions must be regarded as very tentative.

The *Epistle of Barnabas* may be from the mid-second century C.E. The crucial Johannine christological confession finds a parallel in 5.9-11; 12.10 (cf. 1 John 4:2; 2 John 7); 14.5 (cf. 1 John 3:4, 7, 8).

The *Second Epistle of Clement*, though disingenuously attributed to Clement of Rome, must date from the mid-second century C.E. In 6.9 there is a reference, "Who shall be our advocate (*paraklētos*)," which might allude to 1 John 2:1. Given that in the NT *paraklētos* is used only by the Gospel and 1 John, there seems to be a prima facie case. But there is a problem in that 1 John appeals to the advocate for the situation "if we sin," whereas 2 *Clement* implies that the advocate is effective only for those having "pious and righteous works."

From the middle of the second century phrases and themes similar to those in 1 John become more common in works like the *Shepherd* of Hermas. In Herm. *Man.* 3.1 "in him there is no lie" perhaps echoes 1 John 2:27, and Herm. *Man.* 12.3.5 may echo the assertion that "his commandments are not burdensome" in 1 John 5:3. In Herm. *Sim.* 9.24.4 reference to receiving the Spirit might reflect 1 John 4:13. The proposed allusions are not particularly persuasive.

The writings of Justin also contain parallel phrases. That reference to Christ's blood in *1 Apol.* 32.7 might echo 1 John 1:7 is supported by *1 Apol.* 32.8, which refers to the seed of God, the Word dwelling in the believer, cf. 1 John 2:14; 3:9. *Dialogue with Trypho* 123.9 might express ideas found in 1 John 2:3; 3:1, 22; 5:3 where we find the association between keeping the commandments and being called children of God. The *Epistle to Diognetus* 10.2-3 is close to 1 John 4:9, 19 in expressing the idea of the sending of the Son as an expression of the love of God to which human love is the response. Reference to the Word as the one who was from the beginning (*Diogn.* 11.4) echoes 1 John 1:1; 2:13-14.

Polycarp's *Epistle to the Philippians* (not later than 140 C.E.) contains a number of passages almost certainly dependent on both 1 and 2 John. He speaks of false brethren (6.3) and says that "everyone who does not confess Jesus Christ to have come (perfect infinitive) in the flesh is Antichrist," and goes on to say that they belong to the devil (7.1). The comparison is with 1 John 4:2-3, which uses the perfect participle, and 2 John 7, which uses the present participle. Both texts also refer to the Antichrist. 1 John 3:8, 10 also speaks of children of the devil. In addition, Polycarp speaks of the Word that is from the beginning (7.2), which echoes the common theme of 1 John 1:1; 2:7, 24; 3:11. That Polycarp knew at least 1 John is supported by the evidence of Eusebius concerning Papias, the bishop of Hierapolis and contemporary of Polycarp, that Papias made use of the testimonies of the First Epistle of John (*HE* 3.36.1-2; 3.39.17).

The most important witness to the Johannine Epistles in the second century is Irenaeus, a native of Asia Minor who became bishop of Lyons and wrote circa 180 C.E. The evidence of Irenaeus (*Adv. haer.*) is often repeated by Eusebius (*HE*): *Adv. haer.* 3.1.1 = *HE* 5.8.4; *Adv. haer.* 2.22.5 = *HE* 3.23.3; *Adv. haer.* 3.3.4 = *HE* 4.14.3-8 and 3.23.4; *Ep. ad Flor.* = *HE* 5.20.4-8. See also *Adv. haer.* 1.8.5; 1.9.1-3; 2.2.5; 2.22.3; 3.31.3 (cf. *HE* 5.25.1-7); 3.8.3; 3.11.1-4, 7, 9; 3.15.2, 5, 8; 3.16.5, 8; 3.22.2; 4.2.3; 4.6.1; 4.10.1; 5.18.2; 5.33.3; *Epideixis* 43.94. From these references it is clear that Irenaeus identified John, the disciple of the Lord, with the Beloved Disciple as author of the Gospel and Epistles, published in Ephesus in the reign of Trajan. He claimed to have this information from the elders of Asia Minor of whom he names Polycarp of Smyrna and Papias of Hierapolis (See *Ep. ad Flor.* = *HE* 5.20.4-8; *Ep. ad Victor of Rome*; *Adv. haer.* 2.22.5; 3.1.1, 4; 5.33.3-4.).

Irenaeus had grown up around Ephesus where he had come to know
Polycarp and Papias.

Nevertheless, Irenaeus' use of the Johannine Epistles is sparse and reveals some puzzles. In *Adv. haer.* 1.16.3 he refers to 2 John 11 as from John
the disciple of the Lord. He also refers to 1 John 2:8-19, 21-22 in *Adv. haer.*
3.16.5 and 2 John 7-8; 1 John 4:1-2; 5:1 in *Adv. haer.* 3.16.8. Thus it is clear that
Irenaeus knew both 1 and 2 John, but the form of the quotation in 3.16.8
refers back to the epistle already quoted (in 3.16.5), and after quoting
2 John 7-8 continues by reference to "this epistle" before quoting 1 John
4:1-2; 5.1. Thus it seems that the form in which Irenaeus knew 1 and 2 John
did not distinguish the two Epistles. The reason for this may be that
2 John was originally the covering letter for 1 John and it was in that combined form that 1 and 2 John were known to Irenaeus in Asia Minor. See
also *Adv. haer.* 1.9.5, which may allude to the "spirit of error" of 1 John 4:6;
and *Adv. haer.* 5.1.1 may allude to 1 John 1:1-4, "hearing with our own ears
. . . we have communion with him."

To this point there is evidence of allusion to and quotation of 1 John. In
addition, Irenaeus quotes from 2 John 7-8 but seems to attribute this quotation to the same epistle as the other quotations. If the earlier uncertain
allusions to 2 John 7 can be accepted, they too support a knowledge of
1 and 2 John, but we have no way of knowing whether they were known
as two separate Epistles at the time. We have no evidence of the use of
3 John. This evidence is consistent with the view that 2 John was a covering letter for 1 John. This being the case, 2 John did not exist separate from
1 John. Because 1 John was also used by the author in his own church
where it needed no covering letter, 1 John did exist without 2 John. While
2 John is a short letter, like 3 John, it was an official letter directed to one or
more (house) churches that were in relation to the author's (the Elder's)
own church, but 3 John was a personal letter addressed to Gaius. That
could account for the evidence suggesting that it was more slowly accepted into common use in the churches than either 1 or 2 John.

The Muratorian fragment (the so-called "Canon") is in Latin and
comes from the eighth century. Because of its barbarous Latin it is thought
to be the translation of a Greek original perhaps dating from the late second century. Traditionally it is located in Rome. While evidence of a Greek
original does not preclude this, as Greek was common in Rome until well
into the third century, it does not make the Roman case secure. Thus
Albert C. Sundberg ("Canon Muratori: A Fourth Century List") argues for
an Eastern origin in the fourth century. Whatever its origins, it is not clear
that it is an official list, and so it is misleading to refer to it as a canon. The
text deals with the conditions that gave rise to the writing of the Gospel of
John and makes reference to Johannine Epistles. The latter reference is unclear. The most probable rendering of the rather obscure text finds in it the

acceptance of two Johannine Epistles in the Catholic Church. This is probably a reference to 1 and 2 John. As 1 John 1:1-2 had been quoted already in defense of the Gospel, it was certainly known, and other evidence supports the recognition of 2 John as the second Epistle in view. A less likely alternative is that the earlier reference to 1 John in relation to the Gospel implied its place there with reference to 2 and 3 John, the two (other) Johannine Epistles following. But, although there is evidence placing the Johannine Epistles after the Gospel and before Acts in later Western manuscripts (such as Codex Bezae), the Epistles are not separated. All three are placed at this point. Consequently the Muratorian fragment also supports the acceptance of 1 and 2 John, further raising a question about the history of 3 John.

From the end of the second century there is evidence of widespread and frequent use of 1 John in both West and East. Tertullian cites 1 John almost fifty times and Clement of Alexandria frequently cites 1 John (*Stromata* 3.5.44; 3.6.45 cite 1 John 2:4, 18-19, and *Quis dives salvetur* 37.6 cites 1 John 3:15), naming it "the greater Epistle" (*Strom.* 2.15.56), thus implying that he knew at least one other Johannine Epistle, which is confirmed by his commentary on 2 John in his *Hypotyposes*. Although this work is lost, there is a Latin translation of part of it entitled *Adumbrationes*, attributed to Cassiodorus (circa 540 C.E.). By the middle of the third century there is evidence of the use of 3 John also. Eusebius attests Origen's use of both 2 and 3 John (*HE* 6.25.10). Dionysius of Alexandria knew that John wrote the Gospel and Epistles but rejected the Johannine authorship of Revelation (*HE* 7.25.7-8, 11). The seventh council of Carthage recognized 2 John as well as 3 John. The thirty-ninth Festal Letter of Athanasius (367 C.E.) listed the Catholic Epistles in order including 1, 2, and 3 John, and the Synod of Hippo (393 C.E.) and Council of Carthage (397 C.E.) acknowledge the three Epistles as Johannine. Didymus the Blind (d. 398 C.E.) wrote a commentary on the three Epistles. Thus by the end of the fourth century acceptance of the three epistles was more or less complete in East and West.

It is not surprising, however, that the evidence attests an uneven rate of acceptance. 1 John was known and accepted in the second half of the second century with evidence of the use of 2 John following. The early use of 2 John does not distinguish it from 1 John, suggesting that it was first known as a covering letter for 1 John. Only in the third century does evidence of the use of 3 John appear and doubts about the authorship and authority of 2 and 3 John continue throughout the third and much of the fourth centuries. Raymond E. Brown notes that 1 John was associated with the Gospel and, like it, attributed to the authorship of the apostle John. But 2 and 3 John name their author as the Elder. Eusebius' reading of Papias distinguished the Elder from the apostle (*HE* 3.39.4). Thus, not only because they were short letters and, by comparison with 1 John, seemingly insignificant, but also because they lacked apostolic authorship, their road to acceptance was more difficult than it was for 1 John (Brown, *Johannine Epistles* 12). Although 2 John is first evidenced in connection with 1 John, it became disconnected, perhaps because the assumed author of 1 John was the apostle and the declared author of 2 John was the Elder.

FOR REFERENCE AND FURTHER STUDY

Brooke, Alan England. *A Critical and Exegetical Commentary on the Johannine Epistles*, lii–lxx.
Brown, Raymond E. *The Epistles of John*, 3–13.
Dodd, Charles Harold. *The Johannine Epistles*, xi–xvi.
Parker, David C. *Codex Bezae. An Early Christian Manuscript and its Text.*
Schnackenburg, Rudolf. *The Johannine Epistles*, 46–47.
Strecker, Georg. *The Johannine Letters*, xxix–xxxv.
Sundberg, Albert C. "Canon Muratori: A Fourth Century List," *HTR* 66 (1973) 1–41.

## 5. AUTHORSHIP

The task of identifying the author of 1 John is complicated. Because 1 John is not a letter or an epistle, the author does not identify himself. Nevertheless, the tone of authority with which the author writes is consistent with the use of the title "the Elder" in 2 and 3 John. Common language, style, and point of view make clear that these three writings stand in some close relationship to each other. Part of the complication is to unravel precisely what that relationship is in each case. That the Gospel has a close relationship to 1 John was also recognized in the earliest extant references to the writings, but these references are not as precise as we might hope nor are they early enough to provide assurance that they are based on accurate evidence. At the same time even the modern reader is aware of the general similarities that exist between these works. They are set out in some detail elsewhere in the Introduction. Here we note that 1 John shares with the Gospel a significant vocabulary and style that distinguish the Johannine literature from other early Christian writings.

The claim that the Gospel embodies eyewitness testimony seems to be indicated by John 1:14; 19:35; 21:24-25. While it might be said that "to see the glory" is not to see an object with the eye (1:14), what John has in mind seems to be based on firsthand believing experience, the vision of faith (2:11). Thus it is a reference to what is actually seen and understood from the perspective of belief. The witness of 19:35 is probably to be identified with the Beloved Disciple (13:23; 19:26; 20:2). The Beloved Disciple can also be identified with "the other disciple" of 18:15 (cf. 20:2) and the un-named disciple of 1:40. If this reading catches the implications of the nar-rative, then an eyewitness provides a basis for the narrative from the earliest moments of Jesus' ministry. Yet confidence in these details is under-mined because evidence of this testimony is found in John alone and it is difficult to reconcile the distinctive Johannine perspective with the Synop-tic narratives.

In John 21 the Beloved Disciple is identified as the author of the Gospel (21:7, 20, 24). There is no hint of this throughout chs. 1–20, and ch. 21 is a self-indicated addition (*"we* know that *his* witness is true"). But who is in this group that adds its seal of approval to the witness of the Beloved Dis-ciple? Would the Beloved Disciple need the supporting testimony of an anonymous group? If his witness needed support, why is it that the wit-nesses have not identified themselves? Their testimony in support of the Beloved Disciple is perplexing. It leaves the reader none the wiser as to the identity of the author because the Beloved Disciple remains a mysteri-ous enigma. It may be that the first readers knew his identity. This need not be the case because if the readers had known him he would not have needed the testimonial support of 21:24.

Neither 1 John nor the Gospel identifies an author. The Gospel (20:31) refers to its having been written (passive voice), a resonance suggesting scriptural status. The author of 1 John refers to writing, once in the first person plural present tense (1:4), six times in the first person singular present tense (2:1, 7, 8, 12, 13 [2x]), and six times in the first person singu-lar aorist tense (2:14 [3x], 21, 26; 5:13). The statement of purpose using "I wrote to you" (5:13) gives the sense of a personal communication in some contrast to the abiding presence of what *is written* in the Gospel. The first person plural "we write" (1:4) occurs in the context of a series of first person plural statements affirming firsthand testimony (1:1-5). Thus the "we" who write purport to do so from the perspective of a firsthand rela-tionship to the subject of their message.

Alongside this impressive opening there is a widespread use of the first person plural "we" throughout 1 John (1:6-10; 2:2-3, 5, 28; 3:1-2, 14, 16, 18-19, 21-25; 4:6, 7, 9-14, 16-17, 19; 5:2-3, 14-15, 18-20). In these in-stances it is often difficult to know whether this use is similar to 1:1-5, where the author associates himself with other authoritative witnesses. There are times when the author is speaking inclusively of himself and his readers (2:18-21, 24-25; 3:19-24). At other times "we" and "you" (plural) *seem* to be clearly distinguished (3:14, 15, 16; 4:4-6). Although the address to the readers ("you") clearly distinguishes them from the author (5:13), the recurrent "we" does not necessarily exclude the readers. The ambigu-ity of the first person plural throughout 1 John weakens the force of "we" as an expression of an exclusive source of authority. If the author has used this technique to bolster his own authority and "to strengthen his readers' confidence in the message" (Kruse, *Letters* 61), this seems to indicate the author's awareness of his own precarious position with his readers.

The Gospel and 1 John make no claims to common authorship. While style and language certainly show there is some relationship between the two works, there is not enough evidence to determine that they are by the same author. The similarities are explicable if the two authors were members of the same school or if the evangelist was the founding teacher of the Johannine school, of which the author of 1 John was a member. What then is the relationship of 1 John to those who bore that testimony in 21:24?

The closest comparison between the "we" of 1 John 1:1-5 and the Gospel is found in John 21:24, "we know his witness is true." Ostensibly these are not the words of the "author" of the Gospel but of those who give testimony to his witness. Apparently anonymous witnesses attempt to shore up the authority of the Beloved Disciple, as if his credibility were in question. There is something implausible about this. Even if the reader knew no more than is in the Gospel, the role of the Beloved Disciple would be secure. If he is the foundation witness of the Johannine community, then the attestation of 21:24, "we know that his witness is true," is extraordinary. To identify the Beloved Disciple as the author is one thing. To bear witness to the veracity of his testimony is quite another! Given this perplexing problem we may question whether the attestation is correct. Is the Beloved Disciple (whoever he may be) the actual author of the Gospel? Or is he the source of the tradition or the one who caused the Gospel to be written?

However we answer these questions, there is the obvious problem of the relationship of the "we" of 1 John 1:1-5 to the "we" of John 21:24. We may accept that the author of 1 John stands in a close relation to the author of the Gospel, perhaps as one of the group that sends the Gospel finally on its way with their support. That this group was responsible for the final editing of the Gospel also makes sense. That being the case, the author of 1 John writes with intimate knowledge of the Gospel tradition but without the literary skills of the author of the Gospel and perhaps without a total grasp of the profundity of the message of the Gospel.

At the same time, 1 John shares a close relationship to 2 John in terms of style and vocabulary and 2 John is closely related to 3 John, which is not so closely related to 1 John in terms of language, style, and content. While 2 and 3 John also share the address from the author who calls himself "the Elder," this is absent from 1 John, which lacks the formal address of a letter. The absence of that address may explain the absence of the title "the Elder." 1 John seems to be dealing with the same situation as 2 John (see 2 John 7 and 1 John 2:18-19, 22; 4:1-3). The language and style of 1 and 2 John bear a marked resemblance to each other, as do 2 and 3 John. Though the evidence is explicable in terms of writings from a closely-knit school, the weight of probability is that 1–3 John are the work of a single author. But this leaves us no clearer about the identity of the author.

Because the writings themselves do not identify the author of the Gospel or the Epistles, we must turn to external evidence. Certainly the earliest evidence of authorship attributes both the Gospel and 1 John to John the disciple of the Lord. But the earliest evidence is not very early. There is, first, the evidence of Papias of Hierapolis (writing circa 140 C.E.) which is indirectly relevant because, although it does not mention the Gospel or Epistles of John, it provides important references to John. Eusebius quotes Irenaeus (*Adv. Haer.* 5.33.4):

> To these things Papias, who had listened to John and was later a companion of Polycarp, and who lived at a very early date, bears written testimony in the fourth of his books; he composed five. (*HE* 3.39, in Williamson, 101)

Eusebius understands this to be a reference to the apostle John but objects that Papias himself in the Preface to his work makes it clear that he was never a hearer and eyewitness of the holy apostles, and tells us that he learned the essentials of the Faith from their former pupils. The quotation from Papias then follows:

> I shall not hesitate to furnish you, along with the interpretations with all that in days gone by I carefully learnt from the presbyters and have carefully recalled, for I can guarantee its truth. Unlike most people, I felt at home not with those who had a great deal to say, but with those who taught the truth; not with those who appeal to commandments from other sources but with those who appeal to the commandments given by the Lord to faith and coming to us from truth itself. And whenever anyone came who had been a follower of the presbyters, I inquired into the words of the presbyters, what Andrew or Peter had said, or Philip or Thomas or James or John or Matthew, or any other disciple of the Lord, and what Aristion and the presbyter John, the disciples of the Lord, were still saying. For I did not imagine that things out of books would help me as much as the utterances of a living and abiding voice. (*HE* 3.39, in Williamson, 102)

Nowhere here does Papias assert that he had not seen or known the apostles. Nor is it altogether clear that two different Johns are mentioned. Each of the two groups is referred to as presbyters (elders). What distinguishes them is not that the first is described as apostles. Rather, reference is to what the first group *had said* and to what those in the second group *were still saying*. That the same John might fit both groups is possible if he alone of the first group remained alive at the time of Papias' inquiry. It is notable that Papias does not refer to John as a follower of the presbyters.

Rather he says he inquired of the followers of the presbyters concerning the words of the presbyters. Eusebius notes that the name John is used twice, once with the apostles and the second time after Aristion, calling John "the presbyter." From this he confirms the story that there were two Johns in Asia, the first the evangelist and the second the Elder and author of Revelation. These are the conclusions of Eusebius, writing in the first quarter of the fourth century. We assume that Eusebius had access to the whole of the *Expositions* of Papias, now lost apart from the fragments he quotes. He makes no reference to Papias to establish the apostolic authorship of the Gospel or Epistles of John, though he includes Papias' testimony to the origin of Matthew and Mark. This suggests that no such testimony was to be found in Papias. All that Eusebius could find there was a dubious testimony that *might* mean that there were two notable Johns in Asia, though it can be read as an indication that, of the apostles, only John was long living.

Later Jerome (*Lives of Illustrious Men* 13) makes reference to the same words of Papias, drawing the same conclusion as Eusebius: that there were two Johns. Indeed, he may well have drawn his reference to Papias from Eusebius. Where Jerome differs from Eusebius it is not because he shows an independent reading of Papias. Rather he departs from Eusebius by noting that many conclude that the second John, the Elder, is the author of 2 and 3 John. It may be the case that Jerome thought both the Gospel and 1 John to be the works of John the disciple of the Lord (apostle). But the basis for this distinction seems to be the fact that the author of 2 and 3 John identifies himself as the Elder. This is not based on any evidence from Papias, nor is it a solid ground for distinguishing the authorship of the small letters from 1 John. Because 1 John is not a letter, like 2 and 3 John, it has no form of address. Nothing in what Jerome writes suggests that he has any more evidence upon which to base his views than was available to Eusebius.

Nevertheless it is clear that Irenaeus (circa 180 C.E.) attributes both the Gospel and 1 John to John the disciple of the Lord.

> As John the Lord's disciple affirms, saying, "But these things are written that you might believe that Jesus is the Son of God, and believing might have eternal life in his name": foreseeing these. . . . Wherefore also in his Epistle he has borne this witness unto us: "Little children, it is the last hour: and as you have heard that Antichrist comes, now many Antichrists have appeared, whereby we know that it is the last hour. They went out from us but they were not of us; for had they been of us they would have remained with us; but that they might be revealed as not being of us. Know therefore that every lie is foreign and is not of the truth. Who is the Liar but he who denies that Jesus is the Christ? This is the Antichrist." (*Adv. haer.* 3.16.5)

Here Irenaeus quotes both from the Gospel (20:31) and 1 John (2:18-19, 21-22) and attributes both to the one and same John. Shortly after, he quotes from 2 John 7, attributing it to the same Epistle:

> These both our Lord forewarned us of, and his disciple John in the afore-mentioned Epistle bade us fly from them, saying, "Many deceivers have gone out into this world who do not confess Jesus Christ come in the flesh. This is a deceiver and an Antichrist." Take heed of them that you lose not what you have wrought. And again he says in the Epistle, "Many false prophets are gone out into the world. Hereby know the Spirit of God. Every Spirit that confesses Jesus Christ to have come in the flesh is of God. And every Spirit that denies Jesus is not of God but is of the Antichrist." Now these things are like what is said in the Gospel, that "the Word was made flesh and dwelt among us." Wherefore in his Epistle again he cries out, "Every one who believes that Jesus is the Christ is born of God." (*Adv. haer.* 3:16.8)

Evidently Irenaeus knew 1 and 2 John in some combined form. Here 2 John 7, 8 is quoted alongside 1 John 4:1-3 and 5:1 as if they were all part of the same epistle. If 2 John had been a letter accompanying 1 John, this might explain how the two could be combined and thought of as one epistle.

The appeal of Irenaeus to 1 and 2 John as if they were a single Epistle does not inspire confidence in his knowledge about their origin. Rather he is drawn to them as a source to be used in overcoming his theological opponents. He provides no actual evidence for his view that John the disciple of the Lord was the author of the Gospel, 1 John and by implication 2 John also. Nevertheless, the writings of Irenaeus were pervasively influential from circa 180 C.E. onwards. Thus it is not surprising to find Tertullian (circa 220 C.E.) accepting the Johannine authorship of the Gospel, 1 John, and also of Revelation. Certainly Tertullian's Montanist leanings will have made him sympathetic to Revelation.

> There is a certain emphatic saying by John: "No man has seen God at any time"; meaning, of course, at any previous time. . . . But the very same apostles testify that they have both seen and "handled" Christ. . . . John says "That which we have seen with our eyes, which we have looked upon, and our hands have handled, of the Word of Life." (*Adversus Praxias* 15)

> To whom would he [Christ] have made known the veiled import of his own language, than to him to whom he disclosed the likeness of his own glory—Peter, John and James, and afterwards to Paul, to whom he granted participation in (the joys of) Paradise too, prior to his martyrdom? Or do they write differently from what they think—teachers using deceit, not truth? . . . John, in fact, exhorts us to lay down our lives even for the brethren, affirming that there is no fear in love: "For perfect love

> casts out fear, since fear has punishment; and he who fears is not perfect
> in love." . . . And if he teaches that we must die for the brethren how
> much more for the Lord,—he being sufficiently prepared, by his own
> Revelation too, for giving such advice! For indeed the Spirit had sent the
> injunction to the angel of the church in Smyrna: "Behold, the devil shall
> cast some of you into prison, that you may be tried ten days. . . . But the
> fearful (John says) . . . will have their part in the lake of fire and brim-
> stone." Thus fear, which, as stated in his epistle, love drives out, has pun-
> ishment. (*Scorpiace* 12)

While Tertullian followed Irenaeus in accepting the Johannine authorship of Revelation, showing no awareness of the interpretation of Papias
as a basis for two Johns in Asia, Dionysius of Alexandria (circa 260) distinguishes the author of Revelation from the author of the Gospel and
Epistles.

> I do not, therefore, deny that he [the author of Revelation] was called
> John and that this was the writing of one John, and I agree that it was the
> work, also, of some holy and inspired man. But I would not easily agree
> that this was the apostle, the son of Zebedee, the brother of James, who is
> the author of the Gospel, and the catholic epistle bears his name. But
> I conjecture, both from the general tenor of both, and the form and com-
> plexion of the composition, and the execution of the whole book, that it
> is not from him. For the evangelist never prefixed his name, never
> proclaims himself, either in the Gospel or in his epistle. (Dionysius of
> Alexandria quoted by Eusebius, *HE* 7.25.6)

Interestingly, Dionysius shows no knowledge of the passage quoted from
Papias and its interpretation in terms of two Johns in Ephesus. He acknowledges that the distinction between the author of the Gospel and
Revelation is his own proposal. It is based on two critical observations.
The character of Revelation is incompatible with authorship by the same
person who wrote the Gospel and 1 John. Second, the author of the
Gospel and Epistles does not reveal his name as does the author of Revelation (1:1, 4, 9; 22:8). Dionysius appeals to no traditional evidence for his
views. Eusebius provides the first evidence of the reading of the Papias'
quotation as indicative of two Johns.

The earliest evidence of the identification of a single Johannine author
comes from Irenaeus, who attributes the Gospel, 1 John (and 2 John by implication), as well as Revelation to John the disciple of the Lord. The earliest evidence of different authors comes from Dionysius of Alexandria. But
he shows no knowledge of traditional evidence of independent authorship. Nevertheless, he distinguishes the authorship of Revelation from the
Gospel and Epistles on critical grounds.

At the end of the scrutiny of the external evidence we are left with no
solid grounds for making a decision about the common authorship of the

Gospel and Epistles. Certainly this is not impossible, but neither is there solid evidence that this is the case. While the three Epistles might have been written by separate authors, a strong case can be made for reading them in relation to the same crisis in the Johannine circle of churches, and this provides a basis for understanding them as the work of a common author. The internal evidence points to some close relationship between the three Johannine Epistles. The differences between them do not preclude common authorship.

FOR REFERENCE AND FURTHER STUDY

Beutler, Johannes. *Die Johannesbriefe*. Regensburg: Friedrich Pustet, 2000, 29–31.
Brooke, Alan England. *A Critical and Exegetical Commentary on the Johannine Epistles*, lxxiii–lxxix.
Brown, Raymond E. *The Epistles of John*, 14–35.
Culpepper, R. Alan. *The Johannine School*. Missoula: Scholars, 1975.
Dodd, Charles Harold. *The First Epistle of John and the Fourth Gospel*. Manchester: Manchester University Press, 1937.
_____. *The Johannine Epistles*, xlvii–lvi.
Gerhardsson, Birger. *Memory and Manuscript: Oral Tradition and Written Transmission in Rabbinic Judaism and Early Christianity*. Uppsala: Gleerup, 1961.
Howard, Wilbert F. "The Common Authorship of the Johannine Gospel and Epistles," *JTS* 48 (1947) 12–25.
Kruse, Colin G. *The Letters of John*, 9–14, 36–37, 42.
Painter, John. *The Quest for the Messiah*. Edinburgh: T & T Clark, 1991, 2nd ed. Nashville: Abingdon, 1993, 36–47, 50–52.
Rensberger, David. *1 John, 2 John, 3 John*. Nashville: Abingdon, 1997, 17–20.
Salom, A. P. "Some Aspects of the Grammatical Style of 1 John," *JBL* 74 (1955) 96–102.
Schnackenburg, Rudolf. *The Johannine Epistles*, 40–41.
Wilson, W. G. "An Examination of the Linguistic Evidence Adduced against the Unity of Authorship of the First Epistle of John and the Fourth Gospel," *JTS* 49 (1948) 147–56.

## 6. RELATIONSHIP OF THE EPISTLES TO EACH OTHER

Detailed discussion of the evidence concerning the relationship of the Epistles to each other is provided in the Notes and Interpretation. The position adopted in this commentary is that 2 John stands in a close relationship to each of the other Johannine Epistles but that 3 John seems to be more independent of the language and subject matter of 1 John. That 2 and 3 John belong together is indicated by their common letter form, authorial address and subject matter. Both deal with the issue of the practice of hospitality in the mission. Georg Strecker thinks the literary evidence points to their independence of 1 John and argues that they are earlier than 1 John (*The Johannine Letters* 3). While this is possible, because the Elder does not identify himself as the author of 1 John, Strecker underrates the connections with 1 John, especially between 1 and 2 John. He also fails to take account of how far the differences arise from the letter form of 2 and 3 John that is not shared by 1 John. Here it is argued that it is likely that the three Epistles were written by the Elder about the same time, perhaps in canonical order. 1 and 2 John may have been sent out to a circle of churches at the same time with 3 John following a little later.

The self-identification of the author(s) of 2 and 3 John as the Elder sets these works apart from the rest of the Johannine writings. Within the limits of the two short letters (2 and 3 John being 245 and 219 words respectively) they share significant vocabulary and ways of expression with 1 John. This statement needs to be elaborated: 1 John stands closer to 2 John than 3 John, and 2 John is closer to 3 John than 1 John. Thus 2 John is the link connecting 1 and 3 John. Unlike 1 John, however, 2 and 3 John clearly comply with the features of the Greco-Roman personal letter in length, form of address, opening greetings, and farewell. The author of each of the two short letters identifies himself as the Elder, which sets them apart from 1 John. It may be that when each of these factors is related to the other their significance is diminished. Because 1 John is no letter in the ordinary sense, the letter form and some clear identification of the sender are hardly to be expected.

Self-identification of the author as "the Elder" is meaningful only if the author was well known to the readers by this designation. This we must assume unless the letter form of 2 and 3 John is a cloak for some more general "publication." Given the independent insignificance of these letters, such a theory seems unlikely. Their relative insignificance is attested by the flimsy evidence of their use in the first two centuries. This appears not to have been because of controversy concerning them but more because they had not become widely known. We might guess that one reason for their limited circulation was their apparent insignificance. Nevertheless, the author's identification of himself as "the Elder" implies a sense of his recognition as an authoritative leader.

2 and 3 John are specifically addressed, apparently to individual readers. 3 John is written to "Gaius the beloved, whom I love in truth." There is no reason to think that Gaius is anything but an individual believer known to the Elder. He is perhaps one of his protégés, included among those referred to as "my children." Given that "the Elder" writes to him, it is implied that he lives at some distance from him. Gaius seems to occupy a position of leadership alongside Diotrephes and Demetrios. They may

be leaders in the same community or, more likely, in neighboring communities. While Diotrephes opposed the Elder, Demetrios was a supporter. This letter aims to clarify the lines of conflict, to ensure that Gaius is not corrupted by Diotrephes. It signals that, so far, Gaius has supported the right side, but the Elder's underlying anxiety is apparent.

A major issue is the offering of hospitality to those in fellowship with the Elder. This was provided by Gaius but was refused by Diotrephes, who would not receive what the Elder wrote to the church (3 John 9). Diotrephes also spread false charges against the Elder and those associated with him (*hēmas* seems to include *tous adelphous*, 3 John 10). This group is referred to as "fellow workers" (*sunergoi*) in 3 John 8, reminiscent of the Pauline use of this term to describe his close associates. Here, in 3 John, it is both similar and different in that the Elder uses it of himself and his associates as "fellow workers with the truth" (*sunergoi tȩ̄ alētheią*). The latter gives a Johannine character to the use of the term. Diotrephes also refused hospitality to supporters of the Elder, forbade others from providing this, and excommunicated them (*ek tēs ekklēsias ekballei*) if they did not comply with his wishes. Interestingly, the description of this practice is close to what the Gospel of John says the Jews/Pharisees did to the believers in Jesus, casting them out of the synagogue (9:22, 34; 12:42; 16:2). In the time of Jesus *synagōgē* and *ekklēsia* were used without distinction. Compare the use in Rev 1:4, 11, 20; 2:1, 7, 8, 9, 11, 12, etc., and see also James 2:2. By the end of the first century the former was used of a Jewish gathering while the latter became the distinctive term to describe the gathering of believers in Jesus. Perhaps because of his mission to the nations, already in the 50s Paul used the term *ekklēsia* of the Christian community.

What was it the Elder wrote to the church? Most likely this is a reference to 1 John. If this is right, 1 John was written prior to 3 John and the conflict with Diotrephes could well be an expression of the schism reflected in 1 John 2:18-27; 4:1-6. That need not mean that Diotrephes was one of those who separated from the community of the writer of 1 John. Before we can assess the implications for this issue, the relation of 2 John to the schism must be discussed.

Further, what are we to understand by "the church" (*ekklēsia*) in 3 John 3, 6, 9, 10? This term is not used in the other Johannine letters or in the Gospel. It is used in Rev 1:4, 11, 20; 2:1, 7, 8, 9, 11, 12, etc. Reference to something (*ti*) written to the church (*tȩ̄ ekklēsią*) suggests that what was written was not addressed simply to the believers in the locality in which the Elder customarily moved. Yet it is difficult to imagine that it was not also addressed to his own local community. Thus *tȩ̄ ekklēsią* does not refer to a local church. More likely it refers to a group of house churches scattered throughout a region and in fairly close communication with each other. Thus the use of *ekklēsia* in 3 John lies somewhere between the Pauline use in 1 and 2 Corinthians and the reference to the universal church found in Eph 1:22; 3:10; 5:23-25, 27, 29, 32. Perhaps in Ephesians *ekklēsia* is a theological concept rather than an empirical church, local or otherwise. Thus Ephesians is not addressed to the church in Ephesus but to the saints in Ephesus. 1 John was addressed to a circle of house churches in a region in which the Elder exercised authority. The schism mentioned in 2:19 might have occurred in one local community. It obviously had repercussions throughout the whole network of believing communities which the Elder collectively designates the *ekklēsia*.

1 John is addressed to *eklektę kyrią kai tois teknois autēs*. Two interpretations seem to cover the probabilities: The elect lady is the head of a house church, or the expression is itself an analogy for a local church with the reference to her children indicating the individual members of that local church. The latter view seems to be confirmed by reference to the greetings from "the children of your elect sister," which is apparently a reference to the members of the author's community. This confirms the probability that the Johannine Epistles were addressed to a network of local churches in some region. As in 3 John (5-8, 10), the issue of hospitality is at the heart of 2 John 10. This confirms the mobility of missionaries within the network of Johannine churches. 2 and 3 John together show that there was a mutual rejection of missionaries by the Elder and his opponent Diotrephes.

2 John 7 should be looked at in relation to 1 John 2:18-24; 4:1-6. Reference to many deceivers *(planoi)* who have gone out into the world is reminiscent of 1 John 2:18, which mentions that many antichrists have appeared. They deny that Jesus is the Christ, which the author says is a denial of the Father and the Son (1 John 2:22-23). This finds further elaboration in 4:1-6 where the antichrist is recognized by the refusal to confess Jesus Christ come in the flesh *(en sarki elēlythota)*. 2 John 7 adds to the perception of the close connection between 1 John 2:18-27 and 4:1-6. In this way it becomes clear that 4:1-6 and 2 John 7 deal with the issue of the "secessionists." In 2 John 7 the many deceivers are recognized by their failure to confess Jesus Christ "coming" in the flesh *(erchomenon en sarki)*. The context of each passage concerns confession or failure to confess Jesus Christ in flesh.

There is a difference in the description of those who refuse to confess that Jesus is the Christ. They are antichrists in 1 John 2:18-25 and deceivers *(planoi)* in 2 John 7. But 1 John 2:26 is probably referring to the antichrists of 2:18 when it says "I write these things to you concerning those who would deceive you *(tōn planōntōn)*," and 2 John 7 identifies *ho planos* with the antichrist. The fluidity with which these two letters express agreement suggests the freedom of a common author rather than the stereotyping of a copyist. The same freedom is to be seen in the way each letter expands the singular deceiver/antichrist into the plural, many deceivers/antichrists. Given the lack of any known precedent for use of the term "anti-christ," this overlapping use of the term and the freedom with which this common understanding emerges are impressive evidence of the close connection between the two letters. Both letters appear to have moved to the plural use of a term in relation to the expectation of a singular figure. They did this because of the contemporary crisis faced, a crisis involving many deceivers (1 John 2:26 and 2 John 7), many false prophets (1 John 4:1). See the excursus in Georg Strecker, *The Johannine Letters* 236–41.

The main difference in language is between the tenses of *elēlythota* (1 John 4:2) and *erchomenon* (2 John 7). The present participle of 2 John 7 has been taken as a reference to the future coming in the *parousia*. (Thus Strecker, *The Johannine Letters* 232–36.) If that were the case, the issue of 2 John 7 is quite different from 1 John 4:2, which refers to the Incarnation (compare John 1:14). It is more likely, however, that 2 John 7 also refers to what we have come to call "the Incarnation." In 1 and 2 John it is Jesus Christ who has come (or comes) in the flesh. We should not expect exact agreement of language in each case, as if a precise formula with the au-thority of some church council was in view. Rather, the language is more fluid and becomes the basis of a more uniform formulation in a later cen-tury. The language of 2 John 7 probably presupposes 1 John 4:2. If that is correct, those letters belong together. Given that 2 John 7 summarizes a central issue for 1 John and overlaps discussion of the new command-ment, abiding in the Father and the Son, and uses the language of the con-fession of faith *(homologein)*, all in the space of thirteen verses, a good case can be made for recognizing 2 John as an accompanying letter introducing and commending 1 John to a specific community or circle of communities.

If 1 John was written to deal with the crisis of the schism (2:19), which threatened to disturb and fragment the believers in a network of house churches in a region in which the Elder had exercised some authority, then 2 John is addressed to a specific situation and not to Christians gen-erally. The contents of 1 John demand to be recognized as addressed specifically, yet the letter lacks a formal specific address such as we find in 2 and 3 John. If "the elect lady and her children" of 2 John is a reference to a local church and its members, this short letter provides that personal ad-dress and at the same time concisely introduces the main issues of the longer letter. 2 John might have been one of a number of letters addressed specifically to individual local churches. More likely its general form of address meant that it could be sent with 1 John as a covering letter to each of the churches in the network, except the sender's own church. The evi-dence that Irenaeus knew 1 and 2 John as a single letter lends support to this view. If the Elder wrote to "the elect lady and her children" (2 John 1), at the end he sends greetings from "the children of your elect sister" (2 John 13). The change of address from third person, "her children" (2 John 1), to second person, "your sister" (2 John 13), is necessitated by the direct form of address in the final salutation, *Aspazetai se.* . . . These greetings come from the members of the local church of the Elder.

In 2 John one issue not mentioned in 1 John finds important focus. Here the Elder directs his readers not to offer hospitality to anyone who comes with a teaching other than what they find in his letter. Such a one is identified with the deceiver/antichrist, and those who welcome such a one participate in his evil deeds. The issue of hospitality is first raised by the Elder. The person implied by reference to one who does not accept the teaching of the Elder's letter represents those who separated from the community of the Elder. They refused to make the Johannine christological confession (1 John 4:2). It is evident that they continued to have a disturbing influence within the network of churches. Because of this they continued to be the "opponents" of the Elder. But he was not concerned to persuade them of the errors of their way. Rather the aim was to neutralize, or at least minimize, the effects of their influence. Here the strategy was to limit their opportunities by strongly arguing against offering any hospitality to them (2 John 10-11).

3 John is also concerned with the issue of hospitality. It acknowledges the hospitality Gaius has provided for the supporters of the Elder (3 John 5-8) so that he and they become coworkers with the truth. Note the contrast with those who provide hospitality with the deceivers, who come to share in their evil works (2 John 10-11). Though Gaius is addressed as a supporter, it is clear that the Elder is anxious and concerned that he might waver from this resolve. The reason is that Diotrephes rejects the authority of the Elder and refuses hospitality to his supporters, excommunicating from the church any who resisted his wishes. Given that he could do this, Diotrephes must have exercised considerable authority in the community with which Gaius had some connection. But the Elder was not without support, as the letter to Gaius shows. Not only was Gaius a supporter, it seems that there were others, who were part of the community where Diotrephes exercised authority, who wished to offer hospitality to those who came to their church from the Elder. The action of Diotrephes opposed the exhortation of the Elder, excommunicating those who dissented from his policy. The Elder was content to use strong exhortation. It is a moot point whether this "softer" course of action is an indication of an inability to enforce excommunication rather than the deliberate choice of persuasion. Yet the opponents of 1 John 2:19 were not excluded. They separated themselves from the community of the Elder.

Diotrephes should not be seen as one of the secessionists/opponents mentioned in 1 John 2:19. Rather he seems to be the/a leader of one of the churches in the network in which the Elder sought to exercise authority. Diotrephes refused to recognize that authority. Because 3 John was a letter subsequent to the sending of 1 John with its covering letter (2 John), the issue of hospitality had become central. By refusing hospitality to those associated with the Elder, Diotrephes isolated his church from the influence of the Elder. Whether by design or not, this opened his church to the influence of the secessionists, unless Diotrephes refused hospitality to them also.

3 John was written to bolster the support of those, like Gaius, who were inclined to acknowledge the Elder's authority in spite of the authoritarian action of Diotrephes. Though he writes of Diotrephes in threatening terms, the best he can do is warn what will happen "if I come" (3 John 10). Even what he foreshadows is not particularly forceful: "I will call attention to what he is doing in spreading false charges against us." He goes on to draw attention to the policy of excommunication practiced by Diotrephes to neutralize support for the Elder. Gaius was probably the leader of a house church in the same locality as Diotrephes. The Elder feared the influence that Diotrephes might have on him.

Thus it seems that Diotrephes, though not one of the secessionists, plays into their hands by rejecting 1 John and cutting ties with the Elder and his supporters. The refusal to give hospitality to supporters of the Elder might have been a response to the policy of 2 John 10-11, which advocates refusal of hospitality to the false teachers. Diotrephes may have been sympathetic to secessionists and unwilling to reject them as antichrists and deceivers. Alternatively, Diotrephes may have resented the intrusion of the Elder's authority into the churches (including his own) in the surrounding area. However we read this, it seems clear that the disturbance caused by the schism was far from over in the network of the churches addressed by the Elder. He was concerned to neutralize the influence of the secessionists on those who remained in his network of churches. One of the consequences of the schism was the widespread trauma, anxiety, and uncertainty of those who remained. It was for this reason that 1 John was written and sent out under the cover of 2 John to each of the churches in the network. 3 John was later sent to one of these churches to deal with the specific secondary crisis caused by the enforced policy of Diotrephes.

## FOR REFERENCE AND FURTHER STUDY

Brown, Raymond E. *The Epistles of John*, 14–19, 30–35.
Dodd, Charles Harold. *The Johannine Epistles*, lxvi–lxxi.
Kruse, Colin G. *The Letters of John*, 7–8.
Lieu, Judith. *The Second and Third Epistles of John*. Edinburgh: T & T Clark, 1986.
Strecker, Georg. *The Johannine Letters*, 3–4.

## 7. RELATIONSHIP TO THE GOSPEL OF JOHN

The relationship of the Epistles to the Gospel of John is complex. Some kind of relationship is obvious, but it is necessary to work through complex evidence of similarities and differences if that observation is to be made more precise. Certainly the Johannine Epistles (especially 1 John) and the Gospel are closer to each other with respect to language, style, and theology than either of them is to any other early Christian writing in the New Testament. Because some form of relationship is so obvious, scholars have concentrated on differences with a view to discussing the tradition of common authorship.

### 7.1. Common authorship?

For the first half of this century the preoccupation was with the question of whether a common author wrote the Gospel and 1 John. In many ways the assembly of evidence and argument against common authorship reached a watershed in the 1937 paper by C. H. Dodd, "The First Epistle of John and the Fourth Gospel." The conclusions of his paper appeared in more summary form in his 1946 commentary, *The Johannine Epistles*. In these studies Dodd built solidly on the work of A. E. Brooke, *A Critical and Exegetical Commentary on the Johannine Epistles* (1912). But Dodd did not have it all his own way. The publication of his commentary provoked a series of responses defending the unity of authorship, first by W. F. Howard, "The Common Authorship of the Johannine Gospel and Epistles," then by W. G. Wilson, "An Examination of the Linguistic Evidence Adduced against the Unity of Authorship of the First Epistle of John and the Fourth Gospel," and A. P. Salom, "Some Aspects of the Grammatical Style of 1 John."

Dodd argued that differences between the two writings indicated different authors. About forty words in the Epistle were not used in the Gospel while groups of important words in the Gospel were not used in the Epistle. Then there is the matter of substantial differences in thought where Dodd argued that 1 John is closer to primitive Christianity and more naïvely open to Gnosticism than was the Gospel. For a brief discussion of these arguments see my *John, Witness and Theologian* 103–108. It is sufficient to say here that the relationship to emerging Gnosticism is more apparent in 1 John because the author is specifically confronting the position of his opponents. The language of the opponents has made an impact on the language of the letter as the author responds to the position of the opponents, but the author of 1 John is critical of emerging Gnosticism.

Those elements of primitive Christianity that, according to Dodd, separate 1 John from the Gospel concern eschatology, the Spirit, and the death of Jesus. While the imminent future emphasis might be more prominent in 1 John, it is not absent from the Gospel (see 5:21-29; 6:39, 40, 44, 54; 12:48; 14:3; 17:24). Attempts to reinterpret the evangelist's eschatology wholly in realized terms are only possible by excluding such passages. At the same time, a recognition of fulfillment in the present is not absent from 1 John (2:8; 5:20). There are differences between the Gospel and 1 John on the teaching concerning the Spirit and the death of Jesus. The Gospel nowhere uses the expression *hilasmos peri tōn hamartiōn hēmōn* (1 John 2:2; 4:10) of Jesus, though this motif is not incompatible with the Gospel. On the other hand, 1 John does not speak of the Spirit as the Paraclete or develop the role of the Spirit along lines found in the Farewell Discourses in the Gospel. Instead, the Spirit inspires the true confession of faith in the confrontation with false prophets understood as antichrists. John 15:26-27 implies a prophetic witness inspired by the Spirit. This suggests an inspired confession like that of 1 John 4:2. Thus even these differences are not so sharp that they rule out common authorship.

The linguistic evidence adduced to argue for separate authorship is neutralized to a degree by noting that 1 John is only about one sixth the length of the Gospel and the two are very different kinds of book. Size, genre, and subject matter have a marked bearing on the language used. The Gospel is predominantly narrative concerning the mission of Jesus. This is quite different from the discursive nature of 1 John, which has more in common with the language of the discourses of the Gospel, especially the Farewell Discourses. Linguistically the Gospel and 1 John are no more different from each other than the variations we find amongst the Pauline letters.

The evidence, linguistic and theological, concerning the relationship of 1 John to the Gospel is somewhat inconclusive. As early as we can trace evidence about the order of the Gospels, the Gospel of John was regarded as the Fourth. Evidence within the Gospel itself suggests that it is the product of a process of composition, and in that process more than one hand can be discerned (see John 20:30-31 and 21:24-25). From this perspective the possibility of a Johannine School emerges. Jesus gathered disciples around him, founding what can be understood as a school, though perhaps not as tightly organized as was argued by Birger Gerhardsson in his important book, *Memory and Manuscript* (1961).

Examples of schools that studied and handed on teaching traditions are to be found in the philosophical schools and, in the Jewish context, in the "house (school) of Hillel." There is evidence too that Philo of Alexandria formed a school that might have influenced the formation of the catechetical school best known under the leadership of Clement and then Origen in Alexandria. No exact parallel with any of these schools is claimed for the Johannine school, only that there were ample precedents for such a

development. See Alan Culpepper, *The Johannine School* 258–59, and the
discussion below.

While it is important to distinguish the Johannine school from the
community or communities it sought to influence, it should not be distanced from those communities. The school developed its teaching not for
its own benefit but in order to teach the Johannine community. The evidence of the Gospel suggests that in its development this process was
sometimes open-ended so that mission to the world outside was promi-
nently in view. At other times both the school and the community were
suffering trauma: after the struggle with the synagogue and after the se-
cession of 1 John 2:19. There is evidence that through the struggle with the
synagogue the Johannine community became increasingly isolated from
the broader Jewish community.

The survival of the school was threatened by the death of the founder.
It may not have survived long after the deaths of the leaders who directly
followed him. The school seems to have depended on the vitality and inspiration of the founder. Those who followed him may have been lesser
figures. This is suggested by the rich and creative use of symbolism in the
Gospel, where a relatively limited vocabulary is used with mastery and to
good effect. Of the Epistles, 1 John stands closest to the Gospel. By comparison, its syntax is so unclear that problems confront the reader in almost every verse. In spite of this, the author of 1 John has his moments.
"This is the message that we have heard from him and report to you, 'God
is light and in him there is no darkness at all'" (1:5). "This is the message
that you heard from the beginning, 'Let us love one another'" (3:11). "By
this we know love, he gave his life for us and we ought to give our lives
for the brethren" (3:16). "Beloved, let us love one another, because love is
of God, and every one who loves is born of God and knows God" (4:7).
See the whole passage 4:7-12 as well as "God is love, and the one abiding
in love abides in God and God abides in him." The love for the brethren is
not allowed to remain in the ether. Rather, it is tied down to Christian
charity in the deepest sense (see 3:17-18). Where the Gospel stands out is
in the clarity of the message as against the often conflicting and unclear
statements of 1 John.

While the evidence does not exclude the possibility of a common author,
it does not make common authorship probable. The evidence of 1 John
and the Gospel leads us to a view of common authorship only in the light
of tradition that we can trace back, at the earliest, to the late second century. The gap between that evidence and the origin of the Johannine
Gospel and Epistles is too great to inspire confidence in the reliability of
the evidence.

The position argued in this commentary is that the evidence makes it
unlikely that the evangelist wrote 1 John. Such a possibility cannot be

ruled out categorically. Such matters as the length of the Gospel and the brevity of 1 John (one sixth the length of the Gospel), the different nature of the writings—a Gospel and whatever 1 John is—provide a basis for explaining differences. It is also true that 1 John is closer to certain parts of the Gospel than others, especially to the Farewell Discourses. If the Gospel is the culmination of a lengthy process of composition, 1 John may well be closer to some later stage of its development.

## 7.2. Literary and thematic evidence

The author of 1 John lacks the fundamental literary skills manifest in the Gospel. All commentators note textual problems and the lack of clear meaning in verse after verse of 1 John. By comparison the meaning of the text of the Gospel is largely free from problems. The first four verses of 1 John constitute a single sentence and provide the unsuspecting reader with fair warning of the difficulties to be faced in untangling the meaning of what follows. Thus while there are so many connections with the language and thought world of the Gospel, the author of 1 John rarely rises to the literary heights of the Gospel. Care must be taken here in talking of the evangelist's literary skills. Certainly he writes clear and correct Greek. But the artistry does not inhere in the command of a substantial vocabulary and a sophisticated use of syntactical constructions. Rather it is in the impressive use of a limited vocabulary to tell a dramatic story, full of surprises and layered with levels of meaning. The discourses too provide an interpretation of the story that illuminates the various layers of meaning. Through this there emerges what we recognize as the Johannine interpretation of the Gospel. This can be seen as making explicit what is, at best, implicit and undeveloped in the Gospel tradition. Alongside this achievement the author of 1 John appears to be somewhat inept. Nevertheless, it is argued that he was working with the tradition of the Gospel of John and interpreting it against the position of his opponents. Perhaps the difficulties of this task led the author to be less than fully coherent from time to time.

One of the most striking shared perspectives between the Gospel and the Epistles is summed up by the term "dualism"—between light and darkness, truth and error/falsehood, God and the devil, love and hate. These polarities determine the view of reality expressed in the writings. Thus they are particularly significant. Talk of dualism must be carefully qualified when using it of the Johannine writings. This I have attempted to do in *The Quest for the Messiah* (2nd ed. 1993, 36–47). Briefly, the understanding of God as the creator of all things is held in tension with a recognition of the reality of the power of evil that is opposed to God and seeks to frustrate God's purpose. Human life is lived between God and evil, light and darkness, truth and falsehood, love and hate/murder. Although the present world is God's creation, it is dominated by the power of evil. However, it will not remain, because God has ordained an end to evil. Indeed, God has already acted and the true light is already shining. Nevertheless, evil has not been vanquished finally and there remains a struggle before the power of evil is brought to an end. The signs of the impending great struggle are recognized in the appearance of many false prophets, antichrists. But the victory is assured because the Son of God has already appeared and the belief he evoked is the power to overcome the evil of the world. Nevertheless, the final victory awaits the appearance of the Son of God in judgment.

This dualism, which also defines the sons of light and the sons of darkness, is on the one hand an explanation for why some people believe and others reject the message of the Gospel. From this perspective dualism appears to imply a deterministic understanding whereby everything is determined by its origin, in the light or the darkness. In one sense this may be true. In practice the dualism works quite differently because people are called on to recognize and thereby choose their origin, in the light or the darkness. It is for this reason that Bultmann aptly described the Johannine dualism as "a dualism of decision."

It is important to remember that Johannine language operates within the dualistic framework described above. With this perspective in mind we can examine the shared language of the Gospel and Epistles, comparing it with the usage of the Synoptics, Paul, and the NT as a whole.

| | Matt | Mark | Luke | John | JohnEp | 1 John | 2 John | 3 John | Paul | NT |
|---|---|---|---|---|---|---|---|---|---|---|
| *agapan* | 8 | 5 | 13 | 36 | 31 | 28 | 2 | 1 | 33 | 141 |
| *agapē* | 1 | 1 | – | 7 | 21 | 18 | 2 | 1 | 75 | 116 |
| *aiōn* | 8 | 4 | 7 | 13 | 2 | 1 | 1 | – | 38 | 123 |
| *aiōnios* | 6 | 3 | 4 | 17 | 6 | 6 | – | – | 21 | 70 |
| *alētheia* | 1 | 3 | 3 | 25 | 20 | 9 | 5 | 6 | 47 | 109 |
| *alēthēs* | 1 | 1 | – | 4 | 3 | 2 | – | 1 | 4 | 26 |
| *alēthinos* | – | – | 1 | 9 | 4 | 4 | – | – | 1 | 28 |
| *alēthōs* | 3 | 2 | 3 | 7 | 1 | 1 | – | – | 1 | 18 |
| *hamartanein* | 3 | – | 4 | 3 | 10 | 10 | – | – | 17 | 42 |
| *hamartia* | 7 | 6 | 11 | 17 | 17 | 17 | – | – | 64 | 173 |
| *archē* | 4 | 4 | 3 | 8 | 10 | 8 | 2 | – | 11 | 55 |
| *gennan* | 45 | 1 | 4 | 18 | 10 | 10 | – | – | 7 | 97 |
| *ginōskein* | 20 | 12 | 28 | 56 | 26 | 25 | 1 | – | 50 | 221 |
| *graphein* | 10 | 10 | 21 | 21 | 18 | 13 | 2 | 3 | 12 | 190 |

|  | Matt | Mark | Luke | John | JohnEp | 1 John | 2 John | 3 John | Paul | NT |
|---|---|---|---|---|---|---|---|---|---|---|
| *diabolos* | 6 | – | 5 | 3 | 4 | 4 | – | – | 8 | 37 |
| *oida* | 25 | 22 | 25 | 85 | 16 | 15 | – | 1 | 103 | 321 |
| *entolē* | 6 | 6 | 4 | 11 | 18 | 14 | 4 | – | 14 | 68 |
| *ergazesthai* | 4 | 1 | 1 | 8 | 2 | – | 1 | 1 | 18 | 41 |
| *ergon* | 6 | 2 | 2 | 27 | 5 | 3 | 1 | 1 | 68 | 169 |
| *echein* | 75 | 69 | 77 | 86 | 34 | 28 | 4 | 2 | 159 | 705 |
| *zēn* | 6 | 3 | 9 | 17 | 1 | 1 | – | – | 59 | 140 |
| *zōē* | 7 | 4 | 5 | 36 | 13 | 13 | – | – | 37 | 135 |
| *thanatos* | 7 | 6 | 7 | 8 | 6 | 6 | – | – | 47 | 120 |
| *theos* | 51 | 48 | 122 | 83 | 67 | 62 | 2 | 3 | 548 | 1314 |
| *Iēsous* | 150 | 81 | 89 | 237 | 14 | 12 | 2 | – | 213 | 905 |
| *hina* (gr.S) | 41 | 65 | 46 | 147 | 27 | 20 | 5 | 2 | 249 | 673 |
| *kathōs* | 3 | 8 | 17 | 31 | 13 | 9 | 2 | 2 | 84 | 178 |
| *kosmos* | 8 | 3 | 3 | 78 | 24 | 23 | 1 | – | 47 | 185 |
| *logos* | 33 | 24 | 33 | 40 | 7 | 6 | – | 1 | 84 | 331 |
| *martyrein* | 1 | – | 1 | 33 | 10 | 6 | – | 4 | 8 | 76 |
| *martyria* | – | 3 | 1 | 14 | 7? | 14 | – | – | 2 | 37 |
| *menein* | 3 | 2 | 7 | 40 | 27 | 24 | 3 | – | 17 | 118 |
| *misein* | 5 | 1 | 7 | 12 | 5 | 5 | – | – | 4 | 39 |
| *monogenēs* | – | – | 3 | 4 | 1 | 1 | – | – | – | 9 |
| *nikan* | – | – | 1 | 1 | 6 | 6 | – | – | 3 | 28 |
| *nyn* | 4 | 3 | 14 | 28 | 5 | 4 | 1 | – | 52 | 148 |
| *homologein* | 4 | – | 2 | 4 | 6 | 5 | 1 | – | 4 | 26 |
| *onoma* | 22 | 15 | 34 | 25 | 5 | 3 | – | 2 | 21 | 228 |
| *horan* | 13 | 7 | 14 | 31 | 8 | 7 | – | 1 | 10 | 114 |
| *hoti* | 141 | 101 | 173 | 271 | 78 | 75 | 2 | 1 | 282 | 1285 |
| *houtos* (gr.S) | 147 | 78 | 230 | 237 | 48 | – | – | – | 268 | 1388 |
| *parrēsia* | – | 1 | – | 9 | 4 | 4 | – | – | 8 | 31 |
| *patēr* | 64 | 18 | 56 | 137 | 18 | 14 | 4 | – | 63 | 415 |
| *peri* (gr.S) | 28 | 22 | 45 | 66 | 11 | 10 | – | 1 | 52 | 331 |
| *peripatein* | 7 | 9 | 5 | 17 | 10 | 5 | 3 | 2 | 32 | 95 |
| *pisteuein* | 11 | 14 | 9 | 98 | 9 | 9 | – | – | 54 | 241 |
| *planan* | 8 | 4 | 1 | 2 | 3 | 3 | – | – | 6 | 39 |
| *pneuma* | 19 | 23 | 36 | 24 | 12 | 12 | – | – | 146 | 379 |
| *poiein* | 84 | 47 | 88 | 110 | 16 | 13 | – | 3 | 82 | 565 |

| | Matt | Mark | Luke | John | JohnEp | 1 John | 2 John | 3 John | Paul | NT |
|---|---|---|---|---|---|---|---|---|---|---|
| *ponēros* | 26 | 2 | 13 | 3 | 8 | 6 | 1 | 1 | 13 | 78 |
| *sarx* | 5 | 4 | 2 | 13 | 3 | 2 | 1 | – | 91 | 147 |
| *skotia* | 2 | – | 1 | 8 | 6 | 6 | – | – | – | 17 |
| *skotos* | 6 | 1 | 4 | 1 | 1 | 1 | – | – | 11 | 30 |
| *sōtēr* | – | – | 2 | 1 | 1 | 1 | – | – | 12 | 24 |
| *teknion* | – | – | – | 1 | 7 | 7 | – | – | – | 8 |
| *teknon* | 19 | 9 | 14 | 3 | 9 | 5 | 3 | 1 | 39 | 99 |
| *teleios* | 3 | – | – | – | 1 | 1 | – | – | 8 | 19 |
| *teleioun* | – | – | 2 | 5 | 4 | 4 | – | – | 1 | 23 |
| *tērein* | 6 | 1 | – | 18 | 7 | 7 | – | – | 7 | 70 |
| *typhloun* | – | – | – | 1 | 1 | 1 | – | – | 1 | 3 |
| *hydōr* | 7 | 5 | 6 | 21 | 4 | 4 | – | – | 1 | 76 |
| *phaneroun* | – | 3 | – | 9 | 9 | 9 | – | – | 22 | 49 |
| *phobos* | 3 | 1 | 7 | 3 | 3 | 3 | – | – | 15 | 47 |
| *phylassein* | 1 | 1 | 6 | 3 | 1 | 1 | – | – | 8 | 31 |
| *phōs* | 7 | 1 | 7 | 23 | 6 | 6 | – | – | 13 | 73 |
| *chairein* | 6 | 2 | 12 | 9 | 4 | – | 3 | 1 | 29 | 74 |
| *chara* | 6 | 1 | 8 | 9 | 3 | 1 | 1 | 1 | 21 | 59 |
| *Christos* | 17 | 7 | 12 | 19 | 12 | 9 | 3 | – | 379 | 529 |
| *pseudos* | – | – | – | 1 | 2 | 2 | – | – | 4 | 10 |
| *pseustēs* | – | – | – | 2 | 5 | 5 | – | – | 3 | 10 |

Whether or not the Gospel and Epistles have a common author, it is important to note the main lines of contact between 1 John and the Gospel. The main common vocabulary has been set out with a view to showing the way the language of the Gospel and Epistles looks in relation to the rest of the New Testament. There is a good case for recognizing characteristic Johannine language. The force of the evidence is strongest when we take account of the way the Gospel and 1 John use this language. This has been well set out by A. E. Brooke (*Commentary* i–x), who shows that the similarities and differences are best weighed when the use of common words is seen in phrases. His work makes free use of the 1882 studies by H. J. Holtzmann (*Das Problem des 1 Johannesbr. in seinem Verhältnis zum Evang. Jahrbuch für Protestant. Theologie* 1882). His comparisons, based on the Greek words and phrases, should be consulted by anyone seriously concerned to understand the relationship between these two works and to gain a firm grasp of the nature of the Johannine tradition. Simply to list the parallel texts side by side provides a preliminary analysis, making some observations fairly obvious. Some of the more notable parallels are set out below. Attention is drawn to the use of common and significant words in similar phrases. Specific examples are also related to broader Johannine syntax and style. As far as possible, translation agreement in the comparisons reflects a common use of vocabulary and syntax.

| 1 John | Gospel of John |
|---|---|
| 5:20 that we may know the one who is true | 17:3 that they may know you the only true God |

In each text we have the use of *hina* followed by *ginōskein* in the subjunctive. In each case the object of knowledge is expressed using *alēthinos*. Thus we have a complex web of similarities at the levels of syntax as well as shared vocabulary. The frequent use of *hina* clauses is a Johannine characteristic (147 times in John and 27 times in the Johannine Epistles; see the list above).

| 1 John | Gospel of John |
|---|---|
| 4:9 he has sent his only begotten Son | 1:14 as the only begotten from the Father |
| | 1:18 only begotten God (Son) |
| | 3:16 he gave his only begotten Son |
| | 3:18 of the only begotten Son of God |

Five of the nine uses of *monogenēs* in the NT are found in the Gospel and 1 John. Interestingly, although the Gospel says God gave *(edōken)* his only begotten Son, 1 John expresses this motif using the characteristically Johannine verb *apostellein*, which, with *pempein*, is used to express the Father's sending of the Son, but without using *monogenēs*. John 1:14 comes close when describing "the only begotten from the Father." Here "sent" may be implied. This is another constellation of significant Johannine characteristics. It is one in which the author of 1 John has freely and appropriately brought together two important Johannine words that do not appear together in the Gospel.

| 1 John | Gospel of John |
|---|---|
| 4:6  the Spirit of truth | 14:16-17  another Paraclete, the Spirit of truth (cf. 15:26) |
|  | 16:13  he, the Spirit of truth |
| 1:6  we do not do the truth | 3:21  but the one who does the truth |

The phrase "do the truth" (in 1 John 1:6 and John 3:21) is intelligible as a Semitism meaning "to act faithfully." Use of it in the NT is a Johannine characteristic. The use of the participle with the definite article in John 3:21 is a characteristic of 1 John and there is a concentration of this use in John 14–16. Here, as with other aspects of 1 John, similarities are stronger in relation to the Farewell Discourses of the Gospel than to the narrative sections.

| 1 John | Gospel of John |
|---|---|
| 1:8  the truth is not in us | 8:44  truth is not in him |
| 2:21  he is not of (*ek*) the truth | 18:37  everyone who is of (*ho ōn ek*) the truth |
| 3:19  we are of the truth |  |
| 3:8  he is of the devil | 8:44  you are of your father the devil |
| 3:10  he is not of God (cf. 4:1-4, 6; 5:19) |  |
| 2:16  it is of the world | 8:23  you are of this world (cf. 18:36) |
|  | 15:19  if you were of the world (cf. 17:14, 16) |
| 2:29  is begotten of him | 1:13  those begotten of God |
| 3:9  everyone begotten of God (cf. 5:4, 18) | 3:8  everyone begotten of the Spirit |

In both 1 John 3:9 and John 3:8 the authors write *pas ho gegennēmenos*. Throughout the passages listed above, "of" translates the preposition *ek*, which indicates the sense of the source or origin.

| 1 John | Gospel of John |
|---|---|
| 3:1 that we should be called children of God | 1:12 he gave them authority to be children of God (*tekna theou*, cf. 10:52) |
| 3:2 now we are children of God (cf. 3:10; 5:2) | |
| 2:11 he walks in the darkness (cf. 1:6) | 8:12 shall not walk in darkness (cf. 11:9, 10; 12:35) |
| 4:20 he is not able to love God whom he has not seen | 6:46 not that anyone has seen the father |
| | 1:18 no one has seen God |
| 3:16 he gave his life for (*hyper*) us | 10:11 gives his life for (*hyper*) the sheep (cf. 10:15, 17, 18; 13:37, 38; 15:13) |
| 1:8 we have no sin (guilt) | 9:41 you would not have sin |
| 5:13 that you may know that you have eternal life | 3:15 that everyone who believes in him may have eternal life (cf. 3:16, 36; 5:24, 39; 6:40, 47, 54) |
| 3:14 we have passed from death into life | 5:24 he has passed from death into life |
| 5:4 conquers the world; and this is the victory which conquers the world (cf. 5:5) | 16:33 I have conquered the world |
| 5:9 if we receive the witness of men | 3:33 the one receiving his witness (cf. 3:11) |
| | 5:34 but I do not receive the witness of man |
| 3:5 he was revealed to take away sin | 1:29 the one who takes away the sin of the world |
| 5:6 the one who came through water and blood | 19:34 immediately came out water and blood |
| 2:28 abide in him | 15:4, 7 abide in me (and cf. 14:10; 6:56) |
| 4:12 God abides in him (cf. 4:13, 15, 16) | |

| 3:4 everyone who does sin (cf. 3:8, 9) | 8:34 everyone who does sin |
|---|---|
| 4:16 and we have known and believed | 6:69 and we have believed and known that |
| 2:3 if we keep his commandments (cf. 2:4; 3:22, 24; 5:3) | 14:15 you will keep my commandments |
| 3:23 even as *(kathōs)* he gave *(edōken)* me | 14:31 even as the Father gave commandment to us to |
| | 12:49 the Father who sent me has given *(dedōken)* commandment to me |
| | 13:34 a new commandment I give to you |
| 2:17 the one doing the will of God abides forever *(menei eis ton aiōna)* | 8:35 the Son abides forever |
| | 12:34 the Christ abides forever |
| 3:3 he sanctifies himself | 11:55 to sanctify themselves |
| 2:6 even as he walked *(kathōs ekeinos periepatēsen)*, cf. 3:3, 5, 7, 16; 4:17 | 2:21 but he *(ekeinos)* spoke concerning the temple of his body |
| | 3:30 he *(ekeinos)* must increase |
| | 4:25 when he *(ekeinos)* comes |
| | 9:27 the one speaking to you is he *(ekeinos)* |

In the Johannine writings *ekeinos* is not invariably used of Jesus, as John 1:8 shows. Nevertheless, there is a tendency to do so in both the Gospel and first Epistle.

A. E. Brooke (*Commentary* ix) quotes Holtzmann (*Das Problem des ersten Johannesbriefes* 134) with approval: "In the whole of the first Epistle there is hardly a single thought that is not found in the Gospel." The similarities between the two writings are closer than those between Luke and Acts or 1 and 2 Thessalonians. While there are differences between the Gospel and Epistle, Brooke thinks that none of these precludes common authorship. Reference to 1 and 2 Thessalonians raises the question of imitation. Brooke rejects the possibility that a writer of the power and originality of the evangelist would copy himself or another. He argues that an author "who had steeped himself in the thought of the Fourth Gospel might produce the First Epistle." Perhaps John 21 is the work of the same imitator. Nevertheless, Brooke thinks that the tradition of common authorship "remains the most probable explanation known to us" (xviii).

I do not doubt that the author of 1 John was steeped in the thought of the Fourth Gospel. The adaptation of the tradition to meet the crisis caused by the secessionists was a creative achievement, though not of the same order that we find in the symbolic transformation of the Gospel. The adaptation of the tradition to deal with a specific crisis in the Johannine circle of churches calls attention to the relationship between 1 John and the Gospel. Brooke concludes that the Epistle is later in composition than the Gospel and that it was written to clarify the situation caused by the opponents. This accounts for the limitations of the Epistle when compared with the Gospel and for the change in viewpoint in 1 John. It does not adequately take account of the tangled Greek of 1 John and its consequent lack of clarity. This, more than differences of thought in the Gospel and 1 John, poses a problem for the view of common authorship. At the same time there are striking similarities, particularly in their openings and closings. The Prologues of the Gospel (1:1-18) and 1 John (1:1-5) are by no means identical but they stand together against anything else in the NT, sharing a large number of common features in a short space. Raymond E. Brown (*Epistles of John* 179) sets out the following similarities, including 1 John 1:5 as a relevant transitional verse.

| John 1:1-18 | 1 John 1:1-4(5) |
|---|---|
| 1a  In the beginning was the Word | 1a  What was from the beginning |
| 1b  The Word was in God's presence | 2de  Eternal life which was in the Father's presence |
| 4a  In him (the Word) was life | 1f  The word of life |
| 4b  The life was the light of men | 5d  God is light |
| 5ab  The light shines in the darkness, for the darkness did not overcome it | 5e  and in Him there is no darkness at all |
| 14a  The Word became flesh | 2a  This life was revealed |
| 14b  and made his dwelling among us | 2f  and was revealed to us |
| 14c  and we looked at his glory | 1d  what we looked at |

| 16ab Of his fullness have we all received<br><br>17a  through Jesus Christ<br><br>18b  God the only Son | 3de  The communion we have is with the Father and with His Son, Jesus Christ |
|---|---|

The parallels are quite marked and significant, though they do not follow the Gospel in the same order. The rearrangement of order confirms a free working with the tradition. Thus, for example, the parallel with 17a and 18b in the Gospel is found in a reversal of order in the last two lines of 3de from 1 John.

What does this comparison of the Prologues reveal? A copyist is more likely to follow a text rather mechanically. At the same time, a more creative use of a source does not provide evidence of a common author. Authors frequently used sources creatively. Brown does not argue for common authorship on the basis of the parallels. Rather he argues that 1 John's use of the Gospel's Prologue manifests the author's literary ineptness by comparison with the evangelist. Nevertheless, Brown argues that this reinterpretation attempted to clarify the meaning of the Gospel in opposition to the interpretation of the secessionists. Thus the recognition of the hand of an independent author does not signal the work of a copyist. The evidence suggests rather the work of an authoritative interpreter.

Alternatively, Georg Strecker suggests that the authors of the Gospel and 1 John independently drew on a common tradition (*Johannine Letters* 9, n. 8), which he describes as "the independent language and world of ideas of the Johannine school." While this view cannot be ruled out, it is made less likely by the recognition that 1 John also shares the form of closure found in the Gospel. The language of the concluding statements of purpose (John 20:30-31; 1 John 5:13) is similar in each writing, but with some differences. What is particularly impressive is that in each case the closure comes before the end! So conclusion-like is John 20:30-31 that many scholars think it was the original ending to the Gospel, perhaps taken over by the evangelist from a source used. I am inclined to think that it is a Johannine composition, strongly manifesting distinctive Johannine characteristics. If 20:30-31 was once the conclusion, it seems that ch. 21 has been added by other members of the Johannine school (see 21:21-24, especially v. 24), making use of Johannine tradition. Be that as it may, our task is to look at 20:30-31 in relation to 1 John 5:13.

> Jesus performed many other signs in the presence of his disciples, which are not written in this book; but *these things (tauta)* are written that you may *believe* that Jesus is the Christ *the son of God* and that believing *in* his *name* you may *have life*. (John 20:30-31)

I wrote *these things (tauta)* to you that you may know that you *have* eternal life, who *believe in* the *name of the Son of God.* (1 John 5:13)

The comparison of 1 John 5:13 is mainly with John 20:31. There are striking points of contact and agreement, though the stated purpose of 1 John is certainly not exactly the same as indicated in John 20:31. It can be said to build on that purpose. Both refer to the purpose of *writing* using a common verb (different tenses of *graphō*) and concerning a common subject. For both, what is written is referred to as *tauta*, though what this refers to is the Gospel, encompassing a collection of signs, on the one hand, and the Epistle, on the other. For both, the purpose is stated using *hina* with the following verb in the subjunctive mood. The content, with some variation, is in terms of believing and having eternal life. If they were not written by the same person it is difficult to resist the conclusion that both statements of purpose are drawn, at close range, from a common tradition or that one conclusion was based on the other. If literary dependence is suspected, this evidence implies the use of the Gospel by the author of 1 John. The placing of 1 John 5:13 prior to the end of the Epistle seems to presuppose the comparable conclusion of the Gospel prior to its actual end. Because ch. 21 appears to have been added by a hand or hands other than those of the evangelist, this implies that 1 John presupposes the final form of the Gospel including ch. 21.

The dependence of 1 John on the Gospel is also implied by a comparison of the stated purposes. The Gospel was written in order that the readers may come to believe and thus have eternal life. The evangelist simply asserts that those who believe have eternal life. The objective is to lead the readers to believe and the strategies of the Gospel are designed to achieve this end. Whether the evangelist used a present or an aorist subjunctive *(pisteu[s]ēte)* in 20:31, he wrote to promote believing, because such believing opened the way to eternal life. It need not be shown in detail that such belief assumes the christological content proclaimed by the Gospel because the point to be made here is simply that the purpose of the Gospel is to lead readers to believe. But 1 John is written to those who already believe and the purpose of the letter is to assure those who believe that they have eternal life. It is to provide assuring knowledge (5:13).

To this point differences in content have been ignored in order to draw out the strong connections between the two passages. Some of the differences are a consequence of the genre of the Gospel and the kind of writing 1 John is. While the evangelist was aware that the Gospel was a book (20:30), both authors refer to their writings as "these things" *(tauta),* John 20:31 and 1 John 5:13. In each writing something different is in view. The evangelist has in mind, in using *tauta,* the signs *(sēmeia)* narrated in the Gospel, while the author of 1 John refers more straightforwardly to what he has written. The language of the Gospel, using the passive *(gegrammena . . . gegraptai),* is suggestive of a reference to scripture. The author of 1 John unpretentiously says, "I wrote *(egrapsa)* these things to you."

The evangelist wrote "that you may believe that Jesus is the Christ . . . that believing in his name you may have life." 1 John (5:13) assumed that truth but needed to concentrate on another problem. The assurance of eternal life had been shaken among the Johannine believers, or some at least. 1 John is written to assure, "that you may *know* that you have eternal life, who believe in the name of the son of God." This difference of purpose is explicable as a consequence of the confusion and uncertainty produced by schism involving the departure of a significant group from what had been the believing community (1 John 2:18-19).

That the community left behind was destabilized by the schism was at least the perception of the author of 1 John. His writing is preoccupied with the task of reestablishing confidence and community. His strategy was twofold, to make his readers aware (that you may *know*) (1) that the opponents were in error and (2) that those who believe have eternal life. To this end it was crucial that the object and content of belief be "correct." Both the Gospel and 1 John focus on the correct content, using *hoti* clauses to clarify the content of belief and knowing. The use of *hoti* is concentrated in the Gospel (271x) and Johannine Epistles (78x). Elsewhere it is used 141 times in Matthew, 101 times in Mark, 173 times in Luke, 120 times in Acts, 282 times in Paul including the deutero-Paulines, 62 times in Revelation. Thus there is a far greater concentration in the Johannine Gospel and Epistles than in any other part of the NT. Even here, however, there are differences in the midst of a profound common perspective. In the Gospel, believing and knowing seem to be interchangeable to a large degree, so that those who believe have eternal life (3:16) as do those who know (17:3). The order of believing and knowing (8:31-32) can be reversed to knowing and believing (4:53). On this subject see the celebrated article in *TDNT* 1:689–719 by Rudolf Bultmann and my summary treatment in *John, Witness and Theologian* 71–100. In 1 John 5:13 knowing is the self-conscious awareness of believing and of eternal life as its consequence. It is a more reflective response to the reality of believing than is to be found in the Gospel. To know or believe is one thing. To reflect, that is, to know that you know or believe is another. From this perspective the position of 1 John seems to be logically dependent on that of the Gospel.

Believing on the name *(eis to onoma)* is an important expression (1 John 5:13, and see John 1:12; 2:23; 3:18). In this one phrase we have two important Johannine characteristics: *pisteuein* followed by *eis* and the use of this expression with the name *(onoma)* as the object of believing. Eternal life, as a consequence of believing and knowing, is characteristically Johannine. The theme separates John from the Synoptics, where kingdom of God (heaven) terminology dominates while "eternal life" is rarely mentioned. In John it is kingdom of God language that is rare while eternal life is a common theme as in 1 John. Knowing is central to both the Gospel and Epistles but the noun (*gnōsis*, "knowledge") is not found at all in the Johannine Gospel and Epistles. The similarities between the openings and closings of the Gospel and 1 John strongly suggest some kind of relationship between these two writings. The similarities draw attention to distinctive Johannine characteristics in terms of both dominant Johannine vocabulary and idioms.

## 7.3. Priority of the Gospel

Which came first, the Gospel or the Epistles? Or are they all contemporary, written more or less at the same time? The evidence is inadequate to settle the question when the alternatives are put in these terms because it suggests a developing gospel tradition that goes back, in some form, to Jesus. The Epistles are the fruit of some relationship to that developing tradition in written or oral form, perhaps at an early stage of its development. On the other hand, the similarities between the two endings may imply that the Gospel was known complete with ch. 21. Thus 1 John 5:14-21 follows the conclusion in 5:13 just as John 21 follows the conclusion of John 20:30-31.

The finished Gospel is generally dated around 85–90 C.E. The overall evidence of the Gospel confirms the implications of ch. 21. That chapter appears to have been appended to an earlier version of the Gospel that concluded at 20:30-31. It is not only the evidence of 20:30-31 that implies that ch. 21 is an addition. John 21:21-24 indicates that a hand or hands other than the primary author added the whole of ch. 21 and perhaps other material as well. Discussion of the purpose of this addition is complex. First, the addition implies the death of the evangelist (Beloved Disciple) and seeks to provide a rationale for it. That rationale includes setting out a working relationship between the Beloved Disciple and Peter. Chapter 21 also modifies the Gospel's Jerusalem orientation by adding the return to Galilee where Jesus meets with apparently disillusioned disciples and regathers and recommissions them via the recommissioning of Peter.

Chapter 21 suggests that the primary evangelist was not the single author of the final Gospel. Thus the relationship of the Gospel to the Epistles might be explained via someone other than the evangelist. The hands responsible for the completion of the Gospel are effectively what is meant by the Johannine school. It was made up by the disciples of the evangelist, teachers who recognized the authority of the evangelist and sought to establish his understanding of the tradition. Although a uniform interpretation of the tradition may not have developed in the school, a high degree of agreement is to be expected.

If scholars in the first half of the twentieth century were concerned with the question of the common authorship of the Gospel and 1 John, those of today generally reject common authorship. The debate now concerns whether the Gospel has a single author and the Epistles a common author. In this new awareness of complexity it is a question of the relationship of the Epistles to each other and to the Gospel.

It is generally recognized that a breach between Johannine believers and the synagogue had already taken place by the time the Gospel was published, though some critics think that the failure to establish the enforcement of *birkath ha-minim* as a datable event invalidates this hypothesis. Some of those who accept that the evidence in John establishes a breach, at least for the Johannine community (Lieu, *Epistles* 187 n. 44), think of it as past and minimize its impact on the shaping of the tradition in the Johannine Gospel (Lieu, *Epistles* [1986] 168, 212). What is not always taken into account is the evidence of the shaping of the tradition in the Gospel at various earlier stages of its history. If the Gospel was published around 90 C.E. the tradition was in a process of being shaped between 30 and 90 C.E. It is likely that 1 John was written toward the end of that period or perhaps soon after it. While the publication of the Gospel was the consequence of a lengthy transmission of tradition, the Epistles were written in a relatively short space of time in response to a single significant crisis.

FOR REFERENCE AND FURTHER STUDY

Beutler, Johannes. *Die Johannesbriefe*, 18–20.
Brooke, Alan England. *A Critical and Exegetical Commentary on the Johannine Epistles*, i–xxvii.
Brown, Raymond E. *The Epistles of John*, 32–35, 86–92.
Dodd, Charles Harold. *The First Epistle of John and the Fourth Gospel*.
_____. *The Johannine Epistles*, xlvii–lvi.
Howard, Wilbert F. "The Common Authorship of the Johannine Gospel and Epistles," 12–25.
Kruse, Colin G. *The Letters of John*, 5–7.
Lieu, Judith. *The Second and Third Epistles of John*. Edinburgh: T & T Clark, 1986.
Rensberger, David. *1 John, 2 John, 3 John*, 20–21.
Salom, A. P. "Some Aspects of the Grammatical Style of 1 John," 96–102.
Schnackenburg, Rudolf. *The Johannine Epistles*, 34–39.
Wilson, W. G. "An Examination of the Linguistic Evidence Adduced against the Unity of Authorship of the First Epistle of John and the Fourth Gospel," 147–56.

## 8. MARKS OF THE JOHANNINE SCHOOL

Of the Gospels, only John has a closely related group of Epistles written to a network of house churches. That network can be thought of as the Johannine community in its broadest sense. Within the network some of the churches were likely to have been more in accord with the Johannine point of view than others. We may take the church of Diotrephes (3 John 9-10) as an example of a more distant relationship, but even in that church there were those sympathetic to the Elder and his cause. The church of Gaius, to whom 3 John was written, was more closely a Johannine church. 1 John is probably addressed to a group of churches. Thus the broad Johannine community provides a spectrum of responses to the Johannine vision. The Epistles are the instruments used to realize the Johannine vision more effectively within that broad community.

The existence of the Epistles alongside the Gospel of John suggests the activity of a Johannine school. 3 John provides evidence of a group closely associated with the Elder in his work of disseminating the Johannine vision. First, there is Gaius (v. 1), whom the Elder implies is one of his children, that is, one of his protégés (v. 4). Then there are "the brothers" (3 John 3, 5, 10) who traverse the network of churches bearing letters from the Elder. Demetrios (3 John 12) is also a member of this team, whom the Elder describes as "fellow workers with the truth" (3 John 8). While this description relates the worker to the truth, it is clear that they share in this work together and with the Elder. To this we can add those who produced the Johannine writings. John 21:24 reveals a circle, the Beloved Disciple who bore witness and wrote, and the group that added ch. 21 attesting the veracity of what was witnessed and written. This certainly shows a nucleus of the Johannine school. If the Johannine Epistles were written by another author or authors the web of the Johannine school has been spread even further.

What are we to make of the Johannine school? First we can say that it was a tightly knit group (but not without differences) that was responsible for the shaping and dissemination of the Johannine vision. Its achievement was the creation and shaping of the Johannine community, yet the members of the group stand in the shadows. Even those we can name, like Gaius and Demetrios, remain unknown to us because these names do not identify known persons. 2 and 3 John name their author as the Elder and 1 John provides no explicit indication of authorship. The Gospel identifies no author, although John 21:24 refers to the Beloved Disciple in an active role. Because the Beloved Disciple is not identified, this takes us little farther.

Even if the Beloved Disciple is identified with John, John 21:24 seems to rule out the straightforward authorship of the Gospel and Epistles by this John. Nor does anything in John 1–20 and 1 John imply that John was the author of either work. Other identifications are possible on the basis of the evidence. Irenaeus may be right in associating the Johannine writings with the apostle John, but few scholars today think this can be done in a straightforward fashion. They tend instead to think in terms of a Johannine school in which John the apostle may or may not play a defining role. The evidence of a school producing and disseminating the Johannine writings is strong. Such evidence is found in the common language and perspective of these writings, which appear alongside significant differences. The hypothesis of a Johannine school provides a reasonable basis for understanding this balance of agreement and difference. The plural attestation of John 21:24, "we know that his witness is true," adds weight to the perception of a school as the source of the Johannine writings.

R. Alan Culpepper (*The Johannine School* 258–59) defines a school in relation to the following characteristics: (1) The school gathers around a founding figure; (2) the founder is a teacher and exemplar of wisdom or goodness; (3) members of the school are disciples (pupils) of the teacher and loyal to his teaching; (4) teaching and learning are the focal activities of the school; (5) common meals commemorate the role of the founder; (6) there is an emphasis on *philia* and *koinōnia*; (7) rules define the life of members; (8) the school is distanced from wider society; (9) institutional structures (routinization) provide a basis for the perpetuation of the school. The relevance of this profile of an ancient school to the Johannine school is readily apparent though it needs to be nuanced to fit the particularities of the Johannine situation. Other evidence of the perpetuation of the school tradition can be seen in the catechetical school of Alexandria, which probably has its roots in a school tradition going back to Philo (Wilhelm Bousset, *Jüdischer-Christlicher Schulbetrieb in Alexandria und Rom* 267).

The Johannine Epistles confirm the actuality of both the Johannine school and a broader Johannine community made up of a network of Johannine house churches. While these were in a single region, they were spread widely enough to require special journeys to visit the different churches. For this reason the Elder was in closer and more intimate contact with some of the churches than others. He probably felt that those situated remotely from him were more exposed to the dangers of false teachers than his own community. On the other hand, 1 John might indicate that the schism that tore apart the Johannine community began in the author's own community (1 John 2:18-19). Even if this is true, it is clear that the waves generated by the schism threatened the whole network of churches. The threat called the Johannine school into action (not, of course, into existence). This group was responsible, at least, for the final editing and "publication" of the Gospel as we know it (John 21:24, and see my *John, Witness and Theologian* 4 and *The Quest for the Messiah* 33 n. 3) and for the Johannine Epistles. The distinction between school and community is also important for Raymond E. Brown (*The Community of the Beloved Disciple* 101–102; *The Epistles of John* 96 n. 221).

FOR REFERENCE AND FURTHER STUDY

Beutler, Johannes. "Krise und Untergang der johanneischen Gemeinde: Das Zeugnis der Johannesbriefe," in Jean-Marie Severin, ed., *The New Testament in Early Christianity*. BETL 86. Louvain: Leuven University Press 1989, 85–103.

Bousset, Wilhelm. *Jüdischer-Christlicher Schulbetrieb in Alexandria und Rom; literarische Untersuchungen zu Philo und Clemens von Alexandria, Justin und Irenäus*. Göttingen: Vandenhoeck & Ruprecht, 1915.

Culpepper, R. Alan. *The Johannine School*.

Kruse, Colin G. *The Letters of John*, 4–5.

Painter, John. *John, Witness and Theologian*. London: S.P.C.K. 1975, 2nd ed. 1978; 3rd ed. Melbourne: Beacon Hill, 1980.

_____. *The Quest for the Messiah*, 63–79.

Strecker, Georg. *The Johannine Letters*, xxxv–xlii.

## 9. STYLE AND LANGUAGE OF THE LETTERS

The letters display a semitizing Greek. Language is always influenced by the culture of the author. It can also be shaped by the author's intention to use language appropriate to the envisaged readers. Culturally versatile authors have the facility to do this. Does the semitizing Greek of the Johannine Epistles reflect the author's cultural context or was it carefully chosen for the readers? Because the characteristics of this Greek are found both in the Gospel and in the Epistles, a good case can be made for arguing that the Semitic character of the language tells us more about the author of the Epistles than about their intended readers.

A number of clues suggest that the Epistles are directed to a dominantly Gentile readership. As distinct from the Gospel, arguments in the Epistles are not supported by appeals to the Scriptures. The point is not that Gentile believers did not use the Jewish Scriptures. The force of the argument comes from the opposite direction. It is inconceivable that a Jewish believer (the author) would not appeal to the Scriptures when seeking to persuade other Jewish believers of the truth. It is no real help to assert that "Old Testament language and thought permeate our text." (Thus Ruth B. Edwards, *The Johannine Epistles*, 77.) Edwards here appeals to the work of Judith Lieu, "What was from the beginning," *NTS* 39 (1993) 458–77. Just what constitutes OT language and thought is difficult to establish where the evidence falls short of quotation or specific allusion. Even if an author has used OT language it is not like an appeal to the authority of the Scriptures to deal with issues. Nothing in the letters confirms that the readers would have recognized "OT language and thought."

The letter is characterized by a stylistic duality. This was identified by Rudolf Schnackenburg in his *Die Johannesbriefe* of 1953. (See the English translation: *The Johannine Epistles*, 5, 13–15, especially point 2 on page 14: "The change in style in the text of 1 John is in itself well observed and susceptible of a positive explanation, in part from the dual purpose of the document. For it is both a didactic and a polemical work directed against the heretics [e.g., 1:6-10], and at the same time a homiletical and paraenetic work addressed to the community [e.g., 2:1-2].") Here we need to note that although the polemical passages are directed against the opponents, they are addressed to the community with a view to dissuading them from following the secessionists into schism. The paraenetic material also deals with the issue, but as a form of encouragement in the face of the trauma caused by the schism. That trauma can be understood in terms of emotional pain resulting in confusion and uncertainty. A major aim of 1 John was to rebuild certainty and the joy of a confident faith, all of which had been undermined by the schism. The duality is recognized in the swing from passages of a polemical tone to those of pastoral concern. "The double nature of the material is not the result of the author commenting on a source, but is the consequence of the author's double purpose for writing. He wrote to oppose the heretics and to encourage the believers" (ibid.) The reason for this is that the community (or communities) for which 1 John was written was/were in turmoil following a controversial and bitter struggle that had ended in a schism. 1 John was written to deal with the aftermath. "Though the heretics had withdrawn, the community was in turmoil and continued to be threatened by the false teaching. . . . 1 John was written to bring the assurance of faith to those who had been troubled by the heretical teachers. . . . Thus the confession of true faith and active love for the brethren have become the tests which expose the heretics and provide the believers with the assurance of faith" (ibid.). See my *John, Witness and Theologian*, 112, 116, 124, 125.

While one strategy was to deal with the position of the opponents in a polemical way, exposing the error, 1 John was not written to the opponents. It was written to the traumatized and disturbed community whose assurance of faith had been undermined. The aim of the letter was to restore that assurance and to place it on a solid basis. To this end we find the many assurances, "By this you know . . ." *(en toutō ginōskete)* and the like. These are supported by the strong pastoral concerns of 1 John. See the Introduction to the Exegesis of 1 John.

FOR REFERENCE AND FURTHER STUDY

Brooke, Alan England. *A Critical and Exegetical Commentary on the Johannine Epistles,*
    i–xxvii.
Edwards, Ruth B. *The Johannine Epistles.* Sheffield: Sheffield Academic Press, 1996.
Kilpatrick, G. D. "Two Johannine Idioms in the Johannine Epistles," *JTS* 12 (1961)
    272–73.
Klauck, Hans-Josef. *Die Johannesbriefe,* 41–50.
Schnackenburg, Rudolf. *The Johannine Epistles,* 6–11.

## 10. THE "IMPLIED" CONTEXT OR SITUATION

Reference to the "implied" context reminds us that almost all we know specifically is drawn from the Johannine writings. Two difficulties need to be kept in mind. The first is that none of the writings explicitly refers to any of the others. Because external evidence concerning their relationship to each other is imprecise, inconsistent, and too late to be drawn on confidently, the only way ahead is to seek to clarify that relationship from the evidence of the writings themselves. That evidence makes the recognition of some form of relationship inescapable. To read each writing as if it had no relationship to the others is obviously wrong. To discern the actual relationship of the writings to each other is a task to be undertaken tentatively and with caution. But it is a task that no commentator should avoid. The task is made more difficult because the recipients of the letters knew the situation into which these writings were sent. We do not. Thus the writings do not deal specifically and fully with the situation. Nevertheless the issues with which the writings deal often throw considerable light on the situation.

Two aspects can be noted here though the details can only be set out in the commentary in the discussion of the text. The final warning, "Little children, guard yourselves from idols," makes more sense in a predominantly Gentile context (1 John 5:21). The suggestion that reference to idols is metaphorical is based on the Qumran expression of "the idols of his heart" found in 1QS 2.11. (Thus Edwards, *Epistles* 43.) But 1 John warns "guard yourself from idols." There is no mention of the idols of the heart. Paul's letters remind us that idolatry was pervasive in the Roman empire and Jewish Christianity was concerned to avoid the contamination of idolatry. See 1 Cor 8:1–10:33 and note also Acts 15:20, 29; 21:25. Further, the wording that follows in 1QS 2.12-14 is dependent on Deut 29:17-19 where the words "I shall be safe, though I walk in the stubbornness of my heart" (see 1QS 2.13-14) are an expression of turning away to serve the gods of the nations (Deut 29:18). Thus even in 1QS 2.11 the warning is against actual idolatry and its consequences in the community. The Jewish view that idolatry was accompanied by moral decline and the judgment of God (see Wisdom 13–14) is to be found also in Paul's letters; see Rom 1:18-32.

The pressure to find a more acceptable contemporary meaning for the warning must be held in check. There is evidence of the pervasive reality of idolatry in the Roman Empire and continued Jewish abhorrence of it. The prominence of idolatry is clear enough. It was one of the four issues forbidden to Gentile Christians in the so-called "Jerusalem decree" according to Acts 15:20, 29; 21:25. In each case the issue of idolatry is mentioned first. That this continued to be a problem is clear enough from Paul's first letter to the Corinthians, where the subject is dealt with in a number of chapters beginning at 8:1, "Concerning food offered to idols." In what follows, Paul twice directly and specifically warns against idolatry: "Do not be idolaters as some of them were . . . therefore, my beloved, shun the worship of idols" (10:7, 14). The latter warning is comparable to what we have at the end of 1 John: "Little Children, guard yourselves from idols."

In 1 Corinthians what follows each of these warnings is an exposition of the theme of the judgment of God on idolatry based on the example of the people of Israel who submitted to the attraction of idolatry. The warning against idolatry in 1 John 5:21 may seem to us to come unexpectedly, from out of "left field." That is because we live outside the pervasive reality of idolatry in the Roman empire.

Two passages, closely connected to each other in 1 John, call for close attention in relation to an important aspect of the context in which they were written (1 John 2:18-25, 26-27, and 4:1-6). The inseparable connection between these two passages is important because it is clear enough in 1 John 2:18-19 that a schism is at the heart of an unsettling disturbance addressed by 1 John.

> Little children, it is the last hour, and as you have heard, "antichrist comes," and now many antichrists have come, from which we know it is the last hour. They went out from us but they were not of us; for if they were of us, they would not have separated from us; but [they went out] that it may be revealed that all [of them] are not of us.

The syntax is awkward, but the separation of the negative from "all" *(pantes)* by the verb *(eisin)* means that the negative should be taken with the verb and not with "all." Thus the meaning is that "all (the antichrists) are not of us." While there is no significant rejection of the view that a schism has occurred within the community of Johannine believers, there is room to debate whether this issue is central to 1 John or peripheral, perhaps one of many issues. The evidence as construed in this commentary supports the view that the schism was the immediate reason for the writing of 1 John. The schism is not simply a falling out as a consequence of a conflict of personalities. Those who went out are characterized as "antichrists." Our author appeals to what his readers know (have heard) about the coming of [the] antichrist. He goes on to assert, "many antichrists have come." Although reference to [the] antichrist assumes a common knowledge, the term is used in the New Testament only in the Johannine writings (five times: see 1 John 2:18 (2x), 22; 4:3; 2 John 7) and we know of no prehistory of its use. Yet it must have a prehistory because the use in 1 John assumes the readers know of it in the singular and the author wishes to use it in the plural to describe his opponents. A general background of associated motifs is to be found in various apocalyptic writings. Two perspectives become clear in the discussion by our author.

First, the antichrist (antichrists) is an eschatological figure whose appearance heralds the end time (2:18). Second, unlike the figures of Mark 13:5-6, 21-22 (and parallels), we are not dealing with pseudo-messianic figures (false Christs). Rather, here the "anti" signals opposition to the identification of Jesus as the Christ, involving the denial that, in truth, Jesus *is* the Christ (1 John 2:22-23). Unless our author has grossly distorted the views of his "opponents" these differences should not be glossed over in terms of the rhetoric of a leadership struggle or the like. If our author was writing to people familiar with those who had separated from the community it would not have been helpful to portray their teaching in terms wildly different from the position they adopted. Reference to the antichrist reappears in 4:3 where our author is concerned to distinguish the spirit of truth and the spirit of error. The criterion is the confession "Jesus Christ is come in the flesh." This confession marks those who have the spirit of truth, while refusal to make the confession reveals the spirit of error, alternatively described as the spirit of the antichrist. Here it is explained that the antichrist comes, indeed is already present in the world (4:1-6). The opponents provide evidence of this and, perhaps because of their number, it is explained that there are many antichrists (2:18).

FOR REFERENCE AND FURTHER STUDY

Beutler, Johannes. "Krise und Untergang der johanneischen Gemeinde: Das Zeugnis der Johannesbriefe," 85–103.

Brooke, Alan England. *A Critical and Exegetical Commentary on the Johannine Epistles,* xxx–xxxii.

Brown, Raymond E. *The Epistles of John,* 47–68.

Edwards, Ruth B. *The Johannine Epistles.*

## 11. IMPLIED AUTHOR

The opening of 1 John (1:1-4) implies that the author stands with a select band of firsthand witnesses of the ministry of Jesus, communicating their message to another generation. Two things modify this impression. First, the content of the message communicated in 1:1-4 is less than completely clear. The neuter relative pronoun does not easily lend itself to being understood as a personal content. Were it not for the *logos* of John 1:1, 14 it is likely that the opening of 1 John would be interpreted in terms of the message although there are signals that suggest overlap with the content of the message in 1 John 1:1-4. But this is further confused by 1:5, where the content of the message is stated, "God is light and in him there is no darkness at all" (cf. 1:3). The certainty that the reference must be to a firsthand witness of the ministry of Jesus is undermined by the lack of clarity in 1:1-4 and the statement of the message in 1:5. Even this reservation needs to be qualified by the way the message is introduced. It is "the message that we heard from *him.*" Here "him" might refer to the Father or to "his Son Jesus Christ" (1:3). Most likely we should understand it as a reference to the latter. If that is the case, the notion of a select band of witnesses is maintained.

Second, the first person plural, "we write these things" in 1:4 gives way to the singular "I write" (2:1, 7, 8, 12, 13 [2x]) and "I wrote" (2:14 [3x], 21, 26; 5:13) in the remainder of the letter. At the same time the author reverts to "we" in various other contexts (1:5-10; 2:2-3, 5, 28; 3:1-2, 14, 16, 18-19, 21-25; 4:6, 7, 9-14, 16-17, 19; 5:2-3, 14-15, 18-20). It is often difficult to know whether this use is similar to 1:4 where the author associates himself with other authoritative witnesses in writing 1 John, or whether he is speaking inclusively of himself and his readers (2:18-21, 24-25; 3:19-24). There are times when "we" and "you" (plural) *seem* to be clearly distinguished (3:14, 15, 16; 4:4-6). Although the address of the readers ("you") clearly distinguishes them from the author, the recurrent "we" does not necessarily exclude the readers. The result is that the implied author is less than clearly defined.

Nevertheless, the author speaks in authoritative tones, addressing his readers as "little children" (*teknia*, 2:1, 12, 28; 3:7, 18; 4:4; 5:21; *paidia*, 2:14, 18; 3:7). This is the most common form of address in 1 John. It implies a fatherly authority. But the tone of the letter is one of persuasive rhetoric rather than the commanding tone of one who expects to be obeyed without question. Alongside this form of address we find "beloved" (*agapētoi*, 2:7, 3:2, 21; 4:1, 7, 11). The concentration of this address in ch. 4 is explained by the theme of love in that chapter. Nevertheless, this form of address links 1 John with 3 John (1, 2, 5, 11) though it is used in the singular there because the letter is addressed to Gaius. There is also one address of the readers as "brothers" (3:13) in the context of the discussion of Cain as an example of the children of the devil who hate their brothers (3:10-18).

### FOR REFERENCE AND FURTHER STUDY

Brooke, Alan England. *A Critical and Exegetical Commentary on the Johannine Epistles,* lxxiii–lxxix.
Beutler, Johannes. *Die Johannesbriefe,* 29–31.
Brown, Raymond E. *The Epistles of John,* 14–35.
Schnackenburg, Rudolf. *The Johannine Epistles,* 40–41.
Rensberger, David. *1 John, 2 John, 3 John,* 17–20.

## 12. IMPLIED READERS

The implied readers' lives have been established by the foundational message delivered by the author and the tradition bearers associated with him. That message is now considered to be old. Together with the love commandment, it is the foundational message. Yet the author is aware that the love command stands in the tradition under the title of "the new commandment." Probably because the opponents now appear to the author as innovators, he is at pains to establish the traditional nature of the message and the commandment. Nevertheless he acknowledges the eschatological newness of the commandment because the darkness is passing away and the true light already shines. In 1 John "the light" has taken on a strongly ethical sense and does not simply speak of revelation. Rather it asserts the nature of revelation in terms of the love revealed in the sending of the Son and in the giving of his life as an expiation for the sins of the world.

While the author again and again asserts that the readers know these things, he is at pains to clarify and provide tests to demonstrate the true faith and life of those who know God and abide in God. The author's affirmation of confidence in the faithfulness of the readers coupled with his exhorting and setting out tests to assure them that they are walking in the truth can be misleading. His affirmation of confidence turns out to be a rhetorical strategy to encourage the readers to meet his expectations. Thus the affirmation of 2:20-21:

> And you have the anointing from the Holy One and you all know. I did not write to you because you do not know the truth, but because you know it . . .

In what follows, the author is keen to distinguish the truth from the lie. Indeed, he goes on, "I wrote these things to you concerning those who lead you astray" (1:26). The whole point of 1 John seems to be to deal with a situation that has disturbed the readers. They are part of a community made up of a circle of house churches that has been rent asunder by a schism (2:18-19). Whatever authority the author of 1 John has, it is not such that he can deal with this problem by an authoritative pronouncement. Instead he must persuade and cajole, always seeking to keep his readers on his side. The author seems to be aware that there is a real danger that at least some of the readers may follow those who have separated from the group "loyal" to the author. Indeed, the letter suggests that the author perceived their loyalty to be somewhat wavering. It may be this that explains the character of 1 John.

FOR REFERENCE AND FURTHER STUDY

Kruse, Colin G. *The Letters of John*, 14–15, 37–38, 43.
Schnackenburg, Rudolf. *The Johannine Epistles*, 39–40.

## 13. POLEMIC AND THE PURPOSE OF 1 JOHN

I have referred to the "opponents." An alternative nomenclature could have been used without prejudice to this study. Raymond Brown *(The Epistles of John)* prefers the term "secessionists" (69, 70, 70 n. 156, and elsewhere); he also refers to "adversaries" (415, 574, 618), "opponents" (x), "deceivers" (358–59), and "propagandists" (429). They could also be called "schismatics" or "heretics." Each of the terms can be justified as representative of the author's point of view. Certainly he wrote against those he viewed as adversaries. We conclude that the opposition was mutual. Clearly also he spoke of those who had broken away from his own group and hence from his point of view they were "schismatics" or "secessionists" (1 John 2:19). From his point of view also the schism was rooted in false practices, but more important, in a false confession of faith. The latter is more important because 1 John implies that the false confession gave rise to the false practices. Hence from his point of view they were "heretics." If such titles are pejorative that is no more than our author intended.

A profile of the opposition is complicated by the lack of agreement among scholars concerning the extent of reference to the opponents in the Johannine Epistles. Commentaries following the influential work of Robert Law *(The Tests of Life*, 1909) have tended to follow this line of interpretation. Recently, however, Law's observation that although controversial allusions are limited to two passages (2:18-19; 4:1-6) "there is no New Testament writing which is more vigorously polemical in its whole tone and aim" (p. 25) has been challenged. A tendency has emerged to restrict reference to the opponents to these specific texts. Other texts, which Law and other commentators read with reference to the polemical situation, are now treated as evidence of the author's rhetorical style (thus Judith Lieu, *The Theology of the Johannine Epistles* 5–6, 13–16, 66; Ruth B. Edwards, *The Johannine Epistles* 37–38, 57–60, 64–65). It is also argued that 1 John is not to be read as a polemical text. Rather its concern is pastoral. Here there is a misunderstanding of what has been argued in significant treatments of 1 John in relation to its polemical purpose. The confusion is contained in such statements as "Its purpose is not first of all to engage in polemic with outsiders or with their views . . ." (Lieu, *The Theology of the Johannine Epistles* 22). And Edwards says (*The Johannine Epistles* 67): "it is more likely the author of 1 John is directing his thoughts to his own community rather than outsiders or particular adversaries . . . but 1 John is probably less polemical than often assumed (3 John contains no theological polemic)."

First, none of the Johannine Epistles is directed to the opponents. The polemic is not addressed to outsiders. Lieu has covered this by reference to "polemic with outsiders or their views." By combining the two positions, critics may proceed as if they were one. My assumption is that the Johannine Epistles are directed to the continuing Johannine community. 1 John is directed to the situation subsequent to the schism referred to in 2:18-19. It is addressed to those who have been confused and made unsure by the departure of the schismatics who were, until recently, members of the Johannine community. The purpose of 1 John is to address the confusion and heal the trauma caused by the schism. A concise statement of purpose is given:

> I wrote these things to you (plural) that you may know you have eternal life, you who believe in the name of the Son of God. (1 John 5:13)

The Gospel provides a statement of purpose that is formally comparable:

> These things are written that you may believe that Jesus is the Christ, the Son of God, and that believing in his name you may have life. (John 20:31)

The Gospel was not written as a tract to convert unbelievers. It is directed toward believers, to lead them into Johannine belief and consequent eternal life. Such belief has a specific content, "that Jesus is the Christ, the Son of God." That confessional formula presupposes the meaning unfolded in the Gospel. 1 John was also written to believers, but 5:13 makes no reference to modifying their belief. The Gospel assumes that those who (truly) believe have eternal life. 1 John does not question that. Rather the problem seems to be that believers are uncertain whether they have eternal life. The aim of 1 John was to reassure believers that they have eternal life. The purpose of 1 John is assurance. This is certainly a pastoral concern. What made it urgent was the crisis caused by the opponents. They had undermined the stability of the Johannine community. Explicit references to the schism are few, but those that are present make clear the serious nature of the event. In a community that believes itself to be a manifestation of the unity of the divine love, a schism threatens disaster. Something like this is true of the Johannine community.

The textual duality of 1 John provides an effective response to a schism that has left those who remain in a state of shock. 1 John sets out reassuringly to deal with the shock. All of the "tests" referred to in Law's title assure those who remain that they are in the truth, in the one who is true, that they have eternal life. To do this it was necessary to show that the opponents were in error, that they did not know God, and that their position was destructive and deceptive, opposed to Christ. The aim was to assure believers that they were already in the truth and that the opponents must be deceivers, false prophets, antichrists, and of the devil. The description "antichrists" puts the opponents in an eschatological frame, affirming the coming of the last day (1 John 2:18-19).

The effects of this schism have impacted pervasively on 1 John. Both the specific evidence of the schism and the pervasive evidence of the author seeking to reassure his reader attest its impact. Robert Law described the latter as "The Tests of Life." Interestingly, this perspective is used by Judith Lieu (*The Theology of the Johannine Epistles* 51–54) even though elsewhere she minimizes the role of the opponents and the polemic of 1 John. Law rightly notes that these tests are aimed at assuring the readers that they have life, but they can only do this by showing that the opponents are in error. Assurance of the believers and polemic against the views of the opponents are thus two strands running through 1 John. The result is a positive and coherent message even if there are numerous unclear and difficult passages.

### FOR REFERENCE AND FURTHER STUDY

Beutler, Johannes. *Die Johannesbriefe*, 20–24.

Brooke, Alan England. *A Critical and Exegetical Commentary on the Johannine Epistles*, xxxviii–lii.

Brown, Raymond E. *The Epistles of John*, 32–35, 86–100.

Klauck, Hans-Josef. *Die Johannesbriefe*, 127–49.

Kruse, Colin G. *The Letters of John*, 27–28, 39–40, 47–48.

Law, Robert.*The Tests of Life: A Study of the First Epistle of St. John*. Edinburgh: T & T Clark, 1909.

Lieu, Judith. *The Theology of the Johannine Epistles*. Cambridge: Cambridge University Press, 1991.

Painter, John. "The Opponents in 1 John," in idem, *The Quest for the Messiah*, 427–64.

Robinson, John A. T. "The Destination and Purpose of the Johannine Epistles," in idem, *Twelve New Testament Studies*. SBT 34. London: S.C.M., 1962, 56–65.

Smalley, Stephen S. *1, 2, 3 John*. WBC. Waco, Tex.: Word Books, 1984.

Whitacre, Rodney A. *Johannine Polemic: The Role of Tradition and Theology*. SBLDS 67. Chico: Scholars, 1982.

## 14. THE RHETORIC OF 1 JOHN

The struggle to define the genre of 1 John has produced no clear results and the attempts to outline its structure have fared no better. One reason for this can be seen by reference to the character of 1 John in terms of the rhetoric of the time. Hans-Josef Klauck argues that 1 John is an example of *deliberative* rhetoric, which is strong in exhortation and dissuasion, seeking to influence decision and action. Certainly 1 John does this. Alternatively, Duane Watson makes a case for recognizing the marks of *epideictic* rhetoric in 1 John. Also known as demonstrative rhetoric, this is designed to advance knowledge by setting out accepted views that establish and maintain group unity. Two things seem to support this case. First, from the beginning the author is attempting to nurture the bonds of community and to reassert the values that have bound the community together prior to the schism. Seen as a response to schism, 1 John readily fits the category of epideictic rhetoric. In particular, Watson draws attention to the multifarious uses of *amplification* in 1 John. To demonstrate his position, he argues that 1 John uses a full range of the methods of amplification. But this need not mean that other forms of rhetoric are excluded from 1 John. There is ample evidence of exhortation and attempts to dissuade the readers from following the schismatics out of the community. The author has utilized skills of rhetoric to reinforce the art of persuasion that he brings to bear on his readers. The stakes are high. The urgency of the task lifts the level of communication. The author reveals his concern in his exhortations and recalls the readers to commitment to the common Johannine tradition as the foundation of their *koinōnia*, their community (1:5-10).

### FOR REFERENCE AND FURTHER STUDY

Brown, Raymond E. *The Epistles of John*, 92–100.

Edwards, Ruth B. *The Johannine Epistles*.

Kennedy, George A. *New Testament Interpretation through Rhetorical Criticism*. Chapel Hill: University of North Carolina Press, 1984, 19–20, 24, 36–37, 39–85, 91–92, 116–38, 142, 145–52.

Klauck, Hans-Josef. "Zur rhetorischen Analyse der Johannesbriefe," *ZNW* 81 (1990) 205–24.

Kruse, Colin G. *The Letters of John*, 28–32.

Watson, Duane F. "1 John 2:12-14 as *Distributio, Conduplicatio, and Expolitio*: A Rhetorical Understanding," *JSNT* 35 (1989) 97–110.

_____. "Amplification Techniques in 1 John: The Interaction of Rhetorical Style and Invention," *JSNT* 51 (1993) 99–123.

Watson, Duane F., and Alan J. Hauser. *Rhetorical Criticism of the Bible: A Comprehensive Bibliography with Notes on History and Method*. Leiden: Brill, 1994.

## 15. A PROFILE OF THE OPPOSITION

This profile builds on my article "The Opponents in 1 John" (1986), which is an elaboration of *John, Witness and Theologian* (1975) 115–25. The paper carries on a running dialogue with Raymond E. Brown's commentary. His treatment of the opponents is marked by caution (*The Epistles of John* 47–48). He more often than not refers to them as secessionists but also uses other terms to describe them, including "adversaries" (ibid. 47–68). Brown was aware that Pheme Perkins (*The Johannine Epistles*. Wilmington, Del.: Michael Glazier, 1979 xxi–xxiii) was critical of the focus on the adversaries. She argues that the apparent polemic in 1 John was a function of the author's rhetoric and warns against identifying it with the historical situation. Brown considers some of the language to be far too pointed and extreme to be reduced to rhetoric (*The Epistles of John* 48–49). Nevertheless, with growing interest in Hellenistic rhetoric the position advocated by Perkins has gained momentum and it is taken further by Judith Lieu, who refers to Perkins's position (*The Theology of the Johannine Epistles* 13 and n. 17). My detailed exegesis of the text now seeks to establish that the rhetoric is an expression of the polemical situation. The rhetoric is designed to persuade the readers, the Johannine believers spread throughout the circle of Johannine churches. The aim of the persuasion is to bring reassurance that those who believe the Johannine gospel have eternal life. Such assurance is the basis for the recovery of a stable Johannine community.

Methodologically, producing a profile of the opponents begins by noting that they are explicitly revealed in the text. Scholars widely acknowledge the evidence of their activity in 2:18-25 (26); 4:1-6. Some scholars restrict what we know of the opponents to these texts or parts of these two texts. This decision is based on three kinds of evidence or argument. First, the opponents are not explicitly mentioned until 2:18-19 (Lieu, *The Theology of the Johannine Epistles* 13; Edwards, *The Johannine Epistles* 64–65). Arguing that the reference is *held back* to the middle of 1 John can then be taken to mean that the schism was not the critical event I have depicted. Yet when the schism is mentioned it is in apocalyptic terms, signaling the last hour. Further, it is held back only if reference to the event is restricted to the two self-contained passages mentioned. Lieu, who adopts this approach, recognizes the schism as a recent event (*The Theology of the Johannine Epistles* 5, 13, 25). That being the case, can it be as peripheral to 1 John as this interpretation suggests?

The second line of argument is that other passages of polemical tone can be attributed to the writer's rhetorical style without reference to any polemical situation. Lieu refers to the work of Pheme Perkins who "emphasizes the rhetorical nature of the language and warns against taking it too literally as a reflection of the actual historical situation" (ibid. p. 13 and n. 17, as well as p. 16). The same point is made by Edwards (*The Johannine Epistles* 64–65). Both Lieu and Edwards refer to the same pages in Perkins' commentary on the *Epistles* (xxi–xxiii) as Brown had noted (*The Epistles of John* 48–49). But is it likely that polemical language is merely rhetorical when we know that a schism had occurred recently and that those involved in it are called false prophets and antichrists, while in 2 John they are called deceivers? In the mind of the author(s) of 1 and 2 John this hardly looks like a storm in a tea cup. In discussing the schism Lieu perceptively says of 2:26; 3:7: "This implies some continuing relationship or dialogue, and it is not clear whether the separation is as absolute as the author would like" (*The Theology of the Johannine Epistles* 13). This is precisely the situation that makes unlikely the containment of the polemic to the two christological passages (2:18-22; 4:1-3). The community that remained was open to the influence of the opponents. They were in danger and the author attempts to set up defenses, tests that would expose the false teaching and reveal the truth, tests of life.

The third line of argument is that the christological error should be separated from the moral dilemma dealt with in 1 John, which is nowhere associated with the opponents (Lieu, *The Theology of the Johannine Epistles* 14–16; Edwards, *The Johannine Epistles* 65). If this is the case, why is 1 John at pains to root the command to love one another in the revelation that is summed up christologically (3:16-18, 23; 4:7-12, 19-21)? Indeed, for 1 John the giving of the Son as the foundation of the love command involves his coming in the flesh.

> By this we know love, he gave his life for us; and we ought (*opheilomen*) to give our lives for the brothers. (3:16)

What follows confirms that this giving of life is a manifestation of love, and 3:16-17 applies it in very practical terms. In 4:7-12 the ground of love is taken back to God, who is love. But the love is revealed in God's sending of the Son into the world "that we might live through him" (4:10-11).

The obligation *(opheilomen)* to love one another is grounded in this. This argument is integral to the exegesis and is dealt with in some detail there. Recognition that the opponents do not love one another (their brothers), is not based on a theological deduction. It arises from an analysis of the polemical material. An evaluation of the force of this analysis is given in the commentary.

Developed from the work of Robert Law and Alan E. Brooke, Rudolf Schnackenburg's literary analysis (see *The Johannine Epistles* 3 n. 3, and 77) led me to recognize seven slogan-like assertions. These assertions encapsulate the "truth *claims*" of the opponents. They are grouped in sayings introduced by quotation formulae: a threefold "if we say . . ." in 1:6, 8, 10; a threefold "he who says . . ." in 2:4, 6, 9; and a final "if anyone says . . ." in 4:20. Given their content (see below and the discussion of the passages), these assertions form an important strand of evidence. Two of the sayings are opposed outright. The others are subjected to tests to show what validates or falsifies the claim. Given the recent schism, it seems unlikely that the author was making up problems that were of no present danger to the community. One objection to the attribution of these claims to the opponents is that the first three sayings are not attributed to them but are introduced by "if we say . . ." (Edwards, *The Johannine Epistles* 58). Judith Lieu's recognition that the separation of the opponents was not as clear as the author would like (*The Theology of the Johannine Epistles* 13) makes precisely the right point. As long as these assertions could be contained among the opponents, now outside the community, no more damage would be done. The danger lay in the continuing influence of the opponents within the community.

The claims begin to provide a coherent pattern of the position of the opponents. This coherence is something of a confirmation that the claims are not simply a random selection of rhetorical statements ungrounded in the life of the community. In dealing with them the author builds his own coherent response. The shape of the response was chosen by our author to deal with the claims of the opponents on his own terms. If the response is the expression of our author's coherent theology, it was nevertheless crucial that he respond fully and adequately to the claims of the opponents in their christological position and the seven assertions recorded in 1 John.

Six of the seven assertions are concentrated in 1:6–2:11 (17?). Thus the first section after the Prologue is a concentrated response to the claims of the opponents. The first three assertions are introduced with "If we say. . . ." This formulation makes us aware that the opponents were, until recently, members of the community. It also alerts us to the threat that they continued to pose within the community. Our author is concerned that they may continue to make serious inroads within the community. These three warnings concentrate on the ethical area. Two of them are about the claim to be sinless (1:8, 10). Clearly these are considered to be false claims. The first claim concerns "communion" with God. While the claim is expressed in the terms of the opponents, our author does not repudiate it in principle. Rather he provides a statement about God that enables him to falsify the claim to have communion with God. Because God is light, in whom there is no darkness at all, it is self-evident that those who walk in the darkness do not have communion with God. What is not yet clear is that the light symbolizes the love of God and the darkness is the realm of hatred of the brother or sister (2:8-11; 4:7-12, 16b). For the opponents the claim to be sinless is not an ethical claim. It has nothing to do with the love of the brother. For the opponents the claim to be sinless relates to communion with God without reference to or consequence for social relationships.

The second group of three assertions is introduced by the formula "The person who says . . ." (2:4, 6, 9). The claim to know him (God) is false when it disregards God's commandments. Keeping the commandments is related to the fulfillment of the love of God. Again the ethical test falsifies the claim made by the opponents. Already there is a clue to suggest that God's commandments can be encapsulated in the command to love the brother, which is grounded in the event that reveals God's love (see 3:23). The claim to abide in him is tested by walking as he walked, another formulation of the ethical test. Then the claim to be in the light is falsified by hating the brother or sister, behavior that exposes a person who is in the darkness. The person loving his or her brother or sister is in the light (2:9-11).

From this point 1 John deals with two major issues, the true confession of faith and the necessity of love for the brother in the authentic response of faith. If the treatment of the sixth claim ends with the test of loving the brother, the seventh claim, "I love God" (4:20), is shown to be false by the failure to love the brother. Much of chs. 3 and 4 concerns the theme of love. The Father is the source of love, and love is defined in terms of God's love for us. Failure to love the brother or sister falsifies the claim to love God. In 4:20 our author shows that the opponents claimed to love God and sets out to falsify their claim using the test of love for the brother or sister.

The other major area in which 1 John confronts the opponents is in their denial of what our author considered to be the true christological confession (2:18-23; 4:1-6). Here 1 John does not tell us what the opponents affirmed, only that they denied what our author affirmed. They denied that Jesus Christ has come in the flesh. This was a denial of the Incarnation, a denial that the divine Son was to be identified with the human Jesus, the denial that Jesus is the Christ, that Jesus is the Son of God. This denial struck at the heart of our author's theology. The separation of the human Jesus from the divine Son or Christ meant that the life and work of

Jesus could not be seen as the revelation of the divine life and love. Crucial for 1 John was the extrapolation of the love of Jesus in giving his life for us, for the world, so that it was not merely the human love of Jesus but the love of the Father in and through Jesus. The christological difference between 1 John and the opponents meant that ultimately they had different views of God. They also were opposed on the understanding of love, ethics, and relationship to God.

While there is much other data in 1 John concerning the opponents, the seven assertions focus attention on the ethical failure of the opponents to understand God's love as the basis for the love command. Their denial of the author's christological confession shows that their faulty christology was the basis for their defective understanding of God and their failure to acknowledge the obligation to love the brother.

In one of the explicit references to the opponents, the author calls them false prophets (4:1-6). Here he distinguishes between the spirits inspiring true and false confessions of faith, describing them as the spirit of truth (spirit of God) and the spirit of *error* or *deception (to pneuma tēs planēs)*. Elsewhere (2 John 7) the Elder speaks of the opponents, saying that many deceivers *(polloi planoi)* have gone out into the world. In 1 John 4:1 it is many false prophets who have gone out into the world. In each case what marks the false prophets and the deceivers is the refusal to make the true confession of faith. What they denied is as important for the profile of the opponents as the claims they made. The confession is worded slightly differently in each place, but the parallel is unmistakable. Thus the spirit of error is encountered in deceivers. When, following 2:18-25, the author of 1 John writes (2:26),

> I wrote these things to you concerning those who would deceive you
> *(peri tōn planōntōn hymas)*

this is patently a reference to the opponents. Verse 27 is the author's response to those who would deceive his readers, and it resumes verse 20 where the author affirms of his readers,

> . . . and you have the anointing from the holy one and you all know.

Verses 20 and 27 are difficult to understand. They seem to be a response to the opponents' appeal to the Spirit as the inspiration of their utterances. Against this the author asserts his own teaching of the Spirit. But there seems to be a reluctance to stay with teaching about the Spirit. Rather there is a tendency to turn attention to the word. The opponents might have developed their claims to have Spirit-inspired teaching on the basis of the tradition of the Spirit Paraclete in the Farewell Discourses of the Gospel. Clearly the author of 1 John was uncomfortable with the direction taken in their use of this tradition. To deal with this he identifies the Spirit of Truth with the confession of Jesus Christ come in the flesh while identifying the rejection of this confession with the Spirit of Error (4:6).

The author proposes a whole series of antithetical statements in which he sets his position over against what is not true in his view. It is unlikely that the author opposed purely theoretical positions just because he had a liking for antithetical statements. It is probable that the statements were used to oppose actual rather than purely theoretical problems. All the problems with which 1 John deals are intelligible in relation to the known crisis. Consequently scholars have tended to agree that 1 John confronts one set of opponents.

It would be a mistake, however, to think that a single set of opponents will have held a single tightly logical position. It is commonly recognized that there are divergent positions evident in the texts from Qumran, even in individual texts like 1QS. It is probable that there were tensions within the continuing Johannine community. It was the function of the Epistles to attempt to hold those tensions together and direct them along the line of the author. Thus the recognition of one group of opponents need not mean that we will have no loose ends in our understanding of their position, even if we had full knowledge of them. As it is, we have only what we learn from their implacable opponent, the author of 1 John, and the Elder, if he is to be distinguished from him.

Recognizing that 1 John is a response to the threat of the opponents does not mean accepting that 1 John is intelligible entirely in the light of the threat of the opponents. The author's response to this crisis is called forth from his own coherent and powerful understanding of the gospel. It is distinctively Johannine, and if the author is not the evangelist he has drawn deeply on the Johannine gospel tradition. Even if 1 John is preoccupied with the life and faith of the community, that life and faith are founded in Jesus Christ come in the flesh as the ground of faith and of the obligation to love one another. As the ground of faith, the Son who gave his life for us reveals the God who is love. There is in this complex an authentic grasp of what is essential to the gospel, which is ultimately the gospel of God revealed in God's Son Jesus Christ.

### FOR REFERENCE AND FURTHER STUDY

Beutler, Johannes. "Krise und Untergang der johanneischen Gemeinde: Das Zeugnis der Johannesbriefe," 85–103.

_____. *Die Johannesbriefe*, 20–24.

Brooke, Alan England. *A Critical and Exegetical Commentary on the Johannine Epistles*, xxxviii–lii.

Brown, Raymond E. *The Epistles of John*, 32–35, 86–100.

Klauck, Hans-Josef. *Die Johannesbriefe*, 141–49.

————. "Internal Opponents: The Treatment of the Secessionists in the First
    Epistle of John," (translated by Robert Nowell ) in Wim Beuken, Sean Freyne,
    and Anton Weiler, eds., *Truth and its Victims. Concilium* 200. Edinburgh: T & T
    Clark, 1988, 55–65.
Kruse, Colin G. *The Letters of John*, 15–27, 38–39.
Painter, John. "The Opponents in 1 John," in idem, *The Quest for the Messiah*, 427–
    64.
Schnackenburg, Rudolf. *The Johannine Epistles*, 17–34.

## 16. THE THEOLOGY OF 1 JOHN

The theology of the Johannine Epistles poses problems. Inevitably the theology of 1 John overwhelms the theologies of the smaller letters. On its own each of the smaller letters provides only fragments of theology. These fragments are dealt with independently in the commentary. As this commentary reads them, those fragments fit into and fill out the theology of 1 John. Thus the theology of 1 John is treated here, reinforced by the evidence of 2 and 3 John.

**16.1. God.** Following the Prologue the reader might be forgiven for expecting that 1 John is about to launch into an exposition of christology. But this is not what follows. Rather, the point is made by 1 John 1:5:

> And this is the message that we have heard from him (Jesus) and we report to you, "God is light and there is no darkness at all in him."

1 John places the initial focus on the message of Jesus concerning God. This is consistent with the final statement of the Prologue of the Gospel (John 1:18):

> No one has ever seen God; the only begotten *[monogenēs]* God/Son (textual variant) who is in the bosom of the Father, he has made him (the Father) known.

The point of John's christology is to make God known. Although christology is prominent, the point of Johannine christology lies somewhere else. In the Gospel this is reinforced by the dominant imagery of God as the Father who sent Jesus and Jesus as the sent one whose mission is determined by the sender.

In 1 John Jesus is also the one sent by God (4:9, 10), sent by the Father (4:14). These references fall in a section of 1 John that deals with the grounding of the obligation to love one another *(allēlous)* in God who is love (4:7-21). This obligation is also expressed in terms of the command to love the brother or sister. The grounding of the obligation in God depends on the affirmation that God is love (4:8, 16). Awareness of the character of God is recognized in a specific revelation of God's love "for us" (4:9). God "sent his only begotten son into the world that we may live through him." Here the phrase "that we may live through him" has the meaning of "eternal life" (5:13). This corresponds to the use of the verb *(zēn)* in the Gospel (5:25; 6:51, 57; 11:25, 26; 14:19) where "life" *(zōē)* is shorthand for "eternal life" (John 1:1; 3:15, 16, 36; 4:14; 5:24, 29, 39-40; 10:10; 20:31; see especially 5:24, 29, 39-40). The Son came "that they may have life" (10:10). "God loved the world like this, he gave *(edōken)* his only-begotten Son so that everyone who believes in him may have eternal life" (3:16). All of this is the substance that 1 John builds into a more specific statement about God. The giving of life in the sending of the Son is understood to reveal the very character of God, so that twice in this passage the affirmation is made: "God is love" (1 John 4:8, 16). The second affirmation is prefixed by the testimony that provides its foundation (4:14).

> And we have seen and bear witness that the Father has sent the Son as the savior of the world.

Reference to Jesus as "the savior of the world" resonates with John 4:42, again confirming the development of the central themes of the Gospel in 1 John. But it is in 1 John that the theme is given extensive treatment directly in relation to the Johannine understanding of God. Here it becomes clear that the love of God for the world is the motive power expressed in the sending of the Son. The scope and purpose are clear in the phrase "savior of the world." The scope of the mission is the world. The purpose is to save. Clearly the context of 1 John 4:7-21 confirms that God's love has the world in view (compare John 3:16). Clearly the sending of the Son is to give life, to save. Clearly also those who believe, who receive life from God find themselves under obligation to love one another as God had loved them.

The understanding that "God is love" recalls the initial announcement of the message (1:5), "God is light." More clearly than the Gospel, in 1 John the message that "God is light" affirms the moral content of the revelation. Certainly the notion of revelation is fundamental to John's use of the symbolism of light. To affirm that God is light is to assert that it is of the very nature of God to reveal. That is what light does. But the formulation that "God *is* light" makes God himself the subject of the revelation. This revelation certainly has content. The content is the action of God, which reveals the character of God. That action is motivated by love and is itself the fundamental loving action of God. The giving or sending of the Son reveals the heart of God in love for the world. That love is expressed in dealing with the sin of the world (2:1-2; 4:10). The language of "expiation" used in these texts alerts us to the place where that action is to be seen. In the death of Jesus, God's Son deals with our sins, "and not ours only but also the sins of the whole world."

Reference to sin draws attention to the darkness exposed by the light. The light is understood to be God's love for the world expressed in the sending of the Son to be the savior of the world. That light determines the lives of believers who abide in it and walk in it. But sin remains a force and people continue to walk in the darkness. The darkness is constituted by the rejection of the light, and it means to walk in hatred, in the rejection of love. Thus if the revelation is motivated by the love of God, the love of God is also the content of the revelation because "God is love." The message "God is light" affirms this in the context in which the darkness of hatred rules. "God is light, and in him is no darkness whatsoever." Like the Gospel, 1 John provides no solution to the origin of the darkness. At the same time the prevailing presence and influence of the darkness are recognized as antithetical to the being and purpose of God.

**16.2. Christology.** Christology is the point at which the revelation of God encounters the world of darkness. The concentration of the christological focus in 1 John is the historical intersection of the divine and the human in Jesus. This intersection is asserted in the confessions "Jesus is the Christ" (2:22; 5:1), "Jesus [Christ] is the Son of God" (4:15; 5:5), and "Jesus Christ has (is) come in the flesh" (4:2; 5:6; 2 John 7). In the first of these confessions "Christ" has the same meaning as "Son of God" in the second confession and refers to the divine Son sent by the Father/God. At the same time "Jesus" signifies the historical human person. The affirmation that Jesus *is* the Christ/Son of God also finds expression in the use of the double name "Jesus Christ" (1:3; 2:1; 3:23; 4:2, [15]; 5:6, 20; 2 John 3, 7). The use of the double name is rare in the Gospel, being found only at John 1:17; 17:3, and both of these references fall in passages often thought to belong to later strata of the Gospel. In the Gospel "Christ" elsewhere retains its Jewish sense of "Messiah" and is not construed as a personal name (see John 1:20, 25, 41; 3:28; 4:25, 29; 7:26, 27, 31, 41, 42; 9:22; 10:24; 11:27; 12:34; 20:31). This makes the exceptional use in John 1:17; 17:3 the more marked and suggests connections with the use of the double name in 1 and 2 John.

In 1 and 2 John coming in the flesh (1 John 4:2; 2 John 7) is in both instances unequivocally affirmed/denied of Jesus Christ. To affirm that Jesus has come in the flesh would not have served the author's purpose because "Jesus" signified the human flesh-and-blood person. To say that the human flesh-and-blood person has come in the flesh is a tautology. But to affirm that Jesus Christ has come in the flesh identified the human and the divine in the one flesh-and-blood person. In 1 John this confession is controversial and there are those who refuse to make it. Their refusal marks them as those who are inspired by the spirit of the Antichrist. They are opponents of the author of 1 John.

The development of the use of the double name in the Johannine writings was motivated by the crisis caused by the opponents. The schism they initiated had a christological basis. Thus the use of the double name has a different meaning than in Paul and the rest of the New Testament. The difference is signaled in 1 John 4:2 and 2 John 7 and, once seen in these texts, is evident elsewhere in these writings. In the early church christological developments were a response to perceived false teaching. This is also the case in the Johannine Epistles.

The identity of the human and the divine in the flesh-and-blood person Jesus Christ is crucial for the christology of the letters and has clear implications for the understanding of God. To deny that Jesus is the Christ is to deny the Father and the Son, because the person who denies the Son does not have the Father and the person who confesses the Son has the Father also (2:22-23). As in the Gospel, christology is the way in which 1 John speaks of God where existing understandings are being modified. This is especially true in relation to the understanding of the world in terms of the darkness and the purpose of God to overcome the darkness with the light of God's presence (2:8, 17; 3:8, 14). Because the whole world lies in the power of the evil one (5:19), God sent his Son to be the savior of the world (4:14). The power of the evil one is the power of darkness, which has blinded the eyes of those who do not believe (2:11, and see 2 Cor 4:4). The means of deliverance is found in the coming of the Son of God to bring knowledge of the one who is true, "and we are in the one who is true, in his Son Jesus Christ. This is the true God and eternal life" (5:20). Here 1 John echoes John 17:3, "This is the eternal life, to know you, the only true God, and Jesus Christ whom you sent." In John the distinction between the Father and the Son (Jesus Christ) is maintained more clearly than in 1 John, although the unity of action is affirmed (John 5:17; 10:30). But it is less than clear whether 1 John 5:20 refers to the Father as the one who is true, or to the Son, or to both Father and Son. This may be a consequence of the more tangled Greek of 1 John, though this could itself be a consequence of imprecise thought. It could be argued that such imprecision is a theological advance because of the unity of presence and action of the Father in the Son.

Christology also has implications for understanding the way God encounters the world of darkness for it is the point at which the revelation of God encounters that world. In a world where death reigns, it is the work of the Son to give life (4:9; 5:13) and it soon becomes clear that this involves dealing with the problem of sin (1:7; 2:2; 3:5; 4:10, 14). Relevant to this subject are the references to "the *blood* of Jesus his son [that] *cleanses* us from all sin" (1:7) and to Jesus Christ the righteous as the "*expiation* for our sins" and "the sins of the whole world" (2:2), and defining what love is: "in this is love, not that we loved God but that he loved us and sent his Son as an *expiation* for our sins" (4:10). The term translated "expiation" is *hilasmos*. In relation to sin(s) it has the sense of "expiation," the appropriate means of dealing with sin(s). Used in relation to God the term means "propitiation." In the Johannine literature this language is invariably used in relation to sin(s). This is generally true in the New Testament, including Paul. In 1 John the reference to blood and expiation suggests that God's way of dealing with sin is bound up with the death of Jesus. His death deals with the problem of sin(s) by providing expiation and cleansing. As Jesus Christ the righteous he is also the advocate sinners have with the Father, but that advocacy presupposes both expiation of sins and the cleansing of the sinner.

Two other related aspects have a bearing on christology. First there is the reference to "the message we have heard from him" (1:5). This is the message of the sent one, Jesus Christ. The message is "God is light." It is unclear whether what follows is part of the message or the elaboration of it by the author of 1 John. The message concerns God. This is consistent with the preaching of Jesus in the Synoptics. Jesus' proclamation found its focus in "the kingdom of God." Here in 1 John the message that "God is light" is opposed to the darkness, so that the rule of God is opposed to the powers of the world. The power of the light is manifest in the sending of the Son. His mission is motivated by the love of God, reveals God's love, and actualizes it in the world. As a result of his coming the true light already shines (2:8-10). The commandment also comes from Jesus Christ. Just as 1:5 said that "This is the message that we have from him," so now it is said, "and this is the message that we have heard from the beginning, that we love one another" (3:11). Almost certainly the reference to the commandment that "we love one another" refers to the commandment given by Jesus (John 13:34). There it is spoken of as "a new commandment." In 1 and 2 John there is reference to it as an old commandment (2:7-8; 2 John 5, 6). What was once new has become the old foundational commandment. Thus the message concerns God and the love commandment, expressed in reciprocal terms. Following the idiom of 1:5; 3:11 is "This is the commandment that we have from him" (4:21, and cf. 3:23). Here the commandment is addressed to those who claim to love God, telling them it is necessary to "love [one's] brother [and sister] also." The truth that God is light and the command to love one another form the message of Jesus Christ in 1 and 2 John.

1 John also presupposes the *parousia* of the Son of God. This is to take place at the end, bringing judgment. Those who believe in him may have confidence on the day of judgment (2:28; 4:17). The christological emphasis of 1 John is weighted to the past: "Jesus Christ has come in the flesh"

(4:2), "the Son of God has come" (5:20), "the darkness is passing away and the true light is already shining" (2:8). Nevertheless, the presence of the power of darkness remains, and sin continues to be a problem (5:16-17). 1 John remains oriented to the coming of Jesus and the day of judgment for a final resolution of the struggle with evil.

**16.3. Believing, confessing, and knowing.** Much of the theology of the Epistles is concerned with the response to God in the sending of his Son. In the Gospel the world is divided by belief and unbelief. It is true that the Gospel is concerned about authentic belief and the content of such belief is indicated by the verb "to believe" followed by a construction indicating the content of belief *(pisteuein hoti)*. Belief that does not yet attain this authenticity nevertheless is on the way and stands over against unbelief. In 1 John the problem is not unbelief but false belief. Consequently the whole weight of the treatment of belief falls on the correct content.

The focus on believing is complex in the Gospel, where the verb is used 98 times, 76 of which are in chs. 1–12 where the great concentration of use falls. It is in these chapters that Jesus challenges the world to believe and the struggle between belief and unbelief is fought out. In chs. 13–21 the verb is used 22 times. When length of chapters is taken into account this is proportionately closer to the nine uses in 1 John than to the concentration in John 1–12. Only in 1 John is the noun "faith" *(pistis)* used (5:4). In 5:4-5 "our faith" is identified with believing that Jesus is the Son of God. Thus in 1 John "our faith," correct belief, has become the dividing line for the world. This also finds expression in terms of those making or refusing to make (deny, 2:22, 23) the true christological confession (2:23; 4:2, 3, 15; 2 John 7). In 1 John the struggle with the false teachers has determined the perspective rather that the outright unbelief of the world. Nevertheless the world is redefined, to a degree, in terms of the false teachers (2:15-17; 3:1, 13, 17; 4:1, 3, 4, 5; 5:19; 2 John 7). The identification of the false teachers with the world is especially clear in 4:1, 3, 4, 5; 5:19; 2 John 7.

The true confession of belief, our faith, is the means and evidence of victory over the world, over the power of darkness, over the evil one. The whole world lies in the power of the evil one who obstructs the true confession of faith. But "the Son of God has come and has given us a mind *(dianoian)* that we should know the one who is true" (5:20). Knowledge of the one who is true breaks the tyranny of falsehood so that it is both the means and expression or evidence of victory over the world. Thus the true faith is itself the victory.

The true faith is also the means and expression of eternal life: "This is the true God and eternal life" (5:20). 1 John was written so that those who believe in the name of the Son of God may know that they have eternal life (5:13). Both 5:13 and 5:20 are framed to emphasize the importance of those who believe, knowing that they have eternal life. But believing is only one aspect of the evidence of eternal life. The twin evidence is loving one another (3:23). The authentic confession of faith is inseparably tied to the realization of the love command. Believing rightly and loving one another are two aspects of the one reality grounded in the one who is true.

In the Gospel the two verbs "to know" (*ginōskein* and *eidenai*) are used 56 and 85 times respectively. The same two verbs are used 25 times and 15 times in 1 John. The choice of verb seems to be determined grammatically rather than because the verbs convey different shades of knowing. But there is something of a difference in their use in the Gospel and 1 John. In the Gospel the theologically significant uses signify the cognitive *content* of belief. In 1 John there is an emphasis on knowing the *consequences* of believing (see 5:13). Another characteristic use in 1 John concerns the formula of testing the authenticity of claims, "by this you know," all of which use *ginōskein*.

**16.4. Mutuality.** The stress on mutuality in the Johannine writings is to be seen first in the use of the reciprocal pronoun *allēlōn*. Meaning "one another," this word is used 100 times in the New Testament (including three uses in Matthew, five in Mark, and eleven in Luke). A greater concentration is found in the Gospel of John (fifteen). 1 John uses the term six times and 2 John once. More important than the number of uses is the concentration of the command "love one another" in John 13:34 (2x), 35; 15:12, 17; 1 John 3:11, 23; 4:7, 11, 12; 2 John 5. The formulation "love *one another*" is exclusive to the Gospel and Epistles of John in the New Testament. We should add to these references John 13:14, "you *ought (opheilein)* to wash one another's feet." In John the action of Jesus in washing the disciples' feet is both the motivation for the action of the disciples and the model for what loving one another should mean. The mutuality of love is grounded in the love command, but the love command is itself grounded in Jesus' loving action. 1 John treats the theme more fundamentally by grounding the obligation to love one another in God: "Beloved, if God loved us like this, we *ought* also to love one another" (4:11). The grounding action of God is in sending the Son as the expiation of our sins (4:10). On the obligation and its grounding see also 1 John 2:6; 3:16; 3 John 8. The obligation is grounded in God's loving action in Jesus and is expressed in the love command *(entolē)*; see John 13:34 and note the importance of commandment(s) in John 10:18; 12:49, 50; 14:15, 21, 31; 15:10 (3x); 1 John 2:3, 4, 7 (3x), 8; 3:22, 23 (2x), 24; 4:21; 5:2, 3; 2 John 4, 5, 6 (2x).

Because the mutuality of love is grounded in God's loving action in his Son Jesus Christ, those who bear the message of that love assert that acceptance of the message is the means by which the love of God becomes effective, creating community *(koinōnia):* 1 John 1:3, 6, 7. Community with God does not bypass community with believers, and that community is expressed in love for one another. The obligation to love one another is thus grounded in the gospel. Because of this the commandment can be expressed in terms of the fact "that we believe in the name of his son Jesus Christ and love one another" (3:23). Although the word "church" is not used in the Gospel and Epistles of John, the believers are described in terms of the community of mutual love, which is grounded in God's love.

This community is also an expression of a mutual *abiding (menein)* with God. The verb "to abide" is used 117 times in the New Testament (3 times in Matthew, twice in Mark, 7 times in Luke, 40 times in John, 23 times in 1 John, and 3 times in 2 John). In these Johannine writings we find over half the uses in the New Testament and the distinctive sense of God's word, seed *(sperma),* anointing *(chrisma),* spirit abiding with the believer and reciprocal abiding of the believer in the light, in God, in the truth (see 1 John 2:6, 10, 14, 17, 24, 27, 28; 3:6, 9, 14, 15, 24; 4:12, 13, 15, 16; 2 John 2, 6). The reciprocity of abiding is explicit in 3:16. The believer abides in God and God in the believer. The concentration of this theme in 1 John is pronounced. Not only is the verb used 23 times in five short chapters, but almost all uses there fit into this theme.

Because the theme of mutual abiding suggests an emphasis on interiority rather than externals, Edward Malatesta argues that 1 John is to be interpreted in terms of the new covenant of Jer 31:31-34. In asserting this he must contend with a complex of evidence that seems to run contrary to his thesis. First, the term "covenant" *(diathēkē)* is nowhere used in the Gospel and Epistles of John. Indeed, the term is rarely used in the New Testament, only 33 times, of which 17 are in Hebrews. In Hebrews the theme of the new covenant is clearly important. The word is used four times in the Synoptics (one each in Matthew and Mark and two in Luke); two in Acts; one in Revelation; nine times in the Pauline corpus (two in Romans, one in 1 Corinthians, two in 2 Corinthians, three in Galatians, one in Ephesians). There are points at which God's covenant with Israel is important for Paul, but this is not consistently expressed in his letters. It emerges when the place of Israel in God's purpose is raised. But the Gospel and Epistles of John show no explicit interest in the covenant, old or new.

Malatesta also confuses John's focus on mutual abiding with the interiority of the law in the new covenant, "I will write my law on their hearts." Not only is there no reference to covenant, there is no allusion to these words. Rather, the evidence of mutual abiding is to be found in the confession of the true faith and in mutual love in the community. "Covenant" deals with the ground rules governing the relationship of God with God's people. It is, however, a case of category confusion to read covenant into any discussion of relationship with God. Had it been the point of 1 John to deal with relationship with God in terms of covenant it could easily have been done. If the readers of the Epistles were not Jewish, this might have made little sense. Even in the Gospel, which reflects the struggle of Jewish believers with the synagogue and unbelieving Jews, there is no sign of the author's direct use of covenant. Associated themes are developed instead.

**16.5. Sin.** Teaching about sin in 1 John is complex. Because christology is the point at which the revelation of God encounters the world of darkness, we may expect that christology encounters the problem of sin head on (3:5, 9). This is apparent in the first references to sin in 1:7-10. Here, paradoxically, walking in the light is accompanied by cleansing from all sin. In this first discussion walking in the light, at first glance, might seem to exclude the possibility of sin. This clearly is not the case. Only those who walk in the light have the promise of reciprocal community *(koinōnia met' allēlōn)* and cleansing from all sin through the blood of Jesus, God's Son, because to walk in darkness is to hate the brother (2:9). Thus to walk in the light is to enter reciprocal love for one another and to experience cleansing from sin. Cleansing is one metaphor alongside the description of forgiveness. Acknowledgment and confession of sins are presupposed as a basis of forgiveness and cleansing from all sin. If it can be said that the blood of Jesus as God's Son cleanses us from all sin, it is also said that God is faithful and just to forgive us our sins and to cleanse us from all unrighteousness. Fundamental to 1 John is the view that what Jesus is and does is grounded in God and what God does. While this is implicit in the Gospel, 1 John makes it emphatically explicit in a number of places.

1 John 2:1-2 begins with an exhortation: "Do not sin." Immediately the author presumes the possibility of sin and outlines the way sin is to be dealt with. Just as God was described as faithful and righteous, so now our advocate with the Father is named "Jesus Christ the righteous." An isolated reading of 2:1-2 could be taken to mean that only reluctantly could the Father be persuaded to forgive and cleanse us. But God seems to be in view in 1:9, and 4:10-11 is quite explicit in making God and God's love for us the ground of the sending of the Son as the expiation for our sins. Further, 2:2 makes quite clear that the Son was sent to deal with the sins of the whole world.

1 John 3:4-10 begins by identifying sin with lawlessness. It follows that the Son of God was revealed to take away sins, to destroy the works of the devil. The children of God and the children of the devil are contrasted: the one does righteousness and the other sins. Doing righteousness is identified with loving the brother or sister, implying that sin is hating the brother or sister. In this contrast between the children of God and the chil-

dren of the devil several claims are made about not sinning. "Everyone abiding in him does not sin" (3:6). "Everyone born of God does not commit sin, because his seed abides in him and he is not able to sin, because he is born of God" (3:9). "Everyone who believes that Jesus is the Christ is born of God" (5:1). "Everyone born of God conquers the world; and this is the victory that has conquered the world, our faith. Who is the one who conquers the world if not the one who believes Jesus is the Son of God?" (5:4-5).

At a glance 3:4-10 is in serious conflict with 1:7–2:2. The author has modified his view of sin in the life of the children of God in the context of the contrast between the children of God and the children of the devil. One way to handle this is to limit the scope of sin in 3:4-10 to the refusal to confess Jesus is the Christ, the Son of God, come in the flesh, and the failure to love one another as an obligation grounded in the revelation of the love of God. The refusal to make this confession and the failure to love one another is the sin unto death mentioned in 5:16-17. This is the sin committed by the false teachers and their supporters. But there is a sin that is not mortal. It is mortal sin that those born of God do not commit, and the seed of God keeps them so that the evil one cannot touch them. The coming of the Son of God has delivered them from the power of the evil one (5:18-20). But there is a sin that is not mortal and believers may commit such sins; hence prayerful intervention is sought on behalf of such in order that they may receive life. But the false teachers and their followers have committed mortal sin and revealed that they "are not of us" (2:18-19). Their separation from the community, their refusal to love the brothers and sisters, and their rejection of the confession of faith bear the mark of mortal sin and identify them as children of the devil. This evaluation of the opponents is harsh and finds expression in terms like "children of the devil," "deceivers," "false prophets," "antichrists." See the discussion in the Appendix to the Interpretation of 2:2.

**16.6. The world (*kosmos*).** Of the 185 times the "world" is used in the New Testament, 78 occur in John, 23 in 1 John, and 1 in 2 John. Only 1 Corinthians has a significantly similar use where "world" is used 21 times. As in the Gospel of John, but more emphatically so, in 1 John the whole world lies in the power of the evil one (5:19). For this reason the mission of the Son of God was to destroy the works of the devil, to take away sins (3:5, 10). Jesus Christ the righteous is God's way of dealing with the sins of the world (2:2); he was sent to be the savior of the world (4:14). Nevertheless the world currently remains in the power of the evil one and the false teachers belong to it and express its values. For this reason the world listens to them (4:1-5). The values of the world remain a seductive attraction to believers so that they must be warned against them (2:15-17). Nevertheless, the coming of the Son of God provides the assurance that the world and its values will pass away (2:17). The mission of the Son of God carries within it the grounds for the overcoming of the world, dealing with sins, bringing a knowledge of the one that is true as the ground of the confession of the faith. The overcoming of the world is manifest in "our faith," and the victor is "the one who believes" (5:4, 5). The overcoming of the world is also manifest in the mutual love for one another that is grounded in the love of God. This love overcomes the hatred of the world. See the discussion in the Interpretation of 2:2.

### FOR REFERENCE AND FURTHER STUDY

Beutler, Johannes. *Die Johannesbriefe*, 26–29.
Boer, Martinus C. de."The Death of Jesus Christ and His Coming in the Flesh (1 John 4:2)," *NovT* 33 (1991) 326–46.
Bultmann, Rudolf. *Theology of the New Testament*. 2 vols. Translated by Kendrick Grobel. London: S.C.M., 1955, 2:3–92.
_____. "Is Exegesis without Presuppositions Possible?" (1957) in idem, *Existence and Faith: Shorter Writings of Rudolf Bultmann*. Selected, translated, and introduced by Schubert M. Ogden. London: Hodder and Stoughton, 1961, 289–96.
Kruse, Colin G. *The Letters of John*, 33–36.
Lieu, Judith. *The Theology of the Johannine Epistles*.
_____. "'Authority to Become Children of God': A Study of 1 John," *NovT* 23 (1981) 210–28.
Malatesta, Edward. *Interiority and Covenant: A Study of* einai en *and* menein en *in the First Letter of Saint John*. AnBib 69. Rome: Biblical Institute Press, 1978.
Rensberger, David. *1 John, 2 John, 3 John*, 20–21.

## 17. JOHANNINE THEOLOGY: ITS CONTINUING INFLUENCE

Unlike the Gospels of Matthew, Mark, and Luke, which are featured successively in the three-year cycle of liturgical reading, the Gospel of John has no year of its own. It is a slight consolation that at Christmas and Easter readings from John are featured and there are some readings from 1 John at Easter also. Featuring John at Christmas and Easter has given prominence to the Prologue of the Gospel with its proclamation of the Incarnation of the Word. Because Incarnation is also an important emphasis in 1 and 2 John, the Gospel and Epistles have reinforced each other in public consciousness. From the Johannine tradition belief in the Incarnation became central to Christian faith.

The Incarnation of the divine Word *(logos)* was affirmed in the terms of the Gospel Prologue. When, in the second century, Justin Martyr interpreted the *logos* in terms of Platonic/Stoic doctrine, the divine rational mind expressed in nature and history was identified with the divine Incarnation in Jesus Christ. In this perception, room was made for the recognition of God in the world at large and the revelation in Jesus Christ became the key for understanding the world better than it understood itself. But this *logos* doctrine is not found in the Epistles.

It is frequently noted that the confession of the Incarnation in 1 and 2 John is used to exclude those who fail to make the confession. Where Justin's interpretation of the Johannine Incarnation of the *logos* was inclusive, in the Johannine Epistles the confession of the Incarnation was the ground for division and exclusion. This divisive and excluding perspective calls for attention, but before turning to it we need to make clear what it was that the Epistles excluded by the confession that Jesus Christ has come in the flesh. What this means is that the human (Jesus) and divine (Christ) are united in the flesh in one Jesus Christ. The opponents had rejected the identification of the divine Christ with the human Jesus. The importance of this for an understanding of the relationship of God to the world and the character of Christian ethics grounded in theology is clear.

The importance of the Johannine confession for a constructive theology is the recognition that God is known, insofar as humans may know God, in the human life of Jesus. From this perspective the Incarnation is the "coming down of God" to be encompassed in human terms and to be apprehended by human minds. The insistence that *Jesus* is the Christ, the Son of God locates the revelation and saving action of God in the life of a first-century Galilean Jew. The Incarnation also affirms the value of the created world for God and is an expression of God's will to bring the world into a relationship of reciprocal love with God's very self. Thus the Johannine understanding of the Incarnation is a basis for the development of theology and ethics.

The particularity of the christological confession is matched by the specific nature of the love command. It is the command to "love one another" or to "love the brother [and sister]." It is frequently noted that the more comprehensive commands known in the Synoptic Gospels, to love the neighbor and the enemy, are missing from the Johannine writings. Given the manifest acrimony expressed toward the opponents in the Epistles, a case has been made for arguing that the Epistles restricted love to the Johannine group while expressing hostility to those outside the group. There is an element of truth in this criticism, but the aim of the love command is to bring all into the sphere where the divine mutual love operates.

The Johannine tradition provides the clearest basis for the development of the classical christology of Athanasius. It would be anachronistic, however, to read Athanasius back into John. Nevertheless, it is the Johannine tradition that most clearly stands in the way of any attempt to interpret Jesus in purely prophetic terms and lays the foundation for an incarnational christology.

Liturgical reading from the Johannine Epistles is restricted to 1 John. This adds weight to Judith Lieu's complaint that 2 and 3 John have been unjustifiably ignored. Yet these two small letters throw a good deal of light on the situation addressed by the Epistles. Even 1 John is used sparingly: only in the season of Easter, when six readings are drawn from the Epistle in the three-year cycle of readings: 1:1–2:5; 3:1-8; 3:14-24; 4:7-21; 5:1-9; 5:9-15. While the readings cover much of 1 John, they are concentrated in Year B and are read in Easter weeks 2 to 7. Given this concentration and the selection of the readings, the focus is on Jesus' death in relation to the problem of sin. Thus 1 John 2:1-2 speaks of Jesus Christ the righteous as the sinner's advocate with the Father and as the expiation of our sins and the sins of the whole world.

At the same time, 1 John accentuates the role of the Father (God) in dealing with the problem of sin. It is God who sent the Son as the expiation for our sins (4:10). Indeed, the point of 4:7-21 is that the sending of the Son "that we might live through him" (4:9), "as the expiation for our sins" (4:10), "as the savior of the world" (4:14), is because "God is love" (4:8, 16). In this way 1 John establishes the principle that Jesus the Son reveals the Father. The loving action of the Son reveals the love of God, that God is love. Paul, like 1 John, interprets the death of Jesus "for us" as the revelation of God's love for us (Rom 5:8). In fact John goes further in the passage bounded by the inclusion of 4:8 and 16. The sending of the Son as an expiation for sin involves the blood of Jesus Christ (1:7), that is, his death: "he gave his life for us" (3:16). It is this event that reveals the depth of God's love for the world. It is christologically significant that what happens in Jesus reveals God's love. It is also theologically significant that the fundamental understanding of the being of God is established in the giving of Jesus' life. But for the giving of Jesus' life to reveal that God is love it is necessary to perceive that the giving of his life dealt with the problem of our sins, indeed, the sins of the whole world.

There is a second great affirmation of the being of God in 1:5: the message that we heard from him (Jesus). That message is "God is light." This is to affirm that God is self-revealing. But 1 John elaborates the message further by insisting: "in him is no darkness at all." In this way it becomes clear that the revelation has specific content. The person who loves the brother or sister walks in the light, but the one who hates the brother or sister remains in the darkness. The light of God is the light of God's love, and to walk in the light is to walk in love. To say that God is light is to acknowledge the necessity of walking in the light. To acknowledge that God is love is to acknowledge the obligation to love one another. In 1 John ethical obligation is theologically grounded. The theological grounding is not self-evident, but is dependent on belief in Jesus Christ as the Son of the Father (3:23).

In 1 John there is no danger that anyone might think of a christology with its own independent significance. What Jesus is and does reveals what God is. What God is and does is the ground of the ethical obligation for believers living in God's world. While much of the Johannine language operates at a level of generality, speaking of love and hate, 3:16-18 becomes quite specific. Love is known in the giving of Jesus' life for us. Thus we ought to give our lives for the brothers and sisters. Such giving implies responding to the physical needs of the brother/sister (fellow believer) and is incompatible with turning away from the obligation to the fellow believer.

The acknowledgment of obligation to the fellow believer, arising out of the love of God revealed in Jesus, raises the question of the broader obligation to the neighbor or even the enemy. 1 John does not explore, as Paul does in Romans 5, that God's love reaches us while we are sinners and at enmity with God. From such a basis 1 John might have been constrained to argue that the obligation is not restricted to the fellow believer. But this step is not taken. At the same time there is no implied instruction to hate those who are not believers. The instruction (in 2 John) not to aid those whose teaching differs from the author's is not a call to hatred. There is no suggestion that such teachers are in a life-threatening situation. The call is to refuse to assist a work that the author sees as destructive to the life of believers.

The Johannine Epistles reveal a pastoral context in which the understanding of the message provides the ethical basis for living together in a community of love for one another. The theological grounding of love has as its counterpart clear ethical obligations. But there is a need to work out in detail what this might mean for the life of a believing community and for the mission of believers living in the world.

1 John is concerned with the problem of sin. It was the work of Jesus to deal with sin, and believers need to confess their sins and be cleansed from all unrighteousness. Within the community it seems that the problem of sin is to be understood in terms of the failure to love. Such a problem is made intelligible by the repeated emphasis on the obligation to love one another, to love the fellow believer. But if 1 John insists that the way to deal with sin is to confess and be cleansed, there are also the passages that insist that those born of God do not sin (3:9-10; 5:18), and that those who abide in God do not sin (3:6).

Because of these passages 1 John has provided a basis for the Holiness Movement and for the development of teaching that affirms the possibility and necessity for the believer to be sinless. Indeed, from the nineteenth century onward there has been a Wesleyan holiness tradition that appeals to these texts. At the same time it is necessary to notice the emphatic rejection of sinlessness in 1:6, 8. Just how to resolve these two perspectives is an issue dealt with in the commentary. Here we note the way 1 John has provided a basis for a holiness teaching that affirms sinless perfection. In that tradition there is a danger that the individual will become so preoccupied with personal holiness that the ethical obligation of love for the other person is overlooked. In 1 John it is not possible to think of holiness in strictly individual terms. Rather, holiness language is notable for its absence and the model believing response is expressed in relation to God and one another. It is not an issue for the unrelated self. For John, holiness is not so much a separation from as it is commitment to "the other."

In dealing with the opponents 1 and 2 John describe them as false prophets and the antichrist(s). This language has gripped the imagination of Christian groups down through the ages. Many individuals and movements have been identified in this way. The danger of so labeling those who differ from us is now widely recognized. At the same time the Epistles bring into sharp relief the problem of those whose words and actions are destructive to the life of the believing community. The figure of the Antichrist also alerts us to those destructive forces in the world at large. There are evil forces that need to be opposed, though to brand them as the Antichrist perhaps unfairly strips them of any grace and excludes any hope of reconciliation. Certainly there is no hint in 1 John that the opponents might be won over to the truth, and this constitutes something of a problem in the context of the understanding of God, who is love.


## GENERAL BIBLIOGRAPHY

Barrett, Charles Kingsley. *The Gospel According to St. John*. London: S.P.C.K., 1955, 2nd ed. 1978.

_____. *The Gospel of John and Judaism*. London: S.P.C.K., 1975.

Betz, Hans Dieter. *Galatians: A Commentary on Paul's Letter to the Churches in Galatia*. Hermeneia. Philadelphia: Fortress, 1979.

Beutler, Johannes. *Die Johannesbriefe*. Regensburger Neues Testament. Regensburg: Friedrich Pustet, 2000.

_____. "Krise und Untergang der johanneischen Gemeinde: Das Zeugnis der Johannesbriefe," in Jean-Marie Severin, ed., *The New Testament in Early Christianity*. BETL 86. Louvain: Leuven University Press 1989, 85–103.

Boer, Martinus C. de. "Jesus the Baptizer: 1 John 5:5-8 and the Gospel of John," *JBL* 107 (1988) 87–106.

_____. "The Death of Jesus Christ and His Coming in the Flesh (1 John 4:2)," *NovT* 33 (1991) 326–46.

Bogart, John. *Orthodox and Heretical Perfectionism in the Johannine Community as Evident in the First Epistle of John.* SBLDS 33. Missoula: Scholars, 1976.

Borgen, Peder. *Logos Was the True Light, and other essays on the Gospel of John.* Trondheim: Tapir, 1983.

Bousset, Wilhelm. *Kyrios Christos; Geschichte des Christusglaubens von den Anfängen des Christentums bis Irenaeus.* Göttingen: Vandenhoeck & Ruprecht, 1913. English: *Kyrios Christos; A History of the Belief in Christ from the Beginnings of Christianity to Irenaeus.* Translated by John E. Steely. Nashville: Abingdon, 1970.

_____. *Jüdisch-Christlicher Schulbetrieb in Alexandria und Rom; literarische Untersuchungen zu Philo und Clemens von Alexandria, Justin und Irenäus.* Göttingen: Vandenhoeck & Ruprecht, 1915.

_____. *Der Antichrist in der Überlieferung des Judentums, des Neuen Testaments und der Alten Kirche.* Göttingen: Vandenhoeck & Ruprecht, 1895. English: *The Antichrist Legend: A Chapter in Christian and Jewish Folklore.* London: Hutchinson, 1896.

Brooke, Alan England. *A Critical and Exegetical Commentary on the Johannine Epistles.* Edinburgh: T & T Clark, 1912.

Brown, Raymond E. *The Gospel According to John.* AB 29/29A. Garden City, N.Y.: Doubleday, 1967.

_____. *The Community of the Beloved Disciple.* New York: Paulist, 1979.

_____. *The Epistles of John.* AB 30. Garden City, N.Y.: Doubleday, 1982.

Bultmann, Rudolf. "Analyse des ersten Johannesbriefes," in *Festgabe für Adolf Jülicher zum 70. Geburtstag.* Tübingen: J.C.B. Mohr, 1927, 138–58.

_____. *Das Evangelium des Johannes.* Göttingen: Vandenhoeck & Ruprecht, 1941. English: *The Gospel of John.* Translated by G. R. Beasley-Murray. Oxford: Blackwell, 1971.

_____. "Die kirchliche Redaktion des ersten Johannesbriefes," in Werner Schmauch, ed., *In Memoriam Ernst Lohmeyer.* Stuttgart: Evangelisches Verlagswerks, 1951, 189–201.

_____. "Johannesbriefe," in *RGG³.* Tübingen: J.C.B. Mohr, 1959, 837–40.

_____. *Theologie des Neuen Testaments.* Tübingen: J.C.B. Mohr, 1948–1953. English: *Theology of the New Testament.* 2 vols. Translated by Kendrick Grobel. London: S.C.M., 1955.

_____. "Is Exegesis without Presuppositions Possible?" (1957) in idem, *Existence and Faith: Shorter Writings of Rudolf Bultmann.* Selected, translated, and introduced by Schubert M. Ogden. London: Hodder and Stoughton, 1961, 289–96.

_____. *Die drei Johannesbriefe.* KEK 7th ed. Göttingen: Vandenhoeck & Ruprecht, 1967. English: *The Johannine Epistles; A Commentary on the Johannine Epistles.* Translated by R. Philip O'Hara with Lane C. McGaughy and Robert Funk. Philadelphia: Fortress, 1973.

_____. "The Interpretation of the Fourth Gospel." Review of C. H. Dodd's *The Interpretation of the Fourth Gospel.* NTS 1 (1954–55) 77–91. English translation by W. C. Robinson in *Harvard Divinity Bulletin* 27 (1963) 9–22.

Carroll, K. L. "The Fourth Gospel and the Exclusion of Christians from the Synagogue," BJRL 40 (1957–58) 19–32.

Court, John. "Blessed Assurance," *JTS* 33 (1982) 508–17.

Culpepper, R. Alan. *The Johannine School.* SBLDS 26. Missoula: Scholars, 1975.

————. "1–2–3 John," in Gerhard Krodel, ed., *The General Letters.* Proclamation Commentaries. Revised and enlarged ed. Minneapolis: Fortress, 1995.

Dahl, Nils, A. "Letters," *IDBSupp* (1976) 538–41.

Deissmann, Adolf. *Licht vom Osten : das Neue Testament und die neuentdeckten Texte der hellenistisch-römischen Welt.* Tübingen: J.C.B. Mohr, 1908; 4th ed. 1923. English: *Light from the Ancient East. The New Testament Illustrated by Recently Discovered Texts of the Graeco-Roman World.* London: Hodder and Stoughton, 1927.

Dodd, Charles Harold. "*Hilaskesthai,* Its Cognates, Derivatives and Synonyms in the Septuagint," *JTS* 32 (1931) 352–60.

————. *The First Epistle of John and the Fourth Gospel.* Manchester: Manchester University Press, 1937. Reprinted from *BJRL* 21/1 (1937).

————. *The Johannine Epistles.* MNTC. London: Hodder and Stoughton, 1946.

————. *The Interpretation of the Fourth Gospel.* Cambridge: Cambridge University Press, 1953.

Donfried, Karl P. "Ecclesiastical Authority in 2–3 John," in Marinus de Jonge, ed., *L'Evangile de Jean: sources, redaction, theologie.* BETL 44. Gembloux: Duculot, 1977, 325–33.

Doty, William G. *Letters in Primitive Christianity.* Philadelphia: Fortress, 1973.

Dunn, James D. G. *The Partings of the Way between Christianity and Judaism and their Significance for the Character of Christianity.* London: S.C.M.; Philadelphia: Trinity Press International, 1991.

————, ed. *Jews and Christians: The Parting of the Ways, AD 70–135: The Second Durham–Tübingen Research Symposium on Earliest Christianity and Judaism, Durham, September 1989.* Tübingen: J.C.B. Mohr [Paul Siebeck], 1992.

Edwards, Ruth B. *The Johannine Epistles.* Sheffield: Sheffield Academic Press, 1996.

Ehrman, Bart D. "1 John 4:3 and the Orthodox Corruption of Scripture," *ZNW* 79 (1988) 221–43.

Funk, Robert W. "The Form and Structure of 1 & 2 John," *JBL* 86 (1967) 424–30.

Gerhardsson, Birger. *Memory and Manuscript: Oral Tradition and Written Transmission in Rabbinic Judaism and Early Christianity.* Uppsala: Gleerup, 1961.

Goodenough, Erwin R. *By Light, Light; The Mystic Gospel of Hellenistic Judaism.* New Haven: Yale University Press, 1935.

Grayston, Kenneth. *The Johannine Epistles.* NCB. Grand Rapids: Eerdmans, 1984.

Häring, Theodor. "Gedankengang und Grundgedanke des ersten Johannesbriefes," in Adolf Harnack, et al., *Theologische Abhandlungen Carl von Weizsäcker zu seinem siebzigsten Geburtstage, 11. December 1892.* Freiburg: J.C.B. Mohr [Paul Siebeck], 1892, 173–200.

————. *Die Johannesbriefe.* Stuttgart: Calwer, 1927.

Harnack, Adolf. "Über den dritten Johannesbrief," *TU* 15/3 (1897) 3–27.

————. "Das 'Wir' in der Johanneischen Schriften," *SB* (Berlin) 1923, 96–113.

Hengel, Martin. *Die johanneische Frage: ein Lösungsversuch.* Tübingen: J.C.B. Mohr [Paul Siebeck], 1993. English: *The Johannine Question.* London: S.C.M., 1989.

Hills, Julian. "'Little Children, Keep Yourselves from Idols': 1 John 5:21 Reconsidered," *CBQ* 51 (1989) 285–310.

_____. "A Genre for 1 John," in Birger A. Pearson, A. Thomas Kraabel, George W. E. Nickelsburg, and Norman R. Petersen, eds., *The Future of Early Christianity: Essays in Honour of Helmut Koester*. Minneapolis: Fortress 1991, 367–77.

Holtzmann, Heinrich J. *Evangelium des Johannes*. Hand-Commentar zum Neuen Testament 4:1. 3rd ed. Tübingen: J.C.B. Mohr [Paul Siebeck], 1908.

_____. *Das Problem des 1 Johannesbriefes in seinem Verhältnis zum Evangelium*. *Jahrbuch für Protestant. Theologie* 1881, 1882.

Houlden, James Leslie. *A Commentary on the Johannine Epistles*. HNTC. New York: Harper & Row, 1973.

Howard, Wilbert F. "The Common Authorship of the Johannine Gospel and Epistles," *JTS* 48 (1947) 12–25.

Jonge, Marinus de. "To love as God loves" (1 John 4:7) in idem, *Jesus: Inspiring and Disturbing Presence*. Translated by John E. Steely. Nashville: Abingdon, 1974, 110–27.

Käsemann, Ernst. "Ketzer und Zeuge: Zum johanneischen Verfasserproblem," *ZTK* 48 (1951) 292–311.

Kilpatrick, G. D. "Two Johannine Idioms in the Johannine Epistles," *JTS* 12 (1961) 272–73.

Kim, Chan-Hie. *Form and Structure of the Familiar Greek Letter of Recommendation*. SBLDS 4. Missoula: Scholars, 1972.

Klauck, Hans-Josef. "Internal Opponents: The Treatment of the Secessionists in the First Epistle of John" (translated by Robert Nowell) in Wim Beuken, Sean Freyne, and Anton Weiler, eds., *Truth and its Victims. Concilium* 200. Edinburgh: T & T Clark, 1988, 55–65.

_____. "Brudermord und Bruderliebe. Ethische Paradigmen in 1 Joh 3:11-17," in Helmut Merklein, ed., *Neues Testament und Ethik: für Rudolf Schnackenburg*. Freiburg, Basel, and Vienna: Herder, 1989, 151–69.

_____. "Zur rhetorischen Analyse der Johannesbriefe," *ZNW* 81 (1990) 205–24.

_____. *Die Johannesbriefe*. EdF. Darmstadt: Wissenschaftliche Buchgesellschaft, 1991.

_____. *Der erste Johannesbrief*. EKK 23/1. Zürich: Benziger; Neukirchen-Vluyn: Neukirchener Verlag, 1991.

_____. *Der zweite und dritte Johannesbrief*. EKK 23/2. Zurich: Benziger; Neukirchen-Vluyn: Neukirchener Verlag, 1992.

Kruse, Colin G. *The Letters of John*. Grand Rapids: Eerdmans, 2000.

La Potterie, Ignace de. *La vérité dans saint Jean*. 2 vols. AnBib 73-74. Rome: Biblical Institute Press, 1977.

Law, Robert. *The Tests of Life: A Study of the First Epistle of St. John*. Edinburgh: T & T Clark, 1909.

Lieu, Judith. "'Authority to Become Children of God': A Study of 1 John," *NovT* 23 (1981) 210–28.

_____. *The Second and Third Epistles of John*. Edinburgh: T & T Clark, 1986.

_____. "Blindness in the Johannine Tradition," *NTS* 34 (1988) 83–95.

_____. *The Theology of the Johannine Epistles*. Cambridge: Cambridge University Press, 1991.

_____. "What was from the beginning," *NTS* 39 (1993) 458–77.

Malatesta, Edward. *Interiority and Covenant: A Study of* einai en *and* menein en *in the First Letter of Saint John.* AnBib 69. Rome: Biblical Institute Press, 1978.

Malherbe, Abraham J. "The Inhospitality of Diotrephes," in Jacob Jervell and Wayne A. Meeks, eds., *God's Christ and his People: Studies in Honour of Nils Alstrup Dahl.* Oslo: Universitetsforlaget, 1977, 222–32.

_____, compiler and translator. *Ancient Epistolary Theorists.* Sources for Biblical Study 19. Atlanta: Scholars, 1988.

Martyn, J. Louis. *History and Theology in the Fourth Gospel.* New York: Harper & Row, 1968, 2nd ed. 1979.

Okure, Teresa. *The Johannine Approach to Mission: A Contextual Study of John 4:1-32.* WUNT 2nd ser. 31. Tübingen: J.C.B. Möhr [Paul Siebeck], 1988.

O'Neill. John C. *The Puzzle of 1 John.* London: S.P.C.K., 1966.

Painter, John. *John, Witness and Theologian.* London: S.P.C.K. 1975, 2nd ed. 1978; 3rd ed. Melbourne: Beacon Hill, 1980.

_____. "The Opponents in 1 John," *NTS* 32 (1986) 48–71. Now revised in idem, *The Quest for the Messiah.* 2nd ed. Nashville: Abingdon, 1993, 427–64.

_____. "C. H. Dodd and the Christology of the Fourth Gospel," *JTSA* 59 (July 1987) 42–56.

_____. *The Quest for the Messiah.* Edinburgh: T & T Clark, 1991, 2nd ed. Nashville: Abingdon, 1993.

_____. "The Quotation of Scripture and Unbelief in John 12.36b-43," in Craig A. Evans and W. Richard Stegner, eds., *The Gospels and the Scriptures of Israel.* JSNTS 104. Sheffield: Sheffield Academic Press, 1994, 429–58.

Parker, David C. *Codex Bezae. An Early Christian Manuscript and its Text.* Cambridge: Cambridge University Press, 1992.

Parkes, James. *The Conflict of the Church and the Synagogue: A Study of the Origins of Antisemitism.* London: Soncino, 1934; repr. New York: Atheneum, 1969.

Perkins, Pheme. *The Johannine Epistles.* New Testament Message 21. Wilmington, Del.: Michael Glazier, 1979.

_____. "Koinonia in 1 John 1:3-7: The Social Context of Division in the Johannine Letters," *CBQ* 45 (1983) 631–41.

Porter, Stanley E., ed. *Handbook of Classical Rhetoric in the Hellenistic Period 300 B.C.–A.D. 400.* Leiden: Brill, 1997.

Rensberger, David. *1 John, 2 John, 3 John.* ANTC. Nashville: Abingdon, 1997.

Richter, Georg. "Blut und Wasser," *MThZ* (1970) 1–21; reprinted in idem, *Studien zum Johannesevangelium.* Regensburg: Pustet, 1977, 120–42.

Robinson, John A. T. *Twelve New Testament Studies.* SBT 34. London: S.C.M., 1962.

_____. "The Destination and Purpose of the Johannine Epistles," in ibid., 56–65.

Salom, A. P., "Some Aspects of the Grammatical Style of 1 John," *JBL* 74 (1955) 96–102.

Schnackenburg, Rudolf. *Die Johannesbriefe.* HThK 13/3. Freiburg, Basel, and Vienna: Herder, 1953. English: *The Johannine Epistles.* Translated by Reginald and Ilse Fuller. New York: Crossroad, 1992.

Schwartz, Eduard. *Über den Tod der Söhne Zebedaei. Ein Beitrag zur Geschichte des Johannesevangeliums.* Berlin: Weidmann, 1904.

Sekki, Arthur Everett. *The Meaning of* Ruaḥ *at Qumran.* SBLDS 110. Atlanta: Scholars, 1989.

Smalley, Stephen S. *1, 2, 3 John.* WBC. Waco, Tex.: Word Books, 1984.

Stowers, Stanley K. *Letter writing in Greco-Roman Antiquity.* Philadelphia: Westminster, 1986.

Strecker, Georg. *Die Johannesbriefe.* KEK 14. Göttingen: Vandenhoeck & Ruprecht, 1989. *The Johannine Letters: A Commentary on 1, 2, and 3 John.* Translated by Linda M. Maloney. Hermeneia. Minneapolis: Fortress, 1996.

Sundberg, Albert C. "Canon Muratori: A Fourth Century List," *HTR* 66 (1973) 1–41.

Vermes, Geza. *The Dead Sea Scrolls in English.* 3rd ed. New York: Penguin, 1987.

Wahlde, Urban C. von. *The Johannine Commandments: 1 John and the Struggle for the Johannine Tradition.* New York: Paulist, 1999.

Watson, Duane F. "1 John 2:12-14 as *Distributio, Conduplicatio,* and *Expolitio*: A Rhetorical Understanding," *JSNT* 35 (1989) 97–110.

_____. "A Rhetorical Analysis of 2 John According to Greco-Roman Conventions," *NTS* 35 (1989) 104–30.

_____. "A Rhetorical Analysis of 3 John: A Study in Epistolary Rhetoric," *CBQ* 51 (1989) 479–501.

_____. "Amplification Techniques in 1 John: The Interaction of Rhetorical Style and Invention," *JSNT* 51 (1993) 99–123.

Watson, Duane F., and Alan J. Hauser. *Rhetorical Criticism of the Bible: A Comprehensive Bibliography with Notes on History and Method.* Leiden: Brill, 1994.

Westcott, Brooks Foss. *The Epistles of St John: The Greek Text, with Notes and Essays.* London: Macmillan, 1883.

White, John Lee. *The Form and Function of the Body of the Greek Letter: A Study of the Letter-Body in the Non-literary Papyri and in Paul the Apostle.* SBLDS 2. Missoula: Scholars, 1972.

_____. "New Testament Epistolary Literature in the Framework of Ancient Epistolography," *Aufstieg und Niedergang der römischen Welt* II.25.2 (1984) 1730–56.

Whitacre, Rodney A. *Johannine Polemic: The Role of Tradition and Theology.* SBLDS 67. Chico: Scholars, 1982.

Wilson, W. G. "An Examination of the Linguistic Evidence Adduced against the Unity of Authorship of the First Epistle of John and the Fourth Gospel," *JTS* 49 (1948) 147–56.

Witherington, Ben III. "The Waters of Birth: John 3:5 and 1 John 5:6-8," *NTS* 35 (1989) 155–60.

Wurm, Alois. *Die Irrleherer im ersten Johannesbrief.* Biblische Studien 8/1. Freiburg and St. Louis: Herder, 1903.

Yates, Roy. "The Antichrist," *Evangelical Quarterly* 46 (1974) 42–50.

# 1 JOHN

## INTRODUCTION TO THE EXEGESIS OF 1 JOHN

Rudolf Schnackenburg noted that 1 John is characterized by a stylistic duality (*The Johannine Epistles* 77). A duality of tone is recognized in the swing from passages of a polemical tone to those of pastoral concern. "The double nature of the material is not the result of the author commenting on a source, but is the consequence of the author's double purpose for writing. He wrote to oppose the heretics and to encourage the believers" (Painter, *John, Witness and Theologian* 112). The reason for this is that the community (or group of communities made up of a network of house churches) for which 1 John was written was in turmoil following a controversial and bitter struggle that had ended in a schism. 1 John was written to deal with the aftermath.

> Though the heretics had withdrawn, the community was in turmoil and continued to be threatened by the false teaching. . . . 1 John was written to bring the assurance of faith to those who had been troubled by the heretical teachers. . . . Thus the confession of true faith and active love for the brethren have become the tests which expose the heretics and provide the believers with the assurance of faith. (*John, Witness and Theologian* 116, 124, 125)

In doing this 1 John specifically gives a critique of the seven assertions of the opponents (1:6, 8, 10; 2:4, 6, 9; 4:20) and their denial of the central christological confession (*John, Witness and Theologian* 115–25). It also seeks to reassure the readers that they know the truth and have eternal life. The first step in providing this reassurance is to discredit the position of the opponents whose message continued to destabilize the community even though they themselves had separated from it.

Critics of the polemical nature of 1 John tend to think of a polemic addressed to the opponents. My paper for the 1984 SNTS John Seminar, "The Opponents in 1 John," does not clarify this issue because my purpose was to set out as clearly as possible the position of the "opponents" in response to the publication of Raymond E. Brown's commentary, *The Letters of John*. The paper does not give an account of broader issues such as the purpose of 1 John. From this point of view my 1975 treatment was more balanced.

The audience addressed is more clearly expressed in a statement on the purpose of 1 John, written in 1996 and soon to appear in *The Eerdmans Critical Commentary on the Bible:*

> Nevertheless this polemic is not directed to the opponents. They can hardly have been the intended audience. Rather its purpose was to persuade the author's supporters that in remaining loyal to him they were abiding in the truth of the Gospel. This was done first by a critique of the opponents. Because the controversy had unsettled even those loyal in the community, bringing uncertainty and anxiety, our author had to blend his polemic with a sensitive pastoral concern for his readers. His objective was to assure them that they were abiding in the truth, [that] they were children of God walking in the light, and thus restore them to a confident relationship with the Father through faith in the Son. Because of this 1 John manifests a literary duality of polemical and pastoral perspectives.

Raymond Brown was well aware that the polemical nature of 1 John did not mean that it was directed to the opponents. He wrote:

> Let me add here that a theory that gives prominence to the role of adversaries in the background does not automatically mean that 1 John should be classified as a polemical tract. . . . The primary purpose of the work might well be to strengthen the author's own Community in a time when adversaries are causing trouble. (*The Epistles of John* 47)

Thus while one strategy was to deal with the position of the opponents in a polemical way, exposing the error, 1 John was not written to the opponents. It was written to the traumatized and disturbed community whose assurance of faith had been undermined. The aim of the letter was to restore that assurance and to place it on a solid basis. To this end we find the many assurances, "By this you know. . . ." These are supported by the strong pastoral concerns of 1 John.

## OUTLINE OF 1 JOHN

There are considerable problems concerning the structure of 1 John. A. E. Brooke put this down to the "aphoristic character of the writer's meditations," and concludes: "perhaps the attempt to analyze the Epistle should be abandoned as useless" (*Commentary* xxxii). Nevertheless he recognized that Theodor Häring had made the most successful attempt to show the underlying sequence of thought in the Epistle ("Gedankengang und Grundgedanke des ersten Johannesbriefes," 1892) and he followed Häring's analysis generally in his commentary (*Commentary* 34). A summary of Häring's analysis follows, modified by the recognition of the claims of the opponents (1:6, 8, 10; 2:4, 6, 9; 4:20), to which 1 John makes a serious response.

I. Prologue (1:1–5)

II. First presentation of the two tests (1:6–2:27)
Two tests of the claim to have union *(koinōnia)* with God: the ethical (love) and christological theses.

    1. The ethical (love) test. Walking in the light as the true sign of union *(koinōnia)* with God. Refutation of the first two series of lies (1:6–2:17)

        1.1. God is light and the necessity of walking in the light (1:6–2:11)

            1.1.1. Response to the claim to have union with God who is light (1:6–2:2)

                a. First claim (we have union with him) and test (1:6-7)
                b. Second claim and refutation (1:8-9)
                c. Third claim and refutation (1:10–2:2)
                    Christ our advocate (2:1-2)

            1.1.2. Response to the claims to know, abide, be in the light (2:3-11)

                a. Formula of reassuring test (2:3)
                 b. Fourth claim and test (2:4-5)
                 c. Fifth claim and test (2:6)
                 d. The old commandment which is new (2:7-8)
                 e. Sixth claim and test (2:9-11)

        1.2. Preliminary appeal (2:12-14)

        1.3. Admonition: False love (2:15-17)

    2. The christological test. Faith in Jesus Christ as the test of the claim to have fellowship with God: Refutation of the second lie (2:18–27)

III. Second presentation of the two tests (2:28–4:6)

    1. The ethical test. Doing righteousness (= love of the brethren) as the sign by which we may know that we are born of God (2:28–3:24)

        1.1. Acting righteously is the test of abiding in him (2:28-29)

        1.2. Sanctification (separation from the corruption of the world) is the test of the claim to being sons and daughters of God (3:1-3)

        1.3. The incompatibility of sin and righteousness (3:4-10)

        1.4. The incompatibility of love and hate (3:11-18)

1.5. The grounds for confidence before God (3:19-24)
   Emphasizing the connection between the two tests (3:22–24)

2. The christological test. The Spirit from God confesses that Jesus Christ
   has come in the flesh (4:1–6)

IV. Third presentation of the two tests (4:7–5:12)
   Stressing the inseparable relation between the two tests

1. Love based on faith in the revelation of love is the proof of knowing God
   and being born of God (4:7–21)

   1.1. God's love is the source of love for one another (4:7-12)

   1.2. The Spirit is the evidence of abiding in God (4:13-16a)

   1.3. Abiding in love is the ground of confidence before God (4:16b-21)
      Seventh claim and test (4:20)

2. Faith is the foundation of love (5:1–12)

   2.1. Those who believe are begotten of God and love one another (5:1-3)

   2.2. Victory over the world (5:4-5)

   2.3. The witness to the Son is the witness to eternal life (5:6-12)

V. Conclusion (5:13–21)

   1. To reestablish confidence (5:13-15)

   2. Prayer for those sinning (5:16-17)

   3. God and the problem of sin (5:18-20)

   4. Final exhortation (5:21)

Häring's analysis of 1892 is largely followed by Robert Law (1909) although he appears not to have known Häring's article at the time. I have
adopted the term "tests" from Law's title, *The Tests of Life*. He recognized
three tests: righteousness, love, belief, whereas Häring viewed love as the
expression of righteousness. Law failed to distinguish the "Conclusion"
or "Epilogue" from the third cycle. On the substantial differences Häring's
analysis is to be preferred, though Law's work remains a stimulating
interpretation.

This analysis of the letter emphasizes its controversial nature. The tests
of life were necessary because our author perceived that counterfeit claims
were abroad in the church. Recognition of the affirmations and denials of
the opponents is important to the following interpretation, as is the evidence of the antithetical statements in which the author set his position
over against that of his opponents. Their claims needed to be tested so
that the true might be recognized and the false rejected.

FOR REFERENCE AND FURTHER STUDY

Brooke, Alan England. *A Critical and Exegetical Commentary on the Johannine Epistles.* Edinburgh: T & T Clark, 1912, xxxii–xxxviii.

Brown, Raymond E. *The Epistles of John.* AB 30. Garden City, N.Y.: Doubleday, 1982, 116–29.

Häring, Theodor. "Gedankengang und Grundgedanke des ersten Johannes-briefes," in Adolf Harnack, et al., *Theologische Abhandlungen Carl von Weizsäcker zu seinem siebzigsten Geburtstage, 11. December 1892.* Freiburg: J.C.B. Mohr [Paul Siebeck], 1892, 173–200.

Law, Robert. *The Tests of Life: A Study of the First Epistle of St. John.* Edinburgh: T & T Clark, 1909.

Painter, John. *John, Witness and Theologian.* London: S.P.C.K. 1975, 2nd ed. 1978; 3rd ed. Melbourne: Beacon Hill, 1980.

Schnackenburg, Rudolf. *Die Johannesbriefe.* HThK 13/3. Freiburg, Basel, and Vienna: Herder, 1953. English: *The Johannine Epistles.* Translated by Reginald and Ilse Fuller. New York: Crossroad, 1992, 11–13.

Strecker, Georg. *Die Johannesbriefe.* KEK 14. Göttingen: Vandenhoeck & Ruprecht, 1989. *The Johannine Letters: A Commentary on 1, 2, and 3 John.* Translated by Linda M. Maloney. Hermeneia. Minneapolis: Fortress, 1996, xlii–xliv.

# TRANSLATION, NOTES, INTERPRETATION

## I. PROLOGUE (1:1-5)

1. What was from the beginning, what we have heard, what we have seen with our eyes, what we have seen and our hands handled, concerning the word of life 2.—and the life was revealed, and we have seen and bear witness and announce to you the eternal life that was with the Father and was revealed to us 3.—what we have seen and heard, we announce also to you, that you also may have fellowship with us. And our fellowship is with the Father and with his Son Jesus Christ. 4. And we write these things, that our joy may be complete. 5. And this is the message that we have heard from him and announce to you: "God is light and in him is no darkness at all."

### NOTES

1. *What was from the beginning, what we have heard, what we have seen with our eyes, what we have seen and our hands handled, concerning the word of life:* The five

neuter singular relative pronouns ("what") commencing the first four clauses of v. 1 and the first line of v. 3 constitute a puzzle. The neuter agrees with neither the masculine of "word" *(logos)* nor the feminine of "life" *(zōē)*, which is the subject of v. 2. The neuter relative pronouns that are the subject of vv. 1 and 3 make it difficult to identify with either the "Word" of the Prologue of John or the "life" of 1 John 1:2. Perhaps the author chose the neuter to signify the impersonal "message." The reverse process may be used to explain the masculine demonstrative pronoun *(ekeinos)* used of the neuter noun "Spirit" *(pneuma)* in John 14:26; 15:26; 16:8, 13, 14. There the explanation may be an attraction to the masculine "Paraclete" *(paraklētos),* 14:26; 15:26; 16:7. If that is the case "Paraclete" is to be understood as the dominating title alongside *"Spirit* of truth," which is neuter. Against this explanation we note that when the message is mentioned specifically (1:5; 3:11) the feminine *aggelia* is used. It might be suggested that the neuter *euaggelion* (gospel) has influenced the gender of the relative pronouns chosen in 1:1, 3. Against this is the absence of this word group (noun and cognate verb) from the Johannine Gospel and Epistles. See the Notes on v. 5.

*"From the beginning" (ap archēs):* See 2:7, 13, 14, 24 (2x); 3:8, 11; 2 John 5, 6. The expression is used eight times in 1 John, twice in 2 John and twice in John, where the noun "beginning" is used a total of eight times. All uses of "beginning" in 1 and 2 John occur in the phrase "from the beginning."

From these uses four ideas emerge. We may rule out the relevance of the first in 3:8, "because the devil sins from the beginning." There "beginning" may relate to the story of Genesis 3, but more likely with the present tense *(hamartanei)* has the sense that he has always sinned and continues to do so. Cf. John 8:44 where the devil is said to be a murderer "from the beginning" and is also called a liar and the father (source) of the lie. In this way John makes the devil the source of sins and lies and perhaps 1 John suggests he is the source of sin. See also on 3:11-12.

The second idea is that *"what* was from the beginning" is to be understood as a reference to the "Word" more or less in the sense of John 1:1. This is supported by 1 John 2:13, 14. There those addressed as "fathers" are reminded, "you know (perfect tense) the one who *(ton)* is from the beginning." The masculine *(ton)* in 2:13, 14 constitutes a problem for identifying the one from the beginning here with the neuter relative pronouns of 1:1, 3.

Third, there is the idea of the commandment (2:7) or the message (3:11) "which *(hēn)* you have (heard, 3:11) from the beginning." In 2 John 5, 6 the Elder speaks of the commandment "we have had" or "we have heard" from the beginning. Here the problem is identifying the feminine commandment or message with the neuter relative pronouns of 1:1, 3. There is also the problem that in both cases "from the beginning" almost certainly relates to the moment when the commandment, or the message, was received or heard. This beginning seems to be the foundation of the believing community. An improbable alternative is that "from the beginning" refers to the origin of the commandment or message, not the reception or hearing of it. This same unlikely possibility is relevant to 2:24. It is suggested by the use of *ap archēs* in 1:1, 3.

Fourth, there are references to "what *(ho)* you heard from the beginning" that do not specify what was heard (2:24 [2x]) and like 1:1, 3 use the neuter relative pronoun. At first sight these references seem to agree with 1:1, 3. But where 1:1 speaks of "what *was* from the beginning," 2:24 speaks of "what you heard from the beginning." At least these references provide a basis for the argument that the message was understood as neuter. Had 1 John used *euaggelion* an explanation would lie ready to hand. An improbable way of reading 2:24 harmonizes the understanding of "from the beginning" with 1:1, 3. See on the third group of references above.

The first person plural perfect indicative active *akēkoamen* is used in 1:1, 3, 5 and not again in 1 John until 4:3 where it marks the last use of *ēkousate*. The second person plural aorist indicative active *ēkousate* is used in 2:7, 18, 24 (2x); 3:11 and not again in 1 John (see 2 John 6). The third person singular present indicative active *akouei* is used in 4:5, 6; 5:14, 15. The first person singular present indicative active *akouō* is used in 3 John 4. The pattern in 1 John seems planned in that forms of *akouō* fall in groups with one use of *akēkoamen* separating the uses of *ēkousate* from *akouei*.

2. *and the life was revealed, and we have seen and bear witness and announce to you the eternal life that was with the Father and was revealed to us:* Life *(zōē)* is a major theme in the Gospel (36 times plus 16 uses of the verb *zaō*) and also in 1 John (13 times plus a single use of the verb) but not at all in 2–3 John. Given the varied content of the Gospel, where the occurrence of "life" belongs in the discourse material, the use of this term unites 1 John with the Gospel. Both use "life" and "eternal life" as synonyms with reference to the gift of life. Thus "eternal life" *(zōē aiōnios)* occurs seventeen times in the Gospel and six times in 1 John. In each case "eternal life" makes up almost half the uses of "life." But the Gospel does not use "eternal life" of God or Jesus as the source of life. This appears in 1 John 1:2. The life that was revealed (in the Incarnation) was the eternal life that was with the Father.

The verb "was revealed" *(ephanerōthē)* occurs nine times in John (see 1:31; 2:11; 3:21; 7:4; 9:3; 17:6; 21:1 [2x], 14) and nine times in 1 John (see 1:2 [2x]; 2:19, 28; 3:2 [2x], 5, 8; 4:9) and not in 2–3 John. In 1 John the life was revealed (1:2); the opponents were revealed by the schism (2:19); Jesus will be revealed at his *parousia* (2:28; 3:2); what the children of God will be is to be revealed at his coming (3:2); Jesus was revealed to take away sin (3:5 and cf. 1:2); the Son of God was revealed to destroy/take away/remove sin (3:8); love was revealed. While the orientation of sayings about revelation is to the Incarnation, its purpose and consequences (1:2; 3:5, 8; 4:9), there is also a focus on future revelation at Jesus' *parousia*. The only other use is in reference to the opponents, who were revealed for what they were by the schism (2:19).

After the reference to "And the life was revealed" codex B (Vaticanus) adds the relative pronoun *ho* before *heōrakamen*, conforming this reference to "what we have seen . . ." in v. 1 and the resumption in v. 3. This is a scribal addition.

Identifying what was revealed as "the life," the author repeats, still using the perfect tense, "we have seen" *(heōrakamen)*, thus providing a basis for the present witness, "we bear witness" *(martyroumen)*. On this sequence from the perfect to the present tense see 4:14. On the use of the verb "to bear witness" see also 5:6, 7, 9, 10; 3 John 3, 6, 12, and for the noun "witness" see 5:9, 10, 11; 3 John 12.

For references to "the Father" see also 1:3; 2:1, 13, 14, 15, 16, 22, 23, 24; 3:1; 4:14; 2 John 3, 4, 9. As in John, speaking of the Father naturally implies the Son just as speaking of the Son implies the Father. Thus *Gospel of Truth* 38:6 says: "Now, the name of the Father is the Son." In the Johannine writings the "Name" is an important theme: see John 1:12; 2:23; 3:18; 5:43; 10:25; 12:13, 28; 14:13, 14, 26; 15:16, 21; 16:23, 24, 26; 17:6, 11, 12, 26; 20:31, noting especially 5:43; 10:25; 12:13, 28 [in relation to 17:1]; 17:6, 11, 12, 26, all of which closely identify Jesus with the name of the Father. See 1 John 2:12; 3:23; 5:13; 3 John 7.

3. *what we have seen and heard, we announce also to you, that you also may have fellowship with us. And our fellowship is with the Father and with his Son Jesus Christ:* A resumption of v. 1 is signaled by the repetition of *ho heōrakamen* and *akēkoamen* from v. 1, though they appear in reversed order in v. 3. A connection with v. 2 is made by the repetition of *apaggellomen hymin* from v. 2 in v. 3.

The idiom "have fellowship with" uses a noun *(koinōnia)* with the verb "to have" *(echēte)* where the verb *koinōnein* might have been used. This is characteristic of 1 John. See also 1:6, 7, 8; 2:1, 7, 20, 23 (2x), 27, 28; 3:3, 15, 17, 21; 4:16, 17, 18, 21; 5:10, 12, 13, 14, 15. The use of *echein* is much more frequent in John and 1 John than in the average NT book.

*Koinōnia* is used four times in 1 John and nowhere else in the Johannine literature. Elsewhere it is used once in Acts, thirteen times in Paul and once in Hebrews. Though it is not used in John 15:1-8, the use of the term here is illuminated by the image of participation in the vine. See also 1 Cor 12:28-31. Because the conventional translation "fellowship" has been devalued, the notion of "union with" is preferred, though "fellowship" is retained in 1:6 to maintain the idiom of "we have fellowship with him." Because the term is used only in 1 John 1:3, 6, 7 in the Johannine literature it is likely that this is a term used by those who claim "We have fellowship with him" (1:6).

*Patros*: *Patēr* is used 137 times in the Gospel, all but seven of God, and three of which are vocative address to God (17:21, 24, 25). *Patēr* is used fourteen times in 1 John (all but two with reference to God); and four times in 2 John. The importance of this concentration of language is increased by the focus on the Father-Son relationship in such phrases as those used by the Johannine Jesus referring to "the Father who sent me" (see 5:23, 37; 6:44; 8:16, 18; 12:49; 14:24, 26; 20:21). There are many more references to Jesus being sent where it is clear that the Father is the sender. All of this lies behind the use in 1 John 4:14, "the Father sent the Son as the savior of the world."

*Iēsou Christou* is rarely used in the Gospel (1:17; 17:3) but seven times in 1 John (1:3; 2:1; 3:23; 4:2, 15; 5:6, 20) and twice in 2 John (3, 7). In addition 1 John 3:22 says "Jesus is the Christ." This reference shows 1 John has not lost sight of the messianic status of Jesus, though it may be that in 1 John the affirmation that Jesus is the Christ has come to mean something like "come in the flesh." Reference to "his Son Jesus Christ" is found in 1:3; 3:23; 5:20 and cf. 4:15; 5:5, and see "Jesus his Son" in 1:7. 1 John 1:3 and 1:7 are also connected in their treatment of union *(koinōnia)* with God.

For Paul, believers can be called sons of God (Rom 8:14; Gal 3:26; 4:7), though Son of God is much more frequent and characteristic as a Pauline designation for Jesus. But for John and 1–3 John "son" *(huios)* is not used at all of believers. In 1 John the term characteristic of believers is "children of God" *(tekna theou).* (See below on 3:1.) Perhaps for this reason the author does not address his readers as *tekna,* but as *teknia.* (See below on 2:1.) 2 and 3 John depart from this practice, perhaps because: (1) they do not use the phrase "children of God"; (2) the Elder does not address his readers as "Children," as the author of 1 John does, using the diminutive "little children" *(teknia),* which is a more intimate form of address.

4. *And we write these things, that our joy may be complete:* Two pronouns are the subject of textual variants in this verse. In Greek the verb form contains indication of first person (we) without an additional pronoun, but the pronoun can be added for emphasis as here. Thus "We write these things" emphasizes the "we" of the authoritative messengers. A few manuscripts have changed the pronoun to second person (you) plural in the dative case. Because the verb already expresses the first person plural "we" the sense becomes "We are writing these things to you." Although this does not provide a proper letter address, it does give the form of a writer and an addressee (group of readers). That is probably the reason for this scribal modification.

Only this first reference to writing is in the first person *plural.* From here on reference is in the first person singular, "I write" (2:1, 7, 12, 13 [2x]), all in the present tense to this point; then "I wrote" (2:14 [3x], 21, 26; 5:13), all in the aorist.

The same motivation as that given for the first scribal change probably explains the second variant also. The purpose of writing is stated: "that our joy may be complete." The variant, which is quite well attested, is "that your joy may be complete." (Compare 1 John 2:25 and see John 15:11; 16:24.) The probability is that "your joy" is scribal, as it is more what might be expected. Thus in both cases it is likely that the first person plural is original.

"These things" might refer to vv. 1-3, but more likely to what follows (see Brooke, *Commentary* 9). This is supported by the use of the present tense *(graphomen)* rather than the aorist. The use of the first person plural here is in contrast to 2:1, which uses first person singular present tense. Probably there is no intention to draw a sharp distinction between the corporate authorship of ch. 1 and the individual authorship of ch. 2; rather, the singular is used there with the intimate address of readers as "my little children."

5. *And this is the message that we have heard from him and announce to you: "God is light and in him is no darkness at all."* "This *(hautē)* is the message." For the formula "this is . . ." with the feminine demonstrative see 2:25; 3:11, 23; 5:3, 4, 9, 11 (2x), 14; 2 John 6. Just as here "this is the message" (cf. 3:11), so also the phrase is used of the promise, 2:25; the commandment, 3:23; the love of God, 5:3; the victory, 5:4; the witness of God, 5:9; the witness, 5:11; the confidence, 5:14; love, 2 John 6. The phrase "this life is in his Son" is similar. The masculine

is used in a similar way in 2:22; 5:6, 20, and 2 John 7, 9: "This is the Antichrist," 2:22; "This is the one who came through water and blood," 5:6; "This is the true God," 5:20; "This is the Deceiver and the Antichrist," 2 John 7; "This person also has the Father and the Son," 2 John 9. Determined by gender, the statements using the feminine are wholly positive while those using the masculine are a mixed bag.

"Message" *(aggelia)* is used elsewhere in the NT only in 1 John 3:11, where the same phrase occurs but with slight variation of word order. In spite of this the message is stated in different terms in each place: here "This is the message that we heard (first person plural perfect tense) from him (Jesus)," and in 3:11, "This is the message that you heard (second person plural aorist tense) from the beginning *(ap archēs)*." What "we have heard from him" (from Jesus) stands in contrast to what "you have heard from the beginning." The "we" of the tradition bearers is related directly to Jesus, while the recipients of the letter are reminded of the love command they heard when they first became believers. Yet it is surprising that the message that "God is light" is attributed to Jesus while the love command is said to be what "you heard from the beginning."

In 1:5 we first encounter the complex and frequent use of *hoti* in 1 John. We may note five classes of use. First, the epexegetical use gives the content of what is heard, reported, or known: 1:5; 2:3, 5, 18 (2x), 19, 22, 29 (2x); 3:1, 5, 15, 19, 24; 4:3, 10 (2x), 14, 15, 17; 5:1, 2, 5, 9, 11, 13, 15 (2x), 19, 20. Second, after words of speaking it may introduce exact quotation when the words are reported in the first person of the speaker and not in the third person: 1:6, 8, 10; 2:4; 4:20. This is a special case of the epexegetical use and is reserved for the quotation formulae of five of the seven claims made by the opponents. Third is the causal use: 2:8, 11, 16; 3:8, 9 (2x), 11, 12, [20 (2x)], 22; 4:1, 4, 7, 8, 18, 19; 5:4, 6, 7, 9, 10, 14. Fourth, there are ambiguous uses that might be epexegetical or causal: 2:12, 13 (2x), 14 (3x), 21 (3x); 3:16; 4:9. Fifth is the double use, first epexegetical and then causal: 3:2, 14, [20]; 4:13, and one possible case of causal followed by epexegetical in 5:9.

The message has its origin with "him." Here the message is "God is light. . . ." In 3:11 it is "Love one another." That this suggests that "God is light" is the foundation of the love command is borne out by the recognition of the parallel saying, "God is love" (4:8, 16) and the connection between the love of God and the love command in 4:7-11. In the Gospel formulation (13:34) the love command is grounded: "Love one another as I have loved you," and the "as" *(kathōs)* has a double force: "in the same way as I have loved you," thus describing the manner or character of the love. More fundamental is the causative sense, "because I have loved you" *(BDF* §453).

Although this use of "message" is without a qualifying adjective, such as "*good* news," it is clearly used in this sense (see below). It sums up "what *(ho)* was heard" (1:1, 3) and announced *(apaggellomen)* in 1:2, 3. This verb is linguistically connected to the noun "message" and indicates the announcement or proclamation of the message. See Julius Schniewind, "ἀγγελία, κτλ.," *TDNT* 1:56–73. In v. 5 what is announced is explicitly specified as the message *(aggelia)*. In v. 5 the popular Hellenistic form of the verb *(anaggellomen)* is used, while the Attic form *(apaggellomen)* appears in 1:1, 3. In all three cases the meaning is: "we announce *to you*" (plural). Only in vv. 2-3, 5 are these two forms of the verb used in the Johannine Epistles and no change of meaning is implied in the change from the Attic form in vv. 2-3 to the Hellenistic form found in v. 5. Both forms are used in the Gospel, where *anaggellomen* is used in John 4:25; 5:15; 16:13, 14, 15 and *apaggellomen* in 16:25. No distinction of meaning is discernible in John's use, where a preference is shown for *anaggellein*. If an unworthy communication is indicated by John 5:15 (an incriminating report, aorist tense), *anaggellein* is also used (in the future tense) of the Messiah who will announce all things and of the Spirit of Truth who will announce the things to come and from Jesus. The only use of *apaggellō* is also future and expresses Jesus' promise to end parabolic talk and openly to announce [the message] concerning the Father. Interestingly, all the positive uses of these two forms in John are in the future tense. All three uses of the two forms in 1 John are present tense; here a two-to-one preference is shown for *apaggellein*. But given the linguistic connections between hearing and proclaiming in 1:1-3 and 1:5, no distinction of meaning between the two forms of the verb is intended.

Reference to *"what* we have heard" in vv. 1, 3 does not indicate from whom it was heard. This deficiency is met in v. 5, which supplies "which we heard from him." This can only be a reference to Jesus. The idiom "heard from him" *(ap' autou)* is Hellenistic. Generally in the NT "to hear from" uses the preposition *para*.

Again reference to *"what* we have heard" in vv. 1, 3 does not mention specifically *what* was heard. The "life" may be implied by v. 2, but the feminine noun is not readily identified with the neuter relative pronoun. Now in v. 5 what was proclaimed is identified as the "message." But this too is a feminine noun. Perhaps the writer had in mind, when using the neuter relative pronoun in vv. 1, 3, the related neuter noun *euaggelion*. This would fit all references to what was heard and proclaimed, but it does not readily fit reference to what was seen and handled, or what was from the beginning. We are left with the impression that in vv. 1-3 the message and the person who is the subject of the message are inseparably intertwined. The use of the neuter relative pronoun would be explained if the unspoken *euaggelion* lay in the background. It is a puzzle that neither this word nor its cognate verb is used in the Johannine Gospel and Epistles. The noun is used frequently by Paul and, of the Gospel writers, by Mark. It does not appear in Luke and only twice in Acts, but Luke-Acts make frequent use of the cognate verb *euaggelizomai*. Brown (*The Epistles of John* 192–93) persuasively suggests that John's use of "the message" is the equivalent of "the gospel" in texts that use that vocabulary.

The connection of "that we heard from him" with the "we" of 1:1-4 may suggest that we are still dealing with the "we" of the tradition bearers. The alternative is the "we" of the Johannine community. How this question is decided will guide the answer to the question of the "we" in 1:6, 8, 10. Does the author allow that the false teaching may have penetrated the circle of the tradition bearers, the Johannine school? See below on 1:6, 8, 10.

"God is light" *(ho theos phōs estin)*. It is sometimes noted that the word for light *(phōs)* is anarthrous (without the definite article). See also the similar anarthrous use in "God is love" (4:8) and "God is Spirit" (John 4:24). Commentators such as Brooke *(Commentary* 11) and Smalley *(1, 2, 3 John* 20) argue that the anarthrous use expresses quality and is a reference to God's nature. By contrast, reference is made to texts using the definite article in 1 John 1:7; 2:8. Neither of these texts is comparable to 1:5, where God and light are coupled by the verb "to be": "God *is* light." In Greek subject and object are distinguished by case endings, not word order. When subject and object are coupled by the verb "to be," the subject is distinguished not by word order or by case but by the use of the definite article. A good example is John 1:1c, *kai theos ēn ho logos.* The words for both "God" and "Word" are in the nominative case. Although "God" comes first in this clause, it is the object, as is indicated by the definite article with "the Word." Thus it is a statement about the Word. The same is true in 1 John 1:5, where both nouns come before the verb *(ho theos phōs estin).* But of course when used of God, light is a metaphor. This is the point rather than a meaning based on the absence of the definite article.

"In him is no *darkness (skotia)* at all." In the NT this is almost a Johannine term; it occurs elsewhere only in Matt 4:16; 10:27 and Luke 2:3. It is used eight times in John (1:5 [2x]; 6:17; 8:12; 12:35 [2x], 46; 20:1) and six times in 1 John (1:5; 2:8, 9, 11 [3x]). In John the Word and Jesus (the incarnate Word) challenge the darkness, and those who follow Jesus are delivered from its power. This element is developed in 1 John, where the presence and power of the eschatological word are causing the darkness to pass away. Nevertheless the darkness still has power. See the use of the related term *(skotos)* in 1:6.


### INTERPRETATION

Unlike 2 and 3 John, 1 John lacks any form of opening address. It is thus not a genuine letter although there is something like a closing in 5:21. Even this does not qualify as a closing salutation in a letter. In it the writer addresses the readers directly as "little children," a formula used for the first time in 2:1. See also 2:12; 3:7, 18. It may be that 1 John was addressed to a circle of churches accompanied by a specific covering letter such as 2 John. Such a reading does justice to the specific nature of the issues dealt with in 1 John. It is unsatisfactory to read it as a general tract, because it deals with issues that have taken place in the community addressed (see 2:18-19). While the language of 1 John is simple and involves a limited vocabulary, its expression is frequently ambiguous and unclear to the modern reader. We may suspect that the author did not always make his meaning clear, but this sometimes occurs in places where the author seems to be using familiar words and phrases, suggesting the use of "insider" language in such a way that what is said lacks clarity for an outsider. The phenomenon is encountered immediately when we begin to read the text. To what does the first word *(ho)* refer?

Following the Greek word order, our translation places the emphasis on the content of the message and its basis in the firsthand experience of the writer and his colleagues. This is borne out by the parenthetic exposition in verse 2. Verse 1 concentrates on the *word* of life while verse 2 elaborates on the theme of the *life*. The life was revealed. This spells out the implications of *the word* of life. Because it is the word of *life*, the life was revealed. But *revealed* is a more comprehensive image than *word* because the word was not only heard, it was seen and handled. Further, the life announced is the eternal life, because the life that was revealed to us was with the Father. Here, as in the Prologue of the Gospel, where the Word is first related to God (John 1:1), the relationship is ultimately spoken of in terms of the Father (John 1:18).

Overlaps of language and theme between 1:1-4 and the Prologue of the Fourth Gospel (John 1:1-18) imply some relationship. Words shared with the Prologue are noted in the order in which they appear in 1 John: "beginning," "we have seen" *(etheasametha)*, "the word," "life," "to bear witness," "the Father," "Jesus Christ," "fulfilled"—all of this in four verses, overlapping just eighteen verses of the Gospel. Yet there are important differences in the way these terms are deployed. The Gospel, with its focus on the divinity of Jesus, asserts the eternity of the divine Word. The Epistle appeals to the primitive, foundational message, suggesting that a more "progressive" position is opposed (see 2 John 9).

The similarities between the two Prologues suggest that either 1 John is dependent on the Gospel (Houlden, *A Commentary on the Johannine Epistles* 46–47) or that the Gospel develops on the basis of 1 John (Grayston, *The Johannine Epistles* 11–14). Stated this way the relationship can be thought of in terms of a single author or one dependent on another. Yet the evidence may not support a case for direct dependence. An alternative is the independent use of common tradition from the Johannine school. R. E. Brown allows that 1 John might have been written while the composition of the Gospel was still in process. He considers it probable that the fundamental shaping of the tradition had been completed, though not the final redaction and publication of the Gospel (*The Epistles of John* 32–35).

The opening sentence of 1 John runs for three and a half verses, including a parenthesis on "the life" (v. 2). The primitive message concerns "the word of life" or "the Word of life" (see John 14:6). Though less obviously than the "Word" *(logos)* of the Fourth Gospel, the use of "Word" in 1 John also calls for explanation. The Johannine tradition drew on Jewish Wisdom where the creative Word of God had been identified with the Law. Distinctive developments in the Johannine interpretation identified

Jesus with the Word in such a way that he communicates himself in his words (C. H. Dodd, *Interpretation of the Fourth Gospel* 265–68).

In 1 John Jesus is present also in the word that bears witness to him, and there is a studied ambiguity concerning the message and the subject of the message. The message concerns life and the one who is the subject of the message is himself the life. He has the words of eternal life (John 6:68; cf. 17:6-8, 14, 17). "Heard, seen, and handled" indicate an alternation between the message and its subject. The emphasis here is on having seen the subject, which is twice affirmed in v. 1. The subject is here known under the image of "the life." In the Prologue of the Gospel the *logos* is revealed as "the true light" and "the life" (John 1:4). In 1 John the life is further elaborated as "the eternal life which was with the Father." 1 John affirms twice that the life was manifest (cf. "made flesh" in John 1:14); it was seen, witnessed to, and reported. The author associates himself with the authoritative bearers of the tradition while the readers are identified as the prospective recipients of it.

The purpose of the report was to bring the recipients into a sharing relationship ("fellowship," *koinōnia*) with the tradition bearers. As used in 1 John, *koinōnia* defines the nature of the Johannine "community." The term "church" is not used, but *koinōnia* meaningfully interprets the reality of the believing community. Priority is given to the relationship within the community before extending this to include the relationship with (God) the Father and God's Son Jesus Christ. Relationship with God is dependent on relationship with the community (see 5:1-2). The theological focus of the Epistle is signalled at the end of v. 3 where fellowship with the Father is mentioned before fellowship with the Son who, characteristically of the Epistle, is named "Jesus Christ" (see 1:3; 2:1, [22]; 3:23; 4:2; [5:1], 5:6, 20, but in the Gospel only in John 1:17; 17:3). The purpose of the writing is expressed in terms of the fulfillment of "our (your) joy" (see John 15:1-11).

In the Prologue the author lays the groundwork to refute the opponents, setting out the connection between the foundational message and his own (group of) witness(es). He makes fellowship with the foundational witnesses the basis of fellowship with God. In this way it becomes clear that the life of the believing community *(koinōnia)* is grounded in the foundational message. In this message (1:5) God is understood on the basis of the revelation of Jesus Christ, the Son of the Father.

1 John 1:5 forms a transition from the Prologue to the first group of assertions made by the opponents. The message is now described in terms of what "we heard from him," the Son of the Father, Jesus Christ. The message concerns God: "God is light." In the first instance this means that God is self-revealing. But the affirmation goes beyond the assertion that God, like light, reveals. By asserting "in him is no darkness at all" 1 John signals that what God reveals is God's self. Light reveals light; it is self-

revealing. The exposition goes on to affirm that the light excludes the darkness of hatred and is to be understood in terms of love (cf. 4:8, 16). Thus the dual theological affirmations "God is light" and "God is love" appear to be overlapping and mutually illuminating. "God is love" elaborates the meaning of "God is light" in two ways. First, it states the motivation for God's self-revealing activity. It is because God loves that God reveals God's self. Second, what God reveals is God's love, which is opposed to the hatred of the world.

The life of the believing community is grounded in the life of God revealed in the message, "God is light." Some scholars have related the message to the theme of God's covenant with the people of God, especially to the theme of the new covenant (see Jer 31:31-34 and see Edward Malatesta, *Interiority and Covenant*, 1978). The problem for this approach is that the Gospel and Epistles of John nowhere use the word "covenant" *(diathēkē)*! Indeed, the term is rarely used in the NT, a total of only thirty-three times of which seventeen are in Hebrews, nine in the Pauline corpus, four in the Synoptics (once each in Matthew and Mark; twice in Luke), two in Acts, and one in Revelation. Only in Hebrews does the evidence provide a strong case for a covenant theology. To a lesser extent it is important for Paul to show that the gospel is not opposed to God's covenant with Israel. But when dealing with the gospel Paul develops the theme of relationship with God without reference to covenant. This is true also of the Gospel and Epistles of John, making dubious the case for a strong covenantal theology in 1 John. There the theme of community relationships and the relationship of the community to God overlaps aspects of the covenant, but without reference to covenant. It is a conceptual confusion to identify this theme with any discussion of the relationship of the believing community to God simply because this is involved in covenant theology in the Old Testament. The Johannine Gospel and Epistles deal with this theme without reference to "covenant." (See "Theology" in the Introduction.)

The opening of 1 John, written in the first person plural, continues in this mode throughout ch. 1. The first three verses might have described the author's experience among a group, and v. 4 asserts that 1 John (at least ch. 1) was written on behalf of that group. With ch. 2 the mode of address changes to the first person singular, "I write" (wrote): 2:1, 7, 8, 12, 13, 14, 21, 26; 5:13. The force of the "we" in ch. 1 is understood variously. Adolf Harnack ("Das 'Wir' in der Johanneischen Schriften") argues that it is the plural of authority. But how could the author write as if it were the community speaking when he is writing to the community? What is the difference between the "we" who write and the "you" (plural) to whom 1 John is written? See also 4:14.

The straightforward solution is to identify the "we" with eyewitnesses. But neither the Fourth Gospel nor 1 John shows any real interest in establishing the historical facts based on eyewitnesses (*autoptai*, Luke 1:2). If this does not fit, then C. H. Dodd (*The Johannine Epistles* 13–16) suggests that what is in view is the way believers of all times are united with that first generation of eyewitnesses just as later Israelites and Jews identify themselves with those who came out of Egypt (see Josh 24:7; Amos 2:10). But this ignores the clear distinction between the "we" who have seen, heard, touched, who declare and write, and those to whom it is announced and written ("you" plural).

A third way is to see a group of authoritative witnesses who had known and heard the eyewitnesses, the apostles. They considered themselves to be legitimate tradition bearers of the message from the apostles that connected their hearers to the Incarnation of the Word, Jesus Christ come in the flesh, Life revealed. The concrete actuality of the subject of this message affirms the necessity of the humanity of Jesus in the salvation of humanity and the importance of his life for the connection between faith and love in the conflict with those we meet as schismatics and false teachers in 2:18-19; 4:1-6. Thus in this stress on the relation of the tradition bearers to the saving event of Jesus Christ coming in the flesh 1 John is already confronting the threat of the opponents (see Schnackenburg, *The Johannine Epistles* 55–56).

The place of the opening verses in the overall argument of 1 John can now be addressed. The Prologue unites the author with the foundational witnesses. Any ambiguity concerning the foundational message for the believing community and the eternal Word from the beginning works in the author's favor. The eternal Word reinforces the message preached by the foundational witnesses. Union with God is made to be dependent on union with the foundational witnesses, and in 1:5, speaking for the foundational witnesses, the author asserts:

> This is the message that we heard from him and announce to you: "God is light and in him is no darkness at all."

If the message of the foundational witnesses has come to them from the One who is from the beginning, there is a sense in which the message has come from the beginning. The message that comes from those who communicated it as a basis for the foundation of the believing community is the message from the one who is from the beginning. Thus the message they have from him can be said to be from the beginning and the ambiguity can be described as a studied ambiguity.

Concluding the Prologue, 1 John continues, "This is the message . . ." (1:5). Following its Prologue the Gospel continues, "This is the witness . . ." (John 1:19). The message now introduced (1:5) appears to be the means through which fellowship with one another and the Father and the

Son is realized. The statement of the message becomes the opportunity for misleading claims to be dealt with. The first three of these are closely tied to the theme of the opening of 1 John and maintain the first person plural address. If v. 3 says that the announcement of the message *(apaggellomen)* is to lead (purpose) to fellowship with one another and the Father and the Son, v. 5 reveals the message *(aggelia)*: God is light.

The opening verse of 1 John draws attention to the foundational message of the community, which concerns the word of life. The life referred to here is the life revealed in the incarnate *logos* (cf. John 1:4, 14). In the Prologue of the Gospel the Incarnation evokes the response of witness, "and we beheld his glory" *(etheasametha,* see 1 John 1:1), which is followed immediately by reference to John who bore witness *(martyrei,* and see 1 John 1:2, *martyroumen).* The response to the Incarnation is expressed in the first person plural in John 1:14 ("we beheld his glory"). The response to the revelation of the life in 1 John 1:1-4 is also expressed in the first person plural ("what we have heard and seen with our eyes"). The writer strengthens his message by joining himself with the group of foundational witnesses.

The opening verse of the Gospel shares with 1 John 1:1 the important words *archē,* "beginning," and *logos,* "word." A third word used here, *zōē,* "life," quickly emerges as important in the Prologue of the Gospel (1:4). According to the Gospel, in the *logos* was life and the life of the *logos* was the light for humanity. Here we have common language used by the Gospel and 1 John, but in a context of different use. Whereas in the Gospel, to borrow a phrase from the title of a book by Peder Borgen, the Logos was the true light and Jesus is the light of the world (John 1:4-5, 9; 3:19; 8:12; 9:5; 12:35, 46), in 1 John light is used in an affirmation about God, "God is light" (see my *John, Witness and Theologian* 125–26). Thus in spite of the emphasis on the foundational message which is rooted in the Incarnation, 1 John has a tendency to extend a trajectory of the language of the Gospel about the revelation (christology) back to its ultimate source in affirmations about God. But this is no more than we might expect on the basis of the Gospel's claim that Jesus reveals the Father (John 1:18; 14:7-11). He is the one loved and sent by the Father who speaks the Father's words and performs his works (John 3:35; 5:17, 19-20, 36; 8:28, 38; 12:50; 15:15; 16:15).

1 John also devotes a verse (1:2) to expounding the theme of life. The reader gets the sense that, even though there are differences, these Prologues have much in common. The commonality might be explained in terms of a common author working and then reworking the theme. Alternatively one author may make use of the work of another or both may use a common source or tradition. In this commentary it is argued that the Gospel was fundamentally shaped before the Epistles were written, but

the Gospel might well have been published subsequently. Thus the Prologue of 1 John might have been written before the Gospel was published
and before the Gospel Prologue was composed and added.

Even if the two works are not from the same author, they issue from
the Johannine school and we would expect the author of 1 John to be
familiar with the Johannine Gospel tradition in whatever shape it had
assumed at the time. Likewise, if the Prologue of the Gospel had not been
composed already we would expect the evangelist to be familiar with
1 John once it was written. There is some force in the argument that the
Prologue of 1 John is less developed than the Prologue of the Gospel
(Grayston, *The Johannine Epistles* 14), but this is not a conclusive argument
for the temporal priority of the Prologue of 1 John. Its apparently more
primitive form might be accounted for by the specific purpose of 1 John.
Overall the evidence suggests the writing of 1 John subsequent to the
fundamental shaping of the tradition in the Gospel, though perhaps prior
to the Gospel's publication.

The opening verses of 1 John make a grand statement but lack the clarity of progressive thought found in the opening of the Gospel. Meaning is
not clarified by the use of the neuter relative pronoun *(ho)* with which
each of the first four lines begins. Thus *ho* does not agree with "word"
*(logos)*, which is masculine, or "life" *(zōē)*, which is feminine. Grammatically neither the life nor the "word" is indicated by *ho*.

What v. 2 adds to v. 1 is the exposition of "the word of life." The consequences of seeing and hearing are found in the announcement of the
news. The opening of v. 3 is a resumption of the theme of v. 1, signaled by
the repetition of *ho* in a statement summarizing vv. 1-2, "what we have
seen and heard we announce to you." But what is it that is from the beginning and that "we announce to you"?

While some of the actions of v. 1 suggest reference to a person (seen
and touched), reference to what was heard seems to indicate a message.
To deal with this confusion we need to discuss the meaning of "what was
*from the beginning.*" R. E. Brown analyzes six interpretations of *ap' archēs* in
v. 1 (*The Epistles of John* 155–58). Given the lack of consensus concerning
the reference of *ap' archēs* it seems best not to press for too much precision,
but to ask whether the reference is to the preincarnate *logos* or to the foundation of the message in the Incarnation or the ministry of Jesus. (See the
Notes on v. 1). If the foundation of the message is in view, then the Incarnation seems to be the *archē* of the message. This reading has the advantage of leading directly into the first part of v. 2, understood as a reference
to the Incarnation. That "the life was manifest" is expressed in the aorist
tense, appropriate to the event of the Incarnation. In John 1:4 it is said: "in
him (the *logos*) was life." For John the Incarnation is also the manifestation
of the life, and in 1 John 1:2 it is "the life that was with the Father which

was manifest to us." This may suggest that *ap' archēs* refers to the Incarnation as the foundation of the message, the message proclaiming "the life."
The tenses of the verbs used in vv. 1-3 form a revealing pattern:

| | |
|---|---|
| ¹What *was* from the beginning, | imperfect |
| what we *have heard,* | perfect |
| what we *have seen* with our eyes, | perfect |
| what we *have seen* | aorist |
| and our hands *handled* | aorist |
| concerning the word of life | |
| ² —and the life *was revealed,* | aorist |
| and we have seen and bear witness | perfect and present |
| and *announce* to you | present |
| the eternal life | |
| that *was* with the Father | imperfect |
| and *was revealed* to us | aorist |
| ³ —what we *have seen* and *heard,* | perfect (2x) |
| we *announce* also to you, | present |
| that you also may have fellowship with us. | |
| And our fellowship is with the Father | |
| and with his Son Jesus Christ. | |

The opening tense is an imperfect. It is used twice, at the beginning of v. 1 to speak of what was from the beginning and at the end of v. 2 to speak of the life that was with the Father. This language is appropriate as a reference to the Word. The imperfect signifies an ongoing state of affairs in the past, in this case the beginning. (Compare John 1:1.) Thus the imperfect is used to speak of what *was* from the beginning (1:1) and to speak of the eternal life that *was* with the Father (1:2). The use of the two imperfect tenses suggests we have a parallel description,

What *was* from the beginning

. . .

that *was* with the Father.

Though this parallel hides the neuter relative pronoun of v. 1 and the feminine in v. 2, it is attractive to think that here 1 John is playing on the theme of the first verse of the Gospel. "In the beginning" is now "from the beginning," but the variation "in" or "from" might make little difference because of the imperfect "was." In the Gospel the Word was with God *(pros ton theon),* while in 1 John the author speaks of "the eternal life that was with the Father" *(pros ton patera).* By the end of the Gospel Prologue reference to God has become reference to the Father (1:18).

Two of the four uses of the aorist tense emphasize the actual and completed event of the revelation of the life (1:2). Compare the use of the aorist tense in John 1:14 to narrate the Incarnation of the Word. The other two aorist tenses (in 1:1) emphasize the actuality of what the witnesses saw and handled. These two overlap the use of the perfect tense to express the experience of the witnesses. The first two uses of the perfect tense ("heard and seen," 1:1) are repeated in reversed order ("seen and heard") at the opening of 1:3. The fifth use of the perfect again affirms what the witnesses "have seen" (1:2) as a basis of the witness they continue to bear. Because it is ongoing it is expressed in the present tense, "we *bear witness* and *announce* to you." The opening of 1:3 repeats the experience of the revelation ("we have seen and heard"), expressed in the perfect tense, as a basis for the ongoing "we *announce* to you" in the present tense.

Verse 1 deals with the experience of the witnesses, affirming "what we have heard, seen, and touched." Two perfect tenses are followed by an aorist. Verse 3 continues the affirmation of the witnesses concerning "what we have seen and heard" as a basis for the announcement of the ongoing (present tense) "we announce to you." The consequence of the experience (perfect tense) provides the basis for the ongoing witness.

Verse 2 breaks this sequence to make clear that what was heard, seen, and handled was the consequence of an event. "The life was revealed" (aorist tense twice in 1:2). The experience of "we have seen" is repeated as a basis for the ongoing "we bear witness and announce to you." Thus when 1:3 refers to "what we have seen and heard" it is to "the life that has been revealed," and it is to this that "we bear witness and announce to you."

Although the witnesses affirm the one who was with the Father from the beginning, their experience of seeing, hearing, and handling concerns the Incarnate One. It is to this that the perfect tenses refer. The same is true of the use of the perfect in 2:13-14, where those addressed as "fathers" are said to have known the one who is *from the beginning*. The one who is from the beginning has been made known in the Incarnate One. The experience of the Incarnate One leads into the continuing testimony to the word of life.

Thus the best reading of 1:1 allows that "what was from the beginning" may include a reference to the eternal Word, which was from the beginning. That beginning (according to the Gospel) antedates the creation. But what was heard, seen, and handled was the incarnate Word. This is clarified by v. 2. Encounter with the Incarnate One reveals the eternal Word *that* was from the beginning. Nevertheless, the use of the neuter relative pronouns in vv. 1, 3 unsettles the focus on the divine Word and calls attention to the message in which the Word is proclaimed. It is the intertextual resonance with John 1:1 that attunes the ear to hearing the divine Word in the word of proclamation, the gospel message (1:5; 3:11, 24).

The meaning of the phrase *peri tou logou tēs zōēs*, "about the word of life" at the end of v. 1 is unclear. Is "of life" an objective genitive, meaning something like "the word that proclaims life," so that here the *logos* is the message? Or is it a subjective genitive, meaning something like "the word that belongs to the life," or "is the manifestation of the life" (see the opening line of v. 2)? In the latter sense the meaning is closer to the use of *logos* in John 1:1-14.

Throughout v. 1 the author speaks in the first person plural "we," not in the name of all believers but in the name of the foundational witnesses delivering the message to others who are addressed in the second person plural "you" (1:2, 3). Whatever we may think about the author, he presents himself as one of the foundational witnesses out of whose testimony the message is proclaimed.

The author first affirms what *we* have heard (perfect tense). This is natural because he is dealing with the message (word) that has "the life" as its subject. The stress, however, is on having seen, which is mentioned twice in v. 1, the first time in the phrase "what we have seen (perfect tense) with our eyes" to make the point that no metaphor is being used here. Two different verbs of sight are used, the second in the aorist tense. Probably tense determines which verb is chosen to express sight (see Bultmann, *The Gospel of John* 69 n. 2). It is unlikely that these verbs express different kinds of seeing. The final firsthand evidence is given concerning "what our hands handled" (aorist tense). This language, in which the author distinguishes himself and the band of witnesses from his readers, is not amenable to a reading along the lines suggested by Dodd (*The Johannine Epistles* 13–16) in which membership in the believing community provides believers with a community of experience. Indeed, the author carefully distinguishes himself from his readers and emphasizes the physical senses of hands and eyes.

Verse 1 makes best sense as a claim to firsthand testimony. The authority of the author and those who stand with him is that they have firsthand access to the foundational message (1 John 2:24; 3:11). This is meaningful if "we" represents the authoritative heirs to the eyewitnesses to whom the tradition was committed. This is an important point when it comes to dealing with the opponents. The ever-present threat of the opponents perhaps explains why in this letter the commandment, which is new in the Gospel (13:34-35), is now foundational (1 John 2:7 and 2 John 5-6). The threat of the opponents also explains why the author initially joins himself with the foundational testimony, addressing himself to his readers: "*we* write these things to you." Following this address in the plural the author speaks out of that witness even when he addresses himself to his readers in the singular, as he does in the remainder of the letter (see below on 2:1).

With the opening verse the reader is immediately alerted to the repetitious language of the author. The reader gets a general sense that clarification will be offered through repetition and elaboration. This sense is somewhat diminished the moment the reader attempts to discern the precise meaning of what has been written. Here we have a kind of rhetoric that is in some ways impressive but that lacks precision in communication. It is difficult to know how the original readers would have fared with it. Certainly they would have recognized familiar words and phrases, but ambiguous syntax may have been as confusing to them as to the modern reader. On the other hand, it may be that neither they nor the author pressed for the precise distinctions we are accustomed to make.

Verse 2 is sometimes called a parenthesis. Perhaps it would be better to say that v. 1 is the introduction to the main theme, which is life (see 1 John 5:13). The life that was revealed is the source of the eternal life that is at the heart of the purpose of 1 John. Only at the end of the verse is the reader told that the life is the eternal life that was with the Father. In all probability we have here a signal of the source of the life/eternal life. The verse ends where it began with a repetition of the verb "it was revealed," yet even this is slightly elaborated. It is now said that it was revealed *to us*. The "we" referred to throughout 1:1-4 and beyond are identified as the foundational witnesses in whose name the author writes (1:4).

The verb used in the clause "life was revealed" is in the aorist tense. It is repeated at the end of the verse where the life that was revealed is elaborated in terms of the eternal life that was with the Father. "The Father" is a favorite Johannine ascription for God (see the Notes). Reference to the eternal life that was with the Father is reminiscent of "the Word was with God" (*pros ton theon*, John 1:1-2). That the life (eternal life) was manifest is doubly emphasized. The aorist tense expresses a specific completed act that probably refers to the Incarnation. Compare the use of the aorist tense in John 1:14. There the response was "and we beheld his glory." The Gospel goes on immediately to narrate the witness of John (John 1:15), making the connection of language even closer. Here the response is "we have seen and bear witness and announce to you." It makes no sense to discuss whether "we have seen and bear witness and announce to you" refers back to "the life was manifest" or forward to "the eternal life that was with the Father," as the latter is elaboration of the former.

Thus witness is borne to the life. This is further clarified as the eternal life that was with the Father. The Prologue of the Gospel emphatically affirms that the *logos* was with God (1:1, 2), who is later identified as the Father (John 1:18) in whose bosom is the "only begotten God/Son" (1:18). In 1 John "the life that was revealed is the eternal life that was with the Father and was revealed to us." Thus twice, at the beginning and at the end of the verse, the revelation is stressed: first "(the) life was revealed," then "the eternal life that was with the Father was revealed."

In the Gospel "eternal life" is not used of God or of Jesus. It is the gift of God to believers. While the reference here appears to be to the Incarnation of the One in whom was life, use of the term "eternal life" suggests a reference to the gift of eternal life to those who believe. Against this is the double stress on the revelation of life. Thus we need to conclude that for 1 John as well as for the Gospel (1:4-5) the life that was revealed is the life of the *logos*. There is no explanation of how the witnesses know that the life of the Incarnate (the life revealed) is the life that was with the Father.

Having clarified the object as the life, the eternal life that was with the Father and was revealed, the author now (in v. 3) tells of the consequence of having seen and heard. This is a reversal of the order of the same two verbs in v. 1. The sensory perception of the revelation of the life is now (v. 3) concentrated in these two verbs. The next verb is a repetition from v. 2, "we announce to you." The content the announcement elaborated in v. 2 is not mentioned. Progress is made by reference to the purpose of the announcement. Those who hear and receive the announcement come to share the reality of the life that is announced with those who announce it. They share the common life from God, eternal life. Though the language has the ring of orality about it to this point, the objective is to bring the readers into relationship with the writer and those who stand with him under the cover of the authoritative "we" of the custodians of the tradition. In v. 3 for the first time there is the clear distinction between "us" to whom the life was revealed and "you" (plural) to whom those who saw and heard announce the life that was revealed to them. If acceptance of the announcement *unites* the messenger(s) with those who receive the message, this is only because the messengers have already been *united* with the Father and his Son, Jesus Christ. This implies that the life was revealed in the Incarnation and known in Jesus Christ, and that life is from the Father (v. 2). The messengers have already been *united* with the Father through Jesus Christ (the Son).

The term italicized above *(unite)* is an attempt to grasp the meaning of *koinōnia*, a term difficult to translate. The basic sense is to have in common. Here we are dealing with the revelation of life, eternal life, bringing those who believe to *share* eternal life, not in an individualistic way but mutually sharing in eternal life with the Father and the Son. Consequently 1 John argues that those who mutually share the life from God are brought into relationship with each other, and this is the basis of the Johannine understanding of the possibility and obligation of mutual love (5:1-5).

In verse 4 the force of *"We are writing . . ."* is interesting. With whom is the writer associated? From the beginning he has associated himself with those who have heard, seen, and handled what concerns the word of life. It is apparently on behalf of this group that 1 John was written. The first person plural continues to the end of ch. 1. This partly explains the idiom of the claims made in the first person plural in 1:6, 8, 10. Beyond this the author writes in his own "name" ("I write"; see below on 2:1). But even when he does this, he does so out of his own sense and his readers' awareness that he is one of the foundational witnesses. The point is belabored at the beginning and the readers are not permitted to forget it. This is a major defense against the opponents.

The purpose of 1 John, or at least of 1:1-3, is stated in 1:4 using a standard construction to express purpose (*hina* + subjunctive). The purpose is "that our joy may be complete." But surely it should be "that *your* joy may be complete"! So some scribe thought also, and some texts read "your joy." Because this is a likely change, the unexpected "our joy" is almost certainly original. If this sounds self-centered, then we need to notice the relationship of vv. 3-4. The purpose of the communication is to *unite* the readers with the writers, who are united with the Father and his Son Jesus Christ. From this perspective "our joy" includes "your joy" by the inclusion of "you" with "us." But does this mean that all of those so united can say "what we have heard, what we have seen with our eyes, what our hands have handled . . ."? (Thus Dodd, *The Johannine Epistles* 12–16.) This seems unlikely in that the author immediately returns in v. 5 (see 1:3) to the distinction between "we" and "you" (plural). This suggests that the foundational message is tied to the authenticating witnesses even though it joins those who receive their witness in *koinōnia* with them and the Father and the Son. It is fundamental to the message of 1 John that relationship (*koinōnia*) with God (the Father and the Son) is through the relationship (*koinōnia*) with one another: see 4:7-8, 11-12; 4:20-21; 5:1-3.

The message. Verse 5 supplies the subject that was heard (vv. 1, 3). It is now identified as "the message" (*aggelia*). This feminine noun no more agrees with the neuter relative pronoun (vv. 1, 3) than does "Word" or "life." The word for "message" is linguistically connected to the act of announcing it, relating this verse to vv. 1 and 3. But there the announcement concerns "the word of life," which is expounded in v. 2. Now the announcement or proclamation is described as the message that "we heard from *him*." This reinforces the sense of the apostolic witnesses (we) receiving the message from him (Jesus Christ, v. 3), as does the distinction of "us" from "you" (plural). We who have heard (perfect tense) the message from him announce it (present tense) to you.

The content of this message as stated here is not the same as in v. 2. Rather it is: "God is light and in him there is no darkness at all." (On the language used, see the Notes.) We may ask: is the message "God is light," and what follows an elaboration, a clarification? It is impossible to *know*, but that would make good sense. The clarification, in the terms of 1 John, makes the case harder for the opponents. But what is meant by light?

A starting point is to note that here the author affirms a tradition that is rooted in such Jewish Scriptures as Ps 27:1, "The Lord is my light and my salvation; whom shall I fear?" and Ps 36:9, "in your light we see light."

See also Ps 80:1-3, 7, 19; Hab 3:3-4. For the characteristic Johannine anti-thesis of light and darkness note the parallels in the later Jewish documents from Qumran such as 1QS 1:9-10; 3:13–4:26, and underlying the whole of 1QM (see especially 13:10-12). See also *T. Levi* 14:3-5; 19:1; *T. Gad* 5:7; *T. Benj.* 5:3; *1 Enoch* 58:6; 92:4; 108:11-15; *2 Enoch* 30:15; *Odes of Solomon* 11.19; 15.2; 21.3. That the Johannine message, "God is light, in whom there is no darkness at all," gives expression to the Johannine antithesis suggests that the Qumran parallels and those from Second Temple Judaism are linguistically closer to the language of 1 John than is earlier scriptural language (see my *The Quest for the Messiah* 35–52). That does not exclude the influence of Scripture, but it implies that the later tradition may have influenced the way Scripture was understood.

Also of significance is the evidence from Hellenistic religious texts. Some of these are Jewish texts like the writings from Qumran listed above and the writings of Philo (*Somn.* 1.75; *Praem.* 36-40, 45-46). The *Odes of Solomon* may be Christian Jewish texts also exhibiting Hellenistic influence. Then there are Hellenistic texts influenced by Judaism such as the Poimandres Tractate of the Corpus Hermeticum where we read "That light" said he, "am I, Mind *(nous)*, your God" (1.4-6; see also 1.9, 12, 17, 21, 28, 32; 7.2). On this see E. R. Goodenough, *By Light, Light* (1935); Rudolf Bultmann, *The Gospel of John* (1971) 40–45. In such Hellenistic religious texts light carries the sense of spiritual illumination where the mind is the point of identification with the divine reality. While this is not the sense of 1 John 1:5, it may well be precisely what is meant in the assertion made by the opponents, 2.9. This might be a good indication of what the opponents understood by union with God who is light.

Even if the author of 1 John and his opponents were both working from the Johannine Gospel tradition, we need to allow for the different ways the Johannine language might be understood. There is a tradition of interpreting John 1:4, 9 in terms of illumination. Indeed, the christological use of light symbolism ensures that its fundamental meaning there concerns revelation, though not necessarily illumination. But in 1 John there are clear signs that the *content* of the revelation is more directly in focus. One indication of this is the shift of the symbolism from christological statement to theological statement: "God is light." In John, christology is indirect reference to God. Now the message concerns God directly.

The negative statement "and in him is no darkness at all" is also a warning against interpreting the light symbolism in general religious terms. In 1 John the symbolism of light and darkness does not describe coordinates, such as night and day are in Genesis 1. A symbolism that coordinates these two is quite different from 1 John where light and darkness are given irreconcilably opposed ethical meanings. It is important to remember that we are talking of symbolism, so that it is the opposition of what is symbolized that is essentially irreconcilable. From another point of view light and darkness can be seen as positive coordinates (as in Genesis 1).

Nothing in the Prologue has prepared the reader for this statement about God. The reader of the Prologue of the Gospel (John 1:5) and John 3:19-21 is prepared for an antagonism between the light and the darkness, but (in 1 John 1:5) there is no clue as to the specific meaning of these two antithetical symbols. For this we must wait until 1 John 2:9-11. Indeed, there is a case for seeing an inclusion on the theme of the light bounded by 1:5 and 2:9-11. In 2:9-11 the light becomes identified with love of the brothers (sisters implied) and the darkness with the hatred of the brothers (sisters implied). Though this is not apparent from 1:5, the message "God is light" semantically overlaps the other great theistic statement in 1 John 4:8, 16, "God is love." In the sense of love used here, love and hate are as little compatible as are light and darkness.

The Semitic sense of love as choosing and hate as rejecting is somewhat different (see John 3:19 and 1 John 2:15-17). In this sense to love the darkness is to choose it just as to love the world is to choose its values and be conformed to them. But John can also say that God loved the world (John 3:16). In this case, rather than being conformed to the values of the world God's love for it opens the possibility of the world's transformation. The giving of God's Son is the self-giving (love) of God that makes belief and salvation (transformation) possible.

### For Reference and Further Study

Beutler, Johannes. *Die Johannesbriefe*. Regensburger Neues Testament. Regensburg: Friedrich Pustet, 2000, 34–46.

Borgen, Peder. *Logos Was the True Light, and other essays on the Gospel of John*. Trondheim: Tapir, 1983.

Brooke, Alan England. *A Critical and Exegetical Commentary on the Johannine Epistles*. Edinburgh: T & T Clark, 1912, 1–13.

Brown, Raymond E. *The Epistles of John*. AB 30. Garden City, N.Y.: Doubleday, 1982, 151–88.

Bultmann, Rudolf. *The Gospel of John*. Translated by G. R. Beasley-Murray. Oxford: Blackwell, 1971.

Dodd, Charles Harold. *The Johannine Epistles*. MNTC. London: Hodder and Stoughton, 1946, 1–19.

_____. *The Interpretation of the Fourth Gospel*. Cambridge: Cambridge University Press, 1953.

Goodenough, Erwin R. *By Light, Light; The Mystic Gospel of Hellenistic Judaism*. New Haven: Yale University Press, 1935.

Grayston, Kenneth. *The Johannine Epistles*. NCB. Grand Rapids: Eerdmans, 1984.

Harnack, Adolf. "Das 'Wir' in der Johanneischen Schriften," *SB* (Berlin) 1923, 96–113.

Houlden, James Leslie. *A Commentary on the Johannine Epistles.* HNTC. New York: Harper & Row, 1973.

Law, Robert. *The Tests of Life: A Study of the First Epistle of St. John.* Edinburgh: T & T Clark, 1909.

Malatesta, Edward. *Interiority and Covenant: A Study of* einai en *and* menein en *in the First Letter of Saint John.* AnBib 69. Rome: Biblical Institute Press, 1978.

Painter, John. *The Quest for the Messiah.* Edinburgh: T & T Clark, 1991, 2nd ed. Nashville: Abingdon, 1993.

Perkins, Pheme. "Koinonia in 1 John 1:3-7: The Social Context of Division in the Johannine Letters," *CBQ* 45 (1983) 631–41.

Rensberger, David. *1 John, 2 John, 3 John.* ANTC. Nashville: Abingdon, 1997.

Schnackenburg, Rudolf. *The Johannine Epistles.* Translated by Reginald and Ilse Fuller. New York: Crossroad, 1992, 48–76.

Smalley, Stephen S. *1, 2, 3 John.* WBC. Waco, Tex.: Word Books, 1984.

# II. FIRST PRESENTATION OF THE TWO TESTS (1:6–2:27)

There are two tests of the claim to have fellowship with God (the ethical and christological theses):

## 1. THE ETHICAL TEST. WALKING IN THE LIGHT AS THE TRUE SIGN OF UNION WITH GOD. REFUTATION OF THE FIRST TWO SERIES OF LIES (1:6–2:17).

### 1.1. God is light and the necessity of walking in the light (1:6–2:11)

Raymond Brown (*The Epistles of John* 191) makes a good case for recognizing a division of 1 John at the end of 2:2. This takes in the statement of the message that provides part of the basis for the response to the first three claims (slogans) of the opponents (1:5–2:2). Three assertions are introduced with "if we claim . . ." (1:6, 8, 10), and are matched by three correcting conditional statements introduced by "but if . . ." (1:7, 9; 2:1). The third of these (2:1b-2) is more than a response to the third claim. It sums up the response to this first group of claims. Cleansing by "the blood of Jesus his Son" (v. 7) is associated with the forgiveness of sins and cleansing from every unrighteousness (1:9) and with "the expiation of our sins" (2:2). The first three claims are formally bound together by a common quotation formula ("if we claim . . .") and the responses are united by their rebuttal form in their exposition of the author's treatment of the way God deals with human sin. Certainly Brown is right in seeing the coherence of 1:5–2:2.

Yet there is a case for treating this as part of a larger section bounded by an inclusion formed by the statement of the message that God is light (1:5) and the sixth slogan of the opponents who claimed to be in the light (2:9). Response to this claim continues in 2:10-11. The essential connection between the statement of the message and the sixth claim calls for recognition. Only at this point does the antithetical nature of light and darkness become apparent in relation to love and hate of the brother. Although the fourth, fifth, and sixth claims have a different quotation formula ("The one who claims . . ."), our author continues to deal with the recognition of sin in the exposure of false claims. Sin is exposed in the failure to keep "his" commandments/word (2:4-5), in the failure to follow his example (2:6), in the failure to keep the love commandment, which goes back to the foundational message (2:7-11). The response to the second group of claims gathers them together in the focus on the command to love the brother. That this is the dominant issue is suggested by the connection between 1:5 and 2:9-11 (really 2:7-11). Indeed, the love command lies barely hidden beneath the surface in 2:3-6 (compare 2:6b with 3:16; 4:11). To walk as *(kathōs)* he walked is to love as *(kathōs)* he loved: see John 13:34. For this reason our analysis keeps the first six claims (lies) together. Indeed, the seventh claim returns to this issue as well (4:20).

### 1.1.1. *Response to the claims to have union with God who is light* (1:6–2:2)

6. If we claim: "We have fellowship with him" and walk in the darkness, we lie and do not do the truth; 7. but if we walk in the light as he is in the light, we have fellowship with one another and the blood of Jesus his Son cleanses us from every sin. 8. If we claim: "We have no sin," we deceive ourselves and the truth is not in us. 9. But if we confess our sins, he is faithful and righteous to forgive us our sins and cleanse us from every

wrongdoing. 10. If we claim: "We have never sinned," we make him a liar and his word is not in us. 2:1. My little children, I write these things to you: Do not sin. But if anyone sins we have an advocate (Paraclete) with the Father, Jesus Christ the righteous; 2. and he is the expiation for our sins, not for ours only but for [the sins] of the whole world.

## NOTES

6. *If we claim: "We have fellowship with him" and walk in the darkness, we lie and do not do the truth:* The first of seven claims inspired by the opponents (1:6, 8, 10; 2:4, 6, 9; 4:20) appears here. The first three of these are introduced by the formula "If we claim . . ." *(Ean eipōmen).* The second three are introduced by "The one who claims" *(ho legōn),* and a seventh by "If any one claims . . ." *(ean tis eipē).* The first four (and the seventh) purport to give the claims in the words of the claimants. In these the introductory formula is followed by *hoti* and the following words are reported in the first person ("we" or "I") of the speaker(s), the first three in first person plural and the fourth (and seventh) in first person singular.

Contrary to Brown (*The Epistles of John* 197, and see also 205, 211, 253, 259), who says again and again that "The Greek is in indirect discourse," this is direct discourse, the equivalent of what we put in quotation marks. See BDF §397 (5) and §470 (1). Strangely, Brown himself puts the words of the first four and seventh claims (1:6, 8, 10; 2:4; 4:20) in quotation marks in his own translation!

While *hoti* is also used to introduce indirect discourse, to do so the verb would need to be in the third person. Here it is in the first person in the first four claims. This is more important than the variation between singular and plural quotation formulae. The conditional form of 1:6, 8, 10; 4:20 is not relevant to the distinction between direct and indirect speech constructions. In 4:20 the direct speech is in the text *(ean tis eipē hoti Agapō ton theon).* As indirect speech this would read *ean tis eipē hoti agapei ton theon.* Alternatively, following the indirect speech constructions of the fifth and sixth claims, 1:6 could be expressed as indirect speech, *ean eipōmen hoti koinōnian met autou echein.* Only the fifth and sixth claims are expressed indirectly, not in the words of the claimant.

In discussing the claim of 2:4, Brown (*The Epistles of John* 253) says:

> If there is any difference in the tone between the two sets of three disapproved theses in chapters 1 and 2, it lies in the use of the first person in chapter 1 ("we") and the third person ("one, person") in chapter 2. The false statements here may approach being exact quotations from the secessionists, while those of chapter 1 may have been secessionist-inspired but rephrased in the author's wording.

That this is the wrong distinction may be shown by noting that the construction with *hoti* is used in conditional form with both plural and singular (1:6, 8,

10 and 4:20) as well as the singular with the straightforward statement (2:4). The notion that the second group of claims is a more accurate report than the first group fails to recognize that 2:4 belongs with 1:6, 8, 10 and 4:20 as direct quotations in the first person and is thus rightly put in quotation marks, while 2:6, 9 report only the substance of the claim. This observation weakens Brown's case for suggesting that the author of 1 John has introduced his own term *(koinōnia)* into the first claim.

Verse 6 also supplies a falsification of the claim to have union with God. It is not that such claims are necessarily false. Rather the author shows what would falsify the claim. The use of "walk" as a metaphor for living is characteristically Johannine. The verb *(peripatein)* is used seventeen times in John, five times in 1 John, three times in 2 John, and twice in 3 John. Of these, John 6:66; 7:1; 8:12; 11:9, 10, 54; 12:35; 21:18; 1 John 1:6, 7; 2:6, 11; 2 John 4, 6; 3 John 3, 4 provide evidence of metaphorical meaning beyond the physical act of walking. Especially important for the notion of walking in the darkness are John 8:12; 11:10; 12:35; 1 John 2:11. In the Johannine writings only here and in John 3:19 is *skotos* used for "darkness." Elsewhere *skotia* is used and without any different meaning; see below on 1 John 2:5 and see also 2:8, 9, 11. Cf. John 1:5; 6:17; 8:12; 12:35, 46; 20:1.

"We lie" *(pseudometha)* is a verb used only here in the Gospel and Letters of John (once in Rev 3:9). The cognate noun *(pseudos)* is used in John 8:44 and 1 John 2:21, 27. Related is the reference to the "many *false* prophets *(pseudoprophētai)* who have gone out into the world" (1 John 4:1) and references to the "liar" *(pseustēs)* in John 8:44, 55; 1 John 1:10; 2:4, 22; 4:20; 5:10. The affirmation is a lie only when behavior falsifies the claim that is not false in principle. Communion with God *is* possible: see 1:3, 7.

The lie is not in abstract argument. For the phrase "we do not do the truth" see John 3:21; Gen 32:11; 47:29; Neh 9:33 (LXX) and compare the expression "walking in the truth" in 2 John 4; 3 John 4. Both expressions reflect the influence of Semitic language. Here it has the sense of not telling the truth but lying. The language of truth is prominent in the Johannine literature. "Truth" *(alētheia)* is used 109 times in the NT, of which 45 are Johannine: 25 times in the Gospel; nine times in 1 John; five times in 2 John; six times in 3 John. The adjective "true" *(alēthēs)* is used 14 times in John, twice in 1 John, and once in 3 John; the other adjective with this meaning *(alēthinos)* is used nine times in John and three times in 1 John. See the note on 2:9.

7. *but if we walk in the light as he is in the light, we have fellowship with one another and the blood of Jesus his Son cleanses us from every sin:* Whereas the fulfillment of the condition in 1:6 proved the affirmation to be false of those who made it, fulfillment of the condition in 1:7 proves it to be true. This is the writer's method of dealing with the claims made by the opponents. First the false conditions involved in the opponents' position are stated (v. 6). But there is more to this than showing whether the opponents match their claims in their lives. The author's demonstration of their failure to do so probably shows that he and the opponents understand the claims differently. This is not a matter of inconsistency, of saying one thing and doing another. At the heart of the con-

flict is a different understanding of God, of Jesus Christ, and of the life of the believer in relation to them. Christology and the love ethic are inseparably related in this controversy.

Thus in a similar "if " clause in v. 7 the true conditions are set out. Because this statement is opposed to the false position stated in v. 6 the *de* has adversative force: "*But* if we walk in the light. . . ." Those who walk in the light have fellowship with each other and the blood of Jesus, God's Son, cleanses (present tense) from every sin. The present tense indicates an ongoing cleansing of those walking in the light as a basis for union with God. Thus walking in the light opens up *koinōnia* with each other and with God (see 1:3). On "Jesus his Son" see the notes on 1:3 above.

8. *If we claim: "We have no sin," we deceive ourselves and the truth is not in us:* For the quotation formula see the Note on 1:6 above. The assertion "we have no sin" *(hamartian ouk echomen)* is understood by Brown to refer to the "guilt" of sin (*The Epistles of John* 205–206). The first use of the noun "sin" was in v. 7, also in the singular. There it was used with reference to *cleansing* from every sin, thus to the defilement of sin. The claim to have no sin in v. 8 would seem to assert no defilement from the presence of sin. This is confirmed by 1:8-9 where the author argues that the way to deal with sin is not to deny that we "have sin," which is self-deception, but to confess and be *cleansed* from every act of unrighteousness.

This verse contains the second reference to truth *(alētheia)* in 1 John: "the truth is not in us." The first use is in 1:6. Here a different idiom is used, but with much the same force as in 1:6 where not doing the truth means not telling the truth, but lying. If the truth is not in us, we do not tell the truth.

9. *But if we confess our sins, he is faithful and righteous to forgive us our sins and cleanse us from every wrongdoing:* Although the conditional sentence is not introduced by *kai* or *de*, the adversative force is implied by contrast between vv. 8 and 9. On confession of sin see Lev 5:5; 16:21; Isa 7:19; Ps 32:5; Prov 28:13; Dan 9:20; Mark 1:5 *par.*; Jas 5:16. Confessions of guilt are addressed to God (Ps 51:6; Gen 20:6; 39:9; Lev 5:19; 2 Sam 12:13) or to a priest (Lev 6:5-6) or to others (Josh 7:19). The Qumran covenant renewal involved a confession of sin (1QS 1:16–3:12) in which the whole community may have taken part (CD 20:28-30).

10. *If we claim: "We have never sinned," we make him a liar and his word is not in us:* For the quotation formula see on 1:6 above. On the reference to making God a "liar" see 5:10. On the opponents as liars see 2:4, 22; 4:20.

2:1. *My little children, I write these things to you: Do not sin. But if anyone sins we have an advocate (Paraclete) with the Father, Jesus Christ the righteous:* For the form of address "My little children" see 2:1, 12, 28; 3:7, 18; 4:4; 5:21. In the NT outside 1 John this diminutive of *teknon* is used only in John 13:33; Gal 4:19. The diminutive has an intimate and endearing tone, especially when used in direct address as in 2:1, *Teknia mou.*

Note the move from the plural (1:4, "we write") to the singular "I write to you"; see 2:7, 8. In 2:12, 13, 14 the first three uses are "I write" (present tense) while the next three are "I wrote" (aorist tense). The aorist is maintained in 2:21, 26; 5:13.

The response to the third claim is interrupted by 2:1a: "My little children, I write these things to you: 'Do not sin.'" What follows, "But (and) if anyone sins . . ." (2:1b) matches the pattern of response to the first and second claims in 1:7, 9, "But if. . . ." There is a difference. Whereas the response in 1:7, 9 was "But if we . . . ," in 2:1b it is "But if *anyone (ean tis)* sins we have. . . ." Perhaps the interjection in the first person *singular*, enabling the author to address his readers intimately as *"My* little children" (2:1a), disturbed the first person plural idiom that returns in the affirmation "we have a Paraclete with the Father. . . ." More probably the author felt the greater inclusiveness of "if anyone sins" ("we" being restricted to the Johannine school or Johannine community), in keeping with the view that Jesus Christ the righteous is the expiation for the sins of *the whole world.*

The use of *hina* followed by the verb in the subjunctive mood is epexegetical (*hina* expressing content), that is, it gives the content of what the author writes. The negative *mē* with the aorist subjunctive *hamartēte* expresses a negative command: "Do not sin." Here the aorist in the negative command probably does not mean "stop sinning this instant," a meaning consistent with the use of the aorist tense. Rather, the epexegetical use of *hina* has necessitated the use of the subjunctive mood which, with a negative command, is required in the aorist tense. The command concerns a sustained rejection of sin.

"But if anyone sins" *(kai ean hamartē).* Again the *kai* has adversative force because 2:1b stands against 1:10. The construction of 2:1b expresses the possibility, not the necessity of sin. The verb, an aorist subjunctive, suggests a sinful act rather than habitual sinfulness.

The noun *paraklētos* is used only here in the Johannine Epistles. Elsewhere in the New Testament it is found only in John 14:16, 26; 15:26; 16:7. In 1 John 2:1 the meaning "Advocate" is fairly clear in its use concerning the role of Jesus on behalf of the believer who sins. In the Gospel the term is used alongside "the Spirit of Truth" in reference to the Spirit. There no single translation seems to be adequate in all contexts. Hence we encounter translations like "Comforter" as well as "Advocate," and the roles of "Witness" and "Prosecutor" are also involved. When first introduced by Jesus in John, the Spirit is referred to as "another Paraclete" *(allon paraklēton),* perhaps taking account of the recognition that Jesus himself was the first Paraclete (1 John 2:1). One might then argue that just as Jesus is the believer's advocate with the Father, so the Spirit is Jesus' advocate with us. But such can be only a partial solution for the use in John. In 1 John the sense of Advocate seems clear and is supported by earlier Greek examples with which Philo's use agrees: see Philo, *Jos.* 40; *Mos.* 3.14; *Opif.* 6; *Flacc.* 3, 4. See further A. E. Brooke, *Commentary* 23–27.

2:2. *and he is the expiation for our sins, not for ours only but for [the sins] of the whole world:* Expiation (*hilasmos*), used only in 1 John 2:2 and 4:10 in the NT, is related to a group of words of common root. None of these is frequent in the NT, each being used no more than twice. For this reason clarity is lacking in their use in the NT. See Brown (*The Epistles of John* 217–22). In the NT this group of words is related to God showing mercy; see in addition to 1 John 2:2; 4:10 *(hilaskesthai)* Luke 18:13; Heb 2:17; *(hilastērion)* Rom 3:24-25; Heb 9:5; *(hileōs)* Matt 16:22; Heb 8:12. From the greater frequency of use of forms of the verb in the LXX *(hilasmos* is used only six times!), the following seems clear. The verb is rarely used in relation to God, but when it is it has the sense of propitiation. This is the sense in Zech 7:2 and Mal 1:9, where pagan sacrifice is criticized. But where God is the active agent of the verb, which is generally the case, it has the sense of showing mercy or forgiving. In 1 John *hilasmos* deals with sins. God and Jesus Christ the righteous are the active agents. Thus the meaning seems to be "expiation for our sins." Jesus Christ the righteous is God's means of dealing with our sins. In 1:7 the blood of Jesus implies that his death plays a crucial part in this, and the same seems to be implied in 4:10. The language of expiation may well be based on conceptions related to the Day of Atonement. See Hebrews 9–10 where the ritual of the Day of Atonement is applied to Jesus.

For references to the *world* (23 times in 1 John) see 1 John 2:2, 15 (3x), 16 (2x), 17; 3:1, 13, 17; 4:1, 3, 4, 5 (3x), 9, 14, 17; 5:4 (2x), 5, 19; 2 John 7. As in the Gospel (where the word is used 78 times), the "world" is the object of God's saving action (1 John 2:2; 4:9, 14). Nevertheless, the world is a corrupting power (2:15-17) that failed to recognize Jesus and does not recognize the children of God whom it opposes and hates, but it is overcome by them (3:1, 13; 4:1, 3, 4, 5, 17; 5:4, 5, 19).

INTERPRETATION

The first assertion is made against the background of the message that "God is light." It is the first of three in this passage (1:6, 8, 10). Each is introduced by the quotation formula "If we claim. . . ." The first of these is not necessarily a lie or an error. It is falsified by behavior inconsistent with the claim. The second and third assertions are shown to be outright falsehoods.

Three more assertions are found in ch. 2. These are introduced by the formula "The one who says . . ." (2:4, 6, 9), which is a quotation formula only in the case of 2:4. Like the assertion of 1:6, these are not necessarily falsehoods. The claims are shown to be false by inconsistent behavior. On the stylistic variations and arrangements into units of three and seven see Brown, *The Epistles of John* 116–18, 123. A final claim is made using another quotation formula, "If anyone says . . ." (4:20). Like the previous group of claims, this one is not necessarily false but is falsified by inconsistent behavior.

We might conclude from this survey that the problem 1 John addresses is inconsistent behavior in the network of Johannine churches. The false claims of 1:8, 10 should warn us against hastily adopting that conclusion. Alternatively, those who are portrayed as inconsistent from the point of view of 1 John might have understood the meaning of the assertions very differently from the way the author of 1 John understood them. This may well be the case if we have identified assertions that reflect the views of those opposed by 1 John. Yet, given that the opponents have gone out from the Johannine community (2:18-19), they hardly form a part of the "we" of the Johannine school or community. If this is a reference to the opponents, why would 1 John introduce the first group of these sayings with "If we claim . . ."?

The answer to this question is given in three parts. First, the first person plural idiom was set in vv. 1-4 and continues in vv. 5-10. Indeed, allowing for a momentary break in 2:1a, the plural continues through 2:2. Second, those who had gone out probably included influential members of the Johannine community, perhaps even leaders who until recently were included in the "we" of the witnesses. Third, and most important, the danger of further defections from within the community persisted. In this case the "we" of the foundational witnesses (the Johannine school) has been expanded into the "we" of the Johannine community. The process of this transformation is implied in vv. 3-4. There the communication of the message is expressed in terms of what "we announce to you," with the purpose "that you may be united with us in our union with the Father and his Son Jesus Christ." So the author says, "We write these things that our joy may be complete." In this last sentence the first person plural personal pronoun is used twice. The first ("we") refers to the foundational witnesses. The second ("our") refers to the whole Johannine community.

The author's awareness of the threat to the completion of joy explains the tone of 1 John. The author's worst fear was a continuing drain of defections from within the Johannine network of churches. That being the case, the appropriate way to begin dealing with the threat of the opponents was in language that recognized the danger within the network. If 1 John reveals the wide effects the schism had on the Johannine community, 3 John reveals how deeply into the leadership its effects were felt. The use of "we" in the quotation formulae of 1:6, 8, 10, in close proximity to the use of the "we" of the foundation witnesses, probably indicates the author's awareness of how deeply the schism has bitten into the leadership of the Johannine community.

Brown suggests that the different introductory formulae may indicate different levels of accuracy in quotation, so that the more definite "The person who claims" may approach being exact quotations from the secessionists, while those in ch. 1 may have been secessionist-inspired but rephrased in the author's wording (*The Epistles of John* 232, 253). This is both unnecessary and unjustified. (See the discussion of the quotation formulae in the notes on 1:6.) The use of "we" in 1:6, 8, 10 reveals the author's fear of the continuing influence of the secessionists in the community. The introduction of the first group of claims using "if we claim" shows that the author does not think that the schism has put the problem outside the community. The schism has left the problem seething within it and 1 John is addressing the aftermath of the schism.

Some of the "claims" used by the opponents are opposed forthrightly, but in fact only 1:8, 10 are rejected outright. For the rest it is a question of a conflict of interpretation. The false meaning has to be exposed by tests of truth of the christological confession and ethical behavior understood in terms of love.

**The first claim (1:6-7).** The message that "God is light," which excludes the possibility of darkness in God, prepares the way for dealing with the first of the seven claims inspired by the opponents, the first six of which occur in 1:6–2:11. The first group of three claims is introduced by the quotation formula "If we claim . . ." *(Ean eipōmen)* and is followed by *hoti*, which signals a quotation when what follows is in the first person, as it is here and in the following three claims (1:8, 10; 2:4) and in the seventh claim (4:20). (See the notes.) In indirect speech what follows would use the verb in the third person. In the first three claims the wording shows the author's awareness that the threat of falsehood was harbored within the Johannine community. The threat was not averted by the departure of the schismatics (2:18-19). The "we" might also indicate that the threat was felt even among the leaders of the community.

The first of the claims does not involve a theological or ethical falsehood as such. The claim is not wrong in principle. The lie of the claim is that it is not true of those who made it if they "walk in the darkness." This reading of 1 John suggests that the opponents understood the assertion about having union with God differently from the author of 1 John. What is claimed in the slogan is tested against the relationship with God set out in v. 3. Notably the claim is to have union (fellowship, *koinōnia*) with God. Significantly 1:3 had made union "with us" a condition of union with God. Further, the introduction to this assertion is the affirmation "God is light," clarified by the note that "in him is no darkness at all." Thus "to walk in the darkness" constitutes a problem for the claim to have union with God, whatever that means.

Brown (*The Epistles of John* 252–53) suggests that the first three slogans, introduced hypothetically with "If we claim . . ." (1:6, 8, 10), should be considered as more loosely constructed representations of their position than the second three, which are introduced specifically: "The person who claims . . ." and quote more or less precisely the slogans of the opponents. In support of this position Brown (*The Epistles of John* 186, 232) argues that *koinōnia* was not a "secessionist" term but was introduced by our author. Friedrich Hauck (art. "κοινός, κτλ.," *TDNT* 3:807) adds support to that view by asserting: "In 1 Jn. *koinōnia* is a favourite term to describe the living bond in which the Christian stands."

*The first claim:* "If we claim 'we have *koinōnia with* him (God)'. . . ." If *koinōnia* were a favorite term for our author it would be difficult to show that it was also used, perhaps in a different sense, by his opponents, though that would not be impossible. Brown argues that *koinōnia* was not a term used by the opponents but was an ecclesiastical term by means of which the author of 1 John affirms the importance of the relation to the tradition. He thinks that the "secessionists" used the Gospel terms *menein en* and *einai en,* whereas the author used *koinōnia.* If Brown is right, at least the first of the slogans was constructed in our author's terms.

Against this position it is argued that the introductory quotation formulae of the first four claims imply accurate quotation of the actual words, while the fifth and sixth claims report only the substance of the claims. The first four report *first person* sayings introduced by *hoti,* which in these circumstances signals a quotation. This is more significant than the distinction between the plural claims (1-3) and singular claim (4). The use of "we" (claims 1-3) is a result of the continuation of that idiom from vv. 1-4. More important, it expresses the perceived threat of the opponents' teaching in the midst of the Johannine community, perhaps even threatening its leadership (see 3 John).

Further, the term *koinōnia* is not drawn from the Johannine tradition. It is not used at all in John or 2 and 3 John. The four uses in 1 John are concentrated in 1:3, 6-7. The use in 1:3 prepares for the response to the opponents by providing the author's interpretation of *koinōnia.* There is a case for seeing this as a Pauline term. Thirteen of the fifteen uses in the NT, excluding the four in 1 John, are found in Paul's letters. There is a concentration in 1–2 Corinthians (7x) where *koinōnos* is used four of a total of nine times in the NT. Clearly, in Paul's use these words are closely associated. If we adopt "union" as the translation of *koinōnia,* Paul says the following in 1 Corinthians: "you were called into union of his Son" (1:9); "is it not a union with the blood of Christ? . . . is it not a union of the body of Christ?" (10:16). Using "partners" to translate the plural *koinōnoi* in 1 Corinthians, we read: "are not those who eat the sacrifice partners of the altar?" (10:18); "I do not wish you to be partners of demons" (10:20). References in 2 Corinthians are also illuminating. First, there are four passages with "union": "what union has light with darkness?" (6:14); "the union of service which is to the saints" (8:4); "by sincerity of union with them and with all" (9:13); "the union of the Holy Spirit" (13:13). The following passages in 2 Corinthians use "partners": "as you are partners of the suffering" (1:7); "Titus my partner and for you a fellow worker *(synergos)"* (8:23).

The evidence of this language in Paul and the strong concentration in the Corinthian correspondence is more than suggestive. Both terms imply participation in that with which there is union. The reference in 2 Cor 6:14 uses the language to put in question the union of light and darkness. The

Johannine falsification of the claim to have union with God, who is light, is "to walk in darkness." The message is: "God is light, in whom there is no darkness whatsoever." Thus those who walk in darkness are not in union with God. The Corinthian correspondence also raises the question of idolatry, union with idols and demons. Commentators today generally do not give sufficient weight to the serious threat of idolatry in the first century. Paul's treatment of the subject in 1 Corinthians shows the seriousness of the issue for that fledgling community. The context of Paul's use of this language in 1 Corinthians may be a warning to take the final exhortation of 1 John at face value and as a serious warning: "Little children, guard yourselves from idols" (1 John 5:21).

The following arguments count against seeing *koinōnia* as 1 John's equivalent for the opponents' use of *menein en* or *einai en*. First, these are Johannine terms (*koinōnia* is not); see *menein en* in John 8:31; 14:10; 15:4, 5, 6, 7, 9, 10; 1 John 2:6, 10, 14, 24, 27, 28; 3:6, 9, 14, 15, 17, 24; 4:12, 13, 15, 16; 2 John 2, 9. Second, the use of *menein en* in the fifth claim (2:6) is not in direct speech but reports the substance of the claim. (On this see the Note on v. 6 above.) This suggests that it is *menein en* (and *einai en*) that expresses the author's own language. Third, to adopt *koinōnia* as a means of criticizing the opponents' claim to "be in" or "abide in" God would inevitably miss the mark. Rather, the author critiques the opponents' claim to union with God by arguing that such union involves union with other believers. Fourth, if *koinōnia* were the author's interpretation of the opponents' claim to "abide in God," why did our author also present the slogan in the opponents' own terms in 2:6, where the slogan "to abide in him" *(menein en)* appears?

Not only is *koinōnia* not taken up from the Johannine tradition, it is by no means prominent in the Johannine epistles, appearing in neither 2 nor 3 John (nor in Revelation) and only four times in 1 John, all in the section dealing with the slogan of the opponents, "We have *koinōnia* with him" (1:6; see also 1:3, 7). The evidence suggests that our author took up and used the term because his opponents were using it. However, he modifies the meaning of the term as used in the slogan. The opponents' slogan is "We have *koinōnia* with him (God)." Our author makes the primary reference of *koinōnia* to be *met' allēlōn* (1:7), and this is dependent on *koinōnia meth' hēmōn*, which opens up *koinōnia* with the Father and his Son Jesus Christ (1:3).

In the opponents' slogan of *koinōnia* with God the term is not used in an ecclesiastical sense. It may be that Hellenistic religions provide some sort of clue to what was meant by the opponents (see Hauck's article in *TDNT* 3:799–800) who seem to be claiming some kind of mystical union with God that had no relation to the lives of other believers. That is suggested by the way the theme of *koinōnia met allēlōn* is introduced. The use of *allēlōn* suggests some relation to the love command in the Johannine tradition, *agapate allēlous kathōs ēgapēsa hymas* . . . (John 13:34, and see 1 John 1:7; 4:7, 12). In 1 John these themes are treated in response to the opponents' claims to have fellowship with God and to love God. In each instance the claim is tested in terms of the relationship with one another and the reality of fellowship is tested in terms of love.

Our author used *koinōnia* only in response to the usage of his opponents (four times in 1:3, 6, 7). Thus the view of Edward Malatesta that 1 John is constructed around the theme of *koinōnia* cannot be justified. Characteristically, and in common with the Johannine tradition, 1 John uses love terminology. Indeed, *koinōnia met allēlōn* is *agapan allēlous*. In this way our author has reoriented the theme from a direct relation with God to the believers' relation with each other. The "new commandment" (based on John 13:34, but see also John 17:11, 14, 16, 18, 21, 22; 20:21) provides our author with the model for his *kathōs* ethic (see 2:6; 3:3, 23; 4:17), which is also implied in 1:7; 2:27; 4:11, 19, and is expressed negatively in 3:12. Hence according to John the disciples of Jesus are to live (walk) as he lived. See Brown, *The Epistles of John* 97–98.

The author of 1 John also took up his opponents' affirmation about God. According to 1:5 the message is: "God is light and there is no darkness in him at all." This statement of the message does not come from the Johannine tradition. Rather it is our author's restatement of the message proclaimed by the opponents in order to provide a basis for correcting their claims. It already foreshadows the slogan claiming to be in the light, 2:9. If God is light, in whom there is no darkness at all, having *koinōnia* with God excludes the possibility of being in the darkness. Our author has interpreted being in the darkness as hating the brother (and sister) while the person who loves his brother (and sister) abides in the light *(ho agapōn ton adelphon autou en tō phōti menei)*, 2:9-10. This is to walk in the light and to have fellowship with one another.

Thus *koinōnia* had no ecclesiastical sense when used by the opponents. Our author reinterpreted the term to assert dependence on the tradition bearers and the obligation to love one another. On the basis of his reinterpretation he declares his opponents to be liars when they claim to have fellowship with God but fail to love the brothers and sisters (1:6). The liar also denies that Jesus is the Christ and in so doing denies the Father and the Son; on the liar see 1:6; 2:22; 4:1 (false prophets); 4:20. Thus the first of the claims appears to have been presented in the terms used by the opponents. Our author reinterpreted *koinōnia* and developed criteria that would demonstrate that the opponents did not have *koinōnia* with God. They did not walk in the light, loving the brothers/sisters and being united in fellowship with them.

In v. 6 the claim of the opponents is stated and shown to be false of those who walk in the darkness, that is, who fail to love the brothers/

sisters, though this is clear only in the light of 2:9-10. Then v. 7 shows the condition under which the claim is true. Those who walk in the light, that is, love the brothers/sisters, are united with one another in fellowship and with the Father and his Son Jesus Christ (1:3). Interestingly, here God, who is said to be light (1:5) is said also to be *in* the light (1:7). Yet the phrase "to walk in the light as he is in the light" suggests a connection with "the one who claims to abide in him ought to walk as he walked" (2:6). There the clause "as he walked" *(kathōs ekeinos periepatēsen)* uses the aorist tense, referring to the completed earthly life of Jesus. The use of *ekeinos* is emphatic, distinguishing Jesus from the one who claims, who is referred to by the pronoun *autos*. But it is not the case that *autos* always refers to someone other than Jesus. In 2:2 we read that "he [*autos*] is the expiation for our sins," referring to Jesus. There the emphasis is on "expiation." In 2:6 the emphasis is on walking as *he* walked. But in 2:2-6 there is a lack of clarity about the referents of the third person personal pronouns, whether God (the Father) or Jesus. In 2:2 and 6 reference seems to be to Jesus. In 2:3-5 the three assertions seem to refer to God. The lack of clarity of reference seems to be a consequence of claims about God made by the opponents, which are answered in 1 John by reference to the revelation of God in Jesus Christ. That is, God manifests in action what walking in the light involves. To walk in the light as he is in the light is to love one another as God loves, so that we again return to the recognition that the affirmation "God is light" overlaps "God is love" (4:8, 16). While the light symbolism may express the idea of revelation, the content of the revelation is already in view, and this concerns the love that God is. For this reason those who walk in the light of God's love are cleansed from all sin by the blood of Jesus, his (God's) Son. Cleansing from sin is an expression of God's love (3:16; 4:7-12).

The idea of being cleansed from all sin is introduced because being united in fellowship with one another also involves union with God. God himself cleanses those united in fellowship with him. Here the means of cleansing is said to be the blood of Jesus his Son. It cleanses us from every sin. In 2:2 the author says that Jesus Christ the righteous is the "expiation for our sins" (plural). The term *hilasmos* has the sense of expiation in relation to sin(s) and propitiation when related to a god. In the New Testament this word group is always used in relation to God's dealing with human sin. This is reinforced in 4:10 where the author says "In this is love, not that we have loved God, but that he loved us and sent his Son [as] an expiation for our sins (plural)" (4:10).

In 1:7 "cleansing from every sin" speaks of the removal of what defiles and prevents union with God. Here the use of the singular "every sin" draws attention to the cleansing from each and every one of them. Those who walk in the light are cleansed by God. We shall see in response to other issues how the language of expiation clarifies and fills out the discussion of the way God deals with sin.

The discussion of sin in 1:7 has opened up a tension in the thought of 1 John. Those in union with each other and with God walk in the light and not in the darkness. They are cleansed from every sin, yet to claim to have no sin is self-deception (v. 8). This tension between the call to live in the light and not to sin and the need to confess and be cleansed from every sin runs throughout 1 John (see 2:1; 3:4-10; 5:16-18).

**The second claim (1:8).** The idiom of each of the first two claims is expressed using "We have. . . ." "We *have* union with God"; "We *have* no sin." The reference to sin is singular and the verb "have" is present tense. The talk of being cleansed from every sin might suggest that the one who walks in the light is now sinless. The singular "sin" might imply something like "not a single sin." The present tense "we *have* no sin" may imply "now," subsequent to having been cleansed from every sin (1:7). That this is a false inference is made brutally clear by the sharp correction: "we deceive ourselves" *(planōmen)* if we claim this.

In Judaism the charge of deceiving—that is, leading the people astray—was very serious (see John 7:12, 47). This language is prominent in 1 and 2 John. Here in 1:8 there is reference to self-deception (1:8). There is no reason to think that the opponents, and those attracted to their position, were anything but sincere in their views. Nevertheless, the author of 1 John calls them "deceived" and "deceivers." Concerning the deceivers 1 John provides urgent warnings (2:26; 3:7). 2 John 7 refers to many deceivers *(polloi planoi)* having gone out into the world and identifies the deceiver with the Antichrist. 1 John 4:6 warns of "the spirit of error" *(to pneuma tēs planēs)*. The interrelationship between external deceivers and internal self-deception is complex. For those who assert their sinlessness there is no condition that can make the claim true. It is out-and-out error, and if we make it, 1 John leaves no doubt, "the truth is not in us." (Compare 1:10, which says: "his word is not in us," and see John 17:17: "Your word is truth.")

The use of the language of deception links this charge to the opponents. 1 John's teaching that those who walk in the light are cleansed from all sin (1:7) left those who accepted this position open to be persuaded that they were now without sin. In the teaching of the opponents this seems to have been a consequence of union with God. Those in union with God, who is light, are as a consequence without sin. In the teaching of the opponents this had nothing to do with "the blood of Christ that cleanses us from all sin." This perspective is introduced again and again by the author of 1 John (1:7, 9; 2:2; 4:10), but it was precisely the author's teaching about cleansing from sin that opened the door to a teaching of consequent sinlessness.

While the view outlined is the most likely, it is possible that the present tense "have" is timeless, so that those who claim "we *have* no sin" are making a claim of what is true of them by nature. From this perspective the second claim is not distinct from the third. This has the advantage of identifying one position among the opponents in relation to sinlessness (see 1:10). But two positions on this issue are not inherently unlikely. The notion of being sinless by nature, which seems to be driving the movement of the opponents, might well have been modified by some within the Johannine circle of churches. For them a case could be made for sinlessness subsequent to union with God. Indeed, the author allows at least for the potential of this (see 2:29; 3:6, 9; 4:7; 5:1, 4, 18), and the views expressed on this theme need to be discussed in relation to the present passages (1:8, 10).

Nevertheless, the correction does not state conditions under which the claim to have no sin might be true. Such a possibility is categorically denied and classified as self-deception (v. 8). Rather, v. 9 sets out the right way to deal with sin, namely confession: "If we confess our sins. . . ." Confession *(homologōmen)* has a double sense. The same term is used of confessing or not confessing that Jesus Christ has come in the flesh (4:2-3; 2 John 7; cf. 1 John 2:23; 4:15; John 9:22; 12:42, where it is used of confessing Christ, that is, confessing that Jesus is the Messiah). On this use see below on 2:23. Only here it is used of confessing our sins. The compound *exomologein* is used of confessing sins in Mark 1:5; Matt 3:6, and especially Jas 5:16, "confess your sins to one another," but this form is also used in confessions of faith and of praise in Matt 11:25; Luke 10:21.

But to whom is the confession of sins made? There is no indication of this in the text. Possibly what is in mind is confession to the one against whom the sin was committed (see Jas 5:16 and cf. Matt 5:23-24). Confession of sin is the basis of the forgiveness of sin. "The one who is faithful *(pistos)* and righteous *(dikaios)*" is a reference to God. There has been no change of focus from God who is light (1:5), with whom we are united in fellowship (1:6), the blood of whose Son cleanses us from all sin (1:7). That God, as it were, absolves and cleanses those who confess their sins may shift the balance of probability to God as the one to whom confession is made. There is ample evidence of such confession on the Day of Atonement and at other times. (See the Notes.)

That Jesus Christ is designated "the righteous" *(dikaion*, 2:1) might suggest that he is the one who forgives and cleanses. In 1 *Enoch* 38:2; 53:6 the Messiah is called "the righteous one." As God is righteous, so is God's Son righteous, and what the Son does is at the initiative of the Father (3:16; 4:9-12). That God is faithful *(pistos)* and righteous *(dikaios)* is fundamental to the Jewish understanding arising out of such texts as Exod 34:6-7; Deut 32:4; Pss (LXX) 18:8-9; 32:4-5; 84:12; 88:15; 95:13; 118:160. Such divine qualities are linked with forgiveness: Isa 1:18; Jer 31:34; 33:8; 50:20; Ezek 18:21-23; 33:11, 14-16; cf. Mic 7:18-20; Pss 33:5; 51:4; 119:64. The metaphor used here for forgiveness is the canceling of a debt *(aphienai):* Matt 6:12; 18:27, 32; cf. Exod 32:32; Lev 4:20; 19:22; Num 14:19. See Rudolf Bultmann, article "ἀφίημι, κτλ.," *TDNT* 1:510; Brooke, *Commentary* 21. The idea of cleansing from impurity is also common: Isa 1:16; Jer 40:8; Pss 19:14; 51:4; Prov 20:9; Sir 38:10. In 1 John cleansing obviously has an ethical sense. That God is the referent here is supported by the recognition that God is spoken of, without being named, throughout 1:6-10, and when Jesus is mentioned he is referred to as "his Son" (1:7).

The implications of God as faithful *(pistos)* and righteous *(dikaios)* are spelled out by means of *hina*, using two coordinate epexegetical or explanatory clauses with aorist subjunctive verbs. These assert God's action of forgiving and cleansing as expressions of God as faithful and righteous. Brooke *(Commentary* 19–20) calls this construction the definitive *hina*, which he says is frequent in the papyri; he supplies many examples in John in addition to 1 John (2:27; 3:1, 11, 23; 5:3, 16); 2 John (6); and 3 John (4).

It is interesting to ask whether each of the two characteristics (faithful and righteous) relate to one or other of the actions. Is it God as faithful who forgives and God as righteous who cleanses? Or is the construction chiastic, so that it is God who is faithful who cleanses, and God who is righteous who forgives? More probably the activity of God, who is faithful and righteous, is not to be compartmentalized in this way, especially because we may suspect a degree of overlap in the understanding of "faithful" and "righteous."

The aorist tense suggests that forgiveness and cleansing are viewed as completed actions. Thus the one who confesses is forgiven, is cleansed. By contrast, in 1:7 it is said of the one who walks in the light that "the blood of Jesus his Son cleanses (present tense) from every sin." This suggests a process whereby, in the walk, cleansing is going on.

The form of the slogan "If we claim 'We have no sin'" is matched by the form in which the correct response is expressed, "If we confess our sins. . . ." The result of such confession is forgiveness and cleansing. Such a situation might be described in terms of being free from sin, but not as a state of being. Rather it is understood in dynamic terms on the basis of the confession of sins and consequent forgiveness and cleansing (see the force of the present tense in 1:7).

God forgives our *sins*. God cleanses us from every bit of unrighteousness. The statement of forgiveness views sins as a collective whole. Reference to the cleansing deals with the individual acts of unrighteousness, as does the reference to cleansing from every sin in 1:7 where the blood of Jesus "his Son" is the agent of cleansing. This may suggest that God is the one who cleanses us from every sin and the blood of Jesus his Son is the means God uses. It is clear that in 1 John God is the initiator of human salvation and, indeed, the salvation of the world is the goal (2:2). By dealing with sin and its consequences God maintains the possibility of union with him and with each other.

**The third of the claims (1:10)** introduced by "If we claim . . ." follows. In many ways it seems to be a reiteration of the second. The idiom is different, though any distinction in meaning is unclear. The second claim may be taken as an assertion to have no sin in the present (*echomen*, present tense). It may thus affirm freedom from sin consequent on union with God. If this is correct, then in spite of the affirmation of walking in the light, 1 John asserts, there is no sinlessness! Then 1:10 may go further in asserting "We have not sinned" (*ouch hēmartēkamen*, perfect tense). Whereas the perfect tense asserts a continuing effect from a past action, when it is used with a negative the situation is different. Because the verb is negated there is no event from which effects flow. The sense is thus "We have never sinned." If the opponents were on the way to Gnosticism they might have claimed to be sinless by nature.

That this makes God a liar is an extreme statement. It is a variation on "we deceive ourselves" (1:8) or the accusation in 2:4 that the one making a false claim is a liar. The more normal strategy of 1 John is to accuse the opponents of being liars; see 2:22; 4:20; 5:10, and cf. John 8:44, 55. The variation may have been chosen to connect the statements in the Scriptures testifying to human sinfulness (Gen 8:21; 1 Kgs 8:46; Pss 14:3; 53:2; Job 4:17; 15:14-16; Prov 20:9) to show that those who affirmed their sinlessness did not have God's word (Scripture) abiding in them. By rejecting God's word they implied that God was lying (compare 5:10).

The flow and critique of the claims addressed in the first person plural is briefly interrupted in 2:1 so that the author may directly address his readers. If the author of 1 John is the author of 2-3 John he appropriately addresses his readers as "My little children" (*teknia mou*, see 2:12, 28; 3:7, 18; 4:4; 5:21). This diminutive form is used in direct address to the readers and expresses an affectionate relationship; it would be especially appropriate should the author be the Elder of 2–3 John. Compare the use of *paidia* in 2:14a with *teknia* in 2:12a. It is notable that this form of address is used authoritatively as the writer is about to issue his first command to his readers. Thus the establishment of an authoritative relationship by the use of this title is an astute rhetorical move.

The plural "we write" (1:4) now becomes "I write" (2:1), which is also a move on the part of the author to assert his own authority. This idiom is sustained throughout the rest of 1 John, though the present tense (2:1, 7, 8, 12, 13) is exchanged for the aorist (2:13, 14, 21, 26; 5:13). The function of the new reference to writing is to move from the plural to the singular, yet it does not indicate the beginning of a new section here any more than it does in 2:7 or in the string of references in 2:12-14, or in 2:26. Even though the author from now on asserts his own authority in *writing*, what is written from time to time is expressed in the first person plural, "we," by which the readers are sometimes included with himself. The author may also at times revert to joining himself to the authoritative witnesses of 1:4.

What the author writes now is a negative command: "Do not sin." Having denied the possibility of sinlessness and argued that God forgives and cleanses those who confess their sins, the author now sets out to show that he has not gone soft on sin. "Do not sin" is a command, not an attempt at some persuasive argument against sin. This sharp interjection signals the author's ethical seriousness. Even so, there is no falling away from the denial of sinlessness. Immediately the *possibility* of sin is acknowledged: "If anyone sins. . . ." The aorist subjunctive suggests a lapse into sin rather than a continuing life of sin. Although it is not reiterated here, we may assume that confession of sin is presupposed (see 1:9). That being the case, two further images are now laid alongside the images of God, who forgives and cleanses (1:9) by means of "the blood of Jesus Christ his Son" (1:7).

Returning to the first person plural idiom, the author affirms: "We have a *Paraclete* with the Father, Jesus Christ the righteous." Here the term Paraclete is rightly interpreted as "Advocate." There may be an association with the intercession of Abraham for Sodom (Gen 18:20-33), of Moses for Pharaoh (Exod 8:28-29), of Aaron's role as the blameless intercessor (Wis 18:21), and the role of the righteous person in the writings of early Judaism (Philo, *Migr.* 21.121-22; see John Painter, *Just James: The Brother of Jesus in History and Tradition* [Columbia: University of South Carolina Press, 1997] 254–59). The mention of an Advocate with the Father might suggest that persuasion is necessary to bring the Father to deal mercifully with our sin, but any such suggestion stands in tension with 1:9, and see 4:7-11, 16.

Jesus is here described as "Jesus Christ the righteous." The double name "Jesus Christ" has been used only at the end of v. 3, where union is "with the Father and with his Son Jesus Christ." The next reference to Jesus is also as "his Son" but without using the double name (1:7). Both vv. 3 and 7 deal with *koinōnia*. Both refer to Jesus explicitly as "his Son," but v. 3 uses the double name and v. 7 the single name Jesus.

Then there is the reference to Jesus Christ the righteous as "the *expiation (hilasmos) for our sins*" (2:2). This word is used only twice in the NT, here and in 4:10 where the initiative for this action is attributed to God who "loved us and sent his Son as the *expiation* of our sins." There is no doubt that in this sequence of ideas the author sees God the Father dealing with human sin through the sending of the Son. But what does *hilasmos* indicate about God's way of dealing with sin? The term is used only ten times in the LXX. Related terms and their use in the LXX suggest that when used in relation to sin *hilasmos* has the sense of expiation, especially where God himself is the agent of the action as he is in 1 John 4:10 (and implied in 2:2 as Jesus Christ the righteous is "his Son"). Though not mentioned here, it is the blood of Jesus his Son, according to 1:7, that cleanses us from every sin. It seems that the death of Jesus is God's means of dealing with sins. If the vision of 1 John is sometimes thought to be too narrow in ignoring the obligation to love beyond "one another," the concluding statement of this verse might suggest that an overly restrictive interpretation has been given to the love command. It is affirmed that expiation has been made for the sins of the whole world *(peri holou tou kosmou)*. Elsewhere we learn that "the whole world lies in the power of the evil one" (5:19). Nevertheless, Jesus Christ the righteous is the expiation for the sins of the whole world because "the Father sent the Son to be the savior of the world" (4:14, and cf. John 1:29).

"The world" is an important Johannine term, used 78 times in John, 23 times in 1 John, and once in 2 John out of a total of 185 times in the NT. Only Paul in Romans and 1 Corinthians approaches the Johannine frequency of use. The Johannine use shows a diversity of attitudes to the world. That diversity is expressed in 1 John. Here (2:2), in the first use of the term, we find that the world is the object of God's saving action in his Son, who is himself the expiation of the sins of the whole world. The universality of the scope of expiation is stressed. It is not simply for the sins of the world but "for the sins of the *whole* world." In the same vein 4:14 says "the Father sent the Son [as] the savior of the world," and 4:17 "even as he is, so are we in the world." The world needs a savior because "the *whole* world lies in the power of the Evil One" (5:19). That has been demonstrated by the false prophets, antichrists, and deceivers who have gone out into the world (2:18-19; 4:1, 3, 4, 5; 2 John 7). Because of this the world is characterized by immoral values (2:15-17). It does not recognize the Son of God or the children of God (3:1). Indeed, it hates them (3:13). In spite of this the Father sent the Son to be the savior of the world (4:14), that we might live through him (4:9), that we might be as he is in the world (4:17), and as believers we conquer the world (5:4-5, and cf. 2:13-14; 4:4). In what way do believers conquer the world (5:4-5), the Evil One (2:13-14), and the false prophets (4:4)? In the first place, they conquer the false prophets by confessing that "Jesus Christ has come in the flesh," thus overcoming the christological lie (see 2:22; 4:1-6). Second, they overcome the Evil One by rejecting the values of the world (2:15-17) and by loving the brother, not like Cain, who was of the Evil One (3:11-15). Finally, they overcome the world, the sphere where death reigns, because they have passed from death to life (3:14) and because they are as Jesus is in the world (4:17; see John 17:18) and their presence is the ground of hope that even the world may come to believe and thus be delivered from the power of the Evil

One. On this theme see John 17:6-26. See the discussion of "the world" in the Introduction, 16.6.

EXCURSUS: SIN AND SINLESSNESS

If the second claim asserted a state of sinlessness from the time of *koinōnia* with God, the third claimed absolute sinlessness. Perhaps this asserted that there were those who were sinless by nature while others only became sinless through union with God, presumably at their initiation *(chrisma)*; see my *John, Witness and Theologian* 120. Brown *(The Epistles of John* 82) rejects this view because "children of God by nature" cannot be derived from John. But this is to apply too rigorously the criterion of the derivability of the position of the opponents from John. If the opponents made the heavenly origin of the "Son" the paradigm for their own "sonship," John could provide a basis for such a view, though it would be a misinterpretation of John. Neither John nor 1 John speaks of believers as "sons of God" *(huioi theou)*; rather they are "children of God" *(tekna theou,* 1 John 3:2).

While the claim to be sinless is said to be self-deception, the claim never to have sinned is said to make God a liar and to demonstrate that his Word is not abiding in those who make such an assertion. This would seem to indicate that our author was more sure that he could *demonstrate* the error of those who claimed never to have sinned because this claim runs contrary to the message of forgiveness and cleansing in the gospel, including the Johannine tradition (John 1:29; 13:10; 15:3; 17:17). However, the claim to be sinless consequent to believing in Jesus is not as easily demonstrated to be false. No clear statements in the Johannine tradition exclude the view. Nonetheless, our author was prepared to assert that those who claim such a state of being are deceiving themselves.

Our author's attitude to sin is complex. Sin should be confessed so that it may be forgiven and cleansed (1:9); that cleansing takes place through walking in the light, by means of which the effects of Christ's death cleanse the believer (1:7). Yet he commands his readers, "Do not sin!" Yet again, the believer who sins has the assurance of the advocacy of Jesus Christ the righteous whose death *makes possible* the forgiveness and cleansing of the sins of everyone in the world (2:1-2). Such forgiveness is not automatic. It is dependent on the confession of sins and walking in the light. This suggests two levels of forgiveness and cleansing. There is the initial forgiveness and cleansing for the believer. There is also the recognition that the believer may slip and fall into sin which, if confessed, and if the believer returns to walk in the light, will be forgiven and the believer cleansed and reinstated to a dynamic sinlessness (2:1-2; 5:16-17).

The subject is taken up again in the discussion of the children of God and children of the devil (2:28-29; 3:1-10). In 2:29 the link between God, who is righteous, and God's children, all those who do righteousness, is affirmed. The children of the devil are identified with those who commit sin, who act lawlessly. Further, righteousness is associated with loving the brother and sin is the negation of that. It is hating the brother, the murder of the brother. The characterization of the children of God and children of the devil in terms of their opposite behavior is understandable in a situation in which our author sought to distinguish himself and his adherents from his opponents. He goes on to assert that

> everyone born of God does not sin because his *sperma* abides in him; and he is not able to sin, because he is born of God. This is how the children of God and the children of the devil are revealed (are to be recognized): everyone not doing righteousness is not of God, even (that is) the one who does not love his brother. (1 John 3:9-10)

Our author's aim in this tortuous statement is clear enough, though the opening would be more intelligible in English if translated "no one who is born of God sins. . . ." It was to provide a test to be passed by those who claimed to be God's children. That test was acting righteously, that is, loving the brother. Those who did not do this, and in his view his opponents did not, were not children of God but children of the devil. Moreover, it is argued that God's *sperma* abides in God's children, and they are not able to sin. How is this to be reconciled with our author's earlier rejection of his opponents' claim to be sinless?

Probably the opponents claimed that God's *sperma* dwelt in them and *as a consequence they were sinless.* What our author does is to reverse the function of the argument by changing the question the assertion answers. The question is not, as it was for the opponents, "who is sinless?" Answer: "those who possess God's *sperma*!" Rather the question is "how do you know who possesses God's *sperma*?" Answer: "the one who does righteousness, who loves his brother possesses God's *sperma*!" However, by accepting the language of his opponents at this point the author has adopted a form of words in 3:9 that is difficult to reconcile with 1:8, 10. The language of 3:9 is not drawn from John but is characteristic of the mystery religions; see Siegfried Schulz, article "σπέρμα, κτλ.," *TDNT* 7:545. This, together with the apparent contradiction of 1:8, 10 and the way our author has modified the assertion of 3:9 by setting up a test for the claim in the immediate context of the passage in which it has been embedded, indicates that the claim to possess God's *sperma* comes from the opponents. Reconciliation of the apparent contradiction is made possible by seeing that the overall argument of the passage 2:28–3:24, especially

3:4-10, is about how to recognize the children of God. The *claim* to have the *sperma* is not enough, nor is the *claim* to have the Spirit (4:1-6).

In none of the claims except 2 and 3 (1:8, 10) does our author reject the validity of the wording of the claim. What he does elsewhere is to question whether the claims are true *of his opponents*. In his understanding, the lives of his opponents demonstrate that the claims were not true of them. In thinking that they were, they evidently understood them in some way different from our author. Hence his criteria and critique are unlikely to have made any impression on them. In any case the critique was probably not aimed at them, but at his own adherents who had been disturbed by the schism. For this reason 1 John exhibits both polemical and paraenetic characteristics, because it was written to oppose the "heretics" and encourage the author's adherents. It did this by transmitting and interpreting the Johannine tradition. (See my *John, Witness and Theologian*, 112–13.)

Slogans 2 and 3 (1:8, 10) are rejected outright. Slogan 2, the claim to be sinless, is said to involve self-deception, and slogan 3 could only be held as true if God was a liar. There is no attempt to reinterpret them. For this reason 3:9 and 5:18 should not be understood in terms of the claims denied in 1:8, 10. Both 3:9 and 5:18 assert that "everyone born of God does not sin." According to 3:9 it is because God's *sperma* abides in the one born of God, whereas in 5:18 it is because *ho gennētheis ek tou theou tērei auton.* God's *sperma* is *ho gennētheis ek tou theou* in the thought of the opponents, though our author may have identified *ho gennētheis* with Christ. Perhaps, having used the opponents' terms, our author was arguing that those born of God are not able *to live in sin.* This could be the subtle point of the present tenses rather than the aorist, which would indicate a specific act of sin. The person born of God *hamartian ou poiei* because God's *sperma* is in him and *ou dynatai hamartanein* because he is born of God (3:9). The same point is made in 5:18, where it is asserted that everyone who is born of God *ouch hamartanei.* Such a position does not preclude that a person born of God might lapse into sin, and for such a person the community is urged to pray (5:16-17). In the conditional sentence of 5:16 the present participle is used of a particular sin. The specific act of sin is indicated by the use of the cognate accusative. The present participle indicates that the act was in process at the time of the action of the verb in the conditional clause. The sinner is seen (caught) in the act. Given the proximity of 5:18 to this discussion, it could be suggested that the *ouch hamartanei* there implies *pros thanaton.* But 3:9 is too far away for this assumption to work there. For an alternative solution see John Bogart, *Orthodox and Heretical Perfectionism in the Johannine Community as Evident in the First Epistle of John* (1976).

Bogart argues that perfectionism emerges from the ethical dualism of the Fourth Gospel, which has its roots in a Jewish apocalyptic world view. The world is divided into good and evil, which are defined in terms of those who confess or deny that Jesus is the One from above. Combined with this is the realized eschatology of the Fourth Gospel according to which the believer already was a child of the light and experienced eternal life. In this context the world was divided into the light and the darkness, belief and unbelief, eternal life and abiding death. This is the basis of what Bogart calls the orthodox perfectionism of 1 John. It grows out of the biblical understanding of God, the world as creation, and human beings as part of the creation but destined for eternal life.

Over against this position Bogart sees the emergence of heretical perfectionism, whether by the entry of those whose theology, anthropology, and soteriology were gnosticizing or by the believers' being subjected to gnosticizing influences in these areas. He is inclined to attribute the influences to Cerinthus (docetic christology) and Valentinian Gnosticism (anthropology and theology), while making use of Hans Jonas' understanding of the Gnostic anthropology. Fundamental to this position is the view that within the Gnostic is a divine spark and that the Gnostic is saved by nature. Thus heretical perfectionism is based on a Gnostic anthropology that was opposed by the author of 1 John (see especially 1:8, 10). This form of perfectionism was also susceptible to a disregard for an ethical manner of life because the Gnostic was already perfect by nature.

The author of 1 John denounced this form of perfectionism, restating the Johannine form in 3:6-10. Here the position of the opponents is qualified by the reference to abiding in God and being born of God. In addition, the author introduced the early Christian tradition of Christ's expiation for sin and a casuistic system that differentiates between mortal and non-mortal sins. While this may have dealt with heretical perfectionism, it is Bogart's view that the latter move also brought an end to Johannine perfectionism. The author of 1 John also attacked the docetic views of the opponents, insisting on the confession of Jesus Christ having come in the flesh.

In this way Bogart sees the author of 1 John rescuing the Johannine tradition from a sectarian situation in which the community and tradition were not only divided from the world but also from the mainstream of Christianity. He did this by refuting the Gnostic reading of John and at the same time modifying certain gnosticizing tendencies in the Gospel. Bogart may well be right in seeing interpretative tendencies in 1 John that made the Gospel more acceptable to the wider church. But some of these tendencies are already apparent in the Gospel, though they may belong to later strata of the Gospel tradition. His position is also marred by the use of later (second-century) Gnostic tradition to interpret and explain what is in 1 John. While there is a degree of similarity in the Gnostic texts, the danger of reading back later ideas into 1 John and then reading 1 John in the light of them has not been avoided. This probably means that we need to be satisfied with less precise answers to our questions. Surprisingly, Bogart makes little of the contrast between the Jewishness of the Gospel—not just the story but the assumptions the author makes of readers and their ability to understand a Jewish story and its scriptural context—and the absence of Jewish issues from the Epistles. The total absence of scriptural quotations stands in stark contrast to the Gospel. This evidence from within the Epistles does suggest a change in the makeup of the implied readers of the Epistles. See also the discussion of "sin" in the Introduction, 16.5.

FOR REFERENCE AND FURTHER STUDY

Beutler, Johannes. *Die Johannesbriefe*, 43–53.
Bogart, John. *Orthodox and Heretical Perfectionism in the Johannine Community as Evident in the First Epistle of John*. Missoula: Scholars, 1976.
Brooke, Alan England. *A Critical and Exegetical Commentary on the Johannine Epistles*, 13–29.
Brown, Raymond E. *The Epistles of John*, 191–246.
Dodd, Charles Harold. *The Johannine Epistles*, 19–29.
_____. "*Hilaskesthai*, Its Cognates, Derivatives and Synonyms in the Septuagint," *JTS* 32 (1931) 352–60.
Rensberger, David. *1 John, 2 John, 3 John*, 49–58.
Schnackenburg, Rudolf. *The Johannine Epistles*, 76–88.

## 1.1.2. *Response to the claims to know, abide, be in the light* (2:3-11)

3. And by this we know that we know him, if we keep his commandments.
4. The one who *claims*, "I know him," [and] not keeping his commandments, is a liar, and the truth is not in this person. 5. But whoever keeps his word, truly in this person the love of God is perfected. By this we know we are in him. 6. The one who *claims* to abide in him ought to walk in the same way as he walked. 7. Beloved, I am writing to you no new commandment, but an old commandment which you had from the beginning; the old commandment is the word that you heard. 8. Again I write a new commandment to you, which is true in him and in you, because the darkness is passing away and the true light already shines. 9. The one who claims to be in the light [while] hating his brother is in the darkness even now. 10. The person loving his brother abides in the light and there is no cause of stumbling in it. 11. But the person who hates his brother is in the darkness and walks in the darkness, and does not know where he goes, because the darkness has blinded his eyes.

3. *And by this we know that we know him, if we keep his commandments:* "By this
. . ." *(en toutǭ)* is an idiom found five times in John (4:37; 9:30; 13:35; 15:8;
16:30). Of these, only 13:35 provides a parallel for the ten distinctive uses in
1 John (2:3, 5c; 3:10, 16, 19, 24; 4:2, 9, 13; 5:2). Another five uses of *en toutǭ* in
1 John are not relevant because *en* has the sense of "in" and the phrase is not
made the basis of knowledge (2:4; 2:5b; 4:10, 17a, 17b). In the relevant references to the phrase the *en* is instrumental and should be translated as "by,"
"by this means." Of these, two uses of the phrase "by this means" appeal to
revelation rather than knowledge. But it is assumed that what is revealed is
known. In the first (3:10), "By this the children of God and the children of the
devil are revealed," the adjective *phanera* is used with the verb "to be," *estin.*
In Greek the neuter plural *(tekna)* takes a singular verb, here the third person
singular of the verb "to be." Another (4:9) uses the third person singular aorist
passive *ephanerōthē.* Appeal is made to the basis of the revelation of the love of
God, which also demonstrates the character of God's love. Brown *(The Epistles
of John* 248–49) notes that determining whether the construction points
forward or back to what has been said already depends on whether or not
there is a following subordinate clause or prepositional phrase related to the
*toutǭ.*

To these ten references may be added 4:6, which uses the preposition *ek* in
place of *en.* While the evidence of 1 John is not sufficient to make a rule, the
one case fits the recognition that this construction (using *ek toutou ginōskomen)*
refers back to what has already been written. There is also one instance (2:18)
of a similar use of "from which we know" *(hothen ginōskomen)* pointing back to
what has already been written.

In ten of the twelve relevant references *en toutǭ* [*ek toutou* in one case and
*hothen* in another] is followed by one of the tenses (indicative active) of the
verb "to know" *(ginōskein).* In these a test is provided, demonstrating the basis
and reality of the knowledge claimed. Seven of these ten references use the
first person plural present tense *ginōskomen* (2:3, 5c, 18; 3:24; 4:6, 13; 5:2) while
3:16 uses the first person plural perfect tense *(egnōkamen);* 3:19 uses the first
person plural future tense *(gnōsometha);* and 4:2 uses the second person plural
present tense *(ginōskete).*

Generally this construction comes at the beginning of a sentence (3:16; 4:2,
6, 13; 5:2). Once it follows "and" (2:3) with a possible second (textual uncertainty) following "and" (3:19), both at the beginning of a sentence; twice it follows a major break (semi-colon in 2:5, 18), and once it follows "and" after a
semi-colon break. This placement makes the construction prominent in the
sentence or clause. The prominence and frequency of the construction reinforces the recognition that claims to have knowledge were in dispute in the
historical context of the author. For this reason the author belabors criteria for
the establishment of genuine knowledge and for the identification of false
claims to "know."

There are two elements requiring clarification in the formula "By this we
*know.*" First, what is known needs to be indicated. This can be done straight-

forwardly where the accusative case indicates the object of knowledge: "love" in 3:16 and "the Spirit of God" in 4:2. But the author's dominant method is to use an epexegetical *hoti* clause to indicate what is known (see 2:3, 5; 3:19, 24; 4:13; 5:2). Second, the reference "by this" is often clarified by a second *hoti* clause: see 3:19-20; 4:13; 5:2 (and perhaps by *hotan* = *hoti ean*). Both clauses may be epexegetical, but because "by this" is instrumental, the second *hoti* is translated "because." A simpler alternative is to take the second *hoti* as causal. Either way the test signaled by "by this" is identified. This is true in the cases where what is known is not indicated by a *hoti* clause, so that there is only one *hoti* clause (3:16, and cf. 4:9, 10, 17). An alternative to this is the use of a conditional form (2:3) and once "from this" *(ek)*, 3:24.

The remaining four instances of *en toutǭ* are not followed by the verb "to know" (see 3:10; 4:9, 10, 17). The first of these establishes a criterion for recognizing the children of God and the children of the devil. But instead of saying "by this we know the children of God and the children of the devil," the author writes "in this the children of God and the children of the devil are revealed *(phanera)*." The criterion for distinguishing the children of God from the children of the devil has been built up (3:4-10) in the contrast between "doing righteousness" (3:10) and "doing sin" (3:4). The section concludes by identifying the person who does not do righteousness with the person who does not love his brother (3:10). That this identifies the children of the devil is supported by reference to Cain, who hated his brother and is said to be "of the Evil One," a child of the devil. Thus love of the brother is the mark of the children of God. In the remaining references (4:9, 10, 17) this formulation is used to clarify the nature of love. The focus on love in a controversial way suggests that what constituted love was a matter of dispute, as was the ethical obligation of the child of God to love "his brother."

These formulations straightforwardly state what the test indicated "by this" is about. In 3:10 it is about the way children of God and the children of the devil are revealed. The way itself needs to be identified, and "by this" refers directly to that way. In principle, "by this" can refer back to what has already been written or forward to what is yet to come. In the other three instances of this construction (4:9, 10, 17) the test or way in which "by this" refers is indicated by a following *hoti* clause. Without the *hoti* clause the context is the only guide to identify the test.

In 2:3 "We know (present tense) that *(hoti)* we [have come to] know (perfect tense) him." Here *hoti* follows a verb of knowing and indicates the content of what is known. The writer continues in the first person plural, including his readers with himself. Knowing "him" is not enough. The opponents have undermined any sense of assurance, and so 1 John has been written so that the readers may know that they know (cf. 5:13: 1 John was written "that *they may know* they have eternal life"). The distinct use of the two tenses is deliberate. Assurance depends on ongoing knowledge. We continue to know that we have come to know him. The perfect tense looks back to a moment when knowing him began, but asserts the ongoing effect of that coming to know.

This verb "to know" *(ginōskein)* is used 56 times in John, 25 times in 1 John, once in 2 John. Another verb *(eidenai)* is used 85 times in John, 15 times in

1 John, and once in 3 John. Older commentators argued that the first of these verbs refers to knowledge gained by experience while the latter refers to an immediacy and certitude of knowledge. This is not borne out by the Johannine evidence or the LXX, where the two verbs are used as equivalents. In John there is a preponderance of the use of *eidenai* in narrative. The two verbs are used equally in discourse passages, a total of thirty-five and thirty-six times each. Given the lack of narrative in the Epistles, we would expect that imbalance to be redressed. Because *ginōskein* is used only once in 2 John and *eidenai* once in 3 John, the discussion concerns 1 John, where the imbalance has been reversed. Both verbs are used, followed by *hoti*, to indicate the content of knowledge (*ginōskein hoti:* John 6:69; 8:28; 10:38; 16:19; 17:23, 25; 19:4; 21:17; 1 John 2:3, 5, 18, 29; 3:19, 24, 4:13; 5:2; *eidenai hoti:* John 3:2; 4:25, 42; 8:37; 9:20, 24, 25, 29; 11:22, 24, 42; 13:1, 3; 16:30; 19:28, 35; 20:14; 21:12, 15, 16, 17, 24; 1 John 2:21, 29; 3:2, 5, 14, 15; 5:13, 15 (2x), 18, 19, 20; 3 John 12). See especially John 21:15, 16, 17 for evidence of the interchangeability of the two verbs. Both verbs are used to express knowing the truth (John 8:32; 1 John 2:21; 2 John 1). In 1 John there is a formal difference in use. Only *ginōskein* is used in formulae to produce a test for knowledge expressed in terms of "by this we know" (*en toutǭ:* 2:3, 5; 3:16, 19, 24; 4:2, 13; 5:2), "from whence" = "therefore" (*hothen:* 2:18), or "from this" (*ek toutou:* 4:6). This constitutes the difference between the uses of the two verbs in 1 John.

Even this difference is minimized by constructions like 3:14 using *oidamen:* "We know [that] (*hoti*) we have passed out of death into life, because (*hoti*) we love the brothers." Here the first *hoti* is epexegetical, indicating the content of what "we know," and need not be translated. But the second *hoti* is causal and needs to be translated. This could just as well have been expressed: "By this (*en toutǭ*) we know [that] (*hoti*) we have passed out of death into life, (*hoti*) [because] we love the brothers." No different kind of knowledge or means of knowing is implied by the different verbs. In this construction both uses of *hoti* may be epexegetical, the first indicating what "we know" and the second the means of knowledge, that is, what is meant by "by *this*." Here the use of "by this" (*en* with the dative) is instrumental. Alternatively, the second *hoti* may be causal. Either way the evidence that "we love the brothers" demonstrates that we have passed from death to life. Even the difference in tense between *ginōskomen* and *oidamen* does not seem to be significant in explaining the exclusive use of *ginōskomen* in this formula.

"We have come to know *him*." To whom does this refer? It is either to "God" who is light (1:5), or to Jesus Christ the righteous (2:2). The proximity to v. 2 makes the latter attractive, but the momentum of the construction is to what follows and this could provide the clue to identify "him." Brown (*The Epistles of John* 249) argues that the reference must be to God because "All the secessionist-inspired claims in 1:5–2:11 concern God." He also argues that the opening *kai* (2:3) resumes the previous opening *kai* of 1:5. Thus 1:5 proclaimed the message that God is light, and 2:3-4 now tells how we may confirm that we know God. But *kai* is such a common word that it is not an adequate marker to signal a resumption. Does it follow that God is in view because the claim to know "him" and reference to "his *commandments*" must concern the same person? Certainly in 3:19-24 reference to "his commandments" (3:22, 24) means God's commandments and in both 2:3 and 3:24 the author speaks of keeping *(tērōn)* his commandments. Even this is inconclusive because (in 2:7-8) 1 John moves from "commandments" to "commandment" (as does 3:23), and discussion turns to the foundational command, which is also a "new commandment." That 1 John is here reworking tradition of Jesus' new commandment (John 13:34-35) seems clear (see below on 2:7-11). That the author here is thinking of the commandments/commandment of Jesus is further supported by 2:6, where the claim to abide in "him" is tested. Those who claim to abide in "him" *(en autǭ)* ought to walk the way *(kathōs)* he *(ekeinos* = Christ) walked. See the emphatic use of *ekeinos* of Jesus, *all in the nominative case*, in 2:6; 3:3, 5, 7, 16; 4:17.

Some authors claim that the different pronouns *(autǭ* and *ekeinos)* used here (2:6) confirm that the claims of 2:3, 4, 6, are to know and abide in God, the latter being confirmed by walking as Christ walked. But the language is not as clear as this argument suggests. The emphatic uses of *ekeinos* of Jesus, all in the nominative case, do not preclude non-emphatic references to Jesus using other pronouns, especially in other cases than the nominative. Further, the emphatic use of *ekeinos* in John 8:42 by Jesus to refer to the Father who sent him and in 8:44 to refer to the devil ("he was a murderer from the beginning") makes the point that the demonstrative pronoun is not person particular but emphatic in use. It is coincidental that all uses in the nominative case in 1 John refer to Jesus. The only other use in 1 John (5:16) is feminine genitive (following *peri)* and singular, "concerning that sin." Thus there is no reason to suggest that non-emphatic pronouns may not refer to Jesus in 1 John.

Still, there may be a reason why there is a lack of clarity over who is the object of knowledge and in whom the opponents claim to abide and whose commandments are referred to as "his." Even in John we may get the sense that just as Jesus gave the words, given to him by the Father, to the disciples (John 17:7-8), so he gave the commandment/commandments, given to him by the Father, to the disciples. Some commentators suggest that there is no sharp distinction between God and Christ (Father and Son) in the passage under discussion. Certainly the author has not made any distinction clear. An added reason for this could be that the opponents claimed to know and abide in God, while 1 John located that knowledge and abiding in his Son Jesus Christ.

In 1 John there is a variation of reference to commandment and commandments as there is in John and 2 John. The word *(entolē)* is used 11 times in John (six times singular and five plural); 14 times in 1 John (seven times singular and seven plural), and four times in 2 John (three times in the singular, vv. 4, 5, 6, and once plural, v. 6). A prominent idea is "keeping *(tērein)* the commandments," four times in John (14:15, 21; 15:10 [2x]) and five times in 1 John (2:3, 4; 3:22, 24; 5:3, plus a reference to "whenever . . . we *do* his commandments"). In John, Jesus speaks of having received "this commandment from my Father" (10:18). He refers to the commandment that "the Father who sent me has given to me" so that "precisely as *(kathōs)* the Father has said to me, this is what I say" (12:49, 50). He says, "But that the world may know that I love the Father, even as the Father gave me commandment, that is exactly what I do"

(14:31). If Jesus received a commandment from the Father and demonstrated his love by keeping that commandment exactly, he delivers a commandment to his disciples (13:34), and their love for him is to be demonstrated in *keeping his commandments* (14:15, 21). In John 14:15, 31 and 15:10 Jesus says, "If you keep my commandments you will abide in my love, even as *(kathōs)* I have kept the commandments of my Father and abide in his love." This implies that the giving and keeping of the commandments express mutual love between the Father and the Son and between Jesus and his disciples. In John it is clearly Jesus' commandment/commandments that the disciples are called on to keep (13:34-35; 14:15, 21; 15:10, 12), while in 1 John it is unclear whether it is the commandments of God or of Jesus. It may in fact be the author's strategy to take the commandment given by Jesus during his lifetime and associate it with God. If the opponents disregarded the authority of Jesus' earthly life, this might explain why 1 John blurs the distinction between the Father and the Son. In so doing he claimed the full authority of God for the commandment of Jesus and the example of his earthly life.

4. *The one who claims, "I know him," [and] not keeping his commandments, is a liar, and the truth is not in this person:* For the quotation formula, see on 1:6 above. A. E. Brooke and B. F. Westcott think this formula (2:4, 6, 9) expresses a more specific threat than the three claims of ch. 1. Brown has some sympathy with this view but expresses his position differently. He thinks the three claims of ch. 1 contain the substance of the claims, but not in the words of the opponents and that the case for quotation is more likely in the claims of ch. 2. Contrary to this view, the claims of 1:6, 8, 10; 2:4, and 4:20 are expressed using quotation formulae. See the Notes on 1:6.

*"I know him":* The object of knowledge is uncertain. Is it Jesus, mentioned in 2:1-2, or God, referred to in 1:5-7, 10? On the "liar" see John 8:44, 55 and 1 John 1:10; 2:22; 4:20; 5:10.

5. *But whoever keeps his word, truly in this person the love of God is perfected. By this we know we are in him:* "Whoever keeps his word" is formally like the opening of 3:17. It is separate from the main clause, but by its placement at the beginning of the sentence it gains emphasis. Compare "keeping his word" with "if we keep his commandments," 2:3. The motif of keeping Jesus' word (John 8:51, 52, 55; 14:23, 24; 15:20; [17:6]) or commandments (14:15, 21; 15:10) is prominent in the Gospel. In 1 John every use of *tērein* but one (5:18) is about keeping the commandments (2:3, 4, 3:22, 24; 5:3) or Jesus' word (2:5). 1 John lacks any reference to the community being kept by God or Jesus from the harmful effects of the power of evil (the Evil One) such as we find in John 17:11, 12, 15. This is a little surprising, given the concern that the community was being disrupted by the teaching of the opponents, and the warning about the corrupting power of the world (2:15-17). As an alternative to this, 1 John asserts that "our faith overcomes the world," that is, "the one who believes Jesus is the Son of God overcomes the world," 5:4-5. This is a bold front in the face of the force and threat of the denial by the opponents (2:22-23), which is also expressed as a refusal to confess that Jesus Christ has come in the flesh (4:2; cf. 2 John 7). On the other hand, it is a statement aimed at bolstering the resistance of the faithful.

Reference to "the love *of God*" is ambiguous because the genitive ("of God") can mean God's love for . . . or human love of God. The context must supply the clues to enable the reader to choose which of these meanings is intended.

The love of God "is perfected" *(teteleiōtai)*. The verb is related to *telos*, which refers to the end or goal. It is used four times in 1 John (2:5; 4:12, 17, 18), each time in relation to perfection of love. The adjective is used once in 4:18, "Perfect love casts out fear."

Love terminology is characteristic of the Johannine Gospel and Epistles. While two verbs "to love" are used without distinction in John, only *agapan* appears in the Epistles, 31 times (28 times in 1 John) and the noun *(agapē)* is used 21 times (18 in 1 John) and "beloved" *(agapētoi)* 10 times. This concentration of use marks out the Johannine writings from the rest of the NT and other Greek literature of the period. But it is not just the frequency of use that needs to be noted. The Johannine writings, especially 1 John, make love a theological category derived from the action and character of God. On this basis it becomes an ethical category, placing humans under obligation to love.

6. *The one who claims to abide in him ought to walk in the same way as he walked:* The construction here is an instance of indirect reporting. Unlike 1:6, 8, 10; 2:4, which purport to report the words of those who make the claim, here (and in 2:9) only the substance of the claim is reported. The claim is expressed by the use of the preposition "in" (followed by noun or pronoun in the dative case) with a present infinitive *(en autō menein)*. See the Notes on 1:6.

On "abiding" in God see also 2:24, 27, 28; 3:6. On God abiding in the believer see 4:12, and on mutual abiding see 3:24; 4:13, 15, 16. An examination of all these passages suggests that God abides in those who abide in God, so that even when only one aspect of abiding is mentioned, as here the claim to abide in God, mutual abiding is implied if the claim is true. If, according to 1 John, God abides in those who abide in God, that need not mean that those who claimed to abide in God also claimed that God abides in them. They may not have adopted this aspect of thought, which we find as an expression of the author's view in 1 John.

On the obligation *(opheilei)* to an ethical response see John 13:14; 1 John 3:16; 4:11, and cf. 3 John 8, which uses a different motivation for the obligation. Here there is a link also to the Johannine *kathōs* ethic (John 13:15, 34; 15:12; 1 John 2:27; 3:3, 7; 4:17). On "walking" as a metaphor for the manner of life see 1:6 above. On the use of *ekeinos* see 3:3, 5, 7, 16; 4:17; 5:16 and the Notes on 2:3. All but 5:16 (a genitive reference "concerning that [sin]") are nominative case and refer to Jesus. It would be wrong to conclude that Jesus cannot be referred to by another pronoun, as the nominative use of the demonstrative is emphatic. The use of *ekeinos* in the emphatic nominative case, of the Father (John 8:42) and of the devil (John 8:44) is also a warning against the assumption that the Johannine use of this pronoun is exclusively reserved for Jesus. While the Gospel and 1 John may not be by the same author, the point is that *ekeinos* is emphatic rather than person particular.

7. *Beloved, I am writing to you no new commandment, but an old commandment which you had from the beginning; the old commandment is the word that you heard:* For "beloved" see 2:7; 3:2, 21; 4:1, 7, 11; 3 John 1, 2, 5, 11. It is used a total of 61 times in the NT, but not in the Gospel of John. In each of the Synoptic Gospels it is used three times with indirect or direct reference to Jesus, and there is a dependence on Isa 42:1. This may underlie the description of Jesus as *monogenēs* in John 1:18. More relevant to 1 John is the use of this form of address in other Epistles, especially in opening and closing salutations (seven times in Romans, six times in 1–2 Corinthians, twice in Ephesians, twice in Philippians, four times in Colossians, twice in 1–2 Thessalonians, once in 2 Timothy, twice in Philemon, once in Hebrews, three times in James, twice in 1 Peter, six times in 2 Peter, three times in Jude). On "a new commandment" see John 13:34 and 1 John 2:8. On "I write to you" see above on 2:1. On "which you have from the beginning" see above on 1:1. On "the word that you [have] heard (aorist tense)" see 2:24; 3:11; 2 John 6.

8. *Again I write a new commandment to you, which is true in him and in you, because the darkness is passing away and the true light already shines:* "Again" *(palin)* = from another point of view. On "I write to you" see above on 2:1. The reiteration of this statement in 2:7, 8 reinforces the idea of going over the same ground again, but with a difference.

   The commandment is *kainē*, not *neos*. The latter expresses the idea of the young, while the former stresses a qualitative newness. It is not frequently used, only twice in John, once of the new commandment (13:34) and once of a new tomb (19:41). The latter does not refer to a freshly hewn out tomb, but one in which no one had ever been laid. Both uses in 1 John (2:7, 8) and the single use in 2 John (5) are references to the new commandment. It is in Revelation (nine times) that this word reveals its distinctive character for 1 John. In Rev 2:17; 3:12 (2x); 5:9; 14:3; 21:1 (2x), 2, 5 we read of the "new name," "new Jerusalem," the city of God, "a new heaven and a new earth," and God who says, "Behold, I make all things new."

   *which (ho) is true (alēthes):* The relative pronoun is neuter gender, as is the adjective *(alēthes)*. Of the 26 uses of this adjective in the NT, 14 are in John, two in 1 John and one in 3 John. The neuter gender poses a problem as the relative pronoun probably refers to the new commandment (feminine!). See the problem of the neuter relative pronouns in 1:1, 3. This adjective indicates what corresponds with reality. Given this single use in 1 John we need to look at the more frequent use in John to clarify its meaning. The most frequent use in John is reference to "true witness": 5:31, 32; 8:13, 14, 17; 21:24; see also 3 John 12.

   There is a textual variant that reads "which is true in him and in us *(hēmin)*." This reading is much less well attested than "in you (plural) *(hymin)*." Given that the inclusive use of the first person plural is expected, "in you" as the more difficult and better attested reading is to be accepted.

   *the darkness is passing away (paragetai):* See also above on 1:5. The same verb is used in 2:17 to say that the world is passing away. This suggests that the darkness and the world, in the sense of 2:17, have close to the same meaning.

*the true light already shines (to phōs to alēthinon ēdē phainei):* These words are reminiscent of John 1:5, 9. In John 1:5 there is reference to the light shining *(phainei)* and John 1:9 speaks of the true light *(to phōs to alēthinon).* Of the 28 uses of *alēthinos* in the NT, nine are in John and four in 1 John. Of the four uses in 1 John each has a reference to the revelation of the divine reality. Elsewhere in John *phainein* is used only in John 5:35. The use there is quite different from the close similarity in John 1:5 (especially with the 1:9 connection) and 1 John 2:8.

9. *The one who claims to be in the light [while] hating his brother is in the darkness even now:* For the grammatical construction used to make the claim, see on 2:6 above. The term "brother" as a metaphor for believers is not common in John (20:17; 21:23). Elsewhere in John the word is used of physical family relations, including the brothers of Jesus (see John 1:40, 41; 2:12, 6:8; 7:3, 5, 10; 11:2, 19, 21, 23, 32). Mark 3:35 provides a precedent in the teaching of Jesus for extending metaphors of Jesus' family relations to believers. In Acts and the Epistles the use of the term "brother" for fellow believers becomes common, especially in the plural and in addressing believers directly. In this use 1 John and 3 John stand firmly in the early Christian Epistle tradition. See 1 John 15 times (2:9, 10, 11; 3:10, 12 [2x], 13, 14, 15, 16, 17; 4:20 [2x], 21; 5:16); 3 John three times (3, 5, 10); Romans 19 times; 1 Corinthians 38 times; 2 Corinthians 12 times; Galatians 11 times; Ephesians twice; Philippians nine times; Colossians five times; 1 Thessalonians 19 times; 2 Thessalonians eight times; 1 Timothy three times; 2 Timothy once; Philemon four times; Hebrews 10 times; James 18 times; 1 Peter once; 2 Peter twice; Jude once; Revelation five times. The frequency in 1 John and 3 John is comparable to that in 1 Corinthians and James. In 1 John all references to brothers occur in the context of the discussion of loving and hating the brother, except perhaps 5:16.

   Yet the use of the masculine "brothers" without any equivalent "sisters" poses a problem, especially in 1 John where similarly gender-biased terms are used in address to "fathers" but not "mothers," "young men" but not "young women." We may feel that this is simply an oversight resulting from the time of 1 John. To some extent this is true. Given the place of women in early Christian communities, it is perhaps surprising that their presence is not taken into account in such writings as 1 John. Interestingly, 2 John is addressed to a church, or circle of house churches, under the metaphor of "the elect lady and her children."

   On "hating" *(misein)* see John 3:20; 7:7; 12:25; 15:18 (2x), 19, 23, 24, 25; 17:14; 1 John 2:9, 11; 3:13, 15; 4:20. Thus 15 of the 38 uses in the NT are found in John and 1 John. In John and 1 John hate is almost exclusively the characteristic of the world of darkness. Only John 12:25 falls outside this use: "The person who loves his life loses it and the person who hates his life in this world guards it for eternal life." This is an altogether different use of love and hate. On the "darkness" see above on 1:5 and 1:6.

10. *The person loving his brother abides in the light and there is no cause of stumbling in it:* On "scandal," "cause of stumbling" see the Interpretation. Only here in the Gospel and Epistles of John is *skandalon* used (once in Rev 2:14). The cognate

verb *(skandalizein)* is used in John 6:61; 16:1. It is unclear whether the reference is to a cause of stumbling for "him" or whether the cause in him makes others stumble. Because *autǭ* may be masculine or neuter, the meaning may be "there is no cause of stumbling in it" or "in him." The masculine reading may be suggested by the Johannine use of "to be in," which almost always involves a person as either subject or object. This reading hangs too much weight on "almost always" because the neuter reading is suggested by the proximity of "he abides in the light" *(tō phōti)* and the antithetic parallelism between vv. 10-11. The blinding effect of the darkness leads to stumbling. There is a cause of stumbling in the darkness (2:11). There is no cause of stumbling in it (the light), a sense that finds support in John 11:9, though *ou proskoptei* is used there, not *skandalon . . . ouk estin* (thus Schnackenburg, *The Johannine Epistles* 108).

11. *But the person who hates his brother is in the darkness and walks in the darkness, and does not know where he goes, because the darkness has blinded his eyes:* To be in the darkness has two levels of clarification. It is to walk in the darkness and such a person "does not know where he goes." This clarifies what it means to "walk in the darkness." The darkness has blinded his eyes: see John 12:40; 2 Cor 4:4. On this see my "The Quotation of Scripture and Unbelief in John 12:36b-43" and the Excursus: The Power of Darkness and the Lure of the World below.

    *does not know (ouk oiden):* For the first time this verb "to know" is used in 1 John. See the Notes on v. 3.

## INTERPRETATION

### *The love command as a response to the claims to know him, to abide in him, to be in the light.*

A foundational statement of the (gospel) message (1:5) that focuses on God introduces the first set of claims (1:6, 8, 10). This provides a basis for dealing with those claims. The second set of claims (2:4, 6, 9) is introduced by appeal to the place of the foundational commandment(s) in the life of the community (2:3) as a basis for dealing with the second set of claims. The first group of claims, introduced by the quotation formula "If we claim . . ." implies that the lies are within the community, perhaps even among its leaders. The second group of claims is introduced by the quotation formula "The person who claims. . . ." This formula implies that such claims are actually being made. This is no less true whether the formula is "If we claim . . ." or "If any one claims. . . ." The difference is that the first group locates the claim within the community, perhaps even within its leadership. This is the force of the "we." The conditional "if" does not, in this instance, indicate uncertainty about the occurrence of the claim. Rather it is the first part of a conditional sentence, the second part of which spells out what follows *when* the conditions outlined in the first part occur. The claims introduced by these quotation formulae provide important evidence of the author's opponents and their continuing influence. See the discussion of the profile of the opponents in the Introduction and the Notes on 1:6.

That **2:3** belongs with what follows is generally recognized. A. E. Brooke notes that "By this" *(en toutǭ)* usually points forward (Brooke, *Commentary* 9, 30), a view with which Raymond E. Brown agrees with some qualifications (Brown, *The Epistles of John* 248–49) and certainly adopts in this instance. Apart from grammatical considerations, v. 3 introduces the commandments, mentioned for the first time in 1 John in this verse, a theme that continues in 2:4, 7, 8. See also 3:22-24; 4:21; 5:2, 3; 2 John 4-6. Indeed, 2:7 relates the commandments to the foundational message, hence to the proclamation "God is light," thus confirming the unity of 1:5–2:11. Thus 1:5 is a bridge between the Prologue and what follows.

The fourth claim **(2:4)** is introduced by a test that already shows what falsifies or confirms the claim. For the first time 1 John uses the expression "by this we know" (cf. 2:5), drawing attention to one of the formulae used in developing "the tests of life." In the statement of purpose (5:13) we are told, "I have written these things to you that you may know *(hina eidēte)* that you have eternal life." In this context it is not enough to have eternal life (John 20:31); there is a need to know. Here the author seeks to establish a test so that the readers may know that they know God.

Knowing *God* is the key to eternal life (John 17:3), but this is inseparably bound up with Jesus Christ, as is clear in John 17:3; 20:31, and 1 John 5:13. For this reason 2:3 does not make clear whether God or Christ is in view when it asserts "we know him." If Christ is in view it must be the heavenly Christ, as an affirmation of knowing the historical Jesus makes no sense in this context. See the Notes on 2:3. Nevertheless, the claim to "know him" is tested here by keeping his commandments, and the one in focus was given during Jesus' earthly life. In 1 John there is no demand to keep the commandments of the Jewish Law. Indeed, commandments can narrow to the singular command (3:22, 23) or expand again from the singular (double commandment of 3:23) to the plural (3:24). In 3:23 the double command is to "believe in the name of *his* Son Jesus Christ and to love one another as *he* gave us commandment." This implies that God gave the double commandment concerning *his* Son.

In 1 John the love command is grounded in the belief that Jesus is the Son of the Father and that his earthly human life revealed the Father's love (4:7-12). It is this complex of thought that makes it likely that the author of 1 John also has Jesus in view in 2:3-6. The relationship of the Son to the Father means that to speak of the Son is to speak of the Father and the action of the Son can be spoken of as the action of the Father. According to 1 John 4:2-3 the opponents refused to confess that Jesus Christ has come in the flesh. The probability is that they claimed to know the heavenly Christ and to abide in him but dismissed any significant connection with his earthly life, including the love command.

In John 14:15 Jesus told his disciples: "If you love me, keep my commandments." In John, Jesus' commandment also expands into his commandments, just as commandments here (1 John 2:3-4) contract to a singular commandment (2:7-8), which is clearly the love command (2:9-11). Again (2:6), the claim to abide in him is tested by the way he (*ekeinos* = Christ) walked. The same problem exists here. Is the claim to abide in God or in Christ? If it is in Christ it is obviously a present relationship with the exalted Christ that is in view. That claim too is tested by the way Jesus lived his earthly life. But again the distinction between God and Christ may not be crucial because of the understanding of the Father-Son relationship in 1 John. The one implies the other, but in 1 John this works from the point of view of the Son, implying that the Father is in the action of the Son, that the Father is known in the action of the Son (see 4:7-12).

A more likely alternative is that the opponents claimed to know God and to abide in God (2:3-6), and that the author of 1 John responded by tying the possibility of knowing and abiding in God to the reality of believing God's Son, Jesus Christ, and loving one another. See the notes on 2:3 for a discussion of the evidence in support of this position.

That "we have come to know (perfect tense) him" is affirmed. What has been undermined is the assurance of that knowledge. The tests of life are put forward to confirm it. So we have the expression, "by this we can go on knowing (present tense) that we have come to know God." The test referred to as "by this," is "if we keep his commandments." In principle this has already established the test for the claim that is yet to be stated in 2:4. At the same time, what these commandments involve is yet to be made clear. See what follows in 2:4-5, 7-8; 3:22, 23, 24; 4:21; 5:2, 3 and the Notes on 2:3.

The *fourth* claim is the first in the new series of three introduced by the quotation formula "The person who says . . ." (*ho legōn*), 2:4, 6, 9. In 2:4, as in the first three claims (1:6, 8, 10), the quotation formula is followed by *hoti* and discourse in the first person to mark the quotation as direct speech. The fifth and sixth claims (2:6, 9) lack the following *hoti*, using in its place a present infinitive with the preposition *en* and a noun in the dative case. In these cases only the substance of the claim is apparent.

Whereas in v. 3 the assurance was that "we know him," the claim reported in v. 4 is "I know him" (also perfect tense). The shift to the singular might be critical given that v. 3 developed the test in relation to the community affirmation "we know him." Certainly 1 John implies that the opponents have rejected the tradition upon which the community was established. Hence 1 John appeals to the foundational message. If keeping the commandments is the ground of assurance that "we know him" (v. 3), failure to keep the commandments reveals that the one who claims to know him is a liar. See 2:22; 4:20. The accusation that the opponents are "liars" comes with the charge of self-deception, "we deceive ourselves," in 1:8. In a Jewish context the charge of deceiving the people is very serious. Here the opponents are said to deceive themselves and to be liars. The question might be asked whether, in the view of the author of 1 John, they willingly deceived themselves or, on the contrary, whether the author knew that what he called lies they believed to be true. This is almost certainly the case whether or not the author of 1 John recognized it. The connection with 1:8 may suggest that he did. In each case, with the liar and the self-deceiver, the author says "the truth is not in us/this person."

Having stated the negative results of the test, the author now **(2:5)** states the positive results with "whoever keeps his word." Placing this relative clause at the beginning gives emphasis to the condition to be fulfilled if the love of God is to be perfected. It is also the condition to be fulfilled to provide a proper ground for knowing that "we are in him."

The phrase "whoever keeps his word" is quite indefinite (cf. John 3:16). There is no condition required other than to "keep his word." The same verb for keeping is used as in v. 3, but the object of keeping there is "his commandments." Although "his word" probably has the sense of the ethical demands or commandments, the use of "his word" again opens the question: who is in view, Jesus or God? Keeping his commandments, his word, soon becomes the foundational commandment. From the perspective of 1 John this is not new, though in John 13:34-35 it is introduced as new and 1 John 2:7 shows awareness of this. Here too that commandment is said to be "the word that you heard." Indeed, 1 John also recognizes that the foundational commandment continues to be new in that it is being realized and kept as the darkness disintegrates and the true light shines. The shining of the true light is the realization of the command to "love one another as I have loved you" (John 13:34; cf. 15:12). The shining of the true light is seen in the reality of love, while the disintegration of the darkness is evidenced as love overcomes hatred (2:7-11).

As for the one who keeps his word (command, see 2:7) truly *(alēthōs)*, the love of God *(hē agapē tou theou)* is perfected *(teteleiōtai)* in that person. The actuality of the fulfillment is stressed, as is the particularity of the person in whom it is fulfilled. It is "in this person," the one who keeps his (God's or Jesus') word. That word is the foundational command: "Love one another as *(kathōs)* I have loved you." An important question is whether the genitive in "the love *of* God" is objective (love for God) or subjective (God's love for us). From the phrase itself it is not possible to answer the question. Only the context can help. The immediate context shows that the evidence 1 John is looking for is love for the brother (2:9-11). In the broader context the foundational commandment grounds the love command (the imperative) "love one another" in the affirmation (the indicative) "as *(kathōs)* I have loved you." The use of *kathōs* here has a double sense, indicating the manner of love in the love command but also the ground of the love command, "because I have loved you." But in 1 John the loving action of Jesus is taken to be the revelation of the love of God, 4:10-12. God's love in sending his Son as the expiation of our sins is then said to be the ground of the love command. "Beloved, if God loved us like this, we also ought *(opheilomen)* to love one another. No one has ever seen God; if we love one another God abides in/with *(en)* us and *his* love is perfected in us *(teteleiōmenē en hēmin estin).*" The connection is clear. God's love for us is perfected, it reaches its proper goal when we love one another.

"By this we know we are in him": see the Notes on 2:3. The *hoti* following verbs of knowing is normally epexegetical, indicating what is known. It does not need to be translated. There is no second *hoti* or relative clause following the formula "by this we know" because the ground of this knowledge is given in what precedes the statement. It is in keeping his word that God's love is made perfect in this person. This is the evidence that demonstrates that "we are in him." The test of the fifth claim, to *abide* in him, also seems to be relevant to the claim to *be in* him, but linguistically it is linked to the fifth claim. The proximity of this test to the fifth claim provides a transition from the fourth claim to the fifth. What validates the claim "I know him" provides assurance so that "we know we are *in* him." Is the fifth claim *"to abide* in him" simply a restatement with a new test, or does the addition of "to abide" add a new dimension?

The *fifth* claim **(2:6)** is expressed using the quotation formula followed by an infinitive with the preposition "in" *(en)*. While the test that verifies the claim is clear, there is no statement of what falsifies it, which we have come to expect from the pattern set up by the previous four claims. But the falsification is clear. It is the failure to pass the test of walking as he walked.

"The person who claims to abide in him *(en autǭ)* ought to walk in the same way as he *(ekeinos)* walked." Here Jesus' life is certainly the point of reference *(ekeinos)*. The test is "to walk (present infinitive) in the same way as he walked (aorist)." The aorist tense draws attention to the historical life of Jesus in the past, leaving an example to be followed. The present infinitive implies a continuous emulation of the example of Jesus. The argument that the claim to abide in him *(autǭ)* must be a reference to God, distinguished from Jesus *(ekeinos)*, is shaky. (See 3:5 where both *ekeinos* and *en autǭ* refer to Jesus.) The use of the demonstrative *(ekeinos)* is for emphasis and does not exclude the identification of the person in other prepositions. See the Notes on 2:3, and compare 3:3, 6, 7. In these passages it is not clear that God is spoken of in addition to Jesus. The theme of abiding in Jesus is found in the Gospel (15:4), and the opponents' claim to abide in God or the exalted Jesus might be met by a call to walk as he (Jesus) walked during his earthly life.

An important theme emerges in this verse: it is the grounding of Johannine ethics in God's love revealed in Jesus. That love lays the recipient under obligation, and this is expressed in 1 John in "we ought" (*opheilomen*, 4:11); or "he ought" (*opheilei*). Further, the character of the obligation is demonstrated by the life of Jesus, "to walk as *(kathōs)* he walked" and is summed up in the love command, "love one another as *(kathōs)* I have loved you." The command has left its mark on 1 John, which has developed a *kathōs* ethic, 2:6; 3:3, 7; 4:17. In that ethic *kathōs* draws attention to both the motivation—love one another *because* I have loved you (see 4:11)—and the manner: love *in the same way as* I have loved you (see BDF).

Instead of treating the fifth claim, vv. 7-8 prepare the way for the sixth claim, which is dealt with extensively in vv. 7-11. Thus 2:7 is a departure from the form of dealing with the opponents' claims to this point. Both here and in 2:1 the direct address to the readers in endearing terms reminds us that the polemic against the views of the opponents is actually addressed to those who remained loyal to the author. A new form of address is introduced here. "Beloved" (*agapētoi;* see also 3:2, 21; 4:1, 7, 11) is used in the plural form in addressing members of the Johannine circle of house churches (in the singular see 3 John 1, 2, 5, 11, addressed to Gaius). The suitability of this transition soon becomes clear as the subject turns explicitly to the love command, which uses the cognate verb *(agapan)* related to the noun "beloved." That the author clarifies the status of this command may help to explain the emphasis on the foundational, what is from the beginning, in 1 John. Though it was *instituted* as the new commandment by Jesus (John 13:34), 1 John asserts that it is not new but old, "which you have had from the beginning; the old commandment is the word that you heard." What was new from the perspective of Jesus' ministry is now deemed old, part of the foundational tradition upon which the life of the community was built. They know it, they have heard it. It is not new. The reason for this emphasis is almost certainly that the opponents are "progressive"; they are introducing what is new. Against such a position 2 John 9 asserts that "Every one going beyond *(proagōn)* and not abiding in the teaching of Christ does not have God." The teaching about the Spirit of Truth, the Paraclete (John 14:15-18, 25-26; 15:26-27; 16:7-11, and especially 16:12-15) suggests new teaching (see especially 16:12-13), and the opponents might have been led on by this emphasis. But 1 John returns to a more conservative position, focusing on the life (2:6) and word (2:7) of Jesus as a correction to a teaching that was new. Compare the focus in John 17 on the word of Jesus, which is to keep them from the corrupting power of the world. There is no reference to the Spirit in John 17. See my *The Quest for the Messiah* 428–35. Consequently there is an emphasis on the origin of this commandment in the past, in the ministry of Jesus. It is nothing new. It is the command, the word that "you (plural) have already heard (aorist tense)."

Yet (again), the commandment is new (2:8). The author knows that in the tradition this commandment is transmitted as "a new commandment." Having established that the commandment belongs to the foundational period of the community, our author now sets out to show what is always new about it. What is new is that the command is realized "in him," that is, in Jesus, and "in you (plural)," in the life of the believing community. The form of the new command proclaims the actuality of love in the life of Jesus. 1 John treats that love as the eschatological revelation of the divine reality. The revelation of that love in Jesus is the ground of the obligation to love one another. It is more than that: it is the source that actualizes the fulfillment of the command. So it can be said that it is true, that is, it is realized in him and in you. This reaffirms in a new way what is said in 2:5. "Whoever keeps his word, truly in this person God's love reaches its true goal." It finds expression in love for one another. This is the evidence that the darkness is being dissolved (see 2:17) by the shining of the true light. We are yet to learn that the darkness is identified with hating the brother and the true light is manifest in the love for the brother (2:9-11). Thus the author of 1 John sees the life of love in the community as evidence of the eschatological work of God in making all things new.

The *sixth* claim **(2:9)**, like the fifth, is not a quotation. The substance of the claim is expressed in a construction using the infinitive of the verb "to be." It is the claim "to be in the light." Given that we have already encountered the claim to have union with God (1:6; 2:6), who is light, it is not surprising to find a claim to be in the light. From this perspective what is surprising is that 1 John uses the test of walking in the darkness to falsify the claim of union with God. It might be noted that the message that God is light is no part of the claim to have union with God, but was introduced earlier by the author, perhaps to provide a basis for falsifying the claims of the opponents to have union with God. This proposal might work on an isolated reading of 1:5-6, but it is ruled out by 2:9. The opponents also claimed to be in the light. If this is the case, how can they be shown to be walking in darkness and thus falsify their claim? The falsification of the sixth claim is the key to working this out. "The one claiming to be in the light and at the same time hating his brother is in the darkness even until now."

It is clear that the language of loving and hating **(2:10-11)** is chosen to express very clearcut and opposite positions. In this regard, failing to love is hating. There is no intermediate position. The language is specific in both cases. It is loving or hating *his* brother. The one is evidence of being in the light, the other is the evidence of being in, or walking in the darkness (cf. 1:6-7).

This interpretation of the implications of light and darkness is the work of the author of 1 John, not the view of the opponents. In other words, the author tests the claims of the opponents against the standard of his understanding, hoping to carry his readers with him. It is not at all clear that the opponents understood light and darkness in this way. To be in union with God, who is light, meant to be in the light. With this *language* both sides could agree. But for the opponents this seems to have been understood exclusively in terms of union with God. It may express an understanding of sharing in the "light nature" of God.

Even though the darkness is passing away, the person who hates his brother is in the darkness (2:8, 9) and walks in the darkness (2:9). The *power* of darkness is manifest in the hate. Those who hate are blinded by the darkness. The power of darkness is aggressive and active, with the consequence that they do not know where they are going. That is what it means to walk in darkness. The person who hates, in one sense, does not know what he or she is doing. Such a person is described in 1 John as deceived (1:8) and a deceiver (2:26; 3:7; 2 John 7).

In 1 John the darkness is depicted as a power. The verb "to blind" *(typhloun)* is used just three times in the NT, in John 12:40; 1 John 2:11; and 2 Cor 4:4 where Paul says that the god of this world has blinded the eyes of those who do not believe. The sense is similar here and in John 12:40: blinded eyes produce unbelieving behavior. For John and 1 John the god of this world is encountered in the power of darkness.

The person who loves his brother abides in the light. It is not easy to say whether loving the brother enables the person to abide in the light, or whether it manifests the reality of abiding in the light, or again whether it is in itself abiding in the light. Perhaps this is to press for clarity on too fine a point. Given the nature of the tests, perhaps loving the brother is best understood as the evidence of abiding in the light. Nevertheless, some responsibility for hating the brother seems to be attributed to the darkness (2:11).

The intentional contrast in 2:10-11 raises the question of how 2:10 is to be understood. Is it that there is "no cause of stumbling *(skandalon)* in" the person who abides in the light? That is to take the pronoun *autǭ* as a masculine referring to a person. On that reading, the person who loves his brother does not cause others to stumble. According to the Gospel, love for one another is the mark of Jesus' disciples (John 13:34-35; 15:12). In the Johannine sense as well as the modern sense the failure to love the brother is a scandal. It misrepresents, distorts, and destroys the reality of the witness to Jesus in the lives of his disciples, causing others to stumble.

While this meaning is quite Johannine, a simpler reading is to take *autǭ* as a neuter referring to the light. The person loving the brother abides in the light and there is no cause of stumbling in it. In stark contrast, the person hating the brother is stumbling about in the darkness. There is cause of stumbling here (2:11). Indeed, the darkness has blinded the eyes of such a person. The argument seems to suggest that the person who hates his brother has chosen a way that reinforces the blindness of hatred.

What are we to understand from 1 John's charges that his opponents did not love but hated the brothers/sisters? First, it means that we must take account of the schism (2:18-19). Those whom the author of 1 John called brothers/sisters were supporters of the one with whom the opponents were in conflict. In 2 and 3 John we may well get a view of what "hating" (not loving) meant. In 2 John 10-11 the Elder counsels his readers not to provide hospitality for missionaries who come with a teaching at variance with his own. According to 3 John 9-10, Diotrephes responded by refusing hospitality to supporters of the Elder. But this does not seem to be the point of 2:10-11. In each case the author refers to "the one who loves *his* brother" and "the one who hates *his* brother." This implies either that the opponents remain brothers, or that they recognized no obligation to those of their own group.

Second, from the treatment of the love command in 1 John it seems likely that the opponents did not accept the authority of this command arising from the life and example of Jesus. For 1 John the command expressed the reality of the message (gospel truth) and fulfillment of the command was evidence of a genuine response to the message. The opponents do not seem to have recognized the roots of the reciprocal love command in the reality of the message (gospel).

When the seventh claim emerges in 4:20 it is the claim to love God without loving the brother. The claim is embedded in 4:7–5:3, which embodies by far the longest response to any of the lies. In this response the love obligation is grounded in Jesus Christ coming in the flesh (4:10-11), which is the evidence of God's love for us and the basis of the affirmation, "God is love" (4:7, 16). It is no accident that this section (4:7–5:3) immediately follows the response to the opponents' refusal to confess that "Jesus Christ has come in the flesh" (4:1-6). The cumulative evidence is overwhelming that the opponents not only refused to make this christological confession but also failed to acknowledge the authority of the love command that was grounded in the confession. See further the discussion of 4:7–5:3.

EXCURSUS: LOVE OF THE BROTHER/SISTER AND LOVE OF ONE ANOTHER

It is well known that neither in the Gospel nor in the Epistles of John do we find Jesus' instruction to love the neighbor, let alone the enemy. Given the absence of this perspective, and the expression of a sectarian consciousness whereby Jesus and his followers are set over against the Jews and the world, the oft-repeated commands to love one another or the brother can be read in a very negative or exclusive fashion. This probably does not do justice to the Johannine understanding of love.

First, it should be noted that both the Gospel and 1 John are to be understood in a context of the recognition of God's love for the world, which involves a mission to save the world (John 3:16; 4:42; 17:20-26; 20:21; 1 John 2:2; 4:14). This may pose problems of its own for those who think that such a frame of mind betrays an attitude of superiority. That may be the case. If such criticism is leveled, the authors of the Johannine Gospel and Epistles may simply have to accept it. They may plead that such an attitude is well-intentioned, indeed that it arises out of concern for the well-being of the "world."

Second, the mutual love between the Father and the Son is the foundation of God's love in the world. Thus there is a stress on the mutuality of love between believers (John 13:34-35). At the same time, that love is inclined to inclusiveness and oriented to the transformation of the world (John 17:20-26).

Third, 1 John 2:15-17 is not about hating those who are not believers. It is about the clash of values within the believing community in relation to the "world." The same clash of values is reflected in John 17:11-19. Jesus prays that the disciples will be kept from the corrupting power of "the world." But this is not a statement of hatred of the world. The transformation of the world is dependent on the disciples' maintaining a life that manifests the revelation of the Father in the Son through the disciples. So Jesus prays that the disciples will be kept by the power of the name and word of God. The viability of their mission into the world, as an extension of the mission of Jesus into the world, is dependent on maintaining a life that may challenge the world to be different from the way it is. The challenge is rooted in the life that fulfills the command, "love one another because I have loved you"; "love one another in the same way as I have loved you."

In 1 John the love command remains rooted in the life of Jesus. The author takes a step that is implied but not quite taken in John: "Beloved, if God loved us like this, we also ought to love one another" (1 John 4:11).

Nevertheless, the love command from John poses an added problem in 1 John. Here it becomes, on occasion, love for the brother (2:9-10). The author has not perceived the problem of this gender-specific language, reminding us of the culture-specific context of this writing. The author addresses "young men" *(neaniskoi)* and fathers *(pateres)* in the community in 2:13-14. There is no comparable address to "young women" or "mothers." On the masculine forms of address without comparable feminine forms there can be no response except to admit the author's blindness to the issue of gender equality in addressing sectional groups of his readers. Even here, this judgment must be qualified by the recognition that, when addressing his readers collectively, his preferred form of address was "my little children" (*teknia mou:* see 2:1, 12, 28; 3:7, 18; 4:4; 5:21 and the Notes on 2:1). Outside 1 John the use of the diminutive *teknia* is rare in the New Testament. See also the comparable use of *paidia*. Perhaps this neuter noun was used of small children until gender differences became more important. As a neuter noun, used symbolically and endearingly of adults, it is no more directed to men than to women. This is an advantage. It may or may not have been recognized by the author.

In 1 John we also find the command to love the brother. There is no comparable command to love the sister! In the Epistles "sister" is used only in 2 John 13 and there probably as a reference to a sister house church. More characteristically Johannine is the command to "love one another" (3:11, 23; 4:7, 11, 12; 2 John 5 and John 13:34; 15:12, 17). Reference to love of the brother seems to be developed on the basis of the example of Cain who hated his brother and murdered him. Thus Cain becomes the example of the children of the devil over against the children of God and the language of loving the brother occurs in contexts where love and hate stand over against each other, revealing the children of God and the children of the devil. (See 3:10-18 and 2:9-11.)

### FOR REFERENCE AND FURTHER STUDY

Beutler, Johannes. *Die Johannesbriefe*, 54–63.
Brooke, Alan England. *A Critical and Exegetical Commentary on the Johannine Epistles*, 29–40.
Brown, Raymond E. *The Epistles of John*, 247–92.
Dodd, Charles Harold. *The Johannine Epistles*, 29–36.
Kilpatrick, G. D. "Two Johannine Idioms in the Johannine Epistles," *JTS* 12 (1961) 272–73.
Lieu, Judith. "Blindness in the Johannine Tradition," *NTS* 34 (1988) 83–95.
Painter, John. *The Quest for the Messiah*. Edinburgh: T & T Clark, 1991, 2nd ed. Nashville: Abingdon, 1993.
_____. "The Quotation of Scripture and Unbelief in John 12.36b-43," in Craig A. Evans and W. Richard Stegner, eds., *The Gospels and the Scriptures of Israel*. JSNTS 104. Sheffield: Sheffield Academic Press, 1994, 429–58.
Rensberger, David. *1 John, 2 John, 3 John*, 58–69.
Schnackenburg, Rudolf. *The Johannine Epistles*, 89–114.
Wahlde, Urban C. von. *The Johannine Commandments: 1 John and the Struggle for the Johannine Tradition*. New York: Paulist, 1999.

## 1.2. Preliminary appeal (2:12-14)

12. Little children, I write to you: your sins have been forgiven on account of his name.

13. Fathers, I write to you: you have come to know the one from the beginning. Young people, I write to you: You have conquered the Evil One. 14. Little children, I wrote to you: you know the Father. Fathers, I wrote to you: you have come to know the one from the beginning. Young people, I wrote to you: you are strong and the word of God abides in you and you have conquered the Evil One.

NOTES

12. *Little children, I write to you: your sins have been forgiven on account of his name:* On the address "little children," here *teknia*, which becomes *paidia* in 2:14, 18, see the general comments above. That the name manifests the reality of a person is evident in the OT. Thus in Genesis there is attention to the naming of all things: see Gen 2:11-14, 20; 3:20; 4:17, etc. There is also concern over the name of God: Exod 3:13, 15; 6:3; 20:7; Deut 5:11. In Deut 12:11 there is reference to God making his name to dwell in a place (see also 12:21; 14:23, 24; 16:2). In the NT there is close attention to the naming of Jesus (Matt 1:21, 23, 25; Luke 1:31; 2:21), and just as prophets spoke in the name of God (Deut 18:18-22), so there are those who prophesy in the name of Jesus (Matt 7:22).

For the use of "the name" of Jesus in the Johannine literature see John 1:12; 2:23; 3:18; 14:13, 14, 26; 15:16, 21; 16:23, 24, 26; 20:31 (and see 1 John 3:23; 5:13). But Jesus also makes reference to the name of the Father (John 5:43; 10:25; 12:28; 17:6, 11, 12, 26). Then there are references in which it is unclear whether what is in view is the name of the Father or the Son (John 12:18; 1 John 2:12; 3 John 7). The Son makes known the Father's name (17:26) and in doing so is revealed as the Son.

13. *Fathers, I write to you: you have come to know the one from the beginning. Young people, I write to you: You have conquered the Evil One:* For "the one from the beginning" in 2:13-14 see above on 1:1. The "Evil One" *(ton ponēron)* is mentioned in John 17, where Jesus prays that the Father will keep *(hina tērsēs)* the disciples from the Evil One *(tou ponērou)*. Elsewhere in John it is said that those who perform "evil works" hate the light and do not come to it lest their works be exposed (3:19), and Jesus bears witness against those who hate him, that their works are evil (7:7). Then (1 John 3:12) Cain, whose works were evil (cf. John 3:19; 7:7) is said to be "of the Evil One" *(ek tou ponērou)*, that is, a child of the Evil One (cf. the charges in John 8:44). In 5:18-19 the author says that although the whole world lies in [the control] of the Evil One, he cannot touch the one born of God. The young men too have conquered the Evil One. The full elaboration of this is given only in the second round of sayings in 2:14 where the same affirmation of victory over the Evil One is made.

The verb "to conquer" *(nikan)* is used once in John (16:33) and six times in 1 John (2:13, 14; 4:4; 5:4, 5). Elsewhere it is used once in Luke, three times in Romans, and 16 times in Revelation. Here as in some important other places Revelation shares distinctively Johannine language and perspective.

14. *Little children, I wrote to you: you know the Father. Fathers, I wrote to you: you have come to know the one from the beginning. Young people, I wrote to you: you are strong and the word of God abides in you and you have conquered the Evil One:* On the address "little children," here *paidia*, which is more frequently expressed using *teknia*, see the Interpretation.

## INTERPRETATION

In this passage there are six forms of address in which three groups are addressed twice. The form of address is identical except that in the second round the verb "I write" (present tense) gives way to the aorist tense. In the Greek the word order is "I write (second round: wrote) to you (plural)" followed by the name of each group in order. The names of the three groups are repeated in the second round with the exception that the initial *teknia* becomes *paidia*.

The two rounds of address suggest that *paidia* in the second round is a variation on *teknia* with no change of group or meaning involved. Likewise, the change to the aorist tense in the second round (v. 14) is not likely to indicate that reference is being made to a previous writing. Rather, the aorist draws attention to the repetition of address to the same three groups (vv. 12-13). Before 2:14, 1 John uses the present tense of *graphō* (1:4; 2:1, 7, 8, 12, 13). From 2:14 onward the aorist is always used (2:14, 21, 26; 5:13). This suggests a stylistic turning point in the letter at 2:14.

Two aspects of the three groups are puzzling. First, prior to this and following 2:14 the letter is addressed to the *teknia* (2:1, 28; 3:7, 18; 4:4; 5:21; *paidia* in 2:18). Now (2:12) they seem to be just a part of the group addressed. Second, the order—little children, fathers, young people—does not make sense. It seems more likely that the whole group continues to be addressed as "Little children" and that *paidia* is just a variation (see 2:18; 3:7 [variant reading]). Thus elsewhere in 1 John the whole group is addressed using each of these words, and that seems to be the case here. The other two forms of address then make sense in the present order, giving priority to seniority. Thus all readers are addressed as "little children." They are then divided into older and younger groups.

Each of the six statements made to the three groups is introduced by *hoti*. How is this to be translated? It could be rendered as "because," giving the reason why the author addresses/writes to each group. Brown (*The Epistles of John* 301) rightly notes that this reading gives a confident tone to 1 John that seems to be lacking elsewhere. That does not seem to be why the author is writing. Rather, *hoti* in these verses functions much as it does in 1:6, 8, 10; 2:4, where it marks the words spoken, like opening quotation marks. While we are not dealing with the spoken word here, we may understand the function as marking out what the writer has to say. Perhaps this style is inclined to be a little pompous. Why does the author have to reiterate again and again, "I write to you"? Why did he not simply write, "Little children, your sins are forgiven on account of his name"? It is the use of "I write to you" that calls for the use of *hoti*, which has an epexegetical function, setting out what was written. The difference of 2:1 from this is that there the author uses the epexegetical *hina* and writes a negative command using *mē* with the aorist subjunctive. Alternatively he might have written *hoti* followed by the same negative command construction. Understood in this way the statements made by the author reassure those who have been shaken by an event that he is soon to speak about (2:8-19).

In each of the six affirming statements the verb is in the perfect tense, implying that an action in the past has achieved the status or situation of the present. The readers as a whole, addressed as "little children," are said to have been forgiven and have come to know the Father. Fathers are twice said to have come to know the one from the beginning. Young people are twice said to have conquered the Evil One, though the second time the means of their victory are set out.

The author affirms each group addressed in a statement introduced by *hoti*. The affirmation of the first round to the *teknia* is altogether different from the one to the *paidia* in the second round. The affirmation to fathers is the same in each round. The first affirmation to young people is included in the second round *after* two new statements. The two additional statements there provide the grounds that make the affirmation true. There seem to be two grounds, but in fact the second ground explains the first so that there is only one ground (*hendiadys*).

Besides the sixth affirmation, only the first indicates the basis for the claim it makes. This does not appear in a separate statement but is part of the affirmation. Thus the group of affirmations is enclosed between the two (first and last) that provide statements of the grounds for them, grounds that assure the truth of the affirmations. The sixth affirmation brings this section to a climax by providing two additional statements, though the second is the basis of the first, of the truth that assures the reality of the affirmation. This affirmation leads naturally into the next section with its warning about the world.

Given that "little children" **(2:12)** is the author's way of addressing his readers (see 2:1, 28; 3:7, 18; 4:4; 5:21), we may assume that they were in need of assurance that their sins were forgiven. This is expressed using the perfect passive: "They have been forgiven" and are therefore forgiven. See John 20:23 (also using the perfect passive) where Jesus tells the disciples, "If you forgive anyone's sins, they are forgiven" (see C. K. Barrett, *The Gospel According to St John* 571). Here in 1 John we are probably to think of a reassuring statement rather than an act that produces forgiveness at that moment. They are forgiven "for his name's sake," "on account of his name." To whose name does this refer, and what is the significance of an appeal to "his name"?

In Jewish Scripture "the name" is thought to reveal the reality of the person. In Genesis careful attention is paid to the naming of everything, and the revelation of the name of God is a sacred moment because the name must not be defiled or taken in vain. (See the Notes for details.) For this reason the name of God ceases to be spoken and conventions were developed to make oblique reference to God. The technical term for this practice is *Nomina Sacra*. (See Robert F. Hull, "Nomina Sacra," in Everett Ferguson et al, eds., *Encyclopedia of Early Christianity* [2nd ed. New York and London: Garland, 1997] 2:818.) One of these was to use "the name" *(ha-shem)* as a reference to God. The NT, and especially John, develops the language of the name of Jesus. This is recognized in early Christianity, where Jewish scribal practices in dealing with the name of God are applied to Jesus in recognition that he is now the bearer of the name (John 17:11).

What makes 1 John 2:12 troublesome is first that the Johannine tradition refers to both the name of Jesus and the name of God (the Father). (See the Notes.) Second, the subsequent two references to "the name" in 1 John are specifically to "the name of his Son" and "the name of the Son of God" (3:23; 5:13). It seems strange that the clarified uses follow the unclarified text. The 3 John 7 reference is also unclarified and made problematic by the reference to doing well by sending on "the brothers . . . worthily of God because they went out for the sake of the name." Proximity to the reference to God, and the place of the sacred name of God in the tradition, make complex what is probably a reference to the name of Jesus.

While 1 John 2:12 is grammatically ambiguous ("his" does not identify the person), references to forgiveness "on account of his name," like "belief in his name," are probably to Jesus, not God. The primary evidence is the early Christian (including Johannine) use of "the name" to refer to Jesus. Thus 2:12, like 1 John 2:22 and 3 John 7, is probably a reference to the name of Jesus. (But see the comment on 3 John 7.)

But what is the name of Jesus? One answer is to suggest that "Jesus" is the name of Jesus. In Phil 2:9-11 Jesus "is given the name above every name, that at the name of Jesus every knee shall bow. . . ." At the same time what is confessed is that "Jesus Christ is Lord *(kyrios).*" That may be the case, but there is no suggestion here that either "Jesus" or "Lord" is in view. In the LXX the use of *kyrios* was one way of speaking of God while avoiding the divine name. This appears to be of no help as the only other references in 1 John are to "the name of his Son," and "the name of the Son of God" (3:23; 5:13 and see John 3:18). An interesting reading is found in *Gospel of Truth* 38:6-7, "Now the name of the Father is the Son." This might be a meditation on the name of the Father in John 17. What we can say is this: In John and 1 John references to "the name" generally refer to Jesus and in doing so identify him with the name of God. Jesus as the incarnate *logos* is God revealed. In him God's name has been made known. In him the name of God is revealed in the work of forgiveness. Consequently the author affirms: "your sins are forgiven, on account of his name."

Fathers are now addressed **(2:13)**. This appears to be an address to the senior members of the circle of churches. That no senior women are mentioned is a reflection of the attitudes of the time. (See the notes on 2:9 and the excursus after 2:11.) The author assures "You (plural) have come to know (perfect tense)." The same tense is used in first person plural (v. 3) and in the first person singular of the claim of v. 4. That claim is not wrong in principle, though the author set a test to check its validity. Here the author attests the validity and assures his readers it is true. What they know is "the one who is from the beginning." The words "from the beginning" are identical to the words at the opening of 1 John, but there a neuter relative pronoun is used, while here the definite article is masculine, so the meaning is "the one from the beginning" whereas the meaning in 1:1, which also uses the verb "to be" in the imperfect tense, is "that which was from the beginning."

Here, where the reference to "the one from the beginning" is personal, only God or God's Son can be intended. If "his name" in 1:12 refers to the Son we have every reason to think that the one from the beginning is the Son. It is not impossible that the reference is to the Father. It is appropriate to address those called fathers, affirming that they have come to know the Father. If this is true, they have come to know the Father through the Son. Yet if "from the beginning" refers to the beginning of John 1:1, being older is not particularly relevant. This does not involve the ones who have come to know being in the beginning themselves.

The third group addressed is "young people." The term used is masculine *(neaniskoi).* (See the notes on 2:9 and the excursus after 2:11.) Appropriate to young men is the image of victory in the conflict. The verb is in the perfect tense. Here the conflict is with the Evil One. In 1 John, even more than in John, the world is portrayed as in the power of the Evil One (5:19). (See the Notes on 2:13.) This can only be a reference to the devil (John 6:70; 8:44; 13:2; 1 John 3:8, 10), called Satan in John 13:27 and "the prince of this world" in John 12:31; 14:30; 16:11. The devil comes to prominence in the post-exilic period, growing out of the role of Satan in the heavenly court (Job 1–2) into the role of the adversary of God as in the Johannine writings. See also Matt 6:13; 13:19, 38-39; Eph 6:16; 2 Thess 3:3.

"The victory over the Evil One" in 1 John finds its only verbal echo in the Gospel in John 16:33. There Jesus reassures his bewildered disciples that though in the world they will have tribulation, "Be of good cheer, I have conquered the world." Such a context removes the sense of crass triumphalism because the statement is addressing those whose confidence has been shaken. From this perspective the victory of the young men is reassuring. (See also John 12:31.) For the full statement of the victory see v. 14.

The second round of assuring affirmations **(2:14)** uses the aorist "I wrote," probably taking account of what was written in 2:12-13. The diminutive for children *(paidia)* is really a synonym of the earlier title *(teknia)*. That it is said of them "you have come to know the Father" may count against understanding *ton ap' archēs* as a reference to the Father. John uses the title "Father" of God 120 times; it appears twelve times in 1 John and four times in 2 John. What John and 1 John make clear is that God is known as Father in relation to Jesus as the Son. It is the Son who makes the Father known.

The message addressed to "Fathers" in 2:14 is identical to 2:13a. The address to the "young people" repeats what was said to them in 2:13 but first provides an explanation of the means of their victory over the Evil One. First it is said: "you are strong." Strength is a virtue of youth and may be applied to them for this reason, though physical strength is clearly not in view. The real source of their strength is revealed in the affirmation, "the word *(logos)* of God abides in you." Here it is likely that there is an interplay between the word as the message and the Word as Jesus. The abiding word/Word is the source of their strength and the ground of their victory. Cf. John 15:7, though there Jesus' words *(ta rhēmata mou)* are plural and expressed using a different noun (neuter) not susceptible to interplay with Jesus as the Word *(logos)* of God (cf. Rev 19:13). In Revelation, where the theme of victory is also prominent, the context is a persecuted and suffering church. There the aim of the book is to encourage faithfulness to the end (death if necessary), a faithful witness to Jesus (see Rev 2:7, 10-11, 17, 26-29; 3:5-6, 12-13, 21-22, and see further the Notes on v. 13).

The references to victory in 1 John (2:13, 14; 4:4; 5:4 [3x]) are illuminating and strengthen the resonance with the references in John and Revelation. In particular, 4:4 deals with the coming of the antichrist (representative of the Evil One of 2:13, 14; cf. 4:3). Interestingly, 4:4 in affirming victory (perfect tense as in 2:13-14) says, "you have conquered them *(nenikēkate autous)*." The antichrist, the Evil One, is encountered in a multiplicity of phenomena so that we are to understand that the false prophets of 4:1 are representative of the antichrist, the Evil One (cf. 2:18 and 1 John 7). Because the one is manifest in the many, the one can be expressed in terms of the many antichrists. There the ground for confidence of victory over them is: "Greater is the one in you than the one in the world." This suggests that the Evil One (antichrist) is the real opponent in the many *(autous)* and perhaps weight is given to taking "the Word of God" in a christological sense. What confuses the issue is 4:6, which expresses the contrast between the Spirit of Truth and the Spirit of Error. Even here we may think that the Spirit of Truth is the new mode of presence of the Word and the Spirit of Error is the mode of presence of the Evil One.

Here the discussion of the relationship of the Evil One/antichrist to the "world" prepares the way for 2:15-17. Treatment of the "world" is followed by the introduction of the theme of the last hour, the appearance of the antichrist/antichrists, and reference to the schism, all of which is connected to 4:1-6. The negative treatment of the world that follows ought not to be taken as a full picture. Primarily in view is the schism and its causes as seen by our author.

### 1.3. Admonition: False love (2:15-17)

> 15. Do not love the world or the things in the world. If any one loves the world, the love of the Father is not in him; 16. because every thing that is in the world—the lust of the flesh and the lust of the eyes and ostentatious boastfulness of the possessions of life—is not of the Father but is of the world. 17. And the world and its lusts is passing away, but the person who does the will of God abides forever.

#### NOTES

15. *Do not love the world or the things in the world. If any one loves the world, the love of the Father is not in him:* The use of *mē* with the present imperative *agapate* expresses a negative command, a prohibition. The present tense implies a sustained response, not merely a momentary restraint. Thus the meaning is not "stop this instant," but "do not love the world," a command with continuing effect. See the discussion of the negative command in 2:1.

On love see the discussion on 2:5. Here, in 2:15 (contrary to Brown, *The Epistles of John* 323–25), love has a somewhat different meaning. Although the verb used is *agapan,* it does not have its characteristic sense. That is because the love spoken of here has a character that is prohibited: "do not love. . . ." To some extent this is determined by the object of love, in this case the world. On "the world" see above on 2:2.

Brown's objection is based on the assumption that the secessionists were advocating, "Love the world," arguing that they are unlikely to have a radically different understanding of love because they were (or had been) Johannine Christians. First, I see no indication that the author says the opponents were advocating this. The threat of worldliness is fairly clear in 2:15-17. It may be that the opponents, having gone out into the world (2 John 7), had adopted a more accommodating relationship to the world. There was probably an attraction to this way of life for the readers of 1 John. It is hardly appropriate to illuminate the command not to love the world by saying "ultimately Jesus refused to pray for the world" (John 17:9), implying a change. Though God loved the world (3:16), Jesus refused to love the world. Brown explains this on the basis that the world had rejected Jesus. So he understands 2:16 in world-rejecting terms. Small twists of language can work marvels. In John Jesus does not say, "I refuse to pray for the world" but, "I do not ask concerning the world." The request concerning the disciples is precisely in terms of a strategy to lead to the world coming to believe and to know. Praying for the disciples was a specific act of love to be understood within overall love for the world. This is especially clear in John 17:20-26. The command not to love the world (2:15) is to be understood in relation to John 3:19. There it is said reprovingly that people loved the darkness rather than the light. Love of the darkness, like love of the world in 2:15, is choosing the values of the world.

Here again God is referred to as Father (see 1:2-3). Father is an especially appropriate Johannine title to use in relation to the theme of the love of God; see 2:22, 23, 24; 3:1; 4:14.

16. *because every thing that is in the world—the lust of the flesh and the lust of the eyes and ostentatious boastfulness of the possessions of life—is not of the Father but is of the world:* Many attempts have been made to identify the three "vices" listed in this verse. The problem with the first two categories is in the term "lust" or "desire," which is used only here and in v. 17 in 1 John and in John 8:44 in the Gospel, where Jesus charges his critics with being willing to perform the desires of their father the devil. A generally (but not inevitably) negative sense is carried by this word in Romans (1:24; 6:12; 7:7, 8; 13:14). When it is combined with "the flesh" in what probably is a subjective genitive, a negative sense is certainly given. Desires arising from the flesh are fleshly desires. In the LXX the command prohibiting covetousness is expressed as "you shall not desire *(ouk epithumēseis).*" It is precisely this command that Paul discusses in Romans 7.

While there may be good desires (Phil 1:23), fleshly desires are the problem; see Rom 7:18; Gal 5:16-17, 19; cf. 1QS 11:9, 12; 1QM 4:3. Warnings against carnal desires and those aroused by looking at beautiful women are to be found in the Jewish and Greco-Roman writings of the time (see *T. Jud.* 17:1; Philo, *Post.* 40–135; Polycarp. *Phil.* 5:3; and the catalogue of vices in Gal 5:19-20).

"Life" *(bios)* is used only here and in 3:17 in the Johannine writings, out of a total of ten times in the NT. It may refer to the public image of a person's life and thus to a public "biography." There is nothing negative about the term in itself. Here a problem is raised by the nominative *hē alazoneia,* (used only here and in Jas 4:16 in the NT), which covers a range of meaning such as boastfulness, pride, arrogance, ostentation. See Hab 2:5, which describes the boastful man in terms related to the desires of the flesh and the eyes. The noun *alazōn* is used only in Rom 1:30 and 2 Tim 3:2 in the NT. Together with the genitive *tou biou* the phrase probably has the sense of something like "the boastful possessions of life." In 3:17 something like the possessions of life (livelihood) is implied, but without the sense of arrogant boasting implied here by *hē alazoneia*. The genitive *tou biou* is probably objective, so that the boasting is focused on the life, perhaps the luxurious lifestyle. Alternatively it can be taken as boastful self-confidence in the ability to secure one's own life (see Luke 12:16-21).

On the world and its values as confronted here in 1 John and its relationship to the individualistic values of the Hellenistic world of the time see C. H. Dodd, *The Johannine Epistles* 39–43. He argues that the world as portrayed is the pagan society within which the readers moved. The *alazōn* "is a conceited pretentious humbug" who "came to the front in the irresponsible, acquisitive, individualistic society of the Hellenistic world" (*The Johannine Epistles* 42).

17. *And the world with its lusts is passing away, but the person who does the will of God abides forever:* Just as 2:8 said "the darkness is passing away," so now it is said, "The world is passing away" *(paragetai)*. The noun *thelēma* is used seven times of the will of God in John and is also used again in this sense in 1 John 5:14. "Abides forever" *(eis ton aiōna)* is a phrase from the LXX that occurs 26 times in the NT, 12 of which are in John and one in 2 John 2. In the OT, God and his truth abide forever, as does the son of David (Ps 89:37[36]; on this see John 8:35; 12:34). But here it is the one who does God's will who abides forever. Old Latin texts add words to the effect "as also he himself [God] lasts forever." The addition is quite Johannine in style but has inadequate textual support, being unattested by any Greek manuscript, and was not adopted by Jerome in the Vulgate. For the writer of 1 John it was unnecessary to assert that God abides forever. That is not in question.

INTERPRETATION

The first use of "the world" in 1 John (2:2) portrays it as the object of God's saving activity in Jesus Christ (cf. 4:10-11). In both 2:2 and 4:10 Jesus is described as the expiation for our sins. Only in 2:2 does the writer extend this to "for the sins of the whole world" and only in 4:10 does he tell us that the initiative for this act was that God loved *(ēgapēsen)* us. This perspective needs to be kept in mind as we read 2:15-17, which is not necessarily in conflict with John 3:16 where we are told that God loved *(ēgapēsen)* the world. Now, in 2:15, the reader is instructed: "Do not love *(mē agapate)* the world." This seems strange at first, especially as linguistically there is no difference between the love God has for the world and the love for the world prohibited by the command.

It is clear that God's love for the world seeks to transform the world, to save it. The kind of love for the world that is prohibited is the kind of love for the world that seeks to possess it. The result of that kind of love is that the one who loves the world is transformed by the world. Here 1 John reveals awareness of the powerful attractions of "worldly values." J. B. Phillips paraphrased Rom 12:1: "Don't let the world squeeze you into its mold." The recognition of the need for the world to be transformed by the love of God is consistent with recognition of the corrupting power of worldly values. This is a dominant theme of Jesus' prayer in John 17:6-19. While 17:9 can be isolated and understood to indicate a negative view of the world, and in one sense it is, it is not an indication of Jesus' lack of concern for the world. Rather, the separation of the disciples from worldly values is precisely what continues the possibility of the transformation of the world, and this comes to focus in 17:20-26.

When the world is the object of love and the character of the love is determined by its object, then such love is prohibited by the author's understanding of the gospel (2:15). It is prohibited by the love of God revealed in the gospel. The point is made in both John 3:16 and 1 John 4:11: "For God loved the world in this way *(outōs)*, he gave . . . in order that . . ." (John 3:16); "If God loved us in this way *(outōs)* . . ." (1 John 4:11).

In John 3:16 *outōs* looks forward to "he gave. . . ." In 1 John 4:11 *outōs* looks back to "he sent his Son . . ." (4:10). The nature of love is exemplified in the giving/sending, which is (purpose) "to save the world" (John 3:16) or for the sake of the whole world (1 John 2:2). The love for the world that is here forbidden is the love that wishes to possess the world *as* the world. But in this way the world possesses the person and takes control. That it is this kind of possessive love is made clear by reference to "the things in the world." Here love has a quite different sense. It means choosing the world of possessions so that they become life-determining. On love in the sense of choosing, see John 3:19. Where possessions become a first priority the Q saying found in Matt 6:24 becomes operative. Love for the world in this sense is incompatible with the love of the Father. Given the saying that "no one can serve two masters," this might dispose us to think that "the love *of the Father*" means "love for the Father." This may be the case. But here, as in v. 5, we have an ambiguous genitive case. The words "of the Father" are in the genitive. We have to choose between a subjective genitive, which is understood as "the Father's love," or an objective genitive, "love for the Father." Is the choice between love for the world and love for the Father? This makes good sense in the light of Matt 6:24, but that saying is not part of the context.

Perhaps more determinative for the use here is the character of the love of the Father in giving and sending the Son. Love here has the sense of self-giving and graciousness. This sense too finds support in the use of the noun *(agapē)* and reference to "the love of God in him." This suggests that God's love is perfected in the person. Of course v. 15 expresses the negation. The love of God is not in the person who loves the world and its things. The choice of the subjective genitive here implies a specific character in the divine love expressed in the life of the person. Love for the world does not have this character. Love for the world in this sense does not come from God.

"Every thing that is in the world" **(2:16)** is first to be understood as creation, and as important, but not of the first order of importance. The descriptions that follow provide three statements using genitives, "the lust *of the flesh*" and "the lust *of the eyes*" and "ostentatious boastfulness *of the possessions of life.*" Neither of the first two seems capable of being persuasively or straightforwardly interpreted as objective genitives. Rather we are dealing with the desires that arise from the flesh. This need not imply a Pauline understanding of the flesh but may well reflect an understanding of the LXX reading of the tenth commandment. The lust of the eyes is well captured by Qoh 4:8, which describes the person "whose eyes are never satisfied with riches." To see it is to desire it; these are people whose "eyes are bigger than. . . ." The third genitive should probably be understood as objective. It most likely refers to possessions: see 3:17. There it refers to a person who has worldly possessions (the possessions of the world) and sees his brother in need. It is likely that the attitude expressed in 2:16 leads to failure to show compassion as described in 3:17.

The language of this third attitude may well point toward the Greco-Roman cultural challenge to Johannine Christianity. It is related to the boasting *(kauchēsis, kauchēma, kauchasthai)* culture we meet in Paul, especially in 1–2 Corinthians where the nouns are used 13 times and the verb 25 times. Encountering the boasting culture at Corinth induced Paul to the foolishness of boasting (2 Cor 11:1, 16-18, 21-33; 12:1-10, 11-13), but in doing so he overturned traditional values. Boasting and ostentation are a part of the honor culture with which Johannine Christianity was forced to struggle.

Not only the three specific examples but "every thing in the world is not from *(ek)* the Father but is from *(ek)* the world." This use of "from" describes source or origin (see John 3:31). "From the world" and "from God" are set in opposition. In 1 John 2:21; 3:19 we also find the expression "from the truth." Clearly, then, the world is not here used in the sense of God's creation. Rather we have an expression of the Johannine dualism in which the world *as it now is* manifests the power of the Evil One (1 John 5:19), the prince of this world (John 12:31).

Reference to the world passing away *(paragetai,* **2:17)** looks back to 2:8 and implies that the world is the world of darkness that is shattered by the shining of the true light, the light of the revelation of God that has the content of God's love. The desire/lust of the flesh and the eyes are now subsumed as its (the world's) desire/lust. While this present is transitory, the situation in view is eschatological. The true light already shines (2:8). The point is not the inherent and always transitory world but its dissolution under the impact of the events of the last time; see 2:18.

Nevertheless, the author assures his readers, "the person doing the will of God abides forever." The motif of "doing the will of God" is not distinctively Johannine (see Mark 3:35). We might have expected "the person who does the truth" or "walks in the light" or "the person who loves his brother." But the will of God is a more important Johannine theme than is at first obvious. For example, reference to "nor the will of the flesh, nor the will of man but of God" might imply "by the will of God" in John 1:13. More important are Jesus' references to *doing* "the will of the one who sent me" (John 4:34; 5:30; 6:38, 39). There are further references to "the will of my Father" (6:40) and more importantly concerning those who "seek to do his will" (7:17; 9:31). The only other reference in 1 John shows the importance of asking "according to his will" (1 John 5:14). Thus we might say that, if not distinctive, it is nevertheless a characteristic Johannine idiom. It arises out of the discussion of the commandments in 2:7-11. Doing the will of God involves keeping God's commandments, which come to sharp focus in the command to love the brother.

Those who do the will of God *abide* for ever. Here the contrast is with the world (the darkness) that is passing away. Just as God, his name, his justice, his truth, his word, his will abide forever (Pss 9:8[7]; 102:13[12]; 111:3; 117:2; Isa 40:8; Prov 19:21), so do those who do the will of God. They belong to another reality. Abiding "to the age" is an expression that belongs to the doctrine of the two ages, which is fully developed in 4 Ezra. Though this book is probably from ca. 100 C.E., the teaching is presupposed in the writings of Second Temple Judaism and the writings of the NT, especially Paul and John. The two ages, this age and the age to come, are in tension, even in conflict. The age to come represents the new age God brings in to overcome the problems of the old age. Consequently it is associated with the life of God, and so those who abide in the new age are those who come to share in the life of God.

The life of the age to come is spoken of as "eternal life." The expression occurs only once in the OT, in Dan 12:2 (LXX). About half of the uses of "life" (17 of 36) in John occur in the phrase "eternal life," that is, the life of the age to come. Because of the strength of the connection in John, many of the references to life clearly mean "eternal life." To have eternal life is to abide in the coming age. See C. H. Dodd, *The Interpretation of the Fourth Gospel* 144–50. Thus we have here a synonym for the more characteristic Johannine phrase "eternal life"; see 1 John 1:2; 2:25; 3:15; 5:11, 13, 20. Clearly in the other instances where "life" *(zōē)* is used alone, eternal life is in view (see 1:1, 2; 3:14; 5:11, 12 [2x]). In John "life" occurs so frequently in the phrase "eternal life" *(zōē aiōnios)* that we have the signal: when you see "life," read "eternal life."

Verses 15-17 deal with inappropriate attraction to the world. See the Excursus: The Power of Darkness and the Lure of the World below. At one level this is made clear by drawing attention to the transitory nature of the world alongside that which abides. The world should be treated appropriately, and possession of it and the things that belong to it should not be an ultimate concern. Part of what constitutes the world as the darkness is its power to elicit "desire." Perhaps it is better said that by their desire people constitute the creation as the world of darkness. Yet under the impact of the light of the gospel the world is passing away, the darkness is passing away, but the one who does God's will abides forever. Doing God's will is a proper ultimate concern. It is to love the brother/sister.

## 2. THE CHRISTOLOGICAL TEST. FAITH IN JESUS CHRIST AS THE TEST OF THE CLAIM TO HAVE FELLOWSHIP WITH GOD: REFUTATION OF THE SECOND LIE (2:18-27)

18. Little children, it is the last hour, and as you heard, Antichrist is coming, and now many antichrists have appeared; from which we know it is the last hour. 19. They went out from us, but they were not of us; for if they were of us, they would have remained with us; but that they may be revealed, because not all are of us. 20. But you have an anointing from the Holy One and you all know. 21. I did not write to you that you do not know the truth, but that you know it, and that every lie is not of the truth. 22. Who is the liar if not the person who denies, [saying] the Christ is not Jesus? This person is the Antichrist, the person who denies the Father and the Son. 23. Every person who denies the Son does not have the Father; the person who confesses the Son has the Father also. 24. Let what you heard from the beginning abide in you; if what you heard from the beginning abides in you, you also will abide in the Son and in the Father. 25. And this is the promise which he promised to us, eternal life. 26. I wrote these things to you about those who deceive you. 27. But you, the anointing which you received from him abides in you, and you have no need that anyone should teach you; but as his anointing teaches you about all things, and it is true and not a lie, and even as it taught you, abide in him.

### NOTES

18. *Little children, it is the last hour, and as you heard, Antichrist is coming, and now many antichrists have appeared; from which we know it is the last hour:* "Little children" here translates *paidia*. (See above on 2:14.) The variation from *teknia* in 2:12, in the first group of three addresses, to *paidia* in the second group might explain the continued use of the latter in 2:18 before returning to *teknia* in 2:28.

"Last hour" *(eschatē hōra)* occurs only here in the NT. Though there is no definite article, the eschatological element is stressed by reference to the coming of Antichrist. In John the expression "on the last day" *([en] tȩ̄ eschatȩ̄ hēmera̧)* occurs seven times, though 7:37 is not strictly relevant (6:39, 40, 44, 54; 11:24; 12:48). The definite article is always used, and the reference is always to the day of resurrection. This clearly differs from the "last hour," which seems to refer to a short period of time immediately leading up to the last day. In a more general sense 2 Tim 3:1 and 2 Pet 3:3 speak of the "last days" and Jude 18 of "last times" *(eschatou chronou)*, all without the definite article. This use seems closer to "last hour" in 1 John. It is also a time when bad things happen, leading up to the last day.

On "from this we know" see above on "by this we know" in 2:3. The content of what "we know" is introduced by *hoti*, which need not be translated. Compare its use after "I write" in 2:12, 13, 14.

20. *But you have an anointing from the Holy One and you all know:* See 2:27, which is a resumption, expansion and clarification of this verse.

*But you:* In 2:18-27 three sentences begin with the second person plural "you." The first and third of these concern the "anointing" and begin with *kai hymeis* (2:20, 27). This statement, repeated with variations and expansions in 2:27, suggests an adversative statement: *you*, not those mentioned in 2:18-19, have the anointing from the Holy One, and *you* all know. The second sentence, begun with the emphatic "You" (plural), is sandwiched between the other two (2:24). It is an exhortation to "Let *abide* in you what you heard from the beginning." This suggests some connection between what was heard and the "anointing." In 2:20 it is said "You have the anointing . . ." and in 2:27 "but you, the anointing which you received from him *abides* in you." Thus "abide" has been introduced into 2:27 perhaps on the basis of the abiding word of 2:24. This suggests a close connection between the word and the anointing.

*You have an anointing (chrisma) from the Holy One (apo tou hagiou):* Here "anointing" is anarthrous, without "the" *(to)*. In 2:27 it is "the anointing" that confirms that we need to understand this as definite, "the anointing from the Holy One." First, what is the "anointing"? In the OT anointing is characteristic in the appointment to office of priests (Exod 29:7; 40:13, 15; Lev 6:22), kings (1 Sam 9:16; 10:1; 15:1; 16:3, 12; 1 Kgs 19:15, 16), and prophets (1 Kgs 19:16; Isa 41:1). The word translated "anointing" occurs only three times in the NT: once in 2:20 and twice in 2:27. The cognate verb "to anoint" is used five times, four to refer to the anointing of Jesus and once of the anointing of Christians (1 Cor 1:21).

Jewish usage of *chrisma* (LXX) suggests that the translation "anointing" is correct, rather than a reference to the oil or ointment. The question then is: Does this describe a physical act of anointing or is a symbolic meaning intended? In the context of 1 John it seems that the anointing is related to that which abides (see the discussion of 2:20, 24, 27). Some reference to the Spirit cannot be ruled out in light of the quotation of Isa 61:1 by Jesus soon after his baptism (Luke 4:18): "The Spirit of the Lord is upon me, because he has anointed me to preach good news to the poor. . . ." But such an anointing is to a task, a mission; it is not the basis of knowledge and it uses the verb and not the noun *chrisma*. Thus the abiding word of 2:24 seems to be the basis of knowledge. That being the case, it probably is figurative speech, but it may have reference to baptism. If that is so, the opponents, no doubt, could also appeal to this. Thus whether or not baptism is in view, the foundational message (2:24 and see 1:1) is the primary focus, and this is precisely what the opponents had moved away from. It may be that in the thought of 1 John it is the word of Jesus illuminated by the Spirit (John 14:26; 16:13-15). There are, however, indications that claims about the Spirit may have been central to the opponents. The approach of 1 John was to tie the teaching activity of the Spirit to the foundational word of Jesus.

That *chrisma* is used nowhere else (only 2:20, 27) in the NT may suggest that here, as with *koinōnia*, we have one of the terms coined by the opponents. For them it might have involved some form of initiation into knowledge. If that is the case, 1 John redefines anointing in terms of the foundational message that all (remaining in the community) have received, but that was rejected by the opponents.

Then to whom does "the Holy One" refer? God? Jesus? the Spirit? Surprisingly, there is little scholarly support for identifying this title with the Spirit, although the *Holy* Spirit is a reasonably common designation (John 1:33; 14:26; 20:22 just to mention the Johannine references). There is also the tradition of the descent of the Spirit on Jesus at his baptism, which could be thought of as messianic anointing. But this position has won little favor. Perhaps this is because the anointing is "from *(apo)* the Holy One," allowing for the intermediate agency of the Spirit. It could be implied that the anointing is by the Spirit from the Holy One. But this would need to relate the activity of the Spirit to the foundational message of 2:24, which is connected to 2:20, 27 by the opening emphatic "you" (plural) of these three sentences.

Certainly there is ample evidence for reference to God as "the Holy One" (see Hab 3:3; Bar 4:22, 37; Sir 23:9 [LXX] and very frequently in the rabbinic literature, suggesting a significant pool out of which this use came; see also Isa 1:4; 5:16; 27:7, 8; 30:12, 15; 37:23; 41:20; Hos 11:9). While the NT does not use this title of God, Jesus uses the adjective in addressing God as "Holy Father" (John 17:11; see also Rev 3:7; 6:10). Paul speaks of "God who anointed us," and this seems to be related to "giving the earnest of the Spirit in our hearts." But this falls short of saying that the Spirit is the "anointing." In John 14:16, 17, 26, which resemble 1 John 2:20, 27, the Father sends/gives the Spirit. But the context of 1 John 2:20, 27 does not support this view.

If the Spirit is thought of as the anointing rather than the anointer, then the Spirit comes from Jesus, according to John (15:26; 16:7), and Jesus is called "the Holy One of God" in Mark 1:14; Luke 4:34; John 6:69 (cf. Acts 3:14; Rev 3:7; *1 Clem.* 23:5; *Let. Diogn.* 9:2). Here (2:20) and in 2:27 "the anointing is *from (ap')* the Holy One" or "from him." This can only be a reference to Jesus, who must be in view in 2:25 ("the promise which *he* promised to us") and in the latter part of 2:27 ("even as he taught you, abide in him"). Thus it seems most likely that the anointing is from Jesus. Three sentences begin with "you" in Greek (2:20, 24, 27). Thus 2:20, 27 form an inclusion on the anointing, while the middle sentence appeals, "let what you heard from the beginning abide in you." In 2:27 it is the anointing that "abides in you." Thus the case is persuasive for recognizing Jesus as the Holy One from whom comes the anointing with the Word.

The question remains: Is the result of anointing that "you all *(pantes)* know" or that "you know all things *(panta)*"? The textual evidence is divided. Supporting *pantes* are Sinaiticus (‭א‬), Vaticanus (B), the Sahidic and Jerome, as well as some later mss. Supporting *panta* are Alexandrinus (A), Ephraemi Rescriptus (C), the Old Latin, Syriac Peshitta, Bohairic, Ethiopic, the Byzantine tradition, and the Vulgate. The weight of the versions strongly favors the neuter plural *(panta)*, but without evidence of early papyri the weight of the two great fourth-century codices (‭א‬ and B) balances the fifth-century witness of A and C and the supporting evidence. Thus context and internal evidence must decide this issue. If *pantes* is adopted, what is known is left unspecified and "know" *(oidate)* is used absolutely, without an object. If *panta* is adopted as an accusative neuter plural, the text supplies what is known. Thus this is an easier reading because it supplies what a reader might expect to find. It is also suggested by 2:27, where it is said that "the anointing teaches you concerning all things." According to John 14:26 Jesus says that the Paraclete "will teach you all things and bring to memory all that I said to you" (cf. 16:13). All of this suggests that it is more likely that *pantes* has been changed to *panta*. Further, the threat of the opponents makes the assurance that "you all know" meaningful in the historical context of 1 John. This is not a factor likely to have influenced a copyist, whose concern was more for the meaning for the readers of his time. For 1 John the content of knowledge is supplied in the verses that follow: "the truth" (2:21); "Jesus is the Christ" (2:22-23).

The expression "you all know" uses the second person plural *oidate;* see also 2:21 (2x), 29 ("if you know"); 3:5, 15; 5:13 ("that you may know").

21. *I did not write to you that you do not know the truth, but that you know it, and that every lie is not of the truth:* In "I did not write" *(ouk egrapsa)* the aorist tense of the verb is continued from 2:14, and for the rest of 1 John. Thus this seems to be a stylistic choice referring to the whole of 1 John rather than an indication of an earlier writing or a reference to the earlier part of 1 John. The reintroduction of the reference to writing does not here introduce a new section. Compare 2:1, 7 and the string of references in 2:12-14; 2:26. The writer's penchant for introducing references to writing is misleading because it suggests something of a new beginning; hence the misleading chapter division at 2:1.

The translation of *hoti* continues to be a problem in the three instances in this verse. Should it be translated "that," indicating the content of what is written, or should it be translated "because," stating the reason for writing? It is not easy to decide, but the statement of content seems more consistent with the author's style and fits best into his reassuring approach.

On "you know" *(oidate)*, used twice in this verse, see above on 2:20. Characteristic of the author's style is the phrasing "every lie is not of the truth," where we might have said "no lie is of the truth." (See also 2:23.) On the "lie" see also "to lie" (1:6 and 2:22).

**22–23.** *Who is the liar if not the person who denies [saying] the Christ is not Jesus? This person is the Antichrist, the person who denies the Father and the Son. Every person who denies the Son does not have the Father; the person who confesses the Son has the Father also:* The construction "Every person who . . ." is characteristic of 1 John. It expresses the use of *pas* followed by the definite article (here *ho*) with a participle (here *arnoumenos*). These often appear in opposing pairs or opposed to the truth or error, expressing the Johannine dualism. See 2:23, 29; 3:3, 4, 6 (2x), 9, 10, 15; 4:7; 5:1 (2x), 4, 18; 2 John 9.

On the language of "denial" (*arneisthai*) and "confession" (*homologein*) see further in the Interpretation of 2:23. The language of denial is used in John 1:20; 13:38; 18:25, 27. The prediction and description of the denial of Peter is interesting but different from the denial of a christological confession in 1 John 2:22, 23. The language of confession is found in John 1:20; 9:22; 12:42. The last two references concern intimidation to prevent the confession of Christ (= Jesus is the Christ). In 1 John 1:9 the confession of sin is not relevant, but christological confession is in view in 2:23; 4:2, 3, 15, and in 2 John 7.

In the Greek text "Jesus" is without the definite article that is used in "the Christ." The same construction is used in the confession "Jesus is the Son of God" in 4:15. Because with the verb "to be" subject and object take the same case, and word order can be varied, the object normally is anarthrous (without the article). Thus a case can be made for reading "the Christ is Jesus," the Son of God is Jesus. This suggests that "the Christ" was known but the identification of this identity with Jesus was controversial. The same is true of the confession of "the Son of God" in 4:15. In 2:22 the denial took the form "the Christ is not Jesus."

The denial that the Christ is Jesus has been taken to be a rejection of the messiahship of Jesus and to identify the problem confronted in 1 John as a Jewish Christian problem. This does not sufficiently take account of identification of the denial that Jesus is the Christ with the denial of the Father and the Son (2:23) and the connection with the confession that "the Son of God is Jesus," "that Jesus Christ has come in the flesh" (4:2-3). This language is not that of Jewish messiahship. It is not a denial that Jesus meets the criteria of Jewish messiahship, but a denial that the human Jesus can be identified with the lofty claims of Johannine christology. It is not a rejection of those lofty claims but a rejection of their identification with Jesus.

**24.** *Let what you heard from the beginning abide in you; if what you heard from the beginning abides in you, you also will abide in the Son and in the Father:* For "what you have heard from the beginning" see above on 1:1. On mutual abiding see John 15:7, and cf. 8:31; 15:4, 5, 9-10. (See the Notes on 1 John 2:6.) John 15 provides a basis for understanding mutual abiding in 1 John. Here the themes of abiding in Jesus, allowing Jesus' words to abide, abiding in Jesus' love, and keeping Jesus' commandments are intertwined in ways suggestive of developments in 1 John. In 1:5 "This is the message we have heard from him" resonates with "This is the message which you heard from the beginning: Love one another" (3:11). Here message (word) and commandment are one, united in the love command, which is grounded in the revelation of God's love (4:9-

11). To abide in the word (command) is to abide in love. To confess that Jesus is the Christ, in terms of the foundational message, is to confess the Son, which is to have the Father also, that is, it is to abide in the Father and the Son. For 1 John "Father" and "Son" are reciprocal terms, so that the one cannot be without the other. (See on 2:12 on "the name.") "The name of the Father is the Son" (*Gospel of Truth* 38:6-7; see John 17:11).

25. *And this is the promise which he promised to us, eternal life:* The "promise" (*hē epaggelia*) which he "promised" (*epēggeilato*). These words are found only here in the Johannine writings. The noun is found 52 times in the NT: once in Luke, eight times in Acts , eight times in Romans, twice in 2 Corinthians, ten times in Galatians, four times in Ephesians, once each in 1 and 2 Timothy, fourteen times in Hebrews, once in 2 Peter, and once in 1 John. The verb is used once each in Mark, Acts, Romans, Galatians, Titus, 2 Peter, and 1 John; twice each in 1 Timothy and James; four times in Hebrews. The concentration of the noun and verb in Hebrews is notable.

   The best textual evidence supports the reading that the promise was given to "us," yet the reading "to you" (plural) does have the support of Vaticanus (B). For a similar statement see 1:5, "This is the message we heard from him." On eternal life see above on 1:2.

26. *I wrote these things to you about those who deceive you:* Is this a reference to what has been written in 1:1–2:25, or to the whole letter? On the change of tenses see above on 1:4. Because present tenses (I write) are used until 2:14, when the author begins to use the aorist (I wrote), no firm conclusion can be drawn from the tense. Nevertheless, in this instance there is a strong case for seeing this as a reference to 2:18-25. What follows immediately in 2:28–3:3 has little direct reference to those described as "the people who would deceive you." A case can be made for taking it as a reference to the whole letter, but "these things" (*tauta*) indicates something more specific than the whole of 1 John.

   On the "deceivers" see above on 1:8, and see also 3:7 and John 7:12, 47. In each reference in John, Jesus is accused of leading people astray, a serious charge in the Jewish context. The cognate noun has both a feminine form (4:6) and a masculine form (used twice in 2 John 7). Apart from this, only Revelation (in the Johannine writings) contains any of this language; Revelation uses the verb eight times. In the apocalyptic setting of Revelation deceivers are prominent. Their appearance in 1–2 John is evidence of the last day.

27. *But you, the anointing which you received from him abides in you, and you have no need that anyone should teach you; but as his anointing teaches you about all things, and it is true and not a lie, and even as it taught you, abide in him:* On the expression "you have no need that" see John 2:25; 16:30. Though this precise expression is not found elsewhere in the Greek Bible, it is a particular example of the epexegetical use of *hina* with the subjunctive (*hina* expressing content). See 2:1, where it gives the content of what 1 John says: "I write."

   The verb "to teach" is used three times in this passage (twice in the present tense: the first a subjunctive, the second an indicative, the third an aorist indicative) and nowhere else in the Epistles. It is used nine times in John, six times of Jesus teaching the disciples and once for the Spirit Paraclete teaching the disciples. What the anointing teaches is true *(alēthes)*, not false *(pseudos)*. (For this antithesis see above on 1:6.) While the previous *menei* is indicative, asserting that the anointing *"abides* in you," what that abiding anointing teaches is what Jesus taught. This 1 John reports in the third person. Here, in 2:27, *menete* is to be read as an imperative ("abide in him"), as is shown by the repetition in 2:28 (cf. John 15:4). The command to abide shows that, for all the author's assurances, he is anxious about the resolution of his readers in the face of the challenge of the opponents.

### INTERPRETATION

A new section is signaled by a new address, "Children" *(paidia)*. (See 2:1.) The new subject is introduced by the announcement of the last day, which is marked by the appearance of the Antichrist. The relationship of the one Antichrist to the many antichrists and to those who separated themselves from the author and his supporters is a major problem. The impression given is that the reality of the schism has been imprinted on what the readers had heard about the coming of Antichrist. The reality of the schism reveals many antichrists. To this point 1 John has dealt largely with the ethical dilemma caused by the schism, the challenge it posed to an understanding of the central obligation to love the brother. The previous section concluded with a presentation of the clash of values between those who do the will of God and the world. The values advocated in 1 John are grounded in the understanding of God revealed in Jesus Christ.

The disturbance caused by the schism unsettled those who remained and the aim of 1 John is to reassure them. To do this the author must also attack the position of his opponents, which he does, branding it as "the lie," and the person who holds it as "the liar." The lie is the denial of the confession that Jesus is the Christ, the Son of God. This passage has close connections with 4:1-6. There what the opponents refused to confess is "Jesus Christ has come in the flesh." Against this denial the author holds up the foundational message that contains the promise of eternal life. About this we might add the words, "I wrote these things to you so that you may know that you have eternal life" (5:13).

Addressing the readers afresh as "Children," 1 John **2:18** introduces a new theme, announcing that it is the last hour. The connection between the last hour and the coming of the Antichrist is assumed knowledge. Thus the evidence is called to mind: "and as you have heard, Antichrist comes," with the implication "at the last hour." No doubt what is in mind is tradition like Mark 13:6 and 2 Thess 2:3, but in those texts there is no specific use of the word "antichrist." How a variety of traditions came to be gathered together under that title is hidden from us by an absence of evidence.

Verse 18 begins with a reference to the prophecy of the coming of Antichrist. The fact that "now many antichrists have appeared" is not presented as in conflict with the tradition the readers already knew. On the contrary, having indicated the plurality of antichrists, 1 John affirms even more emphatically, "From this we know it is the last hour." It is likely that the antichrist tradition concerned a particular figure that is here interpreted in terms of antichrists, under the impact of the schism and in the face of the activity of those who were, according to 1 John, false teachers, false prophets, deceivers. The tradition in 2 John 7 begins from the reality "that many deceivers have gone out into the world." These are specifically identified with those who do not confess Jesus Christ coming in the flesh. Then it is concluded, "This is the Deceiver and the Antichrist." The point is probably the same as in 1 John 2:18.

Possibly the contraction from the many to the one (in 2 John 7) suggests the principal leader of the schismatics; see 2:19. It is almost unthinkable that the schism did not involve a leadership struggle. While 1 John does not name a leader, read in the light of 2 John 7 the fluidity of the one Antichrist and the many antichrists suggests a leader and his schismatic followers. In the context of the characteristic "every person who . . ." sentences (2:23; cf. 4:3), 2:22 poses the question: "Who is the liar if not the person who denies that Jesus is the Christ; this person is the Antichrist. . . ." These names seem to focus on the leader of the opponents: The Deceiver; The Liar; The Antichrist. But all his followers are characterized in similar terms.

Though it is not specifically said here, the last hour immediately precedes "the last day." This is apparent from the connections with Mark 13 and parallels; 2 Thess 2:3-11; Rev 12:18–13:18. In those texts the Antichrist is not named. Indeed, 1–2 John provide the first evidence of the use of this term. The use of the preposition *(anti)* in this way gives two possible senses: one who takes the place of Christ or one who opposes Christ. It was probably understood in both ways in different contexts. In 1–2 John there is no suggestion that the opponents claimed to be Christ (contrast Mark 13:6, 21-22). The reference to "false prophets" (cf. "antichrists") points to a similarity with the false prophets of Mark 13:21-22. But the teaching of the false prophets of 1 John was not an error of eschatology but an error of christology (1 John 2:22-23; 4:2-3; 2 John 7). Thus 1–2 John do not call the opponents "false Christs" *(pseudochristoi,* Mark 13:22), but Antichrist and antichrists, and that alongside reference to "false prophets" (1 John 4:1, 3; see Mark 13:22). 1 John certainly sees them as opposed to Christ, but the opposition seems to have taken the form of the rejection of the christology of 1–2 John rather than outright opposition to Christ. There is no sign of the oppressive political Antichrist.

The coming of the Antichrist marks the arrival of the last hour. In fact many antichrists have appeared. This suggests that the antichrist tradition has been reshaped by the circumstances of the schism. The author identifies their work with the teachers who oppose the teaching of 1 John.

The tests that 1 John provides to assure the readers that they know God and the Spirit of God, the essential tests that demonstrate the reality of eternal life, are formulated with "by this we know . . ." (generally *en toutǭ ginōskomen* but also *ek toutou ginōskomen*). On this see the notes on 2:3. The evidence in this case does not concern essential, life-giving knowledge. Rather it is evidence of the arrival of the "last hour." Perhaps by coincidence a different formula is used here, translated as "from this we know" but quite different in Greek *(hothen ginōskomen)*. This phrase is used nowhere else in the NT, though *hothen* is used a total of fifteen times, of which six are in Hebrews, four in Matthew, three in Acts, and one each in Luke and 1 John. The idiom used here has been shaped by the author's interests. The appearance of the antichrists identifies the last hour. Such an explanation gives the antichrists an intelligible place in the scheme of things. In this way 1 John begins to control the damage he is about to describe.

Commentators are agreed that these words **(2:19)** provide evidence of a schism. That "they went out" *(exēlthan)* implies that "they" were once part of the community and that they left of their own accord. The precise circumstances were known to the readers and are not described in 1 John. The argument that those who left were never truly part of the community is used to lessen the impact of the schism on those who have been shaken by it. It is made to assure those who remain that they are secure. The schism revealed those who did not belong. The argument should not be extended outside the concern with which it was dealing. There is no suggestion that any of the opponents remain within the community, but there is a great deal of evidence that the author is fearful that the effects of their work may yet cause more damage in the community. For this reason, in addition to sharp criticism of those who have withdrawn, the author is strongly affirming of those who remain.

While 1 John repeatedly appeals to what the readers know, it continually instructs them in the path of true knowledge and identifies what is false. It may be that 1 John supplies no new knowledge, and in that sense assumes that the readers already know the truth **(2:20)**. But 1 John exhibits an anxious uncertainty about whether the readers will continue in the truth. They are assured, "and you have the anointing *(chrisma)* from the Holy One and you all know." The anointing is the ground of knowledge. In this section of text (2:18-27) three sentences begin with an emphatic "You" or "But you" (2:20, 24, 27). In Greek the indication of first, second, or third person, singular or plural, is expressed by the form of the verb. An additional personal pronoun, "You" (plural) is unnecessary. When it is used, as it is here, at the beginning of the sentence, it is for emphasis. Here in 2:20 *kai hymeis* has the sense of "But you. . . ." Thus the emphasis is on the group of readers addressed in 1 John. It is they who have been anointed by the Holy One (2:20, 27). The connection between these three sentences turns our attention to the middle sentence of 2:24. Here the emphasis is on the role of what was heard from the beginning; it is to *abide* in them. In 2:27 the anointing received is to abide in them. The structure of the three sentences makes an inclusion of 2:20-27 focused on the anointing. In the middle (2:24) what was heard from the beginning is described in terms similar to the anointing in 2:27. This suggests that the foundational message upon which the faith of the community grew is in view.

The result of the anointing is that "you all know." Although *ginōskomen* is used in 2:18 to express the way "we know it is the last hour" (see above on 2:3), the affirmation "you all know" uses *oidate* (see above on 2:11). The assurance that all the readers know is important in light of the uncertainty created by the schism. The textual variant supplies the missing content of knowledge, but this is given in what follows, in 2:21 and afterward. (See also on 2:27 and the Note on 2:20.)

In reassuring style 1 John continues to affirm the knowledge of the readers while at the same time clarifying the issues. If the author did not write because his readers did not know the truth (**2:21**, and see John 8:32 and the discussion of 1:6, 8; 2:4 above) but because they know it, he nevertheless makes sure that what is true and what is false is clearly stated. For this author truth and falsehood are black and white, starkly clear, and opposed. This language continues to make the reader aware of the presence of the opponents. That they went out shows that they did not belong because falsehood (a lie) does not come out of truth. The argument is an expression of the dualism of 1 John.

Mention of a lie raises the question of the identity of the liar (**2:22-23**). The question is, "Who is *the* liar?" The question implies a particular identification. In 2 Thess 2:8-9 there is reference to "the lawless one" who comes in the power of Satan with lying signs and wonders. See also reference to "the man of the lie" at Qumran in *CD* 20:14-15; 4QpPs 37 1:17-19; 4:13-14.

1 John at first gives a rhetorical answer in the form of a question. Who is it, if it is not the person who denies that Jesus is the Christ? The question is not answered; it is rhetorical. All that remains to be done is to identify the liar with the Antichrist. Earlier the Antichrist had been identified with antichrists who had separated from the community, the opponents of the author. Nevertheless, the significance of the many antichrists is gathered together and focused in the figure of the Antichrist.

The opponents deny that the Christ is Jesus. This opposition to Christ gives a basis for the identification of the opposition with the Antichrist. The reader already knows that "the Antichrist" is encountered in antichrists.

But in what sense does 1 John understand that Jesus is the Christ, and in what sense was it denied? Several scholars think that the problem arose because some Jewish believers came to question whether Jesus did fit the expectations concerning the Messiah (thus Teresa Okure, *The Johannine Approach to Mission* 235–81, especially 263, 268, 273–81). But most scholars recognize that in 1 John the confession that "Jesus is the Christ" has come to mean much the same as "Jesus is Son of God." The debate does not appear to be about Jewish messiahship. Along the same lines it is argued that the opponents denied that the Messiah was divine. This does not seem to be the point of dispute in 1 John. Rather the argument concerned the reality or relevance of Jesus' humanity (having come in the flesh) to his work of revealing God and bringing eternal life to believers.

While maintaining a Jewish perspective and a common context for 1 John and the Gospel, Martin Hengel argues that the introduction of the docetic teaching of Cerinthus, a Judeo-Christian influenced by popular philosophy encountered in Hellenistic synagogues, created the crisis addressed (*The Johannine Question* 59–63, 73, 105–106, 176–77). Hengel thus recognizes the evidence of a significantly different problem than a debate over whether Jesus fulfilled Jewish messianic expectations. This position recognizes the point at which christological debate occurs in 1 John. The identification of the confession, "Jesus is the Christ," with "Jesus is Son of God" suggests that the divine status is not in question in 1–2 John. Rather conflict has emerged over the humanity of Jesus Christ, at least over the significance of the humanity. Hengel's analysis of the problem in terms of docetism is on the right track. But the Johannine Epistles give no hint of a connection with Cerinthus. This Hengel has drawn from tradition. There seem to be grounds for recognizing a differentiation between Jesus and the Christ, but the identification of Cerinthus with Judaistic elements on the basis of Epiphanius (*Pan.* 28.2-5) is questionable (see Strecker, *The Johannine Letters* 69–76, especially 72). Careful analyses (from Brooke to Brown, 1912–1982, and beyond to Strecker, 1989) of the Cerinthus traditions have failed to find a basis for a confident identification of the teaching of the opponents with Cerinthus. It is better to restrict what we know of the opponents to what we can learn of them in the Johannine Epistles, though what we find there leaves many gaps and puzzles.

The reciprocity between Father and Son is expressed in the formula that the one who denies the Son does not *have* the Father and the one who confesses the Son *has* the Father *also*. Compare 2 John 9, which says that the person who abides in the teaching *has* the Father and the Son. In 1 John 5:12 "The person who has the Son has life." In the Son the Father is made known as the Father, and the Son is known in relation to the Father. Perhaps John 17:3 lies in the background: "This is the eternal life, to know you, the only true God, and Jesus Christ whom you sent." "Father" and

"Son" involve interrelated identities and, because the one implies the other, to deny the one is to deny the other. But because it is the Son who makes the Father known, confession or denial of the Son is the touchstone of faith. For this reason in 1 John the sending of the Son reveals the Father's love (4:9-11; see John 3:16 and on 1 John 1:3).

Had the personal pronoun "you" (plural) not been placed first for emphasis, this sentence **(2:24)** would have looked more like the opening of 1 John. The next word is the neuter relative pronoun, like the opening of 1 John. But in place of "what *was* from the beginning" we have "what *you* heard from the beginning." The "you" is made emphatic by placing an unnecessary personal pronoun at the head of the sentence, unnecessary except, that is, for emphasis. The emphasis is on the "you" who heard from the beginning. The third person singular present imperative active *(menetō)* is used to call on the readers to let the foundational message *(ho ap' archēs)* abide in them. The consequence of doing this is expressed in a conditional sentence: "If [the foundational message] abides in you, you will abide in the Father and the Son." The argument places the responsibility on the readers of 1 John. They are called on to let the message abide. Only if they do this will the condition be fulfilled, and as the message abides in them they will abide in the Father and the Son.

This motif of mutual abiding is Johannine (see John 15:4). The foundational message is identified with Jesus' word(s) (John 15:7). In 1 John the consequence of receiving that message (letting it abide) and keeping that message is to "abide in the Son and the Father." The order is somewhat surprising, being the reversal of what we find in 2:22. Perhaps the Son is here placed first because the controversy with the opponents concerns him.

The argument gives prominence to the foundational message, "the message which we heard from him" (1:5), "the message which you heard from the beginning" (3:11). The message that God is light is the foundation of the message "that we love one another" (3:11).

"This is the promise" **(2:25)** is formally like "this is the message" of 1:5; 3:11, and is probably intended to resonate in the reader's mind with these two texts. The promise is the same as the word for "message" with the addition of *ep(aggelia)*.

"*This* is the promise . . . ." apparently refers to the promise of "eternal life." The abrupt introduction of this theme has led some scholars to seek a backward reference for "this" in the content of some part of v. 24. But the word translated "this" is nominative feminine singular and seems to be the subject of the sentence of which "eternal life" (accusative feminine singular) is the object. The only real objection to this obvious reading is the abruptness of its introduction. So we can say that the foundational message ("what you heard from the beginning") looks back to 1:1-3, and in particular to 1:2, which deals with the revelation of life, the eternal life that was with the Father. Nevertheless, "this" does not refer back to 2:24; rather the theme is suggested by reference to the foundational message.

The foundational message suggests that the "he" who promised eternal life is Jesus. The controversy with which this passage deals concerns the Son. This confirms the reference to Jesus here. As elsewhere in 1 John, the author has not written in a way that makes his meaning unmistakably clear.

Eternal life is the central theme of 1 John. The gospel message can be described as "the message of life, the eternal life that was with the Father and was revealed to us." The overall purpose of 1 John was to ensure that the readers know that they have eternal life through believing in the name of the Son of God (5:13).

"*These things* . . . concerning the ones who [would] deceive *(tōn planōntōn)* you" **(2:26)** refers to 2:18-25. This reference confirms that the whole passage concerns the opponents, depicted here as deceivers. In 2 John 7 many deceivers *(polloi planoi)* are focused down to one in the assertion: "This is the deceiver and the Antichrist." This verse obviously runs parallel to 1 John 2:18, which first speaks of the coming of Antichrist but quickly moves to assert that many antichrists have actually appeared. Thus both 1 and 2 John show how the antichrist tradition has been modified by the actual situation, where the problem is not one single person but many who have gone out. The profile of that group is given in 2:18-25 and filled out by another reference to "the Antichrist" in 2:22. Connections between 4:1-6 and this passage as well as with 2 John 7 confirm that we are dealing with the same group there. The use of the participle with the article to describe "those who would deceive you" reveals another connection with 2 John 7. There Antichrist remains singular, as a description of the many deceivers, but "antichrist" is clearly used to characterize the many.

Verse **27** is a resumption, expansion and clarification of 2:20. Like 2:20, which follows the reference to the Antichrist/antichrists "who have gone out from us," 2:27 follows the reference to "those who would deceive you." As in 2:20, *kai hymeis* is adversative: *you* have the anointing, not the antichrists, not those who would lead you astray. Here, unlike 2:20, "the anointing" is with the definite article, which had to be supplied in 2:20. In place of "but you have an anointing from the Holy One" (2:20), here it is said, "but you, the anointing you *received* from *him* abides in you. . . ." That 2:20 implies that they received the anointing is clear. They did not anoint themselves. It is now made clear that it is *from him,* the Holy One. The present tense "you *have* the anointing" (2:20) implies continuing possession and does not simply refer to a past act (2:27: you received). This point is made in 2:27 by saying that the anointing "abides in you." Again

2:24 is called to mind with its appeal to "let [the foundational message] *(ho ap' archēs ēkousate) abide* in you."

Reference to the Spirit is suggested by "his anointing teaches you concerning all things" (2:27). In John 14:26 Jesus says of the Paraclete/Spirit of Truth, "he will teach you all things and will bring to your memory all that I told you." Thus the anointing involves the foundational message (all that I told you) and the activity of the Spirit, in continuing to teach and to bring to memory. 1 John assures the readers: "you have no need for any person to teach you." The use of *hina* here is explicatory. It gives the content of the need. As the need is negated, it means "you have no need that any one teach you," because his anointing "teaches you." But it is *what* his anointing teaches that is now in view, not simply the fact of the anointing. "As his anointing teaches *(didaskei)* you concerning all things . . . and just as *(kathōs)* he taught *(edidaxen)* you, 'Abide in him.'" The historic teaching of Jesus in the past is indicated by the aorist tense, "he taught," and the ongoing teaching of the anointing is expressed with the present tense, "it teaches." But the important point is the correspondence of the two in the one word of Jesus, "abide in him," or in Jesus' own words, "Abide in me." (See John 15:4, and cf. 15:5, 6, 7.) In 2:27 this is to be read as an imperative, not an indicative, as a command, "Abide in him," not a statement of fact, "you abide in him." This is borne out by the relation to John 15:4, but more importantly by 1 John 2:28.

The conflict with the opponents is still in view, and the author affirms that the teaching he refers to is true *(alēthes)* and not a lie *(pseudos)*. This expression of the Johannine dualism contrasts the teaching of 1 John with the teaching of the opponents; cf. 2:21, and see on 1:6. The noun *alēthēs* normally refers to statements or specific matters that can be true or false. In 2:27, as in 2:21, the truth is opposed to the lie, but it is now explicitly more comprehensive in its scope: "His anointing" teaches you concerning *all things.* While this involves the framework of the knowledge of faith, it finds its focus in knowing the Father in the Son. In the background is the innuendo that the opponents are liars. (See 2:22.)

In the struggle with the opponents the correspondence between the words of Jesus and a renewed word in the anointing has become an issue. The opponents had taken the line that the Spirit brought new words, appealing to tradition such as we find in John 16:12-15. This suggests that the Spirit not only brings to memory the words of Jesus but brings new words that Jesus was not able to speak, leading those anointed into all truth. Against this 1 John reasserts the power and normative character of the foundational message.

Something similar is described in John 17. There is a concentration in John 14–16 on the role of the Spirit as the one who takes the place of Jesus. In the prayer of Jesus in ch. 17 there is no mention of the Spirit in spite of the focus on the theme of Jesus' departure, leaving the disciples in the world (17:10). Where we might expect the prayer for the Spirit to comfort and lead them, Jesus asks, "Holy Father, keep them in your name which you gave to me" (17:11); "sanctify them in your truth; your word is truth" (17:17). John 17 may reflect something of the same crisis we see in 1 John. To deal with the opponents 1 John turns to the foundational message, not to the experience of the Spirit.

EXCURSUS: THE ANTICHRIST

"Antichrist" occurs only in 1 John 2:18, 22; 4:3, and 2 John 7 in the NT. These are the first known uses of the word. The earliest patristic reference is Polycarp, *Phil.* 7:1, which is dependent on 1 John 4:2-3. In 1–2 John the reference is to those who deny that Jesus Christ has come in the flesh, and it is thus identified with false prophets and deceivers. The power of such people comes from the devil, who is the model and source of the Antichrist. That the tradition of the coming of the Antichrist was known to the readers of 1 John is indicated by "even as you have heard, Antichrist is coming" (2:18). The interpretation of the situation of the schism of those who refused to confess Jesus Christ having come in the flesh in terms of the Antichrist (2:22 and 4:1-3) seems to have been the work of the author of 1–2 John. But "now many antichrists have appeared" (2:18). They are "the people who would deceive you" (2:26), described in 2 John 7 as "many deceivers," the "many false prophets" (1 John 4:1). Thus though the devil (Satan) inspires the Antichrist, in the NT the two are distinct. Outside the NT, in the post-NT period, the Antichrist becomes identified as the incarnation of Satan: *Sib. Or.* 3.63-74; *Asc. Isa.* 4.1-18.

Connections between the Antichrist of 1–2 John and the wonderworking false messiahs and false prophets (Mark 13:6, 22), "the abomination of desolation" (Mark 13:14), "the lawless one" (2 Thess 2:3-12), and the disastrous world ruler of Revelation 12–13 all draw attention to dependence on Jewish apocalyptic writings, especially the book of Daniel. Mark 13:14 depends on Dan (8:13; 9:27; 12:11) which refers to Antiochus IV Epiphanes (174–164 B.C.E.). Antiochus erected an altar to Zeus in the Temple (1 Macc 1:54; 2 Macc 9:12; Dan 8:11, 25). Mark 13:14 has interpreted the perfect participle *(estēkota)* translated as "standing" ("whenever you see the abomination of desolation *standing* where it must not") as a reference to the Antichrist.

Thus in Mark 13 there is a combination of two traditions related to the Antichrist: the world ruler who tramples down the nations (13:14) and the false Christs and false prophets (13:6, 22), the latter throwing light on the plural "false prophets" in 1 John 4:1 and the "antichrists" in 1 John 2:18 (cf. 2 John 7). The two traditions stand side by side in Mark 13. They are more closely united in 2 Thess 2:3-12 where "the man of sin," "the lawless one," "the one destined for destruction," is based on the depiction of the evil world ruler of Daniel who "sets himself" in the place of God (2 Thess 2:4 and cf. Dan 11:36). At the same time, the description of him as coming in the power of Satan with "counterfeit miracles, signs and wonders and with *every sort of evil* that *deceives* those who are perishing" (2 Thess 2:9-10) is related to the tradition of Deut 13:2-6 on the false prophets. See also the tradition in *Did.* 16:4 ("and then shall appear the deceiver of the world *[kosmoplanos]* as a Son of God, and shall do signs and wonders . . ."), which is dependent on Daniel and Deuteronomy. This has clear associations with the antichrist tradition as it appears in 1–2 John. The different developments of the antichrist tradition may be a consequence of whether they are in response to a political crisis (Revelation) or an internal religious crisis (1–2 John).

The diversity of the evidence in the NT witnesses to the development of traditions in the Second Temple period. When the NT writers drew on Daniel they did so through the filters of other traditions that were also working with the motifs found in Daniel. Nevertheless, in Jewish writings unaffected by Christian influence the figure of the Antichrist, named or unnamed, cannot easily be traced, though there are motifs that clearly contribute to the antichrist tradition. For example, in *Pss. Sol.* 17:27 the Messiah destroys his foes by the word of his mouth. In 2 Thess 2:8 the author speaks of the Man of Lawlessness, clearly an eschatological figure, in league with Satan (2:9), who sets himself up against God (2:4) and whom "the Lord Jesus will slay by the *breath (tō pneumati)* of his mouth at his coming." This comes close to antichrist language, but does not adopt it explicitly. Given the parallelism between word and spirit in Ps 33:6, it might be suggested that the author of 2 Thessalonians is working with a parallel tradition. It is in the early Christian tradition, Jesus' apocalyptic discourse in Mark 13 (and parallels), the discussion in 2 Thessalonians 2, and Revelation, particularly chs. 12–13 and 17, that the clearest lines are to be seen. See Wilhelm Bousset, *The Antichrist Legend*; A. E. Brooke, *Commentary* 69–79; Rudolf Schnackenburg, *The Johannine Epistles*, Excursus 7, 135–39; and Georg Strecker, *The Johannine Letters* 236–41, and the Interpretation of 2 John 7 below.

## For Reference and Further Study

Beutler, Johannes. *Die Johannesbriefe*, 63–77.
Bousset, Wilhelm. *Der Antichrist in der Überlieferung des Judentums, des Neuen Testaments und der Alten Kirche.* Göttingen: Vandenhoeck & Ruprecht, 1895. English: *The Antichrist Legend: A Chapter in Christian and Jewish Folklore.* London: Hutchinson, 1896.

Brooke, Alan England. *A Critical and Exegetical Commentary on the Johannine Epistles,*
    40–79.
Brown, Raymond E. *The Epistles of John,* 293–377.
Hengel, Martin. *Die johanneische Frage: ein Lösungsversuch.* Tübingen: J.C.B. Mohr
    [Paul Siebeck], 1993. English: *The Johannine Question.* London: S.C.M., 1989.
Okure, Teresa. *The Johannine Approach to Mission: A Contextual Study of John 4:1-32.*
    WUNT 2nd ser. 31. Tübingen: J.C.B. Mohr [Paul Siebeck], 1988.
Rensberger, David. *1 John, 2 John, 3 John,* 69–84.
Schnackenburg, Rudolf. *The Johannine Epistles,* 114–50.
Strecker, Georg. *Die Johannesbriefe.* KEK 14. Göttingen: Vandenhoeck & Ruprecht,
    1989. *The Johannine Letters: A Commentary on 1, 2, and 3 John.* Translated by
    Linda M. Maloney. Hermeneia. Minneapolis: Fortress, 1996.
Watson, Duane F. "1 John 2:12-14 as *Distributio, Conduplicatio,* and *Expolitio:* A
    Rhetorical Understanding," *JSNT* 35 (1989) 97–110.
Yates, Roy. "The Antichrist," *Evangelical Quarterly* 46 (1974) 42–50.

# III. SECOND PRESENTATION OF THE TWO TESTS
## (2:28–4:6)

## 1. THE ETHICAL TEST. DOING RIGHTEOUSNESS (= LOVE OF THE BRETHREN) AS THE SIGN BY WHICH WE MAY KNOW THAT WE ARE BORN OF GOD (2:28–3:24).

### 1.1. Acting righteously is the test of abiding in him (2:28-29)

> 28. And now, little children, abide in him, so that we may have confidence when he appears and not be shamed from his presence at his coming. 29. If you know that he is righteous, you also know that every person who does righteousness is born of him.

#### NOTES

28. *And now, little children, abide in him, so that we may have confidence when he appears:* "And now . . ." marks a transition. "Little children" *(teknia)* returns to the form of address in 2:1 (cf. 2:12). In the second list of the two forms of address to three groups (2:14), an alternative word for "little children" *(paidia)* is used and continues to be used in 2:18. See the Interpretation on 2:12-14.

Whereas the aorist indicative passive *ephanerōthē* was used of the Incarnation (see on 1:2), *ean* with the aorist passive subjunctive *(phanerōthē)* describes his future coming *(parousią)*.

*and not be shamed from his presence at his coming:* The expression "be shamed from his presence" is somewhat awkward. The problem is the first person plural aorist subjunctive, *aischunthōmen*, followed by *ap' autou'*. This and the previous expression with *schōmen* express coordinate purpose or result clauses, introduced by *hina*, but it has been separated from its following verbs by an intervening subjunctive construction introduced by *ean*. To make the sense clearer the translation has placed "when he appears" at the end of the first clause. This creates a greater sense of parallelism between the two clauses than exists in the Greek where a more chiastic structure might be seen. But even there the *hina* introducing the coordinate purpose/result clauses comes first. Brown (*The Epistles of John* 381) treats *aischunthōmen* as a middle rather than a passive (although the aorist subjunctive middle and passive do not take the same form) and suggests a chiastic structure. The sense suggested by the translation is to "be shamed by him at his coming" (see BDF §210.2). The sense is similar to Mark 8:38, which uses the accusative of the one of whom the Son of Man will be ashamed *(epaischunthēsetai)* when he comes. Matthew 10:33 and Luke 12:9 use the active "deny" rather than the passive "be ashamed of" in the parallel accounts. In Mark the idiom is different from 1 John in that it is the Son of Man who will be ashamed of the one who is ashamed of Jesus in this life. Perhaps in 1 John 2:28 *ap'* has the sense of being sent from Jesus' presence in shame, so that to be shamed by him is to be sent from his presence (cf. Prov 13:5).

For "we may have confidence" *(parrēsian)* see 3:21; 4:17; 5:14. This now becomes an important theme. "Confidence" is a prominent word in John, being used nine times (7:4, 13, 26; 10:24; 11:14, 54; 16:25, 29; 18:20) and only 16 times in the rest of the NT. Confidence and assurance are closely related.

Reference to (his) "coming" *(parousia)* is found only here in the Johannine writings but the word is used 24 times in the NT. There may be a play on the sound of *parrēsia* and *parousia*.

29. *If you know that he is righteous, you also know that every person who does righteousness is born of him:* 1 John does not say "As you know . . ." but "If you know. . . ." Nevertheless the conditional form need not imply uncertainty about the first statement. It is laid down as a condition to establish the second statement. On the use of the second person plural *eidēte*, see above on 2:20, though the use here is in the subjunctive mood after *ean*.

The verb *(gennan)* "to beget" is used 10 times in 1 John and 18 times in John. In 1 John the dominant use is with the passive voice, with *ek* to speak of those begotten of God, and only once in the active to refer to God as the begetter. Use in the Gospel is more varied. While the verb is used with *ek* six times, only once is God the begetter (1:13). Other sources of begetting are water and the spirit (3:5), the flesh (3:6), the spirit (3:6, 8), and sexual immorality (8:41). In a similar sense the passive is used with *anōthen* (3:3, 7). Another passive use occurs with the preposition *en*, "to be born in sin" (9:34). With the preposition *eis* see "I was born for this" (18:37). Other passive uses meaning "to be born" occur in 3:4 (2x); 9:2, 19, 20, 32, 34, 16:21 (2x). None of the uses in John deflects the evidence of 1 John from the obvious conclusion that in 2:29 "begotten of him" means begotten of God, so that those so begotten are children of God (3:1).

INTERPRETATION

Because the manifestation of the opponents signaled the arrival of the last hour, 1 John now calls on the readers to be prepared for the coming of Jesus. This leads into the theme of "the children of God" and its relation to the love command.

The transition to a new section is introduced by a renewed address, "And now, little children" **(2:28)**. The instruction, "abide in him" repeats the last words of the previous section, making a connection. Linking the "appearance" *(phanerōthē),* using the language of revelation, with the "coming" *(parousią)* of Jesus provides an incentive for abiding in him. That both of these terms here refer to the eschatological future coming is implied by the earlier declaration that it is the last hour (2:18). The description implies a scene of eschatological judgment.

The scene of coming judgment is the context for the command to "abide in *him,*" which must be a reference to Jesus, as mention of "his coming" confirms. The incentive for abiding in him is expressed in coordinate purpose/consequence clauses. The purpose/result is "that we may have confidence before him," that "we may not be sent in shame from his presence at his coming" (see Matt 25:41-46). The "we" expressed here is inclusive of writer and readers.

The parallel uses of the two verbs meaning "to know" ("if you know *[eidēte]* . . . you know [or the imperative, "know"] *[ginōskete]* that . . .") show that 1 John employs them without distinction of meaning **(2:29)**. The same kind of knowledge is involved. There may be grammatical reason for the choice of the different words at times. Here *eidēte* is a perfect subjunctive while *ginōskete* is a present indicative or imperative. The conditional form of the sentence implies that the second part is instructional whether the verb is indicative or imperative. Older commentaries (A. E. Brooke, *Commentary* 67–68) distinguished between intuitive, immediate knowledge *(eidēte)* and knowledge gained through experience *(ginōskete).* The distinction is not justified in the Johannine writings.

For the Johannine use of *dikaios* see above on 1:9. There it refers to God who is faithful and righteous. 1 John 2:1-2 speaks of Jesus Christ the righteous as the expiation for our sins and the sins of the whole world (cf. 5:19). Nevertheless it seems to be God, who is righteous, who is in view here because "born *from* him" and the end of v. 29 must refer to God (see 3:9 [2x];

4:7; 5:1 [3x], 4, 18 [2x]). See also John 1:13 where to be born of God *(ek theou)* follows reference to believers being given authority to be children of God *(tekna theou)*. In particular the expression of begetting with the preposition *ex* or *ek,* indicating source or origin, is commonly used in relation to God, but never with Jesus. Of the ten uses of the verb in 1 John, nine use this preposition. In the one use without *ek* the verb is active and not passive and refers to the begetter in a verse that twice uses the passive with *ek* (5:1). Of the ten uses in 1 John, the other nine clearly indicate that God is the one from whom believers are begotten. Further, the continuation in 3:1 refers to the Father and to believers as children of God *(tekna theou).* It seems clear that those who do righteousness are begotten of God.

How are we to account for the concentration on having been begotten by God in 1 John? All ten uses are focused on this theme, while the eighteen uses of the verb in John are less concentrated, given the length of the Gospel. Further, there nine of the eighteen uses deal with matters other than divine begetting. In the nine uses that remain, only one concerns precisely being "begotten of God" (1:13). There are two uses of "begotten from above," which use *anōthen,* not *ek* (3:3, 7); one reference to being begotten of water and the Spirit (3:5); and two concerning being begotten of the Spirit (3:6, 8). Where the Gospel is concerned to open the possibility of being so begotten of God, from above, of water and spirit, of the Spirit, 1 John is interested in laying down tests that demonstrate who is begotten of God and who is not. This suggests that 1 John is addressing claims to be begotten of God from those whose lives the author does not think conform to the reality of the claim. The tests are aimed at the position of the opponents with a view to assuring his readers of the validity of the teaching in 1 John.

The motif (born of God) seems to be Johannine, drawn from Jewish tradition. Its use in the Gospel shows no sign of internal conflict, but it seems to have been taken over by the opponents in 1 John. We may ask about the sources of the Johannine use and the impact of the opponents' use of being begotten of God. Given Israel's struggle with the fertility cults of Canaan, it is not surprising that the image of being begotten by God is not common in the OT. There are, however, a few important instances such as Ps 2:7, which speaks of the divine begetting of the Davidic king. This is especially important because at Jesus' baptism the voice from heaven pronounces the opening words of the verse, "You are my son" (Mark 1:11; Luke 3:22; cf. also Acts 13:33; Heb 1:5; 5:5). Though the quotation is cut before "this day have I begotten you," the Western text of Luke 3:22 treats Jesus' baptism as his begetting. It may be for this reason that Matt 3:17 adopts the language of the heavenly voice at the transfiguration, "This is my Son," which breaks the link with Ps 2:7 (see Mark 9:7; Matt 17:5; Luke 9:35). Of course, for Matthew and Luke, Jesus was divinely begotten at his conception (Matt 1:20; Luke 1:35), but the words of Ps 2:7 associated with the baptism of Jesus are evocative of divine begetting. We have another Western reading that treats John 1:13 as singular, "who was begotten, not of the flesh, nor the will of the flesh, nor of man, but of God." In the singular this must be a reference to Jesus, harmonizing the Incarnation tradition of 1:14 with virginal conception by divine begetting. This is clearly a secondary reading, whereas the Western reading of Luke 3:22 simply makes the allusion explicit.

Other texts worth noting (Ps 110:3 [109:3 LXX]; 1QSa 2:11-12) suggest that God may beget the Messiah. More important is the small sample of early Christian uses that shows that the Johannine use is drawn from a wider Christian tradition. See 1 Peter, which says that God "has begotten us anew *(anagennēsas)* to a living hope through the resurrection of Jesus Christ from the dead" (1:3), and "having been begotten anew *(anagegennēmenoi)*, not of corruptible seed but incorruptible, through the living and abiding word of God" (1:23), the readers are exhorted to "desire pure spiritual milk as newborn babes *(artigennēta)*." See also Titus 3:5, which refers to "the washing of regeneration *(paliggenēsias)*," and James 1:18, "he chose to give us birth *(apekuēsen)* through the word of truth." While not an overwhelming collection, it is diverse enough to show the spread of this way of thinking in early Christianity. The concentration in 1 John suggests that the use of this language became a problem in the encounter with the opponents. The tests provided suggest that the opponents did not make a connection between being born of God and an ethical response in doing righteousness.

The construction in 2:29 is conditional and need not imply uncertainty about whether the readers know that God is righteous. "If you know that God is righteous," *ginōskete* may be read as an indicative or an imperative. The meaning with the indicative is "you know that every person who does righteousness is born of him." With the imperative the meaning is "know that every person who does righteousness is born of him." The imperative clearly stresses the need to know that those who do righteousness are born of God. This is explicit. It is implicit in the conditional form with the indicative also but in a less forceful way. There we should understand the conditional sense as "If you know this, then you should know that." Either way, 1 John seeks to provide a criterion for recognizing who is born of God. Either way the condition implies that the author is not certain the readers know that "only those" and "all of those who do righteousness are born of God." Thus the argument makes a strong case for doing righteousness.

What does it mean to do righteousness? The analysis of Theodor Häring subsumes righteousness under the fulfillment of the love command. Robert Law maintains a threefold set of criteria, adding righteousness to love of the brother and a true confession of Jesus Christ having come in the flesh. Yet it is difficult to find what righteousness refers to in 1 John if it is not covered by the love command. This question needs to be addressed in the remainder of 1 John, for example, in 3:10.

## 1.2. Sanctification (separation from the corruption of the world) is the test of the claim to sonship of God (3:1-3)

> 1. See what love the Father has given to us that we should be called children of God; and we are. Because of this the world does not know us, it did not know him. 2. Beloved, now we are God's children, and it has not yet been revealed what we shall be. We know that when he is revealed we will be like him, because we will see him as he is. 3. And everyone who has this hope in him purifies himself even as he is pure.

### NOTES

3:1. *See what love the Father has given to us that we should be called children of God; and we are. Because of this the world does not know us, it did not know him:* "See" is the second person plural aorist active imperative meaning "Look!" It is used in the singular in John 1:29, 36, 47; 19:14, 26, 27. Normally it is a call to see something remarkable, and in John is a revelation formula.

Here, as with the use of *houtōs* in John 3:16 and 1 John 4:11, reference to "what *(potapēn)* love" draws attention to its character and extent. On love in 1 John see above on 2:5. God's love is expressed in giving, and here the perfect tense *dedōken* is used. In John 3:16 we find the aorist tense *edōken*, which may account for that variant here. In 1 John 4:10 the aorist *apesteilen* is used although the perfect tense *apestalken* was used to express the same act in 4:9. In 1 John aorist and perfect tense may be used without clear distinction, though the aorist may stress the event itself while the perfect emphasizes the ongoing consequences.

Codex Vaticanus (B) says "has given to *you*" rather than "to *us*," which is almost certainly the original reading. The influence of the language of 2:29 has been carried through, but the author has characteristically become inclusive in his language at this point.

God is appropriately referred to as Father in relation to children begotten of God; see 2:29 and the reference to "children of God" in this verse (3:1). On "Father" see above on 1:3.

The use of *hina* with the first person plural aorist passive subjunctive *klēthōmen* is epexegetical or definitive, expressing the content of the love given. This is the only use of "to call" *(kalein)* in the Johannine Epistles. This verb is used twice in John in two quite different ways from the use in 1 John: once (second person future indicative) when Jesus says to Peter, "you will be called Kephas" (1:42), and a second time (third person singular aorist passive) to indicate that Jesus was invited to the wedding at Cana (with his disciples).

On "children of God" see especially John 1:12 and also 11:52. In 1 John see also 3:2, 10; 5:2. In 2–3 John the phrase "children of God" is not used, though "children" is in 2 John 1, 4, 13; 3 John 4. Where the image of "being begotten" is used in 2:29, here it is said that the gift of love is "to be called children of God."

"Because of this" *(dia touto)* is used only here, in 4:5, and in 3 John 10 in the Johannine Epistles, and 15 times in John. There, as here, when followed by an epexegetical *hoti* (expressing the content of *touto*), "because of this" points to what follows (see John 5:16, 18; 8:47; 10:17; 12:18, 39). The following *hoti* determines this meaning. When there is no following *hoti,* then *dia touto* points back to a preceding statement (see 1 John 4:5; 3 John 10; John 1:31; 6:65; 7:21-22; 9:23; 12:27; 13:11; 15:19; 16:15; 19:11).

With "the world . . . did not know him" *(auton ouk egnō)* John 1:10 is echoed in this text *(ouk egnō auton).* On the "world" see 2:15-17.

2. *Beloved, now we are God's children, and it has not yet been revealed what we shall be. We know that when he is revealed we will be like him, because we will see him as he is:* For "beloved" see above on 2:7. For reference to "not yet" *(oupō)* see Mark 13:7; Rev 17:10, 12. The language connection between the "not yet" of the revelation *(oupō ephanerōthē)* and "what we shall be" "when he is revealed" *(ean phanerōthē,* 2:28, 3:2) is dramatic. At the same time he was revealed *(ephanerōthē,* 3:5, and see 1:2 [2x]; 3:8; [4:9]). The "now" of the present reality (3:2) is a consequence of the past when he was revealed *(ephanerōthē):* "to take away sin," 3:5; "to destroy the works of the devil," 3:8. The future revelation is expressed by constructions using the aorist passive subjunctive, while the past is expressed by the aorist passive indicative. On the use of *phaneroun* see 1:2. For "we know" *(oidamen)* see also 3:14; 5:15 [if we know], 18, 19, 20 and above on 2:3, 4.

3. *And everyone who has this hope in him purifies himself even as he is pure:* The construction "everyone who" followed by an articular participle, here *pas ho echōn* (see also 3:4, 6 [2x], 9, 10, 15; 4:7; 5:1 [2x], 18) is favored in 1 John. In 3:3 this construction allows the author to use a noun *(tēn elpida)* in place of a verb *(elpizein),* a practice to which the author is also inclined. The noun is used only here in the Johannine literature, and the verb is used only in John 5:45; 2 John 12; 3 John 14. In none of these three uses is "the Christian hope" the subject. In 2 and 3 John the Elder expresses his hope to visit and in John 5:45 Jesus speaks of Moses as the one in whom the Jews have hoped.

Reference to "this hope *in him (ep autǭ)*" might be distinguished from "even as *(kathōs)* he *(ekeinos)* is pure." But to distinguish the person on the basis of the use of a demonstrative pronoun is precarious; see 2:6. The demonstrative pronoun is used for emphasis rather than to identify different persons. On "purifies" *(hagnizei)* and "purity" *(hagnos)* note that these terms are rare in the NT and only the verb is used in John (11:55). The terms "holy" *(hagios)* and "sanctify" *(hagiazein)* are more common: see John 17:19. The purity terminology normally has a ritual context. See the references to the dual dealing with sin in terms of forgiveness and cleansing in 1:9. The language might be associated with baptism, though there is no positive indication of this. On the expression "even as he is," see above on 2:6. On *ekeinos* see on 2:3 and the references in 2:6, 3:3, 5, 7, 16; 4:17.

INTERPRETATION

Reference to being begotten by God **(3:1)** leads the discussion to the theme of the fatherly love of God for his children. Thus God is called Father and believers are called "children of God" (see also 3:2, 10; 5:2). The extent and character of the love is expressed in the gift that we should be called children of God. As neuter nouns *tekna* and the diminutive form *teknia,* used for familial address, have the advantage of being non-gender-specific when referring to people. The use of the other forms of address in 2:12-14 does not suggest that the author was conscious of a gender problem with his use of language. This is especially a difficulty in the love command, to love the *brother* (2:7-11; 3:10, 14, 16; 4:20, 21; [5:16]), though at 1 John 3:11, 23; 4:7, 11 the command is expressed in Johannine terms of "love one another" (see John 13:34-35).

The gift "that we should *be called children of God*" is a metaphor different from "being begotten of God" and more like the expression of John 1:12. To those who believe in his name (the name of Jesus) he gave (aorist tense) authority *(exousian)* to become children of God. Such authority implies something like adoption rather than begetting (though John too can use this metaphor: John 3:3, 5). To "be called children of God" in 1 John 3:1 also implies adoption. But the author of 1 John quickly adds, "and we are": we (writer and readers) are children of God. This might lead the modern reader to think that something more than adoption is in view. But all the references to the use of the term for "adoption" are from Pauline Epistles (see Rom 8:18, 23; 9:4; Gal 4:5; Eph 1:5) and the term is not used in John or 1 John. Indeed, there is no evidence of the use of the word prior to Paul and the five uses in the Pauline Epistles exhaust the evidence of the NT. Nevertheless, the metaphor of adoption can be implied without using the term, which the Pauline Epistles employ so powerfully on the few occasions it is called into service. The affirmation "and we are [children of God is implied]," in no way negates adoption. In the ancient world an adopted son was fully a son and heir. This was as true in the Roman Empire as in Israel. This is the point of Gal 3:26-29, which probably implies adoption: "For you are all sons of God through faith in Christ Jesus . . . and if you are of Christ you are seed of Abraham, heirs according to the promise," sons and heirs by adoption. In Johannine terms here they are children by adoption, and yes, really, children of God.

The final sentence of v. 1 would have been far clearer had the author simply left out the words translated "because of this." It is an example of the author's love of this kind of construction: "by this," "from this," now "because of this." This formula refers to the words following the epexegetical *hoti* that need not be translated. Its function is to signal that the following words give the content of "because of this." "Because of this the world does not know us, it did not know him." Thus it is implied that had the world recognized Jesus as Son of God it would have recognized the children of God. Of course, had it done this it would no longer have been the world in the Johannine sense.

The same verb "to know" is used in each case, though the first time in the present tense and the second in the aorist. Distinct meanings are found in these tense changes. For the writer it was a continuing reality that the world "does not know us," but the failure to know "him" now lies in the past. In each case "know" has the sense of recognize. The failure to recognize the Son of God in the past guarantees that the children of God are not recognized in the present.

Here it is "the world" that did not recognize "him." The world is constituted as the world precisely by its failure to recognize "him," the failure to know "him." But to whom does "him" refer, to the Father, or the Son? Certainly the Father is most recently mentioned. But in v. 2, without any indication of a change of subject, the reference to "if he appears [is revealed]" is surely a resumption of the reference to the "parousia" in 2:28, which implies a reference to Jesus. Further, the distinction of tenses makes the failure to know him (aorist) a past act. It is true that in John 8:19; 16:3 Jesus uses aorist tenses of the failure to know "the Father or me." This is a precarious base for arguing that the aorist here refers to the Father. The point of the aorist in those texts is precisely the historic failure to recognize the Father in Jesus; see John 14:8-11. Here, if the reference were to the Father apart from Jesus, a present tense would be appropriate: "The world does not recognize us because it does not recognize him." Rather the argument is that the continuing failure to recognize the children of God is a consequence of the failure to recognize the Son. See John 1:10, which uses this language of failure. Of course, for 1 John it is true that the Son is Son in relation to the Father. It is for this reason that the failure to recognize the Son definitively constitutes the world within the realm of darkness. Reference here to the Son is confirmed by the assertion that at his revelation/coming we will be like *him*, 3:2.

If to be called "children of God" is an expression of the Father's love, to address the readers as "beloved" **(3:2)** is entirely appropriate, as it was in 2:7. That the author once again affirms: "we are children of God" (see v. 1) shows there is need for this reassurance. To the assurance of v. 1 is added *"now,"* "now we are children of God." This may be a response to three things: (1) denial by the opponents and the world at large; (2) some suggestion that to be called children of God is not necessarily to be children of God; (3) preparing the way for the declaration that we are "not yet" *(oupō)* what we will be. Here 1 John gives concise and clear expression to the eschatological tension that permeates the NT (including, for example, John 5:24-29; 6:39, 40, 44, 54). The already is expressed in the "now" so emphatically affirmed. It is a result of the past revelation of Jesus Christ come in the flesh, revealing life and divine love, dealing with sin and destroying the works of the devil (1:2; 3:5, 8; 4:9). But it is not yet revealed what we shall be! The not yet is connected to "when he is revealed," "at his coming" (2:28; 3:2).

What we know *(oidamen)* is indicated by the first *hoti* clause (epexegetical). It is expressed in a conditional sentence (see 2:28). In both of these sentences (2:28 and 3:2) the construction *ean phanerōthē* is used to express the condition. This condition does not depend on any action of the readers, but on "if he appears (is revealed)." While 3:2 is a straightforward conditional sentence, 2:28 involves a second implied condition that the readers need to fulfill, that is, to abide in him. The condition there is expressed by the command to abide in him followed by a construction expressing purpose/result. It is really with this issue that 2:28 is concerned. Fulfillment by the readers is the point at issue. In 3:2 there is no such complication. It is simply a conditional sentence. That being the case, the "if" does not express uncertainty. It lays down the condition to be fulfilled if we are to be like him. The grounds for this conviction are then given in a second *hoti* clause that expresses cause: "because we shall see him as he is;" see 2 Cor 3:18; Col 3:4. We should ask whether this *hoti* clause provides the ground of our knowledge that we shall be like him or the means of the transformation. This may be a false alternative because to know the means of the transformation is the basis of knowing we shall be like him.

More important is the question of why the author thought that to see him is to be like him. It may be no more than the assumption that like is known by like (see Philo, *Gig.* 2.9 and E. R. Goodenough, *By Light, Light*). Philo sought to show that the ability of the mind to perceive the spiritual is based on affinity. That does not seem to be the point here. Alternatively there may be some thought that the object of vision has a transforming effect on the visionary. Or perhaps the thought is that, as only the pure in heart may see God, the knowledge that we shall see God also assures us that we shall be like God. What is clear is that, although a transformation has already taken place, "we are children of God," the *parousia* brings more change. Interestingly, if we do not know what we shall be, but we will be like him, there must be something about him that we do not know. Nevertheless, the point is to affirm that amid all the transformation there is more to take place at his coming.

"Everyone who has this hope" **(3:3)** refers to the hope of seeing him as he is and being made like him. If his coming is to be life-transforming, so is the interim before the coming. In the meantime those who have this hope purify themselves even as *(kathōs)* he is pure. It is tempting to take *kathōs* in both its senses: because he is pure and in the same way as he is pure. See 2:6, where *ekeinos* is also used to refer to Jesus, and the Notes on

2:3. No indication is given as to what purity means. Although it is a ritual term, no ritual is indicated. It is possible that baptism somehow lies in the background. This seems unlikely because the present tense *(hagnizei)* seems to apply to an ongoing process of purification.

## 1.3. The incompatibility of sin and righteousness (3:4-10)

> 4. Every person who commits sin commits lawlessness, and sin is lawlessness. 5. And you know that he was revealed to take away sins, and sin is not in him. 6. Every person who abides in him does not sin; every person who sins has not seen him or known him. 7. Little children, let no one deceive you; the person doing righteousness is righteous, even as he is righteous. 8. The person committing sin is of the devil, because the devil sins from the beginning. For this purpose the Son of God was revealed, that he might destroy the works of the devil. 9. Every person born of God does not commit sin, because his seed abides in him; and he is not able to sin, because he is begotten of God. 10. By this are revealed the children of God and the children of the devil: every person not doing righteousness is not of God, even the person not loving his brother.

NOTES

4. *Every person who commits sin commits lawlessness, and sin is lawlessness:* For "every person who . . ." see above on 2:23. This is a favorite expression of 1 John. See especially 2:29, "every person who acts righteously." But there is no good reason to think that these similar constructions have been taken from a source or should appear together in 1 John. They give expression to the author's stylistic tendencies and set the Johannine dualism in antithetical statements. On this use of *ho poiōn* see on 2:29; 3:4, 7, 8, 10. The object of the participle is "righteousness" in 2:29; 3:7, 10. In 3:4, 8 the object is "sin."

In Judaism sin is lawlessness by definition: the disregard for and breaking of the Law. Such an explanation seems unnecessary, or would have to Jewish readers. The word *anomia* is used in this verse in 1 John and fourteen times in the NT. In the LXX it is a synonym for "sin" *(hamartia)*, and the two words are often used in parallel (see Pss 32:1; 51:5 [31:1; 50:7 LXX]). Alternatively, given the eschatological perspective of the author (see 2:18), *anomia* may be related to "the man of lawlessness" of 2 Thess 2:3-8. But then it is difficult to see how sin in general is the eschatological iniquity. Attractive as this line of interpretation is, it seems better to take this argument as a straightforward explanation to readers who do not understand that sin is lawlessness. The problem with this reading is that there is no use of "law" *(nomos)* in 1 John. But there are frequent references to commandments (fourteen times in 1 John and four times in 2 John). Very likely "lawlessness" is understood as disregard for the commandments as set out in 1 John.

5. *And you know that he was revealed to take away sins, and sin is not in him:* For "you know that " *(oidate hoti)* see 2:29 and the Notes and Interpretation on 2:20, and cf. also the use of *ginōskomen hoti* in 2:3. The two verbs seem to be used without difference in meaning, though there may be grammatical reasons for choosing one or the other depending on tense and other formal matters. See also on 2:21. Here "you know" conveys the sense of the shared knowledge that is about to be conveyed. There is a variant (Sinaiticus [א] and some Sahidic mss), "we know." 1 John contains a bewildering series of changes from "we" to "you." That might account for variants. The use of *hoti* is epexegetical, indicating the content of what is known, and need not be translated. On *ekeinos* see above on 2:3 and references in 2:6, 3:3, 5, 7, 16; 4:17. The coming of the Son *(ekeinos)* was to deal with sins; see "cleanses," 1:7; "expiation," 2:1-2; 4:10. But a new term is used here to describe dealing with sins, "to take away sins." Compare John 1:29 and see 1 John 3:8. On "he was revealed" *(ephanerōthē)* see above on 1:2.

6. *Every person who abides in him does not sin; every person who sins has not seen him or known him:* For "every person who . . ." see above on 2:23. On the claim to "abide" see above on 2:6.

7. *Little children, let no one deceive you; the person doing righteousness is righteous, even as he is righteous:* The third person singular present imperative *planatō* means "let no one lead you astray." 2 John 7 speaks of "many deceivers" *(polloi planoi)* and "the Deceiver" who is identified with the Antichrist. See above on 2:18, and see 4:1-6.

   On "righteousness" see John 16:8, 10; 1 John 2:29; 3:7, 10; and for "righteous" see above on 1:9; 2:1, and see John 5:30; 7:24; 17:25. While these are not frequent Johannine terms they are nonetheless very important when they are used.

   The "devil" *(diabolos)* is used four times in 1 John, three times in this verse, and once in v. 10. See also John 6:10; 8:44; 13:2. 1 John 3:12 refers to Cain "who was of the Evil One and murdered his brother," and 5:19 says that "the whole world lies in [the power] of the Evil One." The Gospel refers to "the prince of this world" (John 12:31) and to the role of Satan in the betrayal by Judas (John 13:27). The Johannine dualism features strongly in this perspective.

8. *The person committing sin is of the devil, because the devil sins from the beginning. For this purpose the Son of God was revealed, that he might destroy the works of the devil:* On "from the beginning" see above on 1:1. Here there can be no doubt that "from the beginning" refers to the action of the verb "he sins." What makes this difficult is the use of the present tense *(hamartanei).* The aorist *(hēmartēse)* or perfect tense *(hēmartēke)* would have been more appropriate. The use of the present tense almost defies a beginning unless it is read as an historical present. In that case it is unclear whether the beginning refers to the early chapters of Genesis or to some primordial act. Alternatively the clause can be read as meaning "he always has been sinning." But then there is no beginning!

9. *Every person born of God does not commit sin, because his seed abides in him:* "Every person who has been begotten of God" *(pas ho gegennēmenos ek tou theou')* "does not commit sin" *(hamartian ou poiei),* but see 1:8, 10. The *hoti* here is

causal, giving the reason why he does not commit sin, "because his seed is in him." But what is the "seed" and who is it in?

(1) That the seed is Jesus ("seed" here = descendant) abiding in every person begotten of God is unlikely. First, this understanding of "seed" places Jesus with those begotten of God, yet he abides in everyone so begotten. That Jesus abides in believers is Johannine (John 6:56; 15:4, 5). The problem is understanding him as the "seed" of God alongside others spoken of as begotten of God. The identification also seems unlikely in the context.

(2) The believer is the seed of God, abiding in God. Again seed is taken in the sense of descendant, the one begotten of God; thus everyone begotten of God is the seed and abides in God. There is ample evidence of "seed" being used of descendants. In John "seed" always refers to physical descendants, and Paul speaks of believers as Abraham's seed. While this sense is not impossible, it does not fit this context. It seems odd to say that the one begotten of God is the seed because the seed is also the generative agent in begetting. Thus to say that God's seed abides in himself leads to an unhelpful line of thought. The image suggests infertility.

(3) The seed *(sperma)* is God's sperm. Obviously this is used as an image and not biologically. Biology suggests the image. Just as the male sperm generates new life, so does God's sperm. But to what does this analogy refer? There are three possible understandings of this imagery.

a. The seed is the word of God. There is precedent for arguing this in Luke 8:11 ("The seed *[sporos]* is the word of God"); Jas 1:18 ("By his will he begot us by the word of truth"); 1 Pet 1:23 ("being begotten not of corruptible but of incorruptible seed *[sporas]*, through the living and abiding word of God"). See also 1 Pet 1:3. There is thus good precedent for this identification. There are two problems. We find no such identification in the Johannine writings. This is not fatal because these writings are not isolated from other early Christian writings. More serious is that all of the texts that identify the seed with the word use *sporos* and not *sperma*. But there is no doubt that both words can be used in this way. Certainly Justin Martyr uses *sperma* of the word, "Those who believe in him are people in whom there dwells the *sperma* of God, the Word" (*1 Apol.* 32:8). This might show dependence on 1 John. If so, it is evidence of an early interpretation.

b. The seed *(sperma)* is the Holy Spirit. Those who adopt a covenantal interpretation of 1 John (but not Malatesta) refer to the promise of a new heart and a new spirit in the new covenant of Ezek 36:26-27. More directly, the Spirit is related to birth *anōthen* (John 3:3, 5), and the Spirit seems to have a role in the anointing of 1 John 2:20, 27.

c. The lack of clarity in identifying the "seed" suggests that the author has not clearly distinguished the word from the Spirit. In 2:20 Jesus is the Holy One from whom the anointing comes, but the anointing itself seems to involve both word and Spirit. Here the generative "seed" seems to involve both word and Spirit.

*and he is not able to sin, because he is begotten of God:* The clause "he is not able to sin" is made up of three words in Greek, the negative *ou*, the third person singular present indicative active verb *dunatai,* and the present infinitive "to sin" *(hamartanein).* The verb *dunasthai* is used elsewhere in 1 John only at 4:20, but appears 36 times in John. It is normally followed by an infinitive. None of these Johannine cases provides a basis for the statement about not being able to sin.

Clearly part of the context of these statements is the author's intention to strongly deter sin; see 2:1. Thus there is the hope, perhaps even the expectation, that his readers will not sin. It might even be argued that the meaning in 1:6 is that a person does not sin while abiding in him. To sin is by definition to cease to abide in him because there is no sin in him (1:5). There is no consideration of sins of ignorance in 1 John. That would have introduced a further complication.

Further, in 3:6 the saying "everyone sinning" uses the article with the present participle, as in the previous statement about "every person abiding." Both refer to more than single actions. They imply characteristic modes of being. In v. 6 those abiding are contrasted with those sinning, just as the person doing righteousness is contrasted with the person doing sin in vv. 7-8. In each case the article with the present participle is used *(ho poiōn).* Again more than a single action is implied by this construction. Verse 9 then brings this analysis to a conclusion. It does so by affirming that the person begotten of God, in whom God's "seed" abides, cannot sin because he is begotten of God.

10. *By this are revealed the children of God and the children of the devil; every person not doing righteousness is not of God, even the person not loving his brother:* For "by this" *(en toutō)* see above on 2:3. This is a variation on the idiom "by this we know," which could have been used here without change of meaning: "By this we know the children of God and the children of the devil." The second half of v. 10 provides an initial statement of the evidence indicated by the phrase, "By this." Formally this is taken up in the *hoti* clause of v. 11. Both the second half of v. 10 and 3:11-18, introduced by the *hoti* clause, interpret "doing righteousness" as "loving his brother." The author also might have used the verb *ephanerōthē* (see above on 1:2) but instead has used the third person singular of the verb "to be" *(estin)* and the adjective *phanera.* The neuter plural takes a singular verb in Greek. On the devil see above on 3:8. "Every person not doing righteousness is not of God" is a Johannine idiom (see 2:16, 21, 23; 3:6; 4:3).

## INTERPRETATION

Verses 4-10 are closely connected to 2:28–3:3 and 3:11-18, which also deal with "children of God" and how to recognize them. Having introduced the theme, 1 John now sets out to distinguish the children of God from the children of the devil. The theme is closely related to John 8:31-47, especially 8:40-41, 44. There Jesus accuses the Jews of being children of the devil because they sought to kill him. The children are like their father, who was a murderer from the beginning *(ap' archēs)*. (See 1:1; 2:7, 13, 14, 24; 3:8, 11.) That makes the devil the archetypal murderer and the father of all murderers; see 3:12. In 3:8 the devil is depicted as the archetypal sinner. It is unclear whether the sin of murder is in view, thus making 3:8, 11 parallel statements.

In this subsection (vv. 4-10) the person who does righteousness is set against the person who does sin. This is done formally by constructing statements using the article with the present (or perfect) participle in antithetical parallelism. The pattern of the statements is "every person who does . . ." *(pas ho poiōn . . .*; see above on 2:23); or "the person doing . . ." *(ho poiōn . . .*; see John 3:21). The construction is used to speak of "every person doing sin," 3:4; "the person doing sin," 3:8; "the person doing righteousness," 3:7; "the person not doing righteousness," 3:10. It is used with other participles: "every person abiding in him" *(ho . . . menōn*, 3:6); "every person who is born of God" *(pas ho gegennēmenos*, 3:9); "the person not loving his brother" *(ho mē agapōn*, 3:10). This use should be distinguished from the simple use of the verb in the indicative active: *hamartanei*. The latter describes an action, while the article with the participle describes a way of being. This use *(ho poiōn . . .)* should also be distinguished from the negative "we do not do the truth" *(ou poioumen*, 1:6).

The motivation to purity based on the purity of Jesus (v. 3) remains important in the present section (3:4-10). Here, again using the characteristic construction "every person who . . ." plus present participle, 1 John defines sin as lawlessness. Such a definition would hardly be necessary in a Jewish context. That the author presupposes non-Jewish readers is supported by the absence of references to the Jewish Law or any quotation and discussion of the Jewish Scriptures. Thus lawlessness is a disregard for "his commandments," 2:3. The parallelism between law and commandments is common in Scripture (see Ps 119:6-7, 18-20), so that this use of "lawlessness" is not inappropriate. Disregard of the commandments, as set out in 1 John, seems to be one of the charges brought against the opponents. The only commandments specified are described as "his commandment": (1) to believe in the name of his Son Jesus Christ, and (2) to love one another as he gave *(edōken* without a pronoun) us command (3:23). Though the initial reference to "*his* commandment" seems to be a reference to God, it is difficult to think that the command "to love one another" is not a reference to Jesus' commandment in John 13:34-35. See the discussion of 3:22-23. In 3:23 the love command seems to be grounded in belief in the name of his Son Jesus Christ.

The author appeals to common knowledge: "you know" **(3:5)**. What is known seems to be the basis of a creedlike statement: "he was revealed to take away sins." The purpose of the revelation is stated in a *hina* clause with the verb in the subjunctive (aorist active). The same construction is used in 3:8 to state the same purpose but in different terms; there it is "to destroy the works of the devil." The same verb is used here *(arē)* as in John 1:29, though the construction is quite different: "Behold the lamb of God who *takes away (ho airōn)* the sin of the world." For the one epitomized as "the lamb of God" it is of the essence of his being to take away the sin of the world. This seems to be true, though we do not know the background of the imagery concerning "the lamb." But in 1 John 3:5 *hina* with the aorist subjunctive is used to emphasize the purpose of his coming (not the present participle with the article used as a verbal noun, which focuses on the doer of the action). Where John 1:29 uses the singular "sin," 1 John regularly speaks of "sins" in connection with the work of Jesus (see 1:7, 9; 2:2, 12; 4:10). The singular "sin" in John 1:29 may be understood as a collective noun having no significantly different meaning from the plural. The collective singular views the multiplicity as a whole, whereas the plural retains a focus on the multiplicity. Alternatively, the singular might suggest a translation of "guilt" rather than "sin."

The aorist tenses in 3:5, 8 describe the purpose of his coming as a decisive action. It implies that sins have been taken away, that the works of the devil have been destroyed.

Given the reference to the revelation of Jesus *(ekeinos)* to take away sins, what are we to make of the statement "and sin is not *in him"(en autō)*? This is certainly a continuing reference to Jesus. When the sinlessness of Jesus is affirmed, the singular "sin" is used. The claim of the opponents, "We have no sin" (also singular in 1:8), is self-deception, but the author affirms of Jesus, "sin is not in him." The opponents' claim to have no sin might have been developed from the teaching of the sinlessness of Jesus. The opponents may have claimed for themselves what 1 John teaches about Jesus.

In light of the rejection of the opponents' claims to have no sin and "we have not sinned" (1:8, 10), **3:6** seems a bit surprising. The statement is made alongside the affirmation that "there is no sin in him." It follows that "every *person abiding* in him does not sin." The use of the present participle with the article *(ho menōn)* to describe the person abiding implies the characteristic way of being for that person. The present tense of the verb "does not sin" *(ouch hamartanei)* may suggest more than a single act of sin, which might have been indicated by an aorist. In the antithetical parallel statement, "every person who sins has not seen him or known him," the use of the present participle with the article completes the definition of the two groups of people: "every person abiding in him" and "every person sinning." Each group is defined by either "abiding in him" or "sinning." The constructions suggest a state of being rather than an act. 1 John does not say, in full antithetical chiastic parallelism with the first statement, "everyone sinning does not abide in him," but introduces two different aspects of the relationship with Jesus. Using perfect tenses, he says that every person sinning *"has not seen* or *known* him" (see 2:4). 3 John 11 says that "the person doing evil *(ho kakopoiōn) has not seen (ouch heōraken)* God." In Johannine terms, to see Jesus is to see God (John 14:9).

The renewed address of the readers as "little children" **(3:7)** does not mark a new section but introduces a direct appeal to them after an exposition begun in 2:28. The appeal is in the form of an exhortation, "let no one lead you astray" or, to maintain the language, "let no one deceive you." Deceivers are abroad (2:26, and see 2 John 7). The language calls attention to the opponents, who are dubbed "deceivers" in 2 John 7 and "false prophets" in 1 John 4:1; the Liar and the Antichrist in 2:22; cf. 2:18.

The remainder of v. 7 forms an antithetical parallel statement with the first part of **3:8**. The person doing righteousness is set over against the person doing sin and the implications of the way of being of each is set out. Again we note that the article with the present participle is like a verbal noun describing the characteristic way of being of a person. It is not simply the description of a single act but the description of the characteristic way of acting. In each case the characteristic way of acting is described using the present participle of *poiein* with the definite article *(ho poiōn)* and the nouns "sin" *(tēn hamartian)* and "righteousness" *(tēn dikaiosunēn)* respectively, instead of the more direct *ho hamartanōn*. Thus the person doing righteousness, on the one hand, and the person doing sin, on the other, are described in antithetical parallelism. In each case "righteousness" and "sin" are expressed in the singular with the definite article, unlike in 3:5 where it is said that "he was revealed to take away *sins,* and *sin* is not in him." Here "sins" has the definite article but "sin" does not.

The person doing righteousness is said to be righteous as *(kathōs)* he *(ekeinos)* is righteous, but "the person who does sin is of *(ek)* the devil;" see John 8:44. Because the discussion from 3:1-2 onward has been about the children of God it did not need to be said that the person doing righteousness is of God. Instead, 1 John identifies this person with Jesus Christ the righteous (see 2:2), though it is also said that God is righteous (1:9). Certainly the use of the demonstrative *ekeinos* suggests that Jesus is in view (see on 2:6), though other prepositions may be used of him, especially in a nonemphatic way. In 1 John all uses of the demonstrative pronoun *(ekeinos)* in the nominative case refer to Jesus. The only other use is genitive and feminine, *ekeinēs* (5:16) in a phrase "concerning that [sin]." The use of *kathōs* in this construction also points to Jesus and perhaps arises from the language of the love command of John 13:34, though there are other notable *kathōs* sayings such as 13:15; 15:12; 17:11, 18, 21, 22; 20:21. The use of this word suggests that Jesus is the source and mode of the believer's righteousness.

The devil is said to sin *(hamartanei)* from the beginning *(ap' archēs)*; see John 8:44, where it is said "he was a murderer from the beginning" *(ekeinos anthrōpoktonos ēn ap' archēs)*. In John the devil is also marked by the emphatic use of *ekeinos.* Perhaps this should be seen as an expression of the opposition between the two (see 1 John 2:8). That the present tense *(hamartanei)* is used suggests that reference is not to a single act. Rather (used with *ap' archēs*) it is to say that the devil sins and always has. Reference to "the beginning" may have Genesis in mind, as is confirmed by John 8:44. The only allusion (there is no quotation) to the OT in 1 John (3:12) is to Cain, "who was of the Evil One and murdered his brother."

The statement "he was revealed to take away the works of the devil" (v. 5) does not specifically identify Jesus. In a parallel statement at the end of v. 8 the Son of God is named: "because of this the Son of God was revealed to destroy the works of the devil." "Because of this" draws attention to the following reason or purpose of the revelation of the Son of God. That purpose, expressed by *hina* with the verb in the subjunctive mood, was "to destroy sin." This is confirmed by the parallel statement of purpose in 3:5, "to take away sins." Added to the purpose of taking away sins is now the destruction of the works of the devil. The idea of taking away sins is illuminated by 1:7; 2:2; 4:10, while 5:19 provides a context for understanding the destruction of the works of the devil, and victory over the world is promised to those who believe that Jesus is the Son of God (5:4-5).

Chapter 3 begins with the announcement that we are called children of God: "and we are . . . now we are children of God." If this language suggests adoption, **3:9** speaks of "every person who has been begotten of God." To speak of being "of God" refers to the origin and source of being. To speak of being begotten tells of the means of establishing that origin. But how does God beget children, and what is the consequence? In keeping with this imagery 1 John speaks of God's *sperma* as the agent of the begetting. The *sperma* symbolizes the dynamic activity of the word of the gospel, the word of God in creating new life (see Luke 8:11; Jas 1:18; 1 Pet 1:23). But in the Johannine tradition word and Spirit act in concert so that it is a living and life-giving word. In 1 John that word is anchored in the foundational message. This is stressed again and again by reference to what was heard from the beginning (1:1, 2:7, 13, 14, 24; 3:11; and cf. 2 John 5, 6).

Thus it seems that those begotten of God have God's "seed" abiding in them. These are alternative descriptions. It is argued that the person begotten of God does not commit sin *(hamartian ou poiei'*, v. 9a). How can this be so? "Because God's seed *abides* in him" (present indicative active). But there is a development in v. 9b: "he (the person in whom God's seed abides) is not able to sin" *(ou dunatai hamartanein)*. How can this be so? "Because he is begotten of God." This clarification moves from "does not" to "is not able" (to sin). In the latter case the present infinitive used in conjunction with *dunatai* does not indicate a change of meaning. The infinitive is normally used with *dunatai*. The identification of "everyone begotten of God" with the one in whom "his seed abides" means that "does not sin" becomes "is not able to sin" with no further clarification or explanation.

Further descriptions suggest that the imagery of being begotten of God and having God's "seed" abiding are not the only ways 1 John deals with this theme. 1 John 3:6 says, "Every person abiding in him does not sin" *(ouch hamartanei)*. This seems to be the equivalent of 3:9a. There are two linguistic differences. 1 John 3:6 uses the negative *(ouch)* with the verb "to sin" *(hamartanei)*, while 3:9a uses the noun "sin" with negative *(ou)* and the verb "he does." Then 3:6 speaks of "every person abiding in him," while 3:9a says "every person begotten of him." The formal similarity of the beginning of each sentence confirms that we have equivalents, so that "abiding in him" is the equivalent of "being begotten of him" (3:9a), and "hav[ing] his seed abide in him" (3:9b). That this reading and recognition of equivalence is correct is confirmed by 5:18. The reciprocity of abiding becomes clear in these overlapping texts. The believer abides in him (3:6) and his seed abides in the believer (3:9b). For either reason, the believer does not sin.

"Every person who is begotten of God does not commit sin" *(hamartian ou poiei*, 3:9a) and "every one abiding in him does not sin" *(ouch hamartanei*, 3:6) confirm that in 1 John *ouch hamartanei* has the same meaning as *hamartian ou poiei*. Reference to the *sperma* of God is elaborated in the explanation of how the one begotten of God does not sin (3:9b), but without clarification. Indeed, the argument is taken further: "he is not able to sin." Why? "Because he is begotten of God" (3:9d). From the explanation of "does not sin" on the basis of "being born of God," the argument turns to "not able to sin" for the same reason. Further discussion must be postponed until 5:18.

The generative "seed" that makes the believers children of God is the word of the gospel enlivened by the activity of the Spirit. Through this activity believers come to belong to the family and likeness of God as children of God. But in the light of 1:8, 10, how are we to understand the statement that such a person is not able to sin *(ou dunatai hamartanei)*? To deal with this apparent contradiction, scholars have suggested a variety of solutions. Some posit the use of conflicting sources. There is no evidence of this. Others suggest that the author addresses the needs of different groups. This hardly overcomes the conflict. That he is dealing with different problems may be true, but the answers remain in conflict. There is some plausibility to the argument that the language used suggests that the problem finds a partial solution in recognizing that the author is frequently talking about a mode of behavior (using the definite article with a present participle) rather than single actions. Thus we can say that those "abiding in him" do not characteristically live in sin. But this hardly gets around the problem of 3:9, "he is not able to sin."

In 3:4-10 two groups are being contrasted, those doing sin and those doing righteousness. Verse 10 is a concluding summation. The point has been to set out in stark clarity a typology of the children of God and the children of the devil. There is no room in this task for overlapping or blurring of distinctions. This helps to throw light on the increasingly clear-cut distinctions between the two groups as we approach the conclusion. It is here too that the author finally gives content to his understanding of sin. Both final statements concern those who are not of God, which by implication means they are children of the devil. Everyone not doing righteousness is not of God. Not doing righteousness is the same as doing sin (see 3:7-8a). There the contrast is between righteousness and sin and it is said that "the person doing sin is of the devil." In 3:10 by implication the one not doing righteousness is a child of the devil. Thus to do sin is not to do righteousness. To fail to do righteousness is also sin. And who is it who fails to do righteousness? It is the person who does not love his brother.

We return to the difference of opinion between Theodor Häring and Robert Law. Are there two or three tests applied in 1 John? Does the author have a christological test, a love test, and a righteousness test? Or are righteousness and love two ways of speaking of the one reality? There are justice issues that go beyond the explicit scope of the love command in 1 John. It may be that this command is more comprehensive in terms of the Johannine community than is sometimes recognized. Admitting to the wider scope of issues does not mean that they are treated in 1 John. We are hard put to find any concrete actuality for righteousness beyond the love command in 1 John. There is a sense in which it is true to say that divine love encompasses justice, but it cannot be said that justice encompasses divine love. Where 1 John falls down is in the apparent restriction of love to "the brother," or to one another. Even here we should be careful to note that there is no command to hate those who do not belong to the community, not even the opponents.

Given the stark contrast between the children of God and the children of the devil, it is likely that the critique of failure to love is aimed at the opponents. If the author refers to them as deceivers, false prophets, and antichrists it is of a piece that he should describe them as children of the devil. Even here we should note that it is the one described as a child of the devil who is charged with not loving *his* brother, 3:10. This may mean that love for the brother, including members of the schismatic group, was not a foundational commitment for the opponents. The critique given in 1 John suggests that the refusal to confess Jesus Christ come in the flesh led to a devaluation of Jesus' earthly life and the foundational love command that he gave. This explains the emphasis on the foundational nature of the command in 1 John 2:7-11 and its connection to the christological confession in 3:23. This theme appears again in 3:11-18.

The form of 3:10 (see the Notes) is designed to make starkly apparent the difference between the children of God and the children of the devil. This is consistent with the pervasive antithetical parallelism throughout 1 John. "By this is manifest" is not followed by a *hoti* clause or some relative clause. To what then does "By *this*" refer? If 3:9 identifies those who are born of God as those who do not sin, the second part of 3:10 identifies the one who does *not* do righteousness, who does *not* love his brother, as *not* of God and, by implication, a child of the devil. This theme leads naturally into the reference to Cain as the archetypal child of the devil.

## 1.4. The incompatibility of love and hate (3:11-18)

> 11. For this is the message that you heard from the beginning: love one another; 12. not as Cain who was of the Evil One and murdered his brother; and why did he kill him? because his works were evil, but the works of his brother were just. 13. Do not be surprised, brothers, if the world hates you. 14. We know that we have passed out of death into life, because we love the brothers; the person not loving abides in death. 15. Everyone who hates his brother is a murderer, and you know that every murderer does not have eternal life abiding in him. 16. By this we know love, he laid down his life for us; and we ought to lay down our lives for our brothers. 17. But whoever has the wealth of the world and sees his brother having need and shuts off his compassion from him, how does the love of God abide in him? 18. Little children, let us love neither in word nor tongue but in deed and truth.

### Notes

11. *For this is the message that you heard from the beginning: love one another:* The "for" or "because" *(hoti)* that opens this verse begins the explanation of why the person who does not love his or her brother/sister does not do righteousness and is not of God (3:10). It is because of the foundational message embodying the commandment that we love one another. The language "love one another," as distinct from reference to loving the brother, clearly looks back to the love command of John 13:34. Only this connection can explain the idiom "one another" in a context that deals with Cain's failure to love his brother.

  "This is the message:" see above on 1:5. Here a variant reading, "this is the promise," is probably the result of a careless scribal error because "message" *(aggelia)* is found only here and in 1:5 in the NT, while "promise" *(epaggelia)* is found 51 times, though only once (1 John 2:25) in the Johannine writings.

The use of *hina* is epexegetical, that is, the clause it introduces provides the content of the message. It has the same force as *hoti* in 1:5. The difference is that 3:11 expresses a command using *hina* with the subjunctive. This would not have been appropriate for a straightforward (indicative) statement.

12. *not as Cain who was of the Evil One:* The negated use of *kathōs* in *"not like* Cain" *(ou kathōs)* is found in the NT elsewhere only in John 6:58; 14:27 and 2 Cor 8:5. For "from the beginning" see above on 1 John 1:1 and 3:8.

Reference to Cain does not depend on a scriptural quotation but rather develops on the tradition found in John 8:39-44. The Johannine treatment of Cain goes beyond the story of Gen 4:1-16, possibly as a result of the Johannine dualism. Cain is of the Evil One, and the slaying of his brother (Abel is not mentioned by name in 1 John) is a manifestation of his own evil deeds. Thus 1 John treats Cain and his brother as examples of the children of God and children of the devil (the Evil One, 3:10). Cain's evil works identify him with the Evil One, just as his brother's righteous works *(dikaia)* identify him as one of the children of God.

The influence of Jewish tradition on the understanding of Cain is exemplified by Philo. His most sustained treatment of Cain is gathered in the first four works of the second volume of his collected writings in the Loeb Classical Library. In the second part of "On the Cherubim," Adam (= mind) "knew" Eve (= sense perception), who bore Cain (= possession), the impious idea that what we have is our own and not God's. The other three works are "On the Sacrifices of Abel and Cain," "The Worse Attacks the Better," and "On the Posterity and Exile of Cain." Josephus also *(Ant.* 1.52-62) contrasts the *righteousness* of Abel with the *evil* of Cain, in common with the wording of 1 John 3:12. The *Apocalypse of Abraham* 24:5 explains that "Cain acted lawlessly under the influence of the Adversary [Satan]." For Cain in early Christian tradition see Heb 11:4; Jude 10-11. Thus in Jewish and early Christian works Cain epitomizes the impious and unbelievers. Here there is no neutrality because unbelief is violently opposed to the children of God. Compare also *T. Benj.* 7:5, which describes the punishment in store for "those who are like Cain in the envy and hatred of brothers."

*and murdered (esphaxen) his brother:* This verb *(sphazō)* is used twice in the aorist tense in this verse. Elsewhere in the NT it is found only in Revelation (5:6, 9, 12; 6:4, 9; 13:3, 8; 18:24). It always expresses violence. It is used of the lamb slain and of those slain for their witness to the word of God. In the LXX it is most frequently used in relation to sacrifice (see Gen 22:10; Exod 29:11; Lev 1:5; Num. 11:22). On the use of "brother" see above on 2:9.

*and why did he kill him? because his works were evil, but the works of his brother were just:* "And why did he kill him?" (literally "for the sake of what?") is an idiom found only here in the NT (see BDF §216.1). Cain's slaying of his brother shows his origin as "of the Evil One," who was a murderer "from the beginning" (John 8:44). Thus just as he is the father of all liars, so is he the father of all murderers. Similarly, in John, Satan enters into Judas for the act of betrayal (John 13:27), and Jesus describes him as a devil (John 6:70-71). Although 3:11 turns to the idiom of the commandment, to love "one another," here, as in

3:10, the idiom of loving or not loving the (his) brother is in view because of the context of the Cain and Abel story.

13. *Do not be surprised, brothers, if the world hates you:* The sentence probably began with "And" *(kai),* which is supported by א (Sinaiticus), C (Ephraemi Rescriptus), and the Peshitta, Armenian, and Ethiopic versions. The omission is probably a careless accident due to the placing of *dikaia* as the last word of v. 12. The eye of the scribe saw the *kai* in *dikaia* and omitted the following *kai.*

All references to hating are related to the brother(s): 2:9, 11; 3:13, 15; 4:20. On the place of the "world" see above on 2:2. Here the world is depicted in terms common to the Farewell Discourses in John, especially 15:18-19; 17:14-16.

14. *We know that we have passed out of death into life, because we love the brothers; the person not loving abides in death:* Codex Ephraemi Rescriptus (C) reads, "the person not loving *the brother* abides in death," while 𝔓⁶⁹ adds "his brother." Both of these are scribal additions. Had either reading been original there would be no reason for omission. Scribes expecting to find "the brother" have made the addition.

The "we" in "we know" is made emphatic by the use of the personal pronoun before the verb. On the use of the two verbs *oidamen* and *ginōskomen* see above on 2:3. While *oidamen,* the verb here, is not used in the construction, "by this we know . . . ," the construction used here provides just such a test. Again, as in 3:2 (another construction begun with the use of *oidamen,* but there without the additional first person plural pronoun), the verb is followed by a double use of *hoti,* the first being epexegetical, indicating the content of what is known (we have passed out of death into life), and the second causal, giving the proper ground for such knowledge (because we love the brothers). What is known is demonstrated to be true by the evidence to which appeal is made. Love for the brothers demonstrates the reality of having passed from death to life, and might have been expressed using the formula common with *ginōskomen.* "By this we know that we have passed out of death into life, because we love the brothers." Thus love reveals life, while hatred reveals death.

Grammatically it could be argued that the meaning is "we have passed from death to life, because we love the brothers," taking love for the brothers as the means or cause of the transition from the realm of death to the realm of life. This is clearly not the intention of the writer, who is setting out a series of tests to assure the readers that they know the truth (see 5:13, "I write these things to you that you may know . . ."). Further, loving the brother is set out as evidence of life, a test of life, not the genesis of it (see 2:29; 3:9; 4:7; 5:1, 4, 18). In each case being begotten of God is anterior to the effect. In 5:4 "every person begotten of God overcomes the world." Clearly this is an outcome of being begotten of God. In each case the evidence of being begotten of God is in view.

The transition from death to life is expressed by the first person plural perfect *metabebēkamen;* see especially John 5:24 where the third person singular perfect tense is used. The perfect tense expresses an event of transition in the past and a new state of life in the present. The terminology related to life, the verb used in 4:9 and the thirteen uses of the noun *(zōē),* are to be distinguished from the use of *bios* in 2:16 and *psychē* in 3:16 (cf. 3 John 2). In particular, the latter refers to the self rather than life. Both the Gospel and 1 John teach that Jesus gave himself for us and call for such self-giving from those who follow him (1 John 3:16). Reference to the "life" *(bios)* in 2:16 is to the public appearance of life.

15. *Everyone who hates his brother is a murderer, and you know that every murderer does not have eternal life abiding in him:* Codex Vaticanus (B) uses the genitive of the reflexive pronoun *(heautou)* in place of the genitive of the personal pronoun *(autou)*, "his own brother" in the place of "his brother."

On "you know that" *(oidate hoti)* see 2:29 and the Notes and Interpretation on 2:20. The *hoti* is epexegetical, indicating the content of what "you know." It does not need to be translated. For the form "every murderer does not have eternal life . . . ," which is better translated into English as "no murderer has . . . ," see above on 2:22-23. Here, as in 5:11, 13, 20, "eternal life" appears without the definite articles that are used in 1:2; 2:25. Elsewhere 1 John uses "life" as if "eternal life" had been written, as John does also (see 1 John 1:1-2; 3:14; 5:11, 12, 16). This is clear because of the frequent and interchangeable uses of "eternal life" and "life."

16. *By this we know love, he laid down his life for us; and we ought to lay down our lives for our brothers:* Some Vulgate mss read: "by this we know the love of God." This is obviously scribal. In a few texts the preposition *"for (hyper) the brothers"* is *peri.* The influence of the use of *peri* in 2:2 and the LXX sacrificial texts might be a factor here. Alternatively it might be an attempt to distinguish what "we ought to do" from what Jesus did. A minority of texts use the present infinitive *(tithenai)* in place of the aorist infinitive *(theinai),* which is clearly original.

"By this we know . . .": see above on 2:3. The object of "we know" is given as a straight object (accusative), "we know *love.*" The epexegetical *hoti* clause identifies the means by which love was made known. "*He* gave his life for us" uses the demonstrative *ekeinos* to identify Jesus (see on 2:6) and, like Mark 10:45, uses *tēn psychēn* of Jesus' self-giving. In Gen 2:7, when God breathes the breath of life "the man became a living soul" so that, in this sense, the *psychē* is the self. But the verb in Mark 10:45 is *dounai* (aorist infinitive) whereas John (10:11, 15, 17, 24; 13:37, 38; 15:13) regularly uses the verb used here in 1 John *(tithenai).* This verb is used twice, only here, in 1 John. Both uses are in the aorist and denote a specific act of giving ("he gave . . . we ought to give"). "*We* ought," here as in 3:14, is made emphatic by the use of the first person plural personal pronoun ("we"). For "we *ought*" *(opheilomen)* see John 13:14 and 1 John 2:6; 3:16; 4:11. The word is used to bring out the ground of an obligation.

17. *But whoever has the wealth of the world and sees his brother having need and shuts off his compassion from him, how does the love of God abide in him?:* On "whoever has . . ." see above on 2:5. The word *bios* here has something of the sense of "the means of livelihood" or "wealth." The verb used in "and *sees* his brother having need" is *theōrein,* one of five verbs denoting seeing that are used to cover a range of meaning in the Johannine literature. They are not distinguished from each other in terms of meaning, though choice of one verb or another may be dependent on the particular tense. Each of the verbs is used to describe (1) seeing natural objects; (2) seeing supernatural objects; and (3) in a metaphorical

use related to the perception of faith. (See Rudolf Bultmann, *The Gospel of John* 69 n. 2.) Though *theōrein* is used 26 times in John it appears only here in 1 John. The verb is a present subjunctive after the indefinite particle *an*. The rather literal translation "closing his bowels of compassion *(splagchna)* against his brother" needs reinterpretation today in terms of the heart of love, which is equally metaphorical. Here, as elsewhere in 1 John, "brother" needs to be understood inclusively.

18. *Little children, let us love neither in word nor tongue but in deed and truth:* Some texts read "*My* little children," which is original in 2:1. But the manuscript evidence makes clear that it is a favored scribal addition here. The exhortation to love has also been affected by scribal attempts to balance the negative and positive elements. Given that it is a negative expressed in the first person plural present subjunctive, it is a hortatory subjunctive, an exhortation in its form: "let us not love" in way a, but instead in way b. This form, with the authority implied by the address to the readers as "little children," has more or less the force of a command. The use of the present subjunctive rather than the aorist shows that the author has in mind the durative force of the positive command, though the verb is not repeated, rather than the negative prohibition. It is not so much that love in word and the tongue need to be stopped. Rather the writer is urging an ongoing active love for the brothers in need. It is the positive exhortation, where the verb is not repeated, that has determined the mood and tense of the verb ("let us love"), not the negative *mē*, which introduces a qualification.

### INTERPRETATION

The affirmation that we are children of God (3:1-2) led to the contrast between the children of God and the children of the devil (3:4-10). The two families came into sharp contrast on the issue of loving the brother (3:10). The present passage sets out to make clear what loving and not loving the brother means.

The opening "for" *(hoti)* provides the basis for the assertion that the person who does not love his brother is not of God (3:10). The case depends on recognizing that failure to love the brother is a failure to do righteousness (keep the commandments). The foundational message was "that we love one another." This is a reference to the commandment of Jesus (John 13:34). Surprisingly, the resumption of the theme, "this is the message" (see 1:5), which now has the commandment in view, is not said to be "from him" (as in 1:5) but "from the beginning." At the same time "the message we heard from him" is "God is light" (1:5). But there is no precedent for this in the gospel tradition. Indeed, in John "the light" is the light of the *logos* and Jesus is the light of the world (1:4, 5, 7-9; 3:19-21; 8:12; 9:5; 11:9-10; 12:35-36, 46). Certainly there is precedent in the OT for the message that God is light (Ps 27:1). What is surprising is the attribution of that message to Jesus, while the command to love one another is not specifically attributed to him in 1 John. But this is in keeping with the tendency to blur the distinction between God and Jesus when commandment(s) are spoken of. (See 2:3, 4, 7, 8; 3:22, 23, 24; 4:21; 5:2, 3.) In 2 John 4-6 the love command is attributed to the Father. Because the theme of "children of God" is the subject here it is also appropriate that the commandment be related closely to God. It remains the foundational commandment.

This expression *(ap' archēs)* is ambiguous in 1 John. (See the discussion on 1:1.) The context probably indicates that the message "*you* heard from the beginning" (see 2:24 and 2 John 6) is a reference to the beginning of the life of faith for those to whom 1 John is written. It thus distinguishes the message "*you* heard from the beginning" from "what *we* heard from the beginning" (1:1) and "the message *we* heard from *him*" (1:5). While the tradition bearers claim to have heard "from him," the readers of 1 John heard the message at the beginning of their lives as believers and nothing is said of the means by which they heard.

The message is closely related to the gospel. But the focus is on the love command, omitting its grounding in the gospel, "as I have loved you." Here we have only the message "that we love one another." Because the command is binding on all believers, although 1 John speaks of the message *you* heard, the command includes the writer, "that we love one another."

To this point the love command has been expressed in terms of loving the brother (see 3:10). Here, although the author is about to allude to Cain, who failed to love his brother, murdering him, the love command is expressed in the idiom of John 13:34, "love one another." This now becomes a common idiom in 1 John (3:23; 4:7, 11, 12; cf. 2 John 5), though reference to loving the brother(s) continues (3:14; 4:20, 21).

The writer continually clarifies his argument by setting the way of falsehood over against the way of truth, the way of hatred over against the way of love (**3:12** and see 2:9-11). Thus here the example of Cain is exactly the opposite of the fulfillment of the love command. It is a negative example: "do not be like Cain." Just as the Jews of John 8:44 show that they are of the Evil One, that is, their father is the devil, so Cain by murdering his brother showed he was of the Evil One. 1 John here seems to be dependent on the tradition in John 8:41, 44 where the devil is portrayed as a liar and a murderer from the beginning, to which 1 John 3:8 adds that the devil sins from the beginning. Slaying his brother revealed that Cain was of the Evil One. But that act only confirmed what was apparent from his evil works in contrast to his brother's just works. And why did he do this? It is an expression of the Johannine dualism: Cain killed his brother because the evil is implacably opposed to the good, the righteous, the just; see John 3:19-21. Thus the two brothers are used to further the discussion of "children of God" and "children of the devil" and how to recognize them. This also intimates that Cain represents the opponents and his brother represents the children of God. The illustration suggests that the charge that the opponents failed to love the brothers might have involved violent action against them and not merely a failure or refusal to act. This may be to press the illustration too far, but the illustration itself implies violent action.

"And" **(3:13)** connects the following verses to the discussion of Cain. The author addresses his readers as "brothers" only here. He exhorts them, "Do not be surprised." Elsewhere this idiom, using *mē* with the verb *thaumazein,* is found only in John (3:7; 5:28) in the NT. There it is followed by *hoti* because in 3:7 a statement of fact follows and in 5:28 Jesus refers to the certainty of a coming event. The use of "Do not be surprised *if (ei)* the world hates you" (1 John 3:13) may indicate that while this is characteristic of the world (supported by the use of the present imperative) it is not inevitably so. This interpretation takes account of the conditional state implied by "if" and the present imperative of the verb *thaumazete.* The negative command uses *mē* with the present imperative or the aorist subjunctive. Compare John 5:28 for the same construction using the present imperative but followed by *hoti,* while in John 3:7 *mē* is used with the aorist subjunctive *thaumasēs* followed by *hoti* to identify the specific cause in a saying of Jesus. It is possible that no clear-cut difference in meaning between the tenses is found in this construction. Similarly, it may be that John uses *hoti* while 1 John 3:13, in common with Attic Greek, uses *ei,* but this seems less likely because the author of 1 John does not seem to be speaking of the present hatred of the world. Rather he seems to be preparing the readers for what is to come. The point of the argument is to encourage the readers to love one another, and the command is supported by the argument that those who love the brothers are born of God and know God. Indeed, they have passed out of the realm of death into the realm of life (3:14; 4:7-8, 12; 5:1).

In the midst of a discussion of loving the brothers and the world's hatred of them, Cain becomes a representative of the world. This need not put in question the identification of Cain as a representative of the opponents who "went out" from the community (2:18-19); indeed, they "went out into the world" (4:1; 2 John 7). Read in the context of John 15:18-19; 17:14-16, this verse reveals the awareness that the believing community is called to an alternative way of being in the world that may provoke violence against it precisely because of its difference (see 1 John 2:15-17). At the same time, John 17:18-19 reveals the call to mission into the world, a mission that is dependent on the community retaining its alternative way of being in the world. Only in this way does the transformation of the world from the darkness to the light remain a possibility (see 17:20-26).

While the mission of the believing community is not central to 1 John, because of the struggle for community survival it has not altogether vanished from the horizon. Even here the author notes that Jesus is the expiation not only for our sins, but also for the sins of the whole world (1 John 2:2). Consequently God's love in sending his only begotten Son into the world "that *we* might live through him" (4:9) potentially includes all people. So also does the reference to the truth that "he loved *us* and sent his Son as an expiation for *our* sins" (4:10).

The stress on *"we* know" **(3:14)** is made emphatic by the use of the first person plural pronoun before the verb. That this is an inclusive use of "we" is clear because of the test to demonstrate who knows. What we are said to know is that "we have passed from the realm of death into the realm of life." The evidence for this reality is, "because we love the brothers." Loving the brothers is not the means of passing from the realm of death to the realm of life; it is the evidence of such life. Love for the brothers is a sign of life, not the cause of it. Nevertheless, love is the cause of life. "In this the love of God is revealed among us, he sent his only begotten son into the world that we might live through him" (4:9). God's love is the genesis of "life" *(zōē)*, and our love for the brothers/sisters is the sign or evidence of it.

Passing from death to life is expressed in terms of a transition *(meta-bebēkamen)* from one realm to another, "out of death" and "into life." Life and death are one pair of the significant set of dualistic terms in the Johannine writings. The most dominant pair is light and darkness, and we also find truth and falsehood, God and the devil, the children of God and the children of the devil. In this context the realm of death may well be understood as the realm of the devil; see 5:19, "we know we are of God and the whole world lies in [the power of] the Evil One." The transfer from the realm of death to the realm of life is also expressed in terms of victory over the Evil One (2:13, 14; 4:4) and victory over the world (5:4, 5 and cf. John 16:33). The life revealed in Jesus overwhelms the death of the Evil One and his realm (1:2) and it is faith in Jesus that brings the victory (5:5). For the Johannine dualism see John 3:19-21; 8:12; 12:35, 46.

In 1 John "death" *(thanatos)* is used six times (eight times in John), twice in 3:14 and four times in discussing the sin that leads into death (5:16-17). Thus if faith leads out of death into life, sin leads out of life into death. But life is the dominant theme. We have already noted that the Father's love is the ground of life. He sent his Son "so that we may live through him *(hina zēsōmen di' autou)*" (4:9). This is the only use of the verb in 1 John (it is used 16 times in John). But the noun *(zōē)* is used 13 times (36 times in John). Proportionately 1 John has a much greater emphasis on death than the Gospel, largely because of dealing with the sin that leads to death (5:16-17). But in both the Gospel and 1 John the orientation is to life and the purpose of 1 John is that the readers, "who believe in the name of the Son of God, may *know* that you have eternal life" (5:13). Here in 3:14 it is the inclusive "we know," based on the evidence that "we love the brothers." Such love is a sure and certain sign of life. Codex Sinaiticus (‭א‬) reads "because we love *our* brothers." This is clearly a textual emendation, though not incorrect. It makes explicit what is already implicit because "brothers" *are* "our brothers."

While our author addresses his readers as "brothers" in 3:13, in five references to loving the brother this is the only use of the plural, that we love the brothers (see the singular use in 2:10; 3:10; 4:20, 21). The singular form occurs in contrast to hating the brother (2:9, 11; 3:12, 13, 15; 4:20). It is unclear why the plural "because we love the brothers" is used here unless it is a consequence of the address to the readers as brothers.

The contrast of those who have not passed from death to life is first set out in negative terms. Naturally the author does not continue in the first person plural but now moves to his customary third person singular, using the articular participle (see 2:4, 6, 9, 10, 11; 3:7, 8). The person who does not love abides in death. Here loving and not loving form the antithesis. In 3:15 we see that not loving is the equivalent of hating. Just as loving was described as a sign of life, so now not loving is a sign of death. The person not loving abides in death. Interestingly, here the absolute use of not loving appears (as also in 4:8) just as the absolute use of loving appears in 4:19. Whereas not loving is grounded in not knowing God (4:8), loving is grounded in God's prior love for us (4:19). There is no more suggestion here that hating is the cause of death than *our* loving is the cause of life. Death is grounded in the failure to know God. To abide in death is to abide in the darkness where death holds sway. According to John 3:36 it is the realm of the *wrath* of God. But this term, used only once in John, does not occur in 1 John. The evidence that the language of judgment is virtually absent from 1 John runs contrary to the trend of interpretation. The verb *(krinō)* is absent from the Epistles (19 times in John), and of the nouns *krisis* is used only in 1 John 4:17, while it is used 11 times in John. Though 1 John 2:28 reflects the situation of judgment, the explicit vocabulary is not used. The other noun, *krima*, is not used at all in 1 John and only at 9:39 in John. In 1 John it may be a mistake to identify the realm of death with the realm of the wrath of God. More likely death is the mark of Cain and the work of the Devil, whose realm the world presently is because "the whole world lies [in the power of] the Evil One."

The author now **(3:15)** goes on to clarify the implications of not loving. The common formulation expressing "every person who . . ." is here used to identify the person who hates his brother as a murderer. This immediately looks back to Cain, who murdered his brother (3:12), and leads our author to remark: "Brothers, do not be surprised if the world hates you." Now the discussion of the one who hates leads back to the identification of such a person as a murderer (see above on 3:12). That the one who hates is identified as a murderer seems noncontroversial, perhaps because this is a variation on the theme of Matt 5:21-22, which notes the relation of anger and contempt to the command "Do not murder." Hatred is perhaps a more extreme form of the anger and contempt of Matt 5:21-22.

The idiom "we know" (3:14) now returns to the second person plural address of 3:13. The one not loving, that is, every one hating his brother, is a murderer. Now the reader is addressed with "and you know." If the person not loving "abides in death," the murderer who hates his brother does not have eternal life abiding in him. The death sentence is passed on murderers (see Gen 9:6; Rev 21:8).

The expression "he does not have eternal life *abiding in him*" is awkward. It would have been much smoother had the text said simply, "he does not have eternal life." While in John 5:38 Jesus says, "you do not have his [God's] word abiding in you," the notion of eternal life abiding or not abiding in a person is unusual. It is true that "the person not loving abides in death." Had the text said: "every murderer does not abide in eternal life," it would have been less awkward. Nevertheless, 1 John speaks of the many things abiding: the word of God (2:14), [the truth, 2 John 2], what was heard from the beginning (2:24), the anointing (2:27), God's seed (3:9). Because it is said that the love of God (3:17) and eternal life (3:15) do not abide in those *out of* fellowship with the author, it is implied that they do abide in those *in* fellowship with him. Awkward though the saying about "eternal life abiding in him" appears to be, this seems to be what the author meant to write. It implies the gift of life from God as distinct from a "natural capacity," as well as the enduring nature of that gift.

Using the characteristic formula "by this we know (aorist tense) love" 1 John **(3:16)** sets out the nature of love. The aorist ("we know") might have been chosen here because this knowledge is based on the historic self-giving of Jesus. See the use of the future tense "we will know" in 3:19, and the present tense "we know" in 3:24.

The formula "by this we know" is frequently used to provide a test of knowledge or of a claim. Here it is designed to emphasize the basis of the author's understanding of love. "This" refers to the following *hoti* clause, which is epexegetical. That "he" is a reference to Jesus is clear not only from the use of the demonstrative pronoun but also from the action described: he laid down (gave) his life (himself) for us. According to 1 John this act defines what love is. In 4:10 the logic of this statement is taken a step further. 1 John ultimately grounds what love is in God, who "sent his Son as the expiation for (*peri*, see 2:2) our sins." In 4:10-11, as in 3:16, the revelation of what love is becomes the ground for the obligation "to love one another" (4:10-11), or "to give our lives for the brothers." Both here and in 4:10-11 the obligation arising from the recognition of God's love for us is that we love one another. Here that love is given concrete meaning in terms of laying down our lives for the brothers. If that is a somewhat dramatic form, it is based on the actual self-giving of Jesus, whose self-giving, 1 John insists, was God's giving of his Son.

Nevertheless, 1 John is concerned to give love a more everyday and less dramatic meaning also **(3:17)**. Like 2:5, 3:17 begins with a relative clause from which flow three further statements that have their cumulative force on the basis of the opening relative clause, "whoever has the wealth of the world." Everything follows from this. The test of love assumes this reality. Such a person sees his brother having need. It is characteristic of 1 John to use the present participle "having" *(echonta)*. This implies an ongoing need rather than a momentary crisis. But his response is to shut off his compassion from him. We would say "he closes and locks his heart against him." If he does this, our author asks, "how does the love *of God* abide in him?" The words "of God" are in the genitive case and may be understood as an objective genitive (God is the object) meaning love for God, or a subjective genitive (God is the subject), meaning God's love for us. Both 3:16 and 4:10-11 define love as God's love for us, and make God's love the basis for the obligation to love one another. This perspective and the flow of the argument in the context, which deals with failure to love the brother, strongly support a subjective genitive. If in 4:19 the author writes "we love because he first loved us," our failure to love is a demonstration that his love does not abide in us. For the love of God to abide in us seems to mean that the reality of God's love for us determines the manner of our lives. Consequently, we love because God first loved us. This is consistent with defining what love is in terms of God's love for us and not our love for God. Our love is responsive to the primary source of all love. Those who do not love have not passed out of the realm of death into the realm of life, which is characterized by love for the brothers/sisters and arises out of being loved by God.

To drive the message home **(3:18)** the author again addresses his readers directly, not now as "brothers" as in 3:13, but asserting his authority and addressing them endearingly, yet also subordinately, as "little children" *(teknia)*. This form of address is preliminary to the issuing of a strong exhortation with virtually the force of a command (see 2:1). But the command to love is no ordinary commandment. It needs to be grounded in the source of love (see 3:16-17) and nourished by the community of "let us. . . ." While the drift of the exhortation is clear enough, the precise meaning of each of the terms, negative and positive, is less than clear. There are several possible readings. First, there may be no clear distinction between the two words in each part. Thus "word" and "tongue" may have the same meaning, just as "deed" and "truth" can be understood as "reality," "actuality." An alternative is to take the second pair in a single sense, meaning "doing the truth" (see John 3:21; 1 John 1:6), "acting faithfully," and giving active aid to the brother in need. This interpretation assumes the contrast between the two parts set up by the first word in each part, "word" and "deed."

The two parts are not fully in antithetical parallelism. All the nouns are anarthrous (without the article) except "the tongue," and only the positive form is introduced by the preposition *en* even though deed *(ergǭ)*, as little as word *(logǭ)* needs the preposition.

According to Ignace de la Potterie *(La vérité dans saint Jean* 2:663–73) the tongue is the source of the word, and the truth is the source of the deed. Given that the truth is the determining word in the second part, the use of the preposition *en* has been determined by truth rather than the first word, *work*. It is Johannine idiom to use the preposition *en* with truth (four times in John; only here in 1 John; three times in 2 John and three times in 3 John). That this is the only use in 1 John weakens the case, especially as it does not appear directly before *alētheia*. Certainly John 4:23-24 *(en pneumati kai alētheią)* shows that the case is possible. References to "deeds of truth" from Qumran make quite good sense of the idiom: see 1QM 13:2; 1QS 1:19; 1QH 1:30. Nevertheless, I have the impression that this reading of the construction has too little basis in 1 John and is rather too clever and precise to be persuasive.

The lack of formal balance between the two pairs suggests that we do not have a straightforward antithesis or rejection of the first pair of terms. Though the two pairs are joined by an adversative use "but" *(alla)*, word and tongue are not rejected in themselves. They are unsatisfactory if they do not lead to action and embodiment in reality. This much seems clear. It does not explain why "the tongue" *(tē glōssē)*, alone of the four nouns, has the definite article. One possibility is that it refers to ecstatic utterance. This suggests the ecstatic outpouring of love toward God. But without action such ecstatic utterance is as worthless as a pious wish, "be warmed and filled" (see 1 Corinthians 13; Jas 2:16).

## 1.5. The grounds for confidence before God (3:19-24)

19. By this we shall know that we are of the truth, and reassure our hearts before him 20. because if our hearts condemn us, God is greater than our hearts and knows all things. 21. Beloved, if our heart does not condemn, we have confidence in relation to God, 22. and whatever we ask we receive from him, because we keep his commandments and do what is pleasing before him. 23. And this is his commandment, that we believe in

the name of his Son Jesus Christ and love one another as he gave commandment to us. 24. And the person keeping his commandments abides
in him and he in him; and by this we know that he abides in us, because
of the Spirit that he has given to us.

## NOTES

19. *By this we shall know that we are of the truth, and reassure our hearts before him:* The
obscurity of 3:19-21 has led to a series of textual emendations as scribes have
sought to clarify a difficult passage. The difficulties start at the beginning of
3:19. Here "and" *(kai)* has been introduced by Sinaiticus (ℵ), Ephraemi Rescriptus (C), and the Peshitta and Byzantine tradition. It is almost certainly an
attempt to clarify 3:19 by connection to 3:18, thus making love of the brothers
the basis of knowing that "we are of the truth." Omission by Alexandrinus
(A), Vaticanus (B), the Old Italian, Vulgate, Coptic, and Clement of Alexandria
supports the harder reading. There is every reason to add "and," and no reason
to omit it.

 "By this" *(en toutǭ)* has as a variant "from this" *(ek toutou):* see 1 John 4:6,
where this is the original reading. The weight of textual evidence is against the
variant here. Because "by this" is more characteristic, it is the easier reading.
But the sense is not different if the variant is accepted. The same is true of the
verb "we will know" (future), which has as a variant "we know" (present).
The variant is supported by the Vulgate, Syriac, and Byzantine tradition, and
by Augustine. That the future is uncharacteristic of this construction and
therefore the more difficult reading together with the stronger textual support
make the future tense likely. However, in a statement of general truth such as
this there is little difference from the present tense (see BDF §349.1).

 The singular "heart" is attested in Vaticanus (B) and the Peshitta, while
Sinaiticus (ℵ), the Latin, and the Byzantine tradition support the plural
"hearts." The evidence that all other Johannine uses of "heart" are singular,
including those in 3:20-21, suggests that the plural is the more difficult reading. Nevertheless, a scribal slip might have introduced the variant here. In
English certainly a plural is required and has been used in our translation.

 God is intended by the reference "we comfort our heart before him" *(emprosthen autou),* which looks forward to the reference to God in v. 20. Here "before" *(emprosthen)* means "in the presence of." The word is used only here in
1 John, but five times in John (1:15, 30; 3:28; 10:4; 12:37); it has the same sense
as *enōpion* in 1 John 3:22 (see John 20:30 and 3 John 6).

20. *because if our hearts condemn us, God is greater than our hearts and knows all things:*
The opening *hoti* is omitted by Alexandrinus and *f*[13] Greek mss. This is a
scribal attempt to smooth the text by the removal of the first of two uses of *hoti*
in a short space. It is no clarification. The problem is to know how to take the
two *hoti* clauses. Is the first epexegetical and the second causal, as is frequently
the case in 1 John? This does not seem possible, as the second appears to be
epexegetical, setting out what we persuade our hearts, that is, "God is greater

than our hearts and knows all things." On the other hand the first *hoti* may well be causal and the second epexegetical of "we persuade" *(peisomen)* from 3:19. No clear identification of the referent of *toutǭ* (3:20) is evident.

Here, and in v. 21, "the heart" needs to be translated as "our hearts," as we are dealing with the first person plural.

21. *Beloved, if our heart does not condemn, we have confidence in relation to God:* The opening "beloved" is the correct reading (see on 2:7), though "brothers" has been introduced in Sinaiticus (ℵ), probably because of its use in 3:13 and the following theme (3:14-17). Hence the introduction of "and" at the beginning of 3:19 in ℵ. Verse 21 has many minor variations of wording and word order. The text followed by most scholars is that of Vaticanus (B) and Origen. The value of noting the textual variants is to show that from earliest days reading these verses presented serious problems. Modern scholars too have continued to emend the text of these verses in order to make sense of them.

22. *and whatever we ask we receive from him, because we keep his commandments and do what is pleasing before him*: In the NT *ho ean* often replaces the Ancient Greek *ho an:* see John 15:17; 3 John 5. The *hoti* clause is causal. We receive what we ask *because* we keep his commandments.

23. *And this is his commandment, that we believe in the name of his Son Jesus Christ and love one another as he gave commandment to us:* Sinaiticus (ℵ); Alexandrinus (A), and the Byzantine tradition have smoothed the double command by making the command to believe present tense to conform to the tense of the command to love. The aorist tense takes account of the decisive nature of coming to faith. No growth in belief is envisaged because to believe "in the name of his Son Jesus Christ" is to grasp the truth. This belief is the foundation for the ongoing life of loving one another.

*Hina* (epexegetical) governs two verbs in the subjunctive mood, the first in the aorist, "that we believe," the aorist indicating the decisive nature of belief, and the second in the present tense, "that we love," indicating the continuous nature of the loving life. It would be a mistake to think that believing is not meant to be ongoing also, but the aorist tense does not make a point of this. Instead, the authenticity of faith is indicated by the indirect object of believing.

This is the first of nine uses of *pisteuō* in 1 John. The noun is used once in 1 John 5:4. Neither the noun nor the verb is used in 2 or 3 John. In John only the verb is used, 98 times out of a total of 239 in the NT. By contrast, Paul uses the verb 54 times and the noun 142 times out of a total of 244 times in the NT. Thus Paul makes up for the absence of the noun from the Johannine writings. For a discussion of the use of this language in the Gospel see my *John, Witness and Theologian*, "The way of faith," 77–85; and "Eschatological Faith" in *The Quest for the Messiah* 383–416, especially 383–88 in the second edition of 1993. Here we should note the preponderance of use in John 1–12 (76 of the total of 98 uses). The reverse tendency is to be seen in the use of love terminology. The noun *agapē* is used only once in John 1–12 of the total of seven uses, the remainder being in John 13–17. The verb *agapān* is used seven times in John 1–12 of a total of 37 times. Apart from one use in John 19 and four in John 21, the remaining 25 uses are in John 13–17. The verb *philein* is used four times in John 1–12 of a total of 13 times. Thus in John there is a *dramatic* shift of emphasis from believing in 1–12 to love and loving in 13–21. From this perspective of language use the Johannine Epistles, especially 1 John, fit the tendency of John 13–17. The nine uses of the verb "to believe" and the one use of the noun "faith" are to be compared with 18 uses of the noun "love" and 27 uses of the verb *agapān* in 1 John. *Philein* is not used in the Johannine Epistles.

In 1 John 3:23 *pisteuein* is used with the dative case. But this cannot be understood as believing the witness or words of a speaker. Here the reference is to the command to believe in the name of his (God's) Son Jesus Christ. This use with the dative case should be compared with the use of the same verb followed by the preposition *eis*, which takes the accusative case, in 5:13. Here the object of the verb is "the name of the Son of God." It is unthinkable, in Johannine terms, that the command should be in terms different in meaning from those required to comply with the purpose of 1 John. Thus believing in the name, expressed using the dative case, is not different from the expression using *eis* followed by the accusative case. In these constructions we see that the true object and content of faith are crucial. Grammatical constructions do not in themselves determine the meaning of believing.

1 John 4:1 is a good case of the verb followed by the dative case, indicating believing what is said. In this case the command is "Do not believe every spirit." See also the second of the three uses in 5:10, where the dative case is used in reference to the one not believing *God*. God is in the dative case, which here confirms that the reference is to not believing what God says. Interestingly, in the third use it is said of the one who does not believe God "that he has not believed *in the witness*," a construction using *eis* with the accusative where we might have expected to find the dative case without a preposition. Only in the first use in 5:10 do we find the common Gospel use of *pisteuein* with *eis* and the accusative in relation to Jesus, "the person who believes in the Son of God." Even here there is concern to state the precise content of faith and not simply to express personal commitment.

There are two instances of *pisteuein* followed by epexegetical *hoti*, thus emphasizing the content of belief, which is the case also in the references to believing in the name. The other use of *pisteuein* is linked with the verb "to know" *(ginōskein)*. Both verbs are in the perfect tense, and the first person plural personal pronoun is used for emphasis, "we have known and believed the love that God has in us." Here "the love" is the object of the verb and is in the accusative case. If, as seems likely, it is argued that the love came to be known and believed in God's sending of the Son, then this profound content of belief and knowledge is expressed in the accusative case. To gain a fuller picture of the content of belief, some discussion of the language of the *confession* of faith and its denial needs to be undertaken; see 2:22-23; 4:2, 3, 15; 2 John 7.

24. *And the person keeping his commandments abides in him and he in him; and by this we know that he abides in us, because of the Spirit that he has given to us:* Like the formulations beginning "every person who," this construction uses the article (the) followed by the present participle to characterize approved and disap-

proved positions that often appear in antithetic parallelism. Here only the positive position is set out.

In the formula of mutual abiding (3:24; 4:13, 15, 16) the verb *(menei)* only occurs once and is implied in the second aspect of mutual abiding. The implied use of the same verb in the second of the parallel statements is normal in Greek and more elegant than the repetition.

The second part of the verse begins with a connected test using the formula "and by this we know," which is followed by the epexegetical *hoti*. What we know is that "he abides in us." The second *hoti* (found in 4:13) is absent from 3:24 and the parallel reads *ek tou pneumatos hou hēmin edōken,* "of his Spirit that he has given us." The parallel with 4:13 is obvious and in each case provides the test to which "by this" refers (contrary to my view in *John, Witness and Theologian* 124). In 3:24 an explanation is provided in a statement introduced by the preposition *ek.* This might introduce a partitive genitive, indicating that the gift did not wholly contain the Spirit; or a genitive of origin, indicating that the Spirit was the source of the gift. Such a gift might be understood in the sense of the *charismata* of 1 Cor 12:4. Indeed, the imprecision (characteristic of 1 John) might involve both senses. There is a parallel with 4:13. There the use of a second *hoti* clause indicates a causal connection, *"because* he has given us of his Spirit." This implies that *ek tou pneumatos hou hēmin edōken* in 3:24 is also to be understood much like the causal *hoti* clause of 4:13, "because of the Spirit he has given us" or "because he has given us of the Spirit." Because 4:13 uses *hoti* followed by *ek,* the function of *ek* cannot be reduced to the causal sense. Either or both partitive and genitive of origin senses must also be involved. No significant difference between 3:24 and 4:13 is indicated by "the Spirit" (3:24) and "his Spirit" (4:13). In neither case is there any indication of the way in which the Spirit manifests the abiding presence of God.

INTERPRETATION

"By this we will know" (future tense) states what will be known in the following epexegetical *hoti* clause **(3:19)**. This is not in question. We will know we are of the truth. When this will be is not a matter of time but of the fulfillment of the conditions to which "by this" points. Frequently those conditions are indicated in a second *hoti* clause that is epexegetical. Here there is a series of two further *hoti* clauses in 3:20, but neither of these provides a basis for what we will know. Rather, this is to be found in the preceding verses. The evidence that we have passed from death to life (3:14-18) is also the basis upon which we will know we are of the truth. In this instance the instincts of the scribe(s) who inserted "And" at the beginning of 3:19 were correct. It is easier to explain the insertion of "And" than its omission. In this, loving the brothers in deed and truth, we will know we are of the truth. On the basis of this evidence we will persuade and so reassure our hearts. (See the Notes for the justification of "hearts" in place of the Greek singular.)

The clause "because if our hearts condemn us" **(3:20)** makes sense if the heart is understood as the seat of moral decisions that may also be described as the conscience *(syneidēsis)*. There is ample evidence of the heart operating like the conscience (see Pss 7:9-11; 12:2; 32:11; 38:8; 51:10; 73:1, 13, 21). It is the disquieted and accusing heart that is to be persuaded and reassured. The disquieted heart is closely associated with the disquieted soul (Pss 42:5, 11; 43:5). The condemning and accusing heart is to be persuaded that "God is greater than our hearts and knows all things." The greatness of God is specifically demonstrated here by reference to God's knowing all things. While this might suggest that God therefore has more reason to accuse us than our hearts, that argument runs contrary to the drift of this passage. Rather, 3:19 has drawn attention to the evidence that demonstrates that we are of the truth. That evidence is to be found in loving action for the sake of the brothers/sisters. God, who knows all things, knows this, and although the world might not recognize the children of God (3:1), God certainly does.

The renewed address, "beloved" **(3:21**, and see on 2:7), confirms that we are still dealing with the command to love the brother(s) (see 2:7-11). Verse 20 raised the question "if our hearts condemn us," and v. 21 has the antithetic parallel, "if our hearts do not condemn us." The question is: do verses 20 and 21 provide alternative scenarios or a sequential situation? A sequence seems more likely in that the accusing heart is persuaded and reassured in 3:20. Thus assured, on the basis of the evidence of loving the brothers/sisters, we have confidence *(parrēsian)* in relation to God *(pros ton theon;* see John 1:1, 2 and 1 John 2:1).

The interpretation of these verses (3:19-21) we have adopted is reassuring to those whose hearts have been troubled. This passage needs to be related to the overall purpose of 1 John (see 5:13), which is to reassure the readers that they have eternal life, "that you may know that you have eternal life." The tests of life running throughout 1 John reveal the author's concern for the community that has been destabilized and traumatized by a recent schism. Thus 1 John seeks to reestablish assurance while grounding it in his understanding of the true faith and the revelation of the "life" in the self-giving of Jesus. His life is the source and model for the believer's life in the world that can be summed up in terms of loving one another or loving the brothers/sisters. Those whose lives express that love for the brothers/sisters may reassure their hearts that they are indeed the children of God, and this is a sure and certain defense against the accusations of the opponents to the contrary.

While a more negative interpretation is possible, it does not fit the overall purpose of 1 John nor, in my view, does it deal as well with the specific context of 1 John 3:19-21. The more negative interpretation takes the affirmation that "God is greater than our hearts and knows all things" in a threatening sense. If our hearts accuse and condemn us, how much more will God do so? This then becomes the spur to urgent ethical action. Such a spur is unlikely to bring reassurance because, however much is done, "God is greater than our hearts and knows all things." What we do not know then becomes a threat. This is not in the drift of the passage or the purpose of 1 John.

The opening "and" **(3:22)** connects this verse to the theme of "boldness before God" in 3:21. That boldness is now expressed in the encouragement of confidence in making requests, "that whatever we ask we receive from him." The language of asking in the Johannine writings dominantly prefers the verb used here (*aitein;* see John 14:14-16; 15:7, 16; 16:23-26 where it is used eight times and *erōtan* is used once). In 1 John a similar pattern emerges. In addition to the present passage, *aitein* is used four times in 5:14-16, and *erōtan* is used once. Though there is a preference for the use of *aitein* there is no discernible difference in the meaning of the words in this usage.

Here the theme is the assurance that whatever is asked will be received from God (see 3:20-21). Asking and receiving is a prominent theme in the references to the Farewell Discourses of John given above. But this theme is common elsewhere in the teaching of Jesus in the gospel tradition; see Matt 7:7; Mark 11:24; see also Jas 1:5-6. The ground for this confidence in asking, which is an expression of more general confidence in relation to God, is now said to be because (*hoti*) we keep (*tēroumen*) his commandments. Here the commandments are the commandments of God, as 3:23 makes clear. But does the last clause add additional requirements? What is it that "we do [that] is pleasing (*ta aresta*) in relation (*enōpion*) to him," that is, in his sight? (See the use of *emprosthen* in 3:19.) The word used here for what is pleasing is found only four times in the NT. One of those uses is in John 8:29, where Jesus says that he always does the things that are pleasing (*ta aresta*) to the one who sent him. This is another way of affirming the keeping of God's commandments. In a similar way, those who fail to obey God are described in the synonymous parallelism of 3:10, which describes the children of the devil, that is, those who are not of God, as "every person not doing righteousness, even the person not loving his brother."

His commandments are now **(3:23)** specified surprisingly with "and this is his commandment. . . ." The "and" makes clear the continuation from 3:22. Because the commandment refers to "his Son Jesus Christ" there is no doubt that reference to God's commandment is intended. The perplexing element is the change from keeping God's commandments (plural) in 3:22 to the identification "this is his commandment" (singular) in 3:23. The wording of John 15:12, "this is my commandment," is identical, even to the order of words, except that Jesus' "my" replaces "his" (God's) in 3:23. This similarity sharpens our awareness of an interesting difference between the Gospel and 1 John. Some aspects of John's christology become aspects of the theology of 1 John. In John, Jesus is the light, in 1 John, God is light. In John, Jesus gives his commandment to the disciples. In 1 John the commandments are dominantly God's commandments. There is also the puzzling failure to distinguish clearly between Jesus and God in 1 John.

The command turns out to be a double commandment, introduced by a single *hina* that governs two clauses using verbs in the subjunctive mood. The *hina* is epexegetical, indicating the content of the commandment, which is first of all that we believe. Here the aorist subjunctive is used to indicate the decisive nature of believing. The content of belief is indicated by the indirect object expressed in the dative case. It is to believe "in the name of his Son Jesus Christ." This can have no difference in meaning from believing in the name of the Son of God (5:13 and see John 1:12; 2:23; 3:18). Believing *in the name* is an important Johannine motif. In addition to the references to believing in his name, 1 John 2:12 says "your sins are forgiven because of his name." Other references in John make clear the importance of *the name* given to Jesus: see 5:43; 10:25; 12:13, 28; 14:13, 14, 26; 16:23, 24, 26; 17:6, 11, 12, 26; 20:31. In 17:11-12 Jesus addresses the Father and asks, "keep them in your name which you gave to me." Perhaps as a gloss on this and other aspects of John's treatment of the name, *The Gospel of Truth* 38:6 says, "The name of the Father is the Son." It is in relation to the Father that Jesus is known as "the Son," and John teaches that the Father is known in the Son. Thus to believe in his name, or in the name of his Son Jesus Christ, is to believe that God is known in the human life of Jesus, that God acts to deal with human sin in the life and death of Jesus, and that the human life of Jesus is the model for the life of faith.

The second part of the double command is "that we love one another." The expression *allēlous*, rather than "the brothers" (see 2:9-11; 3:10, 12, 14, 15-17; 4:20-21), arises from the tradition of the new commandment (John 13:34; 15:12), which is also reflected in 1 John 3:11. This is confirmed by the use of *kathōs*, "as he gave commandment to us." Thus it is Jesus who gave the commandment to love one another even though this is one aspect of God's commandment. In 1 John God and Jesus are not always clearly distinguished and this is true in the theme of the commandments.

That the two elements are presented as a single commandment is striking, especially after 3:22 has referred to keeping "his *commandments*." The reason seems to be that the first element is the ground of the second. In other words, the love command issues from the human life of Jesus, understood to be the revelation of the Father and the Father acting in the human life of Jesus. That 1 John brings out the connection suggests that the failure of the opponents to "love one another" was a consequence of their rejection of the confession that "Jesus Christ has come in the flesh." Thus for them the revelation of the love of God was not recognized in the human life of Jesus.

The writer characteristically **(3:24)** describes the way of life he affirms using a present participle with the definite article. He sets the way of life he opposes alongside the way he affirms, forming passages of antithetic parallelism. In 3:24 only the position affirmed is outlined and the alternative is clearly just the negative of this (see 2:4). In 3:22 keeping the commandments was the ground of assurance that those who ask will receive. Now the one keeping the commandments is assured of mutual abiding with God. If on the one side the person keeping the commandments abides in God [and God in him], on the other side the person not loving abides in death (3:14) and does not know God (4:8; cf. 2:4).

In this reference to *keeping*, "commandments" is plural. Indeed, throughout the Gospel and Epistles *tērein* is used with the plural "commandments" (see John 14:15, 21; 15:10; 1 John 2:3-4; 3:22, 24; 5:3). But the same verb is used to refer to keeping the word (singular) of Jesus, or of the Father, or of the disciples (John 8:51, 52, 55; 14:23, [24 is plural]; 15:20; 17:6; 1 John 2:5). Other uses of this verb in John refer to keeping the good wine (2:10) and not keeping the Sabbath (9:16). The meaning in 12:7 is obscure; 17:11, 12, 15 deal with the keeping of the disciples by God. In 1 John only 5:18 falls outside the scope of keeping the commandments or word. If the verb is used with word and words, why is it used only with the plural commandments? The plural is used in 1 John 2:3, 4; 3:22, 24; 5:2, 3. The singular is used in 2:7-8; 3:23; 4:21. In 2 John the singular is used in vv. 4-5, but v. 6, like 1 John 2:22-23, speaks of "commandments" only to go on to assert, "this is the commandment." All of this takes place in the context of the commandment to love one another, where love is defined as keeping the commandments and the commandment is identified as "what you heard from the beginning."

It is no explanation to say that the plural "commandments" is always used when reference to keeping them is the theme, because this does not explain why 3:23 reverts to the singular, especially as the double command is in view there. The same complexity is involved in 2 John 6. Yet the purpose of the complexity may be explicable. God's commandment is to believe in the name of his Son. Such belief entails the love commandment that is bound to Jesus' human life both in terms of the giving of the commandment (John 13:34) and of its meaning (see 1 John 4:9-11). Thus the single commandment is complex, containing other obligations within its fulfillment.

But if keeping the commandments is a ground for recognizing mutual abiding, it is now affirmed that the basis for knowing that he abides in us (the second aspect of the mutual abiding outlined in the first part of the verse) is that he gave us (aorist tense) of his Spirit. Here, in the test "by this we know" (present tense), the content of *what* is known is given in the epexegetical *hoti* clause, "he abides in us." But *how* is this known? It is known "because he gave us of his Spirit." The causal relationship is confirmed by the parallel with 4:13. There the use of *ek tou pneumatos* confirms that "of the Spirit" or "of his Spirit" implies there is more to the Spirit than what is given, that the gift originates with the Spirit much in the sense of the *charismata* of 1 Cor 12:4. But neither 3:24 nor 4:13 specifies how the gift of the Spirit is manifest or recognized. If keeping the commandments is the basis for knowing that we abide in him, the fact that he gave us of his Spirit is the evidence that he abides in us. There are dual criteria for mutual abiding. Again, according to 4:12, God abides in us if we love one another, and in 4:13 the test shows that "by this we know that we abide in him and he in us because *(hoti)* he has given us (perfect tense) of his Spirit." Further, "the one abiding in love abides in God and God abides in him" (4:16) because God is love. This suggests that we have a cumulative argument to demonstrate mutual abiding with God.

### FOR REFERENCE AND FURTHER STUDY

Beutler, Johannes. *Johannesbriefe*, 78–100.

Brooke, Alan England. *A Critical and Exegetical Commentary on the Johannine Epistles*, 79–106.

Brown, Raymond E. *The Epistles of John*, 378–484.

Bultmann, Rudolf. *The Gospel of John*, 69.

Court, John. "Blessed Assurance," *JTS* 33 (1982) 508–17.

Goodenough, Erwin R. *By Light, Light; The Mystic Gospel of Hellenistic Judaism.*

Klauck, Hans-Josef. "Brudermord und Bruderliebe. Ethische Paradigmen in 1 Joh 3:11-17," in Helmut Merklein, ed., *Neues Testament und Ethik: für Rudolf Schnackenburg.* Freiburg, Basel, and Vienna: Herder, 1989, 151–69.

Lieu, Judith. "'Authority to Become Children of God': A Study of 1 John," *NovT* 23 (1981) 210–28.

Rensberger, David. *1 John, 2 John, 3 John*, 84–109.

Schnackenburg, Rudolf. *The Johannine Epistles*, 151–95.

## 2. THE CHRISTOLOGICAL TEST. THE SPIRIT FROM GOD CONFESSES JESUS CHRIST HAS COME IN THE FLESH (4:1-6)

1. Beloved, do not believe every spirit, but test the spirits [to discern] if they are of God, because many false prophets have gone out into the world. 2. By this you know the Spirit of God; every spirit that confesses Jesus Christ has come in the flesh is of God, 3. and every spirit that does not confess Jesus is not of God; and this is the [spirit] of the Antichrist, which you have heard comes, and is now already in the world. 4. You are of God, little children, and you have conquered them, because greater is the one who is in you than the one who is in the world. 5. They are of the world; because of this they speak from the world and the world hears them. 6. We are of God; the person knowing God hears us; who[ever] is not of God does not listen to us. From this we know the Spirit of truth and the Spirit of Error.

### NOTES

1. *Beloved, do not believe every spirit, but test the spirits [to discern] if they are of God, because many false prophets have gone out into the world:* The address "beloved" was first used in 2:7 and has been repeated in 3:2, 21. It is also used in 4:7, 11. In 2:7 it opens a discussion of the love command. In 3:2 it introduces the announcement of the children of God. Now three paragraphs begin with "beloved": 3:21; 4:1; and 4:7. The third paragraph, beginning at 4:7, contains a second use of "beloved" in 4:11. See also 3 John 1, 2, 5, 11. In 4:7-12 we find the most concentrated treatment of love in 1 John, though 4:16b-21 comes a close second.

   Two commands, negative and positive, are introduced. "Do not believe . . . but test." The negative command (prohibition) uses *mē* with the present imperative *pisteuete*, which may imply that the author thought the readers were inclined to believe every spirit. The positive command is also a present imperative. In 1 Cor 12:10 the discernment of spirits is depicted as one of the *charismata*. That this was a problem in the early church is also evident in the treatment of this subject in *Did.* 11:6-8; 12:1.

   The command "do not believe every spirit" places three words beginning with *pi* after the initial negative *mē (mē panti pneumati pisteuete).* This may be deliberate alliteration showing clever use of language. The *hoti* is causal, "because."

2. *By this you know the Spirit of God; every spirit that confesses Jesus Christ has come in the flesh is of God:* Codex Sinaiticus (א*) reads "By this *we know (ginōskomen)*." This is a scribal change to the first person that is common in this formula. (See above on 2:3.) The second person plural is strongly supported and is the uncharacteristic reading. The third person singular passive *(ginōsketai)* is supported by the Byzantine tradition, Peshitta, and Vulgate, which rarely justifies

serious attention without support from early papyri or the great fourth- and fifth-century codices (for example A, ℵ, B).

A small minority of texts read "Christ Jesus" for "Jesus Christ." Although it is the uncharacteristic reading, it has too little support to be accepted. It is characteristic of Paul and also found in Acts.

The perfect participle *elēlythota* (*"having come* in the flesh") is strongly attested, but Vaticanus (B) reads the perfect infinitive *"to have come* in the flesh." Vaticanus probably incorporates a stylistic improvement without changing the meaning.

The opening phrase "by this you know" is followed by words in the accusative case that tell what is known (see on 2:3). This is more straightforward than the author's normal practice, yet even here there is ambiguity because *ginōskete* could be indicative or imperative. Only context can clarify the issue. Almost all commentators read this as indicative, giving reassuring and vital information to those who need it, not as an order or instruction. In this formula statement we generally find *ginōskomen* followed by *hoti*. This is not the case here, where the accusative case supplies the object of knowledge and implies the meaning "recognize."

While the form of the statement does not indicate in the normal way that the test follows the formula, this is in fact the case and the test is stated positively and negatively in straightforward terms in 4:2b-3.

3. *and every spirit that does not confess Jesus is not of God; and this is the [spirit] of the Antichrist, which you have heard comes, and is now already in the world:* The text adopted here has the support of the Greek manuscript tradition including Sinaiticus (ℵ), Alexandrinus (A) and Vaticanus (B), many of the church fathers and versions. Some additions make what is not confessed conform to what is confessed, making explicit what is implicit in the refusal to confess Jesus. This is obvious shorthand for the full statement given in 4:2. The expansions do not agree with each other and are clearly secondary.

The variant that calls for closer attention is the replacement of "does not confess" *(mē homologei)*, which merely negates the "confesses" of 4:2, with *lyei*. The alternative *lyei* is supported by Irenaeus (circa 180 C.E.) and the Alexandrians Clement and Origen (though Origen is also a witness for the commonly accepted reading) and other later Fathers. The main thing to be said in favor of this reading is that it is easier to explain the introduction of the majority reading because it merely negates the statement of 4:2. On the other hand, many scholars reject *lyei*, seeing it as a refutation of second-century heretics who distinguish the Jesus of the flesh from the spiritual Christ. Here *lyei* is understood as "divides." It makes as much sense of these positions to say that they *annul* or *destroy* Jesus if what they were affirming was the distinct heavenly element named Christ while they rejected the earthly Jesus. At the same time this may connect some of the later "heresies" with a phenomenon Paul encountered at Corinth. (Naturally there it is less developed.) Paul refuted a position similar to that opposed by 1 John. In 1 Cor 12:3 he contended: "No one speaking in the Spirit of God says, 'Jesus is accursed'" *(Anathema Iēsous).* Instead, he argued, "No one is able to say, 'Jesus is Lord' *(Kyrios Iēsous)*, except by the Holy Spirit." Here Paul is offering criteria for the testing of the spirits. We might say, in Johannine terms, "every spirit that confesses Jesus is Lord is of God" to bring out the similarity of the two points of view. We should also notice that in 1 Cor 1:23 Paul's preaching of "Christ crucified" *(Christon estaurō- menon)* corresponds to "Christ is accursed" (Gal 3:13). Paul did not preach "Jesus crucified," but "Jesus is Lord," and not "Christ is Lord" *(Kyrios Christos)*, but "Christ crucified!" Paul identified the human name with the divine glory, and the name that came to be associated with the divine with the suffering of the cross. In this interchange we find the insistence that Jesus is the Christ (see 1 John 2:22-23). This is also the point of the test in 1 Cor 1:23. From this perspective *lyei* need not be seen as an anachronistic reading.

The *hoti* following "which you have heard" is epexegetical and need not be translated.

4. *You are of God, little children, and you have conquered them, because greater is the one who is in you than the one who is in the world:* The use of the masculine definite article *(ho)* to signify "the one" in you and "the one" in the world rules out identifying the Spirit of Truth and the Spirit of Error. Rather, the reference must be to God and the Antichrist (thus Strecker, *The Johannine Letters* 137).

The comparative particle *ē* is used with *meizōn* instead of the genitive case to express the comparison "greater than."

5. *They are of the world; because of this they speak from the world and the world hears them:* In this case "because of this" refers back to the first half of v. 5, which provides a clear cause. What follows "because of this" states the consequence, not the cause. The verb "to hear" *(akouei)* takes the genitive of the person heard and the accusative of his or her voice or words. Nevertheless, the context implies that hearing here and in v. 6 involves attentive listening, indeed taking notice and obeying.

6. *We are of God; the person knowing God hears us; who[ever] is not of God does not listen to us. From this we know the Spirit of Truth and the Spirit of Error:* Codex Alexandrinus (A) omits "who[ever] is not from God does not hear us." While the antithetic parallelism with the clause dealing with those "who hear us" is not perfect, this is no reason to reject the authenticity of the clause. The imperfect parallelism might account for its omission. The positive statement, which is not in question, implies the negative so that even if these words were rejected nothing much is at stake.

"From this" *(ek toutou)* looks back to the first part of v. 6. See the "by this" *(en toutǭ)* in 4:2, which has reference forward to the second half of 4:2. This idiom *(ek toutou)*, which is similar to that used in 4:2 *(en toutǭ)*, is found only here in 1 John, though it is used twice in John (6:66; 19:12).

"We know" *(ginōskomen)* has the object in the accusative case, like the second person plural *(ginōskete)* in 4:2. There, as here, it deals with knowledge as recognition: "we recognize the Spirit of Truth and the Spirit of Error." There it is "you recognize the Spirit of God."

INTERPRETATION

This section briefly treats the christological error espoused by the opponents. It is closely connected to the preceding and succeeding paragraphs, both of which are also introduced by directly addressing the readers as "Beloved." The previous paragraph succinctly connected the true [confession of] faith to the ethical response of loving one another. The present paragraph deals with the true confession of faith before turning to the nature of love as the source of faith, and faith as basis of the command to love one another. From this perspective the true confession of faith is crucial.

The author again **(4:1)** addresses his readers directly: "Beloved," as he had just four verses earlier (3:21) and will again in 4:7. This concentration makes sense because 3:21-24 connects the true confession of faith with the love command (3:23); 4:1-6 clarifies the true confession of faith and 4:7-11 shows how God's love is the source of faith and the response of faith is the ground of the obligation to love one another. Having addressed his readers as "beloved," the author exerts some heavy pressure, commanding them: "do not believe every spirit, but test the spirits." The continuing influence of the opponents was a matter of concern, and so the author tells the readers, in effect, "Stop believing every spirit." Testing the spirits involves a careful and critical attitude. The verb *(dokimazete)* is used in a variety of contexts including the testing of metals. The idea of testing implies criteria for identifying evidence of the Spirit of God.

While a multiplicity of spirits might be implied here, in 4:6 the range is reduced, or perhaps the focus has been sharpened, to recognize two, the Spirit of Truth and the Spirit of Error. The crisis of the schism seems to have led to the reference to many spirits. In the schism apparently many had separated from the author and his network of house churches. The author warns that "many false prophets have gone out into the world," which is surely a reference to the schismatics, now his opponents. "Many false prophets" might imply many spirits leading to falsehood. The association of the false prophets with the schism is confirmed by 2:18-19, 22-23. False prophets *(pseudoprophētai)* are identified with the liar *(pseustēs)* who denies "Jesus is the Christ," and the author affirms: "This person is the Antichrist." In 2:18-19 the appearance of many antichrists revealed that it is the *last hour*. Expectation of the coming of Antichrist appears to have been modified in the light of many opponents who separated from the Johannine network of churches. In 4:3 the false prophets are identified as manifestations of the Antichrist because every spirit that does not confess Jesus (in terms acceptable to the author of 1 John) is the Spirit of the Antichrist (4:3), and evidently the Spirit of Error (4:6). A variant reading of 4:3 reads *lyei*, which means "negates," "divides," or "destroys" Jesus. (See the Notes on 4:3.) This makes sense of 2:22, where "the liar" denies that Jesus is the Christ and is identified as the Antichrist.

The author's view of the seriousness of the situation is evident in the eschatological terms used to describe the situation. In 2:18 he moves from the expectation of the Antichrist to the actuality of the appearance of many antichrists, apparently those energized by the spirit of the Antichrist. For this see the discussion of 2:18 and in particular the discussion of the Antichrist there. Further light is shed on the situation by 2 John 7. There too we see reference to many *deceivers* who have *gone out into the world*. That this is a reference to the opponents seems clear. In 2:19 the schism is described in similar terms: "they went out from us . . ." and 4:1 says "many false prophets have gone out into the world." Elsewhere the author refers to "those who would *deceive* you" (2:26) and warns, "let no one *deceive* you" (3:7). Thus the opponents are depicted as many (4:1; 2 John 7), as false prophets, deceivers, and antichrists who can be embodied in the single figure of "the deceiver" (2 John 7) or the Antichrist (2:18; 4:3; 2 John 7).

We are dealing with the view that the Spirit of the Lord inspires prophets (2 Chr 15:1; Isa 61:1-2; Ezek 2:2; Mic 3:8; Zech 7:12). In the OT false prophets are those who speak without the Spirit and without being commissioned or sent by the Lord (Jer 23:21). There is reference in 1 Kgs 22:22-24 to false prophecy as the product of a "lying spirit." This description, which is analogous to the Spirit of Error that inspires the false prophets in 4:1-6, lacks the eschatological dimension of the Spirit of the Antichrist. This dimension is best understood in the context of Jewish apocalyptic writings and the apocalyptic writings of early Christianity, including Mark 13; Matthew 24; Luke 21; and especially 2 Thessalonians 2 and Revelation. Though these writings provide many components of the Johannine description of the last hour, nowhere outside 1 and 2 John is there mention of the Antichrist.

That the false prophets have gone out into the world means, in the first instance, that they have separated themselves from the author and those who continue to support him (2:18-19). That they considered this to be an empowered mission is possible. It may be that those who went out were more concerned about mission to the world than those left behind. 1 John seems to be preoccupied with community rebuilding. No attention is given to issues outside the community. There is no indication of a vision of mission to the world, even though recognition remains that "Jesus Christ the righteous is the expiation for the sins of the whole world" (2:2); "that the Father sent the Son [to be] savior of the world" (4:14). Nevertheless, 1 John says that those who separated from the Johannine community of faith never really belonged to it (2:18-19), and thus implies that they really belonged to the world, whose values are depicted in 2:15-17. Thus

already in 4:1 "the world" has the sense of the power and values opposed
to God, a view confirmed by 4:4-5.

"By this you know the Spirit of God" **(4:2)**. Here *ginōskete* has the meaning of "you recognize." The criterion for such recognition (*"By this* you
recognize") is stated straightforwardly: "every spirit that confesses Jesus
Christ has come in the flesh is of God." Obviously the discussion is not
about disembodied spirits; rather the assumption is that the confession
of the true faith is inspired by the Spirit of God (see 1 Cor 12:3). Further,
just as the Antichrist becomes antichrists because there are many false
prophets, many deceivers, and yet they all represent the one Deceiver, the
one Antichrist (see 2:18; 2 John 7), in the same way every spirit confessing that Jesus Christ has come in the flesh represents the one Spirit of
Truth.

In **4:3** the author asserts that "every spirit that does not confess (or
"looses" / "negates" / "destroys," cf. 3:8) Jesus is not of God; and this is
the Spirit of the Antichrist." The import of the variant reading is that the
Spirit of the Antichrist is attacking Jesus with the same intent as that embodied in the revelation of the Son of God in relation to the works of the
devil (3:8). Each seeks to destroy or nullify the other.

Here "every spirit," a description reflecting the multiplicity of the opponents in their refusal to make the authentic (according to 1 John) confession of faith in Jesus, becomes "the Spirit of the Antichrist" *(to tou
antichristou)*. The text uses the neuter definite article with "the Antichrist"
in the genitive case. As the subject under discussion is the spirit (and
*pneuma* is neuter), it is natural to supply "spirit," "the Spirit of the Antichrist." On this analogy the Spirit of God is manifest in every spirit that
confesses "Jesus Christ has come in the flesh" and the Spirit of the Antichrist is manifest in every spirit that will not make this confession, or that
negates, divides, or destroys Jesus.

The positive formulation of the confession of Jesus Christ having come
in the flesh is given in full. If the majority reading is accepted, the refusal
to confess that follows is given in summary terms. Reference to "every
spirit that does not confess Jesus" implies "does not confess Jesus Christ
having come in the flesh." If the alternative reading, *lyei,* is accepted as
more difficult to explain and thus original (see the Notes), we may well be
left with an uneasy feeling because of the total lack of support for this
reading in early Greek mss. Yet *lyei* makes better sense of the single name
"Jesus." The meaning is then "every spirit that looses / divides / destroys
/ nullifies Jesus is not of God." 1 John insists that Jesus is the Christ (2:22-
23), and the dividing of Jesus from Christ or negating or destroying Jesus
is the mark of the Antichrist and implies the rejection of the significance of
the human life of Jesus. Other aspects of the true confession of faith are
found in 2:22-23; 3:23; 4:15; 5:1, 5, 6, 20; 2 John 3, 7.

The author continues to speak of the Spirit of the Antichrist by using the neuter relative pronoun *(ho)*. Mention that "you have heard" (perfect tense) that the Spirit of the Antichrist "comes" implies a tradition well known to the readers, though we have only fragmentary awareness of it. Compare "you have heard Antichrist comes" in 2:18. But 4:3 goes further, adding "and is now in the world already." This was the basis for the declaration in 2:18, "it is the last hour." Although that theme is not repeated here, it is implied by "and is now in the world already."

References such as this ("you have heard that Antichrist comes," 2:18 and cf. 4:3) have led scholars to assume that there was a comprehensive and well-known myth of the Antichrist in the first century (see on 2:18). Though this may be true, we do well to remember that the Antichrist is named in the New Testament only in 1 and 2 John.

Whereas the well-known tradition spoke of the coming of the Antichrist (and the Spirit of the Antichrist), it may be that the author(s?) of 1 and 2 John first announce that he has come and is already in the world (see 2:18 and 2 John 7). The presence of the Spirit of the Antichrist in the world is compatible with many antichrists (4:3). That the author continues to speak of the Spirit of the Antichrist, rather than the Antichrist as such, probably means that no single figure could be identified. Nevertheless, 1 and 2 John tend to focus the many into the figure of the one: "the Antichrist," "the Deceiver." The reason for doing this seems to have been the existing tradition or myth of the Antichrist as one manifestation of the power of the Evil One. Because many antichrists are in the world, manifesting the Spirit of the Antichrist, the author affirms, "the whole world lies in the power of the Evil One" (5:19). Thus 1 John reflects an author in a defensive mode, attempting to ward off the attacks of the Evil One. Even so, there is the continued recognition that the message "God is light," "God is love" is the foundation of the possibility for the salvation of the world, salvation that involves the overcoming of the world as it is through the triumph of faith.

The christological confession that Jesus Christ is come in the flesh is variously stated in 1 John. Whether or not the majority reading ("does not confess") is accepted, the point of contention seems to have been the flesh of the one identified as the Christ (see 2 John 7). Because the liar, who is identified as the Antichrist, denies that Jesus is the Christ (2:22; cf. 5:1), it seems that Jesus is identified with the flesh and the Christ is identified in some way with God. Thus 2:22 continues that to deny Jesus is the Christ is to deny the Father and the Son. The confession that Jesus is the Son of God is fundamental for the believer's mutual abiding in God (4:15) and the one who believes Jesus is the Son of God conquers the world (5:5). In the context of 1 John the confession that "Jesus is the Christ" is scarcely distinguishable from "Jesus is the Son of God." Both confessions seem to have been contested by the opponents. These confessions, like that of "Jesus Christ has come in the flesh," have become criteria for the recognition of the true faith of those who enjoy mutual abiding with God. Clearly, for 1 John the human Jesus is the Christ, the Son of God. Thus to deny Jesus is to deny the Son and to deny the Son is to deny the Father. To have the Son is to have the Father also (2:23). The opponents rejected the identification of the human Jesus with the Christ, the Son of God, the Incarnation, that Jesus Christ has come in the flesh (4:2-3). This is to reject the presence of the Son of God, revealing the Father in the human life of Jesus. In 1 John the ethical obligation of faith is grounded in the human life of Jesus (2:6; John 13:34 and 1 John 4:11). Particularly in 4:7-12 the human life of Jesus is seen as the revelation of God's love and the ground of the obligation to love one another.

The same problem is apparent in 2 John 7 in the reference to "the people not confessing *(hoi mē homologountes)* Jesus Christ coming *(erchomenon)* in flesh." This is confirmed by the identification of these people with the Deceiver and the Antichrist. But the present participle "coming" is used in 2 John 7, not the perfect participle as in 1 John 4:2. Georg Strecker (*The Johannine Letters* 232–36) has revived the view that 2 John 7 is an example of chiliasm, the idea that Christ will return in the flesh to reign on earth for a thousand years (the millennial messianic reign). He argues that the issue in 2 John 7 is the denial that Jesus is coming (again) in the flesh, an issue quite different from that in 1 John 4:2-3. Certainly the present participle may be used with future reference. But had this been a reference to the future coming, the writer would surely have made this clear, as was done in 1 John 2:28. We may question too whether formulations that are so close in wording are likely to be dealing with quite different issues. Do the different tenses of the participles rule out the reference to the "Incarnation" in 2 John 7? Strecker (*The Johannine Letters* 134 n. 18) draws attention to the perfect participle in 4:2, an aorist participle in 5:6, and the present participle in 2 John 7, all referring to the *coming* of Jesus. Strecker presses for distinct meanings. Yet we should notice a certain lack of precision in the use of the aorist and perfect tenses in 1 John. Here we are dealing with participles, where tense functions in a distinctive way. Raymond Brown correctly notes that the perfect participle emphasizes the ongoing consequences of the event, so that Jesus' earthly life is in view in 4:2. In 5:6 "this is the one who came through water and blood" uses the aorist participle with the definite article *(ho elthōn)* to speak of "the *one* who came." In this quite different construction the person and the event of the coming are emphasized. In 2 John 7 "Jesus Christ coming in the flesh" emphasizes the identification of Jesus Christ in the flesh without stressing the event or the ongoing consequences of it. In 2 John there is no attempt to build the ethical teaching of the gospel on the basis of the earthly life of Jesus, a task that is fundamental in 1 John. From the perspective of this theme the present participle is not precise enough.

The use of the present participle in 2 John 7 does not look like the work of a copyist using 1 John as a model. Copyists normally copy without innovation. Differences in word order as well as the tense of the participles mark 2 John 7 and 1 John 4:2. If a copyist is responsible for one of the two works it is more likely that 1 John copied from 2 John than the reverse because the perfect participle is an improvement on the present. But the variation of word order has no real point. More likely we have the work of the same author freely composing on the same theme, less likely different authors working out of a common tradition but not copying one from the other.

The next verse **(4:4)** begins a new paragraph, marked by the renewed address, "little children," last used in 3:18 (and see above on 2:1). This breaks a sequence in which the readers are addressed as "beloved," in 3:21; 4:1, 7, 11. It is normal for the address to come at the beginning of the sentence. Here it follows the opening statement. This highlights the importance of the statement: "you (plural) are of God, little children." Not only is this order of words emphatic, but also the placing of *teknia* is suggestive of the theme "children of God," although the diminutive form is not normally used in that context, but rather *tekna theou*. If the theme is there, it is no more than a clarification by innuendo of *ek tou theou* (see 3:1-3).

This emphatic statement has a parallel in 4:6. There is but one change. The opening word in 4:6 is the first person plural personal pronoun "we": "We are of God." We should expect to learn how these two distinct groups, each of which is said to be of God, relate to each other. That such a relationship is implied is the key to distinguishing "you" from "we."

First the author deals with those he has addressed, affirming "and you have conquered *them*." This cannot be a reference to the Antichrist, which requires the singular, "him," nor can it be a reference to "the Spirit of the Antichrist," which would be neuter. Consequently the reference looks back to the false prophets (masculine as "them" is also), confirming that the spirits not confessing Jesus Christ come in the flesh, which can be spoken of as the Spirit of the Antichrist, energize the false prophets. 1 John now assures the readers: "you have *conquered* them." This is an important theme in 1 John (see 2:13, 14; 4:4; 5:4 [2x], 5 and the noun [victory] in 5:4 and John 16:33).

But 1 John does not suggest that his readers conquer the false prophets themselves. Just as the false prophets are empowered by the Spirit of the Antichrist, so also the readers are empowered. The author now asserts: "greater is the one in you than the one in the world." The contrast of the greater (God, see 3:20) with the lesser (the Antichrist, who is in the world, 4:3) assures the victory of the readers. The perfect tense already pronounces the victory. This language is the kind used for celebrating victory in battle, as we can see in 1QM 11:4-5: "Truly the battle is Thine and the power from Thee! It is not ours. Our strength and the power of our hands accomplish no mighty deeds except by Thy power and by the might of Thy great valour" (Geza Vermes, *The Dead Sea Scrolls in English* [3rd ed. New York: Penguin, 1987, 116). In the Johannine literature it is used metaphorically of the moral victory over evil in the life of Jesus and the Johannine community. On the immoral power of the world see 2:15-17, and on the victory of faith over the immoral power of the world see 5:4-5.

The identification of the Antichrist as the one in the *world* opposed to God (who is in the Johannine believers) not only sets the Antichrist in opposition to God, it sets the world in opposition to believers. This confirms that because "many false prophets have gone out into the world" (4:1) the world now "lies in the power of the Evil One" (5:20). If the false prophets are in the world, the Spirit of the Antichrist is in the world; indeed, the Antichrist is in the world.

Reference returns to the false prophets: "They are of the world" **(4:5)**. They were last mentioned in the first half of 4:4, "you have conquered *them.*" The opening of v. 4: "You are of God," stands in contrast with the opening of v. 5: "They are of the world." Thus God and the world are here in antithetic parallelism. On the one hand this guarantees the victory of the believers over the false prophets. Because it is God who stands over against the false prophets, and God is in those who believe, victory over the false prophets is guaranteed. On the other hand, the false prophets are of the world. It could be argued from 4:1 that they became part of the world when "they went out into the world." But 2:19 says: "they went out from us because they were not of us." This implies that they always were "of the world" and that separation from the Johannine believers only revealed the true state of affairs. On the "world" in 1 John see the discussion on 2:2.

To say "they are of the world" means that they are children of the world just as those who are of God are children of God. To call them children of the world is the equivalent of calling them children of the Evil One (3:12-13; 5:19) or children of the devil (John 8:39-45). They are children of the world and "because of this" *(dia touto)* they speak from the determining reality of the world. The subject matter and values expressed in their speech are determined by the world. Naturally the world, whose speech and values are here expressed, listens to them, that is, it receives and approves of what it hears.

Here and in 4:6, 1 John gives expression to the truth of John 3:31 that the person who is of the earth *(ek tēs gēs)* speaks what (subject matter and values) is determined by the earth. Here "the earth" is the equivalent of "from below" *(katō)* as opposed to "from above" (John 8:23), "of this world" (8:23) as opposed to "from heaven" (3:31). There it is implied that those from above would receive the witness of the one from above, from heaven. In saying this the Johannine author shows profound insight into the problem of adequately hearing and taking account of a message that expresses values opposed to the hearer's determining set of values. Because the false prophets reflect the values of the world, the world listens to them, takes notice of their message, and receives it. This suggests that the opponents' mission to the world was successful.

If vv. 4 and 5 dealt with the contrast between "you" the readers and "they" the false prophets, **4:6** affirms at once a solidarity with and difference from the readers. Both "you" and "we" are said to be of God, to be children of God: "now we are children of God" (3:2). Since 2:1 the author has spoken in the first person singular, "I." The author speaks of "I" when addressing his readers as "you" (2:20-21, 25-26; 5:13-14) and alternates between addressing his readers as "you" and inclusively referring to himself with his readers as "we" (see 2:19-20, 24-26, 28; 3:13-14; 5:13-14). Because of this scholars are divided about whether the "we" of v. 6 is inclusive of the "you" of v. 4 or whether the author here has returned to the exclusive "we" of the tradition bearers of 1:1-5.

The case for the return to the "we" of the tradition bearers is that in 4:6 "we" are explicitly distinguished from "the person who knows God," who "hears us." Thus "we" are distinguished from others "who are of God." It is also said that the person who is not of God does not hear "us." Thus others who know God and those who do not are distinguished from "us," who are of God. Hearing "us" is thus the test of the truth of those who claim to know God. In John 8:47 the same test is related to Jesus' words, "the person who is of God hears the words of God," assuming that Jesus speaks the words of God.

While 1 John is intent on *assuring* the readers that they know the truth (2:20-21), at the same time no stone is left unturned in instructing them as to what the truth is. This is done by refuting the errors of the opponents (1:6, 8, 10; 2:4, 6, 9; 4:20) and by providing tests for the recognition of the true and the false; see 3:20 and the Notes on this verse for further references including 4:2-3 and context. All the evidence of 1 John suggests that the author wrote because he feared that the wound caused by the departure of his opponents would continue to bleed as members of the community who presently remained became disaffected and drawn to the opponents. 1 John would not have been written had the author thought his readers were fully and firmly established in the truth. The aim of 1 John is to bring about that stability in the midst of a wave of uncertainty. In 2 John 10 the Elder writes, instructing: "If any one comes to you and does not bear this teaching (of this letter), do not receive him into [your] house and do not speak to greet him." The author of 1 John, like the Elder in 2 John, made his teaching (and that of the tradition bearers) the test of truth for the readers.

The author makes "hearing us" the test for discerning the Spirit of Truth and the Spirit of Error. Obviously to "hear us" is evidence of possessing the Spirit of Truth; see 3:24. Refusal to "hear us" is evidence of the Spirit of Error. There can be little doubt that the Spirit of Truth of 4:6 is the Spirit of God of 4:2 and the Spirit of Error is the Spirit of the Antichrist of 4:3. The term "error" *(planēs)* is linguistically connected to the Deceiver *(ho planos)* who is identified with the Antichrist in 2 John 7. The participle with definite article is used in the context of the discussion of the Antichrist/antichrists in 2:26, where they are described as "those who would deceive you" *(tōn planōntōn);* cf. also 3:7. The Spirit of Error is the Spirit of the Antichrist.

## FOR REFERENCE AND FURTHER STUDY

Beutler, Johannes. *Die Johannesbriefe,* 100–106.

Boer, Martinus C. de."The Death of Jesus and his Coming in the Flesh (1 John 4:2)," *NovT* 33 (1991) 326–46.

Brooke, Alan England. *A Critical and Exegetical Commentary on the Johannine Epistles,* 106–17.

Brown, Raymond E. *The Epistles of John,* 485–511.

Ehrman, Bart D. "1 John 4:3 and the Orthodox Corruption of Scripture," *ZNW* 79 (1988) 221–43.

Rensberger, David. *1 John, 2 John, 3 John,* 109–15.

Schnackenburg, Rudolf. *The Johannine Epistles,* 198–206.

Sekki, Arthur Everett. *The Meaning of* Ruaḥ *at Qumran.* SBLDS 110. Atlanta: Scholars, 1989.

Vermes, Geza. *The Dead Sea Scrolls in English.* 3rd ed. New York: Penguin, 1987.

# IV. THIRD PRESENTATION OF THE TWO TESTS (4:7–5:12)

*Stressing the inseparable relation between the two tests*

## 1. LOVE BASED ON FAITH IN THE REVELATION OF GOD'S LOVE IS THE PROOF OF KNOWING GOD AND BEING BORN OF GOD (4:7-21)

### 1.1. God's love is the source of love for one another (4:7-12)

7. Beloved, let us love one another, because love is of God, and everyone who loves is begotten of God and knows God. 8. The person not loving did not know God, because God is love. 9. By this the love of God is revealed among us: God has sent his only Son into the world that we may live through him. 10. In this is love, not that we have loved God, but that he loved us and sent his Son [as] an expiation for our sins. 11. Beloved, if God loved us in this way, we also ought to love one another. 12. No one has ever seen God; if we love one another, God abides in us and his love is made perfect in us.

### NOTES

7. *Beloved, let us love one another, because love is of God, and every one who loves is begotten of God and knows God:* "Beloved, let us love one another" is three words in Greek, each beginning with *alpha: Agapētoi, agapōmen allēlous.* This might be a deliberate alliteration. It shows a certain skill in the use of words. See also the description of the one who loves as begotten of God and knows God. Both verbs here begin with *gamma.* The ground or rationale for the love command is given in the *hoti* clause, "because. . . ." In this clause *ek tou theou* identifies God as the origin and source of love. Love, as such, comes from God. The use of the singular noun with the article *(hē agapē)* indicates that. "Let us love one another" uses a hortatory subjunctive that softens a command by including the writer within the scope of the instruction. The use of the present tense implies ongoing action, not simply a single act of love. Codex Alexandrinus (A), following a scribal tendency, inserts "God" after "Every one who loves."

8. *The person not loving did not know God, because God is love:* "The one who does not love does not know *(ouk egnō)* God." The aorist is strongly supported, though Alexandrinus (A) reads a present tense and Sinaiticus reads a perfect. The inceptive aorist implies that they have not begun to know God.

Commonly the predicate in a clause using the verb "to be" is anarthrous (without the definite article). The verb "to be" takes the same case in subject and predicate. The subject is identified by the definite article because Greek word order need not place the subject before the verb. The words "God is love" *(ho theos agapē estin)* make very clear that God is the subject by placing God at the very beginning of the sentence with the definite article, while "love" is anarthrous (without the definite article). "God is love," 4:8, 16; "God is light," 1:5; "God is Spirit," John 4:24. The moral nature of the affirmations in the Epistle sets them apart from John 4:24, "God is Spirit," which distinguishes God from "all flesh" as the creator is distinct from the creation.

9. *By this the love of God was revealed among us: God has sent his only Son into the world that we may live through him:* "By this . . . was revealed": see above on 2:3 for the use of "by this," and on 1:2 for "was revealed" *(ephanerōthē)*. The context makes clear that "the love *of* God" *(tou theou)* is here a subjective genitive meaning "God's love" for us. That love was revealed "among us" *(en hymin)*. That is, *en hymin* goes with "was revealed" *(ephanerōthē)*, not with "the love of God." The use of *en* with the dative *plural* pronoun here means "among." Thus it is not "the love of God in us was revealed" but "the love of God was revealed among us." This is borne out by the explanatory clause introduced by *hoti*. The explanation of "by this" is "that God has sent his only Son. . . ." This event happened "among us," according to 1 John 1:1-4 (and compare John 1:14, 9:3).

The verb "has sent" *(apestalken)* is perfect tense, indicating an event in the past with continuing significance, though aorist and perfect tenses are not always clearly distinct in use by this author. Either way the specific event is clearly emphasized. On the theme of the sending of the Son by the Father (God) see 4:9, 10, 14. In John the theme appears much more frequently and *pempō* is used in addition to *apostellō*. For *apostellō* see John 3:17, 34; 5:36, 38; 6:29, 57; 7:29; 8:42; 10:36; 11:42; 17:3, 8, 18, 21, 23, 25; 20:21. For *pempō* see 4:34; 5:23, 24, 30, 37; 6:38, 39, 44; 7:16, 18, 28, 33; 8:16, 18, 26, 29; 9:4; 12:44, 45, 49; 13:20; 14:24, [26]; 15:21, [26]; 16:5, and see my *The Quest for the Messiah* 231–32 n. 67.

For reference to "his only Son" *(ton huion autou ton monogenē)* see also John 1:14, 18; 3:16, 18, and Brown, *The Epistles of John* 516–17. The construction "that we might live" *(hina zēsōmen)* may express purpose or result. Only context can determine the difference. In the NT purpose and result often merge. The construction "through him" *(di autou)* expresses the idea of agency. If God is the source of the saving action, God's Son is the agent through whom the action is performed.

10. *In this is love, not that we have loved God, but that he loved us and sent his Son [as] an expiation for our sins:* Again Codex Sinaiticus (א) adds to "in this is love" the qualifying "of God." Scribes tend to specify what is left ambiguous, but 1 John is talking about love as such and its definitive expression.

In Codex Alexandrinus (A) "we" is contrasted with the emphatic demonstrative *ekeinos*, not the third person pronoun *autos*. Again this is a scribal change to reinforce the contrast.

Codex Vaticanus (B) reads two perfect tenses for "we have loved" and "he has loved," though the textual evidence strongly favors the use of the aorist tense in the latter *(ēgapēsen)*. The aorist refers to a completed action and appropriately pairs with "he sent" *(apesteilen),* which is also aorist. The latter is in contrast with the use of the perfect tense *(apestalken)* in 4:9, which looks to the ongoing consequences of the sending: "that we might live through him." This is also the point of "not that *we have loved (ēgapēkamen)* God" in 4:10.

Codex Alexandrinus (A) has changed the aorist "he sent" *(apesteilen)* to the perfect tense "he has sent" *(apestalken)* to conform to the perfect tense in 4:9. Again we note the smoothing or harmonizing tendencies of scribal activity. The aorist is clearly the original reading.

On the *en toutō* construction followed by *hoti* see 4:9 and the Notes on 2:3. This time it is a double *hoti,* the first negative, "not that," and the second positive, "but that." See 2 John 5 and John 6:38; 12:6; 15:16 for the "not . . . but" construction. Here the *en* is not instrumental, but specifies where to find love: "in this."

*Beloved, if God loved us in this way, we also ought to love one another:* The use of *ei* followed by the indicative does not imply uncertainty, but expresses a condition from which consequences flow: if "A," then "B." The obligation laid *on the believer* by the revelation is expressed using the modal verb *opheilomen.* The action (object) of this verb is normally completed by an infinitive, as here *(agapan):* We ought *to love* one another. (See on 2:6, and note also 3:16.) The use in 3 John 8 is related but different. The command to love one another in 3:23 and 4:7 placed the verb first *(agapōmen allēlous).* Here the order is reversed, because on the basis of the statement that God loved us like this we would expect the obligation that we ought to love God. Consequently the author wrote *allēlous agapan.*

12. *No one has ever seen God; if we love one another, God abides in us and his love is made perfect in us:* The conditional sentence here uses *ean* [not *ei*] and takes the verb in the subjunctive mood. It nevertheless expresses a straightforward condition that, if fulfilled, leads to certain consequences. There is some textual confusion over the word order of the last four words in this verse. This suggests that some scribes had some difficulty with the second half of the verse.

INTERPRETATION

For the third time in a sequence **(4:7)** the author addresses his readers as "Beloved" (3:21; 4:1, 7, and see 4:11 to follow; see also on 2:7 and 3:2). The exhortation, "let us love one another," is a hortatory formula in which the author includes himself in the command to "love one another." This harkens back to 3:23, which reminds the reader of Jesus' command in John 13:34 (and see 1 John 3:11). On "love" see on 2:5. At the same time 4:11 is a resumption of 4:7, repeating the address "Beloved" and restating the obligation to "love one another."

In John 13:34 the command is "love one another" *(allēlous),* as here and in 3:11; 4:11. There the obligation is grounded in "as *(kathōs)* I have loved you." There *kathōs* has a double sense. It means "in the same manner" and "because." The relevant element for our discussion here is the basis of the love command in Jesus' words, "because I have loved you." That is both the moral ground of the obligation *(opheilomen)* and the affective source to move the one so loved to love others. In 1 John 4:7-12 the ground and affective source are taken back to God. So the ground for loving one another is because *(hoti)* love is of God. That is, God is the ultimate source of love. This means that one who loves is living out of the divine source of love, and that is to be begotten of God. Human loving is not the cause but the manifestation of being begotten of God. From the human side, in 1 John believing that Jesus Christ is come in the flesh is the foundation belief that puts the believer in relationship to the divine source of love. The one who loves reveals the reality of that relationship, reveals the divine origin of the life of the one who loves. Divine origin is understood in terms of the metaphor "to be begotten of God." Simply to love is the evidence, and love is defined by God from whom this love comes. Because it is here defined by the divine love it does not need to be qualified in any other way, for example as for "one another."

The one who loves is begotten *(gegennētai)* of God and knows *(ginōskei)* God. Interestingly, this describes the one who loves from a passive perspective (is begotten of God) and an active perspective (and knows God).

Having spoken of "everyone who loves" *(pas ho agapōn),* 1 John now **(4:8)** refers to "the one who does not love" *(ho mē agapōn).* The difference between these two descriptions is the use of "every" in the first and the negative *(mē)* in the second. This balances the antithetical form (see 2:4, 6, 9; 3:7, 8, 24 for the use of the participle with the article meaning "the person who . . ."). The love theme leads naturally to the metaphor of being begotten of God. If the ground for the love commandment is because love is of God, the evidence that the one who does not love does not know God is that God is love; see also 4:16. This is to say that the being of God is expressed in loving. While "God is love," of love it can only be said that "love is *of* God." God is the source of love just as God is the source of life. The life God gives is life that loves.

Thus the divine love defines the nature of the love commanded; see John 13:34 and 1 John 4:11. 1 John 2:15-17 shows that love can be corrupted. But God's love is defined by the event that forms the fundamental gospel revelation. Thus Jesus says "Love one another as I have loved you" (John 13:34), and 1 John 4:11 says "Beloved, if God loved us in this way, we also ought to love one another" (implied: "in this way"). The revelation of God is spoken of in the other "God is . . ." statement in 1 John 1:5, "God is light" (see the Notes on 1:5). The moral nature of the revelation is emphasized. It follows that the person who does not love in this way does not know God or live out of the reality of the life of God.

1 John **4:9** asserts that God's love was revealed in the world "among us," "in our midst" (see 1:1-3). Whether the author intends to include the readers in the reference "among us" is unclear. Certainly here, as in 1:1-3, there is a clear intention to affirm that there is firsthand testimony to the event that happened among us. God's love remains unqualified. God's love is revealed "by this" *(en toutǭ):* "he has sent his only son into the world that we may live through him." The specific event is emphasized here, whether or not the perfect tense "he has sent" is given its distinctive meaning or read as if it were an aorist. The event of the sending of the Son only reveals God's love when the purpose of the sending is grasped. The purpose is "that we may live through him." In light of this the sending of the Son is the evidence of God's love. We are reminded that in John 3:16 the truth that God *gave (edōken)* his only Son is taken to demonstrate the fact and manner of God's love for the world.

In 1 John 4:9 it is said that God sent his only Son *into the world*, not that he came to save the world. Indeed the author says that the sending of the Son into the world was so that "we" should live through him. Does this mean that the purpose of lifegiving was from the beginning intended only for the group included in this "we"? Of course this depends on how the "we" is understood. There is nothing in 1 John to suggest that there is a foreordained group selected "to live through him." Nevertheless the purpose and the consequence is "that we may live through him." The key is in understanding the scope of the "we."

The point may be expressed this way. The "we" potentially includes the world of humanity, but only those who believe effectively live through him. Thus the meaning is not different from John 3:16. There "whoever believes in him" corresponds to the "we" in 1 John 4:9. This perspective is clear in the first use of "world" in 1 John 2:2. (See the Notes there.) There the author affirmed that Jesus Christ the righteous "is the expiation of our sins and not for ours only but for the sins of the whole world." Further, 1 John 4:14 states that "The Father sent the Son as the savior of the world." The Father is thus the source of life, the Lord and giver of life. But the Son is the agent of lifegiving; life is "through him." Because of this 1 John can say "if God loved us like this we ought to love one another" (4:11), and Jesus can say in the Gospel, "love one another as *(kathōs)* I have loved you" (John 13:34). Here *kathōs* has the double sense of "because" I loved you and "in the same way as" I loved you.

If 4:9 deals with the *revelation* of love, **4:10** affirms what love is. "Love," with the definite article *(hē agapē),* is a reference to the nature of love itself. This is not a statement about the way love is revealed (4:4) or known (3:16). It is an affirmation about what love is. It is first defined negatively by what it is not essentially. It is not that we *have loved* God. It would have been inappropriate to use an aorist tense, indicating a completed act of love. A present tense might have been used, but would have been less effective than the perfect tense, which properly implies a commencement and continuation of loving. Inasmuch as believers love God, the perfect tense is most appropriate. The author does not deny that we have loved God (with continuing effect). He denies that this is essentially what love is. It is not that we have loved God but that God loved us. Here love is defined in the act: God loved (aorist tense) us. God sent (aorist tense) his Son. These aorist tenses identify the event that defines what love is. But the sending of the Son is not a bare event. The event is understood as the *Father* sending the Son (4:14). The sending is understood to have a saving purpose, to save the world (4:14), that we might live through him (4:9). Involved in this is the death of the Son as an expiation for sins (4:10; and see above on 2:2; cf. 1:7).

The renewed address of the readers as "Beloved" **(4:11)** marks the summing up and conclusion of the subsection 4:7-12. It is the sixth and last in the series using this form of address (see 2:7; 3:2, 21; 4:1, 7, 11, and cf. 3 John 1, 2, 5, 11). In 4:7-10 the author began with a direct appeal to his readers to love one another, arguing that love comes from God, that love was revealed in the sending of the Son, and that the nature of love is defined by God's love when he sent his Son. God's love is definitive, primary, and the source of all love. In arguing this way the author implies that four issues are at stake. The first is the character of love, which the author insists is defined by the event of the sending of the Son—understood as the sending of the Son by the Father—the sending of the Son to save the world. Second, love has its source in God so that human love is seen to be derivative and responsive. This implies that human love continually needs to be redefined and corrected by divine love because human love in the world has the potential to be corrupted (see 2:15-17). Third, it is because of the potential for corruption that the love command is given. The love command (John 13:34; 1 John 4:7, 11) reminds the believer of the obligation to love, and this is particularly clear in the use of the modal verb in the formulation *opheilomen allēlous agapan:* "we *ought* to love one another." Fourth, the love command is the claim of divine love on all people. But it is also the gift of the divine love: "we love *because* he first loved us" (4:19), and this is reflected in the love command itself. In the command *kathōs* has the double meaning of "in the same way" and "because." "Love one another because I have loved you." "We love because. . . ." The divine love liberates those who recognize and respond to that love. It liberates us to love one another.

The obligation to love is based on a condition: if God loved us in this way *(houtōs).* Because the writer has established the actuality of the condition, with *houtōs* referring back to 4:7-10, the obligation follows. In the recognition and response to the divine love the potential to love is realized.

The opening clause of **4:12** in literal and word order translation is "God no one ever has seen" *(theon oudeis pōpote tetheatai)*. The absence of the article follows John 1:18 *(theon oudeis heōraken pōpote)*. The first two words are identical, but John 1:18 places *pōpote* last. Further, John uses a different verb for seeing. Indeed, in three passages where John denies that anyone has seen God he uses the perfect tense of *horan*: John 1:18; 5:37; 6:46. But 1 John 4:12 uses the perfect tense of *theasthai*. The evidence does not suggest different ideas of seeing with the use of the different verbs. Each of the verbs of seeing is used in John and 1 John to cover the same range of meanings. (See Bultmann, *The Gospel of John* 69 nn. 2 and 4, and see the Notes on 1 John 1:1.)

The reason for the absence of the definite article at the beginning is fairly obvious. For emphasis "God," though the object in the clause, is placed first. Sentences do not normally start with the definite article and a noun. When the noun is the object of the verb, absence of the article is not surprising. But the emphasis is on God. It is *God* no one has ever seen. The use of *tetheatai* as the final word in the clause (rather than another verb of seeing) might be aesthetic, to match the opening word *theon*. This would be especially appropriate in light of supposed etymologies of the word *theos* and its association with *theasthai*. In the Gospel of John the denial that anyone had seen God was anti-Jewish polemic. But there was also Jewish tradition that refuted the idea that individuals had seen God. The denial that anyone had seen God is inserted here rather abruptly. It is unclear that the opponents claimed to have seen God. It is more likely that the denial is made to make clear that the only means of seeing God was in the revelation in the Son. This is also the point in John 14:8-11. It is also fundamental to 1 John 4:7-12 that the love of the Father (God) is made known in the Son. But here 1 John, in the tradition of John 1:18, denies that anyone has seen God.

The alternative to seeing God is "if we love one another." In 3:2 the expectation of seeing him (Jesus) as he is was the ground of the hope that "we will be like him." This is the Johannine version of the vision of God. In the time of Jesus' ministry there were those who saw, heard, touched, and handled. When he is revealed, at his coming (2:28), we will be like him because we will see him as he is. But here, for the moment, loving one another appears to be an alternative to seeing him as he is. Even here it is unclear whether loving one another is God's abiding with us or whether it is the evidence of that abiding. The latter seems more likely in that it is said that "if we love one another . . . God's love is made perfect in us."

Interestingly, this is the only verse in which reference is made to God abiding in us that does not refer to mutual abiding: see 3:24; 4:13, 15, 16.

On the other hand, statements about abiding in God are found in 2:6, 24, 27, 28; 3:6. But here the stress on God abiding in us if we love one another supports the recognition that the genitive, which may be translated as "his love" (subjective genitive) or "the love of him" (objective genitive), should be recognized as a subjective genitive. If God abides in us, God's love is active in us and is perfected when we love one another. Thus the mutuality formula is indirectly preserved by reference to love for one another.

In 2:5 and 4:17 we also find the motif of the love being perfected. In particular 2:5 refers to "the love of God," and the genitive may be subjective or objective. The context of 2:6-12, dealing with Cain, who hated his brother, supports the recognition of a subjective genitive there. This conclusion is borne out by reference to the truth that "his love is made perfect" here in 4:12. In context it is unlikely that this means love for him. (See the discussions of 2:5 and 4:17.)

## 1.2. The Spirit is the evidence of abiding in God (4:13-16a)

13. By this we know we abide in him and he in us, because he has given us of his Spirit. 14. And we have seen and bear witness: the Father has sent the Son [as] savior of the world. 15. Whoever confesses Jesus is the Son of God, God abides in him and he in God. 16a. And we have known and have believed the love that God has in us.

### NOTES

13. *By this we know we abide in him and he in us, because he has given us of his Spirit:* For "by this we know . . ." see above on 2:3. That "he has given us *of (ek)* his Spirit": here "of" gives expression to *ek* with a partitive genitive. The gift does not exhaust the Spirit. The genitive might also indicate that the Spirit is the source of the gift. See the *charismata* of 1 Cor 12:4. The test of 4:13 is similar to 3:24. Formally they differ in that 3:24 uses only the epexegetical *hoti*, indicating the content of what "we know." Apart from the opening "and" in 3:24, 4:13 follows the same formula wording of "by this we know *hoti*." Then there is the difference of "he abides in us" (3:24) and the mutual abiding formula of 4:13; there is no second causal *hoti* in 3:24 as there is in 4:13. Because abiding in God or God abiding in the believer implies mutual abiding (see the Interpretation) there is no substantial difference of meaning between the two texts on this point. The second *hoti* in 4:13 shows that the test to which "by this" refers is in the second *hoti* clause, "because *(hoti)* he has given us of his Spirit" (4:13). Less clearly the same point is made in 3:24 using *ek* with a partitive genitive,

"of the Spirit that he has given us" (3:24). Thus the *hoti* of 4:13 clarifies 3:24. While the author uses set formulae, he delights in small variations, changes in vocabulary, word order, and the like.

Codex Alexandrinus (A) reads an aorist "he gave" in place of the perfect "he has given" to harmonize 4:13 with 3:24, "he gave us of his Spirit." The aorist is secondary in 4:13.

14. *And we have seen and bear witness: the Father has sent the Son [as] savior of the world:* Codex Alexandrinus harmonizes 4:14 with 1:1 by changing the perfect tense "we have seen" *(tetheametha )* into the aorist *(etheasametha).* This suggests that scribes identified the "we" of 3:14 with the "we" of 1:1-5. For the emphatic use of the first person plural personal pronoun in the nominative case at the beginning of the sentence see 3:14, 20, 24, 27; 4:4, 5, 6, 14, 16, 19. This becomes especially important where there is a play on the contrast between "we" and "you [plural]."

The use of *tetheametha* may have been suggested by the appearance of the same verb in the same tense in 4:12. The perfect tense "we have seen" is appropriate as a basis for the present "we bear witness." This is the first use of "to bear witness" since 1:2. The content of the witness is indicated by an epexegetical *hoti.*

On the variation in use of the different verbs of seeing, see above on 1:1-3 and Bultmann, *The Gospel of John* 69 nn. 2, 4.

15. *Whoever confesses Jesus is the Son of God, God abides in him and he in God:* With regard to "whoever" *(hos ean)* see the more elegant *hos an* in 2:5. 1 John reflects Hellenistic use in the interchangeability of the two forms.

The verb "to confess" [faith] *(homologein)* is used in 2:23; 4:2, 3, 15; 2 John 7. The same verb, "to confess" [sins] is used in 1:9. The *hoti* following "confesses" is epexegetical, indicating what is confessed, and does not need to be translated.

Codex Alexandrinus (A) reads the present subjunctive "confesses" in place of the aorist, which is original. 1 John is referring to the public confession of faith that the author considers to be the foundation of the Christian life. Codex Vaticanus (B) reads "Jesus Christ" for "Jesus." Additions of this sort are scribal inclinations.

In Greek "Jesus" is without the definite article that is used in "the Son of God." Because with the verb "to be" subject and object take the same case, and word order can be varied, the object normally is anarthrous (without the article). Thus a case can be made for reading "the Son of God is Jesus." This suggests that "the Son of God" was a known designation, but the identification with Jesus was controversial. The same is true of the denial in 2:22. The denial took the form, "the Christ is not Jesus." (See above on 2:22.)

16a. *And we have known and have believed the love that God has in us:* Stylistically compare 4:14, "and we have seen and we bear witness." This involves a perfect tense followed by a present. Here in 4:16a "We have known and believed" involves two perfect tenses. On the order "we have known and believed" see John 17:8. Elsewhere in John the order is believe and know; see 6:69; 8:31-32;

10:38. Only in 4:16a do these two verbs occur together in 1 John. Here the order "we have known and believed" means "we have recognized and accepted." On the use of *ginōskein* see above on 2:3, and see 3:23 on the use of *pisteuein.*

INTERPRETATION

In 3:24 the giving of the Spirit is expressed in words close to **4:13**. (See the discussion of 3:24 above.) In 3:24 the relative pronoun "that" is used, while 4:13 uses the genitive of the third person singular personal pronoun, "*his* Spirit." The verb tenses also differ, aorist in 3:24 and perfect in 4:13. Nevertheless, the author clearly resumes the theme of 3:24 in 4:13. In 3:24b the giving of the Spirit is evidence that God abides in us, whereas in 4:13 the gift of the Spirit is evidence of mutual abiding. Yet 3:24a says that the one keeping his (God's) commandments abides in God and God in him. This is mutual abiding. But the test concerns only God's abiding "in us." The reason for this may be that the presence of the Spirit of God with the believer is the mode of God's abiding. What is said about the giving of the Spirit does not *directly* address the believer's abiding in God, but if that is the case, what has changed with 4:13? Further, in 3:24a 1 John speaks about mutual abiding but then makes the gift of the Spirit evidence only that "he abides in us"! Then 4:12 asserts that "if we love one another God abides in us," but 4:13 makes the gift of the Spirit evidence of mutual abiding. (On abiding see the Notes on 2:6.) Thus that God gave or has given us his Spirit is the evidence that he abides with us (in his Spirit?) and of mutual abiding. It is noteworthy that these two tests are embedded in affirmations that broaden the basis of evidence. First 3:24a asserts that "the person keeping his commandments abides in him and he in him" (mutual abiding). Then 4:12 asserts that "if we love one another, God abides in us." Keeping the commandments and loving one another broaden the base of the evidence. It has already been noted that from a basis of mutual abiding in 3:24a the test in 3:24b provides evidence only "that he abides in us," while on the basis of evidence that God abides in us (4:12) the test of 4:13 provides evidence of mutual abiding. Yet the test of 3:24b and 4:13 is the same! This tends to suggest that in the author's thinking there is only mutual abiding, which can at times be spoken of from one side only. Thus God abides in those who abide in God. If we abide in God, God abides in us.

The emphatic use of "we" at the beginning of **4:14** is in conjunction with the verbs of seeing and witnessing. "Witness" is used for the first time since 1:2, suggesting the identification of "we" with the tradition bearers of 1:1-5. There also, having seen (perfect tense of *horan*, not *tetheametha* as here) is made the basis of present witness (present tense *marty-*

*roumen,* as here). In 1:1 the aorist *etheasametha* is used, but the perfect *heōrakamen* is also used in 1:1-2. In 1:2 "what we have seen" becomes the basis of the present tense "and we bear witness." The tenses agree with 4:14 even if the author's love of varying words has led to the use of a different verb of seeing at this point, one used in the aorist in 1:1. There is a strong case then for recognizing an appeal to the tradition bearers here. It is not a valid objection to say that the content of what was seen, and to which witness is borne, cannot refer to physical sight. This is true only in a sense. The witness that "the Father sent the Son as the savior of the world" may well be the conclusion of those who had seen Jesus, and the witness as borne by them could be dependent on what they have seen. Certainly it was not possible to see the Father sending Jesus. There was no visible evidence that was absolutely unique to the savior of the world and was evident for anyone to see and recognize. There was, in what was seen of Jesus, evidence that led to the belief that Jesus is the Son of the Father, sent by the Father to be the savior of the world. The *connection* between what was seen and what is believed and confessed in witness is crucial for 1 John.

That the Father sent the Son is the central Johannine christological motif, though it appears only here and at 4:9, 10. (See the Notes there for the relation of this theme to the Gospel.) Only here in 1 John does reference to Jesus as the savior of the world occur. This confession was used by the Samaritans who came to believe in Jesus according to John 4:42. There "savior," anarthrous here (without "the"), appears with the definite article. But there the title stands alone, not attached to the witness that "the Father sent the Son [as] savior of the world." In 4:14, though "savior" is indefinite, in the phrase "savior of the world" it takes on a definite sense because multiple saviors are not envisaged. Also, given that "the Son [as] savior of the world" is in the accusative case as the object of the verb "to send" *(apestalken),* the definite sense is reinforced by the article with "the Son."

As this is the third and final use of the motif of the sending of the Son (4:9, 10, 14), it may be useful to set out the three statements, all of which use *apostellō:* the first and third use the perfect tense while the second uses the aorist. While all three refer to the sending of the Son, the first and second refer to God as sender while the third refers to the Father. The first use refers to his Son the only one *(ton monogenē).* The first and second make God's love the basis for the sending of his Son. No basis is given in the third. In the first the purpose/consequence of the sending of the Son is "that we may live through him," while in the second his Son is sent as the expiation for our sins (cf. 2:2) and in the third *the* Son is sent as the savior of the world.

Reference to "the savior of the world" draws the obvious comparison with the confession of the Samaritans in John 4:42. While there is ample

precedent in the OT for the use of the title "savior" in relation to God (see
Deut 32:15; Ps 24:5; Isa 12:2), it is the phrase "the savior *of the world*" that
suggests a broader frame of reference. The title "savior of the world" (*sōtēr
tou kosmou*) was used of Roman emperors and is frequently found in in-
scriptions to Hadrian (117–138 C.E.). The title "savior" was applied to many
gods, especially Zeus, Asclepius, Isis, and Serapis. Whether the Johannine
use reflects the Roman imperial situation or a mystery cult context is difficult to say.

"Whoever confesses 'the Son of God is Jesus'" (**4:15**): the confession of
faith is now appealed to as evidence of the mutual abiding of the believer
with God. (On mutual abiding see above on 3:24.) The confession of faith
is expressed in both positive and negative terms; see 2:22-23; 4:2-3, 15;
2 John 7, and the Notes on those passages. The Greek here suggests "the
Son of God is Jesus," just as in 2:22 what is denied is that "the Christ is
Jesus." In 4:2-3 the test confession is that "Jesus Christ is come in the
flesh." When these texts are examined together it seems that the name
"Jesus" is identified with the human Jesus, and the opponents refused to
identify their belief in the heavenly Son of God with Jesus. Likewise, for
them "the Christ" is identified with the Son of God, so that they also denied that "the Christ is Jesus."

While the confession that the Son of God is Jesus is evidence of mutual
abiding, what is it that initiates such abiding? The answer of 1 John is
clearly that it is God's love that initiates this possibility. But because
1 John is preoccupied with the task of discerning who it is who abides in
God and God in him or her, it seems clear that some response on the part
of people is instrumental in moving from potentiality to actuality. If that is
so, there is a case for seeing the confession of faith as the ground of those
other evidences that demonstrate mutual abiding. The difficulty is that
1 John tends to treat all evidence of mutual abiding in the same way without careful attention to the question of the way mutual abiding is initiated.

If 4:7-12 concentrated on God's love as the source of the sending of the
Son and on the sending of the Son as the revelation of God's love, at the
end of 4:13-16a 1 John concludes, "and we have known and have believed
the love that God has for us" (**4:16**). Here the "we," though emphatic like
4:14, is probably not a reference exclusively to the tradition bearers. The
author now gathers his readers with himself in a confident confession of
what "we" have come to know and believe. The perfect tenses imply a
distinct beginning of knowing and believing, but a continuing effect.
What is known and believed is the love God has "for us." This is a common idiomatic use of *en hymin*; see John 13:35. This must be the primary
meaning here, although *en hymin* is also used with other meanings and
probably intimates that God's love is also active "in us" in love for one another. Even so, the emphasis is on "the love" God has for us, its source,

character, activity, and effect. Its source is God, who is love (4:8, 16). Its character is outgoing in sending and giving (4:10). Its activity is self-giving for the sake of the other (3:16). Its effect is the expiation of our sins (4:10), that we may live through him (4:9), the salvation of the world (4:14).

## 1.3. Abiding in love is the ground of confidence before God (4:16b-21)
### Seventh claim and test (4:20)

16b. God is love, and the person abiding in love abides in God and God abides in him. 17. In this love has been perfected with us, that we may have confidence on the day of judgment, because as he is we are also in this world. 18. There is no fear in love, but perfect love casts out fear, because fear has [to do with] punishment, and the one who fears has not been made perfect in love. 19. We love, because he first loved us. 20. If any one says "I love God" and hates his brother, he is a liar; for the person not loving his brother whom he has seen is not able to love God whom he has not seen. 21. And this commandment we have from him: the person who [claims he] loves God ought to love his brother also.

### NOTES

16b. *God is love, and the person abiding in love abides in God and God abides in him:* On "God is love" see above on 4:8. Codex Alexandrinus (A) and the Vulgate omit the last word ("and God [abides] in him"), the third use of *menei* in the sentence. The sentence is complete without this word. Indeed, it is more elegant without it, and 1 John has not previously used the double *menei* in the mutuality formula. Its omission here is probably a scribal attempt to tidy up the text and conform it to the use in 3:24; 4:13, 15. The omission does not change the sense of the sentence at all.

17. *In this love has been perfected with us, that we may have confidence on the day of judgment, because as he is we are also in this world:* The opening *en toutǭ* cannot mean "in this person" (as in 2:5), referring to "the person abiding in love" (4:16b), because the sentence continues, "love is made perfect *in us.*" Rather, the opening words mean "by this . . ." (see above on 2:3, and see 3:10; 4:9, 10, 17). But it is not "by this we *know.* . . ." A straightforward statement follows, setting out the conditions that make it true. Those conditions are indicated by the causal *hoti* clause.

1 John 2:5 says that "the love of God (God's love) has been perfected (*teteleiōtai*) in this person *(en toutǭ)*." The verb is in the same tense as 4:17, but here it is simply "love" *(hē agapē)* that is perfected, and it is perfected *teteleiōtai*

with us *(meth' hēmōn)*. In 4:12 the reference is to "his love" (God's) having been perfected *(teteleiōmenē)* (perfect passive participle) "with us" *(en hēmin)*. The slight variations in language do not signify any difference of meaning. Thus the three statements clarify each other. The love referred to in each case is God's love. (See "his love" in 4:12.) This clarifies the neutral "love" of 4:17 and the ambiguous "the love *of God*" of 2:5, where the genitive could be objective (love for God) or subjective (God's love). The latter is the case, as is confirmed by "his love" in 4:12.

Codex Sinaiticus (ℵ) reads the indicative *echomen,* not noticing the consecutive clause. The *consecutive* clause *(hina parrēsian echōmen)* expresses result or consequence. The consequence is "that we have *confidence* on the day of judgment" (see on 2:28; and cf. 3:2-3, 21).

*En tę̄ hēmerą̄ tēs kriseōs* means "on the day of judgment," not "in relation to the day of judgment," as if the preposition were *eis.* See Matt 10:15; 11:22, 24; 12:36 and cf. 12:36, 41 where *en* certainly means "on" or "at." Interestingly, those references in Matthew do not use the definite article (literally "on day of judgment" *[en hēmerą̄ kriseōs]*). For evidence of the background in Jewish apocalyptic and early Christian writings see *1 Enoch* 10:6; 16:1; *Jub.* 5:10; 24:30; *4 Ezra* 7:113; Rev 14:7; Jude 6.

18. *There is no fear in love, but perfect love casts out fear, because fear has [to do with] punishment, and the one who fears has not been made perfect in love:* Versification of the New Testament in the sixteenth century, slightly modified in 1633 by the Elsevirs who produced the *Textus Receptus,* places "[There is] no fear in love" in v. 18. Some scholars read it as the conclusion to v. 17. This makes little difference. The reader should be aware that chapter and verse divisions are not part of the original text.

The noun *(phobos)* and verb *(phobeō)* for "fear" are used only here in the Johannine Epistles, though both are used in the Gospel, three times and five times respectively, mainly of fear of the Jews.

"*Perfect* love," using the noun *(hē teleia agapē)* is used only here in the Epistles. The verb "to make perfect" is used with "love" in 2:5; 4:12, 17, probably with the same meaning as the noun because the perfect tense refers to love that has been made perfect.

Fear has to do with "torment" or "punishment" *(kolasin).* This term once had a correcting tone much like that implied by the image of the pruning of the vine in John 15:21. Increasingly in the Hellenistic period it took on the sense of destructive punishment, even eternal punishment: see *T. Reub.* 5:5; *T. Gad* 7:5, and Matt 25:46; *Hermas Sim.* 9:18.1.

19. *We love, because he first loved us:* Three ambiguities in this short verse have led to scribal "clarifications." (1) Is *agapōmen* indicative, "we love," or subjunctive, "let us love"? (2) Is "we love" absolute, without object? (3) Should "he first loved" read "God first loved"? The scribal addition of *oun* after *agapōmen* (attested by Alexandrinus [A] and the Vulgate) and the introduction of a direct object (the Byzantine tradition supplies "him"; Sinaiticus [ℵ], the Syriac, Bohairic, and Clementine Vulgate add "God") may reflect scribal judgment in favor of the subjunctive. The subjunctive is supported by the Latin and

Peshitta versions, being indistinguishable from the indicative in Greek. The subjunctive reading finds support in 4:7, "Beloved, let us love one another," but the indicative "we love," without any object, is strongly supported by Vaticanus (B), Alexandrinus (A), the Sahidic, and Jerome's Vulgate. The indicative reading fits well in the overall passage and with 4:14, 16, both of which begin with *hēmeis*, as does this verse. Both Alexandrinus (A) and the Vulgate read "God first loved us" in place of the indefinite "he first loved us." In every case the clarifying additions are secondary.

The personal pronoun *hēmeis* is placed first for emphasis; see 4:14, 16 in the present context, and see also 2:20, 24, 27 and cf. the move from *hymeis* (4:4) to *autoi* (4:5) to *hēmeis* (4:6).

20. *If any one says "I love God" and hates his brother, he is a liar; for the person not loving his brother whom he has seen, is not able to love God whom he has not seen:* In a conditional sentence introduced by *ean* the verbs in the *protasis* (the first part of the sentence) are in the subjunctive mood, as here (*eipē* and *misē*). Because the consequence is stated as a matter of fact, the verb in the second part of the sentence is present indicative *estin*.

The idiom "the person not loving" uses the definite article with the negative and present participle *(ho mē agapōn)*, which describes the person in a way that defines the being of that person as a not-loving (his brother) person.

Some texts read the last part of 4:20 as a question: "how is he able to love?" *(pōs dunatai agapan [or agapēsai];)*. This reading is probably a harmonization with 3:17, which concludes: "how does the love of God abide in him?"

21. *And this commandment we have from him: the person who [claims he] loves God ought to love his brother also:* The opening "and" signals the connection of v. 21 to v. 20. "That the one loving God should love his brother also" *(hina ho agapōn ton theon agapą kai ton adelphon autou)*. The *hina* clause is epexegetical, expressing the content of the commandment.

Alexandrinus (A) and the Clementine Vulgate read "this is the commandment we have from God" in place of "from him." Again this is an attempt to make explicit what 1 John has left open. It is probably a mistaken identification. Brown argues that if 1 John had wanted to identify Jesus the author would probably have used *ekeinos* as in 4:17. But in 4:17 *ekeinos* is emphatically in the nominative case, as it always is in reference to a person (Jesus) in 1 John (see 2:6; 3:3, 5, 7). The only genitive use is after the preposition *peri*, "concerning that sin" in 5:16. The use there is emphatic. There is no example of the use of *ap' ekeinou* in 1 John.

INTERPRETATION

The opening of **4:16b** is a repetition and resumption of 4:8b except that the causal *hoti* is omitted. Causal *hoti* signals an argument explicitly commenced in 4:7. That God is love means that God is the source of love, and that the revealed life and action of God reveal what love is. This is laid out in 4:9-10. The weight of the treatment of the love theme is impressive and the repetition of the words "God is love" marks the importance of this foundational statement. God, who is love, is the source of love, of love defined by the being and action of God. Thus to abide in love is to abide in God, and if a person abides in God it is implied that God abides in that person also (see on 2:6; 3:24; 4:13, 15). This is again affirmed here. We might also say that love abides in the person who abides in love, because God is love. The argument is a response to the claim to abide in God; see 2:6. In response it was argued that the truth of this claim could be tested because such a person ought *(opheilei)* to walk (live) as Jesus walked. The use of the present infinitive expresses the continuous walk of the believer in response to the historic and completed life of Jesus expressed by the aorist tense. This is the first test of the truth of the claim to abide in God. This issue emerges again in 4:13-16a with a fuller series of tests. The second reality test for those who claim to abide in God is "he has given us of his Spirit." Because abiding with God is mutual, the abiding of God's Spirit with us is evidence that we abide in God. But this reality test breaks down because we are given no guide to discerning the presence of the Spirit. It is possible that the *charismata* such as Paul describes are in view (1 Cor 12:4). The third reality test, which reveals the mutual abiding of the believer with God, is the confession "Jesus is the Christ" (4:15). Finally, mutual abiding with God is revealed by those who abide in love (4:16b). But what does it mean to abide in love? Much has already been said about this in 4:7-16 and specific clarification is given in 4:17-21. In the first instance to abide in love is to live out of the reality of the awareness of being loved by God. With 4:16b the theme that God is love is restated as the context in which the reality test of the claim to abide in God is made. The one abiding in love abides in God, and abiding in love is revealed in love for one another. The paradigm for loving one another is found in the Father's sending of the Son that we might live (4:9), to deal with sin (4:10), as the savior of the world (4:14). That God is love is revealed in God's Son, and his life provides the model for our love of one another (2:6; 3:16-17; 4:11-12 and John 13:34-35). Abiding in love, abiding in God who is love, is dependent on the recognition of Jesus as the revelation of the being and character of love, of God. Consequently abiding in love is dependent on the chistological confession of faith (3:23; 4:12, 15, 16b).

The penultimate "by this . . ." statement **(4:17)** sets out to establish the way love has been perfected (perfect passive; see 2:5 and cf. 4:12). The use of the causal *hoti* in the last part of the verse identifies the test. Before turning to that issue we need to make clear what the author is trying to establish.

What is meant by "*love* has been perfected"? From the comparative statement in 4:12 it is clear that "his (God's) love" is in view. The point of the discussion from 4:7 has been to identify God as the source and exemplar of love, and so this is a natural conclusion to draw, and necessary in the light of 4:12. But how can God's love be *perfected*? This verb is related to *telos*, denoting the "end" or goal. The verb here indicates the conditions under which God's love reaches its goal. In 1 John the emphasis has been on love, which originates with God, expressed in the sending of God's Son to be savior of the world, to be the expiation of our sins, that we may live through him. Further, the life that he has revealed is expressed in love for one another. Thus God's love reaches its goal when that love is known/recognized and believed/accepted (4:16a). Thus belief is the basis for loving action because the acceptance of God's love involves love for one another. That is its goal.

The result is "that" *(hina)* when we recognize and accept the love of God (4:16a), and the love of God abides in us (3:17), "we may have bold-ness/confidence on the day of judgment" (see 2:28 and 3:2-3, 21). The expression "the day of judgment" is known from the apocalyptic writings of Judaism and early Christianity.

God's love is made perfect in us "because *(hoti)* even as he is so are we in this world." Here the evidence is clear. "As he is" refers to the Father-Son relationship. The Son abides in the Father's love, so that to abide in the Son is to abide in the Father (2:23-24, and frequently in the Gospel). In this world we abide in the Father and the Son and are children of God though the world does not recognize us just as it did not recognize him (3:1-2). The prayer of Jesus according to John 17 throws light on this pas-sage. There, especially in vv. 9-26, Jesus, on the point of departure from the world, leaves the disciples in the world. He prays: "Holy Father, keep them in your name which you gave to me, that they may be one as *(kathōs)* we are one" (17:11). Even as he is one with the Father, so are we. But he is no longer in the world. Nevertheless, "even as *(kathōs)* he is, so are we in this world." Further, the person who abides in him ought to walk as he walked (2:6), and sanctifies himself even as he (Jesus) is sanctified. Thus even now the life of the person who abides in God, who abides in love, is even as *(kathōs)* he is. The obligation *(opheilomen)* to be like him is stressed in many ways in the love command: "love one another as *(kathōs)* I have loved you" (John 13:34); "if God thus *(houtōs)* loved us we ought *(opheilo-men)* to love one another" (1 John 4:11).

The day of judgment **(4:18)** is related to the great and terrible day of the Lord in the OT, of which Zeph 1:14-18 gives an insight:

> The great day of the Lord is near—near and coming quickly. Listen! The cry on the day of the Lord will be bitter, the shouting of the warriors there.
> That day will be a day of wrath, a day of distress and anguish, a day of trouble and ruin, a day of darkness and gloom, a day of clouds and

blackness, a day of trumpet and battle cry against the fortified cities and against the corner towers.

I will bring distress on the people and they will walk like blind men because they have sinned against the Lord. Their blood will be poured out like dust and their entrails like filth.

Neither their silver nor their gold will be able to save them on the day of the Lord's wrath. In the fire of his jealousy the whole world will be consumed, for he will make a sudden end of all who live in the earth.

That 1 John should deal with fear *(phobos)* in the face of the day of judgment is natural, given the tradition in the OT (see also Isa 2:12-22) and beyond in Judaism and the Hellenistic world. With the mention of the day of judgment the issues have become somewhat more weighty than in 2:28. The fear mentioned here seems to be more than fear of being shamed (cf. 2:28). The noun and the verb used are capable of expressing awesome reverence or raw terror. The imagery of the day of judgment suggests the latter.

But John affirms that there is no fear in love. The noun is used with the definite article so that we are again dealing with love as such. Such love has been described as coming from God (4:7), who is love. Consequently the love we are speaking of is God's love, love that comes from God who is love. To say there is no fear in love means that those who abide in love, in whom love abides (3:17), have no fear. The use of the noun "perfect" probably carries the same weight as the perfect tense in 2:5; 4:12, 17. Love that has been made perfect, that is, that has achieved its goal, is the ground for the driving out of fear. Love that has reached its goal is God's love, reaching out from the Father through the Son to the world. But God's love is not made perfect in the world, because the world does not recognize it, nor does it believe the love that God has for it. Hence God's love is incomplete; it has not reached its goal in relation to the world. But in those who have recognized and accepted the love God has for us (4:16a), in these people God's love reaches its goal and abides in them and they abide in God's love. Here the mutuality formula is: love one another as I have loved you (John 13:34), and "Beloved, if God loved us like this *(houtōs)*, we also ought to love one another [like this]" (4:11). The point is clear in 3:16-17:

> By this we know love: he laid down his life for us and we ought *(opheilo-men)* to lay down our lives for the brothers. But whoever has the wealth of the world and sees his brother having need and shuts off his compassion from him, how does the love of God abide in him?

Clearly, loving the brother in these terms is involved in the mutual abiding of the believer with God. The perfection of love entails not only recognition and acceptance but also active love of the brothers.

In such love the grounds for fear are removed. This does not imply a lack of awe and reverence before God, though even this is tempered by the experience of a loving Father. Perfect love drives out fear because "fear has punishment." This may mean that fear has punishment in view, but probably also means that fear has its own punishment. In Rom 8:15 Paul writes: "For you did not receive a spirit that makes you a slave again to fear, but you have received the Spirit of Sonship. And by him we cry 'Abba, Father.'" In 1 John 3:1-2 the bestowal of love by the Father is the basis for our confidence that we are the children of God, and when we abide in such love there is no fear, no punishment. From this perspective the one who fears has not been made perfect in love. It is not the love that is made perfect, but the believer is to be made perfect in love. Love achieves its goal in this way.

We may ask whether those made perfect in love would be the *teleioi* (see 1 Cor 2:6; 14:20). When this is associated with other language in 1 Corinthians, especially *sarkikoi, psychikos,* and *pneumatikoi* (1 Cor 3:3; 9:11; 2:14; 15:54, 56; 3:1; 12:1), something moving in the direction of Gnosticism seems to be indicated. But 1 John shows no tendency to use that language, although the references to the Spirit in 3:24 and 4:13 could be a response to claims about the Spirit by the opponents. This suggestion is more credible if 2:20 and 2:27 are a response to the opponents, as 2:26 suggests: "I write these things to you concerning those who would lead you astray" *(peri tōn planōntōn hymas)*. The anointing, as understood by 1 John, has become anchored in the foundational message (2:24, 25) with its confession that the Christ is Jesus (2:22-23). This was rejected by the opponents, who denied the essential relationship between Jesus, as the Son, with the Father (2:23; 4:15). Consequently there is some evidence that the opponents disconnected spiritual reality from the human Jesus and as a result recognized no ethical imperatives on the basis of his human life. Because of this 1 John develops, out of the Johannine tradition, an ethic of obligation ("we ought," *opheilomen,* 2:6; 3:16; 4:11) arising from the life and mission of the human Jesus who was at the same time God's Son. In 2:6 this is linked with *kathōs* to make clear that Jesus' life is not only the source or ground of the ethic but also its model. (See also 3:3, 7, [23]; 4:17.) If for others the *teleioi* are made perfect in knowledge, in 1 John they are made perfect in love, abiding in God's love that finds expression in love for one another.

The next verse **(4:19)** is short, seemingly simple, straightforward, and proverbial in character. Like much of 1 John, it is teeming with ambiguities. Consistently 1 John has set out to deal with the nature of love (see 3:16). In many instances scribes have made additions to define love more narrowly in terms of who loved and who was loved. Our reading of the text accepts "*we* love" as correct. This is the remarkable reality that, for 1 John, was not to be taken for granted. The commonplace of the Johannine language has now made this surprising reality prosaic. But if it were commonplace it could hardly have been the distinctive mark of the followers of Jesus! (See John 13:34-35.) Thus it is not the love commandment that marks the disciples (cf. Lev 19:18; "and Hillel said, 'Be of the disciples of Aaron, loving peace and pursuing peace, loving mankind and bringing them nigh to the Law,'" *m. Aboth* 1:12), but the actuality of their love for one another.

Nevertheless, the point is: "we love *because* he first loved us." In the love command of John 13:34 *kathōs* has the force of both "in the same way as" and "because." Here the causal element is clear: "we love *because* he first loved us." The present tense emphasizes the continuing reality of "we love." The causal use of *hoti* makes clear that our love is grounded in the act of love indicated by the aorist tense of "he loved us." The context shows that "he" is God. This second part of v. 19 echoes 4:10-11. There we are reminded that love is not that we have loved God but that "he loved us" (twice in 4:10-11 as in 4:19). The act of love referred to by the aorist tense is "he sent his Son that we might live through him," "as expiation for our sins." In 4:10 love is defined: "not that we have loved God but that he loved us." In 4:19 "we love because he first loved us." Here "first" is *prōtos*, not the comparative *prōteros*. This is probably the result of Hellenistic blurring of the distinction, using *prōtos* as if it were *prōteros* (see John 2:10; 20:4, 8). In the comparative sense this makes our love second and responsive to his. But if the strict sense of *prōtos* is in view, something more like the foundational character of "he first loved us" is stressed. Of course "we love because" remains responsive.

That "he loved" refers to God is evident from the parallels in 4:10, 11. Because "we love" is a response to "he loved," understood as referring to God, the expectation is that the meaning will be "we love God because God first loved us." While 1 John does not rule out that meaning, it maintains a more open understanding of "we love" by refusing to state the object of love. The reason for this soon becomes apparent in 4:20.

Here **(4:20)** we meet the seventh and final claim of the opponents. The first six were introduced within 1:6–2:11. The first three (1:6, 8, 10) introduce a verbatim claim with the quotation formula "If we say. . . ." The second group of three claims (2:4, 6, 9) is introduced "The person who says. . . ." Of these six claims, the first four are seemingly given in the words of the claimants. The quotation is signaled by *hoti* followed by the words quoted in the first person "I" or "we" (see William F. Arndt and F. Wilbur Gingrich, *A Greek-English Lexicon of the New Testament and Other Early Christian Literature. A Translation and Adaptation of Walter Bauer's Griechisch-Deutsches Wörterbuch zu den Schriften des Neuen Testaments und der übrigen urchristlichen Literatur* (BAG) [Chicago: University of Chicago Press, 1957] 593 no. 2, and Walter Bauer, *Griechisch-deutsches Wörterbuch zu* *den Schriften des Neuen Testaments und der frühchristlichen Literatur.* Revised and edited by Kurt Aland and Barbara Aland [6th ed. Berlin and New York: Walter de Gruyter, 1988] 1193 no. 2).

Here in 4:20 the introductory formula is "If any one says" followed by *hoti.* The words reported are in the first person singular: "I love God." This is the claim, apparently in the words of the opponents. But if the person hates his brother, our author says, he is a liar *(pseustēs)* in claiming to love God (see above on 1:6 and 2:4). The author does not repudiate the claim outright as he does regarding the claims of 1:8, 10. This means that the possibility and importance of loving God are not excluded. This could hardly be the case, given the great first commandment (Deut 6:6; Matt 23:37; Mark 12:30, 33; Luke 10:27). It is interesting that Matthew records the command to love God once, but the command to love the neighbor is recorded three times (from Lev 19:18 in Matt 5:43; 19:19; 22:39) and the command to love enemies once more (Matt 5:44). This emphasis on the horizontal element of love rather than the upward vertical element (love for God) is consistent with John and 1 John. In neither John nor 1 John, apart from 4:20 and the problematic 5:2, is there an unambiguous reference to love for God. The reference in 4:20 is in a rather hostile context. The one making the claim is being tested, with the potential result that he might be called a liar. The reference in 5:2 has not left this context behind. Everything suggests that the claim of 4:20 is made by the opponents and that the author indeed thinks it to be a lie in their case. The falsifying test is: if such a person hates his brother, that person is a liar. In the second half of the verse *hating* the brother is equated with "not loving his brother." For our author, not to love is to hate. The world is divided into light and darkness, love and hate. There are no half measures. You are one of the children of God or one of the children of the devil (3:10). Schism within the Johannine circle of house churches meant that battle lines were drawn and the enemy was identified.

The second half of the verse explains the ground upon which the claim to love God and the behavior of hating/not loving the brother are declared incompatible. The author states categorically that "the person not loving his brother, whom he has seen, is *not able* to love God, whom he has not seen." What is in view is not a single spiteful act but a way of being, of being a not-loving person in relation to "his brother." Hating the brother is not a momentary act. The argument here seems to be that if you *do not* do the simpler (loving the brother) you *cannot* do the more difficult. Linking the second part of 4:20 with 3:17 suggests a deeper and more telling critique. There the author asks rhetorically: if one who has the means to help sees his brother having need, yet closes his compassion against him, how does the love of God abide in him? Building on this base with 4:7-19 we may say: God is love, and love comes from God. God's love for us reaches its true goal when we love one another. If we fail to love one another, God's love does not abide in us (we do not abide in his love), because abiding is mutual (see above on 3:24; 4:13, 15, 16). That being the case, the person who does not love his brother, a claim that can be tested, is not able to love God, a claim more difficult to test directly. This is the point of 4:12. No one has ever seen God. Yet God is evidenced when we love one another. The evidence of the love that comes from God demonstrates mutual abiding with God. God's love reaches its true goal in the mutual love of brothers (and sisters), when we love one another.

The seventh claim is the one to which 1 John pays most attention. The issue of love appears for the first time in 2:5 and is never far from the surface from that point onward. The discussion of the old commandment that is new (2:7-11) exposes the person who hates his brother (2:9-11). The announcement of the children of God (3:1-2) leads into the discussion of the children of God and the children of the devil (3:7-10). An example of a child of the devil is given with Cain, who murdered his brother. He is an example of the world's hatred of the children of God. Here everyone who hates his brother is identified as a murderer (Cain). Hatred of the brother is further described in terms of the failure to show compassion to the brother in need (3:11-18). The fundamental commandment enshrines the command to believe in the name of his (God's) son Jesus Christ and to love one another. This is a pivotal statement that roots the obligation to love one another in the recognition and acceptance of and commitment to Jesus Christ as the revelation of the Father's love in saving action. Keeping God's commandments reveals mutual abiding (3:23-24). The christological base of the obligation to love is set out in 4:1-6. What then follows is the most extensive development of a theme in 1 John. Certainly the theme runs throughout the remainder of ch. 4 (vv. 7-21) and overflows into the beginning of ch. 5 (vv. 1-5).

Thus from the fourth claim made by the opponents onward 1 John has begun to deal with the crisis of the opponents' attack on the ethical response to the message. Even more critical than their christological denial was their denial that love for the brothers had anything to do with an appropriate response to God. In response 1 John develops its most sustained argument. That this argument takes a different form from those to which we are accustomed does not mean that it is or was ineffective. Indeed, the proverbial character of many of the sayings has proved to be impressive and memorable, even if variations on the theme are at times repetitious. Nevertheless, it becomes abundantly clear that in our author's understanding the failure to love the brothers demonstrates that such a person has not grasped or been grasped by the love of God, because God's love is directed toward the mutuality of the love of one another.

The variation in language from love for one another *(allēlous)* to love for the (his) brother is interesting. The language of "one another" clearly comes from the love command of John 13:34. Reference to love for the brother comes when there is a contrast between loving and hating (2:9-11), which is developed on the basis of the example of Cain, who slew his *brother* (3:11-18; see 3:10, 11, 14, 15, 16). In this passage we get the only address to the readers as "brothers:" "Do not be surprised, *brothers*, if the world *hates* you" (3:13). Elsewhere it is used only in relation to the motif of not loving/hating the brother in 4:20-21.

The central discussion of loving or hating the brother builds on the example of Cain. It is bounded by the statement of the message heard from the beginning in the form of the commandment "that we love *one another*" (3:11) on the one side and the double commandment to believe and to love *one another* (3:23) on the other. The inclusion is formed by the commandment to love one another! The extensive treatment of love in 4:7-21 begins with the exhortation: "Beloved, let us love one another" (4:7). Then God's love for us is made the ground for the obligation *(opheilomen)* to love one another. If we love one another we show evidence of mutual abiding with God, the source of our love for one another. God's love reaches its goal in the mutual love of one another.

Verse 21 is closely connected to verse 20, continuing the theme of love for "his brother." We return to the love command last mentioned in 3:23. It turns out to be a double commandment from God, the first part being "that we believe in the name of *his* Son Jesus Christ" and the second "that we love one another." Presentation of the commandment(s) is completed by "as he gave us command" (see on 3:23). Because the giving of the new commandment is attributed to Jesus (John 13:34-35), "he" might refer to Jesus. But there is no indication of the change of subject from the mention of "his Son" in the first part to the "he" who gave us the commandment. Formally the case is strong for understanding this as a reference to God (the Father). In 1 John 4, however, we have been given a basis for understanding what Jesus does in terms of what God does.

Now **(4:21)** "this is the commandment that we have from him" is probably to be understood as God's commandment also. The commandment is given to the person who claims to love God. The content of the commandment is expressed by *hina* and the following verb in the subjunctive mood. The command is "that he love his brother also." There is no command to love God here. That the person loves God (or claims to) is the assumption on which the command to love the brother is based. We may suppose that when our author refers to "the person loving God" he has in mind the one who says, "I love God" (see 4:20). Such a person is reminded of the command "that he love his brother also." This is the only instance in the Johannine writings where the love command is expressed in terms of "his brother." Elsewhere it is "love one another" (see 3:23; 2 John 5 and John 13:34; 15:12, 17). What is more, the idiom of loving one another has been dominant since 3:23 (see 4:7, 11, 12), yet reference to "his brother" returns in 4:20, 21. The theme of loving and hating "his brother" first appeared in 2:9-11. The theme was picked up in 3:10 with reference to the marks of the children of God and the children of the devil. The example of Cain, who murdered his brother, exemplifies the hatred of the world for the children of God (3:12-17). Here the opponents stand thinly veiled under the cover of the children of the devil. With the return of the claims of the opponents in 4:20 the author turns from his positive exposition of the source and character of the command to love one another. He now addresses the situation of the one who claims to love God, asserting that such a person should love his brother also.

### FOR REFERENCE AND FURTHER STUDY

Beutler, Johannes. *Die Johannesbriefe*, 107–16.
Brooke, Alan England. *A Critical and Historical Commentary on the Johannine Epistles*, 117–27.
Brown, Raymond E. *The Epistles of John*, 512–34, 542–65.
Jonge, Marinus de. "To love as God loves" (1 John 4:7) in idem, *Jesus: Inspiring and Disturbing Presence.* Nashville: Abingdon, 1974, 110–27.
Painter, John, *The Quest for the Messiah* (1993) 231–32, 383–416.
Rensberger, David. *1 John, 2 John, 3 John*, 116–28.
Schnackenburg, Rudolf. *The Johannine Epistles*, 206–27.

## 2. FAITH IS THE FOUNDATION OF LOVE (5:1-12)

The reason for recognizing a new section here is that the focus has turned more directly to christology, the confession that Jesus is the Christ (5:1; cf. 2:22), that Jesus is the Son of God (5:5), and to the witness borne to him as the bringer of life. But in its attention to the bringer of life, characterized by love, which is both the source of life and the expression of it, the transition to the new section synthetically overlaps the conclusion to the great treatment of love in 4:7-21. The point of this third treatment of the two themes is the inseparable relationship between them. This is already the point of 3:23, which treats as a single commandment "that we believe in the name of his Son Jesus Christ and love one another." This connection is further explored in 4:7–5:12 and is clearly in view in 5:1-12.

### 2.1. Those who believe are begotten of God and love one another (5:1-3)

> 1. Everyone believing Jesus is the Christ has been begotten of God, and everyone loving the one who begat loves the one begotten of him. 2. By this we know we love the children of God, whenever we love God and do his commandments. 3. For this is the love of God, that we keep his commandments; and his commandments are not burdensome.

#### NOTES

1. *Everyone believing Jesus is the Christ has been begotten of God, and everyone loving the one who begat loves the one begotten of him:* On the use of "believing" see above on 3:23. Here as elsewhere in 1 John and in John the focus is christological. Here, as in the denial formula of 2:22, the name "Jesus" is anarthrous (without the definite article) and "*the* Christ" is definite. When coupled with the verb "to be," the subject, not the object, normally has the definite article, as both subject and object are in the same case. It is tempting to translate "the Christ is Jesus" here and "the Son of God is Jesus" in 5:5. In each case the definite article suggests that "the Christ" and "the Son of God" are the important and known titles and Jesus is emphatically being identified with them by placing his name first. This confirms that the opponents denied that Jesus was the Christ and the Son of God. (See also 4:2-3.) The use of the two titles in 5:1 and 5:5 shows that this section is a unity though 5:4-5 introduces the new theme of victory over the world.

In 5:1b Sinaiticus (א), Alexandrinus (A), Peshitta, Clementine Vulgate, Armenian, and Ethiopic add *kai* after the second use of "loves," giving the sense "also loves the one begotten of him," probably influenced by 4:21 where the commandment is "that the one loving God [ought to] love his brother also."

2. *By this we know we love the children of God, whenever we love God and do his com-mandments:* Both the syntax and the meaning of this verse are problematic. This has driven some interpreters to read the text in a way that forces the syntax. It is surprising that there is no evidence of scribal emendation to clarify the meaning. This seems to suggest that they did not share the perplexity experi-enced by modern commentators.

Sinaiticus (ℵ) and the Byzantine tradition read *"keep* his commandments" rather than *"do* his commandments." Because "keep" is the more natural idiom, is also found in 2:3, and fits the scribal tendency to smooth and harmonize the text, *poiōmen,* "do," is to be accepted as the original reading. No scribe will have changed "keep" into "do," which is a favored Johannine verb: see 1:6, 10; 2:17, 29; 3:4, 7, 8, 9, 22; 5:2, 10; 3 John 5, 6, 10. There is probably little difference in meaning. Given the variation in 5:2, 3, the most likely explanation is the author's predilection for very basic terms, and the attempt at a slight modifi-cation of basic formulaic constructions.

The eighth and final testing formula introduced "by this we know . . ." occurs here (see above on 2:3). As usual the content of knowledge is given by the following *hoti* clause. We then expect the means of the test, referred to in "by this," to be indicated by another subordinate clause. Indeed, this appears to follow in the clause introduced by "whenever" *(hotan).* Grammatically this seems to work out quite well, but what seems to be obvious creates a problem. This reading implies the testing of love for the children of God by the evidence of love for God. But this runs contrary to the argument of 3:16-18; 4:11-12, 20-21. The point of those passages is that the invisibility of God makes loving God an unviable test. The syntax of the sentence is also a problem for this reading. The common pattern for the formula "by this we know" is to signal the content of what we know by an epexegetical *hoti* clause (as here). If the test indicated by the phrase "by this" follows, then a second causal *hoti* clause fol-lows the first. The expectation of this has led to the *hotan* clause being read as if it were the causal *hoti* clause or as a second epexegetical *hoti* clause indicat-ing what is meant in the phrase "by *this."*

If *hotan* is related to the opening of the sentence, "by this we *know,"* the connection is to the verb "we know." The syntactical problem might be solved by recognizing that while the *hoti* clause is epexegetical, providing the content of *what* we know, the *hotan* tells us *when* we know. On this reading "by this" specifically refers back to 5:1, which tells us *how* we know. This is a neat solu-tion. It is not altogether satisfactory and calls for clarification.

This use of *hotan* is its only appearance in the Epistles. When used with verbs in the subjunctive mood it is a variant of the much more common *ean,* which is used in 2:28 (altogether 21 times in 1 John and twice in 3 John). In 2:28 *hotan* is a variant because a scribe may have felt that *hotan* was more definite than *ean,* though strictly the point of either (when used with verbs in the sub-junctive mood) is to provide the condition rather than to indicate uncertainty: if "A," then "B" follows. In this construction *hotan* functions in much the same way as *ean* (see BAG 592, 1 and 1.a), though we may translate "when(ever) A, then B." Verbs in the present subjunctive in the *hotan* clause indicate action "contemporaneous with the main clause:" "we love the children of God."

Thus the point of *hotan* is that "when we love God and keep his command-ments," at that very same time "we love the children of God." C. H. Dodd re-arranges the English translation in this way to make the sense clearer (*The Johannine Epistles* 125). This does not mean that the Greek needs to be re-arranged to establish the reading, though this may be a more normal order for a conditional sentence in Greek (see 2:28). Though the *hotan* clause is known as the *protasis*, suggesting it normally comes first, Greek has ways other than word order to indicate the place of components of the sentence. The use of *hotan* with verbs in the subjunctive is one such way. In English we are more dependent on word order and for this reason Dodd's rearrangement is help-ful, though he has not explained the Greek syntax to justify his rearrange-ment. Dodd is also right in noting that "by this" does not refer to anything in v. 2, but refers back to v. 1. Dodd failed to note that "by this" also refers back to 4:21, "and this commandment we have from him, that the one who loves God [should] love his brother also." This is taken up in 5:2: "we love the children of God when we love God and do his commandments."

In the *hotan* clause the Greek places the objects of the two verbs emphati-cally before the verbs: "God we love," "his commandments we do" *(ton theon agapōmen* and *tas entolas autou poiōmen)*. It is emphatically God who is loved and his commandments that are done. When speaking about love 1 John could write: "we love because he first loved us" (4:19), but the object is now important.

On the connection of loving and keeping commandments see John 14:15, 21, 31. In 14:31 Jesus says he *does* what the Father commanded, "even as he gave me commandment [commanded me], that is exactly what I *do*."

3. *For this is the love of God, that we keep his commandments; and his commandments are not burdensome:* The opening of the verse is reminiscent of 4:10, but the dif-ferences are clear. There the discussion concerns "love" *(hē agapē)* without qualification. Here the genitive in the phrase "the love *of God*" is to be inter-preted as an objective genitive. Context always decides this question, and here the context of 5:2 is clear because the author has used the verb there, "when we love God and do his commandments." But in 5:2 doing the command-ments appears to be added to loving God. In 5:3 the love of God appears to be defined as "that we keep his commandments" because "that" *(hina)* is epex-egetical, so the following clause expounds what is involved in love for God. Reference to *doing* the commandments occurs only in 5:2 in the Johannine writings whereas the idiom of keeping the commandments is common: 1 John 2:3, 4; 3:22, 24; 5:3, and John 14:15, 21; 15:10 (2x). The commandments are not "burdensome" *(bareiai)*, a term used only six times in the NT, in Matt 23:4, 23; Acts 20:29; 25:7; 2 Cor 10:10, and here in 1 John 5:3.

## INTERPRETATION

This is the third statement **(5:1)** in the form of "everyone who" *(pas ho +* a present participle) that affirms, "has been begotten of God." "Everyone who does righteousness has been begotten of him (God)" (2:29); "everyone who loves has been begotten of God" (4:7); "everyone who believes Jesus is the Christ has been begotten of God" (5:1). These three statements provide support for Robert Law (*The Tests of Life*, 1909), who argued that there are three tests of the claim to have eternal life in 1 John. Since Theodor Häring's argument ("Gedankengang und Grundgedanke des ersten Johannesbriefes," 1892) that love and righteousness form a single ethical test, the recognition of just two tests has been common. (See 3:10-11.)

All thirteen statements in this form ("everyone who . . .") are related positively or negatively to these three: believing, loving, and doing righteousness. (See the notes on 3:23.) The three examples are presented as evidence of the children of God (having been begotten of God). Probably because of the orientation to provide such tests, the author has not made clear whether belief precedes begetting (supported by John 1:12, 13 if receiving him is understood as a metaphor for believing, and by 20:31) or whether begetting precedes belief. His aim is to show the necessary connection between the two so that it becomes evident that correct belief, along with loving and doing righteousness, reveal the children of God while their opposites reveal the children of the devil (3:10, and see 2:29–3:3).

It is notable that in 5:1, as evidence of being begotten of God, 1 John uses "believing" followed by *hoti* to indicate the content of belief. The confession "Jesus is the Christ" is paired with a similar construction (without *pas*) in 5:4. The content of believing is "Jesus is the Son of God," indicated by *hoti*. In each case the construction makes clear that the confessions "the Christ" and "the Son of God" concern known figures. What is controversial is the identification of Jesus with those figures. The content of correct belief is filled out further by reference to 4:2-3 and 2 John 7. The confession is claimed to be a manifestation of the Spirit of God. The refusal to confess manifests the Spirit of Error.

The argument that follows 5:1 shows that the claim "I love God" (4:20) is still in mind. Consequently there is a close connection between the theme of love in the previous section and the focus on the christological confession in the present section. The argument runs: if everyone with correct belief is begotten by God, the one who claims "I love God," that is, "I love" the one who has begotten all true believers, ought to love those who are begotten by him, who are God's children and the believer's brothers. The argument used here may be illuminated by Plutarch, *Moralia:* "Excellent and pious *(dikaios)* children will not only love each other the more because of their parents, but will also love their parents more because of each other. . . . To love one's brother is a more immediate proof of love for both father and mother" ("On Brotherly Love" 6.480def).

From this we can see that the argument used in 1 John was widespread in the Mediterranean world. There is a familial logic to it. To love the

Father implies loving those the Father loves. In loving each other they will love the Father more. 1 John does not take this step, but affirms that to love one's brother is an immediate proof of love for the Father. In the case of 1 John it is more immediate because the author seems at a loss to know what other kind of proof he might find to verify the claim, "I love God."

The final (eighth) and most problematic use of the "by this we know . . ." construction appears in **5:2**. (For this construction see above on 2:3.) The problem is that it seems to make loving God and doing God's commandments the test of loving the children of God. Such a reading runs contrary to all that 1 John has argued in 3:16-18; 4:11-12, 20-21; 5:1. Certainly "by this" makes good sense as a reference back to 5:1b. The problem is that the construction of 5:2 seems to imply a reference forward to the conditional *hotan* construction. We can say that the test of 5:2 arises out of the conclusion arrived at by 5:1. Can the sense of 5:1b (perhaps even of 4:20–5:1) be discerned in the test of 5:2 without straining the syntax of what is written? Or is the specific reference of "by this" in 5:2a to the *hotan* clause of 5:2b?

Raymond E. Brown (*The Epistles of John* 539) notes that the temporal aspect of *hotan* implies that the two actions go together: "The idea is not that only after (or if) we love God and obey his commandments, do we then love God's children, but that the two actions go together and are simultaneous." Thus "we love the children of God when we love God and do his commandments." The function of the *hoti* is epexegetical, to signal the content of *what* we know. (See BAG 592, no. 1.a.) What we know follows *hoti* in the two clauses in the rest of the verse. This means that there is nothing in 5:2 to indicate *how* we know. Thus "by this" refers to nothing in 5:2 and must refer back to 5:1 (rightly Dodd, *The Johannine Epistles* 125). *Because* "every one who loves the one who begat loves the one begotten of him," *it follows* that we know that "we love the children of God when we love God and keep his commandments." As Brown notes, loving the children of God is not a *consequence* of loving God and keeping his commandments; the actions are simultaneous. Dodd's rearrangement of the English makes the sense clearer and is probably the more common Greek order also: "By this we know that, when we love God, we love the children of God" (*The Johannine Epistles* 125). Dodd omitted "and do his commandments" to make clear that the basis of this knowledge is in 5:1, which makes no mention of doing the commandments. This then means that a hidden ground has been made explicit for knowing that those who love God at the same time love the children of God. Thus "doing his commandments" explicates what love of God involves. (See John 14:15, 21, 31 for the connection.) There is no second and independent element to which "by this" refers. Nevertheless, the addition of "and do his commandments" indicates that this is an important element of loving God in connection with loving the children of God.

This reading of 5:2 tells us *what* we know. "We love the children of God when we love God and keep his commandments." But 5:2 does not tell us *how* we know, to which "by this" points. From this point of view Dodd (*The Johannine Epistles* 125) is right in arguing that the basis for drawing the conclusion that "we love the children of God when we love God and keep his commandments" (5:2) is to be found in 5:1. Thus because "by this" refers to "everyone loving the begetter loves the one begotten of him," "we know that we love the children of God when we love God and do his commandments." Dodd rearranged 5:2 to make the meaning clear in English, adopting a more common Greek order (see the Notes and cf. 2:28). He does not show how the precise reading of the text justifies his meaning. My reading of the Greek of 5:2, set out more fully in the Notes, shows that this is *precisely* what the Greek text means. Evidently the early scribes found no problem with the reading, because they have not emended this part of 1 John. Emendations are common where the text was unclear to them.

Here and in 5:3 there is reference to the commandments (plural), last mentioned in 3:22. There, as here, the reference to "his commandments" means God's commandments, which is true of the plural "commandments" throughout 1 John (2:3, 4; 3:22, 24; 5:2, 3). A case can be made for reading the singular "commandment" as a reference to the love command given by Jesus in John 13:34 (cf. 15:12). But the first use of the singular in 3:23 is clearly a reference to a commandment given by God. This is less clear in the second use in 3:23, which could be a reference to Jesus' command to "love one another" (see 2:7, 8; 3:23; 4:21).

Given that the discussion of loving God was initiated by the claim of the opponents in 4:20, "I love God," it is notable that everything from that point to this has been a test of the claim and a qualification of what it means. The claim is falsified if the person making it hates his brother (4:20). The one who claims to love God is commanded to love his brother also (4:21). Those born of God not only love the one who begat them, but also those begotten by God (5:1). Those who love God and do his commandments love the children of God (5:2). Certainly 1 John does not and could not repudiate outright the claim to love God, but nowhere in 1 John is there any indication as to what this means beyond loving one another (the brothers) and keeping God's commandments. Of course one version of the commandments includes the command to love God absolutely (Deut 6:5) and Jesus' twofold summary of the Law builds on that with the Levitical command "Love your neighbor as yourself" (Lev 19:18): see Matt 22:37-40; Mark 12:29-31. Interestingly, in Luke 10:25-37 it is the lawyer who gives the summary of the Law in these terms, but it is the command to "love your neighbor as yourself" that becomes controversial and the occasion for telling the parable of the Good Samaritan. There too it was recognized that testing love for God in itself was impossible.

Our reading of 1 John 5:2 in its context accentuates the necessity that all those who claim to love God and do his commandments should love the children of God. It does not define loving the children of God in terms of loving God and doing God's commandments any more than loving God can simply be defined as keeping the commandments. In addition there are the gratitude, thankfulness, and bonding *(menein)* that express the relationship out of which doing the commandments arises. Loving the children of God is a response to the commandments (5:2; 4:21) but is also an expression of bonding with the one who begat the children of God (5:1) and kinship *(koinōnia)* with the children of God (5:1; 1:3, 6-7).

1 John 4:7-21 focused on the nature of love, *defined* in terms of its source (God), *characterized* by the definitive *act* of love in the sending of God's Son, and *recognizing* the responsive nature of all human love to the love of God (4:19). In **5:3** "for this is the love of God" is an objective genitive expressing "our love for God" (see 5:2). Further, although there (5:2) loving God and keeping God's commandments appear to be two separate activities, here (5:3) loving God is defined in terms of *keeping* those commandments (cf. John 14:15, 21). Clearly *keeping* here has no other meaning than *doing* in 5:2, though keeping the commandments is the idiomatic phrase and normal in 1 John (see the Notes). In light of 5:3 it is possible that in 5:2 the word translated "and" should be translated "even": "even that we keep his commandments." Otherwise our author presents an obvious conundrum because in side-by-side statements he says that keeping God's commandments is additional to loving God and then says that loving God *is* keeping his commandments. One way out of this would be to see that the command to love God (see the opening of the *Shema*, Deut 6:4, 5; and cf. Matt 22:35-38; Mark 12:28-31; Luke 10:25-28) was consciously included in 5:3 while other aspects of the commandments were in view in 5:2. The problem is that, apart from the love command and the command to believe (3:23), no other commandments are specified.

From this perspective God's commandments are not "burdensome" *(bareia)*. In Matt 23:4 Jesus refers to the teachers of the Law and Pharisees putting heavy *burdens* on people's shoulders. Thus 1 John 5:3 may be in contrast to such imposition. By contrast Jesus, according to Matt 11:30, says: "my yoke is easy and my load *(phortion)* is light." Jesus contrasts the burdensome nature of the Law, as imposed by the teachers of the Law and Pharisees, with the easy yoke and light burden of his teaching. While there was a tendency to multiply demands on the one hand, there was also a move to prioritize and summarize the Law on the other. Jesus needs to be understood in that context. It is unclear just what commandments our author has in mind. He uses the plural as often as the singular (six times each), but only in 3:23 does he specify more than the love command. There, prior to the command to love one another, we find the command to believe in the name of his Son Jesus Christ. To this we need to add, perhaps, the command to love God if that is the solution to the wording of 5:2-3. Simplification of commandments may be one aspect of "not burdensome." A second aspect is suggested by the continuation in 5:4. It is a continuation, yet it has been placed in a new subsection because of the new theme that emerges distinctively there. The new theme suggests a distinctive reason why the commandments are not burdensome.

## 2.2. Victory over the world (5:4-5)

4. because everyone begotten of God conquers the world; and this is the conquering power that has conquered the world: our faith. 5. Who [then] is the one who conquers the world if not the one who believes the Son of God is Jesus?

### NOTES

4-5. *because everyone begotten of God conquers the world; and this is the conquering power that has conquered the world: our faith. Who [then] is the one who conquers the world if not the one who believes the Son of God is Jesus?*: The opening *hoti* is causal, telling why the commandments are not burdensome. 1 John has customarily used the construction "everyone who. . . ." (See above on 2:23.) But here we encounter that construction in the neuter gender: "every*thing* begotten of God. . . ." Compare the masculine "the one begotten of him" in the second half of 5:1. This use of the neuter jars. In 1 John a case can be made for reading the neuter as if it were masculine. Compare the use of the neuter relative pronoun at the beginning of 1:1. Note especially that the use of the neuter in 5:4 where "every*thing* that is begotten of God conquers the world" is followed by the masculine in 5:5: "who is the one who conquers the world . . .?" The Gospel has a number of similar neuter/masculine references. (Compare the pairs of references in John 3:5 and 6; 4:22 and 23; 6:37a and 37b, 39 and 40; 17:2b and 17:2c; 17:9 and 10 [and see BDF §138.1].)

The noun *hē pistis* appears only here in the Johannine Gospel and Epistles (four times in Revelation). It is used here to match "the victory" (*hē nikē*, the power to conquer). Because 1 John says "the victory is our faith," the neat formula is to use *hē pistis hēmōn*, literally "the faith of us."

The verb "to conquer" (*nikan*) is used first of "everything [everyone] begotten of God," of whom it is said: "he conquers the world" (here *nika* is present tense). Then "faith," which is the "victory," is said to have conquered the world. (*Nikēsasa* is an aorist participle.) Finally, "*the one who conquers the world*" is described using the present participle with the article (*ho nikōn*), a formula that matches the answer to the question: "who is *the one who conquers* the world?" The answer is: "*the one who believes* Jesus is the Son of God." Here "the one who believes" *(ho pisteuōn)* is a matching formula alongside "the one who conquers," both using the article followed by the present participle. This is neat verbal matching. The copula verb *estin* is used to identify faith with the victory, the one who conquers with the one who believes. Here is clear evidence of stylistic and rhetorical explanation for the choice and use of language in 1 John. The use of "faith" in 5:4 and "the one who believes" in 5:5 strongly suggests that this single use of the noun in 5:4 is to be understood in no way differently from the use of the verb in 1 John as a whole.

On the construction to express the content of what is believed in 5:5, compare the same construction to express the same content after the verb "to confess" (see 2:22; 4:2-3, 15). To confess is to make a public declaration of faith.

Some mss read "your faith." The weight of evidence clearly supports "our faith." If "your faith" had better support, a case could be made for it as the more difficult reading. Hence its appearance needs to be explained as a scribal slip, writing *hymōn* for *hēmōn*. This was a common scribal error.

### INTERPRETATION

The most important reason why the commandments are not burdensome is now given: "because everyone begotten of God conquers the world." The use of the neuter is jarring, especially as the masculine use in 5:1 is so close (and cf. 2:29; 3:9; 4:7; 5:18). The suggestion that the neuter gives a collective sense provokes the question why the author did not use a plural construction, *panta ta gegennomena*. The suggestion that in this single instance the author is thinking of believers as *tekna theou* and thus uses the neuter does not seem likely. Reference to "his *sperma*" in 3:9 is suggestive. Not only is *sperma* neuter, but it is related to the motifs of being begotten of God and power over sin:

> Everyone who is begotten of God does not do sin because his seed (*sperma*) abides in him, and he is not able to sin, because he is begotten of God.

Yet it is difficult to see how "everything that is begotten of God" can refer to the divine seed. Rather it seems we need to allow that the neuter here is used in the same way as the masculine in 5:1 and other places (BAG 637, g). Otherwise it is used for some mysterious reason that currently eludes us. The expression "everyone" treats a collective individually. Those begotten of God remain in a hostile world environment (see John 17:6, 11, 14-19; 1 John 2:15-17). Here, as Dodd (*The Johannine Epistles* 126) recognized, the threat of pagan values in the Roman world is reflected (see John 17 and 1 John 2:15-17). Because everyone born of God has God's seed abiding in him or her, and "greater is the one who is in you than the one in the world" (4:4), they have conquered the Evil One (2:13, 14) and the antichrists (4:4). They conquer the world (5:4).

The assurance that everyone begotten of God, that is, each child of God, *conquers* (present tense) the world implies that the struggle with the world continues. It is for this reason that we find dualistic language in 1 John, language that characterizes the struggle between truth and falsehood, light and darkness, love and hate, the children of God and the children of the devil, God and the devil, believers and the world. Much of the language has been shaped to give expression to this conflict. Acutely aware of the struggle, the author assures the readers that they conquer the world. He does this by defining what "victory" *(hē nikē)* is. It is understood as "the power to conquer." This is stated with emphasis: "this is the victory." In this specification of the victory one feminine noun *(hē nikē)* is identified with another *(hē pistis hēmōn)*, "our *faith*." To balance the statement stylistically the author has used the noun "faith" for the only time in the Gospel or the Epistles. Elsewhere the characteristic verb "to believe" is used (see on 3:23). The choice of the noun here is stylistic and carries no different meaning. Faith—that is, believing—is the power to conquer the world. Indeed, 1 John says that it is the power *that has conquered* (article with aorist participle, *hē nikēsasa*) the world. The aorist participle looks back to a decisive victory. While it is not specifically mentioned here, according to John 16:33 Jesus said:

> In the world you have conflict *(thlipsis)*, but be of good cheer, I have conquered (perfect tense, *nenikēka*) the world. (Cf. John 12:31.)

John 16:33 speaks of a decisive victory with lasting effects. But this text is not in 1 John. There we do find, however, that "the Son of God was revealed to destroy the works of the devil" (3:8). While this states the purpose of his coming, we may also conclude that a decisive beginning was made by it. That event is also to be seen as the ground of faith, because it generated the witness and the message to which faith is a response (1:1-5). So the coming of faith is a manifestation of the power that overcomes the world, and the one who believes shares in the victory. In John and 1 John the christological content of belief is crucial, and this is signified by the construction using the verb "to believe" followed by *hoti.*

Nevertheless, "the whole world [still] lies in the [power] of the Evil One." Even in this context the power for victory is evident in the affirmation that introduces these words: "we know that we are of God, and the whole world lies in the [power] of the Evil One" (5:19). It is implied that "we" do not lie in the power of the Evil One. This is the victory, the power to conquer the world, "our faith." Our faith has conquered (aorist participle) the world. The occurrence of faith is itself evidence of the power to conquer the world. That victory is affirmed of the young men (2:13, 14), and the readers are assured (4:4): "Little children, you are of God and you have conquered them" (the opponents empowered by the Spirit of the Antichrist).

Just as there was a stylistic balance in the statement identifying "the victory" with "our faith" (feminine nouns with the article), so now there is a balance in identifying "the one who conquers" with "the one who believes." (Each has the article with the present participle.) Just as this motif of "victory" was introduced using the present tense, "everyone begotten of God conquers the world," so it concludes in the present tense, identifying "the one who conquers the world" with "the one who believes Jesus is the Son of God." Beginning and ending with the present tense emphasize that the struggle continues even if the emergence of faith is itself evidence of the victory. Our faith is the power to conquer the world; the one who believes is the one who conquers the world.

That it was right to treat the neuter *(pan to gegennēmenon)* at the beginning of v. 4 as if it were masculine seems to be confirmed by the beginning of v. 5. Here "the one who conquers the world" is identified with "the one who believes." Verse 4 says "everything begotten of God conquers the world." Thus the one who believes is the one who conquers: everyone begotten of God conquers. This conclusion drawn from 5:4-5 is confirmed by 5:1. There is little difference between "the one who believes" (5:5) and "everyone who believes" (5:1).

The rhetorical question concerning "who is the one who conquers the world . . . ?" uses the masculine present participle with the definite article in characteristic Johannine style. The one who conquers is set in parallelism with the one who believes (cf. 5:1). The form of the rhetorical question of 5:5, "who is the one who conquers the world except *(ei mē)* the one who believes that Jesus is the Son of God?" balances the rhetorical question of 2:22, "who is the liar except *(ei mē)* the one who denies, [saying] that Jesus is not the Christ?" The one who conquers is over against the Liar: "This is the Antichrist" (2:22). Nevertheless there is the assurance (4:4): "You are of God, little children, and you have conquered them" (the antichrists inspired by the Spirit of the Antichrist, cf. 4:2-4).

In 5:1 and 5 the verb (article with present participle) is followed by *hoti* to give the content of *what* is believed. The content of faith is also expressed with the use of the verb "to confess" followed by *hoti*. Both constructions stress correct belief over against the false belief of the opponents (see 5:1, 5; 2:22; 4:2-3, 15). The problem there seems to have been that the opponents refused to identify the human life of Jesus with the Christ, the Son of God. Consequently they refused to confess (believe) that Jesus (the human) was the Christ, the Son of God, that Jesus Christ was come in the flesh. Thus the one *correct* faith is seen as the victory, that is, the power that has conquered the world in its appearance and goes on conquering as believing continues. Perhaps the present tense is used in the first instance to emphasize that this was an ongoing process as people came to believe. The content of belief signaled by the use of *hoti* reminds us that "to believe in Jesus" requires a known identity and that Jesus' identity is made known to us in these terms: the Christ, the Son of God, come in the flesh.

## 2.3. The witness to the Son is the witness to eternal life (5:6-12)

6. This is the one who came by water and blood, Jesus Christ; not by water only, but by water and blood; and the Spirit is the one who bears witness, because the Spirit is the truth. 7. Because there are three who are bearing witness, 8. the Spirit and the water and the blood, and the three are in the one. 9. If we receive human witness, the witness of God is greater, because this is the witness of God, that he has witnessed concerning his Son. 10. The one believing in the Son of God has the witness in him; the one not believing God has made him a liar, because he has not believed in the witness that God has witnessed concerning his Son. 11. And this is the witness: God gave eternal life to us, and this life is in his Son. 12. The one having the Son has life; the one not having the Son of God does not have life.

### NOTES

6. *This is the one who came by water and blood, Jesus Christ; not by water only, but by water and blood; and the Spirit is the one who bears witness, because the Spirit is the truth:* There is textual diversity over the wording "by [lit.: through] water and blood." Some late mss. support "spirit" in place of "blood," a reading found also in Ambrose and Cyril. Others read "blood and Spirit," "blood and Holy Spirit," "spirit and blood," and "water, blood, and Spirit." Of these readings only "blood and Spirit" has significant support, being the reading of Sinaiticus (‫א‬) and Alexandrinus (A), the Harclean Syriac, the Coptic, and Origen. The textual evidence in favor of this reading is at least as strong as that in favor of "through water and blood": Vaticanus (B), the Old Latin, Vulgate, Peshitta, and Tertullian. What counts against reading "water and blood and Spirit" is that it cannot explain how the diversity emerged. The only additional change expected on that basis is the addition of "Holy." But the reading "water and blood," which is as well attested as any other reading, makes all other variations intelligible and is to be accepted as original. Almost certainly "spirit" was introduced under the influence of 4:8.

The expression "by water and blood" first appears with the preposition *dia* (expressing agency) and the two nouns "water and blood" connected by "and." Then the preposition changes to *en*, expressing instrumentality. It is used three times and each time the following noun has the definite article, "not by *(en)* the water only but by *(en)* the water and by *(en)* the blood." The differences raise two questions: (1) Is the change from *dia* to *en* simply a stylistic variation or a change of meaning? (2) What difference does the introduction of the definite article make in the references using *en*? At the same time "the one who came" is spoken of using both formulations, "*dia* water and blood" and "not *en* the water only but *en* the water and *en* the blood." Stylistic changes of this sort are characteristic of 1 John. The two formulations refer to the same event, to "the one who came." This suggests that *dia* (expressing agency) and *en* (expressing instrumentality) are used without difference, as is true of the nouns with or without the article.

7–8. *Because there are three who are bearing witness, the Spirit and the water and the blood, and the three are in the one:* The text of the "Johannine Comma," the words added to 5:7-8, is given in the Interpretation. The evidence against the authenticity of these words in the context of 1 John 5:7-8 is overwhelming. No Greek ms. prior to 1400 contains the addition. Only eight post-1400 Greek manuscripts contain the additional words. Of these, four include the words as marginal notes. The words are absent from the Old Latin before 600 and from the Vulgate before 750. The addition is absent from the Coptic, Ethiopic, Arabic, and Slavic versions prior to 1500 and from the Syriac until 1569, when it appeared as a marginal note. No clear reference to these words can be found in the writings of the Fathers before Priscillian (southern Spain ca. 375). The words do not seem to be known by leading Latin Fathers such as Hilary of Poitiers (367), Ambrose (397), Leo the Great (461), and Gregory the Great (604), and knowledge of the words by Augustine (430) is disputed. This is consistent with the common appearance of the words in the Vulgate only in the second millennium. Thus the presence and history of the addition is more important for the history of theology than for the interpretation of the text of 1 John. That history points to North Africa (and closely connected southern Spain) as the source of the Johannine Comma and suggests the demands of trinitarian controversy as the driving force for its creation.

The introductory *hoti* is not easy to translate (5:7). To this point only the Spirit has been mentioned as the one bearing witness. "Because" is not appropriate, as no reason is given for the additional two witnesses. Perhaps "thus there are three who are bearing witness" might do. Though the three witnesses (Spirit, water, and blood) of v. 8 are neuter, the words "three bearing witness" are masculine, probably influenced by the idea of persons bearing witness.

On the language of unity or oneness see John 10:30; 11:52; 17:11, 22, 23. Note that 17:23 uses the same preposition, "into one" *(eis hen).* In 1 John 5:8 the expression may take account of the plurality of the three bearing witness, but it also marks the convergence and agreement of their testimonies.

9. *If we receive human witness, the witness of God is greater, because this is the witness of God, that he has witnessed concerning his Son:* The opening conditional sentence is incomplete. What is expected is "if we receive human witness we should receive the greater witness of God." A more rhetorical apodosis is supplied, implying "we should receive." For the author's fondness for statements introduced by "this is" see above on 1:5.

The second half of the verse has two parts, each introduced by *hoti.* The first is causal ("for"), introducing the witness of God. The second is epexegetical ("that") or a relative *ho ti,* translated as "that" or causal "for" or "because." If causal it would be resumptive. The translation adopts the epexegetical "that," identifying the subject of the testimony.

Some later texts in the Latin tradition make an addition to the end of v. 9 concerning the witness the Son bore on earth "that you may believe." The addition draws on 1:2 and John 20:31.

10. *The one believing in the Son of God has the witness in him; the one not believing God has made him a liar, because he has not believed in the witness that God has witnessed concerning his Son:* Sinaiticus and the Vulgate read "the testimony *of God,*" the scribal addition clarifying the obvious. Sinaiticus has also changed "in him" *(en autou)* to "in himself" *(en heautou).* This is also a clarification. Expectation that the reference to "the one not believing" will balance what is said about "the one believing" has led to scribal balancing by introducing "the Son" (Alexandrinus [A]) or "the Son of God." The original reading is "the one not believing God," supported by Sinaiticus (א), Vaticanus (B), and a broad base of other textual evidence. It is also the reading that best explains the scribal changes.

On the vocabulary of believing see above on 3:23. This is the first of three uses of *pisteuein eis* in 1 John (see also later in 5:10 and 5:13). This construction is used thirty-six times in John and only ten times in the rest of the NT. While *pisteuein* with the dative often means to believe what is said and *pisteuein hoti* draws attention to the content of belief, *pisteuein eis* often portrays a personal commitment, though it need not be full and firm (see John 8:31-32). There is also an overlapping use of *pisteuein en.* These distinctions should not be treated as hard and fast rules, as the second and third parallel uses of *pisteuein* in this verse show. There need be no difference between the use with the dative (the one not believing God, that is, what God said) and *eis* with the accusative (because he did not believe in the witness). This is also a question of not believing what was said. When the witness is to the Son, believing the witness is believing in the Son.

The *hoti* is causal, explaining why not believing has made God a liar. The explanation is little more than a repetition of the witness of God from v. 9 with the indication, now in the perfect tense, that he (the one not believing God) has not believed (perfect tense to match, "has made him a liar") in *(eis)* the witness that *(hēn)* God witnessed concerning his Son. Minor changes have been made to adapt the statement of God bearing witness (5:9) to fit the statement of not believing in the witness (5:10).

12. *The one having the Son has life; the one not having the Son of God does not have life:* There is evidence of variation in word order that may make a slight difference in emphasis.

### INTERPRETATION

The demonstrative "this" **(5:6)** refers back to Jesus in 5:5, "Jesus is the Son of God" (cf. 4:15). That this was denied by the opponents seems clear. Here Jesus is identified as "Jesus Christ." The double name implies that

Jesus is the Son of God, "the one who came through water and blood." Reference to "the one who came" *(ho elthōn)* draws attention to a specific event. The authentic confession "Jesus Christ has come in the flesh" is here called to mind. The use of the double name affirms the identity of the human Jesus and the divine Christ in one Jesus Christ. In all the confessions of faith concerning the *identity* of Jesus, the name Jesus is used alone: Jesus is the Christ (2:22; 5:1) and Jesus is the Son of God (4:15; 5:5). But he is referred to as "Jesus Christ the righteous" and God's command is to believe in the name of his Son Jesus Christ (3:23). Further, the name "Jesus Christ" is used when his coming is spoken of by those who confess "Jesus Christ has come *(elēluthota)* in flesh *(en sarki)*" (4:2) and "Jesus Christ the one who came *(ho elthōn)* by *(dia)* water and blood" (5:6).

The similarity between 4:2 and 5:6 suggests that both texts refer to the incarnation (see Georg Richter, "Blut und Wasser [1970] 1–21). The force of the perfect participle in 4:2 is that the confession (present tense) is based on the event completed in the past, Jesus Christ having come in the flesh. But 5:6 affirms straightforwardly that Jesus Christ is the one who came (article with the aorist participle) by water and blood. What puts this view in question is the variation in the use of the prepositions *dia* and *en* and the use of "by water and blood" in 5:6 in place of "in the flesh" in 4:2.

In 4:2 the meaning is clearly "having come in the flesh." But 5:6 can hardly mean "who came in water and blood" in a sense analogous to "having come in the flesh." The initial statement in 5:6 uses the preposition *dia*, which does not mean "in" but (with the genitive case) means "through" or "by." It is followed by a modified repetition, which has a threefold use of the preposition *en* in place of *dia*. The overlapping use of these two prepositions confirms a common translation of "by" indicating agency *(dia)* and instrumentality *(en)*. Given that the nouns "water and blood" in Greek are neuter the instrumental use of *en* with the dative is normal and the use of *dia* with the genitive is unusual. More puzzling is the single use of *dia* to qualify the anarthrous coordinates of "water and blood," but *en* is used three times, and each time of one of the nouns with the definite article: "not by the water only, but by the water and by the blood." In spite of these differences it is likely that *dia* and *en* here function with the same effect, the one to convey the sense of agency and the other instrumentality. The neuter gender is normally treated instrumentally, so that agency is unusual with two neuter nouns ("water" and "blood"). Although "the one who came" is not repeated in the reformulation, "not by/in the water only but in the water and in the blood," those words are clearly implied by the opening, "not in/by the water *only*." Because the one who came is still the subject, some other reason must be given for the change of prepositions (from *dia* to *en*) and the introduction of the definite article before each noun: "the water and the blood."

That the opponents accepted that Jesus came in/by the water only is implied by the author's protest, "not in/by the water only but in/by the water and in/by the blood." This may suggest that the initial formulation is the author's, using his own words in response to the formula shaped by the opponents in their words. The wording "the one who came through water and blood" is his own, but the formula has been shaped as a response to the wording of the opponents. Given a fresh start, our author might have written "the one who came in flesh," though that too was problematic for the opponents! They rejected this confession, which is not in their terms.

A multitude of interpretations have been spawned by the words of 5:6. It is now commonly accepted that the stylistic variations should not be read as applying to different realities such as that the formulation using "through" refers to the baptism of Jesus and his death, and the other using "in" refers to the sacraments of Baptism and Eucharist. The sacramental interpretation is not attested until the fourth century and no longer has strong support. Tertullian (*Bapt.* 16) makes clear that the sacramental interpretation should not be read into these words, and modern exegesis has followed his view.

Recently Martinus de Boer ("Jesus the Baptizer") and Colin Kruse (*The Letters of John* 174–80) have argued that the water symbolizes Jesus' own baptizing ministry (see John 3:22; 4:1-2; cf. 1:26-27, 32-34). The problem with this is that John, having identified Jesus' baptizing ministry (3:22; 4:1), immediately denies it by saying that Jesus did not baptize anyone, but his disciples did (4:2). The references that make the baptism of Jesus by John a sign that Jesus is "the coming one" (John 1:27, 29, 30), "the Son of God" (1:34), at the same time identify John as the one who baptizes with water and Jesus the one who will baptize in the Holy Spirit (1:33). Thus both 1:33 and 4:2 disassociate Jesus from the administration of water baptism. He is baptized with water, and that is a sign, a witness, but his own baptizing ministry is Spirit baptism. This does not commence until after his glorification or resurrection (John 7:37-39; 16:7; 19:30, 34-35[?]; 20:22). And in what sense does Jesus *come* in or by his baptizing ministry? The argument that it is not by something done to Jesus, his baptism, but something he does as the one who came is not altogether convincing. If being crucified (the meaning of "blood" here according to de Boer and Kruse) can be thought of as something Jesus does, is that not true also of being baptized?

There is another reason for the identification of "water" with the baptism of Jesus. The opponents may have claimed that the heavenly and divine Christ descended, in the form of the dove, on the human Jesus at his baptism. This view is attributed to Cerinthus by Irenaeus:

He represented Jesus as having not been born of a virgin, but as being the son of Joseph and Mary according to the ordinary course of human generation, while he nevertheless was more righteous, prudent, and wise than other men. Moreover, after his baptism, Christ descended upon him in the form of a dove from the supreme Ruler, and that then he proclaimed the unknown Father, and performed miracles. But at last Christ departed from Jesus, and that then Jesus suffered and rose again, while Christ remained impassible, inasmuch as he was a spiritual being.

Those who are called Ebionites . . . their opinions with respect to the Lord are similar to those of Cerinthus and Carpocrates. (*Adv. haer.* 1.26.1-2)

Irenaeus broadens the group that holds these views to certain Gnostics including Valentinus (*Adv. haer.* 3:11.2-3).

Against such views 1 John insists: "This is the one who came by water and by blood, Jesus Christ; not by the water only but by the water and by the blood." The emphatic (demonstrative) "this" draws on 5:5 and 5:1. Jesus is the Christ; Jesus is the Son of God, the one who came through/by water and blood, Jesus Christ.

The most common view is that water refers to the baptism of Jesus and blood to his death, a view partly evident in Tertullian. The case has been made here for the view that 1 John accepted the coming through water as a reference to the baptism. But rather than seeing the Christ descending on Jesus at his baptism, 1 John sees Jesus Christ revealed at his baptism. Jesus was identified as the "coming one" in his baptism; cf. Matt 11:3; Luke 7:20; John 1:27, 29, 30. That Jesus was baptized by John "in water" seems to be assumed in John 1:26, 31, 33. That blood is a metaphor for the death of Jesus is widely attested and in 1 John 1:7; 2:2 relates to Jesus' atoning death.

A variation on this approach is to take baptism as a metaphor for Jesus' death (see Mark 10:38). Thus for 1 John the meaning of the water of Jesus' baptism finds its fulfillment in Jesus' death. Some support is found for this approach in the words of Ignatius: "Jesus was born and baptized that by his suffering he might purify the water" (Ignatius, *Eph.* 18:2). Moving further in this direction, according to John 19:34 at Jesus' death his side was pierced and "blood and water flowed out from his side." This reading takes "water and blood" as a reference to the single event of Jesus' death. It has the advantage of taking seriously the initial "through water and blood," which seems to indicate a single event. Raymond E. Brown (*The Epistles of John* 577–78) notes that Augustine connected John 19:34 and 1 John 5:6. Two nouns, each without the article, joined by "and" and governed by the same preposition, seem to refer to the same event. In John 19:34 "blood and water" are without article and joined by "and." Three serious objections can be raised against this view: (1) In what sense can it be said that Jesus came through, in, or by his death? (2) John 19:34 has "blood and water," but 1 John 5:6 has "water and blood." (3) The final formulation "in the water and in the blood" undermines recognition of a single event "through water and blood."

Certainly the different order can be explained by the evidence that the opponents were claiming the coming in water only. Probably this was a reference to the descent of Christ upon Jesus at his baptism and departure from him before his death (see Irenaeus, *Adv. haer.* 1:26.1; 3:11.3). A view attested later by Epiphanius (*Panarion* 30:3; 34:10) identified the "Christ" descending on Jesus, with the Holy Spirit in the form of a dove, at the Jordan river. Against this view 1 John asserts insistently: "the Christ is Jesus" (2:22; 5:1), "the Son of God is Jesus" (4:15; 5:5), "Jesus Christ has come in the flesh" (4:2-3) and "through water and blood" (4:6). If the opponents used "water" as a reference to the baptism of Jesus, the distinction of "in the water and in the blood" now emphasizes two separate events.

The reader should be aware that precise meaning eludes us here because the author expected his first readers to recognize the subject without explanation. One helpful clue is that the protest, "not by water only," implies that the opponents separated "water" and "blood." This opens the possibility that "water" meant one thing for the opponents, separated from "blood," and "water and blood" meant something else for our author. Again our author may refer to the same event as the opponents in relation to "water" and simply add another event by reference to "blood." On the whole it is likely that the opponents appealed to the baptism of Jesus. What 1 John sets against their understanding of baptism is less clear. An appeal to the one who came in the flesh is certainly in keeping with the Epistle. An emphasis on the real humanity of Jesus and the importance of his death also fits. It could be argued that 1 John accepts the appeal to the baptism of Jesus without disputing the interpretation of baptism because this would be done by appeal to the blood, the death of Jesus. Thus the baptism and death are united in one Jesus Christ coming by water and blood, and not separated as for the opponents. It may be that the stress on three independent witnesses in 5:8 adds weight to the view that water refers to Jesus' baptism as a sign (John 1:33), just as there is testimony attached to his death in John (19:34-35).

Reference to the Spirit bearing witness at this point lends some weight to the view that water refers to the baptism of Jesus. Although John does not describe the baptism, John 1:33 alludes to the sign of the descent and abiding of the Spirit on Jesus at his baptism and to the witness of John the Baptizer identifying "the coming one." The Spirit of Truth is also referred to as a witness in John 15:26. The witness of the disciples too is Spirit-inspired (John 15:27). Here the Spirit is described as the truth. Both the

Spirit and the truth are given the definite article, unlike the assertions "God is Spirit" (John 4:24); "God is light" (1 John 1:5); "God is love" (1 John 4:8, 16). Probably this is a variation on the theme of "the Spirit of Truth" and is related to the view that the Spirit is the agent of God's revealing witness. That witness is to the truth of Jesus: "that Jesus Christ has come in the flesh." Those making this confession manifest the Spirit of Truth (4:2-3, 6).

The need to expand from the single witness to three **(5:7)** may well reflect the law of testimony in Deut 17:16; 19:15; see John 8:17. Witness or evidence could be inanimate objects such as a heap of stones (Gen 31:45-48) or heaven and earth (Deut 31:28). In John 5:36; 10:25 Jesus' works bear witness to him.

Identification of the Spirit and the water and the blood as three witnesses **(5:8)** undermines the attempt to make "water and blood" refer to a single event. Thus there is a case for accepting the baptism of Jesus and his death united in one Jesus Christ and the Spirit as the witness to Jesus Christ coming in the flesh (4:2-3, 6). The agreement of the witnesses was crucial. Where witnesses did not agree, their testimony was undermined and invalidated (see Mark 14:56, 59).

Quite early the threefold reference to "the Spirit and the water and the blood" gave rise to a symbolic interpretation that moved the witnesses out of the context of the ministry of Jesus into the life of the church. Thus Clement of Alexandria (ca. 200 C.E.) says on 1 John 5:6: "There are three that give testimony: the Spirit which is life, the water which is regeneration and faith, and the blood which is knowledge" (*GCS* 17, 214). From the third century a trinitarian interpretation was current in North Africa (Cyprian and Pseudo-Cyprian and leading to Augustine). The trinitarian reading identified God as Spirit (John 4:24), and the Spirit is symbolized by the water flowing in John 7:38-39; 19:34, and from the side of the Son comes blood. Further, God the Spirit and the Son are mentioned in 1 John 5:8-9. Thus Spirit signifies the Father, "water" signifies the "Spirit," and "blood" signifies the Son. The Latin trinitarian interpretations arise from the affirmation that "the three are one."

Questions were provoked by the text, especially when it was translated into Latin *("hi tres unum sunt")*. This eventually led to the introduction of a trinitarian gloss that has become known as "the Johannine Comma." Here "Comma" indicates a sentence or clause. The addition made to vv. 7-8 is indicated below by the words in italics. See the Note for an indication of the secondary nature of the addition.

> Because there are three who bear witness *in heaven: Father, Word, and Holy Spirit; and these three are one; and there are three who bear witness on earth:* the Spirit and the water and the blood; and these three are into one.

*1, 2, and 3 John*

The addition is an excellent example of the way the wording of the text of NT writings provoked theological development in the early centuries. Sometimes, as here, the original text was enigmatic and suggestive. At other times it was the provocation of new contexts and problems that drove theology to find new meanings in the text. Consequently modifications were made to the text. Here the text of 1 John was provocative and suggestive, but the evidence indicates that the pressures of trinitarian controversy, especially in North Africa, led to the addition of the Johannine Comma.

The formulation "the three are one" *(hoi treis eis to hen eisin)* is interesting. Just how to translate it is a tantalizing problem. "The three" is masculine, perhaps because the phrase resumes the 5:7 reference to the "three who are bearing witness" *(treis eisin to martyrountes)*, which is masculine. But when the three are identified it is with three neuter nouns, "the spirit and the water and the blood" *(to pneuma kai to hydōr kai to haima)* and the reference to "the one" is neuter gender. The words "the three" and "the one" are joined by the verb "to be" and should agree in gender. The preposition *eis* is also involved, literally giving the meaning "the three *into* one are." But while the preposition has a bearing on case, it should not modify gender. Philo distinguished between God revealed *(ho ōn)* and God hidden *(to on)*, God in himself. Language like this may have fueled trinitarian thought in the West but is not directly relevant to the language of "three into one."

The suggestion that Spirit is a reference to the Father (John 4:24), the water a reference to the Spirit (John 7:37-39), and the blood a reference to the Son (John 19:34) already shows the power of trinitarian theology driving the interpreter to find it in the text. More likely is the view that Spirit, water, and blood are references to anointing *(chrism,* 2:20, 27), Baptism, and Eucharist. For those who are uncertain of the place of anointing in the Johannine community, the Spirit can be thought of as active in Baptism and Eucharist. While the references to anointing in 1 John are enigmatic, at least they are in the text; the place of the sacraments of Baptism and Eucharist is not explicitly discussed.

Further, there is no evidence that water and blood are being used in a way different from v. 6. It is true that there is now no mention of Jesus who came by water and blood, but equally there has been no signal that the words mean something different. The addition of the Spirit does not explicitly or even implicitly signal a change. Certainly, according to John 1:31-34 the Spirit bore witness to Jesus at his baptism. The association of Jesus giving the Spirit (John 19:30), the effusion of blood and water (19:34), and the witness borne (19:35) is suggestive of the Spirit's witness at the death of Jesus in light of John 15:26-27. The witness to Jesus' death is inspired by the Spirit of Truth. The one bearing witness is the Spirit (5:6);

nevertheless there are three witnesses, the Spirit, the water (Jesus' baptism) and the blood (Jesus' death).

With this enigmatic passage the best that can be done is to weed out what is not possible and then to locate what is more likely. The conclusion cannot be certain. Clearly the trinitarian interpretations are an anachronism. This is probably true also of the sacramental interpretations. Reference to Jesus' baptism is probable because that issue was placed on the agenda by the opponents. Their view of the baptism of Jesus was the basis of this discussion. While accepting their terms, 1 John reinterprets Jesus' baptism and adds the reference to his death, both attested by the witness of the Spirit so that together the Spirit, the water, and the blood converge in agreement.

The argument is now **(5:9)** carried by a piece of proverbial wisdom. So obvious is the conclusion that it is not stated. Instead 1 John simply says: "The witness of God is greater." We have already learned that God is *greater* than our hearts (3:20), that the Spirit "who is in you" is *greater* than the Spirit in the world (4:4). That the witness of God is greater than the witness of human beings is reminiscent of John 5:33-36, where Jesus appeals to the witness of his Father, the witness *greater* than the human witness of John (the Baptist).

When the author says the witness of God is greater than the witness of human beings it is not likely he has in mind the three witnesses of 5:6-8. The contrast in John 5:33-38 makes the witness of John a possibility. Certainly John is portrayed as a witness in John 1:7, 15, 19, 32, and Jesus says he has a witness greater than John (5:36), namely "the works that the Father has given me to complete . . . and the Father who sent me has borne witness concerning me" (5:37). This makes good sense if the opponents appealed to the witness of John to the Spirit's descent on Jesus, the descent of Christ on Jesus at his baptism. But the problem is that the reference is to the "witness of human beings." Thus it seems that here 1 John is making a more general statement true to the proverbial form.

The witness is introduced by a favored "this is . . ." statement. It is the witness of God, the greater witness, the witness to be received. God has borne witness (perfect tense) *concerning (peri)* his Son. This locates the testimony in the past but implies its ongoing effect. The question is: When was this testimony concerning his Son given? In the baptismal testimony of Mark the voice from heaven proclaims: "You are my beloved Son" (Mark 1:11). More appropriate still are the words at the transfiguration: "This is my beloved Son; listen to him" (Mark 9:7). Was something like this known in the Johannine community? The reference in John 5:37 is startlingly suggestive: "the Father who sent me, he has borne witness (perfect tense) concerning *(peri)* me. Neither his voice have you ever heard nor his form have you seen." This is apparently an appeal to the witness of the voice of God, perhaps in the baptism. In Mark those words were concerning God's Son.

As the witness was borne by God to his Son, the one who receives the witness believes in *(eis)* the Son of God **(5:10)**. This is an expression of recognition of Jesus as the Son of God and belief in him as such. Naturally such a belief implies commitment, but the commitment is based on the recognition and acceptance of who he is.

The one who believes has the witness in "himself." This is clearly the meaning of this text, though the Greek probably used the third person personal pronoun that is capable of a reflexive meaning but need not be read that way. Scribes rightly read this text as a reference to the witness within the believer, "in him/herself." The believer has accepted the witness borne (see on 1:2) and therefore has the witness in himself.

The use of *pisteuein* with the dative now indicates the person not believing what God says in his witness. To reject the witness of God is to have made God a liar. While "the one not believing" is a timeless description, the consequence of the action in principle is then viewed as having happened. To have done this is to have made God a liar. This is the very reverse of the idiom of John 3:33, where "the one who receives Jesus' testimony sealed (aorist tense) that God is true." In 1:10 the claim of the opponents, "we have not sinned," makes (present tense) God a liar (see also 2:4, 22; 4:20). Here the one who does not believe "has made" (perfect tense) God a liar. Interestingly, the present tense of the action leads to the perfect tense in the consequence (5:10), whereas the perfect tense in the claim leads to a present tense in the consequence (1:10). This looks a bit like stylistic balancing of present and perfect tenses in each case. The one who does not believe God does not believe the witness God bore in 5:9. Only minor changes are made to adapt the statement of witness to the idiom of non-belief in the witness, using *eis* with the accusative where the accusative alone might have been used.

We now **(5:11-12)** have a repetition: "This is the witness." (See the second half of 5:9, which is repeated in 5:10.) What is now said expands on that statement with attention to the consequence of believing. The gift of eternal life "to us" is obviously to "us who believe in the Son of God" (see 4:15; 5:5). Because the coming of Jesus was the revelation of life, the eternal life that was with the Father (1:2), it is said: "that life is in his Son." In 2:22-23 denying and confessing appear to be public expressions of not believing and believing. Interestingly, the liar is the one who denies that Jesus is the Christ and is identified with the Antichrist, who denies the Father and the Son. Denial is the opposite of confessing or believing that Jesus is the Christ (see 5:1). Thus "the one confessing the Son has the Father also" (in 2:23) implies that the one believing has the Father *also,* and "also" implies that he or she has the Son.

To say that eternal life was revealed in the Son is to say that he reveals the nature of the divine life and is the means of its transmission from God to believers, which is another description of the one who has the Son. To have the Son is to believe in the Son, the revealer and giver of life, the life that was with the Father and was made known to us (1:2). A dominating theme of 1 John is the characterization of the life of God in terms of love. This was the great theme of 4:7-21 and it spills over into much of the rest of 1 John. Because the eternal life that was with the Father is in his Son, to have the Son is to have life. The description of "the one who has the Son" is an alternative to "the one who believes," the christological confession of 5:1, 5, 6, which is an alternative of 2:22-23; 4:2-3, 15. This separates the Johannine believers from the opponents. The lines of division between them and the opponents are deeply drawn. From the standpoint of 1 John the line that separates the two groups is the confession of the true faith, the correct christological confession. On this hangs eternal life, because the very nature of eternal life in the self-giving love of God is inseparably bound to that confession. Break the tie between the life of God and the human self-giving of Jesus and eternal life has vanished.

## For Reference and Further Study

Beutler, Johannes. *Die Johannesbriefe*, 116–26.

Boer, Martinus C. de. "Jesus the Baptizer: 1 John 5:5-8 and the Gospel of John," *JBL* 107 (1988) 87–106.

Brooke, Alan England. *A Critical and Exegetical Commentary on the Johannine Epistles*, 127–41, 154–65.

Brown, Raymond E. *The Epistles of John*, 535–42, 565–603.

Dodd, Charles Harold. *The Johannine Epistles*, 125–26.

Häring, Theodor. "Gedankengang und Grundgedanke des ersten Johannesbriefes" (1892) 173–200.

Kruse, Colin G. *The Letters of John*. Grand Rapids: Eerdmans, 2000, 174–80.

Lieu, Judith. "'Authority to Become Children of God': A Study of 1 John," *NovT* 23 (1981) 210–28.

Rensberger, David. *1 John, 2 John, 3 John*, 128–37.

Richter, Georg. "Blut und Wasser," *MThZ* (1970) 1–21; reprinted in idem, *Studien zum Johannesevangelium*. Regensburg: Pustet, 1977, 120–42.

Schnackenburg, Rudolf. *The Johannine Epistles*, 227–45.

Witherington, Ben III. "The Waters of Birth: John 3:5 and 1 John 5:6-8," *NTS* 35 (1989) 155–60.

# V. CONCLUSION (5:13-21)

## 1. TO REESTABLISH CONFIDENCE (5:13-15)

13. These things I wrote to you that you may know that you have eternal life, you who believe in the name of the Son of God. 14. And this is confidence that we have in relation to him, if we ask anything according to his will he hears us. 15. And if we know that he hears us whatever we ask, we know that we have the requests that we have requested from him.

### NOTES

13. *These things I wrote to you that you may know that you have eternal life, you who believe in the name of the Son of God:* On the use of the epistolary aorist ("I wrote") with reference to the present writing see also 2:14, 21, 26. In 2:26 the author uses the same opening, "These things I wrote to you. . . ." He more often uses the present tense, "these things we write" (1:4), "my little children, these things I write to you" (2:1), and repeatedly "I write to you" (2:7, 8, 12, 13 [2x]). Thus the present tense is used from 1:1–2:13, and from 2:14 onward the aorist *egrapsa* is used.

The use of *hina* with the subjunctive *eidēte* signals a statement of purpose. Does it apply to 1 John or only to part of the writing? While 5:11-12 would be an appropriate reference, coming at the conclusion of 1 John it is a statement of the purpose of 1 John and should be compared with John 20:31. On the use of the second person plural subjunctive "[that] *you may know*" (*[hina] eidēte*) see 2:29 and the Interpretation and Notes on 2:20.

The conclusion, "you have eternal life, who believe in the name of the Son of God" (*zōēn echete aiōnion, tois pisteuousin eis to onoma tou huiou tou theou*) echoes the conclusion of John 20:31, *hina pisteuontes zōēn echete en tō onomati autou.* This suggests that John 20:31 should be translated "that believing in his name you may have life."

Vaticanus (B) and Sinaiticus (א) support the text as adopted, using the dative present participle to resume the reference "to you," and defining the readers as "the ones who believe in the name. . . ." Alexandrinus (A) uses the participle in the nominative case and the Byzantine tradition reorders the sentence in a way that duplicates the reference to those who believe. Both are secondary attempts to clarify the text.

14. *And this is confidence that we have in relation to him, if we ask anything according to his will he hears us:* For "this is" see above on 1:5, and note 5:9, 11. On the use of *pros* with the accusative to describe relationship in the presence of God see John 1:1-2; 1 John 1:2; 3:21; 5:14. Though distinguishing Jesus from God is frequently difficult in 1 John, reference here is to the presence of God, and this is

confirmed by 3:21-22. The *hoti* is epexegetical of "confidence." On "the confidence" *(hē parrēsia)*, see above on 2:28. There it was confidence at the coming *(parousia)* of Jesus, the day of judgment (cf. 4:17). Now it is confidence in prayer before God (cf. 3:21-22). Indeed, the reference to confidence before God in 3:19-22 seems to bridge the theme of judgment and the situation of prayer.

The conditional sentence is introduced by *ean* with the present subjunctive *aitōmetha* stating the condition, and the present indicative *akouei* expressing the consequence when the condition is fulfilled. In a conditional context *ean* does not express uncertainty. It simply lays down the condition to be fulfilled if the consequence is to follow. Here *ean* with the subjunctive seems to have no different meaning from *ean* with the indicative in 5:15.

The verb "to ask" *(aitein)* here and in 5:15 is in the middle voice, which might imply asking for oneself, but the same verb is used in the active voice in 5:15. The clear distinction between active and middle is not always maintained in the NT; see John 16:24, 26, where the same verb is used first in the active and then in the middle with no discernible change of meaning.

15. *And if we know that he hears us whatever we ask, we know that we have the requests that we have requested from him:* The use of the indicative *oidamen* after *ean* in the conditional sentence is probably a result of the author's desire to use the same form of the verb as in the stated consequence. The conditional sense is no different from that in 5:14. On the use of *oidamen* see above on 3:2. Both uses of *hoti* are epexegetical, indicating the content of what we know. The verb "to hear" takes the genitive of the speaker and accusative of what is said (asked). The use of the neuter singular relative pronoun *ho* with *ean* is short for *ho ti ean* and means literally "whatever."

The phrase "the requests that we have requested" employs the cognate accusative, where the noun is used with the verb of the same root. The word translated "we have requested (asked)" is the perfect indicative active of the same verb used in the present middle subjunctive earlier in this verse and in 5:14. The use of the active here confirms that the middle is used in an active sense in 5:14-15.

Sinaiticus and Vaticanus read *apo* (19 times in 1 John) "from him," while Alexandrinus reads the preposition *para*, which is not otherwise used in 1 John.

INTERPRETATION

If the statement of purpose here **(5:13)** did not fit what we find in 1 John we might think that the reference to "these things" was to be found in 5:11-12. But coming, as it does, in the concluding section and fitting the purpose of 1 John as a whole so well, we can scarcely doubt that 1 John as a whole is in view. That the purpose is stated in terms reminiscent of John 20:31 is supportive of this conclusion when the appended nature of John 21 is recognized. Nevertheless, 1 John 5:13, like John 20:31, is followed by the introduction of new material before the book ends.

Both 1 John 5:13 and John 20:31 signal their intentions with a purpose clause. Given the similarity in form, the differences in stated purposes are the more striking. While dissimilarities could be explained by our author's inclination to vary vocabulary and syntactical order, the differences here seem to be more substantial. The Gospel was written that the readers may believe. But there is more to it than that, and the disputed tense of the verb is of little relevance. What is crucial is the content of belief. The author states the purpose of his Gospel as "that you may believe." The verb "believe" is not followed by *eis* with the accusative, but by a *hoti* clause that introduces the content of faith. That content is clearly the distinctive Johannine confession of Jesus Christ as Son of God. It is belief in his name.

While 1 John 5:13 uses many of the same words in similar phrases, the purpose is different. It is written to those who already believe in the *name* of the Son of God. There is no doubt that the content of faith is crucial also in 1 John. The significance and content of that belief are gathered up in the Johannine motif of belief in the name (see John 1:12; 2:23; 3:18; 20:31 and 1 John 3:23), but the purpose is to ensure that those who believe may know that they have eternal life. Here the content of knowledge is introduced by a *hoti* clause. 1 John sets out to confirm that those who believe rightly know that they have eternal life. This purpose is consistent with the way 1 John, from beginning to end, has been determined to establish tests that confirm the status of believers as children of God whose lives manifest the character of the divine life. That character manifests the source of their life in God and is evidence of eternal life. The christological test is also related to this because the eternal life was revealed in Jesus Christ having come in the flesh (1:2; 4:2-3), so that to believe in the Son, to have the Son, is to have life (2:22-23; 5:11-12). Indeed, there is life in his name (John 1:12-13; 20:31); that is, for those who believe in his name.

1 John says **(5:14)** "This is the boldness we have before him" (God, see 3:21-22), that is, in the presence of God. The ground of "confidence" is expounded by means of the epexegetical *hoti*. What follows tells us in what the confidence consists. The basis of the confidence is expressed in a conditional sentence: "If we ask anything according to his will, he hears us." The ground of confidence is that God hears us, though this is qualified by "if we ask according to his will." This is consistent with the confidence before God in prayer in 3:21-22. There the confidence is also conditional, and "if our heart does not condemn us . . . because we keep his commandments and do what is pleasing in his sight."

The next verse, **5:15**, is an elaboration of 5:14. The conclusion of 5:14, "he hears us," now becomes the basis of the condition of 5:15, "if we know that he hears us whatever we ask." The assumption that he hears us has already been made conditional to asking according to his will in 5:14. The new condition builds on that. What follows from this is an elaboration of what it means for God to hear us. It means that "we have the request that we have asked from him." Thus we see that "to hear" means more than simply to be aware of the words. To hear in this sense means to respond positively to what is asked. Thus to know that God hears (5:14) means that God grants the requests: "we know we have the requests that we have asked *from him.*" It is now explicit that the request is made of God and it is implicit that God himself provides whatever it is that has been requested. The hidden assumption is that God is able to provide whatever we ask according to his will.

## 2. PRAYER FOR THOSE SINNING (5:16-17)

16. If anyone sees his brother sinning a sin not to death, he will ask, and he will give life to him to those sinning not to death. There is a sin to death. I do not say that you should ask concerning that. 17. Every unrighteousness is sin, and there is a sin not to death.

### NOTES

16. *If anyone sees his brother sinning a sin not to death, he will ask, and he will give life to him to those sinning not to death. There is a sin to death. I do not say that you should ask concerning that:* This third conditional sentence in three verses is introduced by *ean* with the subjunctive *idē:* "if we ask . . ." (5:14), "if we know . . ." (5:15), "if anyone sees . . ." (5:16). The central second sentence (5:15) uses the indicative mood.

In the space of seven verses 1 John has used three cognate accusatives, "the witness that God witnessed" (5:10), "the requests that we have requested" (5:15), and "sinning a sin" (5:16). The cognate accusative (the verb and its cognate noun in the accusative) is a Semitism. For the idiom "sinning a sin" see LXX Lev 5:6; Ezek 18:24. The sin is not "to death" (*mē pros* and *ou pros* are used without difference in 5:16-17). While the sin "to death" could mean a sin that led to the physical death of the sinner, that is probably not the meaning. Rather the author seems to have in mind a sin so serious that reinstatement is impossible; see Mark 3:28-30.

The future tense has the sense of an imperative: "he will ask." No indication is given of whom he will ask. The context makes clear that these requests are made of God. When this is assumed, the subject of "*he* will give" is also obvious; that is, God, who has been asked, "will give life *to him.*" Obviously this is the brother whose sin is not to death. The one who has not sinned already "has life;" see 5:12. Lack of syntactical clarity is covered by context in this case.

If "to him" is the brother sinning a sin not to death, the following clause, "to those sinning a sin not to death" is expressed by a *plural* present participle in the dative case. This seems to be so, with the dative participle with the article, "the ones sinning," resuming the dative singular "to him" *(autǭ)* in a generalizing fashion. The hypothetical particular example now becomes a general statement.

In referring to the sin that leads to death (see John 11:4 for the use of *pros thanaton*) the author now says, "I do not tell you to ask concerning that sin." Here the feminine demonstrative *ekeinēs* is translated "that sin." The reader has to fill the gap left by an imprecise description to guess what that sin might be. All the reader has are clues implied by the context.

The content of what the author does not tell the readers *(ou legō)* is indicated by an epexegetical *hina* clause using *erōtēsǫ* in the subjunctive mood: "I do *not* tell you *to ask* concerning that sin."

In the cases until now the verb for asking has been *aitein*. The verb now used is *erōtan*. There is no discernible difference in meaning in this context. While *erōtan* covers a wider range of meaning than *aitein*, such as to ask a question, to seek information (see John 1:19; 5:12; 9:2, 15, 16), when used in the context applicable to *aitein* it is used with no discernible difference of meaning, as here. In the Gospel requests made to God introduced by *erōtan* are restricted to those made by Jesus (14:16; 16:26; 17:9, 15, 20).

17. *Every unrighteousness is sin, and there is a sin not to death:* The negative in "not *(ou)* all sin is deadly" is omitted by some late Greek mss and from Tertullian, Vulgate, Coptic, and Syriac versions. This has too little support to be entertained. Tertullian reveals his "rigorist" leanings, "all sin is deadly."

INTERPRETATION

The third conditional sentence **(5:16)** in three verses introduces a new subject, though it still comes under the heading of confidence in prayer. It clarifies what asking according to God's will means in a particular instance. This concerns the policy on prayer in relation to sin. Three matters are specified. It is a sin of a brother, a Johannine believer. The sin is tangible, so that it can be seen. It is a sin *not to death (mē pros thanaton)*. In John 11:4 the expression is used of Lazarus, of whom Jesus says that his sickness is not unto death *(ouk estin pros thanaton)*. For Lazarus that meant it was not a sickness that would lead to his death. In the process of the story the expression takes on a second level of meaning concerning spiritual death. The question is: How is the expression to be understood here in 5:16-17?

Much of the rest of the verse needs to be filled in by the reader. The context makes fairly clear how the gaps should be filled. First, if the outlined conditions are fulfilled, the one who sees *will* ask. The future tense here is an implied exhortation or command. Second, the context of 5:14-15 makes it clear that he will ask God. When God is supplied as the one to whom the request is made it is obvious that "he" who will give life is God. He gives it *to him*. This can only be the brother whose sin is not to death, because the one who sees is a believer who has the Son and already has life (5:12). In an additional clause formed by the plural present participle with the article in the dative case the author resumes reference to the one sinning, but now in a generalizing fashion extending the scope to cover those sinning not to death.

Reference to a sin that does not lead to death implies that there is a sin that does lead to death, and this is soon made clear. The author now intrudes his own personality by saying: "I do not tell you to ask concerning that sin." Throughout this verse we have had to fill in gaps left by the author in order to understand what has been written. We are left with a gap for which the author has laid insufficient clues. What is the sin that leads to death? While the author does not instruct the reader to pray concerning "that sin," does he mean "do not pray concerning the one who commits it?" That seems probable. Is it implied that a brother might commit such a sin? This also seems probable because reference to this sin is introduced by a clause about seeing a brother sinning. The most obvious way to read this is: "if it is a sin not to death, then you will ask (God); but if it is a sin to death I do not tell you to ask God concerning (the one who commits) that sin." The reader fills in the gaps from clues that imply the way to read the text. The modern reader is less well equipped to do this than those for whom 1 John was written.

It is likely that the sin that leads to death is identified with the opponents. They rejected the confession that Jesus Christ has come in the flesh and the obligation of love that flowed from it. The hard line taken against the opponents, naming them as antichrists and children of the devil, is consistent with this. The hard line is a response to the author's fear that the opponents remained a threat to the stability of the community.

Excursus: "A Sin unto Death"

The author's instruction on prayer concerning the brother sinning comes against the background of the Johannine dualism, which leads to the view that "everyone begotten of God does not sin" (5:18; and see 3:9 and cf. 3:6). Yet this runs hard up against the rejection of the claims of the opponents in 1:8, 10. Now the author acknowledges that someone may see a brother sinning. He makes no attempt to deny that such a person is a brother. He enjoins prayer for the brother whose sin is not to death. This may imply that the community did not pray for those who sinned, assuming that sin marked them as those who were not children of God but children of the devil (3:9-10). There is a tension in 1 John concerning sin that allows for the restoration of the brother who sins (2:1-2; 1:7). There is a sin that leads to death, and the author makes no overtures encouraging prayer concerning that. While he does not explicitly forbid such prayer, three contextual elements suggest that was his intent. (1) If we are right in suggesting that the context implies a situation in which the community did not pray for the brother who sinned because sin had put his status as a brother in question, not enjoining prayer concerning the sin unto death leaves it outside the scope of prayerful concern. (2) The discussion of prayer has been bracketed within the condition of asking according to God's will (5:14). Describing the sin as "unto death" implies something of its status before God. (3) The opponents, who have separated from the Johannine network of churches, refusing the fundamental christological confession of the children of God and refusing to love the brothers, probably qualify as those who have sinned to death (see 2:18-19, 22-23). They were brothers, but they have separated from the community of brothers. The author makes no attempt to win them back but brands them as liars, the Antichrist (see also 4:1-6), and children of the devil (3:8-10). Such people do not have eternal life abiding in them (3:12-15). See also 2 John 7.

In the OT there are some offenses that lead to death (Num 18:22). The rapist shall be slain (Deut 22:25-26), but the *victim* "has not committed a sin worthy of death." This could be thought to imply levels or categories of sin. By the late second century of our era there is evidence of the development within Christianity of the category of mortal sins (unto death), such as murder, adultery, and apostasy, distinguished from venial sins, which could be forgiven. Pressure to develop this distinction came in the great persecutions. The threat that apostasy could not be forgiven was a strong deterrent. But the grouping of sins into two such categories does not fit 1 John, and the evidence is rather too late to make probable that this was done at the time 1 John was written. At the same time, the distinction between sins that were and were not unto death is a clear move in that direction. The tradition of the unforgivable sin in Mark 3:28-30 provides a basis for the recognition of a sin that leads to death, for which prayer does not avail. There too the problem is related to the failure to recognize the divine activity in the human life of Jesus.

While Deut 22:30 forbids a man to marry his father's wife, *Jub.* 33:12-18 names incest of a man with his father's wife as "a sin unto death" for which there is no atonement. But 1 John does not speak of enacting the death penalty for certain sins. Acts 5:1-11 deals with the death of Ananias and Sapphira for lying to God. 1 John does not seem to think of perpetrators of this sin being struck down by God. Even the notion of praying concerning this sin implies that the perpetrators are still alive. Further, the likelihood is that in 1 John the sin unto death is related to the refusal to make the Johannine christological confession. It is likely that the opponents are in view. They appear to have been prospering. That is why 1 John was so urgent in dealing with the threat that they continued to pose for

the Johannine network of house churches. In this context the death referred to is spiritual death: it meant failing to have eternal life now and
facing the second death beyond the grave.

Nevertheless, even though believers had passed from death to life
(3:14), the brother who sins could lose life and that life could be restored
(5:16). Such is the case if the sin is not unto death. To describe the sin as
*unto death* implies that no atonement is possible. Such a person is spiritu-
ally dead and headed for the second death. But how are we to understand
this distinction if it is not between serious sins and trivial sins? In the OT
willful sin is distinguished from unintentional sin. Unintentional sins are
classified as sins of ignorance and sins of weakness. For such sins sacrifice
could be offered and atonement made (Lev 4:1-3; Num 15:22-31, and see
1QS 8:21–9:2). But for willful sins, "sins of the high hand," there was no
sacrifice, no atonement. This distinction makes more sense of the Johannine context than one that implies that certain sins are trivial. See Origen,
*Matt.* 13:30 (*GCS* 40, 264).

1 John is referring to sins committed by those described as brothers.
Had a sin to death been inconceivable of a brother, the opening of 5:16
would have been different. It would not have been necessary to explain
that the sin in question was not "to death." If a brother was incapable of
committing a sin to death he would not have needed to tell his readers
that he did not tell them to ask concerning that sin. While 2:18-19 says that
the opponents, who had broken relations with the author and his supporters, revealed that they were never truly part of the community, it is
implied that they were once brothers. Though this can be read systematically as meaning that truly they had never been brothers, this conclusion
goes further than what is actually said and may oversystematize what
was a looser position. It is unsafe to push the thought of 1 John beyond
what it claims simply because logic seems to imply a conclusion.

The reference to a sin unto death, understood in the context of the
schism, probably has to do with rejection of the confession of faith that
formed the basis of the Johannine community (see 2:22-23; 3:23; 4:2-3, 15;
5:1, 5, 6, 13). The author is dealing with the threat of an ongoing influence
by the opponents, draining brothers (and sisters) from the community.
The rejection of the confession of faith was also linked to a refusal to recognize the necessity of loving the brothers (one another) as an essential
element of believing in the name of God's Son, Jesus Christ.

Unrighteousness **(5:17)** is opposed to Jesus Christ the righteous (2:1; cf.
1:9) and those begotten of God, who do righteousness (2:29). To name unrighteousness as sin is an elaboration similar to 3:4. Sin is lawlessness.
That term has a resonance with the man of lawlessness and the mystery of
lawlessness in 2 Thess 2:3, 7. The identification of sin with lawlessness has
much in common with 5:17. By referring to every unrighteousness *(adikia)*

as sin 1 John attends to social justice issues and does not allow any to slip through and escape being critiqued as sin. Nevertheless, 1 John returns to say "there is a sin not to death." The restatement reminds us of the brother sinning a sin not to death. The return of this theme creates a rough edge for the connection with the next statement, but neatly ties up the discussion in 5:16-17.

## 3. GOD AND THE PROBLEM OF SIN (5:18-20)

18. We know, everyone begotten of God does not sin, but the one begotten of God keeps him and the evil one cannot touch him. 19. We know we are of God, and the whole world lies in [the power of] the Evil One. 20. We know, however, the Son of God is come, and has given us a mind to know the One who is True, and we are in the One who is True, in his Son Jesus Christ. This is the true God and eternal life.

### NOTES

18. *We know, every one begotten of God does not sin, but the one begotten of God keeps him and the evil one cannot touch him:* On the use of *oidamen hoti* see 3:2, 14, 15, 18, 19, 20. All uses of *hoti* in this construction are epexegetical and need not be translated. On the construction "everyone who . . ." see above on 2:23. When there is a negative in the "everyone who" statement it is better translated as "no one begotten of God sins" rather than "everyone begotten of God does not sin."

Two Greek miniscules, the Vulgate, and some other evidence support *gennēsis* in place of *gennētheis*, "begetting" for "begotten." While tempting because this would provide a basis for connecting this reading with the *sperma* of 3:9, it looks like a scribal attempt to solve an interpretative problem.

Codices Alexandrinus (A) and Vaticanus (B) and a number of the versions and Fathers read "keeps *him*" *(auton)*, while a corrector of A reads *"himself"* *(heauton)* and is supported by Sinaiticus (א), the Byzantine tradition, and a number of the versions and Fathers. The textual evidence itself is finely balanced. Perhaps the evidence of the correction of Alexandrinus implies a scribal tendency to change "him" to "himself." Again the textual history shows the perplexing ambiguity of 1 John. It also shows theological tendencies at work in the transmission of the text. The passive participle "begotten" is used twice with the definite article, the first time as a perfect tense and the second time as an aorist. Each time it is singular, but on the first occasion it is *"everyone* who is begotten of God," the second "the one begotten." Thus even though each use is singular, the second seems to be distinguished from the first. If that is the case, the likely reading of the next part of the verse is "the one begotten of God keeps him" (everyone begotten of God). This is more likely than a repetition in which "everyone begotten of God" is then spoken of as "the one begotten of God" who "keeps himself." This is the interpretation suggested by Sinaiticus and the corrector of Alexandrinus. The parallelism of the first part of the statement "Everyone who is begotten of God does not sin" with 3:9 suggests that the reason given there will agree with the reason given here. There the reason is that God's *sperma* abides in him (the one begotten of God). Here it is because "the one begotten *(ho gennētheis)* of God keeps him." The problem is that this articular participle is masculine and *sperma* is neuter!

20. *We know, however, the Son of God is come, and has given us a mind to know the One who is True, and we are in the One who is True, in his Son Jesus Christ. This is the true God and eternal life:* Whether the verse begins *kai oidamen* (Alexandrinus [A], Vulgate, and other versions) or *oidamen de* (Vaticanus [B], Sinaiticus [א] and the Byzantine tradition) makes little difference, though minor witnesses omit any particle. Because the use and placing of *de* is stylistically superior, we may suspect it is a scribal improvement.

To the words "he is come" several Vulgate manuscripts and Latin Fathers add "and put on flesh for our sake, and suffered, and rose from the dead; he took us up." This is further evidence of the theologizing tradition of the transmission of 1 John in the West, of which "the Johannine Comma" (5:7-8) is a particular instance.

The use of *hina* with the present indicative *ginōskomen* is a vulgarism (Brooke, *Commentary* 151) later corrected to the subjunctive. Textual tradition favors the indicative as the original reading: Sinaiticus (א), Alexandrinus (A), and uncorrected Vaticanus (B*).

Textual evidence is divided concerning whether the reference is to "the one who is true" *(ton alēthinon:* thus the corrector of Sinaiticus [אᶜ], Vaticanus [B]), to which some have added "God," (thus Alexandrinus [A] and some of the versions and important Fathers). Other witnesses read "that which is true" (the neuter *to alēthinon),* which is supported by Sinaiticus (א*), Coptic, and some Fathers. The latter represents some scribal uneasiness about referring to the unidentified "one who is true."

Some minor manuscripts omit the second *en,* thus running the reference together with the resultant meaning "in his true Son Jesus Christ." Alexandrinus (A) and the Vulgate omit "Jesus Christ." These both seem to be scribal attempts to smooth the text.

## INTERPRETATION

Verses 18, 19, and 20 begin with "we know that" *(oidamen hoti);* see 3:2, 14; 5:15 and above on 3:2. This differs from the formula "by this we know" *(en toutō ginōskomen),* which uses a different verb to express "knowing" and appeals to evidence to substantiate the claim (see on 2:3). The three claims of 5:18, 19, 20 were apparently self-evident for readers, needing no evidential base ("by this"). The verses summarize much that has been addressed so far. Yet the restatement in summary form is not as precise and clear as we might have hoped to find in this conclusion. Indeed, there is an introduction of new terms and expressions that poses problems in a concluding summary, *ho gennētheis, aptetai, keitai, hēkei, dianoian* (see also the new term *tōn eidōlōn* in the last verse!). The three verses also pose problems of ambiguity because the author does not write in such a way as to make his meaning clear. The first two statements concern the children of God and the third is about the Son of God and his achievement. First there is a generalization about every child of God, then an affirmation that "we are children of God," and finally a statement that the Son of God has come and the consequences.

That we know that everyone begotten of God does not sin can be stated straightforwardly because this is a repetition of 3:9, where an explanation is given. The opening, "everyone begotten of God," is identical in 3:9 and 5:18. There are some variations in wording in what follows. In 3:9 the expression is "he does not *do* sin" *(hamartian ou poiei);* indeed, "he is not able to sin" *(ou dunatai hamartanein).* Because two statements of not sinning are given, two reasons are given, one with each statement: (a) because God's "seed" abides in him; (b) because he is begotten of God. The latter repeats the first part of the affirmation ("begotten of God") but now makes it the basis of the second part ("does not do sin"). In 5:18 "he does not sin" *(ouch hamartanei)* because "the one begotten of God keeps him and the Evil One cannot touch him."

First, the parallels between 3:9 and 5:18 seem to rule out giving different meanings to the use of the noun "sin" with the verbs *poiei* and *hamartanei.* Each expression contains a verb in the present tense with the negative *ou[ch],* but 5:18 does not go on to say "he is not able to sin." We need not doubt that, given that the one who does not do sin is not able to sin in 3:9, the same will be true in 5:18. The first reason given in 3:9 is that God's *sperma* abides in him (the one born of God) and the second reason seems to indicate that this is what it means to be "begotten of God." While the language of 3:9 is relatively simple compared to 5:18, there is no clarity of meaning because the referent of the imagery of God's *sperma* is unclear and everything depends on this.

In 5:18 the explanation of why the one begotten of God does not sin is more perplexing. The parallelism with 3:9 suggests that "the one begotten of God . . . keeps every one who is begotten of God." But identifying the agent of the keeping with God's *sperma,* which would make the neatest parallelism with 3:9, is ruled out by the neuter *sperma* and the masculine *ho gennētheis.* A minor textual variant shows that this was an early scribal solution to this problem.

Grammatically, if we take both statements concerning the one born of God as references to the believer, 5:18 then says that the one born of God keeps *himself*. This reading is possible even if the reflexive *heauton* is rejected. In the NT *auton* can be used reflexively (scholars generally read *eis auton* reflexively in Mark 1:10). Nevertheless, it seems unlikely that 1 John would say that the one born of God keeps himself, even if 2:13, 14 says that the young men have conquered the Evil One and the one who believes has conquered the world. The power that gives victory is "our faith," which is not just subjective believing but also the content of faith, that Jesus is Son of God (5:4-5). Nevertheless, this interpretation is attested as early as Origen (third century) and by Sinaiticus (‭א‬) and the corrector of Alexandrinus (A) and cannot be ruled out.

Two other difficult readings introduce God at a point where 1 John is indefinite. The first identifies the indefinite *auton* with God and reads *tērei* as "holds on to." Thus "the one begotten of God holds on to God." This un-Johannine use of *tērein* introduces God in a surprising passive role. Another approach introduces God as the one who keeps the one begotten by God. Though this seems more consonant with the thought of 1 John, neither this nor the previous reading has early support.

Although without such early support, the case for identifying Jesus as the one begotten has some merit. The shift from perfect participle to aorist participle is taken as the clue to identify the latter with Jesus. The opening "everyone who" is obviously a reference to the believer. On this reading, Jesus, the one uniquely begotten, keeps him, that is, everyone begotten of God. With the identification made, this works out well. The identification is the problem. In its favor is that Philo describes the *Logos* as begotten *(gennētheis)* by God *(Conf.* 14.63). But there is no support for speaking of Jesus as begotten of God in the Johannine writings. Even *monogenous*, *monogenēs* (John 1:14, 18; 3:16, 18; 1 John 4:9) is to be understood as meaning "unique," "only" (see Brown, *The Epistles of John* 517). The Gospel and Epistles carefully use language to distinguish Jesus from believers: he is the unique *Son* of God; believers are *children* of God. Elsewhere in 1 John only believers are spoken of as begotten of God (2:29; 3:9; 4:7; 5:1, 4, 18). There is Western support for reading the opening relative pronoun of John 1:13 as masculine singular *(hos)* and the related verb as singular *(egennēthē)*, "*who* [that is, the one born of God] *was born* not of blood nor the will of the flesh nor of the will of man but of God." But this has no Greek manuscript support and is ruled out anyway by the plural *tois pisteuousin*, of which it is epexegetical. The late introduction of the singular is an attempt, motivated by theological dispute, to introduce the divine begetting of Jesus into the Fourth Gospel.

We are left with two possibilities, neither of which is thoroughly persuasive. Jesus is the one who keeps everyone born of God. After all, Jesus says, "when I was with them I *kept (etēroun)* them in your name" (17:12). Does this not make an important connection in favor of this reading? On the contrary, in the prayer Jesus acknowledges that he can no longer keep the believers (17:13) and prays to the Father, "Holy Father, you *keep* them *(tēreson autous)* in your name" (17:11); *"keep* them from the Evil One" (17:15). The parallels with John 17 suggest that God, not Jesus, is the one who keeps the believer "and the Evil One cannot touch him" (1 John 5:18). This connection with John 17:15 seems close enough to lead to the conclusion that somehow 1 John 5:18 means that God keeps the believer.

Reference to the Evil One (see 2:13, 14; 3:12; 5:18, 19) leaves no doubt that the devil is in view, especially in light of 3:8 and 10, dealing with the way the children of God and the children of the devil are manifest. This is illustrated in the story of Cain, who was of the Evil One (a child of the Evil One) and slew his brother (3:11-12). While not mentioning the Evil One, 4:1-6 deals with recognizing and distinguishing the Spirit of God (4:1), the Spirit of Truth (4:6), from the Spirit of the Antichrist (4:3), the Spirit of Error (4:6). We may suspect that the Spirit of Error is also the Spirit of the Evil One. The two Spirits are manifest in the two groups, the Johannine believers and the opponents who refuse to confess Jesus Christ having come in the flesh. Interestingly, here too 1 John says "you have conquered them." In the light of 5:4, 5 we might ask: in what does the victory consist? What is its ground or what is the power that makes the victory possible? The answer is "Greater is the one who is in you than the one who is in the world" (4:4). The Spirit who is manifest in the confession "Jesus Christ has come in the flesh" is the Spirit of God, the Spirit of Truth, the Spirit "in you," and he is greater than the Spirit of the Antichrist, the Spirit of Error who is "in the world" and is revealed in the denial of the christological confession. "In the world" includes and probably finds focus in the opponents. The ground of confidence that the Johannine believers have conquered them (the opponents) is greater because the One who is in you is greater than the One who is in the world. This ties in well with the notion of God's *sperma* abiding in everyone who is begotten of God (3:9), but it is hard to relate to "the one begotten of God" of 5:18.

The assurance that the Evil One cannot touch them is more in keeping with John 17:15 than 1 John 2:13, 14, and even 5:4, 5, where victory over the world implies victory over the Evil One (cf. also 4:4). In 2:13, 14, when the basis of the victory is stated, it is twofold: "you are strong" and "the Logos of God" abides in you." The former sounds like self-reliance, but it is buttressed by "the Logos of God abides in you," which is in harmony with attributing the victory to the fact that "greater is the one who is in you than the one who is in the world" (4:4). But the sense of victory seems far removed from the claim to be kept from the grasp of the Evil One.

While the verb "to touch" *(haptesthai)* does not in itself indicate hostility, in the present phrase it means something like "and the Evil One cannot get hold of you" and is certainly hostile; cf. LXX Gen 26:11; Jer 4:10. On protection from the "touch of Satan" see *Sifre* 42 on Num 6:26, "Satan will not touch him."

The second **(5:19)** of the successive "we know that" sentences moves from a statement about everyone begotten of God to affirm "we are of God." That is shorthand for "we are begotten of God," "we are children of God;" cf. the opening of 4:6. Here in 5:19 the absence of the opening pronoun *(hēmeis)*, used in 4:6, throws the emphasis on "of God we are." This ties in with the contrast with the world that lies "in the [power] of the Evil One." Perhaps even better is to pick up the reference of v. 18. God keeps us from the grasp of the Evil One, but the whole world lies in his grip, completely in his power. Here the sense of being of God includes the awareness that "we belong to him" just as "the whole world belongs to the Evil One." Nevertheless, Jesus Christ the righteous is the expiation "for the sins of the whole world" (2:2). The Father sent the Son as savior of the world (4:14). This suggests that the world is held somewhat unwillingly in the grip of the Evil One. So Jesus came to take away sin (3:5), to destroy the works of the devil (3:8). Over against this view, which depicts the world as a victim in the grip of the Evil One (5:18) and to be delivered (4:14), is the view of the opponents as false prophets, deceivers (2:26; 3:7; 1 John 7), antichrists, in whom the Spirit of the Antichrist abides (4:4). Against this force the author declares: "you have conquered them" (4:4); "everyone who is begotten of God conquers the world" (5:4-5). There is an ambivalence toward the world, as victim to be saved and enemy to be conquered. The latter becomes dominant when the opponents are in view.

The third "we know" in three verses **(5:20)** moves from statements about the children of God to address what we know about the Son of God. We know that he is come. The verb *(hēkei)* is in the present tense but bears a perfect meaning. It implies a coming in the past with a continuing presence, "has come." Elsewhere 1 John uses the aorist passive "was revealed" *(ephanerōthē)* to speak of his coming (see 1:2; 3:5, 8). There he was said to have come with a purpose: to take away sin, to destroy the works of the devil. Here the achievement of his coming is viewed retrospectively. First, he has given us a "mind" *(dianoia)*, a word used only here in the Johannine writings and a total of twelve times in the NT, where it sometimes translates "heart" as in Matt 22:37; Mark 12:30; Luke 10:27; and see Deut 6:5. Luke 1:51 says that God "has scattered the proud in the imagination *(dianoia)* of their heart" (cf. Gen 6:5), making *dianoia* an aspect or function of the heart. That God has given us a *dianoia* suggests that it is a new *dianoia*, a new heart or a renewed mind (see Rom 12:2), a mind to know the one who is true.

This suggests that the grip of the Evil One is on the mind. The coming of the Son of God has given us a mind to know the one who is true. This is the purpose of his coming. If we rule out the neuter reading *(to alēthinon)* on textual grounds we are left with the question: To whom does "the one who is true" refer? Is it God or Jesus Christ? Textual variants provide evidence of attempts to clarify this. First, two variants read "the true God," one simply by adding *theon* after *ton alēthinon* (Alexandrinus [A], most of the Old Latin, Vulgate, Bohairic, Ethiopic, and many of the Fathers) and the other by placing *ton theon* before *ton alēthinon* (not well attested). Then there is the omission of the second *en* in the second part of the verse, which then reads: "and we are in his true Son Jesus Christ" (not well attested, a few miniscules and Fathers). The two parts are then clear. "The Son of God has come, and he has given us a mind to know the one who is true [variant "true God"], and we are in his true Son Jesus Christ." While there is quite strong textual support for the first part, the support for dropping the second *en* is flimsy. Because it is difficult to see the specific reference to God being dropped, that too is to be regarded as a scribal clarification.

The scribal alteration to read "to know the true God" is probably a correct interpretation even if the reading is not original. For many reasons it makes better Johannine sense to say that the Son of God is come and has given us a mind to know the one who is true (God, see Isa 65:16; 3 Macc 6:18; John 17:3; Philo, *Legat.* 45.366) than to say he has come and has given us a mind to know himself. If this reading is correct, it follows that the affirmation that "we are in the one who is true" refers also to God (see the connection of knowing and "abiding in," 2:4, 6).

But how is the final phrase in the sentence to be understood? If "we are in the one who is true" had been understood of Jesus Christ, then the second *en* would be resumptive, repeating the first phrase introduced by *en* and clarifying it; that is, "in his Son Jesus Christ." Grammatically that reading is possible, but it is most improbable if the first reference to "the one who is true" is a reference to God, and this seems to be the case. Then the second phrase introduced by *en* is laid alongside the first: "and we are in the one who is true [and] in his Son Jesus Christ." Reference to Jesus Christ as "his Son" also strengthens the case for taking "the one who is true" as a reference to God. If that were not the case, "his" would hang unattached. This reading fits well with the dual focus of John 17:3, "This is the eternal life, that they may know you, the only true God and Jesus Christ whom you sent."

The final sentence of 5:20 also resonates with John 17:3 and continues to pose problems. To whom does "this" (*houtos*) refer? The last person mentioned prior to this sentence is Jesus Christ. John does not hold back from referring to Jesus as God (John 1:1, 18; 20:28) and so reference to Jesus cannot be ruled out in principle. Nevertheless the reference appears to be to God. God is the one referred to as "the one who is true." When Jesus Christ is referenced in the previous sentence it is as "*his* Son Jesus

Christ," so that God is still the subject. The objection that the final reference to God as "this is the true God" is somewhat tautological is not without force. At the same time, 1 John has a fair share of statements that approach tautology. Here, however, there is a point to the clear statement because "this is the true God" is about to be set over against idols (5:21).

The true God is coupled with eternal life. This could be taken as evidence in favor of identifying Jesus Christ as the one declared here to be "the true God and eternal life" in the light of the revelation of eternal life in his appearance. But the eternal life thus made known and announced is "the eternal life that was with the Father and was revealed to us" (1:2). Throughout 1 John what the Son does is to reveal the Father, so that the self-giving of the Son reveals that God is love. Eternal life revealed in the Son is the life that has its source in the Father. The inseparable connection of eternal life with the true God is emphasized by the clause, "This is *the* true God and eternal life," where eternal life is expressed without the definite article. The Father is the source of eternal life made known in his Son. For this reason, to have the Son is to have life because to have the Son is to have the Father also (5:12; 2:22-23; John 3:36). "This is the eternal life, that they may know you, the only true God, and Jesus Christ whom you sent" (John 17:3).

## 4. FINAL EXHORTATION (5:21)

21. Little children, guard yourselves from idols.

### Notes

21. *Little children, guard yourselves from idols:* The use of the aorist imperative *phylaxate* suggests a response to a particular crisis rather than an ongoing general response. This fits the reference to "the idols" *(tōn eidōlōn),* which is definite and specific. The verb "to guard" *(phylassein)* is used only here in the Johannine Epistles, but see John 12:47 and especially 17:12 where it is used alongside *tērein* with no discernible difference of meaning. Parallelism there raises the question of the relationship of *phylassein* in 5:21 to *tērein* in 5:18. Here (5:21) the reflexive pronoun *heauta* is clearly read. The neuter plural corresponds to the use of the neuter *teknia,* but this difference from 5:18 does not encourage an acceptance of the variant *heauton* in 5:18 as an equivalent of the neuter plural in 5:21. Thus 5:21 in no way alleviates the problems associated with the interpretation of 5:18. Clues to the interpretation of *ho gennētheis* remain as elusive as ever. The use of the preposition *apo* probably reflects the influence of the Semitic *min,* meaning "from" or "away from."

INTERPRETATION

The final warning **(5:21)**, "Little children *(teknia)*, guard yourselves from idols," is introduced in the familiar way (see 2:1, 2, 28; 3:7, 18; 4:4; 5:21). "Little children" is the most familiar form of address in 1 John, followed by *agapētoi*, 2:7; 3:2, 21; 4:1, 7, 11, and in the singular in 3 John 1, 2, 5, 11. The alternative expression for "little children" *(paidia)* is used only in 2:14, 18. With this familiar address in the last verse, 1 John moves a little way toward providing a personal farewell. Even this falls far short of the kind of farewell expected in a letter. Warnings and blessings are common in endings. Here we have a personal warning, but so much is missing from a customary ending.

The warning "guard yourselves from idols" is specific. It is addressed to a particular and known problem, indicated by the aorist imperative *(phylaxate)* and the use of the definite article with "idols" *(tēn eidōlōn)*. This suggests some connection with the problem of the opponents, which has been the issue addressed by 1 John. It would be strange if the final warning now turned to a new problem. Yet the introduction of the reference to "idols" is unexpected, another new word (see on 5:18) used for the first time in 1 John here. What are the idols? Thus with the last word 1 John maintains its record of obscure communication.

The question is: Does "idols" here have a specific reference to pagan idolatry or is the term used metaphorically? Whichever way this is answered, it is likely to have some reference to the opponents. First, we can say that without further explanation this would be a strange way to critique elements of Judaism. It can hardly be a critique of Jewish worship. Second, the use of the aorist imperative (guard) with the definite article with "idols" suggests a specific crisis rather than a perennial problem. Third, reference to idols is suggestive of the context of the Johannine network of churches within the "paganism" of the Roman empire (Asia Minor?). But it is unlikely that 1 John is referring to the crisis in times of persecution when pagan sacrifice was necessary to avoid persecution. There is no suggestion of a crisis of this sort in 1 John. The crisis has come from within, with a schism tearing the community apart. A fundamental cause of the schism was the refusal to confess that "the Christ is Jesus," "the Son of God is Jesus" (2:22-23; 4:15; 5:1; 5:5), the refusal to confess that "Jesus Christ has come in the flesh" (4:2-3). If they would not confess this *about Jesus*, what did they say about him?

It is perhaps interesting that in 1 Corinthians Paul writes of "Christ crucified" (1 Cor 1:23) and that "Jesus is Lord" (12:3) in the face of the saying "Jesus is accursed" *(anathema Iēsous)*. What is more, the discussion in 1 Cor 12:3 is about discerning the Holy Spirit (cf. 1 John 4:1-6). In 1 John what the opponents say about Jesus is not specified. Only what they refused to confess is noted. It is clear that the identification of the human

Jesus with the Christ, the Son of God, was not confessed. What then of the human Jesus: was he "accursed"? If there is some connection between these two problems, it is worth noting that the proclamation of Christ crucified is set in the context of a discussion of the wisdom of the Greeks in 1 Corinthians, and the discussion of the Spirit-inspired confession "Jesus is Lord" is found within Paul's reminder to the Corinthians:

> You know, when you were Gentiles you were carried away to dumb idols as you were led. Wherefore I make known to you that no one speaking in the Spirit of God says "Jesus is accursed," and no one is able to say "Jesus is Lord" except by the Holy Spirit.

Paul connects the confession "Jesus is accursed" with "when you were Gentiles you were carried away to dumb idols." It is interesting that he apparently no longer considers them to be Gentiles! Then what had they become? But it is the association of Gentiles and idols with the confession "Jesus is accursed" that is important for 1 John 5:21. The faulty confession may well have been linked with the worldly values expressed in 2:15-17 as well as the refusal to recognize the obligation to love the brothers. How was this connected with idolatry? This is unclear because the author of 1 John has not explicitly set out to provide a profile of the opponents. He hardly needed to do so, as they were well known to his readers. What seems clear is that the author attributes their errors to their Gentile background and the association of idolatry.

There is no doubt that when Paul spoke to the Corinthians of their Gentile past with its idolatrous associations he was not speaking metaphorically. His letters remind us that idolatry was pervasive in the Roman empire, and Jewish Christianity was concerned to avoid the contamination of idolatry. (See 1 Cor 8:1–10:33, and note also Acts 15:20, 29; 21:25.)

The suggestion (Ruth B. Edwards, *The Johannine Epistles* 43) that reference to idols is metaphorical, based on the Qumran expression "the idols of his heart" found in 1QS 2:11, is unconvincing. When 1 John warns: "guard yourself from idols," there is no mention of the idols of the heart. Further, the wording that follows in 1QS 2:12-14 is dependent on Deut 29:17-19, where the words "I shall be safe, though I walk in the stubbornness of my heart" (see 1QS 2:13-14) are an expression of turning away to serve the gods of the nations (Deut 29:18). Thus even in 1QS 2:11 the warning is against actual idolatry and its consequences in the community (see also 1QH 4:9-11, 15; *CD* 20:8-10). Even at Qumran the actual contamination of idolatry is in view. The Jewish view that idolatry was accompanied by moral decline and the judgment of God is to be found also in Paul's letters (see Rom 1:18-32). Indeed, so serious was idolatry, in the Jewish view, that it was believed to contain within it the seeds of all sins. This is more to the point than to say that idolatry was a metaphor for sin.

The pressure to find a more acceptable contemporary meaning for the warning must be held in check.

There is evidence of the pervasive reality of idolatry in the Roman empire and continued Jewish abhorrence of it. The prominence of idolatry is clear enough. It was one of the four acts forbidden to Gentile Christians in the so-called "Jerusalem decree" according to Acts 15:20, 29; 21:25. In each case the issue of idolatry is mentioned first. That this continued to be a problem is clear enough from Paul's first letter to the Corinthians, where the subject is dealt with in a number of chapters beginning at 8:1, "Concerning food offered to idols." In what follows, Paul twice directly and specifically warns against idolatry: "Do not be idolaters as some of them were" (10:7). "Therefore, my beloved, shun the worship of idols" (10:14). This latter warning is comparable to what we have at the end of 1 John: "Little Children, guard yourselves from idols." These are not metaphors. In 1 Corinthians what follows each of these warnings is an exposition of the theme of the judgment of God on idolatry based on the example of the people of Israel, who submitted to the attraction of idolatry.

The warning against idolatry in 1 John 5:21 may seem to us to come unexpectedly, from out of "left field." That is because we live outside the pervasive reality of idolatry in the Roman empire. The probability is that 1 John relates the problem of idolatry to the opponents. That no "scriptural" arguments are used against them suggests a dominantly Gentile context. In that context "Jesus is the *Christ*" has lost its Jewish messianic sense. It is now wholly understood in its Johannine sense of the divine Son sent by the Father into the world, as Jesus Christ having come in the flesh. Just how the opponents separated Jesus from the Christ is not altogether clear, but the refusal to identify the Christ with Jesus is plain enough, as is the refusal to confess Jesus Christ come in the flesh. 1 John relates this rejection to the idolatrous position of the opponents. See the Excursus: The Power of Darkness and the Lure of the World below.

FOR REFERENCE AND FURTHER STUDY

Beutler, Johannes. *Die Johannesbriefe*, 127–36.
Brooke, Alan England. *A Critical and Exegetical Commentary on the Johannine Epistles*, 141–54.
Brown, Raymond E. *The Epistles of John*, 607–41.
Edwards, Ruth B. *The Johannine Epistles*. Sheffield: Sheffield Academic Press, 1996.
Hills, Julian. "'Little Children, Keep Yourselves from Idols': 1 John 5:21 Reconsidered," *CBQ* 51 (1989) 285–310.
Kilpatrick, G. D. "Two Johannine Idioms in the Johannine Epistles," *JTS* 12 (1961) 272–73.
Rensberger, David. *1 John, 2 John, 3 John*, 137–46.
Schnackenburg, Rudolf. *The Johannine Epistles*, 245–64.

# 2 AND 3 JOHN

## INTRODUCTION TO THE EXEGESIS OF 2 AND 3 JOHN

In the past there was strong support for the view that 2 and 3 John are not genuine letters but were framed like this to give them some authority (see Martin Dibelius in *RGG*² 3:348). Flaws in the evidence for this view are apparent. Unlike 2 Peter or Jude, 2 and 3 John make no pretense to having a universally famous author. By reference to himself as "the Elder" the author of 2 and 3 John claims some authority, but the level is different from that of an apostle or one of the brothers of the Lord. Rather it seems to be a local authority, and the author assumes that his identity is known to the readers. The contents of 2 and 3 John are such that if they were not addressed to a local group or individual it is not easy to see their point. The same sort of specific address, naming individuals, is presupposed by Paul's letter to Philemon. The genuine character of Philemon, 2 and 3 John as letters now finds support in the diverse papyrus evidence of Hellenistic letters. Like 2 and 3 John, the shortest writings in the New Testament (1126 and 1105 letters, 245 and 219 words respectively), such letters are short, fitting on a single papyrus sheet. 2 and 3 John also conform closely to the essential format of Hellenistic letters with address ("from A to B") followed by a greeting and concluding with a final salutation. In between specific issues are dealt with quite concretely and concisely.

The common address of the two letters by one identifying himself simply as "the Elder" implies the common authorship of both letters. Language and style confirm this as the most likely view. Nevertheless, the two letters are concerned with different though perhaps related issues and have distinctive addressees.

2 John takes up two issues of central concern in 1 John. The first of these is the Antichrist deceivers who do not confess Jesus Christ *coming* in the flesh (2 John 7 and cf. 1 John 2:18, 22-23; 4:2-3). Both 2 John 7 and 1 John 4:2 deal with the confession of Jesus Christ in flesh, but each uses a different tense of the participle of *erchomai* to express the motif of coming in the flesh. Because the context of each is true and false confessions of faith, and both

use parts of the verb *homologein,* the commentary argues that 1 and 2 John refer to a common situation. While there is a drive toward a confessional orthodoxy, it is in a very early stage when the form of the verb used to express the coming in the flesh had not become fixed. Indeed, the Gospel expresses the same idea using the aorist tense of another verb, *egeneto.*

The second issue is the place of the command to "love one another" (2 John 5-6, and cf. 1 John 2:7; 3:23; 4:11-12; see also John 13:34). As in 1 John (3:23 etc.), these two elements (the christological confession and the love command) appear to be intimately connected. B. F. Westcott (*The Epistles of St John* 143) notes, "Augustine *(ad loc.)* remarks characteristically that the denial of the Incarnation is the sign of the absence of love." Nevertheless, in 2 John love for one another excludes the offer of hospitality to those who depart from the author's teaching concerning Christ. See 2 John 9, where "the teaching *of Christ*" is understood as an objective genitive (teaching about Christ) referring back to 2 John 7.

It may be that love for one another, understood as love for the brother (sister is surely implied), was specifically more restricted than love of the neighbor. 1 John uses both the commands to love one another (3:11, 23; 4:11) and to love the brother (2:10; 3:14; 4:21). In 2 John 10-11 the readers are exhorted not even to greet those who espouse a teaching concerning Christ different from that found in this letter. When we also recognize the absence of the command to love the neighbor (or enemy), it may be concluded that love for one another (the brother/sister) was exclusive and precluded love for the neighbor. This need not follow. Both 2 and 3 John deal with issues of hospitality. The context of the call to refuse hospitality and greeting presupposes a network of support, making a successful mission possible. If the Elder considered the false teachers to be seriously in error in both their christological teaching and their ethical practice, it was natural that he should call on his supporters not to assist *the rival mission.* The issue does not concern a refusal to aid a helpless and impoverished or suffering group of people.

In dealing with the refusal of aid (hospitality) to a rival mission 2 John 10-11 is taking up an issue not dealt with in 1 John. If, as seems likely, the rival mission is that of the opponents, we may understand why the author or authors of the Johannine Epistles could have been so concerned about the threat of the teaching of the opponents within the continuing Johannine community. Yet 1 John does not address the problem of how to treat false teachers in the community. 1 John addresses the question of how to recognize the false teaching. This was the primary problem. The detailed concentration on this problem is an expression of the author's perception of the confusion that was rampant in the community. First he needed to provide a basis on which error could be detected. This task needed to be done in a persuasive manner and was undertaken in 1 John. Then, on the basis of the recognition of error, a policy needed to be adopted for the treatment of the false teachers. This is the policy advocated in 2 John. It thus fills a gap not dealt with in 1 John. But the Elder, while advocating a policy of the refusal of hospitality to the false teachers, shows no tendency to exclude members of the Johannine network of communities who were wavering; instead, he attempts to win them over. Apparently the danger was that more of those wavering might leave and join the opponents. (Contrast the policy of Diotrephes according to 3 John 9-10.)

The address of the letters (2 and 3 John) by the Elder is discussed in detail in the exegesis of 2 John 1. Use of the title ("the Elder") reflects the local recognition of the author's authority. Here "local" refers to a region rather than a single town or village. This interpretation is indicated by the author's use of this form of address when writing to "churches" in the surrounding area. The assumption is that 2 and 3 John were sent to different churches. The use of such letters presupposes that the author was himself at some distance from those to whom he wrote and his authority was recognized beyond the community within which he normally lived and worked. The evidence of the letters suggests a leader with authority in a local community, but one whose influence had reached out into surrounding towns and villages. The surrounding region was distant enough so that the Elder needed to write rather than being able to meet with the addressees in the normal course of his movements. If he were to see them, a specially planned journey was required (see 2 John 12; 3 John 10).

What model of relationship between the Elder and the surrounding churches is implied? A number of possibilities may be suggested. It is possible that the surrounding churches grew from a mission radiating out from the church of the Elder and that his influence was simply a "hangover" from that beginning. If that were the case, locating the Elder in Ephesus and the churches to which he wrote in the surrounding countryside would make some sense. But what was the nature of his influence? The letters imply precisely that, an influence. There is no suggestion of something like episcopal authority. In relation to 2 John some clarification of the addressees needs to be made before the role of the Elder can be adequately clarified.

Editors of the Greek text (and commentators) have taken the opening words identifying the addressee in four ways. There are two words: *eklektē kyriā*. The question is, are they common nouns or proper names? They can be taken either way. Alternatively, either the first or the second word may be a name. The current editions of the Greek text treat both words as common nouns so that "the Elect Lady and her children" is a reference to a local church and its members. This view seems to be confirmed beyond doubt by the concluding greeting in 2 John 13, where the Elder sends greetings from "the children of your elect sister."

If this reading is correct, it implies a mutuality between the Elder's church and the one(s) to which he writes in 2 John. They are sister churches. Nevertheless, he writes to them as the Elder. If 2 John is addressed to a church rather than to an individual lady and her children there is also the possibility that it was addressed to more than one such community. Given the non-specific address, 2 John could be used as a circular letter, yet the form appears personal and specific. It is because "Elect Lady" is an analogy for a local church that what seems specific has the potential to be used generally. This form of greeting to the Elect Lady from the children of her elect sister maintains reference to the individual believers.

The suggestion that the address to the Elect Lady is to a specific person who was the leader of a house church (Ruth B. Edwards, *The Johannine Epistles* 29) does not commend itself because the Elect Lady is then a specific woman, and also represents the church. The children, however, are not children of the woman, but members of the church. It seems more likely that the imagery of the Elect Lady is used consistently of a local church whose children are its members. Then the children of her elect sister are the members of a neighboring local church. This decision concerning the meaning of the opening and closing forms of address has nothing to do with the question of whether the leaders of such churches might have been women. We know too little of the situation to hazard an informed guess in relation to the church to which 2 John was addressed. Certainly the possibility that the leader of the church addressed was a woman should not be excluded.

The likelihood is that we are dealing with a network of house churches. 2 John has the potential to address each of them individually. This assumes that we are dealing with a group of local churches where the threat of "deceivers" was real (v. 7). If 2 John accompanied 1 John, its relationship to the larger work can be understood readily. 1 John has no form of address at the beginning, though it is replete with words addressing the readers personally and concludes with a statement of the purpose of the Epistle (5:13) and an appeal to the readers (5:21). As an accompanying letter, 2 John identifies the sender (the Elder) and addresses the readers, summarizing the main message of 1 John, identifying the false teaching and warning against it, and reiterating the love command. No more succinct summary of the teaching of 1 John is possible.

Yet 2 John 12 may seem to put this understanding of 2 John in question. Here the Elder indicates that he has much more to write, but aims to visit instead. That "much more" seems to be contained in 1 John. Thus J. L. Houlden has suggested that, in the event that the Elder was not able to visit as he had planned, 1 John might have been written, embodying as it does the fuller treatment of the issues found in 2 John (*A Commentary on the Johannine Epistles* 140). This is certainly possible, and it maintains the close connection between 1 and 2 John. As Houlden notes, this view also preserves a dignity for 2 John, which deals briefly with issues covered more fully in 1 John. If 1 John was not yet written, the brief contribution has its place.

The alternative that 2 John was written to accompany 1 John shares this perspective. It assumes that, as the introductory letter, 2 John would be *read* first. But what of v. 12? We note that sayings about having much more to write and preferring to visit are conventional. We need look no further than 3 John 13 to demonstrate this. The conventional nature of the statement lessens its force. Further, in a letter more personal communication than is found in 1 John might be envisaged as the subject of what the Elder wished to communicate. Such matters would have to wait for his hoped-for visit. Consequently it is possible to view 2 John as the accompanying letter introducing 1 John to a circle of house churches. Whether it was *written* first or second may not be critical. Even if it was written after 1 John and sent as an accompanying letter, the assumption is that it would be *read* first. That in the early evidence of the existence of the letters 2 John is mentioned with 1 John may be taken as supporting evidence of this view.

The situation of 3 John may throw some light on this. First, 3 John is addressed to an individual named Gaius (3 John 1). In addition to Gaius, the Elder mentions Diotrephes (3 John 9), who appears to have some authority in the situation to which the Elder writes. Then there is Demetrios (3 John 12), whom the Elder commends to Gaius. Other unnamed messengers are mentioned (3 John 3-4), and loyal members of each local community are referred to as "friends" (3 John 15); compare the references to the "children" in 2 John 1, 13. The "friends" where Gaius is are to be saluted, not only by the Elder but also by the "friends" associated with him.

Gaius, apparently referred to by the Elder as one of "my children," seems to be a protegé of the Elder (3 John 4). While that alone might explain the letter, it could be that Gaius was the leader of a house church. It seems that he has provided hospitality for traveling missionaries (3 John 5-8). Given that Diotrephes, who was also leader of a house church, refused hospitality and intimidated those who offered it, Gaius manifests some independence of him. Evidently he does not belong to the same house church. Then there is Demetrios (3 John 12), who has a universal testimony, including that of the Elder. Obviously this inclusive claim is something of an overstatement, but it is implied that this testimony is to the good character and conduct of Demetrios. Probably the report of this testimony is to encourage the provision of hospitality for him in the event of his visit. It is also in direct confrontation with the policy of Diotrephes.

The Elder indicates, "I wrote something to the church" (3 John 9). To what does he refer? And how are we to understand "the church" to which he wrote? Given that 2 John is addressed to the Elect Lady, understood as referring to "the church," could this be a reference to 2 John? Less obvious yet more compelling is the suggestion that the reference includes 1 John, with 2 John as a covering letter. If this is right, "the church" for which 1 John was written seems to include a wider audience than that of 3 John. It appears to encompass the circle of churches under the influence of the Elder, including his own house church that, if in Ephesus, might involve a rather large group. The writer of 3 John (v. 10) indicates that Diotrephes puts out of the church those who do not submit to his decision to refuse hospitality to the brethren. The scope of "the church" in this context must be more limited. Though written for a wider audience than the church in which Diotrephes exercised authority, 1 John was also written for that church.

# 2 JOHN

## OUTLINE OF 2 JOHN

1. Prescript
   a. Address and Commendation (1-2)
   b. Greeting (3)

2. Body of the letter (4-11)
   a. The mark of a genuine Christian life (4-6)
   b. Warning against the teaching of the opponents (7-11)

3. Notice of intention to visit (12)

4. Final greetings (13)

While 2 John is made up of 1126 letters and 245 words, C. H. Dodd notes (*The Johannine Epistles* lxi) that it is made up of only 84 different words, about 20 of which are insignificant terms like "the," "and," and "not." Of the remaining sixty-four significant words, two are found only in 2 John (the feminine form *kyria*, "Lady," and *chartēs*, "paper"); one is common to 2 and 3 John (*melas*, "ink"), and one is common to 1 and 2 John ("Antichrist"). Another nine are found also in more than one of the other Johannine writings, and sixteen are in the Fourth Gospel but not 1 John. Given its different character or genre from the Gospel and 1 John, this makes 2 John a strikingly Johannine letter. The language of 2 John is much closer to the Gospel and 1 John than the language of 3 John. Yet the language and content of 2 John are close to 3 John, thus connecting 3 John to the Gospel and 1 John.

It is noteworthy that the manner of the Elder's address to his readers changes in the course of the letter. At the opening he addresses himself to the Elect Lady and her children in the third person (v. 1). The problem of a singular and plural form of address is overcome initially by joining the addressees to himself (and others?) in the first person plural, "us" (v. 2-3). In vv. 4-5 the Elder addresses the Lady directly, using second person singular pronouns, "your" and "you." But in v. 6 the Elder addresses his readers directly, using the second person plural, and this continues to the end of v. 12. From the beginning to this point the Elder has been writing in his own name, though it is not clear if his use of the first person plural includes with the Elder those to whom he writes, or others who join him in addressing his readers, or both. The possibility that others join him in addressing the readers is raised by the concluding greeting. Here the Elder does not write in his own name. Rather he writes in the third person plural, passing on the greeting from "the children of *your* elect sister" (v. 13). Thus he also returns to the second person singular in addressing the Lady directly. What is surprising is that there is no mention of her children in this final greeting as there was in the opening greeting. It is also surprising that the children of the elect sister send greetings but there is no greeting from the sister herself.

# TRANSLATION, NOTES, INTERPRETATION

## 1. PRESCRIPT (1-3)

1. The Elder to the Elect Lady and her children, whom I love in truth, and not only I but also all who know the truth, 2. because of the truth that abides with us and will be with us forever. 3. Grace, mercy, peace will be with us from God [the] Father, and from Jesus Christ the Son of the Father, in truth and love.

Formally 2 John conforms to the format of a Hellenistic personal letter. The opening formula includes both address and a greeting. Typically this pattern was "From A to B, greetings." What puts in question its recognition as a personal letter is the lack of the name of the sender and the suspicion that the person addressed is a symbol for a church, perhaps even adapted to represent several churches individually in a local network of house churches.

## a. *Form of address and commendation* (1-2)

### NOTES

1. *The Elder to the Elect Lady and her children, whom I love in truth, and not only I but also all who know the truth:* The Elder initially addresses himself to his readers in the third person (v. 1). The adjective *eklektos* is used only here (and v. 13) in the Johannine Epistles. There is a contested reading in John 1:34 where "the elect of God" has minority support against "the Son of God." Both 𝔓⁶⁶ 𝔓⁷⁵ have *huios*, and *eklektos* is not used elsewhere in John. Revelation 17:14 describes the called and the elect and the faithful (all in the nominative plural) with the triumphant Lamb. The term is somewhat characteristic of 1 Peter (1:1; 2:4, 6, 9). The verb "to choose" is used in John 6:70, 71; 13:18; 15:16, 19.

   "Whom I love in truth" might be understood as a reference to children only. If the Elect Lady is the church, then the church is the sum of the members (the children) among whom the truth dwells. The relative pronoun *(hous)* is masculine accusative plural, while the Elect Lady is feminine and the children neuter. The use of a neuter term removes any reference to the gender of the persons so described. Compare the reference to Gaius in 3 John 1, "whom I love in truth."

   "All who know the truth" resonates with the language of John 8:32, where "you will know the truth" is held out as a future hope. A different verb is used in 1 John 2:21. The exaggeration is less marked if used of the church.

2. *because of the truth that abides with us and will be with us for ever:* In vv. 2-3 the first person plural "us" might include the addressees with the Elder or others associated with the Elder in writing (see v. 13), or both. The assurance that the truth "will be with us forever" is similar to the promise that the Spirit "will be with you forever" (John 14:16).

### INTERPRETATION

The first two verses constitute a single sentence in which the sender identifies himself and the addressees. The sender's identification is made simply by use of the title, "the Elder." While titles are often used in official letters, the omission of any name is unusual. In the New Testament only 2 and 3 John use a title but no name. The use of name with title is normal in the NT. Only in 1 and 2 Thessalonians, where Silvanus and Timothy (without titles) are joined with him as joint senders, does Paul use his name without a title. Thus the identification of the sender as *the* unnamed Elder is striking. The suggestion that the name of the Elder has dropped out of the text (Eduard Schwartz, *Über den Tod der Söhne Zebedaei. Ein Beitrag zur Geschichte des Johannesevangeliums* 52) is not convincing, especially as the Elect Lady and her children are also unnamed.

The reference to the Elder can be taken broadly in several ways. First, it could refer to the age of the sender. A teacher writing to his students might be referred to affectionately by them as "the old man" and might even refer to himself in these terms when writing to them. If we had only to deal with 3 John, addressed to the beloved Gaius, we might need to take this suggestion seriously. A case could be made for understanding Gaius as a pupil of the Elder. 2 John rather excludes this approach.

This brings us to a second understanding of "the Elder." It cannot be in the sense of "the elders" referred to in Acts such as those in the Jerusalem church or those appointed by Paul (and Barnabas): Acts 11:30; 15:2, 4, 6, 22, 23; 16:4; 20:17; 21:18. Acts refers to elders, but to no singular Elder (*the* Elder). We have something quite different in 2 John 1 (and 3 John 1).

Then there is the suggestion that "Elder" signals the role of the monarchical bishop. But the Elder does not write as one having ecclesiastical authority. Rather he appeals to the tradition in which he and his readers stand. Along similar lines, but reversing the argument somewhat, Ernst Käsemann argues that Diotrephes was the bishop (3 John 9-10) who had excommunicated the Elder and his followers for heresy. The heresy is to be found in what Käsemann argued is the gnosticising teaching of the Gospel of John and 1 John ("Ketzer und Zeuge," *ZThK* 48 [1951], 293–311). Käsemann's position is dependent on his gnosticising interpretation of John, which has received little support, and the assumption of the common authorship of the Gospel and Epistles, both of which Käsemann himself came to question.

The suggestion that readers would have recognized "John the Elder" of Asia Minor mentioned by Papias is hardly convincing (see Eusebius, *Hist. Eccl.* 3.39.3-4, 7, 14, 15; 5.8.8. Compare also Irenaeus, *Adv. Haer.* 1.8.17; 3.36.1; 4.47.1; 4.49.1; 5.33.3; 5.36). Both Papias and Irenaeus mention elders, but it is not clear from Papias that he locates John the Elder in Asia Minor. Because both Irenaeus and Papias speak of a plurality of elders, "the Elder" is hardly a clear indication of John the Elder. It would have been an easy matter to ensure accurate identification by the use of the full identification "John the Elder." Judith Lieu concludes: "That Papias's Elders are relevant to an understanding of the author of 2 and 3 John is therefore highly doubtful" (*Second and Third John* 63). The famous passage from Papias contains all of the problems that provoked C. H. Dodd to conclude:

> We must confess that we do not know who our Presbyter was. It does not greatly matter. He has left us a recognizable self-portrait in his three epistles. If we cannot affix a famous name to the portrait, we know what manner of man he was, what he taught about faith and duty, and what part he played at a critical moment in the history of the Church. (*The Johannine Epistles* lxxi)

The Elder of 2 and 3 John gives no indication of his name. We need to ascertain as precisely as possible what was meant by the use of "the Elder." Certainly "the Elder" implies a distinctive role of leadership even if that role was challenged in some quarters. What did this mean to the readers of 2 and 3 John? Clearly he is not just "the old man." Nor does he speak as one of a group of elders. Rather he addresses his readers as *the* Elder. By so naming himself he claims a unique authority, but it is clear that his authority works as a vantage point from which he may persuade his readers. He does so, first, by uniting himself with all those who know the truth, speaking in the first person plural "we." This is somewhat different from the "we" of 1 John 1:1-4, where the author joins with other authoritative transmitters of the tradition. The latter is analogous to what we might expect from the elders of Asia Minor.

If the addressee is named *(eklektę kyrią)* we may understand either "to the lady Electa" (Clement of Alexandria) or "to the elect Kyria." Though each of these is theoretically possible, only Kyria is a well-attested name, and Rom 16:13 provides precedent for reference to a name with the epithet "elect" *(Rhouphon ton elekton)*. As indicated by the example in Romans, we would expect the article with this form *(tę eklektę kyrią)*. Thus there are grammatical problems with the suggestion that *kyrią* here is a proper name.

The letter is addressed to this lady and *her* children. The form of address is in the third person. The lady seems to have many children (v. 4), and reference there is in the second person, to *"your* children," as it is when the Elder sends farewell salutations from "the children of *your* elect sister" (v. 13). The opening address in the third person is strange if the addressee is an individual woman who has children. Further, at the end of the letter there is no salutation from the sister, only from her children! That would be strange if the Elect Lady and her sister were individual women. The language of vv. 1-3 and 13 is more appropriate to greetings passed between sister communities (churches). If cities and their inhabitants can be addressed in terms of a woman and her children (Isaiah 54; 55; Baruch 4; 5), there is good precedent for understanding the Elect Lady and her children in terms of a church and its members. Perhaps 1 Pet 5:13 provides a useful parallel to the salutation in 2 John 13.

Neither "the Elder" nor any of the people addressed in 2 John is named. Even those in whose name the Elder brings greetings are not named (v. 13).

Thus it is not surprising that the two elect sisters are understood to be local churches whose children are individual members. The main question then is whether the church addressed is one particular local church or whether 2 John might perhaps be a circular letter from the local church in which the Elder was a leading member to the network of churches in which he exercised influence. Perhaps these were churches that had been established by a mission radiating out from the Elder's church.

The form of address now establishes the nature of the relationship between the Elder and those he addresses. A key word ("the *truth*") is introduced and occurs four times in the first three verses. This confirms that the adverbial interpretation of the first use in v. 1 ("whom I love in truth") does not exhaust its meaning. While this means in the first place "whom I truly love," the assertion also signals the authenticity of the love as that which comes from God, not the false (counterfeit) love that comes from the world. Authentic love arises from the truth that is known. That truth is the gospel which, as a message, bears witness to the love of God revealed in Jesus. This love establishes the Elder in a position of favor.

But the love of the children of the Elect Lady is not confined to the Elder alone. This draws attention to the source of this love. All who know the truth love the children of the Elect Lady. This seems to be an exaggerated claim if it is made concerning a particular lady and her children. It seems extreme even with reference to a local church unless we think that the Elder restricted those who know the truth to a particular group of his own supporters. Alternatively, we might reduce the particularity by taking the symbolism to mean something similar to what we find in 1 John 4:21; 5:1-2. If believers are begotten by God they should love each other as brothers and sisters. Does 2 John extend and change the image by describing different local churches as sisters so that those who know the truth in different communities are cousins who love one another? (See v. 13.)

Those who know the truth do so "*because* of the truth that abides with us" (v. 2). The Elder includes those addressed when he refers to "the truth that abides *with* us." This formulation allows the Elder to deny that those who are opposed to him know the truth.

Two different prepositions are used in v. 2. The Elder refers to the truth abiding with us *(en hēmin)*, which will be with us *(meth' hēmōn)* forever. It is the different tenses that are important rather than the prepositions. The Elder affirms that the truth that abides with us now will abide with us forever. In the changing prepositions there is no sense of a developing or greater relationship with the truth. The lives of those who know the truth of the gospel are shaped by the truth enshrined in the gospel, which is "the truth."

## b. *Greeting* (3)

### NOTES

3. *Grace, mercy, peace will be with us from God [the] Father, and from Jesus Christ the Son of the Father, in truth and love:* The common Pauline formula is twofold as in Rom 1:7, "Grace to you and peace from *(apo)* God our Father and the Lord Jesus Christ." (See also 1 Cor 1:3; 2 Cor 1:2; Gal 1:3; Phil 1:2.) This formula is also found in 2 Thess 1:2; Titus 1:4; 1 Pet 1:2; 2 Pet 1:2. As is commonly noted, this blessing combines the Greek "grace" with the Hebrew "peace," *Shalom*, joining West and East, Gentile and Jew. The threefold blessing introduces a third term, "mercy."

   The formula greeting of 2 John is very similar to 1–2 Timothy, but differs in a number of ways. 2 John repeats the theme of "it will be with us" from v. 2, and the ending that adds to the reference to Jesus Christ the words "the Son of the Father, in truth and love." These can be seen as Johannine expansions. In 1–2 Timothy the blessing is not explicitly addressed to anyone, though it is an implied blessing to the readers. In John the blessing is in the form of an affirmation, "will be with *us*." Not surprisingly some texts read "will be with *you*." This is certainly a scribal error. The first person plural "us" is a continuation from v. 2.

   Within the formula, John differs from 1–2 Timothy in the use of the preposition *para* and not *apo,* and in the repetition of the preposition before reference to Jesus Christ, who is spoken of as "Christ Jesus our Lord" in 1–2 Timothy. Perhaps under the influence of 1–2 Timothy, some texts add *"Lord"* or *"our Lord* Jesus Christ" to the Johannine formula. While the textual evidence is somewhat confused, "Lord" is far more likely to be an addition than an accidental omission.

   The characterization of Jesus Christ as "the Son of the Father" is distinctively Johannine. The Father/Son relationship is featured in the Gospel of John. In John it begins (1:14) with the relationship of "the only begotten (unique one) from the Father" *(monogenous para patros).* See also 1:18, where the reference is to the "only begotten God who is the bosom of the Father." Textual variants include the presence or absence of the definite article, *"the* only begotten . . . ," "the only begotten Son," "the only begotten Son of God," and "the only begotten." The last of these has the advantage of agreeing with 1:14, but is weakly attested by some Vulgate and patristic references. From a manuscript point of view the choice is between "the only begotten Son" and "the only begotten God." It is difficult to see what difference the presence or absence of the definite article makes in this case because even without the article the translation of *monogenēs* as *"an* only begotten" does not seem possible. In favor of "only begotten Son" is the context of the "bosom of the Father." But this could explain an editorial change. On the other hand, "only begotten God" is implied by John 1:1, which affirms *kai theos ēn ho logos.* Perhaps this too might explain an editorial change, though the affirmation of the divinity of the revealer at the beginning and end of the Prologue might be a feature of compositional design.

Nevertheless, it is clear that John thinks of Jesus as the only begotten Son of God (3:16, and see 1 John 4:9). The Father/Son relationship is a feature of the discourses in John, especially in those sayings in which Jesus refers to the Father as the one who sent "me" or sent "the Son" or "his Son." See my *The Quest for the Messiah* 224–49. In 1 John, Jesus' relation to God is as God's Son (1:3, 7; 4:10, 14; 5:9, 10, 11, 20), Son of God (4:15; 5:5, 10, 12), the only begotten Son (4:9). In one place reference is made to abiding "in the Son and in the Father" (2:24). This is as close as 1 John comes to describing Jesus as "the Son of the Father." Yet, so frequent is reference to the Father and the Son that "Son of the Father" is implied, though not stated in so many words.

In the Johannine writings, unlike the Pauline letters, believers are not called sons of God. This terminology is restricted to Jesus in the singular form. When believers are spoken of they are described as "children of God" *(tekna theou)*: 1 John 3:1-2, 10; 5:2. The author of 1 John also refers to believers as his children (2:1, 28; 3:7, 18, and compare 2 John 1, 13).

## INTERPRETATION

In the Hellenistic letter the good health wish follows at this point. Because the truth, which already abides with us, will be with those (us) who know the truth forever (v. 2), the Elder's greeting takes the form of a blessing, not a wish. Because the truth is already present, grace, mercy, and peace are also present and are promised for the future as well. The presence of grace, mercy, and peace is grounded in the abiding truth.

The same threefold greeting is to be found in 1–2 Timothy. The formula is used identically in both places and with small variations from 2 John. There (1–2 Timothy) it is "Grace, mercy, peace from God [the] Father and Christ Jesus our Lord." In 2 John, picking up the idiom of "the truth *will be with us*," the Elder writes: "Grace, mercy, peace *will be with us* from God [the] Father, and from Jesus Christ the Son of the Father, in truth and love."

Though it is known only here in John, we have evidence of a stereotypical threefold blessing, as is evidenced by 1–2 Timothy. In the Greek of 2 John the affirmation "it will be with us," a repetition from v. 2, comes at the beginning of the sentence in v. 3. The words that follow, "grace, mercy, peace from God [the] Father and from Jesus Christ . . ." are close to the wording of 1–2 Timothy. In this part of the blessing the only differences are: (1) The preposition in 1–2 Timothy, and normally in Paul in this formula *(apo)*, differs from 2 John *(para)*; (2) It is repeated (in 2 John) before the Son as well as the Father, stressing the twofold source of grace, mercy, and peace; (3) 1–2 Timothy use the distinctive Pauline variation "Christ

Jesus" in place of the more normal "Jesus Christ" found in 2 John; (4) 1–2 Timothy add "our Lord," and this might have influenced the textual tradition of 2 John where some texts add *"Lord* Jesus Christ," others *"our Lord* Jesus Christ."

*Grace, mercy, peace:* "Grace" *(charis)* at this point in the letter suggests the Greek greeting normally expressed with the verb *chairein*. It occurs nowhere else in the Johannine Epistles and only at 1:14, 16, 17 in the Gospel. Following the Prologue, the language of grace in the Gospel is replaced by the language of love. The language of grace describes the foundation of all gifts in the graciousness of God. Love also can describe this (John 3:16), but it is characteristically used to describe the mutuality of the relationship between the Father and the Son and between believers who are to love one another (see my *John, Witness and Theologian* 92–100). This is true also in 2 John. The words that follow in the blessing suggest that "grace" here has a more significant meaning.

Mercy *(eleos)* appears nowhere else in the Johannine literature. In the LXX this term is used in a way that overlaps with *charis* to translate Hebrew words including *ḥesed*. The introduction of "mercy" might be understood as an indication of a more significant use of "grace" than is common in a simple greeting. This understanding is supported by the only other uses of *charis* in the Johannine literature (John 1:14, 16, 17). See Rudolf Bultmann, *The Gospel of John* 74 nn. 1, 2, and idem, ἔλεος, κτλ., *TDNT* 2:477–87, at 483–85.

Peace *(eirēnē)* occurs six times in the Passion and resurrection narratives in the Gospel and nowhere else in the Epistles. See John 14:27; 16:33; 20:19, 21, 26. These three words, which are not otherwise found in the Johannine Epistles, are joined with the Johannine terms "in truth and love." It may be that Jesus Christ is characterized as "the Son of the Father, in truth and love." If we take it in this way we understand the revelation in Jesus to be affirmed as the revelation of the Father. The Son of the Father is a true son of the Father, revealing his character. Consequently the love of the Son can be understood as the love of the Father.

While this is appealing, it is more likely that the final phrase goes with the verb *(estai)*. Taken this way the final phrase implies that grace, mercy, and peace "will be with us in truth and love." They will bring, or produce, truth and love. Where the grace-mercy-and-peace from the Father and from the Son is present (the singular verb *estai* is used), and the blessing affirms *it will be*, the collective presence of grace, mercy, and peace is manifest in truth and love. What makes grace, mercy, and peace present is the abiding presence of the truth. It abides with those who know the truth and is manifest in truth and love. This seems to imply that knowing the truth is a manifestation of the abiding truth. The truth that abides is the gospel, and it is manifest in truth and love, which means the confession of

Jesus Christ coming in the flesh (the true confession) and loving one another (see 2 John 5-7 and 1 John 3:23). At the end this argument looks a little circular. The truth abides with those who know the truth and knowledge of the truth comes from the abiding truth. However we take this, the true confession of faith and love for one another become the twofold test of the claim to know God.

# 2. BODY OF THE LETTER (4-11)

The abiding presence of grace, mercy, peace, terms not used elsewhere in the Epistles, coming from the Father and the Son, is manifest in truth and love. The opening introduces two vital Johannine terms (truth and love). In what follows these two Johannine terms are elaborated in a way that suggests that love is grounded in the truth.

Though the body of the letter opens by speaking about the truth, the first part (vv. 4-6) actually deals with love. The first clue to confirm this is that the Elder speaks of *walking* in truth (see the Notes on v. 1). The notion of "walking" takes "truth" out of the area of ideas and beliefs into the area of action. The second clue is the reference to the commandment received from the Father, which is quickly identified as the command to love one another. But by using the language of truth the Elder has made an inseparable connection between the truth (belief) and action (love). The issue of the truth as the true confession is dealt with in the second part (vv. 7-11).

## a. *The mark of a genuine Christian life* (4-6)

4. I rejoiced greatly because I have found some of your children walking in truth, even as we received commandment from the Father. 5. And now I beg you, Lady, not as writing a new commandment to you but [one] that we have had from the beginning, that we love one another. 6. And this is love, that we walk according to his commandments; this is the commandment, even as you heard from [the] beginning, that you walk in it.

NOTES

4. *I rejoiced greatly because I have found some of your children walking in truth, even as we received commandment from the Father:* The letter now addresses the Lady directly in the second person singular (vv. 4-5) with reference to her children. The letter normally includes a note of praise or thanksgiving at this point. The note here is more in keeping with the Hellenistic letter than is characteristic of the Pauline corpus, where in the opening of eight epistles *chairein* is transformed into thanksgiving to God, using the verb *eucharistein*. See also below on 3 John 3.

The idiom of "walking" as an understanding of living is common in the Epistles (1 John 1:6; 2:6, 11; 3 John 3, 4, etc.). What walking in the truth means is clarified by reference to *doing the truth* in John 3:21. The phrase reveals an author whose idioms are influenced by Semitic language.

On "the commandment" and commandments see vv. 5-6. In this short letter the Elder uses this word four times, a total of almost half as many uses as in the much longer Gospel of John. Here there is mention that "we received commandment from the Father." Compare John 10:18, where Jesus says "this commandment I received from my Father." The notion of receiving a commandment does not occur in 1 John, though the language of commandment(s) is common: 2:3, 4, 7, 8; 3:22, 23, 24; 4:21; 5:2, 3. (Compare also John 10:18; 11:57; 12:49, 50; 13:34; 14:15, 21, 31; 15:10, 12.) 1 John 3:22-24 is especially relevant because of the alternation between "commandment" and "commandments." In 2 John 4-6 the love command is named, leading on to a reference to the commandments before the discussion of the confession of faith in 2 John 7. 1 John 3:23 defines the command in terms of believing and loving.

5. *And now I beg you, Lady, not as writing a new commandment to you but [one] that we have had from the beginning, that we love one another:* Although the Johannine Epistles are full of exhortation, the terms *parakalein* and *paraklēsis* appear nowhere in them. Here the term *erōtō* expresses personal request and entreaty. (See 1 John 5:16, and cf. the use of *aitein* in 1 John 5:14-16; see on 3:22.) The texts in 1 John deal with making requests to God, asking in prayer. The sense of personal request is present in the language of 1 and 2 John. On the contrast of the new and old commandment that is from the beginning see 1 John 2:7.

6. *And this is love, that we walk according to his commandments; this is the commandment, even as you heard from [the] beginning, that you walk in it:* The "we" of v. 6 might or might not include the addressees. If not, it includes others with the Elder in writing the letter (see v. 13).

The opening of v. 6 resonates with 1 John at a number of points. "This is love" *(hautē estin hē agapē):* see 1 John 5:3, "for this is the love of God, that we keep his commandments." Though the two are formally alike (compare 1 John 4:10-11, "In this is love, not that we loved God but that he loved us . . ."), 1 John continues "if God loved us like this, we also should love one another." See also "In this we know love: he laid down his life for us; and we ought to lay down our lives for the brothers" (1 John 3:16). In these texts God's love in giving the Son and the Son's love in laying down his life for us define what love is and create the obligation *(opheilomen)* for us to love one another (the brothers [and sisters]), which is the substance of the commandment. Love is described in terms of action in response to those in need (3:17-18).

INTERPRETATION

The Presbyter notes his rejoicing at finding members of the church to which he was writing walking in the truth (v. 4). Maintaining the form of the letter to the Elect Lady, he refers to them as "your children." Both the perfect tense of the verb "I have found" and the present participle "walking" add weight to the sense that they are continuing to walk in the truth. This is more important than the aorist tense used to describe the Elder's joy. The aorist indicates the event of joy at meeting, while the perfect tense implies that those so found remain as they were then, walking in the truth. The verse indirectly provides evidence of the movement of the Elder and of some of the members of the church to which he writes. In this way they came to meet. This verse implies a Christian *movement* with people crossing each other's paths as they travel around a network of churches. The book of Acts already makes us aware of movements and interaction, and we might also mention the evidence of the *Didache*. Here there is evidence of itinerant ministries supplied by people who travel from one place to the next. So common was the phenomenon that the *Didache* works out rules for dealing with such people.

Still, the mention of having found *some* members of the church walking in the truth looks rather too pointed. It may imply that the Elder has found some others who are not walking in this way (see further on v. 7). If that were not the case, why should he move to introduce the commandment received from the Father? The "commandment from the Father" is puzzling, especially as v. 5 reveals that this is the command to love one another (see John 13:34; 1 John 3:11, but see also 1 John 3:21-23, especially 3:23, which may well refer to God). The probable solution is to see the commandment of the Father delivered by Jesus. Use of the title "Father" for God reminds us that God is revealed in his Son.

Nevertheless, Raymond E. Brown (*The Epistles of John* 661) thinks the Elder would not have called those who had departed from the truth "your children." But if that church continued to recognize such members, it would not have served the Elder's purpose to ignore them. The question rather concerns whether that church was already troubled by the deceivers of v. 7. We may even question whether some of the deceivers had gone out from that church. Whether or not this had happened, it seems certain that the effects of their teaching were evident there.

The Elder now addresses himself directly to his reader (vv. 5-6), calling her "lady" *(kyria)*. The language is personal: "and now *I beg you, Lady*" *(kai nyn erōtō se, kyria)*. The lady is addressed personally, using the second person singular pronoun *(se)*, which returns again in v. 13. In between, the address is second person plural. This change from singular to plural to singular again reflects the reality that the lady is the local church whose reality is to be found in her children. The Elder does not use the language of formal exhortation *(parakalō)*, but of personal entreaty, thus maintaining the idiom of a personal letter even though the lady is an image of the local church. This is appropriate because the Elder understands the church on the analogy of the intimacy of the family (compare 1 John 5:1-3).

The author's rather tangled style is evident in these verses. Having begun to address a request to his reader, he interrupts the request to interject that he is writing no new command but the original one, "that we have had from the beginning." This may be simply a play on the Gospel tradition in which the love command is called "a new commandment" (John 13:34-35). From the perspective of this letter, that command goes back to the origin of the Johannine tradition. It is foundational tradition, not innovation (2 John 9), no new command. Here 2 John is closely connected to 1 John 2:7, 24.

What love is now takes the attention of the Elder. If the commandment is the command to love one another, love is to walk according to the commandment of the Father. Yet his commandment (v. 6) looks back to "the commandment we received from the Father" (v. 4). Reiteration that "we have had this commandment from the beginning" (v. 5), "even as you heard from the beginning" (v. 6) helps to clarify the meaning of "the beginning." It must refer to the original communication of the (Johannine) tradition in that church, perhaps even the event through which the church was established. The command of v. 5 is said to be "that we love one another," and in v. 6 the command seems to be "that you walk in it." But this is probably not right. Rather, when the elder says "This is the commandment, just as you heard from the beginning" we are turned back to v. 5 where we learn that the command is "that we love one another." The last clause of v. 6 looks like a statement of the command. It is a *hina* clause followed by the subjunctive, just like the last clause of v. 5 which defines the old command as "that we love one another." This is confusing. But the content of the command in v. 6 is "what you heard from the beginning," thus referring back to v. 5. The double emphasis of the opening ("that we walk") as well as the last clause of v. 6, "that you walk in it," provide a reminder that love is not just words or feelings. It involves actions (see 1 John 3:17-18). We may now outline the argument of vv. 5-6:

> The original commandment is "that we love one another."
> Love is "that we walk according to his commandments" (plural).
> The commandment (singular) is the original command, "that we love one another."

To this the Elder again adds the reminder "that you walk in it" to emphasize that love involves compassionate action to those in need.

The very complicated path to get to the command: "Love one another," suggests that this command had become problematic. However tangled and fuzzy in detail this might look, the Elder has heavily stressed practice, "that we *walk* . . . that you *walk*. . . ." It is also evident that in this letter, and 1 John 2:7, 24; 3:11; 5:3, as distinct from John 13:34, the command is not from Jesus but from the Father (God); the command is not new, but from the beginning. It is, however, the command "love one another" that, in the Gospel (13:34), Jesus calls his new commandment. In John, Jesus is the emissary of the Father, so that the command comes from the Father. Just why it had become important to insist that the command was not new but from the beginning, a foundational command, not a command from Jesus but from the Father, from God, is nowhere *explicitly* explained. Probably this is because the community had been established on the basis of this commandment, so that it was no innovation for them. Because of the christological controversy it was important to ground the command in God.

## b. *Warning against the teaching of the opponents* (7-11)

7. Because many deceivers have gone into the world, who do not confess Jesus Christ coming in the flesh; this person is the Deceiver and the Antichrist. 8. Watch yourselves, that you do not lose what we have worked for, but you receive a full reward. 9. Anyone going beyond and not abiding in the teaching of Christ does not have God; the one abiding in the teaching, this person also has the Father and the Son. 10. If anyone comes to you and he does not bear this teaching, do not receive him into [your] house and do not speak a greeting to him, 11. for the one speaking a greeting to him has fellowship with his evil works.

### NOTES

7. *Because many deceivers have gone into the world, who do not confess Jesus Christ coming in the flesh; this person is the Deceiver and the Antichrist:* On the appearance of the Deceiver(s) and the Antichrist see 1 John 2:18; 4:1, 3. On the language of confession *(homologein)* see John 9:22; 12:42; 1 John 2:23; 4:2-3, 15; 2 John 7.

   The true confession in 1 John concerns "Jesus Christ having come *(elēly-thota)* in flesh," 4:2. There a perfect participle is used, while 2 John 7 employs a present participle *(erchomenon)*. The question is whether there is any difference of meaning between the two formulations. There are broadly three positions: (1) The two texts have the same meaning, referring to the Incarnation. (2) The present tense of the participle must be taken seriously, so that what is affirmed in the confession is the real presence of Christ in the Eucharist, a view supported by a sacramental interpretation of John 6:53-54 and 1 John 5:6. But there is no sign of this controversy in 2–3 John. (3) Georg Strecker (*The Johannine Letters* 234–36) argues that here the present participle has a future meaning. He argues for a *chiliastic* interpretation that involves a thousand-year reign of Christ on earth. Strecker draws attention to hints of this in Rev 20:1-3 and 1 Cor 15:23-24. Certainly something like this was supposed by the Montanist movement, though we have little direct evidence of what they believed.

Strecker dismisses the possibility that 2 John 7 should be understood in relation to 1 John 4:2-3. The present participle in 2 John excludes this possibility for him because the perfect participle is used in 1 John 4:2.

8. *Watch yourselves, that you do not lose what we have worked for, but you receive a full reward:* The Elder now addresses his readers (the Elect Lady and her children) in the second person plural. This form of address continues through v. 12.

In 1 John 2:18 the appearance of the Antichrist is a signal that it is the last hour. Hence the warning: "Watch yourselves"; see Mark 13:5, 9.

There is a nice literary touch in the double purpose (negative and positive) of the two clauses governed by *hina*, "that you do not lose *(mē apolesēte)* . . . but you receive *(alla . . . apolabēte)."*

There is textual confusion over whether we should read "for what you have worked" *(ha eirgasasthe),* which we might expect, or "for what we have worked" *(ha eirgasametha).* Because the former is expected, it is more likely to have been introduced and is probably a secondary reading. If that is the case, this text provides support for the idea that the Elder had established the church to which he now was writing. On the language of receiving a reward *(misthon . . . apolabēte)* see John 4:36 *(misthon lambanei).*

9. *Anyone going beyond and not abiding in the teaching of Christ does not have God; the one abiding in the teaching, this person also has the Father and the Son:* For "everyone" *(pas)* see on 1 John 2:23. This is a characteristic expression in 1 John, found in 2:16, 23, 29; 3:3, 4, 6, 9, 10, 15, and cf. 4:2, 3, 7; 5:1, 2, 17, 18.

Reference to those "going beyond . . . the teaching of Christ" is subject to some textual confusion, suggesting that the early copyists were not sure how to deal with *proagōn.* Most modern commentators take this to mean that the false teachers were "progressives" or "modernists." In 2 Tim 3:13 the term *prokopsousin* is used alongside *planein.* Such a group is deceiving and being deceived. See Gustav Stählin, *prokoptein, TDNT* 6:703–19. The use of *proagōn* in *Gospel of the Egyptians (N.H.* IV 41.7-8) provides evidence of Gnostic use, but in the sense of "to emanate." Thus the use in 2 John 9 is probably not Gnostic. But this does not preclude the use of the term by the Elder to designate the troublemakers. It is not necessary to suggest that the term represents the self-designation of the group. It is much more likely a designation by the Elder.

Remaining (or "abiding") is a key Johannine term describing the believer's relation with Jesus (John 6:56; 15:4-7; 1 John 2:6, 24, 27) and with God (1 John 2:24). On the expression "remaining in the teaching of Christ" compare John 8:31, "If you remain in my word." For the expression "has the Father" see 1 John 2:23.

10. *If anyone comes to you and he does not bear this teaching, do not receive him into [your] house and do not speak a greeting to him:* On "does not bear" *(ou pherei)* see John 18:29.

11. *for the one speaking a greeting to him has fellowship with his evil works:* In the Johannine literature only 2 John uses the verb *koinōneō* and only 1 John uses the noun *koinōnia.* In 1 John the verbal sense of *koinōneō* is expressed using the noun *koinōnia* with *echō*; see 1:3, 6, 7. 2 John deals with participation in evil deeds, not fellowship between people. The evidence of these differences in language is too slim to justify a theory of the independent authorship of 1 and 2 John. Perhaps the best comparison with the use of *koinōnei* in 2 John 11 is found in 1 Tim 5:22, "Do not share *(mēde koinōnei)* in another man's sins."

The language about "his *evil* deeds *(works)*," referring to the teacher who does not bear the Elder's teaching about Christ, links this critique to the criticism of Diotrephes in 3 John 10. There the Elder criticizes not only his deeds *(works)* but also his *evil* words. Strecker *(The Johannine Letters* 264) rightly believes Diotrephes to have departed from the Elder's teaching of Christ as expressed in 2 John 7.

### INTERPRETATION

Judith Lieu, *Second and Third John* 78, rightly concludes that "It would be difficult to understand this verse (7) without a knowledge of 1 John, and particularly 1 John 2:18ff. and 4:1f." This provides an eschatological context for the discussion. Here, as elsewhere, the relationship between 1 John and 2 John does not seem to be the result of a second author copying a first. There is too much freedom taken with the material. More likely the author is revisiting themes treated earlier.

The Elder turns to the issue of many deceivers *(planoi)* who have gone out *(exēlthon)* into the world. At the end of this verse the deceiver (singular) is identified with the Antichrist.

On the Antichrist see Wilhelm Bousset, *The Antichrist Legend*, and Georg Strecker, "Excursus: The Antichrist," *The Johannine Epistles* 236–41, and the Excursus, "The Antichrist," above in this volume. The term occurs in the NT only in 2 John 7 and 1 John 2:18, 22; 4:3. Early patristic use is dependent on 1 John (Polycarp, *Phil.* 7:1). The Antichrist is opposed to Christ and is a Satanic or diabolical manifestation. The Johannine identification of the Antichrist with deceivers (2 John 7) meant that Antichrists could be recognized in human persons (1 John 2:18-19) such as false prophets (4:1). Mark

13 suggests that Dan 7:25; 8:11, 13, 25; 9:27; 12:1, 11 may have been important in the formation of an Antichrist myth. See the early evidence of 2 Thess 2:4 and later of Rev 13:1-11, which draws on Daniel 7. Thus the probability is that the Elder draws on Jewish and earlier Jewish Christian tradition, so that what is said about the Antichrist here is but the tip of the iceberg of tradition that lies submerged by the drifts of time. Whether or not the Elder coined the term to focus the tradition in a critical fashion we may never know. There is evidence of a diffuse and influential tradition upon which he draws here, and its Jewish sectarian character is attested by 4Q243. Here it is said that the opponent will be worshiped by all as the Son of God and Son of the Most High. Yet it is probable that tradition contained reference to the Antichrist because 1 and 2 John retain the use of the singular form although they wish to use it of a group of false teachers whom 1 John designates as Antichrists and Deceivers.

Reference to deceivers, and the Deceiver who is identified as the Antichrist, immediately calls attention to the relationship of 2 John 7 to 1 John 2:18-26, especially 18-19, 22-23, 26; cf. 4:3. In these passages we have the only references to Antichrist in the New Testament. They are also connected by reference to deceivers (and the deceiver) in 2 John and "those who would deceive you" in 1 John 2:26 as well as the expansion and contraction from singular Antichrist to plural antichrists in 1 John 2:18 and from plural to singular Deceiver, who is identified as the Antichrist, in 2 John 7.

1 John 2:18 identifies the last hour by the presence of many antichrists. But it did not always appear in this light. The Antichrist is identified with those who went out from the community: "they went out from us because they were not of us . . ." (2:19). The Antichrist is described as "the liar who denies that Jesus is the Christ," which entails "the denial of the Father and the Son" (2:22-23). This implies that what is denied is the relationship of the Son to the Father as taught in 1 John. The same phenomenon is described as many false prophets who have gone out into the world. They are detected by their refusal to confess Jesus Christ come in the flesh. This refusal is inspired by the spirit of the Antichrist (4:1-3).

What made the movement confronted by 1 John so dangerous is that "they *went out* from us . . ." (2:19). This language resonates with 2 John 7, "many deceivers *went out* into the world." In both cases it seems that the deceivers were once part of the community. They went out, separating themselves from the Elder and his supporters. From the Elder's perspective, having separated themselves they have gone into the world. The aorist tense of the verb (*exēlthon*) suggests a particular crisis, a schism. If 2 John is a circular letter introducing 1 John to a network of churches it is possible that the deceivers went out from one or some of these, hence the description of their *going out*. Other communities might expect a visit from the deceivers (see v. 10).

In both 2 John 7 and 1 John 4:3 the deceivers, antichrist(s), are identified by their failure to make a true confession of faith. In 2 John 7 "those not *confessing (hoi mē homologountes)* Jesus Christ coming *(erchomenon)* in flesh" are identified as the Deceiver and the Antichrist. 1 John 4:1-3 asserts that "many false prophets have gone out into the world." The spirit that inspires them does not confess *(ho mē homologei)* Jesus Christ having come *(elēlythota)* in flesh, but is of the Antichrist (4:2-3). The circle closes around false prophets who are deceivers and inspired by the spirit of the Antichrist. The multiple phenomena of many false prophets (4:1) or many deceivers (2 John 7), who are all inspired by the spirit of the Antichrist who is the Deceiver, are common to 1 and 2 John (v. 7). But because the spirit of the Antichrist inspires many false prophets (1 John 4:1), 1 John can also speak of many antichrists (2:18).

Evidently the emphasis on the love command in vv. 5-6 was also "because many deceivers have gone out into the world . . ." (v. 7). The opening of this sentence, "because . . ." *(hoti)* connects v. 7 to vv. 5-6, the problem of the deceivers, the Antichrist to the need to stress the application of the love command. Interestingly, 2 John 5-6 does not suggest that the deceivers denied the love command. Apparently they interpreted it in such a way that they did not live (walk) by it. The failure to live by the commandment is linked to the failure to confess Jesus Christ coming in the flesh. This is not surprising in the light of 1 John 3:16. Here the love command is grounded in and defined by Jesus' loving action in giving himself for us.

If 2 John is a circular letter accompanying 1 John, and introducing the main points of 1 John to a circle of churches, each of which is addressed as "the Elect Lady and her children," the Elder would have been uncertain about the reception to be offered to the deceivers. Almost certainly, sympathizers remained within the circle of churches. How they thought of the Elder's opponents is unclear.

The appearance of the Deceiver, the Antichrist is the signal that it is the last hour; see 1 John 2:18. The warning "Watch out for yourselves" (v. 8) fits this eschatological context; compare Mark 13:5, 9, 23. The Elder's concern is that his readers should not lose their reward. On the textual confusion here see the Notes. If we are right in accepting reference to "that for which we have worked," the author implies his own work in establishing the community. Yet they are separate from his own community, suggesting that we have evidence of a mission from one main center into the surrounding areas. Reference to receiving the "full reward" suggests that we are not here dealing with eternal life, which can hardly be had in part. It may be relevant to note the notion of unworthy work *(ergon)* being burned in the fire of judgment, though the person is saved through fire. (See 1 Cor 3:10-15.)

Verse 9 has more in common with 1 John 2:23 than the expression "has the Father." 1 John is dealing with the person who denies the Son and teaches that this person does not have the Father, while the one who confesses the Son has the Father also. 2 John deals with the person who does not abide in the teaching *of Christ*. This person does not have God, while the one who abides in the teaching has the Father and the Son. Crucial here is the meaning of the teaching *of Christ*. There is nothing to suggest that the Elder is appealing to the teaching of Jesus (if we take *of Christ* as a subjective genitive). Rather, since the letter has just dealt with the christology of the true confession, we must understand this to mean what this letter (and 1 John) teaches *about* Christ (an objective genitive). The true confession of faith in Jesus Christ coming in the flesh (see v. 7) is the key to having the Father and the Son.

Given that this letter was addressed to a circle of churches, the deceivers went out from some of them and were likely to arrive in others. Hence the warning, "If anyone comes . . ." (vv. 10-11). That the Elder and his supporters traveled about establishing churches is clear. We now learn that the deceivers also traveled, and their appearance among the churches established by the Elder was anticipated. The connection of vv. 6-7 by *hoti* suggests that the christological problem is linked to the failure to walk according to the commandment to love one another. But the warning comes concerning those who do not bear "this teaching," this christology.

The instruction given here is to be understood against the background of hospitality given to strangers and travelers in the ancient world. It was especially important in Jesus' mission. The instruction given to the Twelve at their commissioning probably reflects Jesus' own practice (see Mark 6:10-11). Hospitality continued to be an important means of mission for the early church. Against this background the instruction by the Elder is startling. Those who do not conform to the teaching of this letter are to be refused hospitality and to be sent on their way without a greeting. (See the evidence of *Did.* 11:1-2.) In 2 John this injunction not only precludes admission of such teachers into the context of the house church, it excludes the possibility of fundamental hospitality. Even a greeting *(chairein)* involves a participation *(koinōnei)* with them in their false teaching. Interestingly, *chairein* is the word used in the normal Hellenistic letter greeting. In this letter the Elder used in its place the word *charis*, which was part of distinctively Christian greetings (see on v. 3 above). Thus the Elder excludes even a secular greeting for such people.

Commentators often note the un-Christian nature of such a teaching and practice. But this instruction does not concern a response to the poor or needy. It is a policy to refuse aid to a rival mission that, in the view of the Elder, was deceived and deceiving in its work. To aid what the Elder evaluated as "evil works" was to participate in the deception and its destructive consequences. Few people will give aid to causes they consider to be misguided and destructive or evil in their consequences. Compare the equally rigorous instruction of Ignatius to the Christians in Smyrna concerning their relationship with docetic heretics (Ign. *Smyrn.* 4:1; 7:2). In dealing with the issue of hospitality 2 John confronts a problem not discussed in 1 John. There the teaching and practice of the opponents is subjected to criticism, but the question of how to deal with them personally is not raised. 2 John leaves no doubts as to the Elder's policy here.

Too little attention is given to the reference to "his evil works." The order of the words stresses their evil nature. The consequence warned against is "to share in his works, the evil ones" *(tois ponērois)*. In Johannine terms this is the word to describe Satan, "the evil one" (1 John 2:13-14; 3:12). According to the Gospel the judgment brought by Jesus is in conflict with this evil and is depicted in terms of the struggle between the light and the darkness; see John 3:19-21; 7:7.

# 3. NOTICE OF INTENTION TO VISIT (12)

12. I have much to write to you. I do not wish to use paper and ink, but I hope to visit you and to speak with you face to face, so that our joy may be complete.

## NOTES

12. *I have much to write to you. I do not wish to use paper and ink, but I hope to visit you and to speak with you face to face, so that our joy may be complete:* The Elder continues to address his readers in the second person plural. Reference here is to writing by means of paper (papyrus, *chartou*) and ink. See the comparable statement in 3 John 13. The idiom of speaking *stoma pros stoma* means speaking face to face, though *stoma* alone means mouth.

   Reference to joy being fulfilled is confused by the textual evidence, where there is support for both "our joy" and "your joy." The same textual confusion exists where the expression is used in 1 John 1:4. But in that instance B (Vaticanus, fourth century) supports ℵ (Sinaiticus, fourth century) against A (Alexandrinus, fifth century) in reading "our joy," whereas both A and B read "your joy" in 2 John 3 against "our joy" in ℵ. The other textual evidence slightly favors "our joy," but the most important evidence is that "your joy" is what the reader would expect to find. Thus it is more likely to be the secondary reading.

On the Johannine expression concerning the fulfillment of joy see John 3:29; 15:11; 16:24; 17:13. The Jewish character of this expression is attested by the rabbinic literature (*Billerbeck* 2:566) where it is the joy of the messianic age (ibid. 2:429–30). Here again we have evidence of the Jewish character of the language of the Elder, even though the community to which he wrote is rooted in the Hellenistic context.

### INTERPRETATION

Reference to having much to write but preferring a personal visit is standard in Hellenistic letters. In this instance it may be a reference to the substance of 1 John, subsequently written because the projected visit mentioned did not take place. This is the view of J. L. Houlden (*A Commentary on the Johannine Epistles* 140) and may not be far from the mark. Houlden notes that 1 John is an expansion of 2 John. But what 2 John has that is lacking from 1 John is the personal address of a letter. If sent as a dispatch, 1 John needs either an introductory letter such as 2 John or a personal delivery that bears all the greetings normally conveyed by a letter. While there can be no certainty in this matter, it seems better to treat 2 John as the accompanying letter for 1 John. The reference to having much more to write is, as Brown has argued, a conventional letter closing (see 3 John 13 and Brown, *The Epistles of John* 693–96). But more to the point it concerns the more personal communication from the Elder to a particular church or group of churches. This is altogether lacking from 1 John. Thus 1 John, though it deals with the substantial issues troubling the Elder, does not address the particularities and persons to whom 2 John is addressed. If 2 John 12 is thought to make this less likely, Houlden's alternative becomes attractive. Either way, 2 John and 1 John remain closely tied in their purpose. If 2 John was written to accompany 1 John it may well have been *written* second, but the intent would have been that it should be *read* first. One strength of Houlden's position is that he recognizes that the significance of 2 John is reduced by the presence of 1 John. 2 John is thus seen as a succinct and to the point introduction to matters dealt with more fully in 1 John.

We have no means of knowing whether the projected visit mentioned by the Elder ever took place or if it was stated simply as a vague hope. Even though 2 John 12 and 3 John 13 express conventional wishes, both letters provide a picture of mobility as teachers move around a network of churches. The Elder was an important figure in these movements.

## 4. FINAL GREETINGS (13)

13. The children of your elect sister greet you.

13. *The children of your elect sister greet you:* In the final salutation the form of address returns to the second person singular, presumably to the Elect Lady. But the Elder now writes in the name of "the children of your elect sister." The children of the Elect Lady have disappeared and the Elder also, which suggests that he considers himself to be one of the children of her elect sister. The final salutation uses the standard term with a neuter plural noun as subject and the verb thus occurs in the third person singular form *aspazetai*.

In the opening greeting the Elder names no persons, but addresses the Elect Lady and her children in the third person. Now at the end the Elder does not greet those to whom he writes in his own name, but addresses the Elect Lady alone, without reference to her children, and not in his own name but in the name of "the children of your elect sister." He uses the personal pronouns "you" *(se)* and "your" *(sou)*. This is almost perfect symmetry. In the opening the Elder alone addressed the Elect Lady and her children. At the conclusion there is a kind of reversal in which the Elect Lady *(se)* alone is greeted by "the children of your elect sister." In the opening the greeting is in the third person. In the closing the greeting is offered directly to "you" in the second person. Where the balance is lacking is in the absence of the elect sister in the final greeting. This is perhaps another clue that these sisters are images of churches whose reality is found in the members, the children.

Various additions occur at the end of the text. They have little bearing on an understanding of the original text, but they throw light on the way the text was read by early readers. The addition of *tēs ekklēsias* is attested by some mss. including some of the Old Latin and Vulgate. This confirms the reading that takes the sisters to be metaphors of local churches. Some mss. go on to add *en Ephesō*, perhaps influenced by the Ephesian tradition concerning John. Editorial additions are completed by a greeting, "Grace be with you" *(hē charis meth' hymōn. amēn* or *meta sou* with or without the *amēn)*. As noted on 2 John 3, the use of *charis* is not characteristic of the Johannine literature, though the appearance of the term in the opening greeting implies the possibility of such a closing greeting. It is the poor textual attestation that rules this out of the original text. The Hellenistic form of the opening is in contrast to this Pauline form in the closing, which has Semitic rather than Hellenistic roots.

### FOR REFERENCE AND FURTHER STUDY

Beutler, Johannes. *Die Johannesbriefe*. Regensburger Neues Testament. Regensburg: Friedrich Pustet, 2000, 147–66.

Bousset, Wilhelm. *Der Antichrist in der Überlieferung des Judentums, des Neuen Testaments und der Alten Kirche*. Göttingen: Vandenhoeck & Ruprecht, 1895. English: *The Antichrist Legend: A Chapter in Christian and Jewish Folklore*. London: Hutchinson, 1896.

Brooke, Alan England. *A Critical and Exegetical Commentary on the Johannine Epistles*. Edinburgh: T & T Clark, 1912, 166–80.

Brown, Raymond E. *The Epistles of John*. AB 30. Garden City, N.Y.: Doubleday, 1982, 645–98.

Bultmann, Rudolf. *Das Evangelium des Johannes*. Göttingen: Vandenhoeck & Ruprecht, 1941. English: *The Gospel of John*. Translated by G. R. Beasley-Murray. Oxford: Blackwell, 1971.

Dodd, Charles Harold. *The Johannine Epistles*. MNTC. London: Hodder and Stoughton, 1946.

Donfried, Karl P. "Ecclesiastical Authority in 2-3 John," in Marinus de Jonge, ed., *L'Evangile de Jean: sources, redaction, theologie*. BETL 44. Gembloux: Duculot, 1977, 325–33.

Edwards, Ruth B. *The Johannine Epistles*. Sheffield: Sheffield Academic Press, 1996.

Houlden, James Leslie. *A Commentary on the Johannine Epistles*. HNTC. New York: Harper & Row, 1973.

Käsemann, Ernst. "Ketzer und Zeuge: Zum johanneischen Verfasserproblem," *ZTK* 48 (1951) 292–311.

Lieu, Judith. *The Second and Third Epistles of John*. Edinburgh: T & T Clark, 1986.

_____. *The Theology of the Johannine Epistles*. Cambridge: Cambridge University Press, 1991.

Painter, John. *John, Witness and Theologian*. London: S.P.C.K. 1975, 2nd ed. 1978; 3rd ed. Melbourne: Beacon Hill, 1980.

_____. *The Quest for the Messiah*. Edinburgh: T & T Clark, 1991, 2nd ed. Nashville: Abingdon, 1993.

Rensberger, David. *1 John, 2 John, 3 John*. ANTC. Nashville: Abingdon, 1997, 147–56.

Schnackenburg, Rudolf. *Die Johannesbriefe*. HThK 13/3. Freiburg, Basel, and Vienna: Herder, 1953. English: *The Johannine Epistles*. Translated by Reginald and Ilse Fuller. New York: Crossroad, 1992, 276–89.

Schwartz, Eduard. *Über den Tod der Söhne Zebedaei. Ein Beitrag zur Geschichte des Johannesevangeliums*. Berlin: Weidmann, 1904.

Strecker, Georg. *Die Johannesbriefe*. KEK 14. Göttingen: Vandenhoeck & Ruprecht, 1989. *The Johannine Letters: A Commentary on 1, 2, and 3 John*. Translated by Linda M. Maloney. Hermeneia. Minneapolis: Fortress, 1996.

Watson, Duane. "A Rhetorical Analysis of 2 John According to Greco-Roman Conventions," *NTS* 35 (1989) 104–30.

# 3 JOHN

## INTRODUCTION TO THE EXEGESIS OF 3 JOHN

The Third Letter of John is addressed to an actual individual. The address is followed by a good health wish that leads into the body of the letter, and the letter concludes with a final salutation. It conforms closely to the Hellenistic letters of the time. 3 John is the shortest book in the New Testament, comprising 219 words and 1105 letters, easily fitting on a single papyrus sheet. Only ninety-nine different words are used (fifteen more than the slightly longer 2 John). Of the ninety-nine different words, seventy-eight are significant. Of these, twenty-three are not found in the Gospel or 1 John, and four are peculiar to 3 John; one is common to 2 and 3 John with a further two common to these letters and other books of the New Testament outside the Johannine writings. Of the rest, five are found in the Gospel but not 1 John and one is found in 1 John but not the Fourth Gospel (C. H. Dodd, *The Johannine Epistles* lxii–lxiii). Dodd concludes that the evidence supports the recognition of the relationship between 2 and 3 John over against the Gospel and 1 John. 2 John includes just under twenty per cent of significant non-Johannine words (not found in the Gospel or 1 John). 3 John has thirty per cent, and is thus less Johannine in vocabulary than 2 John. 3 John has only one significant parallel with 1 John, while there is a series of parallels between 2 John and 1 John. Yet the vocabulary of both shorter letters is closer to the Fourth Gospel than to 1 John, though this is true of 3 John to a lesser degree than 2 John. Dodd concludes that the linguistic evidence is open to a variety of conclusions and in the end opts for authorship of all three Epistles (but not the Gospel) by the Elder. Still, he acknowledges that 2 and 3 John are linguistically closer to the Gospel than to 1 John. Dodd thinks it likely that 1 John was written first, followed quickly by 2 John, because it was on the same subject as 1 John. 3 John deals with a new issue and came somewhat later.

Scholars note, as a matter of course, that there is little overlap between 1 John and 3 John. In 3 John there is no direct evidence of the schism, no mention of the christological error or of the Antichrist, no explicit call to love one another. Yet there is a substantial point of contact with 2 John where the two main issues of 1 John appear. 2 John overlaps 3 John in naming the sender "the Elder" and in the language and form of the opening and closing salutations. If one letter is not dependent on the other in this, we need to conclude that the same author wrote both letters. Because there is also freedom to adapt the opening and closing, it is more likely that the two letters were written by the same author. A copyist would have followed the letter he was copying more closely. Further, 3 John overlaps 2 John precisely where 2 John fills a gap in the defense offered by 1 John. In the strategy of mission, how are the opponents to be treated? 2 John advocates the refusal of hospitality to them so that no aid was given to their mission of error and destruction, or so the Elder saw it. In 3 John the Elder deals with the denial of hospitality to his own supporters by Diotrephes. The refusal of hospitality to the supporters of the Elder appears to be Diotrephes' response to the Elder's strategy set out in 2 John. This raises the question of the relationship of Diotrephes to the "false" teachers of 1 and 2 John.

Abraham J. Malherbe ("The Inhospitality of Diotrephes") provides a pathbreaking study of the significance of Diotrephes in 3 John. He notes that Theodor Zahn and Adolf Harnack saw him as a monarchical bishop. Walter Bauer saw the Elder's struggle with Diotrephes as a struggle between orthodoxy (the Elder) and heresy in the form of docetism (Diotrephes). Ernst Käsemann turned this position on its head, making the Elder the innovator and Diotrephes the orthodox bishop who excommunicated the Elder for heresy and was supported by the majority of his church. Malherbe questions the interpretation based on the theory of theological struggle. He argues rather that the difference between the Elder and Diotrephes concerned hospitality. He demonstrates the importance of private hospitality in the first century and provides evidence for its place in early Christianity. He also demonstrates the development of technical terms to describe hospitable reception, including compounds of *lambanō* and *dechomai* and reference to "sending on" *(propempō)*, terms that are found in 3 John.

Malherbe sets out to interpret 3 John in the light of what is known about the networks of hospitality in the early church. He argues that to provide hospitality for the house church did not necessarily imply leadership of it. If the church met in the house of Diotrephes, that did not make him the bishop. Malherbe also deals with the movement around networks of churches leading to the production of letters of recommendation. These became necessary because hospitality was open to abuse (see 2 John 10; *Didache* 11–12). Given that the practice of writing such letters was common (see Chan-Hie Kim, *The Familiar Letter of Recommendation*), it is not surprising that Paul's letters provide examples of this genre (see Rom

16:1-2, 3-16; 1 Cor 16:15-16, 17-18; Phil 2:29-30; 4:2-3; 1 Thess 5:12-13a; Philemon, especially 8-17). Malherbe interprets 3 John 12 against this background. Through such a letter the person recommended became identified with the letter-writer, so that the reception accorded the emissary reflects on the relationship with the writer. The refusal of Diotrephes to receive the letter of recommendation from the Elder was a rejection of the Elder as well as the emissaries and the letter (see 3 John 9). Malherbe argues that 3 John 9 refers to a previous letter of recommendation. (Thus also Bultmann, *Epistles*, 100; Schnackenburg, *Epistles*, 296; Lieu, *Epistles*, 110.)

Malherbe concludes that the struggle between the Elder and Diotrephes was personal and not theological. Diotrephes was not a bishop excommunicating anyone, but a person who could refuse hospitality to those he did not wish to receive into his own household. This included the emissaries from the Elder and anyone who sympathized with them. He goes a step further than the warning of the Elder in 2 John 10. Where the Elder warned of the implications of sympathizing with those who do not agree with his teaching, Diotrephes excluded those who disagreed with his policy. Malherbe argues that this was not an exercise of ecclesiastical authority but an exercise of the power of a householder.

Malherbe's essay is a good example of the social historian at work, making use of every detail of social evidence at his disposal and limiting theological and sociological interpretation to what is demanded by the evidence. His main conclusions can be summarized:

Neither the Elder nor Diotrephes was a bishop. As the host of a house church, Diotrephes rejected a letter of recommendation from the Elder and the emissaries who bore it (3 John 9) and excluded from his house church those who sympathized with them (3 John 10). In this Diotrephes was enacting a policy similar to "the command given in 2 John 10" by the Elder. The Elder makes no accusations of false teaching about Diotrephes. The only charge is that "he loves to be first of them" (v. 9). The Elder wrote another letter of recommendation to Gaius (3 John, and see v. 12). Gaius was in the same locality as Diotrephes, but not in the same house church. He knew about the dispute between Diotrephes and the Elder because he belonged to a neighboring house church. The Elder wrote to ensure that Gaius would provide an adequate reception for Demetrios, the bearer of 3 John. This would bolster his defenses against Diotrephes in the territory in which he exercised authority.

Malherbe's short study has stood up well to the tests of time because the social evidence has not changed and the understanding of it remains more or less undisputed. Nevertheless, there are points where Malherbe's reading of 3 John can be challenged. There seems to be a determined attempt to remove the controversy from any theological dimension so that it becomes a personal struggle between two leaders over the exercise of power. This is not a new position (see Harnack, *Johannesbriefe* 21; Schnackenburg, *Epistles* 272; Lieu, *Epistles* 145–55). Raymond E. Brown (*The Epistles of John* 738) goes a step further, arguing that Diotrephes shared the Elder's opposition to the "secessionists" as expressed in 2 John 10-11, but took his action against them a stage further by refusing hospitality to all missionaries.

The rejection of any theological conflict ignores the implications of an important observation made by Malherbe toward the end of his study. He notes that Diotrephes' action in 3 John 10 "would have the same effect as the command given in 2 John 10." Two conclusions that might have followed from this observation are rejected by Malherbe. Given this significant connection between 2 and 3 John, might not 3 John 9 refer to 2 John as the "something" written to the church? Is not the action of Diotrephes a response to the recommended policy of the Elder in 2 John 10-11? Both letters deal with the issue of hospitality, revealing that each side in the conflict responded by refusing hospitality to its opponents. The language of 3 John 10 reveals Diotrephes as an opponent in the eyes of the Elder. His account of the action of Diotrephes suggests that this evaluation was not wrong (vv. 9-10).

Recognition of a mutuality of opposition in the responses of the Elder and Diotrephes to each other is important. Otherwise it might be argued that 2 John 10 deals with itinerant teachers, but Diotrephes was resident in a community with a church in his house. That need not mean that Diotrephes had nothing to do with the itinerant teachers. The Elder too was settled in a community, but the brothers associated with him traveled about, as is clear from 3 John 3, 5, 10. The itinerant teacher not bearing the teaching of the Elder may represent Diotrephes just as Demetrios appears to be a supporter of the Elder.

2 John 10 deals with the possibility of a teacher who comes "not bearing this teaching," that is, the Elder's teaching of Christ, his christology (2 John 7, 9). The false teacher goes beyond this teaching and in so doing abandons the Father and the Son. Those who do no more than greet such a teacher participate in his *evil works (koinōnei tois ergois autou tois ponērois)*, v. 11. The placing of *ponērois* at the end, preceded by the definite article, makes "evil" emphatic.

It is no coincidence that (in 3 John) the Elder says of Diotrephes, "if I come I will bring up his *works (autou ta erga)* which he does, slandering us with *evil words*" *(logois ponērois phlyarōn hēmas)*, 3 John 10. Recognizing the linguistic connection between the description of the false teacher in 2 John 10-11 and Diotrephes in 3 John 10 gives weight to the view that the Elder charged Diotrephes with false teaching. The overlap of language concerning evil works and evil words puts a serious dent in the argument that there was no theological difference of opinion between the Elder and Diotrephes. In 2 John the difference of teaching spoken of in v. 9 is the teaching about Christ and seems to refer to those not confessing Jesus Christ coming in the flesh. In 3 John the Elder's language and renewed discussion of hospitality imply that the Elder is treating Diotrephes as one of the false teachers.

The overall line of interpretation laid down by Malherbe has been taken up and developed by subsequent studies of the Johannine Epistles. Judith Lieu's work has the great virtue of highlighting the mission context and the complex of mission-related language hidden in this little letter (3 John). The letter reveals groups of people moving about a network of house churches. It is not possible to say how extensive the network was and how great an area it covered. It must have been great enough to involve quite extensive travel, though this might mean only twenty or thirty miles at that time. However, it might have been much more in this case.

That the brothers moved around the network of house churches is clear enough. But what were they doing? Was their activity directed to the believers, or to extending the mission to those who as yet did not know the "gospel" and did not believe? This is not possible to say. Nothing in 3 John indicates a mission to those who were not believers, though this might be implied by v. 7. Not receiving anything from "unbelievers" might imply that the mission was essentially directed to them. But the gospel was not peddled; it was proclaimed freely. Those who believed bore the cost of the mission. But this is to say more than the Elder tells us, and there is little that might confirm our guess. Alternatively, the brothers might have been traveling about the network of churches seeking to confirm the understanding of the gospel authorized by the Elder. This might explain why Diotrephes, who opposed the Elder and refused to receive what the Elder wrote to the church, also refused hospitality to the brothers and excommunicated those who would do so. In the exegesis that follows these are the issues that will demand our attention.

## EXEGESIS OF 3 JOHN

The reader should note that, in addition to the structural organization of the letter set out in the following outline, the letter is shaped by the reiteration of the address to Gaius as "beloved." The letter is addressed "to Gaius the beloved" in the third person. Following this, Gaius is addressed directly (second person) in vv. 2, 5, 11. In conversations the name of the person addressed can be repeated for different reasons. In the same

way the Elder reintroduces the personal address to Gaius. There is a pro-
gression. The first time it introduces the well wish and commendation.
The second introduces recognition of his actions of love for the brothers.
The third comes after the misdeeds of Diotrephes have been reported and
the Elder calls on Gaius to imitate the good, providing argumentative incentive for him to do so.

## OUTLINE OF 3 JOHN

1. Prescript (1-2)
    a. Address and commendation (1)
    b. Well wish (2)

2. Body of the Letter (3-12)
    a. Praise of Gaius' support of the brethren (3-8)
    b. Conflict with Diotrephes (9-11)
    c. Testimony to Demetrios confirmed by the Elder (12)

3. Final Greetings (13-15)

# TRANSLATION, NOTES, INTERPRETATION

## 1. PRESCRIPT (1-2)

### a. *Address and commendation* (1)

1. The Elder to the beloved Gaius, whom I love in truth.

#### INTERPRETATION

For a discussion of the Elder see 2 John 1. The form of address in
3 John follows the same pattern. The difference is that Gaius, the person to
whom 3 John is addressed, appears to be an actual person. Gaius is a com-

mon Roman first name. That being the case, we have too little to go on to identify this person, though the name appears in Acts 19:29; 20:4; Rom 16:23; 1 Cor 1:14. According to *Apostolic Constitutions* (7.46.9) Gaius was appointed bishop at Pergamum by the apostle John. Origen (*Rom.* 16:23) names Gaius the first bishop of Thessalonica. Neither of these comments is likely to throw any light on the Gaius of 3 John 1.

That Gaius is called "beloved" confirms his Christian status. The meaning of "beloved" is perhaps elaborated by the subsequent statement. He is a person the Elder truly loves, an affirmation common to the opening of 2 John. There, as here, "in truth" bears the adverbial sense of "truly love"; that is, his affirmation is not mere words. It also affirms the authenticity of the love that he has for Gaius. The love expressed in the community is grounded in the love revealed in the sending of the Son (John 3:16; 1 John 3:16). This connection is drawn out in 1 John 4:11; 2 John 4-6.

Reference to "beloved Gaius" in the address is immediately reinforced in vv. 2, 5, 11. This form of address is absent from 2 John but common in 1 John (2:7; 3:2, 21; 4:1, 7, 11). The concentration in 3 John is greater (four times in fifteen verses) than in 1 John (six times in five chapters). In 3 John, which is addressed to Gaius, the singular form is used throughout. The plural is used in 1 John. Used as a courtesy in secular letters of the time, here it has more meaning. This is brought out by the affirmation "whom I love in truth" and by the repeated use of the term in vv. 1, 2, 5, 11.

## b. *Well wish* (2)

2. Beloved, I desire that all may go well with you and that you may enjoy good health, even as I know it is well with your soul.

### NOTES

2. *Beloved, I desire that all may go well with you and that you may enjoy good health, even as I know it is well with your soul:* The use of *euchomai* rather than *proseuchomai* weakens the case for translating "I pray," especially in the opening of the letter. This conclusion is supported by the parallel with the syntax of Hellenistic letters. The verb *euodeusthai* has the sense of "being well." The use of *hygiainein*, "to be healthy" is good Greek and found in letter openings (the cognate adjective being used in John 5:6, 9, 14, 15; 7:23). The construction and vocabulary fit the opening wish for good health in the Hellenistic letter.

INTERPRETATION

The address to Gaius is now picked up in direct address, "Beloved . . .," repeated in 5, 11. Its common use in address is seen in the Pauline letters (Rom 16:5, 8, 9, 12; Phlm 1; 2 Tim 1:2). This verse replaces the blessing of 2 John 3 and follows the pattern of the Hellenistic letter (see R. W. Funk, "The Form and Structure of 1 & 2 John," especially 425). The good health wish, common in Hellenistic letters, does not occur elsewhere in the New Testament. Although *euchomai* can mean "I pray," here it almost certainly expresses the wish for good health. This is signaled by the construction, which has a close parallel in P. Oxy. 292, 11-12 *(pro de pantōn hygiainein se euchomai)*.

The Elder has added to this wish an affirmation. Yet it is a puzzle because in the New Testament generally and in John *psychē* normally indicates the self or the life of a person (see John 10:11; 13:37-38; 15:13; 1 John 3:16, and Eduard Schweizer, ψυχή, κτλ. *TDNT* 9:642). But there are places where the Greek sense of soul seems to have made some impact, and here bodily wellbeing is set alongside the wellbeing of the soul. There may here be some parallel with Paul's contrast between the outer and inner person in 2 Cor 4:16, and compare 4:7. But this is to proceed down a path that has not been illuminated by the Elder.

## 2. BODY OF THE LETTER (3-12)

The body of the letter is in three main parts:

1. It opens with rejoicing and praises the recipient, Gaius. Initially the praiseworthy behavior is spoken of in general terms only (vv. 3-4). The letter then becomes specific in 5-8, making clear that what the Elder approves so strongly is the provision of hospitality to those the Elder calls "the brothers." They must be supporters of the Elder.

2. The issue with Diotrephes is outlined (vv. 9-11). Diotrephes is obviously an opponent of the Elder. But what were his views as distinct from the views of the Elder? What were the grounds for conflict between them? While Käsemann may have gone too far in his analysis of the situation ("Ketzer und Zeuge"), there are reasons for thinking of Diotrephes as one who exercised considerable power in a local church. There is no evidence that he was a bishop or that the people he excommunicated were other

"clergy." Setting the issue up in these terms might be misleading. Perhaps leadership roles were less clearly defined generally, even if the role of Diotrephes was a dominant one.

3. Confirmation of the testimony to Demetrios is important (v. 12). He obviously represents the cause of the Elder in opposition to Diotrephes. Does this mean that the Elder was expecting Demetrios to arrive in the situation he is addressing? If so, Gaius had a crucial role to play to see that Demetrios was not refused hospitality.

### a. *Praise of Gaius' support of the brethren* (3-8)

3. For I greatly rejoiced at the coming of brothers bearing witness to your truth, even as you walk in truth. 4. I have no greater joy than this, to hear that my children are walking in the truth. 5. Beloved, you act faithfully [in] whatever you do for the brothers, and strangers at that, 6. who bore witness to your love before the church. You will do well to send them forward worthily of God; 7. for they went out for the sake of the name, taking nothing from the Gentiles. 8. Therefore we ought to help such as these, that we may be fellow workers with the truth.

#### NOTES

3. *For I greatly rejoiced at the coming of brothers bearing witness to your truth, even as you walk in truth:* For "I greatly rejoiced" see 2 John 4. The prints of the author of 2 John are clearly visible here, confirming common authorship by the Elder. Reference to the "brothers" here and in vv. 5, 10 is to be seen against the common use of *adelphoi* in 1 John 2:9, 10, 11; 3:10, 12, 13, 14, 15, 16, 17; 4:20, 21; 5:16. The word is not used at all in 2 John, and in the Gospel in this sense probably only at 20:17; 21:23. In the Gospel it is possible that Jesus' brothers are in view.

The slight variations in word order between "walking in the truth" in 2 John 4 and 3 John 4—the words "walking in truth" coming after the participle in 2 John and before it in 3 John—manifest an author working freely with his characteristic language. A copier would have replicated the original text.

5. *Beloved, you act faithfully [in] whatever you do for the brothers, and strangers at that:* "You act faithfully" *(piston poieis):* In this clause the languages of faith and action are combined. "Strangers" and hospitality *(philoxenia):* On the obligation to provide hospitality see Rom 12:13; 1 Tim 3:2; 5:10; Titus 1:8; Heb 13:2; 1 Pet 4:9, and compare Hermas *Sim* 9.27; Justin, *Apol.* 1.67. Care of the stranger is also a subject covered in Jewish Scripture.

6. *who bore witness to your love before the church. You will do well to send them forward worthily of God:* In the Gospel and Epistles of John the word "church" *(ekklēsia)*

is used only in 3 John, where it appears three times, in vv. 6, 9, 10. In the first instance it seems to refer to the Elder's community. In v. 9 it may be the church in a wider sense or the community of Diotrephes, which is certainly in view in v. 10.

7. *for they went out for the sake of the name, taking nothing from the Gentiles:* In the New Testament the term *ethnikos* for "Gentiles" is used only here and in Matthew. The Pauline term is *ethnos*, used in the plural *(ethnē)* of the nations or the Gentiles. The term used here by the Elder probably does not mean Gentiles, but may mean "unbelievers."

8. *Therefore we ought to help such as these, that we may be fellow workers with the truth:* On the language of "help" and "fellow workers" see Malherbe's treatment of 3 John as a letter of recommendation ("The Inhospitality of Diotrephes") and the discussion of this in the Introduction to the Exegesis of 3 John above.

## INTERPRETATION

Though it takes the Elder a little longer to tell the cause of his joy in 3 John, the cause is the same as in 2 John 4. In 3 John the Elder first recounts how he knows the situation. Reference to the coming of brothers (3) is unlikely to be gender specific; hence we may think of brothers and sisters. It is they who bear witness to "your truth," which is then interpreted as "even as you walk in truth" (compare 2 John 4). As in 2 John, this formulation makes clear that the ethical command (love one another) is grounded in the revelation (the truth) in which the love of the Father and the Son are revealed (see 1 John 4:10-11; 3:16-18, and see the Notes on 2 John 6). From this perspective 3 John deals with the love command as grounded in the revelation from the Father and the Son.

Having noted his great joy at receiving news of Gaius, the Elder now (v. 4) asserts that there is no greater joy for him than to hear such news. This goes beyond the initial statement that is common to 2 John 4. But there the joy concerned the children of the Elect Lady. What increases the joy here is that Gaius is one of the Elder's children, a metaphor, it seems, for one of his protegés, a convert, pupil, disciple. But then does this mean that the church to which he wrote in 2 John was not established by the Elder? It may mean that in a letter to a church (or network of house churches) the Elder could not assume the more intimate connection for all to whom he wrote. With Gaius it was different. The source of the great joy is expressed with a *hina* clause that is epexegetical in function.

That Gaius is walking in truth means that he is fulfilling the love command (walking) and that his understanding of it is that the obligation is laid on him by the revelation of the Father in the Son (see 1 John 4:10-11; 3:16-18).

Whatever it was that Gaius did for the brothers, their report of this to the Elder was the cause of his rejoicing. Here (v. 5) the Elder stresses that those he calls brothers were strangers *(xenous)* to Gaius. Thus what he practiced was "hospitality" *(philoxenia)*. This is made clear in v. 6.

Reference to "the brothers" provides the perspective of the Elder. To Gaius they were strangers. The brothers bore witness to the *love* of Gaius (v. 6). This confirms that their witness (v. 3) that Gaius was walking in truth is to be understood as fulfilling the love command. This command is based on the revelation of the love of the Father in the Son. Their confession was made before the church *(enōpion ekklēsias)*. This expression has an official ring about it, suggesting a formal report on return from mission. Compare the anarthrous (without the definite article "the") phrase in 1 Cor 14:19, 35; John 18:20. That seems to be the context in which the Elder learned of the love of Gaius for the brothers who were strangers to him. The public context of the report was perhaps an added cause for pride and joy. In this instance the church is apparently the Elder's community. In vv. 9-10, where the word "church" also appears, it is the church dominated by Diotrephes. Though this seems to continue the report, the Elder adopts the future tense, exhorting Gaius, "you *will do* well to send them forward worthily of God." This is somewhat strange, as the brothers have already returned with their report. One can only suppose that the exhortation is meant to encourage Gaius to continue the good work even in a context where Diotrephes is exerting negative pressure to prevent hospitality to the brothers. Reference to "send[ing] them forward" *(propempsas)* goes beyond hospitality to the sponsoring of the next stage of the mission. See Acts 15:3; Rom 15:24; 1 Cor 16:6, 11; 2 Cor 1:16. The language of 3 John obviously presupposes the development of a missionary network based on the kind of hospitality that enabled the missionary to undertake the next stage of mission. The support to be given was to be worthy of God. (See 1 Thess 2:12; Col 1:10.) The language of 3 John reflects a missionary context not evident in the other Johannine letters. More of this is evident in the following verses.

The text returns to the past tense (v. 7), evidently referring again to the brothers of v. 3. In 1 and 2 John "they went out" *(exēlthon)* is used of the deceivers/antichrists. Here it is those who have gone out for the sake of the name. Since the writer has just spoken of sending them forward "worthily of God," we might expect "the name of God," but the idiom "for the sake of the name" suggests the name of Jesus. See Acts 5:41, though there the name of Jesus is supplied in 5:40. See also Rom 1:5 and many other references that use the formula "his name" (e.g., Ign. *Eph.* 3:7). In these it is clear that the name of Jesus is intended. Nevertheless, this seems to be the meaning here also. The reference in 1 John 2:12 does not greatly help, since it is as ambiguous as this reference. See the discussion there. In John 1:12; 2:23; 3:18; 20:31 believing "in the name of Jesus" seems to support the recognition of a reference to Jesus. But throughout John there is reference to Jesus coming in the name of the Father to make known the Father's name. The lack of precision about the name may indicate that, for the Elder, the name of the Father is the Son (*Gospel of Truth* 38:6-7). To put this in more straightforward language, it is as the Son that he makes the Father known. Understanding each name involves the other. Those who have gone out for the sake of the name are worthy of support.

Those who went out received nothing from those who were not believers. They were like Paul who preached the gospel free of charge (2 Cor 11:7), and unlike many of the Hellenistic preachers and popular philosophers who peddled their wares. The Elder declares simply: "we *ought (opheilomen)* to help them" (v. 8). This word takes us back to the grounding of the love command in the revealed love of the Father in the Son (1 John 4:11). But the Elder provides another reason for helping. It is so that we may be fellow workers *(synergoi)* with the truth. This might not be so far away from grounding the obligation in the revelation of the truth of the Gospel (1 John 4:10-11). The term "fellow workers" is characteristic of Paul. In the NT all other uses of this term fall in the Pauline corpus, where they draw attention to the strategy of mission involving many fellow workers. Thus 3 John reveals another glimpse of a mission network of churches independent of the Pauline mission.

As is characteristic of the smaller Johannine letters, these fellow workers are not designated the fellow workers of the Elder, but fellow workers with the truth itself. Nevertheless, that they are brought into relationship with the Elder is implied by the first person plural, "that *we* may become fellow workers with the truth." Here again Gaius is exhorted to love in action those engaged in the mission and, as in a letter of recommendation (see Malherbe, "Inhospitality"), loyalty to the Elder is to be demonstrated in the support of the emissaries of the Elder. Further, in so doing Gaius would fulfill the command (obligation) grounded in the revelation in the Father and the Son. In this way he would be a fellow worker with the truth, the revelation in the Father and the Son.

### b. *Conflict with Diotrephes* (9-11)

9. I wrote something to the church; but Diotrephes, who loves to be first among them, does not receive us. 10. Because of this, if I come, I will call attention to what he is doing, slandering us with evil words; and not

content with this, he does not receive the brethren and forbids those who would and casts them out of the church. 11. Beloved, do not imitate evil, but good. The one doing good is of God; the one doing evil has not seen God.

## NOTES

9. *I wrote something to the church; but Diotrephes, who loves to be first among them, does not receive us:* Reference to the Elder's action, "I wrote," is in the aorist tense, indicating an earlier writing. What was written is indicated by the indefinite *ti*. The textual variants (the omission of *ti* and the introduction of *an*) are probably a result of reluctance to admit that a letter from the Elder was rejected along with his authority and those who supported him. The introduction of *an* could be taken to mean "I would have written," and that whatever had been intended was not in fact written. The *ti* provides no clue to what the Elder wrote. He wrote "to the church." Which church is not specified. By contrast, the action of Diotrephes is in the present tense: "he does not receive us." Malherbe argues that Diotrephes' refusal to receive the letter and the emissaries from the Elder was a rejection of the Elder. Thus the Elder writes: "he does not receive us." The language of reception/non-reception again signals reference to a letter of commendation.

    The name Diotrephes has Greek roots and means "child of Zeus." It was a common name at the time. (See BAGD 199.) Nothing is known of this Diotrephes apart from what we learn in 3 John. We should not expect a sympathetic account of him from the Elder. The Elder attributes his motives to loving "the preeminence." This expression is formed by a present participle with the definite article. There is no precedent for the term, though the cognate adjective is used of a tyrant by Plutarch (*Solon* 95b). Perhaps the Elder suggests that Diotrephes was a tyrant in the way he exercised authority. It may be that he used his authority to remove rivals to his leadership.

10. *Because of this, if I come, I will call attention to what he is doing, slandering us with evil words; and not content with this, he does not receive the brethren and forbids those who would and casts them out of the church:* The language refers to Diotrephes' "works" (*erga*), slandering "us" with "evil words" (*logois ponērois*). This should be compared with 2 John 10-11, where reference is made to the teacher who comes not bearing the Elder's teaching of Christ (see 2 John 7). The Elder warns against receiving or even greeting such a teacher because to do so would be to participate in his evil works (*tois ergois autou tois ponerois*). The linguistic connection makes probable that Diotrephes is connected with the teacher who does not bear the teaching of Christ espoused by the Elder. The Elder was not simply involved in a personal power struggle with Diotrephes.

    In the New Testament only in John (9:22, 34; 12:42; 16:2) is there reference to excommunication from the synagogue, and only in 3 John do we find reference to excommunication from the church (though see also 1 Cor 5:2, 5).

Indeed, the linguistic connections are more than interesting. Malherbe does not think that the Johannine language provides a precedent for excommunication from the synagogue any more than 3 John 10 refers to excommunication from the church. He argues that Diotrephes simply exercised his power as the host of the church in his house. Malherbe may be right in thinking that Diotrephes was exercising his power as the householder, the head of house. But in this case the household involved a house church and the householder had the power to behave quite autocratically. The only line of recourse members could take was to withdraw from the house church, and that might not leave many options open.

11. *Beloved, do not imitate evil, but good. The one doing good is of God; the one doing evil has not seen God:* The language of imitation is more Pauline than Johannine: see 2 Thess 3:7, 9; see also 1 Cor 4:16; 11:1; Eph 5:1; 1 Thess 1:6; 2:14.

The Elder introduces two terms that are not particularly Johannine: "good" (*agathos*, see John 1:46; 5:29; 7:12) and "evil" (*kakos*, John 18:23, 30). Neither term is used elsewhere in the Epistles. He also uses a pair of composite terms, "doing good" (*agathopoiōn*) and "doing evil" (*kakopoiōn*). Neither term is used elsewhere in the Johannine literature. Interestingly, the Gospel uses another term for good (*kalos*): good wine (2:10), good shepherd (10:11, 14), good works (10:32, 33). Reference to the works (*erga*) that Diotrephes does occurs alongside mention of his evil words (*logois ponērois*). The Elder surely meant to convey that his works also were evil. Jesus' good works stand in contrast to the evil works of Diotrephes. In John the particular good work in view was making a lame man whole (*hygiēs*, 5:6, 9, 11, 14, 15; 7:23). The words of Jesus in 10:30, "I and my Father are one," resume the theme of 5:17. The response there was an intensified attempt to kill Jesus (5:18); in ch. 10 his words led to an attempt to stone him (10:31). The charge in 5:18 was "making himself equal with God," and here "you being a man make yourself God" (10:33). This charge followed Jesus' words, "I showed you many good works from the Father (*polla erga kala edeixa hymin ek tou patros*); for which work of these do you stone me?" (10:32). The association makes clear the link with the incident in John 5. The goodness of Jesus' works demonstrates that he speaks from God. The evil words of Diotrephes reveal that his works are evil.

### INTERPRETATION

The Elder wrote to the church (v. 9). The earlier reference to the church is in v. 6. There it seems to refer to the Elder's church, as he heard the witness borne to the church. That Diotrephes would not accept the authority of the Elder or, by implication, what he wrote suggests that it was Diotrephes' church to which the Elder wrote. What was it that the Elder wrote? There are three possible answers: (1) 1 John; (2) 2 John; (3) some writing that has not survived. Scholars in the past were inclined to adopt the second option and think of 2 John. But the trend today is to assume that, whatever the writing was, it has been lost. The reason for this is the assumption that it must have been on the same subject as 3 John. There is general agreement that 3 John is quite different from both 1 and 2 John. Thus what the Elder wrote previously cannot be either 1 or 2 John. The dominant view is that it was a letter of recommendation and that 3 John 12 reiterates that theme. I find this argument unconvincing.

First, what the brothers bear testimony to before the church is Gaius' "love." Love of the *brothers* is consistent with a subject quite central to 1 John (2:10; 3:10, 14; 4:20, 21). Then there are references to loving "one another" that link 1 John (3:23; 4:7, 11, 12) to 2 John 5. Both 2 and 3 John understand the love obligation to be grounded in the love of the Father revealed in the Son (see 1 John 4:11).

Second, 2 John deals with the refusal of hospitality to those whose teaching did not accord with that of the Elder. Not only did Diotrephes not receive that teaching (the letter), the Elder says "he does not receive us." The "us" does not mean the Elder in person. He has not had the opportunity to confront Diotrephes. He threatens to do this in the future (v. 10). Hence it must be a reference to what the Elder wrote that was not received by Diotrephes. To reject what he wrote was to reject him. The same verb, used in the phrase "he does not receive *us*" (v. 9), appears again in v. 10 when he says "neither does he receive the brethren" (see vv. 3, 5). It is this that makes the more commendable the hospitality accorded them by Gaius.

The behavior of Diotrephes may have been provoked by 2 John. His reaction may reveal his sympathy with those the Elder dubbed deceivers and Antichrist(s). This need not follow, though the common language in 2 John 10-11 and 3 John 10 suggests that the Elder made the connection. Alternatively, Diotrephes may have resented the intrusion of the authority of the Elder into his ecclesial area. Given this demarcation dispute, it is not surprising that "church" language *(ekklēsia)* appears in this letter (vv. 6, 9, 10), and nowhere else in the Gospel and letters of John. Here, as in Revelation (1:4, 11, 20; 2:1, 7, 8, 11, 12, 17, 18, 23, 29; 3:1, 6, 7, 13, 14, 22; 22:16), the churches seem to have something of an institutional shape, so that it is not surprising to find evidence of a power struggle in 3 John. The Elder's intervention in 2 John 9-11 already reveals something of this struggle, though the word "church" is not used there.

The Elder reports: "Diotrephes does not receive us." He attributes this behavior to Diotrephes because "he loves the preeminence." But it is hardly true to say that this is the only criticism made of Diotrephes. There is the charge about his works and evil words (v. 10), which connect Diotrephes to the teacher who comes not bearing the Elder's teaching of Christ (2 John 10, 11). There the Elder argues that those who sympathize with such a teacher share his evil works. An ongoing standoff is reported in 3 John 9-10. We have no idea how this turned out. We do know that the Elder's letters were preserved, so that it is unlikely that he lost all support.

Given the approach set out above, can the Elder be referring to 1 John, or to 2 John 9? It is commonly argued that it must be a reference to a lost letter about hospitality (Brooke, *Commentary* 187–88). Today this is referred to as a letter of recommendation or commendation (thus Malherbe, "Inhospitality," and Judith Lieu, *Second and Third Epistles* 110). If 2 John was a letter accompanying 1 John, as has been suggested, the Elder's indefinite reference here may take in both. More probably it was 2 John (in particular 10-11) that ruffled the feathers of Diotrephes (thus also Strecker, *The Johannine Letters* 253–54, 263). After all, 2 John not only instructs in teaching but also directs the action of the readers to refuse hospitality to anyone who does not agree with the Elder's teaching concerning Christ. There is also the connection between 2 John 10-11 and 3 John 10, which suggests a criticism of the evil deeds and evil words of Diotrephes. Refusal of hospitality was thus a natural reaction by Diotrephes to the action recommended by the Elder, especially if what the Elder says about him loving the preeminence is near the mark.

It is because of the refusal "to receive us" that the Elder threatens, "because of this . . ." (v. 10). This threat ends rather weakly: "if I come. . . ." We would expect rather "when I come." What the Elder threatens to do is to remind, to recall for them the works *(erga)* and evil words *(logois ponērois)* of Diotrephes. He deals with the latter first. The term "evil" occurs in John 3:19 concerning those who love the darkness rather than the light because their works are evil. The connection between 3 John 10 and John 3:19-21 is illuminating. The light exposes those who practice evil, and by his coming the Elder threatens to expose the deeds and evil words of Diotrephes. The Elder goes on to speak of the deeds of Diotrephes. He does not specify the words except to describe them as "slandering us." The term translated "slandering" *(phlyarōn)* suggests empty and unjustified charges. But Diotrephes was not content with evil words. His actions are set out in three stages: (1) he does not receive the brothers (compare "he does not receive us," v. 9); (2) he prevents those who are willing to receive them from doing so; (3) he casts the latter out of the church (see vv. 6, 9). This church has to be the one in which Diotrephes exercises authority. It is the church to which the Elder wrote (v. 9) or was included in the scope of the letter.

On the question of whether Diotrephes excommunicated the Elder and his supporters (the brethren of vv. 3, 5, 10) it is rightly noted (thus Judith Lieu, *Second and Third Epistles* 113 n. 158) that *ekballei* is used only of the sympathizers in Diotrephes' church. Indeed, we should note that excommunication was a local discipline in the early church. There was no overarching ecclesiastical authority. If, however, Diotrephes would not receive the Elder and his supporters (vv. 9, 10), that constitutes a form of excommunication in relation to members of another community. Those communities cease to be in communion with each other. To call this excommunication is to state the matter anachronistically, but it deals with the realities even if it uses language that was not yet beginning to cover such situations. The language is used here of the exclusion of members of Diotrephes' own house church who sympathized with the Elder and his supporters. Malherbe rightly notes that the power to do this came from the situation of being the host of the church in his own household. Thus the power to exclude is not vested in some *independent* ecclesial authority.

The Elder addresses Gaius for the third time: "Beloved" (v. 11, and see vv. 2, 5), having called him "beloved Gaius" at the beginning. This third use of "beloved" comes at the point in the letter where the Elder seeks to galvanize Gaius for action. Perhaps the reference to the evil words of Diotrephes *(logois ponērois)* has led to the contrast between good *(agathos)* and evil *(kakos)*. While a different term is used for evil, that is not significant. Both terms denote moral evil. Certainly we remain outside the characteristic Johannine vocabulary where what is good (or righteous, 1 John 3:10) is more characteristically spoken of in terms of love.

Gaius is called on to imitate good and not evil, because the one doing good is of God while the one doing evil has not seen God (cf. John 3:19-21). While the language of good and evil is new, the saying echoes 1 John 3:10 which contrasts the children of God and the children of the devil. The argument there is similar, though stated with double negatives: "everyone who does not do righteousness *(pas ho mē poiōn dikaiosynēn)* is not of God *(ouk estin ek tou theou)*, even the one not loving his brother *(kai ho mē agapōn to adelphon autou)*." In 3 John the double negatives are avoided, and it is the one who does good who is of God *(ek tou theou estin)*. To be "of God" is to be "born of God," "children of God." Doing *good* is now the way the Elder characterizes "walking in the truth" or loving the brothers, which is more characteristic of the Epistles. The introduction of the language of goodness is a significant development here, as it is in John 10:32, though a different term for goodness is used there (see the Notes). Thus it is made clear that moral virtue has its grounding in the character of God (see Ps 136:1).

Gaius is called to choose between the Elder and Diotrephes, who refused hospitality to the brothers and spoke evil, slanderous words about the Elder and the brothers. Diotrephes has shown himself to be on the side of evil and thus demonstrated that he is not of God, and has not seen God. "Everyone who sins has not seen him or known him" (1 John 3:6; compare 3:10).

## c. *Testimony to Demetrios confirmed by the Elder* (12)

12. Witness is borne to Demetrios by all and by the truth itself; and we also bear witness, and you know that our witness is true.

### NOTES

12. *Witness is borne to Demetrios by all and by the truth itself; and we also bear witness, and you know that our witness is true:* While the language of witness is characteristic of the Gospel, the use of the language here differs somewhat from it. Nothing is known of Demetrios except what we learn in 3 John. There is no reason to identify him with the Ephesian silversmith of Acts 19:24.

### INTERPRETATION

The place of Demetrios in the situation described in 3 John is somewhat ambiguous. Clearly the Elder speaks on his behalf. The question is: Is he a member of Diotrephes' church? a traveling missionary? one of the brothers? or the bearer of 3 John? A case can be made for each of these positions. That he was a member of the church of Diotrephes might mean that his position was ambiguous and the Elder sought to clarify it to Gaius. This does not seem likely because one purpose of 3 John appears to be to ensure that Gaius does not waver in his support for the Elder. In this the Elder appeals to Demetrios as an example to be followed by Gaius. The alternatives to this position are difficult to choose between. Demetrios might be one of the brothers, perhaps the leader of the group that Diotrephes continued to refuse to receive. Again, he might have been the bearer of 3 John, which then can be seen as a letter of commendation. Indeed, this is true also if Demetrios was the leader among the brothers. If this is right, the commendation of v. 12 is the main point of the letter and everything prior to this leads up to it (see Malherbe, "The Inhospitality of Diotrephes"). Those who adopt this position often argue that 3 John is more or less a replica of the letter that Diotrephes refused to receive. There is not much evidence for this view. The overlap between 2 John and 3 John is greater than is normally recognized, and if 2 John accompanied 1 John there is a better case for recognizing that their combined message was the "something" written by the Elder (v. 9).

That Demetrios has the testimony of all on his side is obviously an overstatement. The use of the language of witness to refer to Demetrios, not to Jesus as in the Gospel, is un-Johannine. It is a threefold witness (see 1 John 5:7), though there is no reference to the threefold nature here. The use of the perfect passive in the first testimony has more in common with secular use than with the Gospel of John. (For this expression see also *1 Clem.* 44:3.) If it is not an overstatement, "all" may refer to Demetrios' public *persona* outside the church. The second witness is the truth itself, here personified. This looks Johannine (John 14:6; 16:13; 1 John 5:6), but there is no clear indication that this personification is to be identified with the Spirit or Jesus. Rather, here it seems to mean that truth is self-evident in the life of Demetrios. That this means something like "walking in the truth" is possible if it involves love to the brothers arising from a response to the truth (the Johannine gospel). The third witness is the Elder who here speaks in the first person plural, "we." The Elder then asserts: "and you (Gaius) know our witness is true." These words echo the end of John 21 (an epilogue?) where we read

> This is the disciple who is bearing witness concerning these things and has written these things, and we know that his witness is true." (John 21:24)

Interestingly, while a plurality of people attest the truth of a single witness (Jesus) in the Gospel, a single person attests the truth of a plurality of witnesses in 3 John! The self-testimony to speaking the truth in John 19:35 is in a similar idiom, but although the formula of expression is similar it is less closely related to 3 John 12. The appeal to the reader to attest the truth in 3 John 12 actually differs in substance from both of the Gospel testimonies. There the testimony was to bring conviction to the readers. In 3 John the reader is called to recognize his or her acknowledgment of the truth of the witness. Whether the use of the plural "we . . . our" is a ploy on the part of the Elder to attract weight to his own views or is calling attention to those who bear witness with him cannot be decided with certainty. See the variation of singular and plural language in vv. 9-10: "Diotrephes does not receive us. . . . If I come . . . slandering us."

## 3. FINAL GREETINGS (13-15)

13. I have much to write to you, but I do not wish to write to you by ink and pen; 14. I hope to see you soon, and we will speak face to face. 15. Peace be with you. The friends greet you. Greet the friends by name.

NOTES

13–15. *I have much to write to you, but I do not wish to write to you by ink and pen. I hope to see you soon, and we will speak face to face. Peace be with you. The friends greet you. Greet the friends by name:* The similarities and differences between theses verses and 2 John 12 have led to the corruption of the texts of both letters at this point. On the idiom "face to face" see the Notes on 2 John 12.

INTERPRETATION

Given the close resemblance to the wording of 2 John 12, this (vv. 13-15) must have been the way the Elder was accustomed to end his letters. Slight variation indicates common authorship. A copyist is more likely to copy exactly. Thus there is a change of tenses, the variation from "paper and ink" to "ink and pen." Both use the expression "I hope," 2 John "to be present," 3 John "to see you immediately"; in both the object is to speak "face to face" though there is minor variation in the form of the verb. All of this suggests an author who customarily signs off this way.

There is one significant difference between the two endings. 3 John adds a blessing: "Peace be with you." Whether this arises out of Johannine tradition (John 20:19, 26) or existing Christian use (1 Pet 5:14) is difficult to decide. The singular "you" in 3 John is determined by the address of the letter to Gaius and has no bearing on the question of the liturgical origin of the blessing.

The final greeting is somewhat surprising. The letter has spoken of the brothers (vv. 3, 5, 10). Another term and two other groups are now introduced. While "brothers" has a Christian connotation, "friends" has a secular ring about it. The final greeting from the Elder is in the name of "the friends." They greet Gaius. The Elder then directs Gaius: "Greet the friends by name." Thus the friends in one place greet the friends in another. This is another mark of Hellenistic letters. That the letter ends on such a note is both surprising and an anticlimax. Had the final double greeting been followed by the blessing, "Peace be with you," a stronger statement would have been made. That the Elder did not end this way may indicate that the blessing is more of a formality than we might think. But against this, 3 John has the blessing and it is not found in 2 John. On the other hand, 2 John 3 has a significant opening blessing. Can it be that an opening and closing blessing in the same letter are too much for the Elder?

FOR REFERENCE AND FURTHER STUDY

Beutler, Johannes. *Die Johannesbriefe*. Regensburger Neues Testament. Regensburg: Friedrich Pustet, 2000, 175–86.

Brooke, Alan England. *A Critical and Exegetical Commentary on the Johannine Epistles.* Edinburgh: T & T Clark, 1912, 181–95.

Brown, Raymond E. *The Epistles of John.* AB 30. Garden City, N.Y.: Doubleday, 1982, 699–751.

Bultmann, Rudolf. *Die drei Johannesbriefe.* KEK 7th ed. Göttingen: Vandenhoeck & Ruprecht, 1967. English: *The Johannine Epistles; A Commentary on the Johannine Epistles.* Translated by R. Philip O'Hara with Lane C. McGaughy and Robert Funk. Philadelphia, Fortress, 1973.

Dodd, Charles Harold. *The Johannine Epistles.* MNTC. London: Hodder and Stoughton, 1946.

Donfried, Karl P. "Ecclesiastical Authority in 2–3 John," in Marinus de Jonge, ed., *L'Evangile de Jean: sources, redaction, theologie.* BETL 44. Gembloux: Duculot, 1977, 325–33.

Funk, Robert W. "The Form and Structure of 1 & 2 John," *JBL* 86 (1967) 424–30.

Harnack, Adolf. "Über den dritten Johannesbrief," *TU* 15/3 (1897) 3–27.

Käsemann, Ernst. "Ketzer und Zeuge: Zum johanneischen Verfasserproblem," *ZTK* 48 (1951) 292–311.

Kim, Chan-Hie. *Form and Structure of the Familiar Greek Letter of Recommendation.* SBLDS 4. Missoula: Scholars, 1972.

Lieu, Judith. *The Second and Third Epistles of John.* Edinburgh: T & T Clark, 1986.

————. *The Theology of the Johannine Epistles.* Cambridge: Cambridge University Press, 1991.

Malherbe, Abraham J. "The Inhospitality of Diotrephes," in Jacob Jervell and Wayne A. Meeks, eds., *God's Christ and his People: Studies in Honour of Nils Alstrup Dahl.* Oslo: Universitetsforlaget, 1977, 222–32.

Rensberger, David. *1 John, 2 John, 3 John.* ANTC. Nashville: Abingdon, 1997 157–64.

Schnackenburg, Rudolf. *Die Johannesbriefe.* HThK 13/3. Freiburg, Basel, and Vienna: Herder, 1953. English: *The Johannine Epistles.* Translated by Reginald and Ilse Fuller. New York: Crossroad, 1992.

EXCURSUS:
THE POWER OF DARKNESS AND THE LURE OF THE WORLD

Having completed our review of the Johannine Epistles, we are now in
a position to undertake an assessment of their relation to the world of the
Fourth Gospel. 1 John concludes with the call for the readers to keep
(guard) themselves from idols. This exhortation reveals the attraction of
worldly values, represented by idolatry, for the believing community. The
darkness has penetrated deeply into the life of the community and threatens its integrity. In the Gospel the power of darkness is a physical threat
from the outside intimidating rather than attracting believers.

The world of the Fourth Gospel is explicitly made manifest in the
Prologue (1:1-18). The worldview outlined there crystallizes the various
aspects of the description given in the narrative of the Gospel as a whole.
From the beginning the relationship between the darkness and the light
is one of aggressive opposition. The light shines in the darkness and the
darkness seeks to overcome the light (1:4). There is no sense here of harmony between day and night such as is to be found in Genesis 1 where
light and darkness, day and night are perfectly ordered together. Rather,
here the darkness is a malevolent force, opposed to God's creative purpose. But if the darkness opposes the light it is also implied that the light
opposes the darkness, "the light shines in the darkness." The use of the
present tense here *(phainei)* provides no grounds for the assumption that
darkness was the original state of the creation (Gen 1:2). Rather, in John
the light is mentioned before the darkness, though that reference assumes
a conflictual relationship with the darkness, "the light shines in the
darkness." The aggression of darkness against the light is unsuccessful,
a failure *(ou katelaben)*. The light continues to shine in the darkness. To
that extent the power of darkness is bounded and contained within limits.
But there is no suggestion that the light dispels the darkness; "the light
shines in the darkness." This suggests a pervasive darkness in which
there is a point of light emanating. The overwhelming impression is of the
aggressive power of the darkness threatening to overwhelm the light.

It is in this context that the Gospel depicts the story of Jesus. There is
interaction between the darkness and the light when Nicodemus come to
Jesus by night (3:2), and Judas went out from the presence of Jesus, "and it
was night" (13:30). Into that night Jesus goes out with his disciples and the
specific events leading to his arrest, trial, and execution take place. The
Lukan narrative crystallizes the Johannine perspective when Jesus responds to those who arrested him, "But this is your hour and the power of
darkness" (Luke 22:53). The aggression of the darkness is identified with
the arresting forces and they have their moment ("your hour") in which

the darkness seems to have succeeded. But the narrative continues with the bursting light of the resurrection morning.

If the Prologue asserts the continuing shining of the light in the darkness, the Gospel also asserts the coming of the light into the darkness in the ministry of Jesus (3:19-21). That this is a conflictual coming is clearly meant by the reference to the judgment of the light having come into the world. This is, apparently, a new phase in the shining of the light, but it no more rid the world of darkness than the primal shining of the light. People loved the darkness and hated the light. This appears to state the predominant response to the coming of the light. Here the terminology of loving and hating expresses choosing and rejecting. The imagery of loving and hating is used because strong passions are involved in these choices. They are choices that passionately involve the whole person and such passions find expression in violent action. Nevertheless, there are those who act faithfully and come to the light. In this context Jesus is presented as the light of the world (8:12; 9:5). The story of John 9 depicts the conflict as the blind man receives his sight and leaves the darkness for the light only to experience the hostility and rejection of the Jewish authorities. The story is one of browbeating intimidation against him and those around him to deflect them from following Jesus. When that fails, they cast him out (9:22, 34; see 12:42; 16:2).

The intimidation of the power of darkness is apparent in the story of the arrest and trial of Jesus. The resolve of the disciples gives way to flight and denial and after Jesus' death they are to be found behind locked doors "for fear of the Jewish authorities" (20:19). The farewell discourses of Jesus, especially chs. 15–16, warn of the continuing hostility of the Jewish authorities, which at times becomes the hostility of the "world" to the followers of Jesus (15:18-25; 16:1-4a). In all of this there is no suggestion that the darkness represents a seductive temptation to the followers of Jesus. Rather the power of darkness is a brutal and violent force threatening the very existence of the believers in the world. The hostility is aimed at them precisely because of their relationship to the light. Those who love the darkness hate the light, yet in this description there is the glimmer of the attraction of the darkness. "People loved *(ēgapēsan)* the darkness rather than the light, because their works were evil. Every one who practises evil hates the light *(pas gar ho phaula prassōn misei to phōs)* and does not come to the light lest his evil works be exposed." Over against this dominant group there appears to be an exceptional minority. "The person who does the truth *(ho poiōn tēn alētheian)* comes to the light, so that it may be revealed that his works are wrought in (by) God." In the first part it may be the purpose of not coming to the light to avoid exposure while in the latter it is the result/consequence that the works are revealed to have been wrought in God. But if those who practice evil deeds hate the light, that is also a reason for not coming to the light. It is not only the desire not to be exposed in actions of evil. But nothing in the Gospel suggests that the darkness is seductive to believers. Rather the darkness is the context for the practice of evil deeds that are aimed with intent to harm those who live faithfully, walking in the light.

When we turn to 1 John the situation has completely changed. It is true that the darkness has blinded the eyes of those who walk in the darkness (2:11). What is altogether surprising is that the darkness is not an outside power threatening the lives of believers but is a power at work within the believing community. It is those who do not love their brothers (and sisters) who walk in the darkness. The darkness is the darkness of hatred and those who so live reveal that their eyes have been blinded by the darkness. The light of the eye (see Matt 6:22-23) has been extinguished by the darkness of hatred. Reference to the blinding *(etyphlōsen)* introduces a verb used only three times in the New Testament, in John 12:40; 1 John 2:11; and 2 Cor 4:4. In 2 Corinthians it is the god of this world who has blinded the eyes of the unbelievers. The reference is an explanation of the cause of unbelief. This is also the case in the use of the verb in John 12:40. Here John is quoting from Isa 6:10 using his modification of the Hebrew and the LXX. But the one who blinds (third person) is now distinguished from the one who would heal (first person). Origen and Cyril of Alexandria understood this to mean that the prince of this world was the one who caused the blindness. This reading is consistent with the Johannine dualism and makes sense also in 1 John 2:11. Thus we notice that, in the Gospel, the blinding was a result of the intimidation of potential believers, keeping them out of the believing community. Commitment to the values of the world was also a factor leading to the success of intimidation (John 12:40-43).

While there is no absolute difference in understanding the power of darkness in the Gospel and the Epistles, there is a difference of balance. In the Gospel, the weight is on the threat of violence (by those in authority) to those who would identify with Jesus. In the Epistles, the conflict is within the believing community. From the Elder's perspective, it comes from those who will not confess Jesus Christ having come in the flesh and who fail to love their brothers (and sisters). These failures are connected with a love of worldly values, which has penetrated to the heart of the life of the Johannine circle of churches. Those worldly values are intimately connected with the idolatry of the Roman world. Hence the seriousness of the final warning, "Little children, guard yourselves from idols." That warning is intimately connected to the exhortation of 2:15-17.

> Do not love the world or the things in the world. If anyone loves the world, the love of the Father is not in him; because everything that is in

the world—the lust of the flesh, the lust of the eyes and the ostentatious boastfulness of the possessions of life—is not of the Father but is of the world. And the world and its lusts is passing away, but the person who does the will of God abides for ever.

Like 5:21, this exhortation reveals a perspective quite different from anything in the Gospel. The world is no longer the violent power threatening the very physical survival of the believers. Rather the world is the seductive values that attract the longing eyes of believers with the promise of untold pleasures. These are "worldly" pleasures that evoke "desire" or "lust" *(epithumia)*. This word is not characteristically Johannine (appearing only 2:16-17 and John 8:44) but is common in the Pauline corpus, especially the phrase "the lust of the flesh" (Gal 5:16, [17], 24; Eph 2:3). In Rom 7:7-8, Paul explicitly relates "desire" to sin and the command "Do not covet (desire)" *(Ouk epithymēseis)*. In the Johannine writing "desire" is used always in a negative sense and this is also dominant in the Pauline corpus. In 1 John 2:16-17 "desire" is seated in the flesh, operates through the eyes and belongs to the world. It is closely related to boastfulness *(alazoneia)*. This little tirade against attachment to the values of the world is revealing. It seems to be closely connected to the attraction to idolatry. It may well be that the opponents rejected the Elder's countercultural understanding of the implications of the (gospel) message. Rather they affirmed an acceptance of the message that involved no criticism of the social values of the world in which they lived. In this way the values of the world entered the very heart of the life of the Johannine circle of churches. Thus for the Elder the darkness was within the community, threatening the integrity of the life of faith and love. There is no sign of aggressive worldly powers threatening the physical survival of the Johannine believers such as we find in the Gospel.

# INDEXES

## *SCRIPTURAL INDEX*

# INDEX OF ANCIENT WRITINGS

# SUBJECT INDEX

# AUTHOR INDEX